Praise for *The Handbook of Language and Speech Disorders*

Recommended by CHOICE.

"Unique in its comprehensive coverage of language and speech disorders of various aetiologies, a 'must have' resource for students, clinicians and researchers in speech-language pathology and related professions."

Bruce Murdoch, the University of Queensland

"Damico, Müller and Ball have successfully responded to a challenge unanswered since the last revision of Travis' (1971) handbook. They have compiled a work that comprehensively documents how the study of language and speech disorders has changed since then."

Audrey Holland, University of Arizona

"If you've been looking for an accessible reference text on language and speech disorders, written by respected experts, then your search stops here."

Fiona Gibbon, University College Cork

"This handbook is a worthy successor to the classic publication edited by Lee Edward Travis. The editors have recruited capable authors to meet the challenge of assembling a text that is contemporary and comprehensive in its coverage of the field."

Raymond Kent, University of Wisconsin

D0770423

Blackwell Handbooks in Linguistics

This outstanding multi-volume series covers all the major subdisciplines within linguistics today and, when complete, will offer a comprehensive survey of linguistics as a whole.

Already published:

The Handbook of Language and Speech Disorders

Edited by

Jack S. Damico,
Nicole Müller,
Martin J. Ball

WILEY-BLACKWELL

A John Wiley & Sons, Ltd., Publication

This paperback edition first published 2013
© 2013 Blackwell Publishing Ltd except for editorial material and organization © 2013 Jack S. Damico, Nicole Müller, Martin J. Ball

Edition History: Blackwell Publishing Ltd (hardback, 2010)

Blackwell Publishing was acquired by John Wiley & Sons in February 2007. Blackwell's publishing program has been merged with Wiley's global Scientific, Technical, and Medical business to form Wiley-Blackwell.

Registered Office
John Wiley & Sons Ltd, The Atrium, Southern Gate, Chichester, West Sussex, PO19 8SQ, UK

Editorial Offices
350 Main Street, Malden, MA 02148-5020, USA
9600 Garsington Road, Oxford, OX4 2DQ, UK
The Atrium, Southern Gate, Chichester, West Sussex, PO19 8SQ, UK

For details of our global editorial offices, for customer services, and for information about how to apply for permission to reuse the copyright material in this book please see our website at www.wiley.com/wiley-blackwell.

The right of Jack S. Damico, Nicole Müller, Martin J. Ball to be identified as the authors of the editorial material in this work has been asserted in accordance with the UK Copyright, Designs and Patents Act 1988.

Library of Congress Cataloging-in-Publication Data

The handbook of language and speech disorders / edited by Jack S. Damico, Nicole Müller, and Martin J. Ball.
    p. cm. – (Blackwell handbooks in linguistics)
Includes bibliographical references and index.
ISBN 978-1-4051-5862-6 (hardcover : alk. paper) ISBN 978-1-118-34716-4 (paperback: alk. paper)
1. Speech disorders.   2. Language disorders.   3. Communicative disorders.   I. Damico, Jack Samual.   II. Müller, Nicole.   III. Ball, Martin J. (Martin John)
    RC423.H3258 2010
    616.85′5–dc22

                                                                                2009030171

A catalogue record for this book is available from the British Library.

Cover image: Liubov Sergeievna Popova, Painterly architectonic (1918). Costakis Coll, Athens.
© Photo Scala, Florence.
Cover design by Workhaus

Set in 10/12pt Palatino by Toppan Best-set Premedia Limited

Printed in Malaysia by Ho Printing (M) Sdn Bhd

1   2013

Contents

Figures

Notes on Contributors

Hermann Ackermann is a Professor of Neurological Rehabilitation at the Department of General Neurology, Hertie Institute for Clinical Brain Research, University of Tübingen, Germany. His research focuses upon the brain mechanisms of speech motor control and speech sound perception, including the analysis of speech motor and central-auditory deficits in clinical populations as well as functional brain imaging (fMRI, MEG) in healthy subjects.

Martin J. Ball is Hawthorne-BoRSF Endowed Professor, and Co-Director of the Hawthorne Center for Research in Communicative Disorders, at the University of Louisiana at Lafayette. He is co-editor of the journal *Clinical Linguistics and Phonetics*, and the book series *Communication Disorders across Languages*. His main research interests include sociolinguistics, clinical phonetics and phonology, and the linguistics of Welsh, and he is an honorary Fellow of the UK Royal College of Speech and Language Therapists and honorary professor at the University of Wales Institute, Cardiff. His most recent books are *Handbook of Clinical Linguistics* (co-edited with M. R. Perkins, N. Müller, and S. Howard; Blackwell, 2008), and *Phonology for Communication Disorders* (with N. Müller and B. Rutter).

Margaret Lehman Blake is an associate professor in the department of Communication Sciences and Disorders at the University of Houston. Her primary interest is cognitive-communication disorders associated with right hemisphere brain damage. Her research focuses on inferencing, integration, and other processes contributing to discourse comprehension deficits in this population.

Tim Bressmann is an Associate Professor in the Department of Speech-Language Pathology at the University of Toronto. His research interests are in the areas of structurally related speech and voice disorders. The two main foci of his research are head and neck cancer and craniofacial syndromes. A major component of his research is the use of two- and three-dimensional ultrasound imaging for the analysis of tongue function in speech.

Bonnie Brinton is a professor in the Communication Disorders Department at Brigham Young University, Provo, Utah. She recently completed an appointment as dean of graduate studies, a position she held for over 10 years. Her research interests focus on the pragmatic skills of children with language impairment. She is particularly interested in the social competence of these children and in developing interventions that simultaneously facilitate language and social skills.

Steven Cloud is Associate Professor in the Department of Speech and Hearing Sciences at the University of Southern Mississippi. His primary areas of interest include adult neurogenics and diversity.

Chris Code is University Research Fellow in the School of Psychology, Washington Singer Labs, University of Exeter, England, Foundation Professor of Communication Sciences and Disorders (Hon) at the University of Sydney, and past Research Manager for *Speakability*, and is *Speakability*'s National Advisor on Aphasia. He is Patron of *AphasiaNow*. He is also co-founding editor of the journal *Aphasiology*. His research interests include the cognitive neuroscience of language and speech, psychosocial consequences of aphasia, recovery and treatment of aphasia, number processing and apraxia.

Carl Coelho is a speech-language pathologist who has worked clinically and conducted research in the area of neurogenic communication disorders for over 30 years. He is currently Professor and Head of the Communication Sciences Department at the University of Connecticut. Coelho is also an Associate Investigator on the Vietnam Head Injury Study. He is a Fellow of the American Speech-Language-Hearing Association, and President of the Academy of Neurologic Communication Disorders and Sciences.

Truman E. Coggins is Professor and Head of Speech-Language Pathology at the Center on Human Development and Disability (CHDD) at the University of Washington. He also serves as a research affiliate in the Mental Retardation and Developmental Disabilities Research Center at the CHDD. He is a Fellow of the American Speech-Language-Hearing Association and a certified speech-language pathologist. He is an active clinician and researcher with the Fetal Alcohol Syndrome/Diagnostic Prevention Network at the University.

Jack S. Damico is the Doris B. Hawthorne Eminent Scholar in Communicative Disorders and Special Education, and Co-Director of the Hawthorne Center for Research in Communicative Disorders, at the University of Louisiana at Lafayette. He has published widely in applied linguistics, aphasia, language assessment and intervention, literacy studies, diversity education, conversation analysis, and qualitative research methodology. His primary interests are in applications of qualitative research to communicative sciences and disorders, language and literacy, multicultural service delivery, clinical aphasiology, language as social action, ADHD/ADD, and the study of language as a synergistic phenomenon. He has co-authored or co-edited 11 books and manuals, including *Limiting Bias in the*

Assessment of Bilingual Students and *Special Education Considerations for English Language Learners* with Else Hamayan, *Clinical Aphasiology: Future Directions* (co-edited with Martin J. Ball), and *Childhood Language Disorders* with Michael Smith. He has been a keynote speaker at national conferences in Egypt, Zimbabwe, Ghana, Australia, New Zealand, Great Britain, and Canada and he has received several professional awards for clinical research and publishing, and is a Fellow of the American Speech-Language-Hearing Association.

Kathryn Drager is an Associate Professor in the Department of Communication Sciences and Disorders at the Pennsylvania State University. Her primary area of interest is augmentative and alternative communication (AAC) applications for children and adults. Her research interests include augmentative and alternative communication for young children, and for children with autism; listeners' comprehension of synthetic speech; and assessment and intervention for individuals with severe disabilities with challenging behaviors.

Erinn Finke is an Assistant Professor in the Department of Communication Sciences and Disorders at the University of Utah. Her major areas of research interest include investigating outcomes and increasing quality of life for children with ASD and children who require AAC. Before returning for her PhD, she worked for several years in public and private schools in Maryland with children with autism and other disabilities.

Martin Fujiki is a professor in the Communication Disorders Department at Brigham Young University, Provo, Utah. He studies the social and emotional competence of children with language impairment. He is particularly interested in how impaired language skills interact with other aspects of development to impact social outcomes such as friendship and peer acceptance.

Sandra Laing Gillam is an Associate Professor in Communication Disorders and Deaf Education at Utah State University. Her research interests include assessment and intervention for language and literacy impairments, multicultural populations, and processes involved in text comprehension. She has written four book chapters and 18 articles addressing each of these topics. She was a recipient of an American Speech Hearing and Language Association New Investigator Award and received the Outstanding Alumnus Award from the University of Memphis. She teaches courses in language development and disorders, phonological development and disorders, and literacy in school-age children.

Brian A. Goldstein is Chair and Associate Professor in the Department of Communication Sciences and Disorders at Temple University in Philadelphia, USA. His research focuses on speech sound development and disorders in bilingual children. He is a Fellow of the American Speech-Language-Hearing Association.

Archie Bernard Harmon is a doctoral candidate in the Department of Communication Science and Disorders at the Florida State University. His research interests focus on developing measures of the efficacy of voice therapy. He is also interested in perceptual and acoustic descriptions of the effects of singing training on the voice.

Ingo Hertrich is lecturer in Phonetics and Phonology at the University of Tübingen, Germany. His major research areas are various aspects of neurophonetics, including acoustic and kinematic analysis of normal and neurologically disordered speech, and studies on the perceptual processing of acoustic and audiovisual speech and non-speech signals by means of magnetoencephalography and functional magnetic resonance imaging.

Megan Hodge is a professor in the Department of Speech Pathology and Audiology at the University of Alberta. Her primary interests are in linking theory with practice to assess and maximize the spoken language competence of children with motor speech disorders. Her research focuses on measuring speech intelligibility and understanding what factors influence it in children with and without speech disorders.

Ramonda Horton-Ikard is an Assistant Professor in the Department of Communication Disorders at Florida State University. Her research interests focus on the assessment of language development and delay in children from different socioeconomic backgrounds, young children's use of non-mainstream dialects, and multicultural issues in speech-language pathology.

Sara Howard is Senior Lecturer in Clinical Phonetics and Linguistics in the Department of Human Communication Sciences at the University of Sheffield. As well as academic qualifications in phonetics and linguistics, she is professionally qualified as a speech-language therapist/pathologist. Her most recent book is *The Handbook of Clinical Linguistics* (with M. J. Ball, M. Perkins, and N. Müller; Blackwell, 2008). Her research focuses on typical and atypical speech development, with a particular emphasis on connected speech. She is currently President of the International Clinical Phonetics and Linguistics Association and Associate Editor of *Clinical Linguistics & Phonetics*.

Adam Jacks is Assistant Professor in the Division of Speech and Hearing Sciences, Department of Allied Health Sciences at the University of North Carolina at Chapel Hill. He served as a postdoctoral fellow in neuroimaging of speech motor control disorders at the Research Imaging Center, The University of Texas Health Science Center at San Antonio. His research emphasis is on motor speech disorders, specifically examining motor learning and compensation phenomena in individuals with apraxia of speech and brain changes associated with treatment in various motor control disorders, including persistent developmental stuttering, Parkinson's disease, and apraxia of speech.

Laura Jacobson is a doctoral candidate in the Department of Special Education and Communication Disorders at the University of Nebraska-Lincoln. Her major research interests are investigating the outcomes and improving the writing of adolescents with attention deficit/hyperactivity disorder and learning disabilities through strategy instruction. Before returning for her PhD, Ms. Jacobson worked as an assistant professor of special education at Prince George's Community College in Maryland. Prior to that she worked as a teacher of high school students with disabilities.

Alan G. Kamhi is a Professor in the Department of Communicative Sciences and Disorders at the University of North Carolina-Greensboro. His early research focused on linguistic and cognitive abilities of children with specific language impairments (SLI) and mental handicaps. Later research focused on language-learning disabilities, culminating in a book, co-edited with Hugh Catts, on language and reading disabilities (2nd ed., 2005). Other recent books include one on phonological disorders, co-edited with K. Pollock, and one on clinical decision making in developmental language disorders, co-edited with J. Masterson and K. Apel. Current research is addressing how best to assess and improve comprehension abilities.

Laura W. Kretschmer is Professor Emerita from the Department of Communication Sciences and Disorders at the University of Cincinnati. She retired after 41 years of teaching graduate-level audiology courses with special emphasis on audiological assessment, pediatric audiology assessment, and intervention and management of hard-of-hearing children in school settings. Her research interests include infant vocal development, language and communication issues in children who are deaf, and complex interactions of noise and chemicals.

Richard R. Kretschmer is Professor in the Division of Teacher Education in the College of Education, Human Services, and Criminal Justice at the University of Cincinnati. His research interests include language acquisition in typical children, including those who are bilingual, and in children with significant hearing loss. He has taught a graduate course sequence in Theories of Language Development that has been taken by two generations of speech-language pathologists and audiologists. He is a non-certified member of ASHA.

Karen Lé is a speech-language pathologist, and conducts research in the Communication Sciences Department at the University of Connecticut. Her research interests include the study of discourse deficits following traumatic brain injury, the development of sensitive and reliable discourse measures for clinical use, the examination of the effect of cognitive impairments on discourse ability and social interactions, and the role of the frontal lobes in social communication and discourse processing.

Richard Morris is an Associate Professor in the Department of Communication Disorders at the Florida State University. His research has focused in two areas: the acoustics of women's speech and voice, and the acoustics of solo and choral singing.

Jennifer Mozeiko is a speech-language pathologist and conducts research in the Communication Sciences Department at the University of Connecticut. Her research interests include the study of discourse deficits following traumatic brain injury, auditory processing deficits following cerebral vascular accidents, and the role of the frontal lobes in social communication, particularly as relates to discourse processing.

Nicole Müller is Hawthorne-BoRSF Endowed Professor in Communicative Disorders at the University of Louisiana at Lafayette. Her research interests include bilingualism, clinical linguistics, phonetics and discourse studies, and dementing diseases and their implications for communication. She is co-editor of the journal *Clinical Linguistics and Phonetics*, and the book series *Communication Disorders across Languages*. Her most recent books are the *Handbook of Clinical Linguistics* (co-edited with M. J. Ball, M. R. Perkins, and S. Howard), and *Phonology for Communication Disorders* (with M. J. Ball and B. Rutter).

John Muma is Professor in the Department of Speech and Hearing Sciences, University of Southern Mississippi. He has over 90 publications including six books. His major areas of interest are language assessment and intervention, construct validity, rational evidence, and philosophy of science.

Ryan Nelson is an Assistant Professor at the University of Louisiana at Lafayette in the Department of Communicative Disorders. He holds a doctorate in Applied Language and Speech Sciences from the University of Louisiana at Lafayette and a master's degree in communicative disorders. His research interests include literacy in disordered populations and childhood language disorders. He has published a number of articles on eye tracking during literacy tasks in disordered populations.

Rhea Paul is Professor and Director of the Communication Disorders section at the Yale Child Study Center. She is author of over 70 articles in refereed journals, 30 book chapters, and seven books. She has been Principal Investigator on research projects on child language disorders and autism funded by agencies of the National Institutes of Health, as well as several foundations. She has been a Fellow of the American Speech-Language-Hearing Association since 1991.

Michael R. Perkins is Professor of Clinical Linguistics in the Department of Human Communication Sciences at the University of Sheffield, UK. He has published widely in the area of clinical linguistics and has written or co-edited a number of books including *Modal Expressions in English* (1983), *Case Studies in Clinical Linguistics* (1995), *New Directions in Language Development and Disorders* (2000), *Pragmatic Impairment* (2007), and *The Handbook of Clinical Linguistics* (Blackwell, 2008). His research focuses on the relationship between semantics, pragmatics, and cognition in human communication, with a particular emphasis on pragmatic impairment in both developmental and acquired communication disorders. He was a founder member of the International Clinical Phonetics and Linguistics Association (ICPLA) and was its Vice-President from 2000 to 2006.

Robert Reid is a professor in the Department of Special Education and Communication Disorders at the University of Nebraska-Lincoln. His research focuses on strategy instruction and self-regulation.

Donald A. Robin is Professor and Chief of the Human Performance Division at the Research Imaging Center, The University of Texas Health Science Center at San Antonio (UTHSCSA). He has appointments in the departments of Neurology and Radiology and in the Program in Biomedical Engineering at UTHSCSA. He is also a professor in the Honors College and College of Liberal and Fine Arts at The University of Texas at San Antonio. Dr. Robin's research emphasis is on motor control and learning, and understanding neural correlates of treatment outcomes in motor speech disorders.

Jane Russell is Lead Specialist Speech & Language Therapist working with children with orofacial anomalies and velopharyngeal dysfunction at the West Midlands Centre for Cleft Palate based in Birmingham, UK. She has specialized in this field since 1978 and in 1991 completed her PhD with a dissertation entitled "Speech Development in Children with Cleft Lip and Palate."

Kathy Scaler Scott is a speech-language pathologist and Board Recognized Specialist in Fluency Disorders, and has practiced clinically for over 15 years in school, hospital, and private practice settings. Her primary areas of interest are fluency disorders and their relationship to child language disorders and social communication issues. Her research agenda includes investigation of fluency disorders within autism spectrum disorders and developing an evidence-based definition of cluttering. She has lectured nationally and internationally on fluency disorders and social communication disorders. She is currently Coordinator of the International Cluttering Association.

Elizabeth Serpentine is a doctoral student in the Department of Communication Sciences and Disorders at the Pennsylvania State University. Her primary areas of interest are autism, augmentative and alternative communication, and transition and employment. Before returning for her PhD, she worked for five years in public schools in Pennsylvania and has clinical experience with children with autism and other disabilities.

Vesna Stojanovik is a Lecturer in the School of Psychology and Clinical Language Sciences at the University of Reading. Her primary area of interest is language and communication in children with developmental disorders and, in particular, children with Williams syndrome. Her research interests include intonation, language, and communication deficits in children with developmental disorders including genetic syndromes; language abilities in children with reading deficits;

communication in children with sensory impairment; as well as typical language acquisition.

John A. Tetnowski is the Ben Blanco Memorial/BoRSF Endowed Professor at the University of Louisiana at Lafayette. His primary areas of interest are fluency and research methodology. His research agenda includes both qualitative and experimental designs dealing with fluency disorders (both stuttering and cluttering) and concomitant disorders. In addition, his interests include the effects of stuttering in real-world settings. He has spoken and presented papers throughout the world and has published numerous articles, book chapters, and proceedings papers in these areas. He has served as an editor for several texts and journals and is on the Board of Directors for the National Stuttering Association, where he is the Chair of the Research and Professional Relations Committees.

John C. Thorne is a special educator and speech-language pathologist currently studying at the University of Washington pursuant to a doctoral degree. His interdisciplinary program of research is aimed at developing tools for clinical assessment that discriminate typical and atypical populations of school-aged children based on their discourse-level linguistic behaviors. His current focus is on narrative discourse in children with Fetal Alcohol Spectrum Disorders.

Silvana M. R. Watson is an Associate Professor in the Department of Communication Disorders and Special Education (CDSE) at Old Dominion University, Norfolk, VA. Her research interests are in the areas of learning disabilities and culturally and linguistically diverse students with and without disabilities. The main focus of her current research is on cognitive processes and cognitive strategies.

Deborah Weiss is an Associate Professor in the Department of Communication Disorders at Southern Connecticut State University. Her primary areas of interest are child language disorders, reading, multicultural issues, and bilingualism. Her research interests include speech and accent perception in bilingual individuals, interpreter and translator collaboration, and literacy issues.

Carol Westby is a consultant for Bilingual Multicultural Services in Albuquerque, NM. Her interests are in the areas of language/literacy inter-relationships, theory of mind and development of social cognition and self-regulation, and influences of culture and linguistic variations on child socialization, discourse styles, and academic performance.

Tara Whitehill is a Professor in the Division of Speech and Hearing Sciences, University of Hong Kong. Her research focuses on motor speech disorders and cleft palate. She has particular research interests in speech intelligibility, cross-linguistic studies of speech disorder, and measurement issues in the perceptual rating of disordered speech.

Wolfram Ziegler is head of the Clinical Neuropsychology Research Group (EKN), Department of Neuropsychology, City Hospital Munich, and a lecturer in neuro-phonetics at the University of Munich. His major research interest is in motor speech disorders (dysarthria, apraxia of speech) and disorders of phonological processing. Dr. Ziegler's research has an emphasis on understanding how speech motor control is organized, how it disintegrates after brain damage, and how it can be reconstructed through speech therapy.

Introduction

JACK S. DAMICO, NICOLE MÜLLER, AND MARTIN J. BALL

Providing general overviews and updated information on the state of any discipline through the publication of a handbook is a well-accepted practice. In the field of speech-language pathology in the United States, such volumes can be traced to at least the 1940s with the publication of a handbook dealing with speech aspects of the hard of hearing (Bluett, 1947). More familiar, however, is the *Handbook of Speech Pathology* (Travis, 1957) that so many professionals made their primary reference text during the late 1950s through the 1980s. Edited by Lee Edward Travis, a founding father of speech pathology in the United States (Tweedie & Clement, 1976), this text was first published in 1957 having 33 chapters and 27 authors. Within 15 years a new version, the *Handbook of Speech Pathology and Audiology* (Travis, 1971), had been expanded to 50 chapters and 44 authors. At the time of publication, this handbook provided state-of-the-art discussions on the areas believed to be most crucial to the understanding of the discipline of communication sciences and disorders. Since the 1970s, the original volume by Travis has not been updated, and although other texts have been written, there is still a need to provide sufficient and timely content in a comprehensive work. This *Handbook of Language and Speech Disorders* is an attempt to provide such coverage.

Providing a handbook with sufficient and relevant content raises the issue of scope. As the discipline has expanded, particularly with regard to the impact of language and language disorders in the social, educational, and communicative realms (Ball et al., 2008; Duchan, 2008), the need for research, theory, and clinical applications has increased accordingly. Further, researchers and practitioners have realized that in addition to the information on various disorders and conditions, our assumptions and practices themselves must be viewed more circumspectly so that the science of communication disorders and its clinical applications may be advanced in the best possible way. A text that does not carefully consider the most necessary and relevant topics in attempting to accomplish this purpose might be overwhelmed. In his preface to the newer version of the *Handbook*, Travis understood the difficulty in putting together such a reference text and he reaffirmed an earlier statement that no one individual could "react authoritatively to the subject matter of communication disorders" (1971, p. v). Indeed, such a task requires a careful collaboration.

In order to create this handbook, we invited authors from around the world to write articles within their areas of expertise. There are 26 chapters that are divided into four general sections: I: Foundations; II: Language Disorders; III: Speech Disorders; and IV: Cognitive and Intellectual Disorders.

Part I, "Foundations," is oriented toward several issues that are germane to all of the disorders that are covered in the rest of this volume. As the discipline has matured, there have been realizations that the impact of communicative disorders and the roles that professionals may play in their remediation are subject to a host of variables that cross disciplinary boundaries. These variables and the manner in which they are handled create an overall foundation from which appropriate responses to the various disorders detailed in the other three sections are formulated. Issues dealing with cultural responses to the various impairments, the ways that cultural and societal expectations may affect service delivery, even the manner in which the process of identifying communication disorders has been addressed over the past several decades provide this foundational information. Similarly, appreciating the impact of input and output systems on communication functioning overall, and the role of genetics in the discipline, is also pertinent. If work within the human communication sciences and disorders is to be effective, these variables must be considered when addressing the various disorder types and the specific impairments.

In the first chapter, Damico, Müller, and Ball consider the complexity of identifying and labeling individuals as being communicatively disordered. While it is commonplace to employ labels and diagnostic categories as if they were discrete and fixed, this process is actually a social construction that has implications for both the professionals who apply the label or category and the recipients of that label or category. The complexity involved and how it should be addressed is treated in this chapter. Chapter 2 (Goldstein and Horton-Ikard) presents a foundational and operational definition of diversity and then outlines the influence of cultural and linguistic diversity on communicative disorders. The chapter briefly focuses on the role of culture as manifested in communication, on the variation within linguistic systems, how the concept of disability is culturally determined and, importantly, how these diversity issues influence assessment and intervention.

Chapters 3 and 4 deal with some of the basic facets of input and output in communication and how the sensory systems and intelligible output are so crucial to communication even before the various disorders are considered. Kretschmer and Kretschmer (Chapter 3) discuss the primary sensory systems of audition and vision and how they impact language and speech development. They provide information on the impact on language and communicative development of deafness and hearing impairment, and the influence that such sensory impairments may have on interactional abilities. They also review what is known about the impact of blindness on language development and communicative functioning.

In addition, the chapter discusses information crucial to intervention when these sensory systems are impaired. In Chapter 4, Hodge and Whitehill remind us that motoric output is always a primary consideration when determining communicative success, and that intelligibility of speech, as the basic output system, is the actual functional indicator of oral communicative competence. Successful intervention makes it necessary to orient to this basic component of communication. This in turn requires an awareness of the complexity of intelligibility as a process and how various physical, cognitive, and contextual attributes contribute to intelligibility in oral communication. The authors focus on defining the concept and then showing how our conceptualizations affect how intelligibility is rated, measured, and (if necessary) increased.

In Chapter 5, Stojanovik defines genetic syndromes as they are pertinent to communicative disorders and then provides a description of the potential impact that they may have on communication. She discusses several important general patterns noted in meta-analyses of genetic syndromes in communicative disorders and then describes three of the most relevant syndromes and their impact. Importantly, the author also develops a rationale for why professionals in our discipline should focus on genetic syndromes and how such a focus can benefit both the researcher and the clinician.

While many of the chapters in this handbook provide information on assessment and intervention according to the specific disorder discussed, it is also important to have an overall perspective from which to make clinical decisions. Practicing clinicians must be able to look at the disorder-specific clinical suggestions, but they should also be guided by a set of foundational principles. In Chapter 6, Brinton and Fujiki provide this important information. Taking a narrative approach to set up the issue, they discuss five principles they believe are essential for strong and effective service delivery. Ranging from goal setting and planning to the focus on functionality and recognizing the long-term impact of clinical efforts, these principles should assist in making each disorder-specific recommendations more effective.

The eight chapters in Part II, "Language Disorders," deal with various types of recognized language impairments in both children and adults. While Part I was oriented to overall issues, this section is the first of three focusing on pertinent issues within the specific disorder types.

Autism and other categories listed on the autism spectrum have been receiving increased attention over the past several years, and Chapter 7 (Muma and Cloud) addresses some of the more salient issues. Whereas most of the chapters focus on a clinical description and discuss some facets of service delivery, this chapter attempts to address some of the controversies regarding autism such as its perceived increase in incidence, why there are various confusions in the identification and determination of how to best approach autism spectrum disorders from a clinical perspective, and the impact of a behaviorist versus a cognitive approach to this disorder.

Addressing the subset of children identified as having slower-than-normal speech and language growth within the preschool age group, Weiss and Paul

(Chapter 8) provide descriptions and service delivery suggestions for these children with delayed language development and make an important distinction between children with transient problems and those with delayed language development as a chronic condition. In Chapter 9, Gillam and Kamhi address the topic of specific language impairment (SLI) in children, and some of the important clinical themes that adhere to this disorder. Establishing from the beginning that a clinical classification into this subtype of language disorder is often difficult to achieve, they discuss the criteria and how these have been – and may be – applied as well as how SLI may be approached clinically. Highlighting some of the controversies regarding inconsistencies between short- and long-term outcomes, efficacy overall, and the causal explanations that have been given for SLI, they suggest that clinicians have a role in working with these students, albeit not as hopeful as with other areas of impairment (e.g., reading disabilities).

Perkins's ideas on compensatory adaptation (Perkins, 2007) significantly inform the chapter on pragmatic impairment (Chapter 10). Rather than focusing on language issues alone, Perkins makes the point that neurological, cognitive, linguistic, and even sensorimotor deficits may play a role in the behaviors that give rise to this diagnostic category. Recognizing the complexity of what is often termed a pragmatic language disorder enables the clinician to create a different perspective on this disorder. Perkins shows how pragmatic impairment is best addressed as an emergent phenomenon that operates at both the intrapersonal and interpersonal level of communication. Using excerpts from transcripts, he illustrates both the impact of an existing impairment and the role of compensatory adaptation to create the behaviors identified as pragmatic impairment, and demonstrates how there can be both intrapersonal and interpersonal adaptations that may overcome these problems. The review of research linked with the theoretical orientation provided enables a fresh and beneficial conceptualization of pragmatic impairment that has definite clinical applications.

Language as it impacts learning overall, and especially academic tasks, provides the material for the next two chapters. While a significant overlap between language and learning is not universally recognized across the educational field, speech and language clinicians are often expected to address academic problems due to language deficits. Consequently, these chapters were deemed important to the scope of this handbook. In Chapter 11, Reid and Jacobson provide a more traditional perspective on learning disabilities (LD). They provide a definition of the term and a description of the types of problems that are manifested by this disorder. Further, they discuss some of the overlap between language and learning and show how this (and other) relationships make the more traditional definition of LD problematic. By focusing on the types of learning disabilities and some of the factors underlying this disorder category, they construct a frame of understanding for the clinician. This chapter is intervention oriented in that there is a discussion of both response to intervention and the contemporary models of treatment for LD.

Damico and Nelson (Chapter 12) take a less traditional perspective and focus on literacy as a manifestation of language and meaning making. Employing both theoretical arguments and empirical data from the field of emergent literacy, they discuss the central role of language in literacy. They also detail the various conceptions of reading and how these orientations have defined literacy. This provides a basis for a discussion that attempts to explain the "great reading debate" and then suggests a clinically relevant resolution. Adopting a holistic and meaning-oriented perspective, the authors emphasize the complexity of literacy as a process and provide a number of suggestions for the identification, assessment, and treatment of literacy impairments.

Chapter 13 addresses an issue that has seen increased incidence on speech and language clinicians' caseloads: childhood language disorders due to prenatal exposure to alcohol and illicit drugs. Coggins and Thorne provide an overview of this facet of behavioral teratology, including organic responses to these drugs, some performance profiles that result from exposure, and a review of some of the influential environmental factors that exacerbate the consequences of prenatal exposure. The authors focus primarily on Prenatal Alcohol Exposure (PAE) and Prenatal Cocaine Exposure (PCE), and the impact of these drugs on language development and language functioning. By exploring the influences of prenatal alcohol and cocaine exposure on language functioning, they survey the scope of the problem and provide a blueprint for what the clinical response should be when working with these children. Three multifaceted interventions with these clinically complex children are also described.

In the last chapter in Part II (Chapter 14) Code discusses aphasia in adults and its impact on language functioning and communication. After providing a background on the incidence and prevalence of aphasia, the history of medical and clinical aphasiology, and a discussion of some of the primary features of aphasia as opposed to other neurogenic impairments, the author presents current information on recovery from aphasia, and on some of the primary therapeutic strategies that have been successfully employed. To further contextualize this impairment within the social sphere, the psychosocial and emotional impact of aphasia is also discussed.

These eight chapters provide speech and language clinicians and researchers with the necessary background and updated information on the major impairment categories that primarily involve language.

The eight chapters in Part III, "Speech Disorders," focus upon those impairments that are more readily characterized as involving the speech mechanism. The first three chapters in this section (Chapters 15, 16, and 17) focus on articulatory and phonological issues. In Chapter 15, Howard covers the topic of developmental speech sound disorders by providing information on the nature of these impairments and by addressing the heterogeneity of the population of children with speech sound disorders. She also describes the various perspectives that influence classificatory terms and descriptors, and the wide range of theoretical and clinical approaches to developmental speech sound disorders. Her adoption of a more linguistic approach enables effective discussion of the distinctions between phonetic and phonological processes and how these impact assessment and intervention. Ackermann, Hertrich, and Ziegler (Chapter 16) have written a detailed chapter on dysarthria, covering the neural bases of motor speech control in normal speakers, and then using this orientation to discuss and classify the various types of dysarthrias. This treatment is significantly enhanced by the application of research based on auditory-perceptual and instrumental analyses of these motor speech disorders, especially the work with kinematic and electromyographic techniques. Explanation of the various dysarthric deficits is followed by a discussion of the various therapeutic techniques and strategies that are currently being employed within this disorder category. The authors cover behavioral treatment, instrumental aids and prostheses, medication, and surgery. Jacks and Robin (Chapter 17) concentrate their efforts on apraxia of speech by first establishing the distinction between this quintessential disorder of speech motor planning/programming (McNeil, Robin, & Schmidt, 2008) and other neurogenic impairments. Once they establish apraxia of speech as a clinical entity in both adults and children through definitions, descriptions, and etiological distinctions, they provide information on assessment and treatment. Clinicians who have difficulty with the correct identification of apraxia of speech will find the section on differential diagnosis especially useful.

Chapter 18 (Drager, Finke, and Serpentine) is a bit different from other chapters in this section in that it focuses on augmentative and alternative systems that are necessary when a broad range of speech disorders may be involved. Reestablishing communicative functioning in the presence of neurological deficits severe enough to limit effective motor speech functioning is of the highest priority, and the authors provide information regarding AAC systems and their various components (symbol representation, layout and organization, selection techniques, and output systems). They also discuss aspects of assessment and intervention in this complex area of clinical service delivery.

Tetnowski and Scaler Scott (Chapter 19) approach fluency disorders from a clinical perspective, but do not ignore the various controversies that have arisen with this disorder. They state the two primary theoretical orientations (behavioral and constructivist) and the merits and detractions of each. Using these two perspectives, they review information relating to the definition, onset, development, treatment, and theories surrounding fluency and fluency disorders. Especially beneficial in this chapter is the discussion on various approaches to treatment that have arisen from the two theoretical orientations. Chapter 20 (Morris and Harmon) reviews the area of voice disorders, covering prevalence and recent developments in this area. The portions of this chapter involving diagnostics provide instrumental, behavioral, and psychological strategies to best determine the etiology, the extent, and the severity of the voice problem, and then show how these data can be used to plan treatment. A number of direct and indirect treatment strategies are described. Russell (Chapter 21) provides data on the types of orofacial anomalies that occur most frequently, and how they influence speech production and speech development. These descriptions are followed by a clinical section on assessment and intervention strategies and techniques. Bressmann (Chapter 22) discusses the communicative impact of head and neck cancer. Providing essential information on laryngectomy, glossectomy, and velopharyngeal and maxillofacial defects, he first gives an overview of cancer treatments and their impact on speech mechanisms. For each of the defects mentioned previously, he then discusses the effect on communication, how to describe this impact within the individual, and the various rehabilitation options that are available.

The final section of this volume, Part IV, "Cognitive and Intellectual Disorders," deals with other disorders that are relevant to the field of communication sciences and disorders, but are not easily characterized as either language or speech disorders. Indeed, in some of these disorders (e.g., ADHD) cognitive factors may impact both speech and language.

Westby and Watson (Chapter 23) discuss attention-deficit/hyperactivity disorder (ADHD) from a clinical perspective, to offer a justifiable orientation to this disorder. Employing an explanatory mechanism involving poor regulation and inhibition (Barkley, 2006), these authors present clinical data on the nature of the disorder, its impact on language learning, and an extensive discussion on the implications for ADHD in assessment and intervention. In Chapter 24, Lehman Blake provides similar coverage for right hemisphere impairments (RHI). After defining and creating a distinction for this neurogenic impairment, she discusses three primary areas of impact on communication. The first of these involves three themes that affect comprehension in RHI: impairments in activation of less-frequent or less-familiar meanings, difficulties with multiple meanings, and difficulties integrating contextual cues to determine the most appropriate interpretation. The second area is inability to effectively use the context in the complex give-and-take of conversation. The third area of impact concerns discourse production and how its deficits are clinically manifested. Although these three areas of impairment are not always present simultaneously, nor are they the only impairments observed in RHI, they provide a basis for effective assessment and treatment for this population.

Chapter 25 (Mozeiko, Lé, and Coelho) is devoted to the impact of traumatic brain injury (TBI) on communication skills. A major focus of the chapter is the complex and dynamic nature of discourse, and how TBI disrupts discourse in its many facets. The authors suggest that cognitive-communicative impairments such as those seen in TBI may be ascribed to disruptions in cognitive systems, such as attention, memory, and self-regulatory processes. Alternatively, they may be viewed as manifestations of underlying pragmatic impairments. The potential causes are not only of theoretical importance but have clinical implications as well.

Finally, Müller (Chapter 26) reviews the various dementias and dementing conditions that are often noted in medical and clinical contexts, and presents the defining criteria of dementia and the impact of dementia on memory and on communication. A section on dementia categories and dementing diseases provides a background to many of the complexities in determining service delivery in this population. Also contained in this chapter is a detailed discussion of Alzheimer's disease (AD), which Müller refers to as the "poster child" for dementia. Providing the history and the impact of AD on memory, cognition, and communication, the chapter then discusses the processes of assessment and intervention for persons with AD.

REFERENCES

Ball, M. J., Perkins, M. R., Müller, N., & Howard, S. (eds.) (2008). *The handbook of clinical linguistics*. Oxford, UK: Blackwell Publishing, Ltd.

Barkley, R. A. (2006). A theory of ADHD. In R. A. Barkley (ed.), *Attention-deficit hyperactivity disorder* (pp. 297–334). New York: Guilford.

Bluett, C. G. (ed.) (1947). *Handbook for the education of the hard of hearing*. Sacramento, CA: California Bureau of Vocational Rehabilitation, Department of Education.

Duchan, J. (2008). Getting here: A short history of speech pathology in America: http://www.acsu.buffalo.edu/~duchan/1975-2000.html.

McNeil, M. R., Robin, D. A., & Schmidt, R. A. (2008). Apraxia of speech: Definition, differentiation, and treatment. In M. R. McNeil (ed.), *Clinical management of sensorimotor speech disorders*, 2nd ed. (pp. 311–44). New York: Thieme.

Perkins, M. R. (2007). *Pragmatic impairment*. Cambridge: Cambridge University Press.

Travis, L. E. (ed.) (1957). *Handbook of speech pathology*. New York: Appleton-Century-Crofts.

Travis, L. E. (ed.) (1971). *Handbook of speech pathology and audiology*. Englewood Cliffs, NJ: Prentice-Hall.

Tweedie, D., & Clement, P. (eds.) (1976). *Psychologist pro-tem: In honor of the 80th birthday of Lee Edward Travis*. Los Angeles, CA: University of Southern California Press.

Part I Foundations

1 Social and Practical Considerations in Labeling

JACK S. DAMICO, NICOLE MÜLLER, AND MARTIN J. BALL

1 Introduction

When children and adults in our society are perceived as having inordinate difficulty with their speech or language, a natural reaction is to ask whether those individuals have communication disorders (Barsky & Boros, 1995; Brown, 1995; Flower, 1984). More often than not, when this occurs in an educational setting for children or a medical setting for adults, a referral is made to a professional to determine whether there is indeed impairment, and how it should be addressed. If the difficulty is perceived as impacting communication or learning abilities, typically a cognitive, linguistic, or communicative impairment is identified and receives a label. Typically, the label is the product of some evaluative process that results in the assignment of a categorical diagnostic term.

This process of diagnosis is an accepted and even necessary practice when dealing with exceptionalities like communicative disorders. In order to provide services, to access fiscal resources, to obtain accommodations, or even to come to an understanding of how to address disabilities in a remedial process, an official diagnosis, an "objective" label assigned to an individual and his or her difficulty is often necessary. While it is commonplace to obtain these diagnostic labels and to employ them as if they were discrete, concrete, and fixed, this process is actually much more fluid and subjective than many professionals and lay people realize (Aspel, Willis, & Faust, 1998; Augustine & Damico, 1995; Carroll, 1997; Conrad & Potter, 2000; Fraser & Christopher, 2007; Wilson, 2000). The use of diagnostic terms like language disorder, childhood apraxia, dementia, learning disability, specific language impairment, autism, ADHD, auditory processing disorder, and many others, as labels for individuals and their impairments is not always objective or valid and, as a result, there are many possible consequences, some positive and some negative.

The object of this chapter is to demonstrate the impact of labeling via diagnostic categories, and how these labels result in various consequences. If the label or diagnostic category appears valid and is correctly attached to an individual, positive consequences may accrue. Typically, the assignment of a valid diagnostic label enables entry into remedial programs such as special education in the schools, and assignment to therapeutic rehabilitation in medical and other clinical settings. However, there may also be problems. For example, some diagnostic categories themselves are suspect and merely function as mechanisms of current societal values, power, or control (Abberley, 1987; Conrad, 1992; O'Connor & Fernandez, 2006). If the label or category is invalid or if the individual is misdiagnosed, the resulting consequences are frequently negative. This chapter will discuss some of the mechanisms whereby lay, professional, and media claims help establish the practice of assigning diagnostic labels for various perceived impairments; particular aspects of the social context that contributed to the rise of these diagnostic categories and labels and some of the consequences will also be detailed.

2   The Impact of Labeling

Since the early 1960s, but especially since the widespread funding of special education in the United States, there has been a tendency to refer students to special education for language-based learning problems and for communication disorders of various kinds (DOE, 2002; Kretschmer, 1991; Richardson & Parker, 1993). Similarly, adults with various communication problems are also referred in order to initiate rehabilitation (Thompkins, Marshall, & Phillips, 1980). With each of these groups, the referral is followed by an assessment process that is intended to provide a diagnostic label. There have been numerous discussions on the process of evaluation in communication disorders. In general, the process is as follows: (1) a referral is made to the speech and language professional (SLP) by a teacher, nurse, physician, administrator, another professional, or family member; (2) the SLP reviews the referral and determines the types of information that should be collected; (3) an appointment is made for the SLP to evaluate the referred individual in a setting chosen by the professional; (4) a set of tests and other diagnostic procedures are chosen for the assessment session; (5) the assessment is completed at the appointed time(s); (6) the data from the assessment session is combined with any other data obtained by the SLP to provide diagnostic interpretation involving differential and descriptive diagnosis; and (7) a diagnostic label or category is assigned. As previously mentioned, once the diagnosis is assigned, then other decisions addressing educational and/or therapeutic issues are considered and implemented.

2.1   *Positive consequences*

Receiving a diagnosis in the form of a disability label may start a cascade of constructive consequences, if the diagnosis is an accurate one. The first constructive consequence is that the diagnosis may "transform an unorganized and unclear set of complaints and symptoms into a more organized and comprehensible disorder" (Balint, 1957). Once framed with a label, the disorder becomes easier to conceptualize, discuss, and act upon. It is often the case that organized categories help all involved parties achieve greater understanding and communication about complex behavioral entities that are generalized by the labels (Darley, 1975; Leyens, Yzerbyt, & Schadron, 1994). In a study of children with ADHD, for example, one of the authors (Damico & Augustine, 1995) found that parents of many children eventually diagnosed as exhibiting ADHD often had nagging feelings that something was wrong but they could not put their finger on the problem. Indeed, based upon an interviewee's comment, the researchers in the study explained this phase of confusion as a period of "undefined malaise" (Damico & Augustine, 1995, p. 261) in which the parents did not know how to characterize their children's problems or where to turn for assistance. Once a diagnosis was provided, however, the parents felt that they had a better understanding and could proceed in a positive direction.

In line with the first consequence, once a valid and accurate label is obtained it can also "lead to opportunities and extra resources that are not available without a diagnostic label" (Gillman, Heyman, & Swain, 2000; Sutcliffe & Simons, 1993). As previously stated, many governmental regulatory bodies, educational remedial guidelines, and insurance providers require a standard diagnosis before treatment is provided. Federal and state special education regulations, for example, require official diagnoses before intervention is even planned. In the ADHD study just reported (Damico & Augustine, 1995), school systems tended not to orient to the needs of the students studied until a formal diagnosis was obtained. When the formal label was delivered to the schools, however, it acted as a catalyst. Various accommodations and services not previously offered to the child and parents now were provided. The label, therefore, had a reactive power over the schools, the parents, and even the children. This need to employ diagnostic labels to achieve such ends is not unique to ADHD. Numerous researchers have discussed this issue across many of the communicative and cognitive exceptionalities (Gipps, 1999; Glaser & Silver, 1994; Messick, 1984; Rogers, 2002; Rolison & Medway, 1985; Skrtic, 1991; Sleeter, 1996).

Positive impact, however, goes even further with regard to services provided. An appropriate label does not just create reactionary influences to provide service delivery; it also enables a discerning clinician to carefully prepare a treatment plan that is tailored to the needs of the individual now accurately identified and labeled. In doing so, having the valid diagnostic label may lead to specific intervention that will overcome the identified deficits (Archer & Green, 1996; Gross, 1994). In effect, as Brinton and Fujiki (see Chapter 6) have suggested, strong assessment resulting in an accurate diagnosis is essential for good intervention to occur. To use their metaphor, "you must know where you are going to plan your route."

Finally, an accurate diagnosis may have positive psychological and social consequences. For instance, individuals affected by various behavioral or medical symptoms can "legitimate their problems and achieve self-understanding" once an accurate and valid diagnostic label is provided (Broom & Woodward, 1996). The individuals with impairment can address feelings of confusion, isolation, or inadequacy and construct new identities and this, in turn, can assist in dealing more effectively with their problems (Gross, 1994; Gus, 2000; Kelly & Norwich, 2004; Riddick, 2000). Therefore, the diagnostic label can have a substantial positive impact on the lives of the individuals with disabilities (Broom & Woodward, 1996; Damico & Augustine, 1995; Link, et al., 1989).

2.2   Negative consequences

Labels, however, may also have negative effects. This is particularly true if the applied labels are not valid, or if a valid label is inappropriately or incorrectly applied. The most obvious destructive consequence occurs when *an inaccurate label is applied*. There are two ways that this may happen. For instance, a school-child may exhibit communicative or academic difficulties that are not due to actual impairment, but is then misdiagnosed and labeled as disordered. In such a case, the mislabeled individual may be placed in special education or other remedial programs. Often this means that the curriculum is reduced so that more time and effort may be spent on content that is deemed most important and salient, or that specific learning strategies are employed that may be necessary for impaired learners, but that limit learning by average students. In these cases, inappropriate labeling provides poor opportunities for normal learners and the expectations directed toward the inappropriately labeled individuals are reduced (Brantlinger, 1997; Carrier, 1986; Connor & Ferri, 2005; Frattura & Capper, 2006; Rogers, 2002). Such situations often arise in contexts where students have language or learning difficulties arising out of cultural or language differences. When such students are referred for assessment, they are often mislabeled (Artiles & Ortiz, 2002; Cummins, 2000; Trueba, 1988; Wilkinson & Ortiz, 1986). Their difficulties due to differences are categorized as disorders, and they are placed inappropriately in special education (Connor, 2006; Hamayan et al., 2007; Magnuson & Waldfogel, 2005; Trent, Artiles, & Englert, 1998).

The second type of misdiagnosis occurs when an individual with a difficulty due to some actual impairment is identified as having a different impairment. In these instances the genuine impairment is not adequately addressed, remedial plans and the expectations for improvement may be inappropriate, and little positive change occurs. In research focusing on the impact of Asperger's syndrome, for example, Damico and Johnson (2005) found that nearly all of the identified individuals were initially misdiagnosed and their problems were not confronted for several years. These individuals had to endure school suspensions, transfers, and social and institutional isolation due to these misdiagnoses. Similar incidents have been described by numerous researchers across a range of disorders (Connor, 2006; Damico, 1988; Fairbanks, 1992; Fine, 1991; Hood, McDermott, & Cole, 1980; McDermott, 1993; Mehan, 1996). Labeling is particularly problematic in these cases due to the tendency to attach a stereotype to a label, and then to focus on the stereotypic behaviors in the labeled individuals regardless of the presence of other, even conflicting, symptoms (Madon et al., 2006).

Perhaps the most interesting, and potentially most serious, scenario for misdiag-nosis occurs when the actual label applied is suspect, that is, when a diagnostic category itself is invalid. As will be discussed later in this chapter, due to the subjective and fluid nature of labeling and application of diagnostic categories, a number of categories have been challenged in the research literature. These challenges focus on the construct validity of the diagnostic categories themselves, or indicate that the definitions used are too broad or subjective. For example, these claims have been made with regard to the recent definition of autism spectrum disorders (Bishop, 1989; Eales, 1993; Gernsbacher, Dawson, & Goldsmith, 2005; Gross, 1994), dyslexia (Erchak & Rosenfeld, 1989; Riddick, 2000; Weaver, 1998), learning disabilities (Brown et al., 1998; Coles, 1987; Gnys, Willis, & Faust, 1995; Kaufmann, Hallahan, & Lloyd, 1998; McDermott, 1993; Wilson, 2000), auditory processing disorders (Cacace & McFarland, 1998), attention-deficit/ hyperactivity disorder (Bussing, Schoenberg, & Rogers, 1998; Conrad & Potter, 2000; Prior & Sanson, 1986; Reid & Katsiyannis, 1995; Searight & McLaren, 1998), and specific language impairment (Cole et al., 1995; Conti-Ramsden, Crutchley, & Botting, 1999; Dollaghan, 2004; Pena, Spaulding, & Plante, 2006; Ukrainetz McFadden, 1996).

While the most obvious harmful consequences may result from errors in labeling, the negative impact of the process is more complex and insidious. It must be remembered that labels are actually summaries of complex symptoms, a "mental shorthand" that plays into the human inclination to stereotype and make generalizations (Leyens, Yzerbyt, & Schadron, 1994). While this propensity does assist in communicating ideas underlying the labels, there is also the tendency to stop looking at the individual and start assuming that he or she is defined by the label and its characteristics. This assumption enables the professional to stereotype the unique aspects of the labeled individual so that "all children with a particular label are considered to be the same. This results in failure to notice and take into account personal strengths and particular difficulties" (Archer & Green, 1996). The consequence is "a reduction of individual differences and a limitation on the ways in which the individual is perceived and treated" (Lubinski, 2000; Madon et al., 2006).

Another negative consequence of labeling arises from the very practice of assigning a label. If the intent is to label an individual, then often there is an assumption that not only the symptoms but their origins actually exist within the individual being labeled. Consequently, there is a *predisposition to localize the problems within the individual* rather than to search for multiple factors and extraneous variables, including, for example, teaching styles, prior exposure to opportunities to learn and apply the targeted skills, and diversity issues in school children (Brown, 1995; Coles, 1987; Conrad, 2000; Forness, 1976; McDermott, 1993; Rapley, 2004). The decision to focus on intrinsic causal factors rather than extrinsic factors (or at least a combination) is likely a primary reason for the over-representation of various ethnic and socioeconomic groups in some aspects of special education (Cummins, 2000; Damico, 1991; McDermott & Varenne, 1995; McNamara, 1998). Treating labels as verification of intrinsic disability may also be based on the assumption that the source of all educational difficulties is related to causes that are intrinsic to students (Carroll, 1997; Gutkin & Nemeth, 1997). This assumption is exacerbated by the general lack of familiarity that the general public has with the principles of language and learning in academic and communicative contexts.

Unfortunately, this belief in the primacy of intrinsic causal factors, exacerbated by labeling, frequently results in negative consequences. The label is often used to "explain away" the problem, so that if, for example, a child experiences poor teaching or unresponsive therapy, the propensity is to place blame on the child, not the methods or the teacher/therapist. The within-child deficit model makes for an easy and effective excuse (Brechin, 1999; Carrier, 1986; Kelly & Norwich, 2004; MacMillan & Meyers, 1979). As we will discuss later, this tendency to local- ize problems within the individual is a well-studied phenomenon in the sociology of disability. Within that literature it is referred to as the "medicalization" or the "psychologization" of performance and social problems (Conrad, 1992, 2000; Reissman, 1983; Searight & McLaren, 1998) and, because of labeling, there is a dramatic extension of medical and diagnostic psychological boundaries to explain numerous social problems (Barsky & Boros, 1995; Broom & Woodward, 1996).

Since most people are not oriented to the complexity of human meaning making and the importance of systems theory when addressing learning and communicative processes (MacWhinney, 1998; Nelson, 2003; Perkins, 2005; Thelen & Smith, 1998; van Geert, 1998), they are often willing to localize problems in the individual; it is simply easier to do so. To ignore the complexity is often soothing even if it is misdirected. The problem with using the label to reduce the complexity, of course, is that poor results ensue. Even if teachers or rehabilitative professionals are dedicated to the remediation process, their best attempts at assistance often are misguided and ineffective. In fact, research has documented that labeling with a focus on an intrinsic deficit model typically results in overlooking various environmental factors that may have generated or exacerbated the difficulty (Barsky & Boros, 1995; Boxer, Challen, & McCarthy, 1991; Brown, 1995; Coles, 1987; Dudley-Marling & Dippo, 1995). As Brechin (1999) discussed, "If the whole problem, *by definition*, lies *with the* individual [via a label], then our understandings and interventions start and stop with the individual" (p. 1; original emphasis).

Labeling as a process is often discussed within the sociological literature and it is frequently linked with assessment. This is due to the fact that most test development was designed for selection purposes (Glaser & Silver, 1994), that is, to determine who should be admitted to and benefit from what educational opportunity (Carroll, 1997; Glaser & Silver, 1994; Lohman, 1997). In order to cre- ate divisions for selection, however, a label must be supplied. Consequently, labels often become the handmaidens of societal biases and prejudices. Within this function, labeling has particularly damaging consequences. Assessment and the resultant labels assigned to many students are often used to create a kind of social stratification system, a way to keep people in their place (Artiles et al., 2005; Bradley & Corwyn, 2002; Cummins, 2000; Ogbu & Simons, 1998; Ruiz-de-Velasco & Fix, 2000). This labeling process and its resultant placements are a reflection of how power and control is exerted in assessment to fulfill societal roles of cultural and social reproduction (Abberley, 1987; Apple, 1982; Kavale & Forness, 1998; Loseke, 1999). The assignment of a label and the various consequences play a key role in "cultural reproduction and social stratification" (Gipps, 1999). In his discussion of the impact of assessment and labeling theory in education in the United Kingdom, Broadfoot (1996) stated,

> because assessment procedures are so closely bound up with the legitimization of particular educational practices, because they are the overt means of communication from schools to society and . . . the covert means of that society's response in the form of control, assessment may be the most important of the three message systems. Assessment procedures may well be the system that determines curriculum and pedagogy and, hence, social reproduction. (1996, pp. 87–8)

Within the realm of special education, labeling students and placing them in remedial programs – even if only for a half an hour a day – effectively removes these students from "normal" schooling and places them in groups with students of similar ability for instructional purposes; they are socially isolated (Connor & Ferri, 2005; Fine, 1991; Gelb & Mizokawa, 1986; Gill & Maynard, 1995; Irvine & Berry, 1988; Messick, 1980).

Social isolation and stratification often prevents access to equal educational and occupational opportunity. Research in literacy employing a critical interpretivist frame, for example, has found that attaching labels like "intellectually disabled," "mentally retarded," and "dyslexic" significantly reduces the expectations and opportunities for individuals to become literate or to use their literacy skills to improve with practice (Kliewer, Biklen, & Kasa-Hendrickson, 2006). Similarly, Rapley (2004), employing discursive psychology, explored the actual process of limiting opportunity for those individuals labeled "intellectually disabled" through moment-by-moment interaction with care staff and other professionals. This tendency to limit access due to expectations formed by labels is one of the most damaging consequences of this diagnostic process. In education, those professionals who both assign the labels through assessment, and then help prevent access through various means (special education placement, tracking, limiting extracurricular activities) are known as "gatekeepers" (Deyhle, 1987; Mehan, Hertwick, & Meihls, 1986; Ogbu, 1978; Schuster & Butler, 1986; Thoits, 2005). The term is uncomfortably accurate in many instances.

Finally, labels can have *negative consequences for one's psychological health and self-image*. While there are many instances of labeling helping to define individuals and letting them develop a workable self-image based upon identification with a disability label (see section 2.1), an opposite reaction can also occur. Research in "labeling theory" (Heise, 2007; Kroska & Harkness, 2008; Link et al., 1989; Rosenfeld, 1997) demonstrates that when individuals are labeled, the societal and cultural ideas associated with the disability in general and the label in particular become personally relevant to that individual and often foster negative self-feeling. These feelings can have a profound impact on the labeled individual.

An extensive investigation (n = 41) of the impact of labeling on individuals diagnosed as learning disabled, for example, indicated significant changes (Higgins et al., 2002). In this study there emerged a shared set of understandings that involved reaction to the label and then coming to terms with the diagnosis. Conceptualized by the researchers as five stages of acceptance, the labeled individuals struggled with their diagnoses for years. After the second stage of receiving the label, stage three and four involved a long process of trying to understand what the implications of the label was for each person personally and functionally. In stage three, understanding/negotiating, there were struggles to understand the label and how it impacted school and social spheres. Importantly, this was a time when stigmatization was most problematic (Gelb & Mizokawa, 1986; Gergen & Davis, 1985; Goffman, 1964). The fourth stage, compartmentalization, impacted the actual practices of the labeled individuals. Through their actions over a long period of time, these individuals tried to minimize the importance of the label by adapting their preferences and activities so that they could minimize weaknesses and maximize strengths. While this was viewed as a positive adaptive strategy, it nevertheless resulted in reduced opportunities and limited activities. The fifth stage, transformation, indicated a period when the label and disability was reframed into a "positive force in their lives." Interestingly, this stage was not achieved by many individuals, even after a 10-year period.

A number of other researchers have investigated labeling theory or a variant of it once individuals are labeled as "learning disabled" (Bogdan & Kugelmass, 1984; Bos & Richardson, 1994; Foster, Schmidt, & Sabatino, 1976; Hellendoorn & Ruijssenaars, 1998). One study in particular (Forness, 1976) investigated several kinds of behavioral reactions to labeling overall. In these and other studies (Damico & Augustine, 1995; Damico & Johnson, 2005; Higgins, 1980; Hood, McDermott, & Cole, 1980; Klasen, 2000; Livneh & Antonak, 1991; Livneh & Evans, 1984; McDermott & Varenne, 1995) the negative impact of labeling on psychological and social functioning has been demonstrated for many individuals.

3   Concerns with the Process of Labeling

Given the fact that labeling has a long history of application in education, medicine, and the social and psychological sciences, that it arises out of the human propensity to generalize, stereotype, and construct meaning, and that there appear to be both positive and negative consequences of labeling, the process is well ingrained in our sociocultural context. Progressively, however, as social science addresses complexity and has established developmental and epistemological orientations that are less positivistic in nature and focused more on social constructivism (Bruner, 1991; Danziger, 1990; Gergen & Davis, 1985; Goodman, 1978; Iran-Nejad, 1995; O'Connor, 1998; Shuell, 1986), there have been growing concerns about the process of labeling. Within the constructivist framework (see section 4 below), labeling is seen as too subjective and vague, especially given its power in the spheres of social action (see section 2). Foremost in the litany of concern is the linkage of labeling with assessment.

As a widespread practice, assessment is a fairly recent phenomenon (Broadfoot, 1994; Gipps, 1999). In the context of the attempt to develop a more scientific foundation for the discipline of psychology at the beginning of the twentieth century, assessment was seen as a way to demonstrate both scientific principles and practical utility (Gould, 1996; Mills, 1998). When psychometric theory was developed in tandem with the creation of intelligence testing (Bernstein, 1996; Goldstein, 1996; Lohman, 1997), there was an allure of the objective and scientific. This was a time of behaviorism and a belief in positivism and it was taken for granted that the assessment of human abilities, skills, and proficiencies could be effectively accomplished through the development of test instruments. The use of quantification and statistical formulae helped advance this perception. However, to construct testing with sufficient statistical power, especially regarding reliability indices, a strict standardization was required that impacted test design, item selection, administration procedures, and scoring criteria of the tests; these efforts to boost technical reliability often had a negative effect on the construct validity and the practical and clinical impact of the tests (Cronbach, 1988; Damico, 1991; Goldstein, 1996; Lohman, 1997; Lubinski, 2000; Messick, 1984). This resulted in ineffective assessment tools that were, however, typically perceived to be valid and effective.

Especially since the 1970s, research in various fields of education, psychology, and the social sciences has demonstrated that the assessment process, and tests designed to accomplish assessment, are not scientific and objective activities: human assessment is not an exact science. Like other social endeavors, assessment is not objective but, rather, value laden and socially constructed (Broadfoot, 1994; Broadfoot, 1996; Damico, 1991; Greene, 1994; Lohman, 1997). As stated by Gipps (1999, p. 370), "in assessment, performance is not 'objective'; rather, it is construed according to the perspectives and values of the assessor, whether the assessor is the one who designs the assessment and its 'objective' marking scheme or the one who grades open-ended performances." In disciplines and institutions that have traditionally supported assessment with norm-referenced and standardized tests, these tools and their practices of using discrepancy formulae, and procedures and processes that focus on component skills rather than authentic skills have been challenged (Boxer, Challen, & McCarthy, 1991; Fletcher et al., 1998; Greene, 1994; Gutkin & Nemeth, 1997; Lubinski & Humphreys, 1997; Snyderman & Rothman, 1987; Sternberg & Grigorenko, 2002; Wentzel & Wigfield, 1998).

Most significantly, governmental changes are also recognizing the problems with traditional assessment tools and the labeling process. In remedial public education in the United States, the major regulatory instrument is the Individuals with Disabilities Education Act (IDEA). In the most recent re-authorization of IDEA, there have been some rather significant changes that support the need and implementation of different assessment frameworks and processes.

Because of continued disenchantment with the traditional approach to special education, the recent IDEA re-authorization discussed several obstacles to implementing effective special education services (Hamayan et al., 2007). Among the obstacles cited were that implementation of the act has been impeded by a disproportionately high number of referrals and placements of "minority children" in special education, and by the application of discrepancy models using inappropriate tests that often result in these disproportionate placements. To address these and other issues of concern, the 2004 re-authorization requires a number of innovations. For example, the document provides for more specific incorporation of "early intervention services" rather than using assessment tools with discrepancy models to place students into special education. That is, the regulations have been modified to address the needs of the students and to determine eligibility for special education services; pre-referral interventions (a kind of dynamic assessment) rather than tests and other assessments will be employed; the focus directly shifts from evaluation with testing instruments to intervention potential as the primary determinant of placement. Additionally, the new documents do not require test scores to make placement decisions into special education. In fact, in the 2004 version of IDEA, references to "tests" have been changed to "assessment materials" in an attempt to downplay the more traditional testing paradigm.

In addition to the necessity of using testing and assessment procedures that are now suspect in order to obtain a diagnostic label, there are other emerging concerns about the process of labeling. For example, there is now more documentation that labeling within special education functions more as a structural framework for social reproduction than as a remedial model (Carrier, 1986), and that the models used for labeling in the so-called soft diagnostic categories of special education are more influenced and associated with socioeconomic indicators than with proficiency (Gelb & Mizokawa, 1986).

While the perceived difficulties with the use of labels may appear surprising from a positivist and behaviorist perspective, a brief discussion of labeling as a social process may clarify this issue. The remainder of this chapter will focus on labeling as viewed from the social theory of social constructivism.

4   Labeling as a Social Process

Earlier in this chapter (section 1) we claimed that while it is "commonplace to obtain these diagnostic labels and to employ them as if they were discrete, concrete and fixed, this process is actually much more fluid and subjective than many professionals and lay people realize." This is because the assignment of labels based upon clinical and psychiatric diagnoses are historically and culturally situated. That is, they may appear, expand, or contract over time depending on how society and the involved professions form and hold particular beliefs and ideologies (Cooksey & Brown, 1998). To understand this statement, it is beneficial to view labeling from the perspective of social constructivism.

4.1   *Social constructivism*

Social constructivism can provide important insights into the process of labeling. An important assumption is that knowledge does not exist as an external reality; there is no "prefabricated" world of knowledge waiting to be discovered or acquired (von Glasersfeld, 1989). Instead, cognitive development and any subsequent knowledge acquisition is an internal process within both ontogenetic and social dimensions. This starting assumption has informed two strands of social constructivism. One strand focuses on the ontogenetic and personal axis and has been best advanced by two of the leading developmental intellectuals of the twentieth century (Piaget, 1970; Vygotsky, 1978). For our purposes the second strand, focusing on the social dimension, will be discussed. This definition of social constructivism is derived from the sociology of knowledge and focuses on the collective construction of social reality; it is not to be confused with the focus in psychology and genetic epistemology on the influence of social constructivism on the cognitive growth and the creation of a personal epistemological reality.

It can be argued that the primary influence within the sociology of knowledge for the establishment of social constructivism was *The Social Construction of Reality* (Berger & Luckmann, 1967). Recognizing the primacy of systematicity in any successful society, the authors discussed how this systematic and comprehensible social world was created; how a society forms and holds beliefs and social constructs. Unlike the work of many epistemologists, this text focused on the creation of knowledge from the collective perspective, that is, on the construction of what passed for knowledge in a society. Although the individual was, of course, the agent of this creation, it was the knowledge generated by the group that held sway. Berger and Luckmann's book discussed the tendency of individuals to construct meaning in their world; to use their symbolic capacity to create ways to achieve comprehensibility that is constructed, sustained, and transmitted to others in their collective contexts. By constructing meaningfulness and integrating it into their everyday contexts, individuals establish their beliefs, their assumptions, and the understandings of the situations within which they function. Importantly, however, these same meanings, when accepted and agreed upon by a collective of individuals (a society), take on an autonomous reality in the world as social "realities," "facts," and institutions that are maintained over time within this society. That is, subjective meaning constructed by individuals becomes objective social and epistemological "facts" within the society. In effect, the ideas, practices, values, assumptions, and even the institutions of the society, those things accepted as "givens," are constructions that have been established and reified by various social processes and mechanisms.

These same processes operate when institutional and adjunct bodies of knowledge and belief are constructed. Using psychotherapy as an example, Berger and Luckmann discussed how institutional and discipline-specific "realities" are constructed as well. They wrote that, "Since therapy must concern itself with deviations from the 'official definitions' of reality, it must develop a conceptual machinery to account for such deviations and to maintain the realities thus challenged. This requires a body of knowledge that includes a theory of deviance, a diagnostic apparatus, and a conceptual system . . ." (1967, p. 113).

In a similar fashion, the "official definitions," assumptions, and labels used in our related fields of study are also constructed and then mutually agreed upon. As long as the social and institutional "realities" serve our needs and do not

conflict with other social facts and behaviors, we can proceed within our pragmatically constructed reality. The process for accomplishing this task is the thrust
of the Berger and Luckmann text; they analyze the social construction of reality
overall and then demonstrate the impact via numerous specific examples. As they
state, "And in so far as all human knowledge is developed, transmitted and
maintained in social situations, the sociology of knowledge must seek to understand the processes by which this is done in such a way taken-for granted
'reality' congeals for the man in the street" (1967, p. 3). Within this framework,
it is understood that labeling as a process is a conceptual mechanism socially
constructed to accomplish a number of objectives, many of which have been
previously discussed in this chapter.

Those who criticize social constructivism sometimes charge that it denies the
independent reality of anything; that it implies that everything is socially constructed. As O'Connor (1998) states, however, Berger and Luckmann, and other
constructivists, make no such implication. These individuals are not trying to
undermine the physical world or many forms of knowledge; rather, they are trying
to understand the mechanisms that underlie the tendencies and practices of society
and the social world. The recognition and reliance on an external physical reality
can be noted in the following excerpt from *The Social Construction of Reality*:

> Man is biologically predestined to construct and to inhabit a world with others. This
> world becomes for him the dominant and definitive reality. *Its limits are set by nature,*
> but once constructed, this world acts back upon nature. In the *dialectic between nature
> and the socially constructed world* the human organism is itself transformed. In this
> same dialectic man produces reality and thereby produces himself. (Berger &
> Luckmann, 1967, p. 183; emphasis ours)[1]

The process of social construction whereby "facts" and "realities" are created
by the social mechanisms and have an actual impact on the beliefs, assumptions,
and practices of social agencies has been demonstrated in a number of theoretically and research-oriented tests and studies. In *The Social Construction of Literacy*
(Cook-Gumperz, 1986), for example, reality and how it is presented and addressed
in language arts classrooms is examined with a focus on the mechanisms by which
individuals continuously reproduce social order. This affects treatment plans,
pedagogical assumptions, practices, grouping of students, and evaluation. Within
the social constructive framework, learning occurs not by recording information
but by interpreting it. Therefore, instruction must be seen not as direct transmission of knowledge but as a component of the dynamic meaning-making process
(Bruner, 1986, 1991; Cook-Gumperz, 1986; Iran-Nejad, 1995; von Glasersfeld, 1989).
From a constructivist perspective, just as observers construct reality, learners
construct their own knowledge, but always through a dialectic process with their
culture (Airasian & Walsh, 1997; Bruner, 1990; Goodman, 1978; Iran-Nejad, 1995;
von Glasersfeld, 1987).

This focus on the constructive nature of learning has had an important impact
on various facets of education and educationally related fields and it is at the

level of the collective's construction of social reality that the primary implications for education research can be found. For example, issues revolving around what topics and subjects are considered to be most important to teach, what it means to have learned something, who are considered to be the important consumers of education, and how we negotiate the learning process on a daily basis, are all dependent upon our constructive processes (O'Connor, 1998). Mehan, for instance applied a constructivist framework to one of the first detailed analyses of classroom activity. He focused on the impact of social constructivism and ideas and assumptions resulting from it on how lessons and teaching interactions are structured (Mehan, 1979), on the impact of our assumptions and actions, including labeling, on students in special education contexts (Mehan, Hertwick, & Meihls, 1986), and on the construction of learning disability in a special education placement meeting (1996). Similarly, social constructivism has played a role in our changing focus away from behaviorism and toward cognitivism (Danziger, 1990; Mills, 1998; O'Connor, 1998; Shotter, 1993; Shuell, 1986), away from a component-oriented model of literacy instruction (Geekie, Cambourne, & Fitzsimmons, 1999; Goodman, 1994; Smith, 2004; Wells, 1986), and in a current reevaluation of principles underlying special education (Bogdan & Kugelmass, 1984; Dudley-Marling & Dippo, 1995; Gelb & Mizokawa, 1986; Gindis, 1995; Kavale & Forness, 2000; McDermott, 1987; Rogers, 2002).

4.2   Social constructivism and labeling

There are a number of ways that social constructivism is manifested to impact the process of labeling. A brief discussion and several examples will demonstrate the subjective nature of this process.

4.2.1 Medicalization   Perhaps the most salient demonstration of a mechanism of social construction and its impact at the societal level involves what has been termed "medicalization theory" (Williams & Calnan, 1996). This explanatory mechanism involves the impact of society and its values acting through a particular societal institution – medicine – to create new diagnostic categories or to redefine or expand old categories according to current sociocultural values and beliefs (Halpern, 1990; Zola, 1972). In addition to the extension of medical boundaries, in the process of medicalization non-medical problems become defined and labeled as medical problems, usually as disorders or illnesses. For example, over the past 40 years there have been a large number of new medical categories that did not exist before that time. Medical categories and labels like attention-deficit/hyperactivity disorder (ADHD), anorexia, chronic fatigue syndrome, fibromyalgia, and post-traumatic stress disorders have all been established in this time frame and other categories have been redefined to create expansions (Conrad & Potter, 2000; Erchak & Rosenfeld, 1989; Halpern, 1990; Rosenfeld, 1997).

One example of redefinition through medicalization involves cognitive changes associated with high old age. Until a few decades ago, the notion of senility was accepted both socially and medically, and highly "successful" aging, that is, a person living into their eighties or nineties without noticeable deterioration of memory, orientation, or other cognitive skills, was considered the exception rather than the norm. However, a combination of social and medical factors have moved what was formerly understood as senility firmly into the realm of dementia (in public and media discourses more often than not identified with Alzheimer's disease), that is, a disease process, socially constructed as something that is, by definition, not part of "normal" aging (even though the well-established major risk factor for a diagnosis of Alzheimer's disease is old age). While some researchers argue that conflating the low-functioning end of a normal distribution with a genuine disease process may be less than helpful in leading to an understanding of either normal or pathological aging, age-related "dementing" is, in public discourses in the United States and other industrialized nations at present, framed virtually exclusively within a disease model (Fox, 1989; Guendouzi & Müller, 2006; see also Chapter 26).

Conrad and Potter (2000) have provided excellent demonstrations of medicalization for category expansion with Adult ADHD. Their work details a number of societal factors (e.g., emergence of publications aimed at lay readers that heralded the new category, research published with one function but reinterpreted by the media and advocacy groups for their purposes (Zametkin et al., 1990), major news media with their own spin on the issue, popular magazines, organizational stakeholders like Children and Adults with Attention Deficit Disorders (Ch.A.D.D.) and manufacturers of primary drugs for ADHD) to create a perception that is then followed by the medical institutional response. Conrad and Potter detail a set of early claims regarding ADHD in adults that started gaining some attention, and then a strong movement into the public sphere when news organizations began to profile ADHD in adults. Over time, and with the collaboration of sympathetic professionals (Brown, 1995), diagnostic institutionalization occurred through increased attention and support provided by professional publications, research journals, and changes in the medical diagnostic criteria (see below). As detailed by many researchers (Cherkes-Julkowski, Sharp, & Stolzenberg, 1997; Conrad, 1976; Damico & Augustine, 1995; Reid, Maag, & Vasa, 1994; Searight & McLaren, 1998), once the category is institutionalized, the stakeholders then engage in various forms of verification to stabilize this diagnostic category. For example, the condition of Adult ADHD is a convenient way to medicalize academic or occupational underperformance of young adults in a competitive society. In a social context that includes an orientation to drug management of many conditions (Conrad and Potter, 2000, employ the term the "Prozac era"), a focus on genetic foci to explain behavioral and societal tendencies, and the rise of managed care so that a diagnostic label may be needed to receive remuneration for services sought or provided, medicalization is more easily understood.

The problem, of course, is that since this is a constructive process, often more influenced by social rather than biological factors, many of these diagnostic categories may be complicated by ambiguity and subjectivity and this lack of definitional rigor may result in various types of problems. Most relevant to the clinical context is the concern over the authenticity or the construct validity of the various diagnostic categories (see section 2.2). In his book *Illness and Culture in the Postmodern Age*, Morris (1998) has discussed this possibility for a number of illnesses and diagnostic categories. He has suggested that ADHD and some other socially constructed diagnostic categories (e.g., Alexithymia, Gulf War syndrome, chronic fatigue syndrome, multiple personality disorder) may be defined as "postmodern illnesses." This term refers to categories of illness or behavioral states that are vaguely and subjectively defined and that are controversial with regard to their legitimacy as real illnesses. Accordingly, these diagnostic categories often puzzle mainstream medicine, are sensationalized and augmented by the popular media, are confusing to the general public, and have a tendency to be abused (Morris, 1998).

Morris explains this pattern of attention and abuse by suggesting that, rather than being legitimate and objective disease states or disability conditions, these specific illnesses represent changing patterns of human experience and affliction that are shaped by the convergence of biological states, cultural beliefs, and social actions. For example, identification of a child as exhibiting ADHD may often be less the result of a neurological or biological condition and more due to a developing tendency of society to treat teachers' and parents' anxieties regarding childhood by routinely drugging children into good behavior; that is, social control through medication (Damico, Müller, & Ball, 2004). Whether an accurate depiction or not, the constructive nature of these categories and labels cannot be ignored.

The medicalization of social problems is a complex process, rather than a discrete step; it is better conceptualized in terms of degrees of medicalization. Further, this constructive process is usually a collective action. Although various non-professional groups and individuals can propose the creation of new or expanded categories or labels, it usually takes sympathetic professionals for success (Brown, 1995). The final requirement for the establishment and application of socially constructed labels and diagnostic categories does, in fact, rely on professional collaboration and this may be referred to as "legitimization" or "professionalization."

4.2.2 Diagnostic legitimization   The collaborative process of diagnostic legitimization, whether considered a component of medicalization or a separate process in its own right, occurs when professional institutions provide a legitimate cover for the socially constructed categories. Examples of this relevant to our current discussion are some of the diagnostic categories that are enshrined in the American Psychiatric Association's *Diagnostic and Statistical Manual* or the World Health Organization's *International Classification of Diseases*. Once diagnostic legitimization occurs, many lay people and professionals then treat the diagnostic category as an objective "fact" or "reality."

While the American Psychiatric Association's *Diagnostic and Statistical Manual* (DSM) and the World Health Organization's *International Classification of Diseases* (ICD) are often considered as standards for objectivity in medical and behavioral diagnoses – tools that employ rigid standards and objective criteria that are above reproach – many diagnostic categories or labels that are listed and described in the DSM or ICD do not employ objective criteria, nor are they indicators of objective conditions. Rather, like all diagnostic labels, they are social constructions influenced by various social and cultural factors (Coles, 1987; Cooksey & Brown, 1998; Gernsbacher, Dawson, & Goldsmith, 2005; Kroska & Harkness, 2008; Kutchins & Kirk, 1997; Reid & Katsiyannis, 1995; Reid, Maag, & Vasa, 1994; Rutter & Tuma, 1988; Searight & McLaren, 1998). The DSM is a document that has been described as a mechanism that can be used to "secure psychiatric turf" (Kirk & Kutchins, 1992). Numerous researchers have suggested that the DSM is a way of sanctioning the diagnostic categories by providing apparent "objectivity" by using the socially constructed authoritative voice of psychiatry. What is lost in what Cooksey and Brown (1998) referred to as this "diagnostic project" is the reality that the DSM (and ICD) are based upon the same variables that are involved in all social constructions of institutional touchstones: sociocultural values and assumptions, political compromise, scientific evidence, and material for insurance forms.

The subjective and fluid nature of many of these diagnostic categories has been widely discussed in the literature with reference to various diagnostic categories (Aspel, Willis, & Faust, 1998; Augustine & Damico, 1995; Barsky & Boros, 1995; Broom & Woodward, 1996; Brown, 1995; Conrad, 2000; Cooksey & Brown, 1998; Jensen, Mrazek, & Knapp, 1997; Kaufmann, Hallahan, & Lloyd, 1998; Kavale & Forness, 1998; Kirk & Kutchins, 1992; Kutchins & Kirk, 1997; Marshall, 1996; Prior & Sanson, 1986; Reid & Katsiyannis, 1995; Reid, Maag, & Vasa, 1994; Rutter & Tuma, 1988; Scott, 1990). Given recent claims for significant increases in the incidence of autism in the United States, an example for how social construction influences the process of legitimatization in autism and how this very process creates the perception of an "autism epidemic" is especially illustrative (Baker, 2008; Gernsbacher et al., 2005).

Gernsbacher, Dawson, and Goldsmith (2005) convincingly argue that the "autism epidemic" does not really exist, and discuss the role that the DSM and societal influences play in the increased incidence of autism, owing to changes in the DSM diagnostic criteria due to various socially oriented factors, in different editions of this major diagnostic manual. For example, in the DSM-III a diagnosis of autism required satisfying six mandatory criteria ("DSM-III. Diagnostic and Statistical Manual of Mental Disorders," 1980) but in DSM-IV ("DSM-IV. Diagnostic and Statistical Manual of Mental Disorders," 1994) the diagnosis is fulfilled by meeting only 50 percent of 16 optional criteria. Further, the criteria themselves were made more vague and inclusive by changes in the phrasing employed. In the DSM-III one of the criteria was manifestation of "a pervasive lack of responsiveness to other people" (1980, p. 89), while the closest criterion to this in the DSM-IV is that an individual must demonstrate "a lack of spontaneous seeking to share . . . achievements with other people" (1994, p. 70). Similarly, the 1980 mandatory criteria of "gross deficits in language development" and "bizarre responses to various aspects of the environment" were changed to "difficulty sustaining a conversation" and "persistent preoccupation with parts of objects" respectively. Finally, the numbers of diagnostic categories for autism were changed from two in DSM-III (infantile autism and childhood onset pervasive developmental disorders) to five in DSM-IV (autistic disorder, pervasive developmental disorder not otherwise specified, childhood disintegrative disorder, Rhett syndrome, Asperger's disorder). Given these changes to the diagnostic criteria, it is not surprising that there appear to be many more diagnoses of autism over the time period discussed. Indeed, the new and milder categories or variants of autism appear to account for 75 percent of the new diagnoses (Chakrabarti & Fombonne, 2001) and when other socially driven changes (e.g., establishment of threshold and sub-threshold symptoms, a decision to co-diagnose, attempts to identify children at progressively younger ages), are also considered, it is no wonder there appear to be significant increases in incidence. The point, however, is that led by advocacy groups championing more relaxed and inclusive criteria, the "reality" of autism has changed according to social considerations. Discussions on the role of social variables in reconceptualizing autism, its causes, and its incidence may be found in the work of various researchers in the history and epidemiology of autism (Baker, 2008; Fombonne, 2003; Gernsbacher, Dawson, & Goldsmith, 2005; Silverman, 2004).

5 Implications and Conclusion

As professionals, we often operate within our sociocultural milieu without a critical analysis of our practices and the conceptualizations that underlie them. The problem with this, of course, is that we might become blind to our poorly justified practices, or we might ignore new or inconsistent data that could potentially undermine our assumptions about important processes like labeling and its impact on our practices. Since we are agents of our society and, as such, are defined by the same realities, practices, and assumptions as others, this is a natural tendency. Within our sociocultural milieu, however, we must also remember that we fulfill a role as agents of rehabilitation and scholarship. As Brantlinger (1997) has argued, this requires us to be more diligent in how we operate within our sociocultural and political contexts; our priority should not be the sociocultural or epistemological status quo. Rather, our priority should be as advocates and agents of positive change for our patients and clients.

There are at least three implications that should emerge from this realization of our role as advocates when dealing with the social complexity of labeling. First, we should *acknowledge and strive to deal with labels as complex phenomena*. Labels are not simple, direct, or objective. They are powerful sociocultural artifacts that transmit biases, assumptions, and facts. They are also catalysts in the construction of both positive and negative consequences. To effectively elicit the positive consequences and reduce the negative ones, we must recognize the constructive nature of these labels and the fact that they are often context-dependent, and at least partly context-created. For example, a quantifiable impairment such as age-related reduction in hearing (even within "age-normal" limits) may constitute a career-destroying handicap for the conductor of a symphony orchestra, but not for someone in a different walk of life. Consequently, as clinicians we should not simply reify labels and consider them as "absolute," objective categories. Rather, we should carefully consider how important it is to properly identify actual difficulties, determine the severity and context-dependence of the labeled difficulties, and avoid the tendency to label without addressing the complexity and obtaining definite and objective data to support a diagnosis.

Second, we should strive to avoid the most basic negative consequences of labeling that occur when relying solely on the label. Rather, we should strive to *thoroughly describe the difficulties that underlie the label.* This means not only carefully documenting actual behaviors and their impact on the context, but also determining how the context impacts the behaviors and whether there are other emergent factors that must be adequately described and addressed (Perkins, 2005). Rather than orienting to symptoms to determine labels we should orient to the skills, abilities, and strategies that can determine functional adequacy within the relative communicative and learning contexts. Darley (1975) had this in mind when he suggested that, when diagnosing aphasia, we focus on ability not labels, and his chapter "Aphasia without Adjectives" still offers relevant advice nearly 35 years after its publication.

Finally, we must be *circumspect with our current conceptualizations and practices.* By employing a more sociocultural orientation when focusing on diagnosis and labeling, we can turn our analytic powers to the very contexts and assumptions that we often take for granted when working with labels, so that we can better serve the needs of our clients.

The focus of this chapter has been the process of labeling and how it is impacted by sociocultural processes and how, in turn, our practices are then impacted by the labels that we employ. There is, of course, much support in the professional literature for the process of labeling. Such support tends to focus on the positive consequences while downplaying the negative ones. As competent professionals, however, we must consider the potential for both. Certainly, the practicing professional should strive to reduce the negative consequences of labeling whenever possible. As we discussed in an earlier publication (Damico, Müller, & Ball, 2004), we need to be able to contextualize a diagnosis or label, and then we should strive to discover the reality behind the label and the individuality of each client's condition. This will enhance our service delivery in the field of speech and language disorders.

NOTE

1   We may also note in passing that summarizing all of humanity under the label "man" may be considered by many to reflect a social construction of human reality in need of rethinking.

REFERENCES

Abberley, P. (1987). The concept of oppression and the development of a social theory of disability. *Disability, Handicap, & Society* 2 (1), 5–19.

Airasian, P. & Walsh, M. (1997). Constructivist cautions. *Phi Delta Kappan*, February, 444–9.

Apple, M. W. (1982). *Education and power*. Boston, MA: Routledge & Kegan Paul.

Archer, M. & Green, L. (1996). Classification of learning difficulties. In S. Kriegler & P. Englebrecht (eds.), *Perspectives on learning difficulties*. Hartfield, SA: Van Schaik.

Artiles, A. J., Higareda, H., Rueda, R., & Salazar, J. J. (2005). Within-in group diversity in minority disproportionate representation: English language learners in urban school districts. *Exceptional Children* 71.

Artiles, A. J. & Ortiz, A. A. (2002). *English language learners with special education needs: Identification, assessment and instruction*. McHenry, IL: Delta Systems.

Aspel, A. D., Willis, W. G., & Faust, D. (1998). School psychologists' diagnostic decision-making processes: Objective–subjective discrepancies. *Journal of School Psychology* 36, 137–49.

Augustine, L. E. & Damico, J. S. (1995). Attention deficit hyperactivity disorder: The scope of the problem. *Seminars in Speech and Language*.

Baker, J. (2008). Mercury, vaccines, and autism. *American Journal of Public Health* 98 (2), 244–54.

Balint, M. (1957). *The doctor, his patient, and the illness*. New York: International Universities Press.

Barsky, A. & Boros, J. F. (1995). Somatization and medicalization in the era of managed care. *Journal of the American Medical Association* 274, 1931–4.

Berger, P. L. & Luckmann, T. (1967). *The social construction of reality: A treatise in the sociology of knowledge*. New York: Anchor.

Bernstein, B. (1996). *Pedagogy, symbolic control and identity*. London: Taylor & Francis.

Bishop, D. (1989). Autism, Asperger's syndrome and semantic-pragmatic disorder: Where are the boundaries? *British Journal of Disorders of Communication* 24, 107–21.

Bogdan, R. & Kugelmass, J. (1984). Case studies of mainstreaming: A symbolic interactionist approach to special schooling. In L. Barton & S. Tomlinson (eds.), *Special education and social interests* (pp. 173–91). London: Croom Helm.

Bos, C. S. & Richardson, V. (1994). Qualitative research and learning disabilities. In S. Vaughn & C. S. Bos (eds.), *Research issues in learning disabilities* (pp. 178–201). New York: Springer Verlag.

Boxer, R., Challen, M., & McCarthy, M. (1991). Developing an assessment framework: the distinctive contribution of the educational psychologist. *Educational Psychology in Practice, 7,* 30–34.

Bradley, R. H. & Corwyn, R. F. (2002). Socioeconomic status and child development. *Annual Review of Psychology, 53,* 371–99.

Brantlinger, E. (1997). Using ideology: Cases of nonrecognition of the politics of research and practice in special education. *Review of Educational Research* 67 (4), 425–59.

Brechin, A. (1999). Understandings of learning disability. In J. Swain & S. French (eds.), *Therapy and learning difficulties: Advocacy, participation and partnership*. Oxford: Butterworth Heinemann.

Broadfoot, P. (1994). *Educational assessment: The myth of measurement*. Bristol, UK: University of Bristol.

Broadfoot, P. (1996). *Education, assessment and society*. Buckingham, UK: Open University Press.

Broom, D. H. & Woodward, R. V. (1996). Medicalization reconsidered: Toward a collaborative approach to care. *Sociology of Health and Illness* 18, 357–78.

Brown, E., Frederickson, N., Iyadurai, S., Jackson, M., & Kynan, S. (1998). Differences between children with specific learning difficulties (SpLD) and moderate learning difficulties (MLD) on the Phonological Assessment Battery. *Educational and Child Psychology* 15 (4), 18–32.

Brown, P. (1995). Naming and framing: The social construction of diagnosis and illness. *Journal of Health and Social Behavior* (extra issue), 34–52.

Bruner, J. S. (1986). *Actual minds, possible worlds*. Cambridge, MA: Harvard University Press.

Bruner, J. S. (1990). *Acts of meaning*. Cambridge, MA: Harvard University Press.

Bruner, J. S. (1991). The narrative construction of reality. *Critical Inquiry* 18 (Autumn), 1–21.

Bussing, R., Schoenberg, N. E., & Rogers, K. M. (1998). Explanatory models of ADHD: Do they differ by ethnicity, child gender, or treatment status? *Journal of Emotional and Behavioral Disorders* 6, 233–42.

Cacace, A. T. & McFarland, D. J. (1998). Central auditory processing disorder in school-aged children: A critical review. *Journal of Speech, Language, & Hearing Research* 41, 355–73.

Carrier, J. G. (1986). Sociology and special education: Differentiation and allocation in mass education. *American Journal of Education* 94 (3), 281–312.

Carroll, J. B. (1997). Psychometrics, intelligence, and public perception. *Intelligence* 24, 25–52.

Chakrabarti, S. & Fombonne, E. (2001). Pervasive developmental disorders in preschool children. *Journal of American Medical Association* 285, 3093–9.

Cherkes-Julkowski, M., Sharp, S., & Stolzenberg, J. (eds.). (1997). *Rethinking attention deficit disorders*. Cambridge, MA: Brookline Books.

Cole, K., Schwartz, I., Notari, A., Dale, P., & Mills, P. (1995). Examination of the stability of two measures of defining specific language impairment. *Applied Psycholinguistics* 16, 103–23.

Coles, G. (1987). *The learning mystique: A critical look at "learning disabilities."* New York: Pantheon.

Connor, D. (2006). Michael's story: "I get into so much trouble just by walking": Narrative knowing and life at the intersections of learning disability, race, and class. *Equity & Excellence in Education* 39 (2), 154–65.

Connor, D. J. & Ferri, B. A. (2005). Integration and inclusion: A troubling nexus: race, disability, and special education. *The Journal of African American History* 90 (1/2), 107–27.

Conrad, P. (1976). *Identifying hyperactive children: The medicalization of deviant behavior*. Lexington, MA: D.C. Heath.

Conrad, P. (1992). Medicalization and social control. *Annual Review of Sociology* 18, 209–32.

Conrad, P. (2000). Medicalization, genetics, and human problems. In C. Bird, P. Conrad, & A. Fremont (eds.), *The handbook of medical sociology* (pp. 322–33). Upper Saddle River, NJ: Prentice Hall.

Conrad, P. & Potter, D. (2000). From hyperactive children to ADHD adults: Observations on the expansion of medical categories. *Social Problems* 47 (4), 559–82.

Conti-Ramsden, G., Crutchley, A., & Botting, N. (1999). Classification of children with specific language impairment: Longitudinal considerations. *Journal of Speech Language, and Hearing Research* 42, 1195–204.

Cook-Gumperz, J. (ed.). (1986). *The social construction of literacy*. Cambridge: Cambridge University Press.

Cooksey, E. & Brown, P. (1998). Spinning on its axes: DSM and the social construction of psychiatric diagnosis. *International Journal of Health Services* 28, 525–54.

Cronbach, L. J. (1988). Five perspectives on validity argument. In H. Weiner & H. Braun (eds.), *Test validity*. Hillsdale, NJ: Erlbaum.

Cummins, J. (2000). *Language, power and pedagogy: Bilingual children in the crossfire*. Clevedon, UK: Multilingual Matters.

Damico, J. S. (1988). The lack of efficacy in language therapy: A case study. *Language, Speech, and Hearing Services in Schools* 19 (1), 51–66.

Damico, J. S. (1991). Descriptive assessment of communicative ability in limited English proficient students. In E. V. Hamayan & J. S. Damico (eds.), *Limiting bias in the assessment of bilingual students* (pp. 157–218). Austin, TX: PRO-ED.

Damico, J. S. & Augustine, L. E. (1995). Social considerations in the labeling of students as attention deficit hyperactivity disordered. *Seminars in Speech and Language* 16, 259–74.

Damico, J. S. & Johnson, K. (2005). An investigation into the implications of Asperger Syndrome in adolescents, *Annual Meeting of the American Speech-Language-Hearing Association*. San Diego, CA.

Damico, J. S., Müller, N., & Ball, M. J. (2004). Owning up to complexity: A sociocultural orientation to attention deficit hyperactivity disorder. *Seminars in Speech and Language* 25, 277–85.

Danziger, K. (1990). *Constructing the subject: Historical origins of psychological research*. Cambridge: Cambridge University Press.

Darley, F. L. (1975). Aphasia without adjectives. In F. L. Darley (ed.), *Aphasia* (pp. 1–54). Philadelphia: Saunders.

Deyhle, D. (1987). Learning failure: Tests as gatekeepers and the culturally different child. In H. T. Trueba (ed.), *Success or failure? Learning and the language minority student* (pp. 85–108). Cambridge, MA: Newbury House.

DOE. (2002). Twenty-fourth annual report to Congress on the implementation of the Individuals With Disabilities Education Act. Washington, DC: United States Department of Education.

Dollaghan, C. (2004). Taxometric analysis of specific language impairment in 3- and 4-year old children. *Journal of Speech, Language, and Hearing Research* 47, 464–75.

DSM-III. Diagnostic and Statistical Manual of Mental Disorders. (1980). (3rd ed.). Washington, DC: American Psychiatric Association.

DSM-IV. Diagnostic and Statistical Manual of Mental Disorders. (1994). (4th ed.). Washington, DC: American Psychiatric Association.

Dudley-Marling, C. & Dippo, D. (1995). What learning disabilities does: Sustaining the ideology of schooling. *Journal of Learning Disabilities* 28, 408–14.

Eales, M. J. (1993). Pragmatic impairments in adults with childhood diagnoses of autism or developmental receptive language disorder. *Journal of Autism and Developmental Disorders* 23, 593–617.

Erchak, G. M. & Rosenfeld, R. (1989). Learning disabilities, dyslexia, and the medicalization of the classroom. In J. Best (ed.), *Images of Issues*. New York: Aldine de Gruyter.

Fairbanks, C. M. (1992). Labels, literacy, and enabling learning: Glenn's story. *Harvard Educational Review* 62.

Fine, M. (1991). *Framing dropouts: Notes on the politics of an urban public high school*. Albany, NY: State University of New York Press.

Fletcher, J. M., Francis, D. J., Shaywitz, S. E., Lyon, G. R., Foorman, B. R., Stuebing, K. K., et al. (1998). Intelligent testing and the discrepancy model for children with learning disabilities. *Learning Disabilities Research & Practice* 13, 186–203.

Flower, R. M. (1984). *Delivery of speech-language and audiology services*. Baltimore, MD: Williams & Wilkins.

Fombonne, E. (2003). Epidemiological surveys of autism and other pervasive developmental disorders: An update. *Journal of Autism and Developmental Disorders* 33, 365–82.

Forness, S. R. (1976). Behavioristic orientation to categorical labels. *Journal of School Psychology* 14, 90–5.

Foster, G. G., Schmidt, C. R., & Sabatino, D. (1976). Teacher expectancies and the label "Learning Disabilities." *Journal of Learning Disabilities* 9, 111–14.

Fox, P. (1989). From senility to Alzheimer's disease: The rise of the Alzheimer's movement. *Milbank Quarterly* 67, 58–101.

Fraser, L. & Christopher, B. (2007). Is the use of labels in special education helpful? *Support for Learning* 22, 36–42.

Frattura, E. & Capper, C. A. (2006). Segregated programs versus integrated comprehensive service delivery for all learners: Assessing the differences. *Remedial and Special Education* 27 (6), 355–64.

Geekie, P., Cambourne, B., & Fitzsimmons, P. (1999). *Understanding literacy development*. Stoke on Trent, Staffordshire, UK: Trentham Books.

Gelb, S. A. & Mizokawa, D. T. (1986). Special education and social structure: The commonality of "exceptionality." *American Educational Research Journal* 23 (4), 543–57.

Gergen, K. J. & Davis, K. E. (eds.). (1985). *The social construction of the person*. New York: Springer.

Gernsbacher, M. A., Dawson, M., & Goldsmith, H. H. (2005). Three reasons not to believe in an autism epidemic. *Current Directions in Psychological Science* 14 (2), 55–8.

Gill, V. T. & Maynard, D. W. (1995). On "labeling" in actual interaction: Delivering and receiving diagnoses of developmental disabilities. *Social Problems* 42 (1), 11–37.

Gillman, M., Heyman, B., & Swain, J. (2000). What's in a name? The implications of diagnosis for people with learning difficulties and their family carers. *Disability and Society* 15 (3), 389–409.

Gindis, B. (1995). The social/cultural implication of disability: Vygotsky's paradigm for special education. *Educational Psychologist* 30, 77–81.

Gipps, C. (1999). Socio-cultural aspects of assessment. *Review of Research in Education* 24, 355–92.

Glaser, R. & Silver, E. (1994). Assessment, testing, and instruction: Retrospect and prospect. In L. Darling-Hammond (ed.), *Review of research in education* vol. 20 (pp. 393–421). Washington, DC: American Educational Research Association.

Gnys, J. A., Willis, W. G., & Faust, D. (1995). School psychologists' diagnoses of learning disabilities: A study of illusory correlation. *Journal of School Psychology* 33, 59–73.

Goffman, E. (1964). *Stigma: Notes on the management of spoiled identity*. New York: Simon and Schuster, Inc.

Goldstein, H. (1996). Statistical and psychometric models for assessment. In H. Goldstein & T. Lewis (eds.), *Assessment: Problems, developments and statistical issues*. Chichester, UK: Wiley.

Goodman, K. S. (1994). Reading, writing, and written texts: A transactional sociopsycholinguistic view. In R. B. Ruddell, M. R. Ruddell, & H. Singer (eds.), *Theoretical models and processes of reading*, 4th ed. (pp. 1093–130). Newark, DE: International Reading Association.

Goodman, N. (1978). *Ways of world making*. Indianapolis, IN: Hackett Publishing Company.

Gould, S. J. (1996). *The mismeasure of man* (revised and expanded ed.). New York: W.W. Norton & Company.

Greene, M. (1994). Epistemology and educational research: the influence of recent approaches to knowledge. In L. Darling-Hammon (ed.), *Review of research in education*, vol. 20 (pp. 423–64). Washington, DC: American Educational Research Association.

Gross, J. (1994). Asperger syndrome: A label worth having? *Educational Psychology in Practice* 10 (2), 104–10.

Guendouzi, J. A. & Müller, N. (2006). *Approaches to discourse in dementia*. Mahwah, NJ: Lawrence Erlbaum.

Gus, L. (2000). Autism: Promoting peer understanding. *Educational Psychology in Practice*, 16 (4), 461–8.

Gutkin, T. B. & Nemeth, C. (1997). Selected factors impacting decision in prereferral intervention and other school-based teams: Exploring the intersection between school and social psychology. *Journal of School Psychology* 35, 195–216.

Halpern, S. A. (1990). Medicalization as a professional process: Postward trends in pediatrics. *Journal of Health and Social Behavior* 31, 28–42.

Hamayan, E., Marler, B., Sanchez-Lopez, C., & Damico, J. (2007). *Special education considerations for English language learners*. Philadelphia: Caslon Publishing.

Heise, D. R. (2007). *Expressive order: Confirming sentiments in social actions*. New York: Springer.

Hellendoorn, J. & Ruijssenaars, W. (1998). Dutch adults with learning disabilities viewed by themselves. *Thalamus* 16, 65–76.

Higgins, E. L., Raskind, M. H., Goldberg, R. J., & Herman, K. L. (2002). Stages of acceptance of a learning disability: The impact of labeling. *Learning Disability Quarterly* 25 (1), 3–18.

Higgins, P. (1980). *Outsiders in a hearing world: A sociology of deafness*. Beverly Hills, CA: Sage Publications.

Hood, L., McDermott, R., & Cole, M. (1980). "Let's try to make it a good day"

– Some not so simple ways. *Discourse Processes* 3, 155–68.

Iran-Nejad, A. (1995). Constructivism as substitute for memorization in learning: Meaning is created by learner. *Education* 116, 16–31.

Irvine, S. H. & Berry, J. W. (1988). The abilities of mankind: A revaluation. In S. H. Irvine & J. W. Berry (eds.), *Human abilities in cultural context* (pp. 3–59). Cambridge: Cambridge University Press.

Jensen, P. S., Mrazek, M. D., & Knapp, P. K. (1997). Evolution and revolution in child psychiatry: ADHD as a disorder of adaptation. *Journal of the American Academy of Child and Adolescent Psychiatry* 36, 1672–9.

Kaufmann, J. M., Hallahan, D. P., & Lloyd, J. W. (1998). Politics, science, and the future of learning disabilities. *Learning Disabilities Quarterly* 21, 276–80.

Kavale, K. A. & Forness, S. R. (1998). The politics of learning disabilities. *Learning Disabilities Quarterly* 21, 245–73.

Kavale, K. A. & Forness, S. R. (2000). Policy decisions in special education: The role of meta-analysis. In R. Gersten, E. P. Schiller, & S. Vaughn (eds.), *Contemporary special education research: Synthesis of the knowledge base on critical instructional issues* (pp. 281–326). Mahway, NJ: Lawrence Erlbaum Associates.

Kelly, N. & Norwich, B. (2004). Pupils' perceptions of self and of labels: Moderate learning difficulties in mainstream and special schools. *British Journal of Educational Psychology* 74 (3), 411–35.

Kirk, S. A. & Kutchins, H. (1992). *The selling of DSM: The rhetoric of science in psychiatry*. New York: Aldine de Gruyter.

Klasen, H. (2000). A name, what's in a name? The medicalization of hyperactivity revisited. *Harvard Review of Psychiatry* 7, 334–44.

Kliewer, C., Biklen, D., & Kasa-Hendrickson, C. (2006). Who may be literate? Disability and resistance to the cultural denial of competence. *American Educational Research Journal* 43 (2), 163–92.

Kretschmer, R. E. (1991). Exceptionality and the limited English proficient student: Historical and practical contexts. In E. V. Hamayan & J. S. Damico (eds.), *Limiting bias in the assessment of bilingual students* (pp. 1–38). Austin, TX: PRO-ED.

Kroska, A. & Harkness, S. K. (2008). Exploring the role of diagnosis in the modified labeling theory of mental illness. *Social Psychology Quarterly* 71 (2), 193–208.

Kutchins, H., & Kirk, S. A. (1997). *Making us crazy: DSM: The psychiatric bible and the creation of mental disorders*. New York: The Free Press.

Leyens, J. P., Yzerbyt, V., & Schadron, G. (1994). *Stereotypes and social cognition*. London: Sage.

Link, B. G., Cullen, F. T., Struening, E., Shrout, P. E., & Dohrenwend, B. P. (1989). A modified labeling theory approach to mental disorders: An empirical assessment. *American Sociological Review* 54, 400–23.

Livneh, H. & Antonak, R. F. (1991). Temporal structure of adaptation to disability. *Rehabilitation Counseling Bulletin* 34, 298–319.

Livneh, H. & Evans, J. (1984). Adjusting to disability: Behavioral correlates and intervention strategies. *Personnel and Guidance Journal* 62, 363–5.

Lohman, D. (1997). Lessons from the history of intelligence testing. *International Journal of Educational Research* 27, 359–77.

Loseke, D. R. (1999). *Thinking about social problems*. New York: Aldine de Gruyter.

Lubinski, D. (2000). Scientific and social significance of assessing individual differences: Sinking shafts at a few critical points. *Annual Review of Psychology* 51, 405–44.

Lubinski, D. & Humphreys, L. G. (1997). Incorporating general intelligence into epidemiology and the social sciences. *Intelligence* 24, 159–201.

MacMillan, D. L. & Meyers, C. E. (1979). Educational labeling of handicapped learners. *Review of Research in Education* 7, 151–94.

MacWhinney, B. (ed.) (1998). *The emergence of language*. Mahwah, NJ: Erlbaum.

Madon, S., Hilbert, G. S., Kyriakatos, E., & Vogel, D. (2006). Stereotyping the stereotypic: When individuals match social stereotypes. *Journal of Applied Social Psychology* 36 (1), 178–205.

Magnuson, K. A. & Waldfogel, J. (2005). Early childhood care and education: Effects on ethnic and racial gaps in school readiness. *The Future of Children* 15, 169–96.

Marshall, H. H. (1996). Implications of differentiating and understanding constructivist approaches. *Educational Psychologist* 31, 235–40.

McDermott, R. (1987). Achieving school failure: An anthropological approach to illiteracy and social stratification. In G. D. Spindler (ed.), *Education and cultural process. Anthropological approaches*, 2nd ed. (pp. 173–209). Prospect, IL: Waveland Press.

McDermott, R. (1993). The acquisition of a child by a learning disability. In S. Chaiklin & J. Lave (eds.), *Understanding practice* (pp. 269–305). New York: Cambridge University Press.

McDermott, R. & Varenne, H. (1995). Culture as disability. *Anthropology & Education Quarterly* 26, 324–48.

McNamara, B. E. (1998). *Learning disabilities: Appropriate practices for a diverse population*. Albany, NY: State University of New York Press.

Mehan, H. (1979). *Learning lessons. Social organization in the classroom*. Cambridge, MA: Harvard University.

Mehan, H. (1996). The construction of an LD student: A case study in the politics of representation. In M. Silverstein &

G. Urban (eds.), *Natural histories of discourse* (pp. 253–76). Chicago: University of Chicago Press.

Mehan, H., Hertwick, A., & Meihls, J. L. (1986). *Handicapping the handicapped: Decision making in students' educational careers*. Palo Alto, CA: Stanford University Press.

Messick, S. (1980). Test validity and the ethics of assessment. *American Psychologist* 35, 1012–27.

Messick, S. (1984). The psychology of educational measurement. *Journal of Educational Measurement* 21, 215–37.

Mills, J. A. (1998). *Control: A history of behavioral psychology*. New York: New York University Press.

Morris, D. (1998). *Illness and culture in the postmodern age*. Berkeley, CA: University of California Press.

Nelson, K. (2003). The emergence of a consciousness of self. In G. D. Fireman, J. McVay, T. E. & O. J. Flanagan (eds.), *Narrative and consciousness. Literature, psychology, and the brain* (pp. 17–36). Oxford: Oxford University Press.

O'Connor, C. & Fernandez, S. D. (2006). Race, Class, and disproportionality: Reevaluating the relationship between poverty and special education placement. *Educational Researcher* 35 (6), 6–11.

O'Connor, M. C. (1998). Can we trace the "efficacy of social constructivism"? *Review of Research in Education* 23, 25–71.

Ogbu, J. (1978). *Minority education and caste: The American system in cross-cultural perspective*. New York: Academic Press.

Ogbu, J. U. & Simons, H. (1998). Voluntary and involuntary implications for education. *Anthropology & Education Quarterly* 29 (2), 155–88.

Pena, E., Spaulding, T., & Plante, E. (2006). The composition of normative groups and diagnostic decision making: Shooting ourselves in the foot. *American Journal of Speech-Language Pathology* 15, 247–54.

Perkins, M. R. (2005). Pragmatic ability and disability as emergent phenomena. *Clinical Linguistics and Phonetics* 19, 367–78.

Piaget, J. (1970). *Genetic epistemology*. New York: W.W. Norton & Company.

Prior, M. & Sanson, A. (1986). Attention deficit disorder with hyperactivity: A critique. *Journal of Child Psychology and Psychiatry* 27, 307–19.

Rapley, M. (2004). *The social construction of intellectual disability*. Cambridge: Cambridge University Press.

Reid, R. & Katsiyannis, A. (1995). Attention deficit/hyperactivity disorder and section 504. *Remedial and Special Education* 16, 44–52.

Reid, R., Maag, J. W. & Vasa, S. F. (1994). Attention deficit hyperactivity disorder as a disability category: A critique. *Exceptional Children* 60, 198–214.

Reissman, C. (1983). Women and medicalization: A new perspective. *Social Policy* 14, 3–18.

Richardson, J. G. & Parker, T. L. (1993). The institutional genesis of special education: The American case. *American Journal of Education* 101 (4), 359–92.

Riddick, B. (2000). An examination of the relationship between labeling and stigmatisation with special reference to dyslexia. *Disability and Society* 15 (4), 653–67.

Rogers, R. (2002). Through the eyes of the institution: A critical discourse analysis of decision making in two special education meetings. *Anthropology & Education Quarterly* 33, 213–37.

Rolison, M. A. & Medway, F. J. (1985). Teachers' expectations and attributions for student achievement: Effects of label performance pattern, and special education intervention. *American Educational Research Journal* 22, 561–73.

Rosenfeld, S. (1997). Labeling mental illness: The effects of received services and perceived stigma on life satisfaction. *American Sociological Review* 62, 660–72.

Ruiz-de-Velasco, J. & Fix, M. (2000). *Overlooked and underserved: Immigrant students in U.S. secondary schools.* Washington, DC: The Urban Institute.

Rutter, M. & Tuma, A. H. (1988). Diagnosis and classification: Some outstanding issues. In M. Rutter, A. H. Tuma, & I. S. Lann (eds.), *Assessment and diagnosis in child psychopathology* (pp. 437–52). New York: Guilford.

Schuster, T. L. & Butler, E. W. (1986). Labeling, mild mental retardation, and long-range social adjustment. *Sociological Perspectives* 29 (4), 461–83.

Scott, W. J. (1990). PTSD in DSM–III: A case of the politics of diagnosis and disease. *Social Problems* 37, 294–310.

Searight, H. R. & McLaren, A. L. (1998). Attention-deficit hyperactivity disorder: The medicalization of misbehavior. *Journal of Clinical Psychology in Medical Settings* 5, 467–95.

Shotter, J. (1993). *Conversational realities. Constructing life through language.* Thousand Oaks, CA: Sage Publications.

Shuell, T. J. (1986). Cognitive conceptions of learning. *Review of Educational Research* 56, 411–36.

Silverman, C. (2004). "A disorder of affect: Love, tragedy, biomedicine, and citizenship in American autism research." Unpublished PhD dissertation, University of Pennsylvania, Philadelphia.

Skrtic, T. M. (1991). The special education paradox. *Harvard Educational Review* 61, 148–206.

Sleeter, C. E. (1996). Radical structuralist perspectives on the creation and use of learning disabilities. In T. M. Skrtic (ed.), *Disability and democracy: Reconstructing (special) education for postmodernity* (pp. 153–65). New York: Teachers College Press.

Smith, F. (2004). *Understanding reading. A psycholinguistic analysis of reading and learning to read*, 6th ed. Mahwah, NJ: Lawrence Erlbaum Associates.

Snyderman, M. & Rothman, S. (1987). Survey of expert opinion on intelligence and aptitude testing. *American Psychologist* 42, 137–44.

Sternberg, R. J. & Grigorenko, E. L. (2002). Difference scores in the identification of children with learning disabilities: It's time to use a different method. *Journal of School Psychology* 40, 65–83.

Sutcliffe, J. & Simons, K. (1993). *Self-advocacy and people with learning difficulties.* Leicester: NIACE.

Thelen, E. & Smith, L. (1998). Dynamic system theories. In R. M. Lerner (ed.), *Handbook of child psychology: Vol. 1: Theoretical models of human development*, 5th ed. (pp. 563–634). New York: Wiley.

Thoits, P. A. (2005). Differential labeling of mental illness by social status: A new look at an old problem. *Journal of Health and Social Behavior* 46 (1), 102–19.

Thompkins, C. A., Marshall, R. C., & Phillips, D. S. (1980). Aphasic patients in a rehabilitation program: Scheduling speech and language services. *Archives of Physical Medicine and Rehabilitation* 61, 252–4.

Trent, S. C., Artiles, A. J., & Englert, C. S. (1998). From deficit thinking to social constructivism: A review of theory, research, and practice in special education. *Review of Research in Education* 23, 277–307.

Trueba, H. T. (1988). Culturally-based explanations of minority students' academic achievement. *Anthropology & Education Quarterly* 19, 270–87.

Ukrainetz McFadden, T. (1996). Creating language impairments in typically achieving children: The pitfalls of normal normative sampling. *Language, Speech and Hearing Services in Schools* 27, 3–9.

van Geert, P. (1998). A dynamic systems model of basic developmental mechanisms: Piaget, Vygotsky, and beyond. *Psychological Review* 104, 634–77.

von Glasersfeld, E. (1987). Learning as a constructive activity. In C. Janvier (ed.), *Problems of representation in the teaching and learning of mathematics* (pp. 3–18). Hillsdale, NJ: Erlbaum.

von Glasersfeld, E. (1989). Cognition, construction of knowledge, and teaching. *Synthese* 80, 121–40.

Vygotsky, L. S. (1978). *Mind in Society: The development of higher psychological processes*. Cambridge, MA: Harvard University Press.

Weaver, C. (1998). Reconceptualizing reading and dyslexia. In C. Weaver (ed.), *Practicing what we know. Informed reading instruction* (pp. 292–324). Urbana, IL: National Council of Teachers of English.

Wells, G. (1986). *The meaning makers. Children learning language and using language to learn*. Portsmouth, NH: Heinemann.

Wentzel, K. R. & Wigfield, A. (1998). Academic and social motivational influences on students' academic performance. *Educational Psychology Review* 10, 155–75.

Wilkinson, C. Y. & Ortiz, A. A. (1986). *Characteristics of limited English proficient learning disabled Hispanic students at initial assessment and at reevaluation*. Austin, TX: Handicapped Minority Research Institute on Language Proficiency.

Williams, S. J. & Calnan, M. (1996). The "limits" of medicalization: Modern medicine and the lay populace in "late modernity." *Social Science and Medicine* 42, 1609–20.

Wilson, J. (2000). "Learning difficulties," "disability" and "special needs": Some problems of partisan conceptualisation. *Disability and Society* 15 (5), 817–24.

Zametkin, A. J., Nordahl, T. E., Gross, M., King, A. C., Semple, W. E., Rumsley, J., et al. (1990). Cerebral glucose metabolism in adults with hyperactivity of childhood onset. *New England Journal of Medicine* 323, 1361–6.

Zola, I. K. (1972). Medicine as an institution of social control. *Sociological Review* 20, 487–504.

2 Diversity Considerations in Speech and Language Disorders

BRIAN A. GOLDSTEIN AND
RAMONDA HORTON-IKARD

1 Introduction

Individuals from culturally and linguistically diverse (CLD) populations are at risk for both over- and under-identification of speech and language disorders (Roseberry-McKibbin, 2002). They are at risk for over- and under-identification because (1) there is a lack of valid and reliable assessment tools; (2) the data on individuals from CLD populations (in comparison to monolingual speakers from Anglo-European backgrounds) are relatively sparse; (3) there is a lack of speech-language pathologists (SLPs) who have received specific and in-depth pre-service training in such individuals; and (4) few SLPs in the USA (the perspective of this chapter) speak a language in addition to English (e.g., in 2002, only 2,548 ASHA-certified SLPs in the USA designated themselves as bilingual; Beverly-Ducker, personal communication in Roseberry-McKibbin, Brice, & O'Hanlon, 2005). These factors result in SLPs potentially misdiagnosing speech and language disorders in CLD populations. Additionally, an inappropriate assessment could lead to unnecessary intervention services or inappropriate intervention goals.

The purpose of this chapter is to outline the influence of cultural and linguistic diversity on speech and language disorders. To demonstrate how cultural and linguistic diversity influences speech and language disorders, we will focus on the following topics: culture and communication, language variation, language difference vs. language disorder, culture and disability, least-biased assessment, and appropriate intervention. Prior to embarking on this purpose, it is necessary to define *diversity*. The term "diversity" can imply a number of correlates to speech and language disorders (and development). It can refer to gender, race, ethnicity, socioeconomic status and so on. For the purpose of this chapter, however, we are using the term to refer to two specific groups in the USA: (1) speakers of African-American English and (2) speakers who are acquiring a language other than or in addition to English. Some readers (understandably) may take issue with our rather narrow meaning of the term. We are construing the term narrowly because of the relatively large literature on the speech and language development and

The Handbook of Language and Speech Disorders, First Edition. Edited by Jack S. Damico, Nicole Müller, and Martin J. Ball. © 2013 Blackwell Publishing Ltd except for editorial material and organization © 2013 Jack S. Damico, Nicole Müller, Martin J. Ball. Published 2013 by Blackwell Publishing Ltd.

disorders of these groups. Despite the relatively narrow definition of diversity, the issues discussed here have implications beyond these groups.

2 Culture and Communication

According to Anderson and Fenichal (1989), culture is "[t]he totality of socially transmitted behavior patterns, arts, beliefs, institutions, and all other products of human work and thought . . . The predominating attitudes and behaviors that characterize the functioning of a group or organization . . . the cultural framework must be viewed as a set of tendencies of possibilities from which to choose" (p. 8). Speech and language acquisition does not occur in a vacuum but is mediated by the culture from which the child comes. This environment is defined broadly and includes, but is not limited to, parents, siblings, extended family members, peers, teachers, and so on.

Beliefs about communication by these stakeholders may vary across a number of dimensions. Van Kleek (1994) indicates that individuals' beliefs about communicating with their children differ in terms of amount of talk, how teaching takes place, who initiates and directs adult–child interactions, whether parents adapt to children or vice versa, language acquisition (direct facilitation, observation, etc.), and who clarifies when the child is not understood. For example, some families may consider it appropriate to limit verbal interactions between adults and children (e.g., Heath, 1983; Joe & Malach, 2004). Thus, it may be culturally inappropriate for SLPs to ask parents to engage in 10 minutes of free play with their children during an evaluation, because some parents may view this request as unsuitable. This does not mean that there is no verbal inter-action between those adults and their children, but it indicates that the interaction may not be of the variety that many SLPs expect from parents and their children. Likewise, some parents may not see their roles as teachers in the "academic" sense of the word (e.g., Kayser, 1998). That function, many believe, should be left to the formal educational system. Thus, some parents may not be comfortable in serving in that capacity even at the request of a well-meaning SLP. SLPs, then, must work toward cultural understanding by identifying the cultural values in understanding student performance and behavior, determining whether the family values these assumptions, acknowledging and respecting cultural differences, and adapting their cultural values to those of the families they serve (Kalyanpur & Harry, 1999).

The influence of culture continues into school as well. Because children bring to school certain skills that influence communication and then teachers place certain communicative demands on children, a mismatch may occur if the child's communication skills do not meet the teacher's expectations (Iglesias, 1985). Therefore, SLPs must work with children (and their parents) to understand the communication patterns of the classroom. The interaction between culture and communication may include linguistic, sociocultural and sociolinguistic, and training barriers that preclude least-biased assessment and intervention.

An obvious barrier between a client/family and the SLP is dialects and/or languages of the client/family that clinicians do not speak or use. The SLP will need to prepare for delivering culturally appropriate and relevant services. Service delivery that considers the cultural background of the client/family will aid in limiting biases that might be present during the clinical management process (e.g., Goldstein, 2000; Harbin & Hartley, 1978; Roseberry-McKibbin, 2002). These authors argue that it is critical that service providers understand the dialect and language(s) spoken by their clients/families and prepare accordingly.

3   Language Variation

The English language is one in which there exist numerous varieties within the oral system. However, until fairly recently, the treatment of linguistic variation within the context of English language development was a phenomenon relatively ignored. For child language researchers, variation represented a type of noise that could potentially wreak havoc with notions of linguistic universals and characterizations of the normal pathway to English language development (Stockman, 1996). Today, it is recognized that variation due to sociocultural factors does not negate universals. In addition, the politics concerning language use in the USA has made it necessary for linguists to understand the nature of the type of linguistic variation associated with dialect use. US society operates from a system of diglossia. "Diglossia" is a term which implies that two different linguistic varieties of a language are assigned different levels of social status (Ferguson, 1959). In the USA, Standard American English (SAE) is the high status dialect of English, with other vernaculars having been characterized as low status. However, the status and prestige allocated to any dialect of the English language has more to do with who speaks the variety, rather than any linguistic characteristics that might make it a "better" variety. In fact, a great deal of linguistic research within the past 20 years indicates that many non-mainstream varieties of the English language incorporate a systematic and structurally defined organization that is characteristic of mainstream varieties (Wolfram & Schilling-Estes, 1998).

African-American English (AAE) is an example of a non-mainstream dialect of English that has been shown to be systematic and rule governed (Wolfram, Adger, & Christian, 1999). AAE is often cited as one of the most frequently studied varieties of the English language (Baugh, 1999; Crystal, 2001). AAE is also one of the few vernaculars of English in which researchers have been able to characterize observable linguistic patterns and behaviors in child speakers (Stockman, 1996; Washington & Craig, 1994). Investigations on child use of AAE have had a tremendous impact on how psychologists, educators, and linguists characterize the language and literacy development of African-American children (Green, 2002). One primary reason is that, historically, children who used non-mainstream dialects were often misdiagnosed as having a language disorder. In addition, as a unique resource for many classroom teachers, many SLPs have often been placed in the position of educating their colleagues on how language development and linguistic variation might influence the academic success of their students. For these reasons alone, it is important that SLPs continue to receive training and educate themselves on language variation in order to provide effective services to culturally and linguistically diverse populations. SLPs who work with speakers of non-mainstream dialects can do an effective job of providing appropriate services by:

- recognizing dialect specific features used by their clients;
- understanding the nature of language development in children who use a non-mainstream dialect;
- being familiar with assessment strategies that have proven to be especially helpful in evaluating the language performance of non-mainstream dialect users.

The use of non-mainstream dialect by individuals between early childhood and adolescence has been well documented (Horton-Ikard & Miller, 2004; Horton-Ikard & Ellis Weismer, 2005; Isaacs, 1996; Pollack & Meredith, 2001; Stockman, 1996; Washington & Craig, 1994). Parents and adult caregivers shape the linguistic environment of their children simply by using the language of their community. As such, the use of non-mainstream dialect by children is not especially surprising. What is noteworthy is that, although children will adopt the linguistic system of their adult language models, the manner in which they do so produces specific dialectal patterns that may not be seen in the adult version of the dialect. For example, African-American children may produce up to 30 specific forms associated with use of AAE (Craig et al., 2003; Washington & Craig, 1994, 2002). Furthermore, child AAE speakers frequently produce a variety of non-mainstream forms that may not appear in adult descriptions of AAE. Washington and Craig (1994) found that there were several AAE structures that have been identified in adult descriptions that were not used by children 4 to 6 years of age (e.g., remote past "been" in the following sentence: "He BIN ate it" for "He ate it a long time ago"). At the same time, there were forms used by children, such as double modal auxiliary (e.g., "He might can come"), that are not present in adult AAE speech. Oetting and colleagues have also documented that the use of non-mainstream dialect occurs in young children who use other non-mainstream varieties of English, including Southern White English (Oetting, Cantrell, & Horohov, 1999; Oetting & McDonald, 2001, 2002). Speech-language pathologists have a number of resources available to them that will help in recognizing and knowing dialect features of the individuals they serve.

It is important that SLPs not only be able to recognize specific features of a non-mainstream dialect, but that they also understand how general linguistic processes and linguistic variation (dialect use) will interact to create similarities and differences in the development of language. Horton-Ikard and Ellis Weismer (2005) found that dialectal and developmental factors influenced African-American children's early language productions. African-American toddlers, from AAE backgrounds, who were $2\frac{1}{2}$ years of age, produced comparable quantities of non-mainstream speech and language to their $2\frac{1}{2}$-year-old Caucasian peers, from SAE backgrounds. In addition, the amount of non-mainstream speech produced by $3\frac{1}{2}$-year-old African-American toddlers was comparable to the amount of non-mainstream speech/language produced by their younger AAE peers. Perhaps one of the most interesting results from this study was the finding that African-American children from AAE backgrounds demonstrate a very different developmental pathway for acquiring the English language, which seems to be linked to their exposure to AAE. In particular, while older African-American toddlers from AAE backgrounds were increasing their use of non-mainstream speech/language, Caucasian toddlers from SAE-speaking backgrounds were decreasing their use of non-mainstream speech/language. Such a finding has implications for the way in which SLPs assess grammatical development.

Traditionally, it has been established that by the end of the preschool years the mastery of morphological inflections is complete (Brown, 1973; Lahey et al., 1992). The speech-language pathologist who is not aware of such differences in development might believe that the language of a child who uses a great deal of AAE speech is impaired. At the same time, exposure to literacy activities seems to initiate a decline in the use of non-mainstream speech, such that by first grade there is a marked decrease in the use of AAE forms (Craig & Washington, 2004). A second noticeable decrease in the use of AAE occurs around grade three (Craig et al., 2003). In this instance, the speech-language pathologist should be aware of such developmental milestones, as this may play a significant role in how the linguistic competence of AAE speakers is assessed. Other studies have also indicated that the linguistic complexity of speech produced by child AAE speakers interacts with their amount of AAE use. For example Craig and Washington (1995) found that among preschoolers, those children who were high users of AAE were also those who were more linguistically mature. Findings from the National Association of Educational Progress also indicate that even the linguistically complex language produced by adolescent speakers of AAE is linked to their willingness to still use AAE during literacy tasks (Smitherman, 1991, 2000).

Once SLPs are familiar with dialect-specific features of their client population and have gathered knowledge about the interaction of general linguistic processes and dialect variation, they should begin to implement the use of alternative and supplemental procedures to standardized testing. There is overwhelming evidence that the use of standardized tests alone to assess language performance will result in the over-identification and misdiagnosis of language impairment in children who use a non-mainstream dialect (Champion et al., 2003; Qi et al., 2006; Washington & Craig, 1999; Williams & Wang, 1997). SLPs who work with children who use non-mainstream dialects must be willing to incorporate diverse strategies into their assessment protocols. Alternatives or supplements to standardized testing for non-mainstream dialect users include the use of language sample analysis procedures that focus on a variety of linguistic behaviors.

Contrastive and non-contrastive analyses can be completed with or without formalized language sample procedures. These analyses have been advocated for use by SLPs who work with non-mainstream dialect users of any age

(Bland-Stewart, 2005; McGregor et al., 1997; Seymour, Bland-Stewart, & Green, 1998). Contrastive and non-contrastive analysis allows the SLP who is unfamiliar with a specific dialect to examine grammatical and phonological productions produced during naturalistic speech contexts. The SLP uses a list of dialect features (e.g., Washington & Craig, 1994) to separate out those features that are consistent with the targeted dialect from those that are indicative of a language disorder (i.e., variable copula absence vs. inappropriate conjunction use).

Stockman (1996) has suggested that the use of a minimal core competency (MCC) may be an effective tool for differentiating language difference from language delay in young preschoolers. The competency is premised on the assumption that there is a minimal set of phonological, morphological, semantic, syntactic, and pragmatic features that all children, regardless of dialect use, should be capable of producing during naturalistic contexts. The MCC represents "the least amount of knowledge a child may exhibit to be judged as normal in a given age range" (Stockman, 1996, p. 358). Preliminary data indicate that the MCC is a useful tool for screening language delay in 3-year-olds from non-mainstream backgrounds (Schraeder et al., 1999).

A third type of assessment tool that uses language sample analysis that has proven to be useful for identifying language disorders is the evaluation of complex sentence production. Washington and Craig (1998) determined that the frequency of complex syntax produced by preschoolers is age or grade sensitive. In addition, these researchers determined that frequency of complex syntax remains relatively unaffected by the use of AAE dialect. Children with primary or secondary language impairment have deficits in their use of complex sentence structures (Craig & Washington, 2000). All of these characteristics recommend complex syntax indices as a viable option for use with children who use any non-mainstream dialect.

4 Bilingualism and Multilingualism

Speakers vary not only by the number of dialects that they speak but also by the number of languages they speak. The majority of the world's countries are at least bilingual and many are multilingual (Linguistic Society of America, 1996), as exemplified by the facts that almost 60 percent of Europeans have learned a second language and the European Union has more official languages than the United Nations (Sollors, 1998). As indicated previously, relatively few SLPs in the USA speak more than one language. Thus, their ability to provide appropriate services to bilinguals will be a challenge. In order to provide appropriate services, SLPs should note the language history of clients and their families. Bilinguals traditionally have been placed into one of two categories: (1) simultaneous bilinguals are individuals who acquire both languages from birth, and (2) sequential bilinguals are those who acquire a second language after the first. It has been difficult to define these terms precisely (Goldstein, 2004a). That is, there is not agreement in terms of the age at which a child should be considered a simultaneous or sequential bilingual. Some believe children should be considered simultaneous bilinguals only if they are in a bilingual environment from birth (e.g., de Houwer, 1990). Others maintain that the age of 3 is the threshold to distinguish between the groups (e.g., McLaughlin, 1978).

It is less important to place bilingual children into one of two categories but more important to describe their linguistic environment and chart how it changes over time. That environment should be described in terms of input (the amount of time each language is heard), output (the amount of time each language is used), use (with whom each language is spoken), and proficiency (how well each language is spoken). It is likely that these values will change over time given varying linguistic demands (e.g., Kohnert & Bates, 2002). For example, the input and output of some children in the United States may be Cantonese-only until they go to school where English will be introduced. For other children, hearing and using Cantonese and English at home and in the community will be typical. Regardless of the linguistic environment, it is clear that for bilingual children language skills are distributed across the two languages. That is, bilingual children will not have identical linguistic knowledge in both languages (see Goldstein, 2004b for a detailed treatment of this issue). For example, Peña, Bedore, and Rappazzo (2003) found that 4;5 to 7;0-year-old Spanish–English bilingual children showed higher-level skills on certain expressive language tasks (e.g., indicating the function of items) in Spanish but greater skill on certain receptive language skills (e.g., knowledge of similarities and differences) in English. It is important to note that this type of differentiation of skills by language is likely to change over time. Kohnert and colleagues, for example, have examined labeling skills in bilingual students from age 5 to college age and found that, over time, the participants showed greater gains in English than in Spanish (Kohnert, Bates, & Hernandez, 1999; Kohnert & Bates, 2002).

Research on typically developing bilingual children also indicates that their development is similar, although not identical to monolingual peers (e.g., Goldstein, 2006). For example, lexical skill in bilingual children has been shown to be similar to that of their monolingual counterparts, as long as vocabulary items in each language are considered (Marchman, Martínez-Sussman, & Price, 2000). Counting vocabulary items in one language only will result in the lexical skills seeming dissimilar to monolinguals. Moreover, the majority of vocabulary items in a bilingual child's lexicon will be unique to that language. For example, Peña, Bedore, and Zlatic-Giunta (2002) found that the majority of the vocabulary items (approximately 70 percent) produced by 44 Spanish–English bilingual children aged 4;5–7;1 were unique to each language. Similarity in the phonological and morphosyntactic skills between monolingual and bilingual children has also been found. That is, bilingual children go through the same stages and at the same rate as their monolingual counterparts (e.g., Genesee, Paradis, & Crago, 2004; Goldstein, Fabiano, & Washington, 2005).

The bilingual children involved in the studies recounted above were generally those who were acquiring both languages from birth. For children acquiring a second language once entering school, Hearne (2000) outlined a series of stages these children are likely to go through. Stage I, the Pre-production stage, occurs during the first three months or so of second language exposure. It can be characterized by a silent period and a time when children are focusing on comprehension (Tabors, 1997). Stage II, the Early Production stage, occurs 3–6 months after second language exposure. During this stage, children are still focusing on comprehension; however, in terms of expressive language, they are using one- to three-word phrases and may be using formulaic expressions (e.g., "gimme five").

Stage III, Speech Emergence, occurs from 6 months to 2 years after initial second language exposure. During this time period, children show increased comprehension and use simple sentences by expanding vocabulary, although grammatical errors are common. Finally, Stage IV, Intermediate Fluency, occurs 2–3 years after the introduction of the second language. In this stage, children exhibit improved comprehension, adequate face-to-face conversational skills, more extensive vocabulary, and few grammatical errors. It is at this final stage that these children exhibit adequate basic communication skills (i.e., Basic Interpersonal Communication Skills) (Cummins, 1984). However, they still may not have the language skills necessary to succeed in a decontextualized academic environment (i.e., Cognitive Academic Language Proficiency) (Cummins, 1984).

Evidence for the claims about the language skills of bilingual children recounted above comes from typically developing children acquiring more than one language. There is relatively little research examining the language skills of bilingual children with communication disorders. Existing studies show that the prevalence of language disorders is no higher in bilingual children than it is for monolinguals (Paradis, 2005). Additionally, bilingual children with language disorders seem to exhibit similar errors compared to their monolingual counterparts (Gutiérrez-Clellen, Restrepo, Silva, & Del Castillo, 2000 in Restrepo & Gutiérrez-Clellen, 2004; Paradis et al., 2003).

Despite the similarity of language skills between monolingual and bilingual children with language disorders, there is evidence that typically developing bilingual children who are in environments in which both languages are not supported are at risk for the diminution of language skills. Anderson (2004) distinguishes between language shift, language loss, and language attrition. Language shift is "a pattern of language use where the relative prominence or use of the two languages changes across time and across generations" (p. 188). That is, over time the prominence of the community's native language decreases and the importance of the "majority" language increases across a variety of communication settings. This type of language shift is gradual and takes place over generations. For example, by the third generation for immigrant populations, many individuals show fluency only in the majority language but not in the language of the first generation (Anderson, 2004).

Language loss, however, is a rapid decrease of language skills within a generation that takes place in the native language. Language loss describes skills that "change towards earlier linguistic forms, thus the use of the term *loss*. In this context, then, the child evidences reduction in linguistic skill in the L1, as compared to his/her skill at a previous time" (Anderson, 2004, p. 190). Language attrition describes a phenomenon in which the children neither lose nor gain skills in their native language. That is, there may be specific skills that do not develop in ways that are commensurate with monolingual peers (Anderson, 2004). For example, lexical and morphological skills (e.g., deletion of morphological markers, decreased number of different words, increased number of false starts, pauses, hesitation, and decreased referential cohesion) are especially susceptible to undergo language loss (also termed language attrition) (e.g., Anderson, 2004; Restrepo & Kruth, 2000). To help distinguish between language shift, loss, and attrition and a language disorder, Anderson (2004) suggests obtaining information on the language patterns of the home community, the language background and history of the client, changes in the client's receptive and expressive language over time, and relative levels of use and proficiency in all languages as noted by parents and teachers.

There have also been some studies examining phonological and language disorders in languages other than English from a cross-linguistic perspective. The studies listed here are not meant to be exhaustive but merely show the type and range of phonological and language disorders across languages. In terms of children with phonological disorders, Goldstein and Iglesias (1993) examined consonant production in Spanish-speaking preschoolers with phonological disorders and found that stops, glides, and nasals were more accurate than fricatives, flap, trill, and clusters. Bichotte et al. (1993), Goldstein and Iglesias (1996), and Meza (1983) examined the use of phonological patterns in Spanish-speaking children with phonological disorders aged 3–6 and found that patterns such as liquid simplification, stopping, assimilation, cluster reduction, unstressed syllable deletion, velar fronting, tap/trill deviations, and final consonant deletion were exhibited by greater than 20 percent of the children. In a study of preschool children with phonological disorders, Goldstein (2005) found that the children exhibited high frequencies of substitutions for both early-developing sounds (e.g., /k/) and late developing sounds (e.g., trill). So and Dodd (1994) examined the phonological patterns exhibited by 13 Cantonese-speaking children with phonological disorders. The children exhibited assimilation, cluster reduction, stopping, fronting, deaspiration, aspiration, affrication, final consonant deletion, initial consonant deletion, gliding, and backing.

The majority of studies examining language disorders in children have focused on children exhibiting specific language impairment (SLI) (i.e., language impairment in the absence of sensory, neurological, or organic impairments). Cross-linguistic studies indicate that patterns of SLI vary according to ambient language (e.g., Leonard, 1998). One reason for this difference is the relative richness of each language's morphological system (e.g., English has sparse morphology compared with that of Romance languages) (Restrepo & Gutierrez-Clellen, 2004). Although English-speaking children with SLI have most difficulty with verb morphology, Spanish-speaking children with SLI tend to exhibit errors on clitic pronouns and articles (e.g., Restrepo, 1998). For example, Jacobson, Schwartz, and Mosquera (1998) examined 10 Spanish-speaking 4- and 5-year-olds with language impairment and 10 typically developing 4- and 5-year-olds in their ability to produce clitic pronouns. The children with impaired language showed the following atypical patterns: (1) lack of plural inflections, (2) substitution of the indirect pronoun "le" for the direct pronouns "lo, la, los, las," (3) use of infinitive forms when finite forms were required, (4) frequent attachment of clitics to infinitives (e.g., "cortar**lo**" [to cut **it**]), and (5) clitic reduplication (e.g., "se **lo** está poniendo**lo**" [she is putting **it** on]).

It is likely that SLPs will need to assess bilinguals who speak a language (or languages) that they themselves do not speak. Thus, SLPs may need to avail themselves of the use of interpreters (individuals who convey messages orally) and/or translators (individuals who convey messages in written form). Langdon and Cheng (2002) outline a series of steps in which the SLP and the interpreter/translator (I/T) should engage. This procedure is termed the BID (**B**riefing, **I**nteraction, **D**ebriefing) process. *Briefing* consists of planning the session, training the interpreter, and reviewing critical questions/issues. Specific aspects to be discussed would include the goal of the session, the role of the I/T, confidentiality, and legal rights. Responsibilities of the I/T are to maintain linguistic skills (oral and/or written proficiency), knowledge of two cultures, and knowledge of non-verbal communication, ability to convey same meaning in two languages, knowledge of terminology, familiarity with dialect differences, and ability to adapt. Langdon and Cheng counsel never to use an older sibling or family member as your I/T. It is unethical and will most likely confound the results of the assessment. Thus, enlist the help of a trained I/T who is an objective member of the group and who knows what questions to ask and what answers not to give. *Interaction* consists of time with the family in which information is transmitted among the parties through the I/T. During this portion of the process, the interpreter should be introduced along with the SLP, and roles should be established for the entire group. Moreover, the interpreter should interpret all information clearly and exactly as the SLP and all other conference participants present it. Finally, the interpreter should record all responses and ask for clarification when questions arise. All reports should state that an assessment was performed with the assistance of an I/T. *Debriefing* consists of reviewing the outcomes of the session and planning for the subsequent evaluation.

5   Language Difference vs. Language Disorder: Implications for Clinical Practice

Given the similarities and differences that exist between the language skills of children using a variety of dialects and between monolingual and bilingual children, SLPs must differentiate between a language difference (i.e., expected variations in syntax, morphology, phonology, semantics, and pragmatics) and a language disorder (i.e., a disability affecting one's underlying ability to learn a language) (Roseberry-McKibbin, 2002). In children from CLD populations, the appearance of decreased language skills may be a result of experience rather than ability (e.g., Peña, 1996; Peña, Iglesias, & Lidz, 2001). To distinguish a difference from a disorder, SLPs must lower a number of barriers and incorporate those solutions into clinical practice.

One barrier that may preclude an appropriate diagnosis is the SLP's definition of communication disorder. As defined by Taylor (1986), communication is only considered

> defective if it deviates sufficiently from the norms, expectations, and definitions of his or her indigenous culture (or speech community); that is, if it is: considered to be defective by the indigenous culture or speech community, operates outside the minimal norms of that culture or speech community, interferes with communication in the indigenous culture or speech community, calls attention to itself within the indigenous culture or speech community, or causes the user to be "maladjusted" as defined by the indigenous culture or speech community. (Taylor, 1986, p. 15)

Thus, the definition of communication disorder may need to be negotiated between SLPs and the client/family with whom they are working. This type of negotiation is important given that notions of disability vary across individuals and across groups.

Kalyanpur and Harry (1999) suggest that disability must be viewed through the prism of a number of continua along four dimensions:

1   *Disability as a physical phenomenon vs. disability as a spiritual phenomenon.* Believing disability is a physical occurrence will predispose one to allow that it can be remediated, as opposed to a spiritual orientation meaning that it is something that is inherent to the individual and "given" by a more powerful entity. Thus, it cannot and should not be remediated.
2   *Disability as an individual phenomenon vs. disability as a group phenomenon.* Thinking of disability as an individual phenomenon portends that it is an impairment for which the individual has ultimate responsibility. Conversely, tying it to a group may indicate that responsibility for the disability extends beyond the individual.
3   *Disability as a chronic illness vs. disability as a time-limited phenomenon.* Concluding that disability is chronic may result in the client/family questioning the need for intervention, as there would be little reason for receiving services for something that will not ultimately be remedied.
4   *Disability as a phenomenon in need of remediation vs. disability as a phenomenon that must be accepted.* If disability is deemed to need remediation, then the client/family will seek out and be immediately invested in the intervention process. However, if disability is to be accepted, then the client/family will question the rationale for considering any intervention at all.

Ultimately, views on disability must be recognized, discussed, and incorporated into clinical practice.

Another barrier that may prevent SLPs from properly diagnosing speech and language disorders in children from culturally and linguistically diverse populations is a lack of training. For example, Roseberry-McKibbin, Brice, and O'Hanlon (2005) found that in a group of SLPs surveyed in the US, only 13 percent of respondents had a whole course on serving individuals from culturally and linguistically diverse populations, and 38.3 percent had no course at all. Moreover, 77 percent of the respondents cited the need for information on least-biased assessment tools and methods in order to distinguish between a language difference and a language disorder. That is, there is a realization that many, if not most, standardized tests will not be appropriate to assess individuals from culturally and linguistically diverse populations. Thus, as mentioned previously, it is recommended that SLPs use caution in using standardized assessment tools with children from culturally and linguistically diverse populations (e.g., Goldstein, 2000; Roseberry-McKibbin, 2002; Van Keulen, Weddington, & DeBose, 1998; Wyatt, 2002). Such tools may be biased for bilingual children because their norming sample may not match the characteristics of the individuals whom the SLP will test; the items were not developed in ways to minimize bias; and information on sensitivity (i.e., percentage of individuals correctly identified with a disorder) and specificity (i.e., percentage of individuals correctly identified as typically developing) are not reported (Goldstein, 2006).

If those criteria are not met, then alternative methods of assessment will need to be employed. Such methods will decrease bias and increase the likelihood of a least-biased assessment. For example, SLPs may choose to use a standardized assessment in a non-standardized way. Suggestions include repeating directions, providing cues, administering receptive items as expressive and vice versa, providing additional time to respond, going below the basal and above the ceiling, requesting that test takers explain their answers, and adding practice items (Goldstein & Iglesias, 2007). It should be noted, however, that modifying standardized tests in these ways should be done with caution as the altered tests are no longer standardized, and thus, the normative data can no longer be utilized. Using one of these alternative methods also requires that SLPs note in the evaluation report how and why the test was modified (Goldstein & Iglesias, 2007).

In addition to modifying existing tests, SLPs also might consider using a variety of approaches to assessment. As recommended by Gillam and Hoffman (2001), standardized tests should only be one type of assessment completed. In addition to using standardized tests, they propose SLPs should assess functions and activities (e.g., interviews, language samples, and dynamic assessment), participation (e.g., portfolios with homework, class assignments, tests, writing samples), and context (e.g., curriculum measures). Their rationale is that assessment should occur across a number of contexts with a number of conversational partners.

6   Intervention

Once a valid assessment has been completed, then intervention can take place. The purpose of intervention is to systematically improve the communication skills of children by a culturally and linguistically competent professional. As noted above, communication and culture are inextricably linked. Thus, intervention should be commensurate with the families' sociolinguistic practices. If that synergy cannot take place, then the SLP must inform the family why practice is not consistent with culture. That is, SLPs should alert the family as to what they are doing and why they are doing it. Doing so will allow a partnership for intervention. Families are more likely to be engaged in the process if they have an understanding of it and are asked to take some stake in the outcome (Lynch & Hanson, 2004). Thus, conducting intervention as a negotiated process fits directly into the tenets of evidence-based practice (Justice & Fey, 2004) in which such practice combines research findings, clinical judgment, and client goals. These goals should be developed with the following principles in mind:

- Ensure that the goals are of primary importance to the family.
- Modify goals to match the priorities of the family.
- Involve families in the intervention process to the extent that they want to be included.
- Continually provide the family with information about the program and the child's progress, even if they choose to be less actively involved.
- Create goals that fit into the culture of the community from which the child comes.
- Involve leaders from the community into the program. (Lynch & Hanson, 2004, p. 462)

To achieve those principles, a number of intervention approaches and techniques have been suggested for individuals from CLD populations. Kayser (1995) recommends considering sociolinguistic effects by accounting for (1) cognitive load by utilizing holistic patterns of learning and increase amount of observation; (2) participant structure by using individual, peer–peer, and group work; and (3) time by using "wait time" (i.e., increasing the time between question and response) and different "rhythm" (i.e., presenting information in a slow, fluid way). To implement these approaches, Roseberry-McKibbin (2002) suggests that SLPs should use a multi-modal approach; review previous material; rephrase and restate; frequently check for comprehension; emphasize content and use and not just form; encourage students to (a) explain new information in their own words, (b) abstract information, (c) generalize information to new contexts, and (d) analyze new information; and have students be responsible for self-monitoring.

Regardless of the approaches and techniques used in the intervention process, it is critical that SLPs monitor progress to ensure that the intervention is successful in achieving the individual's goals. Three types of progress should be monitored: efficiency, effects, and effectiveness (Williams, 2003). Measuring efficiency answers the questions "How long did it take for the client to achieve the goals?" and "How much effort was needed to facilitate changes?" To answer those questions, the SLP should note the number of treatment sessions; chart the client's learning then examine the slope of the change; examine the child's response level (was there always a need for imitation or was there a move to spontaneous production?); determine the hierarchy needed to produce change (many incremental steps or a few gradual steps); and determine how much cueing was needed to learn the new behavior. Measuring effects answers the question, "Was the change significant?" To answer this question, it will be necessary to graph session data on a regular basis and then inspect the slope of those data; to take pre- and post-treatment measures; and to incorporate broader measures of change such as family/non-family ratings. Finally, measuring effectiveness answers the question, "Was therapy responsible for the changes?" To answer this question, the SLP should do the following: take baseline data, treatment data, and withdrawal data (i.e., examine progress shortly after the intervention is "removed"); administer generalization probes; and finally, collect follow-up data (weeks to months after working on a treatment target).

Beyond identifying, assessing, and treating language disorders, the SLP is a valuable resource in numerous settings. Consultative services can play a key role in helping other professionals understand the difference between a language difference and impairment. SLPs can provide in-services and workshops on the relationship between dialect use and spoken and/or written language. The SLP might also offer to help create a guide for useful strategies that teachers can incorporate for teaching SAE to their students of non-mainstream dialect. Finally, the SLP should be familiar with culturally relevant language and literacy activities and materials that teachers can use within their classroom setting to encourage linguistic growth.

7   Conclusions

The constantly changing demographics of many societies make it likely that the SLP will need to provide services to a population that they may not have previously felt comfortable serving. The appropriate identification, assessment, and treatment of speech and language disorders of children from culturally and linguistically diverse backgrounds is a complex process. It requires that the SLP attain some level of cultural competence to serve clients who may not be from the mainstream US culture. Cultural competence in the field of speech and language implies that the SLP understands how various cognitive, linguistic, social, and cultural factors interact to influence the language and learning behaviors of children. Cultural competence occurs along three primary dimensions: awareness, knowledge, and skills. Once the SLP has an awareness of how cultures differ, and how their own personal biases and values can affect service delivery, they are able to meet the awareness dimension. Knowledge and skills encompasses the understanding that SLPs have about the interactions between language and sociocultural factors and the possession of specific abilities to carry our culturally appropriate and relevant assessment and intervention. A great deal of the material covered in this chapter focused on the knowledge and skills dimension of cultural competence. All three dimensions of cultural competence can be met by continuing to seek out personal, professional, and educational opportunities that address the needs of those individuals who use a non-mainstream dialect or speak languages other than or in addition to English.

REFERENCES

Anderson, P. & Fenichal, E. (1989). *Serving culturally diverse families of infants and toddlers with disabilities.* Washington, DC: National Center for Clinical Infant Programs.

Anderson, R. (2004). First language loss in Spanish-speaking children: Patterns of loss and implications for clinical practice. In B. Goldstein (ed.), *Bilingual language development and disorders in Spanish–English speakers* (pp. 187–211). Baltimore, MD: Paul H. Brookes.

Baugh, J. (1999). Linguistic perceptions in black and white. In *Out of the mouth of slaves* (pp. 137–47). Austin, TX: University of Texas Press.

Bichotte, M., Dunn, B., Gonzalez, L., Orpi, J., & Nye, C. (1993). *Assessing phonological performance of bilingual school-age Puerto Rican children.* Paper presented at the annual convention of the American Speech-Language-Hearing Association, Anaheim, CA.

Bland-Stewart, L. (2005). Difference vs. deficit: What every clinician should know and do. *Asha Leader* (May).

Brown, R. (1973). *A first language: The early stages.* Cambridge, MA: Harvard University Press.

Champion, T., Hyter, Y., McCabe, A., & Bland-Stewart, L. (2003). A matter of vocabulary: Performances of low-income African-American Headstart children on the Peabody Picture Vocabulary Test-III. *Communication Disorders Quarterly* 24, 121–7.

Craig, H. & Washington, J. (1995). African-American English and linguistic complexity in preschool discourse: A second look. *Language, Speech, and Hearing Services in Schools* 26, 87–93.

Craig, H. & Washington, J. (2000). An assessment battery for identifying language impairments in African-American children. *Journal of Speech,* *Language, and Hearing Research* 43, 366–79.

Craig, H. & Washington, J. (2004). Grade related-changes in the production of African-American English. *Journal of Speech, Language, Hearing, and Research* 47, 450–63.

Craig, H., Thompson, C., Washington, J., & Potter, S. (2003). Phonological features of child African-American English. *Journal of Speech, Language, and Hearing Research* 46, 623–35.

Crystal, D. (2001). *A dictionary of language.* Chicago: University of Chicago Press.

Cummins, J. (1984). *Bilingualism and special education: Issues in assessment and pedagogy.* San Diego: College-Hill Press.

De Houwer, A. (1990). *The acquisition of two languages from birth: A case study.* Cambridge: Cambridge University Press.

Ferguson, C. (1959). Diglossia. *Word* 15, 325–40.

Genesee, F., Paradis, J., & Crago, M. (2004). *Dual language development and disorders: A handbook on bilingualism and second language learning.* Baltimore, MD: Brookes Publishing.

Gillam, R. & Hoffman, L. (2001). Language assessment during childhood. In D. Ruscello (ed.), *Tests and measurements in speech-language pathology* (pp. 77–117). Boston: Butterworth-Heinemann.

Goldstein, B. (2000). *Cultural and linguistic diversity resource guide for speech-language pathology.* San Diego: Singular Publishing Group.

Goldstein, B. (2004a). Bilingual language development and disorders: An introduction and overview. In B. Goldstein (ed.), *Bilingual language development and disorders in Spanish-English speakers* (pp. 1–20). Baltimore: Brookes.

Goldstein, B. (ed.) (2004b). *Bilingual language development and disorders in Spanish-English speakers*. Baltimore: Brookes.

Goldstein, B. (2005). Substitutions in the phonology of Spanish-speaking children. *Journal of Multilingual Communication Disorders* 3, 56–63.

Goldstein, B. (2006). Clinical implications of research on language development and disorders in bilingual children. *Topics in Language Disorders* 26, 318–34.

Goldstein, B. & Iglesias, A. (1993). *Phonological patterns in speech-disordered Spanish-speaking children*. Paper presented at the convention of the American Speech-Language-Hearing Association, Anaheim, CA.

Goldstein, B. & Iglesias, A. (1996). Phonological patterns of Puerto Rican Spanish-speaking children with phonological disorders. *Journal of Communication Disorders* 29, 367–87.

Goldstein, B. & Iglesias, A. (2007). Issues in cultural and linguistic diversity. In R. Paul (ed.), *Clinical methods in communication disorders*, 2nd ed. (pp. 283–301). Baltimore, MD: Brookes.

Goldstein, B., Fabiano, L., & Washington, P. (2005). Phonological skills in predominantly English, predominantly Spanish, and Spanish-English bilingual children. *Language, Speech, and Hearing Services in Schools* 36, 201–18.

Green, L. (2002). *African-American English: A linguistic introduction*. Cambridge: Cambridge University Press.

Harbin, G. & Hartley, J. (1978). *Model for identifying and minimizing potential sources of child evaluation bias*. Chapel Hill, NC: University of North Carolina.

Hearne, D. (2000). *Teaching 2nd language learners with learning disabilities*. Oceanside, CA: Academic Communication Associates.

Heath, S. B. (1983). *Ways with words: Language, life, and work in communities and classrooms*. Cambridge: Cambridge University Press.

Horton-Ikard, R. & Ellis Weismer, S. (2005). Distinguishing developmental errors from African-American English in the language production of toddlers. *Applied Psycholinguistics* 26, 597–620.

Horton-Ikard, R. & Miller, J. F. (2004). It's not just the poor kids, age and the use of AAE forms by African-American children from middle SES communities. *Journal of Communication Disorders* 37, 467–87.

Iglesias, A. (1985). Cultural conflict in the classroom: The communicatively different child. In D. N. Ripich & F. M. Spinelli (eds.), *School discourse problems* (pp. 79–96). San Diego, CA: College-Hill Press.

Isaacs, G. (1996). Persistence of non-standard dialect in school-age children. *Journal of Speech and Hearing Research* 39, 434–41.

Jacobson, P., Schwartz, R., & Mosquera, S. (1998). *Morphology in incipient bilingual Spanish-speaking preschoolers*. Seminar presented at the convention of the American Speech-Language-Hearing Association, San Antonio, TX.

Joe, J. & Malach, R. S. (2004). Families with American Indian roots. In E. Lynch & M. Hanson (eds.), *Developing cross-cultural competence: A guide for working with children and their families* (pp. 109–39). Baltimore, MD: Brookes Publishing.

Justice, L. M. & Fey, M. E. (2004). Evidence-based practice in schools: Integrating craft and theory with science and data. *The ASHA Leader* (Sept. 21), 4–5, 30–32.

Kalyanpur, M. & Harry, B. (1999). *Culture in special education*. Baltimore, MD: Brookes.

Kayser, H. (1995). Intervention with children from linguistically and culturally diverse backgrounds. In M. Fey, J. Windsor, & S. Warren (eds.), *Language intervention: Preschool through the elementary years* (pp. 315–31). Baltimore, MD: Brookes.

Kayser, H. (1998). *Assessment and intervention resource for Hispanic children*. San Diego, Singular Publishing.

Kohnert, K. & Bates, E. (2002). Balancing bilinguals II: Lexical comprehension and cognitive processing in children learning Spanish and English. *Journal of Speech, Language, and Hearing Research* 45, 347–59.

Kohnert, K., Bates, E., & Hernandez, A. (1999). Balancing bilinguals: Lexical-semantic production and cognitive processing in children learning Spanish and English. *Journal of Speech, Language, and Hearing Research* 42, 1400–13.

Lahey, M., Liebergott, J., Chesnick, M., Menyuk, P., & Adams, J. (1992). Variability in children's use of grammatical morphemes. *Applied Psycholinguistics* 13, 373–98.

Langdon, H. & Cheng, L. R. L. (2002). *Collaborating with interpreters and translators*. Eau Claire, WI: Thinking Publications.

Leonard, L. B. (1998). *Children with specific language impairment*. Cambridge, MA: MIT Press.

Linguistic Society of America. (1996). *Statement on language rights*. Washington, DC: Linguistic Society of America.

Lynch, E. & Hanson, M. (2004). Steps in the right direction: Implications for service providers. In E. Lynch & M. Hanson (eds.), *Developing cross-cultural competence: A guide for working with children and their families* (pp. 449–66). Baltimore, MD: Brookes Publishing.

Marchman, V., Martínez-Sussman, C., & Price, P. (2000). *Individual differences in early learning contexts for Spanish- and English-speaking children*. Paper presented at Head Start's 5th National Research Conference, Washington, DC, June.

McGregor, K., Williams, D., Hearst, S., & Johnson, A. (1997). The use of contrastive analysis in distinguishing difference from disorder: A tutorial. *American Journal of Speech-Language Pathology* 6, 45–56.

McLaughlin, B. (1978). *Second-language acquisition in childhood*. Hillsdale, NJ: Lawrence Erlbaum Associates.

Meza, P. (1983). Phonological analysis of Spanish utterances of highly unintelligible Mexican-American children. Unpublished master's thesis, San Diego State University, San Diego.

Oetting, J. & McDonald, J. (2001). Nonmainstream dialect use and specific language impairment. *Journal of Speech, Language, and Hearing Research* 44, 207–23.

Oetting, J. & McDonald, J. (2002). Methods for characterizing participants' nonmainstream dialect use in studies of specific language impairment. *Journal of Speech, Language, and Hearing Research* 45, 505–18.

Oetting, J., Cantrell, J., & Horohov, J. (1999). A study of specific language impairment (SLI) in the context of non-standard dialect. *Clinical Linguistics and Phonetics* 13, 25–44.

Paradis, J. (2005). Grammatical morphology in children learning English as a second language: Implications of similarities with specific language impairment. *Language, Speech & Hearing Services in Schools* 36, 172–87.

Paradis, J., Crago, M., Genesee, F., & Rice, M. (2003). French–English bilingual children with SLI: How do they compare with their monolingual peers? *Journal of Speech, Language, and Hearing Research* 46, 113–27.

Peña, E. D. (1996). Dynamic assessment: The model and its language applications. In K. N. Cole, P. S. Dale, & D. J. Thal (eds.), *Communication and language intervention series: Vol. 6. Assessment of communication and language* (pp. 281–307). Baltimore, MD: Paul H. Brookes Publishing Co.

Peña, E., Bedore, L. M., & Rappazzo, C. (2003). Comparison of Spanish, English, and bilingual children's performance across semantic tasks. *Language, Speech & Hearing Services in Schools* 34, 5–16.

Peña, E., Bedore, L., & Zlatic-Giunta, R. (2002). Category-generation performance of bilingual children: The influence of condition, category, and language. *Journal of Speech, Language, and Hearing Research* 45, 938–47.

Peña, E., Iglesias, A., & Lidz, C. S. (2001). Reducing test bias through dynamic assessment of children's word learning ability. *American Journal of Speech-Language Pathology* 10, 138–54.

Pollock, K. & Meredith, L. (2001). Phonetic transcription of African-American vernacular English. *Communication Disorders Quarterly* 23, 47–54.

Qi, C., Kaiser, A., Milan, S., & Hancock, T. (2006). Language performance of low-income African-American and European American preschool children on the PPVT-III. *Language, Speech, and Hearing Services in Schools* 37, 5–16.

Restrepo, M. A. (1998). Identifiers of predominantly Spanish-speaking children with language impairment. *Journal of Speech, Language, and Hearing Research* 41, 1398–411.

Restrepo, M. A. & Gutiérrez-Clellen, V. (2004). Grammatical impairments in Spanish–English bilingual children. In B. Goldstein (ed.), *Bilingual language development and disorders in Spanish-English speakers* (pp. 213–34). Baltimore, MD: Paul H. Brookes.

Restrepo, M. A. & Kruth, K. (2000). Grammatical characteristics of a bilingual student with specific language impairment. *Journal of Children's Communication Development* 21, 66–76.

Roseberry-McKibbin, C. (2002). *Multicultural students with special language needs*, 2nd ed. Oceanside, CA: Academic Communication Associates.

Roseberry-McKibbin, C., Brice, A., & O'Hanlon, L. (2005). Serving English language learners in public schools: A national survey. *Language, Speech, and Hearing Services in Schools* 36, 48–61.

Schraeder, T., Quinn, M., Stockman, I., & Miller, J. (1999). Authentic assessment as an approach to preschool speech-language screening. *American Journal of Speech-Language Pathology* 8, 195–200.

Seymour, H., Bland-Stewart, L., & Green, L. (1998). Difference versus deficit in child African American English. *Language, Speech, and Hearing Services in Schools* 29, 96–108.

Smitherman, G. (1991). Black English, diverging or converging?: The view from the National Assessment of Educational Progress. *Language and Education* 6 (1).

Smitherman, G. (2000). *Talkin' that talk: Language, culture and education in African America*. London and New York: Routledge.

So, L. & Dodd, B. (1994). Phonologically disordered Cantonese-speaking children. *Clinical Linguistics and Phonetics* 8, 235–55.

Sollors, W. (1998). Introduction: After the culture wars; or, from "English only" to "English plus." In W. Sollors (ed.), *Multilingual America: Transitionalism, ethnicity, and the languages of American literature* (pp. 1–13). New York: New York University Press.

Stockman, I. (1996). Promises and pitfalls of language sample analysis. *Language Speech and Hearing Services in Schools* 27, 355–66.

Tabors, P. (1997). *One child, two languages: A guide for preschool educators of children learning English as a second language*. Baltimore, MD: Brookes Publishing.

Taylor, O. (1986). Historical perspectives and conceptual framework. In O. Taylor (ed.), *Treatment of communication disorders in culturally and linguistically diverse populations* (pp. 3–19). San Diego, CA: College Hill Press.

Van Keulen, J., Weddington, G., & DeBose, C. (1998). *Speech, language, learning and the African American child*. Needham, MA: Allyn & Bacon.

Van Kleek, A. (1994). Potential cultural bias in training parents as conversational partners with their children who have delays in language development. *American Journal of Speech-Language Pathology* 3, 67–78.

Washington, J. & Craig, H. (1994). Dialect forms during discourse of poor, urban African American preschoolers. *Journal of Speech and Hearing Research* 37, 816–23.

Washington, J. & Craig, H. (1998). Socioeconomic status and gender influences on children's dialectal variations. *Journal of Speech, Language, and Hearing Research* 41, 618–26.

Washington, J. & Craig, H. (1999). Performances of at-risk African-American preschoolers on the PPVT-III. *Language, Speech, and Hearing Services in Schools* 30, 75–82.

Washington, J. & Craig, H. (2002). Morphosyntactic forms of African-American English used by young children and their caregivers. *Applied Psycholinguistics* 23, 209–31.

Williams, A. L. (2003). *Speech disorders resource guide for preschool children*. Clifton Park, NY: Thomson/Delmar.

Williams, K. & Wang, J. (1997). *Technical references to the Peabody Picture Vocabulary Test*, 3rd ed. Circle Pines, MN: American Guidance Service.

Wolfram, W. & Schilling-Estes, N. (1998). *American English: Dialects and variation*. Oxford: Blackwell.

Wolfram, W., Adger, C. T., & Christian, D. (1999). *Dialects in schools and communities*. Mahwah, NJ: Lawrence Erlbaum.

Wyatt, T. (2002). Assessing the communicative abilities of clients from diverse cultural and language backgrounds. In D. Battle (ed.), *Communication disorders in multicultural populations* (pp. 415–59). Boston: Butterworth-Heinneman.

3 Intervention for Children with Auditory or Visual Sensory Impairments

LAURA W. KRETSCHMER AND RICHARD R. KRETSCHMER

1 Introduction

Speech-language pathologists regularly encounter and provide service to children with sensory impairments. It is well understood that significant impairment in the auditory sensory system will interfere with or even preclude language acquisition, spoken or otherwise, unless early intervention is employed. Visual/signed communication systems are valid alternatives to auditory input, but again, early identification and intervention are necessary for the majority of deaf children if sign language acquisition and development are to occur. There are also demonstrable effects of early blindness on acquisition of some aspects of communication that need to be considered.

This chapter will offer our perspective on ways to positively affect the outcomes of language and communication acquisition and development in children with sensory impairments. For each of these impairments we will also consider best practices for early intervention. Sensory impairments in this chapter will refer to children who are born with or acquire significant loss or impairment of hearing due to genetic or exogenous disruption in the peripheral auditory system[1] as well as children who are born with or acquire significant loss or impairment of vision due to damage to the peripheral visual system.[2]

2 Deafness

In 1990, we wrote an overview of language development practices in education of the deaf for the centennial issue of *The Volta Review* (Kretschmer & Kretschmer, 1990). In that chapter, we wrote about the need to turn from explicit *teaching* of language to focus on deaf children's ability to *learn* language when language-learning principles that work with typical children are applied. In the ensuing 18 years, much has changed with regard to technology (cochlear implants, for example) but sadly some intervention practices and levels of achievement for deaf

The Handbook of Language and Speech Disorders, First Edition. Edited by Jack S. Damico, Nicole Müller, and Martin J. Ball. © 2013 Blackwell Publishing Ltd except for editorial material and organization © 2013 Jack S. Damico, Nicole Müller, Martin J. Ball. Published 2013 by Blackwell Publishing Ltd.

children have not changed dramatically. In the positive vein, there is a renewed appreciation of the importance of early identification to the acquisition of language in deaf children. Increasingly we are learning that language development in deaf children can be parallel to that of normal hearing children who are acquiring their first language. With regard to the acquisition of spoken English, better hearing aids and early use of cochlear implants have emerged as means of dramatically improving access to sound. In addition, there has been an increase in the study of sign language acquisition in young deaf children. Our focus in this chapter will be on development of interpersonal communication. Acquisition of literacy is equally important but we have determined that it is outside the focus of this chapter.

The initial portion of this chapter will focus on deafness with regard to (a) early identification and intervention, (b) the acquisition of spoken English, including those studies reporting on the impact of cochlear implants and Cued Speech, and (c) the acquisition of sign languages with particular emphasis on American Sign Language (ASL), concluding with some comments on effects of marginal, mild/moderate hearing loss on school performance.

2.1   Early identification and early intervention

In 1993, the National Institute on Deafness and Other Communication Disorders released a consensus statement on early identification of hearing impaired children in the United States. This statement concluded that all infants admitted to neonatal intensive care units should be screened for hearing loss before hospital discharge and that universal screening should be implemented for all infants within the first 3 months of life. In 2000, federal legislation mandated implementation of Universal Newborn Hearing Screening (UNHS). Since that time, more than 40 states in the US have mandated UNHS as a first step to early intervention. Although not all states have mandated newborn screening, all states have a newborn hearing screening program in place. Best practices now recommend that all infants both from well baby nurseries and neonatal intensive care units should be provided with hearing screening at birth or soon after, with opportunities for audiological follow-up and, upon confirmation of hearing loss, with placement in a family-centered early intervention program designed to support the communication and audiological needs of the child and their family. This perspective is supported by the 2007 Joint Committee on Infant Hearing Statement (JCIH) and by Early Hearing Detection and Intervention legislation that is pending in the US congress. The Phase II initiative by the JCIH is focused on improving follow-up and early intervention services that are culturally sensitive and family centered. The number of infants who are screened at birth has grown to over 90 percent in the United States, but 2008 data suggest that as many as 60 percent of infants who do not pass initial screening are lost to follow-up because they either do not receive follow-up or their entry into intervention services is not tracked correctly (Al-Mondhiry & Mason, 2008). Since Yoshinaga-Itano and her colleagues (Yoshinaga-Itano, 2003a, 2003b; Yoshinaga-Itano & Sedey, 1998) and other researchers

(Calderon & Naidu, 2000; Moeller 2000) showed that children whose hearing losses are identified with intervention begun by 6 months of age outperformed children who aren't identified until after 6 months of age, in areas ranging from speech perception, speech and/or language abilities to socio-emotional development and parent grief resolution, the ideal of 1-3-6 has been a national goal in the United States.[3]

2.2 Effects of deafness on parent–child interactions

More than 90 percent of children who are born with deafness come into families with no history of deafness while 10 percent or less are born into families where one or both parents are Deaf or there is a significant family history of deafness. Traditional teaching approaches employed with older or even preschool-age deaf children are not viable with infants as young as a few months of age. Consequently, early intervention has become increasingly family centered in order to help families provide the best language-learning environment for their deaf child. We believe that speech-language pathologists and audiologists who work in early intervention programs must understand the effects of deafness on family/parent–deaf child interactions in order to inform their practice.

In families where *the parents are Deaf* there is generally less emotional distress over having a deaf child. Deaf parents from a variety of countries and cultures (Harris et al., 1989; Masataka, 1992) have been shown to make accommodations in their use of sign language when interacting with their children. These modifications can be seen as the adoption of a simplified "motherese" version of ASL, a form that is analogous to the "motherese" used by mothers of normally hearing children who are learning their first spoken language. As with motherese in spoken language, motherese signing is very rhythmic, produced more slowly, and incorporates larger motions than ASL in conversation. Signs are simplified as well, so that the infant or young child can more easily make links between the sign and its referent (Masataka, 1992; Spencer & Lederberg, 1997). Just as normally hearing mothers with typically developing children do, most Deaf mothers establish a conversationally responsive environment in which to learn ASL. Because of the nature of ASL or any sign system, there is more use of physical contact and visual positioning to guarantee that the child is attending and that the topic is within the visual field of the child.

Even though the specific aspects of Deaf parent interactions compared to parents and children with normal hearing will differ in some ways, there is still adherence to the broad principle of an interactive communication environment as a necessary component for language acquisition and development. Deaf mothers expect their children to learn ASL and to become part of Deaf culture.

Normally hearing mothers generally have little experience with deafness. Not surprisingly, they also want their children to become functional members of their (hearing) world. Consequently, they must deal with the grief of having a child with deafness while simultaneously learning about communication modes and the controversies surrounding that choice, and about amplification systems including cochlear implants (Luterman, 2004). Earlier studies on hearing mother–deaf child interactions suggested that such interactions were characterized by a mother who was highly stressed by the presence of a deaf child and was also overly controlling, less responsive to the communication efforts of her child, and who provided less emotional support (Meadow-Orlans, 1997).

Research on the interaction of hearing mothers with their deaf children continues, with new appreciation for maternal behavior emerging. For example, Eddy (1997) matched a sample of mothers with deaf children with two normally hearing groups of mothers and children – one whose children were matched on chronological age and one whose children were matched on linguistic age. She observed that the sample of mothers with deaf children were more intrusive compared to mothers whose normal hearing children were the same chronological age, but there was no significant difference between the "experimental" mothers and the linguistic age-matched comparison group's behavior. She argued that intrusiveness might be a factor of linguistic age, not hearing status per se.

Spencer (2000) found that her sample of hearing mothers with deaf children were able to coordinate joint attention as early as 12 months of age with joint attention events showing dramatic increases over the second year of the child's life. Lederberg and Prezbindowski (2000) also presented data that suggest that deafness per se does not have a negative effect on mother–child social relationships in areas including attachment, quality of maternal affection, and maternal control. Many of their subjects were able to adapt to the affective needs of their children but repeated communicative breakdowns that did disrupt the natural conversational flow between parents and children were observed.

In order to have a meaningful relationship, mothers must be emotionally available to their children. Pressman (1998), using the Emotional Availability Scale (EAS), found that hearing mother–deaf child and hearing mother–hearing child dyads did not differ on this scale. This lack of difference was attributed in part to the early intervention that the mother/deaf child dyads had received. Within the hearing mother/deaf child dyads, positive scores on the EAS were strong predictors of language growth. One conclusion is that mothers who are more emotionally available to their children are better facilitators of language development. Besides the EAS, what else might be measures of emotional availability? Pipp-Siegel (1998) suggested frequency and type of touch as a good candidate. She found that hostile reactions to hearing mothers by their hearing children resulted in more touching, whereas hostile reactions of deaf children to their hearing mothers resulted in less touching by the mother, suggestive of emotional remoteness.

As noted, more recent research paints a positive picture of hearing parent/deaf child interactions and the possibility that reduction of parental stress leads to positive interactions: an outcome of quality early intervention. If parents are provided with quality early identification and family-centered early intervention, the amount of stress decreases (Pipp-Siegel, Sedey, & Yoshinaga-Itano, 2002). Indeed, the stress levels of parents with deaf children were similar to parents whose children had normal hearing. In other words, children cause all parents stress, regardless of their hearing status!

Which aspects of an early intervention program might be most helpful in reducing parental stress and improving parental interactions with their deaf children? Zaidman-Zait (2007) investigated the factors that parents of deaf children reported as helping decrease their stress level about deafness and about future acquisition of cochlear implants in their children. Interviews with 15 Israeli hearing mothers and 13 Israeli hearing fathers yielded several factors that parents cited as helping them to cope. All of the parents reported that when they could identify communication progress their stress decreased significantly. Additional stress-reducing factors included (a) the act of sharing experiences with other parents; (b) professional emotional monitoring, or informational support; (c) family/friend help in seeking out and providing information on deafness, assisting the parent with daily life tasks, and providing emotional support; (d) personal resources such as current profession, past knowledge, religiosity, time available to the child, and family composition; (e) the act of gaining a positive perspective on deafness by realizing that deafness did not mean that the child could not lead an independent life; (f) the presence of an early intervention community and professional support, which was deemed important because it increased parents' feelings of self-efficacy and confidence and decreased their sense of loneliness. These factors seem to be an obvious outline for components to be included in quality early intervention services for families and their deaf children.

In a qualitative study of the interactions of two mothers of children with cochlear implants, Zaitman-Zait and Young (2007) reported on the mothers' attempts to actualize principles given to them by professionals regarding use of a cochlear implant. Home teaching interactions could be ones where maternal emotional support might not be provided. In both of these cases, the interactions were naturalistic and very child-centered. These hearing parents were very sensitive to the emotional and communicative needs of their deaf children and were not acting just as "teachers." Positive interactions in clinics or at home can occur when parents receive support from professionals. It seems a reasonable conclusion that parents who have professional support from the beginning of their journey with their deaf child will be more successful than families who lack support. The major focus of family-centered programs is to provide parents with sufficient information on intervention and communication issues to allow them to make the choices that are best for their family and its goals for their deaf children.

Unhappily, family-centered intervention may not be readily available to minority families or may not always be effective. Steinberg et al. (2003) found that the amount of information provided to Hispanic families of deaf infants was limited. The communication method chosen by these parents was almost always the one recommended by the professional, usually a combination of spoken English and sign language. Rarely were the Hispanic parents in their sample informed about the possibility of using ASL or auditory/oral communication modes. This suggests that there is work to be done to ensure that culturally sensitive family-centered intervention is the rule.

2.3   Acquisition of spoken language in deaf children

We have written consistently that the best framework for understanding language acquisition and development in deaf children is one abstracted from the process of communication development in typical infants, toddlers, and young children (Kretschmer, 1997; Kretschmer & Kretschmer, 1995, 1999). Thus, it should be no surprise that in the following section on acquisition of language in deaf children we will use the typical child language literature as the framework. This section explores the acquisition of speech perception and production skills in deaf children, focusing particularly on the effects of cochlear implants. There will be an emphasis on the following areas: (a) early speech perception, (b) vocalization, (c) early communicative intentions, (d) vocabulary and syntactic development, (e) and some communicative skills acquisition of children who are deaf.

2.3.1   Early speech perception   Cochlear implants (CI) are being placed in younger and younger children to take advantage of the early language learning capabilities of the developing brain. Contemporary research has demonstrated the efficacy of early implantation, if it is appropriate for the child and consistent with the family's goals (Houston et al., 2003). The focus of much of this research is on whether early implantation improves children's speech perception. Speech perception is usually defined as the ability to identify and distinguish among language-specific speech sounds. There is an assumption that more typical speech perception strategies are seen in children who also show typical performance on tasks of phonetic awareness, working memory and complex sentence comprehension (e.g., Nittrouer & Thuente Burton, 2003). Increased abilities in all these areas have been consistently observed after months or years of CI use (e.g., Miyamoto et al., 1999; Nikolopoulos, Archbold, & O'Donoghue, 2006). Early implantation is consistently associated with better performance on auditory-only tasks, while late implantation seems more associated with better performance on visual (speechreading)-auditory tasks (Bergeson, Pisoni, & Davis 2003). Cochlear implants used by children in the context of early intervention do improve both standard test performance and speech perceptual abilities.

One caution needs to be offered about the studies that focus on improvements in auditory skills in isolation from language performance in children with cochlear implants. There is often an assumption by practitioners that when researchers attend to or measure certain behaviors, these behaviors should become the focus of intervention. Although it is important to establish outcome measures that will help to predict which children will fare well with cochlear implants, the complexity of language learning and the effects of other pre-implant variables urge caution in depending solely on the development of speech perception as a primary intervention target. If the basic unit of perception is the syllable, not the sound (Nittrouer, 2002), then the most important goal of auditory/oral intervention is helping the child develop an understanding of how syllables are mapped into words and sentences. Understanding spoken language requires that a variety of cognitive and linguistic knowledge is brought to bear, including acoustic pattern identification of segmental and suprasegmental phonemes that carry meaning. In order to comprehend running speech, the listener, from an early age, must learn how these acoustic events interact with one another to produce meaning. The real test of the effectiveness of cochlear implants (or hearing aids) lies in determining how well such technology improves children's language comprehension and expression and not just their speech perception or bottom-up auditory skills performance.

2.3.2 Vocalization With regard to early *vocalization*, there is an explanation of infant vocalization that uses the Davis and MacNeilage hypothesis (Von Hapsburg, Davis, & MacNeilage, 2008) that the jaw or frame of mouth movements account for the nature of early vocalization better than models that rely on perceptual input (McCaffrey 1999). For purposes of this portion of the chapter, however, the model recommended by Oller (1980) and subsequently researched by Oller and his colleagues will be our focus. Oller's model assumes that infants from the earliest hours of life, if they have normal hearing, attempt to match the phonation, pitch, amplitude, tongue placement, resonance, and timing of the adult speech they hear around them (see Table 3.1).

Oller (2000, 2006) contends that, based on auditory input, infants attempt to master temporal transitions from syllable to syllable, and to explore the full range of their articulators. These activities will lead eventually to vocalizations with the

Table 3.1 Grand Synthetic Stage Model of infant vocal development (Oller & Eilers, 1988)[4]

1.	*Preverbal vocalization and perception* (birth–18 months)
1.1	The PHONATION STAGE (quasivowels with normal phonation) 0–2 months. This stage manifests abilities that will be brought to bear in speech regarding control of phonation with an open vocal tract.
1.2	The PRIMITIVE ARTICULATION STAGE (gooing and protosyllables with glottals) 1–4 months of age, in which closure of vocal tract is combined with phonation; exploration of front and back of the mouth closures.
1.3	The EXPANSION OR EXPLORATORY STAGE (fully vocalic sounds, raspberries, squeals, yells, growls, whispers, and marginal babbling, all of which are non-canonical protophones) 3–8 months, during which the bases of vocal tract control are practiced and contrasted; the full range of phonatory abilities is expressed.
1.4	The CANONICAL STAGE (well-formed syllables with at least one vowel-like, one consonant-like element with rapid formant transition between consonant and vowel) 5–10 months of age, where emphasis is on mastery of the timing or durational aspect of vocalization so that syllable construction and phonetic content of syllables at 6–8 months of age is very similar to syllable content of the integrative stage and to early phonology.
1.5	The INTEGRATIVE STAGE (babbling and speaking together) 9–18 months.

timing and syllable structure of more mature speakers termed "canonical babbling" (CB). CB refers to those well-formed, repeated, and well-timed utterances produced by infants that begin to appear around 5 months of age in typical infants and are well established by 10 months of age. Oller and Eilers (1988) and Eilers and Oller (1994) were the first to caution that the absence of canonical babbling by 10 months of age was diagnostic of significant hearing loss. It appears that congenitally deaf infants will not progress through any of the stages of the Grand Synthetic Stage Model shown in Table 3.1 without intervention.

Research on the effects of deafness on early vocalization has included focus on CB because of its robustness. CB appears predictably in a variety of typical infants, including those from low SES (socioeconomic status) homes as well as those less typical infants with developmental delays such as those with Down syndrome and other developmental conditions. Since these reports by Oller and Eilers, researchers have been interested in how varying degrees of hearing loss might affect the appearance of CB. For example, Nathani, Oller, and Neal (2007) suggested that even in some moderately hearing impaired infants their hearing loss may have a retarding effect on the development of CB, with substantially more variability in CB onset than in infants or toddlers with profound hearing loss. Von Hapsburg and Davis (2006) investigated the emerging vocalizations of 15 infants fitted with amplification whose aided Pure Tone Averages (PTAs) ranged from 25 dB to 120 dB HL. All of these infants, except one, were effectively in the canonical babbling stage during the period of study. They reported a relationship between auditory sensitivity and production of CB. On average, the percentage of utterances containing CB recorded from infants with severe-to-profound hearing loss was much lower than from infants with near normal and mild-to-moderate/severe hearing loss. This was true even though all of the children had the benefit of early amplification. Children with PTAs of 85 dB HL exhibited considerable variation and unpredictable outcomes with regard to canonical development.

Moeller et al. (2007a, 2007b) reported on two longitudinal studies comparing CB and later vocalizations in infants and toddlers with hearing loss who wore amplification to a sample of normally hearing age-matched infants. Their subjects with moderate hearing loss entered the CB stage at ages similar to those of normally hearing infants. Volubility or frequency of vocalizations was not significantly different for the two groups in terms of vocalizations over time. Interestingly, the three deaf subjects who received cochlear implants began CB within 2–3 months of implant activation. The Moeller et al. second study reported on vocal and speech behavior in their samples at older ages (up to 3 years). For both studies, one conclusion was that with early amplification, vocal and early speech development in infants with hearing loss, while delayed, was roughly parallel to that of typically developing infants in most respects.

Other researchers have also reported on how cochlear implants can affect speech development in deaf children. In a 16-month study of a Spanish-speaking child implanted at 20 months, Moore, Prath, and Arrieta (2006) found that their subject exhibited a surge in canonical babbling within 6 months of activation. In addition, there were large syllable strings (8 to 11 units) present throughout the first

5 months after activation. When this child attempted word approximations, the productions were consistent with Spanish phonology. As with typically developing children, the target language will influence the types of word and sound productions produced by children with cochlear implants.

Ertmer and Stark (1995) and subsequently Ertmer and his associates have been particularly active in the measurement and reporting of effects of cochlear implantation on young children's pre-linguistic vocalizations.[5] In their 2007 report, Ertmer, Young, and Nathani used the *Stark Assessment of Early Vocal Development – Revised* to classify post-implant vocalizations of seven children who had received CIs at relatively early ages. With the exception of one child, each of their subjects made greater progress during the third year of cochlear implant use than during the first and second years combined. They concluded that the time course of vocal development in young cochlear implant recipients could provide clinically useful information for assessing the benefits of implant experience.

When researching *later speech development*, Miyamoto et al. (1997) tracked improvement in speech intelligibility in children implanted for an average of 5 years. Speech samples were collected prior to implantation and at 6-month intervals through 90 months of implant usage. The results showed that intelligibility increased gradually to approximately 25 percent during the first three years of CI use, and to 40 percent for children with 3.5 to 7.5 years of use. Although improvements during the first two years were relatively small, subsequent speech intelligibility scores exceeded those of children who used hearing aids (Osberger, 1992). Miyamoto et al. (1999) also found that children who received their implant before age 3 tended to be more intelligible than those who received it after age 3. However, there is great variability in progress depending on variables such as amount of hearing prior to deafness, age at implantation, the quality and type of educational support services, and issues such as monaural versus binaural implants (Ertmer, Leonard, & Pachuilo, 2002).

Yoshinaga-Itano (2006) presented three case studies of early-identified deaf children who received cochlear implants after they had been in a high-quality program emphasizing listening and language acquisition. These case reports are particularly interesting because two of the children received sign language along with auditory instruction, and one was exposed to ASL along with listening. Prior to implantation, all three had impressive sign vocabularies, but exhibited no documented speech perception abilities even after wearing hearing aids for a number of years. However, as Yoshinaga-Itano stressed, these children wore their hearing aids consistently and thus had some auditory experiences, and they did produce some vocalizations, albeit not formal spoken language. After cochlear implantation, all three children appeared to fast map their speech production onto their sign language knowledge so that near chronological age-appropriate spoken vocabulary was acquired within 12–14 months after implantation. Yoshinaga-Itano hypothesized that because the children were receiving simultaneous presentation of auditory messages and sign language, the period prior to implantation involved the development of listening abilities and the acquisition of vowel/ diphthong and consonant knowledge, while the 6–8 months after implantation involved a rapid mapping of those previously learned sounds on to hundreds of signed words.

With regard to *voice quality and intonation contours*, there have been a few studies on the production of suprasegmental aspects of speech in children with cochlear implants. Peng et al. (2007) investigated the ability of children with CIs to produce the rising intonation contour heard in English yes/no questions. Their subjects did not consistently use appropriate intonation contours even after 7 years of implant use. Flipsen and Colvard (2006) examined the conversational speech of six young deaf children, all implanted before age 3, and observed that all had conversational speech that was more than 65 percent intelligible during the evaluation period. Using the same sample of children, Lenden and Flipsen (2007) studied speech and voice characteristics in connected language. Their subjects did not demonstrate any unusual problems with phrasing and pitch, although in several subjects problems with rate, loudness, and laryngeal quality were noted. For the entire sample, accurate use of resonance continued to be a problem, but toward the end of the study two of the children began to demonstrate more appropriate use of stress. Taken as a whole, these findings suggest that prosody and voice quality observed in the conversational speech of children with implants is much less of an issue than has been previously noted in the speech of deaf children using hearing aids.

2.3.3 Early communicative intentions

Explorations of early communication of deaf children show that they express intentions in a manner similar to children with normal hearing but with the difference that proto-imperative and proto-declarative gestures are not typically accompanied by vocal activity (Lichtert & Loncke, 2006). Nicholas (2000) found that the informative/heuristic communicative intent increased in deaf children as their language abilities increased. The heuristic function is one in which children seek out information in interactions with others by making statements, asking questions, and providing answers. In a study of Israeli deaf children and their hearing parents, Dromi and her colleagues (Dromi, 2003; Zaidman-Zait & Dromi, 2007) observed that (a) their sample of deaf children used fewer words than normally hearing children at equivalent ages; (b) gestures and communicative points emerged much earlier than vocalizations and words in deaf children; and (c) deaf toddlers exhibited reduced interest in joint book reading with adults as compared with normally hearing toddlers.

The delay in use of vocalizations by deaf children, even those with early amplification, is entirely expected. The absence of early gestures plus words, in deaf children, suggests that therapeutic intervention with strong auditory/verbal or auditory/oral focus should consider that typical communication development includes gestures paired with utterances and words. Second, and just as importantly, we know that interactions that involve an adult, a child, and an external object (such as a book) are of utmost importance for the establishment of shared reference, for learning new words, and as the basis for development of social interaction scripts. In joint book reading or any joint interactions, the informational/heuristic function plays a key role. We agree with Nicholas (2000) that too many of the therapeutic approaches for young deaf children still center on structured, prescriptive events; events that do not bear a relationship to normal child–parent interactions. We urge that the early intervention focus be placed on supporting families in using interaction-centered approaches as the best avenue for communication progress. In Table 3.2, we summarize the language intervention principles that we have consistently advocated.

Early identification coupled with high-quality family-centered intervention should lead to more typical communication outcomes for young deaf children. Promoting emergence of canonical babbling as soon as possible, in conjunction with communicative gestures, should lead to the same natural cognitive distancing

Table 3.2 Principles governing language intervention as suggested by R. Kretschmer

Step 1
Collect and analyze the communication of the child in real-life situations using actual communication purposes. Focus should be on collecting data on key discourse functions – namely, personal narratives, literary narratives, explanation of physical phenomena, explanation of social phenomena, identification descriptions, photographic descriptions, instruction giving, bargaining for an object or service, and persuading someone to a certain point of view. Samples should be collected, whenever possible, with a variety of communication partners, especially family members, friends, classmates, and teachers.

Step 2
Once the language aspect on which to focus is decided, identify the discourse function in which that principle plays a major role. For example, if trying to improve use of tense, you could use personal narratives, where the story is typically in past tense, but any talk about the story is in present tense, as in "... and we **went** [past tense] on a picnic to Grant Park. Oh, Grant Park **is** [present tense] where they have the dog show ..." Another example could be the conjunction "if." This conjunction is usually used in explanations of social phenomena such as: "... people lie **if** they feel trapped."

Step 3
Tie the form and discourse to be practiced to content areas that are useful to the child. These content areas can be topics being covered in various school subjects, or related to the playground, or occurring at home. For example, the present/ past distinction could be tied to a unit on exploring family roots, a topic often encountered in school. The student could interview older family members about their past and then verify the interview information, as in "... oh you **were** in Normandy on D-Day; Normandy **is** in France, right?" For the **if**-construction, playground bargains could be highlighted, as in "... I'll let you have this swing **if** you pick me first for the team."

Table 3.2   (*Cont'd*)

Step 4

During communication interactions focusing on a linguistic form, begin with expansions of the child's production coupled with extensions. Extensions are used so that the child has some information on which to build in order to extend the conversation, but focus should always be on the conversational exchange, not the syntactic form per se:

CHILD: He lie and he scare.

TEACHER: If he is scared, he will lie [**expansion**]. Why would Johnny be scared about lying? What does he think will happen? [**extension**]

You should provide questions that will prompt the use of the form. Don't be surprised if the child's early use of the form is imperfect; language growth occurs in stages. In most cases the initial imperfect productions will conform to what we know about the development of that form. For instance, initially, **if** often appears early as **and** in the sentence.

Step 5

Provide the child with meaningful practice where he or she can use the linguistic principle and practice its use. For instance, with regard to **if**, the child can present a report to the class as part of a unit in social studies. In this report, he can explore the conditions under which people perform social acts. This can be written out with the child and then practiced with special emphasis on the linguistic targets. During these activities, you can have mini-lessons on its use within that discourse function. This is called situational/focused practice, but it always occurs within the context of the ongoing conversation, not as an activity set aside from the lesson itself. For instance, when discussing people's motivations, you can emphasize the word **if** and, perhaps, have the child practice its use in sentences as you are constructing the report.

Step 6

You should make sure that there is coordination between home and school on these targets. Many of the practice assignments mentioned in Step 5 can be sent home to the parents so that they can rehearse with the child. If the parent is aware of the target, she/he might be interested in helping the child focus attention on that element. Use caution in this practice, of course. The parent should not become a teacher but rather hone their skills as communication partners.

Step 7

You should have a program of evaluation in place to measure growth in the child with regard to a particular form. For example, make the classroom teacher aware of the use of **if**, and ask him/her to track the number of spontaneous uses of this form in a couple of 5-minute periods. The SLP can help to track the same use of forms in two or three brief observation periods as well. Graph or chart the findings for a period of a couple of weeks to help in understanding language growth.

in deaf infants and toddlers that is observed in young normally hearing children. This in turn should lead to greater expansion of communication intentions including the informational/heuristic function.

2.3.4 Vocabulary and syntactic development Studies of the size and complexity of vocabulary of young deaf children show, as one might expect, considerable variability. Deaf children of deaf parents who use ASL have been found to have vocabulary sizes at 12 to 17 months of age that are larger than those of hearing children at the same age (Anderson & Reilly, 2002). This advantage disappears, however, between 18 and 23 months. It is more usual for deaf children who have not received quality early intervention and early amplification to possess lexicons that are more than 2 standard deviations below those of age-equivalent hearing children (Lederberg, 2003). Because there continues to be such heterogeneity in deaf children as a group, disparities in vocabulary size are not surprising. Even with UNHS and efforts to institute early intervention, deaf children continue to vary in terms of actual age of identification, nature, function and consistency of amplification use, access to quality early intervention, family decisions about communication mode and goals for their child, family culture, home language, available assets, and associated disabilities, to name a few factors that affect communication development. While taking all these factors into account, we have tried to synthesize the literature on vocabulary and spoken English syntactic development.

Lexical acquisition in hearing children seems to occur in stages (Lederberg, 2003). Children around 12 months of age slowly retain words after hearing them multiple times. Some time between 16 to 24 months children are able to retain a word after only a few exposures, and, more importantly, they can learn the meaning of a word based on the pragmatic/semantic cues provided by adults. At about $2\frac{1}{2}$ years, typical children have learned to make inferences based on their own world knowledge with much less need for cues from the adult communicator.

The question of where deaf children, in general, fall along the word knowledge continuum has led to a variety of answers. Houston et al. (2003) observed that infants and toddlers with early CIs performed in a pre-word Preferential Looking Paradigm very like typically developing infants and toddlers, while later implanted toddlers did not. In other words, their sample of early implanted deaf children demonstrated that they were more ready to learn words than were later implanted subjects. Lederberg (2003) and associates (Lederberg, Prezbindowski, & Spencer, 2001) examined deaf children's ability to learn words through explicit instructions and/or through novel inference. From two different samples of deaf children, they observed children who seemed to learn new words best through explicit instruction, those who could learn both from explicit instruction and through their own ability to utilize novel mapping strategies from context, and children who did not appear to learn new words through either strategy. In the preschool sample, the mean size of a child's lexicon was predictive of the ease of word learning. Children who had mean lexicons of 308 words were able to learn new words with explicit instruction as well as by inference with and without cues from adults. These results suggest that a variety of approaches to lexical acquisition need to be considered for young deaf children since some will benefit from contextual cues but can also develop meaningful semantic maps in the early stages of acquisition. There are also some who present with very small early vocabularies who can benefit from explicit teaching but, if given the opportunity, are also able to acquire in an interactive communication environment just as typical children do.

In our experience there are still too many intervention/educational programs that focus on the explicit teaching of lexical items even if they espouse an interactive communication philosophy. Young deaf children are still presented with too many "Show me the ball" teaching encounters where the focus is on matching the word to its picture or object referent as a way to control the language environment. In contrast, typical children acquire new words through participating in activities where the language supports the initiation, the implementation, and the completion of the learning. Language should be a means for discussing and explaining a task, not a target in and of itself. To their credit, many communication and family-centered intervention programs do understand and implement an interactive approach to language learning and acquisition. Sadly, just as many programs and professionals use explicit or direct teaching as their standard, with the idea that less language is more helpful for the deaf child. We question that position, since we have found that less exposure usually results in less language learned.

In the realm of *grammatical acquisition*, once typical children acquire a base vocabulary, they begin to combine words and acquire more grammatical elements. Syntactic rules specify the word order and morphological markers also govern the production and complexity of those combinations. Researchers have found that many deaf children implanted later in life continue to have problems with connected language (Geers, Spehar, & Sedey, 2002; Nikolopoulous et a., 2004). Geers (2004) reported that 43 percent of a national sample of 8- to 9-year-old deaf children who received a cochlear implant between 24 and 35 months of age achieved combined speech and language skills close to the average for hearing children of the same chronological age – but obviously 57 percent did not. As we have noted, children implanted at younger ages show a clear trend toward use of a variety of vocalizations, speech production, and speech perception as well as grammatical mastery that are noticeably better than deaf children with hearing aids (Nicholas & Geers, 2007; Spencer, 2004). This advantage is especially noticeable when children have some auditory experience prior to receiving the implant. Yoshinaga-Itano et al. (1998) reported that children identified before 6 months of age with no secondary handicaps and who were enrolled in high-quality early intervention programs outperformed deaf children identified after 6 months of age with similar early intervention. Mayne (1998a, 1998b) observed, however, that this same group of children, despite their strong start, still lagged behind their normally hearing peers. We do not know whether early intervention alone will lead to typical language development, or whether deaf children who are implanted and show early benefits but do not have access to quality education programs will continue to keep pace with typically developing peers.

Tur-Kaspa and Dromi (1998) reported on a sample of deaf children learning Hebrew, none of whom had cochlear implants. The syntactic forms used by their sample were both quantitatively and qualitatively different from those generated by normal hearing peers. Subject–verb–object (SVO) simple syntactic constructions dominated, which was surprising given that Hebrew word order is not that fixed. The subjects' utterances showed a lack of more complex syntactic structures. The primary qualitative difference from typical peers was the omission of central nodes from the sentence, particularly the subject or main verb. It was not clear whether omissions were related to the deaf students being unaware that the missing elements were part of the sentence, or whether the omissions were production errors. Deaf speakers who generate sentences with missing key elements place the listener at a disadvantage, especially with omission of verbs. Verbs act as key elements in establishing argument structures in running sentences, and their omission can make processing sentences difficult at best. No other study containing this amount of detail on the syntactic performance of young deaf speakers could be located.

The next challenge for deaf children as they enter school is learning *with* or *through* language. We know that children with cochlear implants exceed the academic achievement of deaf peers, as shown by reports from the United States (Connor & Zwalan, 2004), the Netherlands (Vermeulen et al., 2007), and Scotland (Thoutenhoofd, 2006). Children who received their implants earlier seem to be closing the gap with normal hearing peers in school performance. It should be understood, however, that children with CIs would continue to need quality educational support, especially if they are in regular education classrooms. It is tempting to declare that a third or fourth grade deaf student who is a CI user, has very fluent conversational abilities, and is achieving at grade level no longer needs educational support. Regular education administrators must be helped to understand that such students are still deaf and can return to that state in an instant if their CI fails.

This assertion is borne out by interviews with samples of CI users, ages 8 to 10 years (Preisler, Tvingstedt, & Ahlstrom, 2005) and 13–17 years (Wheeler et al., 2007), all but two of whom rated the implant as essential and critical to their communication success. Most reported that they wore their implants all day every day, but they were very realistic about the potential disadvantages of the technology. They recognized that it did not help them in certain communication situations, so they knew and used sign language when necessary. Interestingly, most of these students lacked knowledge of how cochlear implants work and, indeed, some were unable to provide any information at all about its functioning.

2.3.5 Communicative skills acquisition   In addition to other facets of verbal interaction, conversations are organized to include (a) initiations or opening sequences; (b) topicalization, where the communication partners agree on and exchange information about a topic; (c) information giving about the topic through extended discourse; (d) clarification sequences that are initiated when there is a breakdown in communication; and (e) closing sequences. No information on closing sequences among deaf children could be located. This section will focus on initiations, topicalization, and clarification aspects of conversation.

There were no studies available that examined *conversational initiations* in authentic and unstructured settings between deaf persons or between deaf and hearing persons, but several studies examined conversational initiations in structured settings. Duncan (1999) assessed the conversational skills of deaf children included in regular classrooms, reporting no significant difference between the initiation attempts employed by these children and their normal hearing peers, although deaf children tended to use more non-verbal rather than verbal attempts. Messenheimer-Young and Kretschmer (1994) tracked the initiation efforts of one hard-of-hearing child attempting to enter play with normal hearing peers. When the child used the strategy of picking up a prop and jumping into play, an approach used by his normal hearing peers, he was successful. He was unsuccessful if he used a teacher's suggestion that he asked to be allowed to play. Professionals working with deaf children in inclusive settings should be aware of both the child's needs as well as the implicit rules governing social interactions among typical children.

In a non-classroom study, Rodriquez and Lana (1996) found that a group of Canary Island preschool deaf children tended to make initiation adjustments according to the age of the communicator, their familiarity with the partner, and the type of communication system employed by their partner. We can assume that deaf children, even at the preschool level, are aware of the style and characteristics of their communication partners. Indeed, Blennerhassett (1984) observed that ability in a 13-month-old deaf child.

There are two studies germane to *topicalization*. Duncan (1999), cited above, also reported that her deaf subjects attempted to maintain conversation at the same rate as their hearing peers, but they tended to use minimal contingent responses and made fewer contributions that actually added new information to extend the conversation. Only 75 percent of the productions by her deaf sample fit the communication partner, the context, and the ongoing conversation. Normally hearing peers observed were appropriate 100 percent of the time. Both groups attempted to shift conversational topics at the same rate but the normal hearing students were more successful. Her deaf subjects were more likely to stay with the topic they had established rather than to shift to a topic established by their communication partner.

In a study of Australian deaf children aged 5 to 16 with their itinerant teacher, Toe, Beattie, and Barr (2007) found very few conversational breakdowns, with the older students demonstrating more talk time, and more introduction of their own topics rather than merely responding to the adult's topics. The youngest deaf communicators relied heavily on simple responses to teacher questions, while all participants asked very few questions of their teacher, a person with whom they were very familiar.

With regard to *information giving*, the only study located that examined the effects of deafness on extended discourse was reported by Crosson and Geers (2001), on the literary narratives of 8- to 9-year-olds who had at least four years of cochlear implant experience. Their subjects generated narrative productions prompted by an eight-picture story sequence. These narratives were compared to narratives generated by 28 normal hearing children. Deaf children with above-average speech perception scores produced narratives that were similar in structure and use of referents to those of normal hearing peers. Their use of subordinate conjunctions as cohesion markers between events was not as well developed as referencing, but it was superior to the deaf subjects who received poorer speech perception scores despite a similar period of implant use. Children with more limited speech perception abilities exhibited significantly poorer narrative structures and poorer use of cohesive devices to connect events. Interestingly, narrative scores were found to contribute heavily to reading scores, suggesting the importance of discourse ability and sentence-level understanding to reading comprehension.

Clear understanding of how deaf children who are developing spoken language, especially with cochlear implants, engage in extended discourse has yet to be documented. How well can they engage in description, both identification and photographic? How well can they engage in expository discourse such as explanation, instruction giving, negotiation, or persuasion? How well can they negotiate or fabricate? We believe that we need to know the routes that deaf children, learning spoken language, take in becoming conversation partners. As we have noted, unless there are large-scale descriptions of actual discourse performance, we will be unable to determine whether we are really making progress in helping deaf children learn to converse.

There have been several studies on deaf children's response to *clarification requests*, all of which studied students using total communication. In a study of 4- to 7–6-year-old children, Ciocci and Baran (1998) found that deaf children's most frequent response was revision of their productions followed by repetitions. Hearing children used revisions and repetitions with equal frequency. Blaylock, Scudder, and Wynne (1995) found that when used with deaf children, a "What?" question yielded reductions or repetitions of comments. "I don't understand" clarification requests yielded more information, while saying "I still don't understand, can you show me?" caused children to act out or show what they were talking about rather than restating or expanding comments. Most (2002) found that when asked for clarification, the most frequent response from both hearing and deaf subjects was to repeat their statements followed by revising an utterance, expanding the utterance into two sentences, and/or adding additional information (cueing). Shortening one's utterance, offering background information, and inappropriate responses in an attempt to discontinue the conversation occurred infrequently.

As with typical students, the ability of deaf students to converse, to provide, and to respond to clarification requests improves with language growth and maturity, but may still not be entirely typical, as demonstrated by a report from Marschark et al. (2007) on the success of pairs of deaf college-age students playing a modified version of Trivial Pursuit. The dyads were pairs of deaf students who used oral English, pairs who used ASL, and pairs of mixed communicators. Three aspects of their conversations were tracked, namely (a) whether the dyads seemed to understand what was being said, (b) the number of requests for question repetition, and (c) the total number of unrequested repetitions. The dyads consisting of participants who both signed understood each other significantly better than those dyads using spoken language, 63 percent to 44 percent of the time. On the other hand, students who used spoken language were significantly more likely to be correct in giving responses to questions. Interestingly, both groups requested clarification only 20 percent of the time. All these dyads seemed to tolerate a considerable amount of ambiguity and made few attempts to resolve it by asking clarification questions even though they were in an ideal communication situation. To determine whether such results are typical, of course, requires that normal hearing dyads be observed.

Collectively, the research shows that deaf children/students are variable in their knowledge of the conventions of conversation, conventions that are best learned by engaging in chats or conversations. Too often, conversations with deaf children have focused on the teaching of specific bits of behaviors, or isolated vocabulary or syntactic structures rather than on transactions about knowledge or provoking real communication (Wood & Wood, 1997). By engaging in conversations about real topics of interest from life or school, children can be exposed to and are encouraged to use the conventions of their oral language. Such an approach has been advocated (e.g., Clark, 2007; Johnson, 1997; Kretschmer & Kretschmer, 1995; Stone, 1988; Tye-Murray, 1994).

2.4   *Cued Speech*

Cued Speech is a system designed by Orin Cornett (1967). It attempts to provide deaf children with additional visual information as a supplement to speechreading. There are two sets of cues, one for consonants and one for vowels. Consonant cues consist of hand configurations, while vowel cues involve placement on or around the face. In English, for example, a finger point signals the presence of a [d], [p], or [ʒ], while placement of that point to the right of the mouth signals [i] or [ɝ]. This combination would signal the syllables [di], [pi], [ʒi], [dɝ], [pɝ], or [ʒɝ] with the particular syllable being referenced resolved by paying attention to lip movements. Since only about 30 percent of speech is visible on the lips and face, the combination of lip movements along with specific cues could increase the amount of information available substantially. Cued Speech was designed to aid in speech reception and not speech production per se. If speech production is the focus in deaf children, then auditory, tactual, and kinesthetic input would need to be employed (Vieu et al., 1998). Cued Speech increases the linguistic information available to the child, which encourages more attention to the speaker in contrast to using speechreading alone (Torres, Moreno-Torres, & Santana, 2006).

Does Cued Speech increase speech reception abilities? Research focusing on either French- or English-speaking children suggests that Cued Speech does increase speech perception abilities when added to speechreading (Alegria & Lechat, 2005; Nicholls & Ling, 1982) or to speechreading and cochlear implants

(Descourtieux et al., 1999). Nicholls and Ling (1982) found that the speech recep-tion scores of profoundly deaf children using Cued Speech for at least 3 years increased from about 30 percent for both syllables and words with speechreading alone, to more than 80 percent with speechreading plus Cues.

Does increasing speech perception abilities translate into increased linguistic and communication understanding? Research suggests that Cues increase under-standing of the morphological system for a particular language. Kipila (1985) tracked the acquisition of Brown's 14 grammatical morphemes in one English-speaking child with a cochlear implant who was taught using Cued Speech. The percentage of correct use was 100 percent for the first seven morphological end-ings (see Brown, 1973 for a list of these morphemes) and varied from 50 percent to 80 percent for the last seven forms acquired.

A study of French-speaking deaf children indicated that Cued Speech aided in the acquisition of gender designations in that language, a form that is somewhat arbitrary in its application to nouns (Hage, Alegria, & Perier, 1991). Children receiving Cued Speech had direct access to this information, whereas children who did not must deduce this information from multiple sources, such as gender markings on the determiners that precede the noun. A study of Spanish-speaking deaf children indicated that Cued Speech aided in the acquisition of prepositions, both those that were semantically meaningful to the sentence such as "ante," meaning "before," and those that function more as a link between words and whose meaning must be deduced from the words surrounding it, such as "con" meaning "with" or "by" (Santana Hernandez, Torres Monreal, & Garcia Orza, 2003).

It appears that Cued Speech can increase awareness of morphological endings in a language. Beyond a variety of persuasive case studies, it is not yet clear whether use of Cued Speech can assist a range of deaf children in understanding syntactically complex utterances of others or whether the receptive language abilities shown in some children will eventually allow those children to be inde-pendent speechreaders without Cues.

2.5 Sign language acquisition

When discussing deaf individuals, one must acknowledge a distinction between those who see themselves as part of Deaf culture and those who do not. Deaf culture communities believe that language ties them together and that language in the US is some variant of American Sign Language (ASL).

Deaf or hearing infants exposed to sign language have been observed to engage in manual babbling (Meier & Willerman, 1995; Petitto & Marentette, 1991) which is analogous to the babbling of typical infants. This babbling is characterized by specific types of hand positions found in the production of ASL (Colin et al., 2000; Manentette & Mayberry, 2000) and is analogous to the Expansion or CB stages identified by Oller (1980).

Previously, we explained that early communication intentions develop prior to the acquisition of spoken language in typical children. Infants learning ASL produce deictic gestures such as "I" and "you" – gestures where pointing precedes the first sign symbol (Folven & Bonvillian, 1991). There is a notion that meaningful signs are acquired at younger ages than first spoken words but Anderson and Reilly (2002) have shown that although children of Deaf parents produce sign-like gestures between the ages of 8 and 11 months, like CB and jargon, they are not real words. Because gestures resemble baby signs, first sign words are often credited when first spoken words are not. In any case, by the end of the second year the so-called sign language advantage is smoothed out so that deaf and hearing children with Deaf parents and hearing children of hearing parents are quite similar in their linguistic milestones (Meier & Newport, 1990).

Sign production varies across three features: location of the sign, the hand configuration of the sign, and movement to and from the body (Klima & Bellugi, 1979). When children transition into meaningful signing, Cheek et al. (2001) found that place of location-restricted forms were rare, but there was a high rate of error or immature production of hand shapes. When placement-restricted forms occurred they were quite consistent for any child, while hand shape-restricted forms were quite variable from one child signer to another. This would seem to suggest that the hand shape feature of ASL word production is more problematic than the location feature.

The content of ASL and English initial vocabularies are quite similar to one another as well. Nouns far outstrip the number of verbs in both early vocabularies. Once deaf children have attained a vocabulary size of approximately 115 words they begin to generate multi-sign combinations, a finding that is consistent with spoken English acquisition (Fenson et al., 1993).

Researchers have noted that Deaf parents often interspersed their ASL productions with fingerspelling, especially in book-reading activities (Kelly, 1995). Deaf parents embed fingerspelling by sandwiching it into ASL strings. An example was a string like: [Duck Duck Q-U-A-C-K] where duck was signed twice, followed by the fingerspelled "sound" produced by ducks. Padden (2006) argues that fingerspelling acquisition involves two understandings. First, the child must learn the skill of fingerspelling itself and then the skill of connecting fingerspelled words to their English alphabetic counterparts. According to Kelly (1995), fingerspelled words appear as young as 24 months with initial attempts to replicate the movement contour of the word, rather than precise production of individual letters. Very little else is known about the actual realization of fingerspelled letters within words, although Wilcox (1992) and Padden (1991) have reported on general aspects of fingerspelling acquisition. Information about the development of fingerspelling seems important since Ramsey and Padden (1998) found a link between awareness that fingerspelling related to English words and measurements of reading. They argue that fingerspelling can be used as a transition from ASL to developing early English literacy.

2.5.1   Sign language discourse   Most (2003) focused on the repair strategies used by seven Israeli children as they attempted to sign a picture description to an adult who knew Hebrew Sign Language. During the course of this interaction, two clarification requests were made, one early in the task and the second later.

In response to the first clarification, they tended to repeat or revise the utterance. In response to the second clarification, they would add new information along with repeating and revising the utterance. Some additional strategies were explanation of specific terms used in the original utterance, use of cueing strategies that provided background information to make words clearer, use of fingerspelling to make sure that the word was clear to their communication partner, and/or simplifying the utterance by shortening it. These children seemed to have a wider range of clarification strategies than previously reported for either spoken language or total communication users. Most importantly, they seemed to be strategic in their use of clarification, depending upon the nature and timing of the clarification request.

Morgan (2002) reported on narrative production in British Sign Language users who were asked to tell a story based on a two-page sequence from the wordless book, *Where Are You?* The first scene showed a boy climbing a tree to look in a hole while a dog disturbs a hive of bees that has fallen from the tree. In the second part, the bees are chasing the dog while the boy has fallen from the tree, surprised by an owl. In the 4- to 6-year-old children's narratives, this scene was retold as a sequence of actions focusing on only one character with no attempt to overlap or encode the simultaneity of events. The syntactic conventions that could have allowed discussion of all the action were present in the children's comments but only at the sentence level. In the narratives of the 7- to 10-year-olds, there continued to be a sequential description of the two parts of the scene, but older students were able to include both characters involved in the episode and switch between them. Children aged 11 to 13 years interconnected the scenes by establishing both characters in space and then switching from space to space to indicate the action, both in terms of cause-and-effect and simultaneity. We would like to see many more studies of children's use of discourse in ASL. It is our experience that children who cannot express a variety of discourse functions have great difficulty in interpreting those functions in interpersonal or academic conversations.

This section demonstrates some important points. Any professional who intends to interact with a Deaf child who uses ASL must be well versed in ASL in order to evaluate the child's competence and determine the directions in which language growth is occurring. Secondly, if ASL is the language of choice, it should be used in a conversational format just as spoken English, or it will not be an effective mode of communication. Third, the child who is a competent ASL user must be assisted to bridge to English print. Musselman (2000) suggests that there are several paths to literacy for deaf students who are ASL users, including from ASL to English-based sign to print and from ASL directly to print. For a complete discussion of literacy issues with deaf students, the reader is referred to Mayer and Wells (1996), Mayer (2007), Paul (2000), and Schirmer (2000).

3   Marginal, Mild, and Moderate Hearing Loss

Children with marginal, mild, and moderate hearing impairments account for about 7–8 million of the 50+ million schoolchildren in the United States. In this category is any child with a bilateral hearing loss of 16 dB HL or greater, with a permanent unilateral hearing loss of 35 dB or greater, with fluctuating conductive hearing loss, a high-frequency hearing loss, or a mid-frequency "cookie bite" hearing loss, all of which could be called minimal or marginal but should be considered educationally significant (Flexer, 1995; Gravel, 1996). These children are routinely included in general education classes, some with supportive assistance from outside professionals and others with no assistance. Based on early studies such as those by Bess (1985) and his colleagues (Bess, Dodd-Murphy, & Parker, 1991; Tharpe & Bess, 1991), it is clear that every child with a hearing loss that falls into these categories should be evaluated carefully for associated learning, language, literacy, and psychosocial problems. More contemporary reports continue to emphasize that the effects of minimal hearing loss are rarely minimal (Goldberg and Richburg, 2004; Kaderavek & Pakulski, 2007).

For example, English and Church (1999) found that 54 percent of children with unilateral hearing loss were receiving assistance from some professional and 24 percent were functioning below average when compared to their hearing peers. Using standardized tests of language, Sikora and Plapinger (1994) found that 22 percent of their sample of children with mild to moderate hearing loss did not perform within normal limits. Anderson (1991) reported that children with marginal to mild or unilateral hearing loss evidenced greater academic and social difficulties than children with normal hearing. Delage and Tuller (2007) investigated the language abilities of 19 French-speaking adolescents, aged 11–15 years with mild to moderate hearing loss. In more than half the sample, major problems with phonology and grammar were found. In another study of 20 hard-of-hearing children, 7–10 years of age, Gilbertson and Kamhi (1995) observed that the students were divided into two groups, one that displayed problems with phonological processing and novel word learning, and one that did not. Most (2004) found that some Israeli children with mild/moderate and unilateral hearing loss were performing less well than children with more severe hearing impairments who consistently used amplification. Taken as a whole, these studies suggest that marginal, mild hearing loss, both sensorineural and conductive, can pose communication problems, particularly in schools.

Given the extent of academic problems, what do teachers know about how to manage these children? Richburg and Goldberg (2005) investigated teachers' beliefs about assisting children with marginal/mild hearing loss. When asked if preferential seating alone was sufficient to manage the effects of the hearing loss, 69 percent of 45 teachers strongly agreed with that statement. The majority of this sample of teachers did not understand that preferential seating alone is rarely sufficient.

A variety of technologies such as sound field amplification, personal hearing aids, or personal FM systems are currently available to assist children with mild hearing loss. The evidence is clear that, in addition to helping children with marginal/mild hearing loss, sound field FM systems reduce teacher absences from school by relieving vocal stress and fatigue. Incidentally, sound field FM systems have also been found to generate positive results when used in classes containing children with learning disabilities, attention deficit disorders, developmental delays, and in classrooms for English Language Learners (Eriks-Brophy & Ayukawa, 2000; Flexer, Millin, & Brown, 1990). Sound field FM systems function best in classrooms with good acoustics, meaning that the background noise for an unoccupied classroom is at 35 dBA SPL with reverberation time in the .4–.6 second range.[6]

As a transition to the section on blindness, it is important to remind the reader that the prevalence of visual problems in persons who are congenitally deaf is approximately twice that of the normal hearing population. Approximately 25 percent of normal hearing school-age students have a visual impairment of some variety in one or both eyes, including problems with visual acuity at near or far distance, muscle balance problems, color blindness, or visual field limitations. The percentage of children and young adults with congenital deafness and visual problems is estimated at 6 percent to 60 percent, with the latter figure supported by Silberman (1981) and Johnson (1991). Conditions such as Usher's syndrome and dozens of other peripheral visual disorders are associated with deafness, which means that all congenitally deaf children must have regular visual examinations. Indeed, it is reasonable that every child with a permanent hearing loss, even of the marginal/mild variety, should be regularly screened for vision problems.

4 Blindness

Research on the status of language, and communication learning in blind children, is not as extensive as the research on deaf children, but it is available. The remainder of this chapter will focus on (a) early mother–blind child interactions, (b) language acquisition, and will conclude with comments about deaf-blind children.

4.1 Mother–child interactions

Literature on language development stresses the importance of the mother–child interactional dyad as a precursor to the fluent development of language in children. As with deafness, there has been considerable research on the question of how, or if, blindness alters communication interactions between mothers and their blind children. It seems logical that establishing joint attention would be difficult since it is so heavily dependent on visual regard of the topic by both partners. Since mobility is also a problem for blind infants, it would seem that the parent must provide prompts – either verbally or tactually – to the infant regarding changes in the environment or the presence of interesting objects. It is not surprising that mothers of blind children are observed to use language to structure interaction with their infants, toddlers, or young children. For example, Andersen, Dunlea, and Kekelis (1993) found that the imperative, especially the request for action, was the highest sentence-type used by mothers to their blind children between the ages of 1;4 years and 1;10 years. This overuse of imperatives was partially related to the blind infant's slowness in initiating actions and topics. Because topic nomination has a high visual component, mothers feel the need to establish topics verbally. Pointing to or looking at objects is not an option for blind toddlers as it is in interactions between mothers and sighted children.

Dote-Kwan (1995) found that mothers of blind children initiated a higher proportion of topics than do mothers of sighted children. Topics nominated by blind children tended to be about themselves. Topics about activities in the here-and-now were rarely mentioned, which is in stark contrast to topic nomination of sighted children at the same age. Instead of being provided with extensive or elaborated descriptions of topics from their mothers, blind children received a restricted sample of language. When a child provided an object label, the mothers rarely extended beyond what the child stated, although they did, on occasion, engage in direct expansion of the child's comment. In two-word utterances, Dote-Kwan's blind subjects usually did not include novel information concerning the qualities of the objects, rather falling back on restricted label-focused speech as their major discourse strategy.

In a second study of mother–child interactions, Dote-Kwan (1995) investigated mother–blind child dyads, ages 20–36 months, interacting in daily routines on two different occasions. She identified two maternal communication moves in the interactions: (a) mother-initiated behaviors, and (b) mother-responsive behaviors as well as a set of child-initiated behaviors. The most common mother-initiation was calling the child's name, followed by facilitating the child's ability to antici-pate activities or acknowledging changes in the child's physical environment. The latter communications can be seen as highly directive interactional utterances such as telling the child that their cup has been moved to the sink, or saying "no" to the child who is touching the television control knobs. Mother-responsive behaviors included (1) encouraging the child's involvement in mobility tasks, (2) complying with the child's request for help with an object, (3) repeating or rephrasing the child's communicative behavior, and (4) pacing the rate of speech and length of pauses between turn taking in vocal interactions. Mother-initiation behaviors were most common with children with less language ability, that is, children in the first word stage, while the mother-responsive behaviors were more characteristic of interactions with children displaying more language facility. Child-initiations dropped dramatically when the mother was not immediately available, demonstrating that young blind children are cognizant of the need for mother's presence in order to have an interaction.

Taken as a whole, these findings suggest that there is an imbalance in the conversations of mothers and blind children. Mothers must, of necessity, be very directive in their management of the conversation both with regard to topic nomination and topic management. They tend to provide blind children with labels for objects rather than rich descriptions of the objects that would be more characteristic of mother and typically developing child. In response to this style, blind children are observed to adopt a fairly passive role in topic nomination, and tend not to provide novel information. The behavior of mothers reported in these studies is entirely realistic due to the fact that the blind child cannot see the objects or animate topics and will not be able to direct attention unless coached about what is in the environment. Further, mothers need to control the action in order to protect the child from potential harm.

Since there are degrees of visual impairment, the question becomes whether the presence of some sight has an effect on mother–child interactions. Moore and McConachie (1994) argue that degree of sight will make a difference in mother–child interactions, based on their study of eight blind children and eight children who had severely impaired but useable vision and their mothers. Children in both groups received more requests for actions than any other utterance type. All mothers made infrequent mention of the attributes of objects. However, mothers of the blind children were far more likely to initiate an interaction with a verbal comment alone, while mothers of the severely visually impaired children were likely to use a verbal statement accompanied by a gesture. Mothers of blind children made fewer references to objects/toys that were the child's current focus of attention and more references to potential objects.

Conti-Ramsden and Perez-Pereira (1999) tracked the interactions of three young children – one who was blind, one who had low vision, and the third who had normal sight – with their mothers. The data revealed an asymmetry between the contributions of the mother–blind child dyad. Although the blind child contributed to the interaction at the same rate as the other two children, that mother used almost three times as many communicative acts. The blind child used a significantly higher proportion of non-verbal turns when compared to the other two children. The blind and low vision children engaged in interactions aided by their mothers who physically helped them to follow instructions by moving their hands to an object. The mothers never used a non-verbal communicative act without accompanying it with language with the blind and low vision children, whereas 2 percent of the interchanges with the sighted child were purely non-verbal. The mother of the low vision child used descriptions as part of her imperative utterances. In agreement with previous findings, the mother of the blind child used the most imperatives; these imperatives or directives tended to be stacked, or came in bursts as if she was trying to repeat or elaborate on the directive each time she presented it. More likely, she was providing the blind infant with a context. In a second study, involving three blind children and one normally sighted twin of one of the blind children, Perez-Pereira and Conti-Ramsden (2001) confirmed the results of their previous study particularly with regard to stacked imperatives by the mothers of the blind children.

4.2 Language acquisition

Language acquisition in blind children has not been heavily researched, neither at early nor later stages, but the information that is available is considered in the next section.

4.2.1 Early language acquisition The early words of blind children are very similar to those of sighted children (Andersen, Dunlea, & Kekelis, 1984; Dunlea,

1989). However, as reported by Andersen et al. (1984), the meanings of words that blind children attach are limited and often not extended to new instances of the same referents. Sixty to seventy percent of the meaning of words of blind children in the single-word period is tied to the original use or context. This contrasts to word learning in sighted children where only 10 percent of the words are tied to their original context. Anderson et al. conclude that blind children are not constructing hypotheses about the nature and meaning of words to the same degree as their sighted peers in the earliest stages of language learning.

Blind and sighted children begin to combine words and to express a range of semantic relationships at about the same age, despite blind children's constrained lexical development (Dunlea, 1989). A closer examination of these early words also reveals some striking differences. First, blind children encode their own agency or possession, while sighted children tend to refer to others as agents and to both themselves and others as possessors (Klincans, 1991). Second, blind children rarely express original descriptive information, whereas sighted children seemed intrigued to discover and talk about new or unexpected qualities of objects and locations (Perez-Pereira and Castro, 1992). Third, blind children's most complex constructions refer to past events, while sighted children's typically describe the "here and now." Consequently, the regular past tense marker is one of the first morphemes to emerge in blind children. Fourth, blind children seem to have particular difficulty with the prepositions "in" and "on." These first appear as verb particles for blind children ("put in box"), but emerge as true prepositions in sighted children ("in the box"). When prepositional use does develop in blind children's language, inappropriate use is very common ("keep your food in your plate," rather than "keep your food on your plate"). Clearly, there are differences between the acquisition of semantics and syntax in blind as compared to sighted children.

4.2.2 Later language acquisition Language facility at older ages requires mastery of discourse forms and the ability to engage in meaningful extended communication exchanges. Rosel et al. (2005) investigated the narrative language of blind Spanish-speaking children and a comparable group of sighted children. They focused on "verbalism" in narrative structure, that is, using words for which there is no specific referent, such as color terms. They found equal use of verbalisms by both blind and sighted children, with verbalism used observed to increase with age in blind children. Use of words without clear referents has been traditionally seen as atypical in blind children, but Rosel et al.'s results suggest that it is a normal process seen in all speakers of a particular language. As blind children mature they seem to acquire and use the full breadth of lexical items available in the language as part of becoming effective communicators.

In narratives, knowledge of the language used to describe social interactions is very important. Pring and Dewart (1998) studied the ability of blind and sighted readers to determine the mental state of characters in stories. The subjects were given two stories examining such mental states as lying, communication misunderstanding, sarcasm, pretense, and persuasion, among others. Both groups easily used mental state verbs, but the explanations provided by blind children for their choices were less correct than those provided by sighted children. Blind children appear to possess less knowledge about social interactions and thus have less information for making judgments about the mental states motivating actions in others. This particular issue suggests that blind students may have problems with academically related materials that require this insight, such as critiquing literature.

In a study on blind college-age students' understanding of expository prose, Tuncer and Altunay (2006) investigated the comprehension levels of four individuals as they attempted to process expository prose that was initially very difficult to understand. The students were taught to summarize the prose as a way of increasing their comprehension of this discourse format. This approach did increase the students' comprehension. Since the focus of this study was on the retention of content, we do not know if this approach might foster understanding of the organization of expository discourse. Does it assist if the learning of that expository prose is organized using clear connections between paragraphs, and syntactic forms such as discourse conjunctions, including "however" and "therefore"?

4.2.3 Knowledge about English conversation The blind child's knowledge of conversation and interaction was also studied by Andersen, Dunlea, and Kekelis (1984), who found that some blind children had difficulty with certain linguistic structures in conversation, particularly the reciprocal pronouns "I" and "you," and deictic pronouns, "this" and "that." Both of these sets of relational terms are dependent on visual cues, namely, the person one is talking to is "you" while the child talking is "I." Similarly, "this" refers to nearby objects while "that" generally refers to distant objects. Perfect (2001) argues that some of these problems may be due to delayed echolalia. In observing one 3-year-old blind child, she found he would echo a phrase or part of a sentence used previously within that or another conversational exchange. By doing this, the child would maintain the pronoun "I" even though it was not appropriate to that specific conversational context. She also found that the blind children in her sample tended to ask questions that mirrored adult statements as a way to maintain open lines of communication and as a way of soliciting information about their immediate environment. She observed that sighted children tend to use questions to relate objects to familiar situations and to ask about past experiences. The question becomes whether this misuse of pronouns is a true misunderstanding of linguistic constructions, a tendency to use echolalia as a conversational strategy, or both (Erin, 1990).

In face-to-face conversation, sighted individuals use gestures as a way of supplementing the semantic content of what they are saying, with three types of gestures used most commonly. First, there are emblems that are gestures with direct verbal translations, for example, the "hang loose" gesture (the extension of the thumb and pinkie and shaking it back and forth) used by Hawaiians and the members of the surfing community. Second, there are illustrators, or gestures that help to describe what is being said. For example, making a size or shape gesture to signal that one object is bigger than another. Third, there are adaptors or gestures that signal emotional states, such as touching one's body (self-adaptors), touching an object (object-adaptors), or other people (alter-adaptors). Blind and sighted adults' gestures were significantly different from one another. Blind adults tend to use more adaptors, while sighted individuals tend to use emblems and illustrators (Frame, 2000). Although it is clear that among blind adults and older children gestural use during conversation is different from that of sighted individuals, it is not clear whether this difference is apparent early in language acquisition of blind children or how it changes over time. Studies focusing on the paralinguistic features of conversation with very young blind children would certainly be a profitable line of research.

Conversational initiations in school (school discourse) are different than those that occur in non-school interactions. McGaha and Farran (2001) investigated the social interactions between blind and sighted preschool children in an inclusive classroom. Both groups of children preferred to play with sighted partners. They found that the number of initiations generated by the blind children was significantly below that of their sighted peers, and, more importantly, those initiations tended to fail. To assist blind children, the researchers recommended that teachers focus attention on helping them learn how to develop effective initiation procedures. While this is a good idea, it is important to remember that initiations in children's play do not parallel that of adults. Teachers need to carefully observe the initiations that are the norm for their classroom and then coach children on how to use those strategies, rather than suggesting entry bids that might work with adults, but not other children.

Depending on whether blind children are developing normally, otherwise, or whether they may have other disabilities, speech-language pathologists may or may not be involved in assessing and/or assisting those children with communication. It would be particularly important to carefully observe the interactions of any blind child in the clinic, preschool or school environment to establish a baseline on communication abilities, particularly their interpersonal interactions. It goes without saying that any child with significant visual problems should have their hearing tested on a regular basis.

5   Deaf-blind

In addition to deaf and blind children, there is a small group of children who are both deaf and blind. Depending on the extent of their hearing and visual losses, this group of individuals may be quite dependent on tactual input for their acquisition of communication and language. There is a small but growing body of research that focuses on communication issues in this group of children. Bruce et al. (2007) investigated the early use of gestures by seven children who were classified as deaf-blind. The types of gestures generated were: (a) contact points where the child touched another communication partner, (b) pushing an object, (c) clapping with another communication partner, and (d) reaching out with one's hand. Four of Bruce et al.'s subjects used gestures primarily to express the function of requesting an action, two to request an object, and one to protest. Some gestures emerged out of a child's emotional state, such as wiggling the fingers and flapping the arms in excitement. Taken as a whole, this sample of deaf-blind children generated from six to 13 different types of gestures per child, with one gesture found to serve up to seven different functions. Just as with deaf, blind, and typical children, early gestures appear to play an important role in the acquisition of language for deaf-blind children. Other than this study, no reports on language acquisition or growth in deaf-blind individuals could be located. This area of study seems particularly important since it is likely that an increasing number of deaf-blind children will be given cochlear implants and will be in need of intervention (Chute & Nevins, 1995).

Communication between deaf-blind individuals and communication partners involve one of three types of interactions. First, there is the Tadoma method, or tactual speechreading, where the deaf-blind individual places a hand over the face and neck of the talker to monitor various facial actions as well as the production of speech. Second, there is fingerspelling, where the letters of the manual alphabet are spelled directly into the hands of the deaf-blind person. Third, there is use of a formal sign system such as ASL or Pidgin Signed English (PSE) that the deaf-person receives by placing a hand (or hands) on the dominant (or both) hands of the signer and passively tracing the motion of the signing hand. Reed and associates (Reed et al., 1982; Reed et al., 1990; Reed & Delhorne, 1995) have determined that experienced deaf-blind adults are able to receive key words in conversational speech at roughly 80 percent accuracy for the Tadoma and fingerspelling modes and 60–85 percent for ASL/PSE, which suggests that all these modes are suitable for deaf-blind adults.

In investigating how one 3;6-year-old deaf-blind child interacted, Vervloed et al. (2006) observed the child in an experienced teacher's special education classroom. The teacher and child established meaningful communicative interactions where both partners contributed equally to the interaction; however, because of the demands of the classroom, the teacher was not always able to engage in sustained interactions. Unfortunately, not all deaf-blind children have continuous access to such highly experienced communication partners, but this interpreter-tutor model should be available to every deaf-blind child during the early intervention stage and during school programs.

6 Summary

Speech-language pathologists and audiologists have important roles to play in early identification and subsequent intervention with deaf and hard-of-hearing infants, toddlers, and young children but they must obtain necessary knowledge about typical language acquisition, technology and communication modes in order to positively contribute to this process. Helping families with deaf children is not a time to engage in debates about mode of communication no matter how strong the professional's bias. The parents or families of the deaf child should decide the issue regarding sign versus spoken language or any combination of modes. Speech and hearing professionals are urged to seek out collaboration with persons who are experienced in working with deaf children, including educators of the deaf, parents, and early intervention specialists, to ensure that deaf children are helped to achieve to their fullest potential.

Deaf children, with and without cochlear implants, will continue to enter general education settings as the least restrictive environment, where SLPs and educational audiologists will have increasing responsibilities for supporting them. Help is also desperately needed for children with marginal/mild/moderate hearing loss who are already in regular educational settings but may not be progressing in ways that are consistent with their potential. SLPs and educational audiologists should not confine their help to improving speech performance or developing "auditory skills" for this group but should identify the interpersonal and school discourse needs of these students.

Blind children are certain to be placed in general education settings these days, since their sensory impairment should not have an effect on language/communication use or school learning. This means that SLPs and educational audiologists will have more traditional roles with blind students, including speech and language therapy and monitoring of hearing status through screening or audiological evaluations.

In either case, interacting with and assisting children with sensory impairments to experience full access to communication and learning is certain to be one of the most rewarding activities speech and hearing professionals can have.

NOTES

1   To save space in this chapter, we will use the term "deaf" to refer to children with significant bilateral hearing loss that is permanent and severe to profound in degree. To be sure, most of the research findings and intervention principles can be applied to children with milder forms of hearing loss but the use of other terminology such as hearing impairment, hearing disorder, or hearing handicap makes writing much more difficult. When reference is made to families or children who define themselves as culturally Deaf, the term will be capitalized.

2   The same point applies to infants or children who are visually impaired. We will use the term "blind" to refer to children who are likely, at least initially, to be Braille readers, require mobility assistance, and generally learn without recourse to vision, although through optical advances the child may be able to read print or use other methods for print reading as they mature.

3   '1-3-6' refers to screening by 1 month of age, evaluation by 3 months of age and early intervention services by 6 months of age. The advantages of intervention by 6 months of age on subsequent communication abilities holds true regardless of gender, socioeconomic status, ethnicity, cognitive status, degree of hearing loss, mode of communication, and presence/absence of other disabilities.

4 Researchers including Kent et al. (1987), Stark (1972, 1980, 1983), Stoel-Gammon & Otomo (1986) and others have also investigated the effects of deafness on vocal behavior.

5 Ertmer edited a Clinical Forum on cochlear implants for *Language Speech and Hearing Services in the Schools*, 33 (3), 2002. The reader is referred to that Forum for a range of information on cochlear implants in young children.

6 There are several excellent monographs explaining the ANSI 12.60-2002 acoustical standards for classrooms, including *Language Speech and Hearing Services in the Schools*, 31, October, 2000 and *Seminars in Hearing*, 25 (2), 2004.

REFERENCES

Ackerman, J., Kyle, J., Woll, B., & Ezra, M. (1990). Lexical acquisition in sign and speech: Evidence from a longitudinal study of infants in deaf families. In C. Lucas (ed.), *Sign language research: Theoretical issues* (pp. 337–45). Washington, DC: Gallaudet University.

Akamatsu, C. (1982). *The acquisition of fingerspelling in pre-school children*. Unpublished doctoral dissertation, University of Rochester.

Al-Mondhiry, R. & Mason, P. (2008). Early hearing detection advances. *The ASHA Leader* 13 (4) (March 25), 1, 37.

Alegria, J., Charlier, B. L., & Mattys, S. (1999). The role of lipreading and cued speech in the processing of phonological information in French-educated deaf children. *European Journal of Cognitive Psychology* 11, 451–72.

Alegria, J. & Lechat, J. (2005). Phonological processing in deaf children: When lipreading and cues are incongruent. *Journal of Deaf Studies and Deaf Education* 10, 122–33.

Andersen, E., Dunlea, A., & Kekelis, L. (1984). Blind children's language: Resolving some differences. *Journal of Child Language* 11, 645–64.

Andersen, E., Dunlea, A., & Kekelis, L. (1993). The impact of input: Language acquisition in the visually impaired. *First Language* 13, 23–49.

Anderson, D. & Reilly, J. S. (2002). The MacArthur Communication Development Inventory: Normative data for American Sign Language. *Journal of Deaf Studies and Deaf Education 7*, 83–106.

Anderson, K. (1991). Hearing conversation in the public schools revisited. *Seminars in Hearing* 12, 340–64.

Bergeson, T. R., Pisoni, D. B., & Davis, R. A. O. (2003). A longitudinal study of audiovisual speech perception by children with hearing loss who have cochlear implants. *The Volta Review* 103, 347–70.

Bess, F. H. (1985). The minimally hearing-impaired child. *Ear and Hearing* 6, 43–7.

Bess, F. H., Dodd-Murphy, J., & Parker, R. A. (1998). Children with minimal sensorineural hearing loss: Prevalence, educational performance, and functional status. *Ear and Hearing* 19, 339–54.

Blaylock, R. L., Scudder, R. R., & Wynne, M. K. (1995). Repair behaviors used by children with hearing loss. *Language, Speech, and Hearing Services in Schools* 26, 278–85.

Blennerhassett, L. (1984). Communicative styles of a 13 month old hearing impaired child and her parents. *The Volta Review* 86, 217–28.

Bowerman, M. & Brown, P. (eds.) (2008). *Crosslinguistic perspectives on argument structure*. New York: Lawrence Erlbaum.

Brown, P. M., Abu Barker, Z., Rickards, F. W., & Griffin, P. (2006). Family functioning, early intervention support, and spoken language and placement outcomes with profound hearing impairment. *Deafness Education International* 8, 207–26.

Brown, P. M. & Nott, P. (2006). Family-centered practice in early intervention for oral language development: Philosophy, methods, and research. In P. E. Spencer & M. Marschark (eds.), *Advances in the spoken language development of deaf and hard-of-hearing children* (pp. 136–65). New York: Oxford University Press.

Brown, R. (1973). *A first language: The early stages.* Cambridge, MA: Harvard University Press.

Bruce, S. M., Mann, A., Jones, C., & Gavin, M. (2007). Gestures expressed by children who are congenitally deaf-blind: Topography, rate, and function. *Journal of Visual Impairment and Blindness* 102, 637–52.

Calderon, R. & Naidu, S. (2000). Further support of the benefits of early identification and intervention with children with hearing loss. In C. Yoshinaga-Itano & A. L. Sedey (eds.), Language, speech, and socio-emotional development of children who are deaf and hard-of-hearing: The early years. *The Volta Review* 100, 53–84.

Carroll, D. W. (2004). *Psychology of Language,* 4th ed. Belmont, CA: Wadsworth.

Caselli, M. C. (1983). Communication to language: Deaf children's and hearing children's development compared. *Sign Language Studies* 39, 133–44.

Cheek, A., Cormier, K., Repp, A., & Meier, R. P. (2001). Prelinguistic gestures predict mastery and error in the production of first signs. *Language* 77, 292–323.

Chute, P. M. & Nevins, M. E. (1995). Cochlear implants in people who are deaf-blind. *Journal of Visual Impairment and Blindness* 89, 297–302.

Ciocci, S. R. & Baran, J. A. (1998). The use of conversational repair strategies by children who are deaf. *American Annals of the Deaf* 143, 235–45.

Clark, M. (2007). *A practical guide to quality interaction with children who have a hearing loss.* San Diego, CA: Plural Publishing.

Colin, K. E., Mirus, G. R., Mauk, C., & Meier, R. P. (2000). The acquisition of first signs: Place, handshape, and movement. In C. Chamberlain, J. P. Morford, & R. I. Mayberry (eds.), *Language acquisition by eye* (pp. 51–69). Mahwah, NJ: Lawrence Erlbaum.

Connor, C. M. & Zwalan, T. A. (2004). Examining multiple source of influence on the reading comprehension skills of children who use cochlear implants. *Journal of Speech, Language, and Hearing Research* 47, 509–26.

Conti-Ramsden, G. & Perez-Pereira, M. (1999). Conversational interactions between mothers and their infants who are congenitally blind, have low vision, or are sighted. *Journal of Visual Impairment and Behavior* 93, 691–704.

Cornett, R. O. (1967). Cued speech. *American Annals of the Deaf* 112, 3–13.

Crandell, C., Smaldino, J., & Flexer, C. (eds.) (2005). *Sound-field FM amplification: Theory and practical applications,* 2nd ed. Clifton Park, NY: Thompson Delmar.

Cross, T. G., Johnson-Morris, J. E., & Nienhuys, T. G. (1980). Linguistic feedback and maternal speech: Comparisons of mothers addressing hearing and hearing-impaired children. *First Language* 1, 163–89.

Crosson, J. & Geers, A. (2001). Analysis of narrative ability in children with cochlear implants. *Ear and Hearing* 22, 381–94.

Davis, B. L. & MacNeilage, P. F. (1994). Organization of canonical babbling. *Journal of Speech and Hearing Research* 38, 341–55.

Davis, B. L. & MacNeilage, P. F. (1995). The articulatory basis of babbling. *Journal of Speech and Hearing Research* 38, 1199–211.

Delage, H. & Tuller, L. (2007). Language development and mild-to-moderate hearing loss: Does language normalize with age? *Journal of Speech, Language, and Hearing Research* 50, 1300–13.

Descourtieux, C., Groh, V., Rusterholz, A., Simoulin, I., & Busquet, D. (1999). Cued speech in the simulation of communication: An advantage in cochlear implantation. *International Journal of Pediatric Otorhinolaryngology* 47, 205–7.

Dore, J. (1974). A pragmatic description of early language development. *Journal of Psycholinguistic Research* 3, 343–50.

Dote-Kwan, J. (1995). Impact of mothers' interactions on the development of their young visually impaired children. *Journal of Visual Impairment and Blindness* 89, 46–59.

Dromi, E. (2003). Assessment of prelinguistic behaviors in deaf children: Parents as collaborators. *Journal of Deaf Studies and Deaf Education* 8, 367–82.

Duncan, J. (1999). Conversational skills of children with hearing loss and children with normal hearing in an integrated setting. *The Volta Review* 99, 193–203.

Dunlea, A. (1989). *Vision and the emergence of meaning: Blind and sighted children's early language*. Cambridge: Cambridge University.

Eddy, J. R. (1997). Mothers' topic-control behaviors during play interaction with hearing-impaired and normally hearing preschoolers. *The Volta Review* 97, 171–83.

Eilers, R. E. & Oller, D. K. (1994). Infant vocalizations and the early diagnosis of severe hearing impairment. *Journal of Pediatrics* 124, 199–203.

English, K. & Church, G. (1999). Unilateral hearing loss in children: An update for the 1990s. *Language, Speech, and Hearing Services in Schools* 30, 26–31.

Eriks-Brophy, A. & Ayukawa, H. (2000). The benefits of sound field amplification in classrooms of Inuit students of Nunavik: A pilot project. *Language, Speech, and Hearing Services in Schools* 31, 324–35.

Erin, E. N. (1990). Language samples from visually impaired four- and five year olds. *Journal of Childhood Communication Disorders* 13, 181–91.

Erting, C. J., Prezioso, C., & O'Grady Hynes, M. (1990). The interactional context of mother–infant communication. In V. Volterra & C. J. Erting (eds.), *From gesture to language in hearing and deaf children* (pp. 97–106). Berlin: Springer-Verlag.

Ertmer, D., Leonard, J. S., & Pachuilo, M. L. (2002). Communication intervention for children with cochlear implants: Two case studies. *Language, Speech, and Hearing Services in Schools* 33, 205–17.

Ertmer, D. J. & Stark, R. E. (1995). Eliciting prespeech vocalizations in a young child with profound hearing impairment: Usefulness of real-time spectrographic speech displays. *American Journal of Speech-Language Pathology* 4, 33–8.

Ertmer, D. J., Strong, L. M., & Sadagopan, N. (2003). Beginning to communicate after cochlear implantation: Oral language development in a young child. *Journal of Speech, Language, and Hearing Research* 46, 328–40.

Ertmer, D. J., Young, N., & Nathani, S. (2007). Profiles of vocal development in young cochlear implant recipients. *Journal of Speech, Language, and Hearing Research* 50, 393–407.

Fenson, L., Dale, P. S., Reznick, J. S., Thai, D., Bates, E., Hartung, J. P., Pethick, S., & Reilly, J. S. (1993). *MacArthur communicative development inventory – Toddlers*. San Diego, CA: Singular.

Flexer, C. (1989). Turn on sound: An odyssey of sound field amplification. *Educational Audiology Association Newsletter* 5, 6–7.

Flexer, C. (1995). Classroom management of children with minimal hearing loss. *The Hearing Journal* 48 (10), 56–8.

Flexer, C., Millin, J., & Brown, L. (1990). Children with developmental disabilities: The effect of sound field amplification on word identification.

Language, Speech, and Hearing Services in Schools 21, 177–82.

Flipsen, P. & Colvard, L. G. (2006). Intelligibility of conversational speech produced by children with cochlear implants. *Journal of Communication Disorders* 39, 93–108.

Folven, R. & Bonvillian, J. D. (1991). The transition from nonreferential to referential language in children acquiring American Sign Language. *Developmental Psychology* 27, 806–16.

Ford, J. & Fredericks, B. (1995). Using interpreter-tutors in school programs for students who are deaf-blind. *Journal of Visual Impairment and Blindness* 89, 229–35.

Frame, M. J. (2000). The relationship between visual impairment and gestures. *Journal of Visual Impairment and Blindness* 94, 155–72.

Fryhauf-Bertschy, H., Tyler, R., Kelsay, D., Gantz, B., & Woodworth, G. (1997). Cochlear implant use by prelingually deafened children: The influence of age at implant and length of device use. *Journal of Speech, Language, and Hearing Research* 40, 183–99.

Gallaway, C. & Woll, B. (1994). Interaction and childhood deafness. In C. Gallaway & B. J. Richards (eds.), *Input and interaction in language acquisition* (pp. 197–218). Cambridge: Cambridge University.

Geers, A. (2004). Speech, language, and reading skills after early cochlear implantation. *Archives of Otolaryngology – Head and Neck Surgery* 130, 634–8.

Geers, A., Spehar, B., & Sedey, A. (2002). Use of speech by children from total communication programs who wear cochlear implants. *American Journal of Speech-Language Pathology* 11, 50–8.

Gilbertson, M. & Kamhi, A. G. (1995). Novel word learning in children with hearing impairment. *Journal of Speech and Hearing Research* 38, 630–42.

Goldberg, L. R. & Richburg, C. M. (2004). Minimal hearing impairment: Major myths with more than minimal implications. *Communication Disorders Quarterly* 25, 152–60.

Gravel, J. (1996). Otitis media: A common but complex condition of childhood. *The Hearing Journal* 49 (10), 60–4.

Guiberson, M. M. (2005). Children with cochlear implants from bilingual families: Considerations for intervention and a case study. *The Volta Review* 105, 29–39.

Hage, C., Alegria, J., & Perier, O. (1991). Cued speech and language acquisition: The case of grammatical gender morpho-phonology. In D. S. Martin (ed.), *Advances in cognition, education, and deafness* (pp. 395–9). Washington, DC: Gallaudet University Press.

Harris, M., Clibbens, J., Chasin, J., & Tibbitts, (1989). The social context of early sign language development. *First Language* 9, 81–97.

Houston, D. M., Ying, E. A., Pisoni, D. B., & Kirk, K. I. (2003). Development of pre-word learning skills in infants with cochlear implants. *The Volta Review* 103, 303–26.

Hudgins, C. V. & Numbers, F. C. (1942). An investigation of intelligibility of speech of the deaf. *Genetic Psychology Monograph* 25, 289–92.

James, D., Rajput, K., Brown, T., Sirimanna, T., Brinton, J., & Goswami, U. (2005). Phonological awareness in deaf children who use cochlear implants. *Journal of Speech, Language, and Hearing Research* 48, 1151–528.

Johnson, C. (1997). Enhancing the conversational skills of children with hearing impairment. *Language, Speech, and Hearing Services in Schools* 28, 137–46.

Johnson, D. (1991). Visual assessment of people who are deaf. *ASHA* 33 (11), 32–35+.

Joint Committee on Infant Hearing (2007). Year 2007 position statement: Principles and guidelines of early hearing detection and hearing intervention. *Pediatrics* 120, 898–921.

Kaderavek, J. N. & Pakulski, L. A. (2007).
Mother–child story book interactions:
Literacy orientation of pre-schoolers
with hearing impairment. *Journal of
Childhood Literacy* 7, 49–77.

Kantor, R. (1982). Communicative
interaction: Mother modification and
child acquisition of American Sign
Language. Reprinted in M. McIntire
(ed.), *The acquisition of American Sign
Language* (pp. 115–72). Burtonsville,
MD: Linstock Press.

Kelly, A. (1995). Fingerspelling interaction:
A set of deaf parents and their deaf
daughter. In C. Lucas (ed.),
*Sociolinguistics in deaf communities:
Volume 1* (pp. 62–73). Washington, DC:
Gallaudet College.

Kent, R. D., Osberger, M. J., Netsell, R.,
& Goldschmidt Hustedde, C. (1987).
Phonetic development in identical twins
differing in auditory function. *Journal of
Speech and Hearing Disorders* 52, 64–75.

Kipila, B. (1985). Analysis of an oral
language sample from a prelingually
deaf child's cued speech: A case study.
Cued Speech Annals 1, 46–59.

Kirkman, M. & Cross, T. (1986).
Conversation between mothers and
their deaf children. In T. Cross &
L. Riach (eds.), *Aspects of child
development* (pp. 217–53). Hillsdale, NJ:
Lawrence Erlbaum.

Klima, E. & Bellugi, U. (1979). *Signs of
language*. Cambridge, MA: Harvard
University Press.

Klincans, L. (1991). The development of
speech acts by a blind child and his
identical sighted twin. Unpublished
MSc thesis, University of British
Columbia.

Koester, L., Traci, M., Brooks, L.,
Karkowski, A., & Smith-Gray, S. (2004).
Mother–infant behaviors at 6 and
9 months: A microanalytic view.
In K. Meadows-Orlans, P. Spencer, &
L. Koester (eds.), *The world of deaf infants*
(pp. 40–56). New York: Oxford
University Press.

Kretschmer, R. R. (1997). Issues in the
development of school and
interpersonal discourse for children who
have hearing loss. *Language, Speech, and
Hearing Services in Schools* 28, 374–83.

Kretschmer, R. R. & Kretschmer, L. W.
(1978). *Language development and
intervention with the hearing impaired.*
Baltimore, MD: University Park Press.

Kretschmer, R. R. & Kretschmer, L. W.
(1984). Language habilitation of deaf
children. In W. Perkins (ed.), *Current
therapy of communication disorders:
Hearing disorders* (pp. 37–46). New York:
Thieme Stratton.

Kretschmer, R. R. & Kretschmer, L. W.
(1990). Language. In S. R. Silverman &
P. B. Kricos (eds.), A centennial review.
The Volta Review 92, 55–72.

Kretschmer, R. R. & Kretschmer, L. W.
(1995). The bases of communicative
classrooms. *Volta Review* 97 (5), 1–18.

Kretschmer, R. R. & Kretschmer, L. W.
(1999). Communication and language
development. *Australian Journal of
Education of the Deaf* 5, 17–26.

Lederberg, A. (2003). Expressing meaning:
From communicative intent to building
a lexicon. In M. Marschark &
P. E. Spencer (eds.), *Deaf studies,
language, and education* (pp. 247–60).
New York: Oxford University Press.

Lederberg, A. & Everhardt, V. (2000).
Conversations between deaf children
and their hearing mothers: Pragmatic
and dialogic characteristics. *Journal of
Deaf Studies and Deaf Education* 5,
303–22.

Lederberg, A. & Prezbindowski, A. K.
(2000). Impact of child deafness on
mother–toddler interaction: Strengths
and weaknesses. In P. E. Spencer,
C. J. Erting, & M. Marschark (eds.), *The
deaf child in the family and at school: Essays
in honor of Kathryn P. Meadows-Orlans*
(pp. 73–92). Mahwah, NJ: Lawrence
Erlbaum.

Lederberg, A., Prezbindowski, A. K., &
Spencer, P. E. (2001). Word-learning

skills of deaf preschoolers: The development of novel mapping and rapid word-learning strategies. *Child Development* 71, 1571–85.

Lenden, J. M. & Flipsen, P. (2007). Prosody and voice characteristics of children with cochlear implants. *Journal of Communication Disorders* 40, 66–81.

Leybaert, J. (2000). Phonology acquired through the eyes and spelling in deaf children. *Journal of Experimental Child Psychology* 75, 291–318.

Leybaert, J. & Lechat, J. (2001). Phonological similarity effects in memory for serial order of cued speech. *Journal of Speech, Language, and Hearing Research* 44, 949–63.

Lichtert, G. F. & Loncke, F. T. (2006). The development of proto-performative utterances in deaf toddlers. *Journal of Speech, Language, and Hearing Research* 49, 486–99.

Luterman, D. (2004). *Counseling for parents of children with auditory disorders.* New York: Thieme.

MacNeilage, P. F. & Davis, B. L. (1990a). Acquisition of speech production: Frames then content. In M. Jeannerod (ed.), *Attention and performance XIII: Motor representation and control* (pp. 452–75). Hillsdale, NJ: Lawrence Erlbaum.

MacNeilage, P. F. & Davis, B. L. (1990b). Acquisition of speech production: The achievement of segmental independence. In W. J. Hardcastle & A. Marchal (eds.), *Speech production and speech modeling* (pp. 55–68). Dordrecht: Kluwer Academic Publishers.

MacNeilage, P. F. & Davis, B. L. (1993). Motor explanations of babbling and early speech patterns. In B. Boysson-Bardies, S. de Schoen, P. Jusczyk, P. MacNeilage, & J. Morton (eds.), *Developmental neurocognition: Speech and face processing in the first year of life* (pp. 341–53). Dordrecht: Kluwer Academic Publishers.

Manentette, P. F. & Mayberry, R. I. (2000). Principles for an emerging phonological system: A case study of the acquisition of American Sign Language. In C. Chamberlain, J. P. Moreford, & R. I. Mayberry (eds.), *Language acquisition by eye* (pp. 71–90). Mahwah, NJ: Lawrence Erlbaum.

Marschark, M., Convertino, C. Macias, Monikowski, C., Sapere, P., & Seewagen, R. (2007). Understanding communication among deaf students who sign and speak: A trivial pursuit? *American Annals of the Deaf* 152, 415–24.

Masataka, N. (1992). Motherese in a signed language. *Infant Behavior and Development*, 15, 453–60.

Mavilya, M. (1969). Spontaneous vocalizations and babbling in hearing impaired infants. *Dissertation Abstracts International* 31 (01), 74. (UMI No. 70-12879). Unpublished doctoral dissertation, Columbia University.

Mayer, C. (2007). What really matters in the early literacy development of deaf children? *Journal of Deaf Studies and Deaf Education* 12, 411–31.

Mayer, C. & Wells, G. (1996). Can the linguistic interdependence theory support a bilingual–bicultural model of literacy education for deaf students? *Journal of Deaf Studies and Deaf Education* 1, 93–107.

Mayer, M. (1969). *Frog where are you?* New York: Dial.

Mayne, A. M. (1998a). Expressive vocabulary development of infants and toddlers who are deaf or hard of hearing. *The Volta Review* 100, 1–12.

Mayne, A. M. (1998b). Receptive vocabulary development of infants and toddlers who are deaf or hard of hearing. *The Volta Review* 100, 29–62.

McCaffrey H. A. (1999). Multichannel cochlear implantation and the organization of early speech. *The Volta Review* 101, 5–24.

McGaha, C. G. & Farran, D. C. (2001). Interactions in inclusive classrooms: The effects of visual status and setting.

Journal of Visual Impairments and Blindness 96, 80–94.

Meadows, K. P., Greenberg, M. T., Erting, C., & Carmichael, H. S. (1981). Interactions of deaf mothers and deaf preschool children: Comparisons with three other groups of deaf and hearing dyads. *American Annals of the Deaf* 126, 454–8.

Meadows-Orlans, K. P. (1997). Effects of mother and infant hearing status on interactions at twelve and eighteen months. *Journal of Deaf Studies and Deaf Education* 2, 26–36.

Meier, R. P. & Newport, E. L. (1990). Out of the hands of babes: On a possible sign advantage in language acquisition. *Language* 66, 1–23.

Meier, R. P., Mauk, C., Cheek, A., & Moreland, C. J. (1998). Motoric constraints on early sign acquisition. *Papers and Reports in Child Language Development* 29, 63–72.

Meier, R. P. & Willerman, R. (1995). Prelinguistic gesture in deaf and hearing children. In K. Emmorey & J. Reilly (eds.), *Language, gesture, and space* (pp. 391–409). Hillsdale, NJ; Lawrence Erlbaum.

Messenheimer-Young, T. & Kretschmer, R. R. (1994). "Can I play?" A hearing-impaired preschooler's requests to access maintained social interactions. *The Volta Review* 96, 5–18.

Miyamoto, R. T., Kirk, K. I., Svirsky, M., & Sehgal, S. T. (1999). Communication skills in pediatric cochlear implant recipients. *Acta Otolaryngologica* 119, 219–24.

Miyamoto, R. T., Svirsky, M., Kirk, K., Robbins, A. M., Todd, S., & Riley, A. (1997). Speech intelligibility of children with multichannel cochlear implants. *Annals of Otology, Rhinology, and Laryngology* 106, 35–6.

Moeller, M. P. (2000). Early intervention and language development in children who are deaf and hard of hearing. *Pediatrics* 106, E43.

Moeller, M. P., Hoover, B. M., Putman, C. A. et al. (2007a). Vocalizations of infants with hearing loss compared to infants with normal hearing: Part I – Phonetic development. *Ear and Hearing* 28, 605–27.

Moeller, M. P., Hoover, B. M., Putman, C. A. et al. (2007b). Vocalizations of infants with hearing loss compared to infants with normal hearing: Part II – Transition to words. *Ear and Hearing* 28, 628–42.

Mohay, H., Milton, L., Hindmarsh, C., & Ganley, K. (1998). Deaf mothers as language models for hearing families with deaf children. In A. Weisel (ed.), *Issues unresolved: New perspectives on language and deafness* (pp. 76–87). Washington, DC: Gallaudet University.

Moore, J. A., Prath, S., & Arrieta, A. (2006). Early Spanish speech acquisition following cochlear implantation. *The Volta Review* 106, 321–41.

Moore, V. & McConachie, H. (1994). Communication between blind and severely visually impaired children and their parents. *British Journal of Developmental Psychology* 12, 491–502.

Morgan, G. (2002). The encoding of simultaneity in children's BSL narratives. *Journal of Sign Language and Linguistics* 5, 127–61.

Most, T. (2002). The use of repair strategies by children with and without hearing impairment. *Language, Speech, and Hearing Services in Schools* 33, 112–23.

Most, T. (2003). The use of repair strategies: Bilingual deaf children using sign language and spoken language. *American Annals of the Deaf* 148, 308–14.

Most, T. (2004). The effects of degree and type of hearing loss on children's performance in class. *Deafness and Education International* 6, 154–66.

Most, T. & Peled, M. (2007). Perception of suprasegmental features of speech by children with cochlear implants and children with hearing loss. *Journal of Deaf Studies and Deaf Education* 12, 350–61.

Musselman, C. (2000). How do children who can't hear learn to read an alphabetic script? A review of the literature on reading in deafness. *Journal of Deaf Studies and Deaf Education* 5, 9–31.

Nathani, S., Oller, D. K., & Neal, A. R. (2007). On the robustness of vocal development: An examination of infants with moderate-to-severe hearing loss and additional risk factors. *Journal of Speech, Language, and Hearing Research* 50, 1425–44.

National Institute on Deafness and Other Communication Disorders. (1993). *National Institutes of Health Consensus Statement: Early identification of hearing impairment in infants and young children.* Bethesda, MD: National Institute on Deafness and Other Communication Disorders.

Neuss, D., Blair, J., & Vichweg, S. (1991). Sound field amplification: Does it improve word recognition in a background of noise for students with minimal hearing impairments? *Educational Audiology Monograph 2*, 43–52.

Newborn Infant Hearing Screening and Intervention Act of 2000: Title VI of the Departments of Labor, Heath and Human Services, and Education Appropriations Act. Public Law, 106–13.

Nicholas, J. G. (2000). Age differences in the use of informative/heuristic communicative functions in young children with and without hearing loss who are learning spoken language. *Journal of Speech, Language, and Hearing Research* 43, 380–94.

Nicholas, J. G. & Geers, A. (2007). Will they catch up? The role of age at cochlear implantation in the spoken language development of children with severe to profound hearing loss. *Journal of Speech, Language, and Hearing Research* 50, 1048–62.

Nicholls, G. & Ling, D. (1982). Cued speech and the reception of spoken language. *Journal of Speech and Hearing Research* 25, 262–9.

Nikolopoulos, T. P., Archbold, S., & O'Donoghue, G. M. (2004). Development of spoken language grammar following cochlear implantation in prelingually deaf children. *Archives of Otolaryngology – Head and Neck Surgery* 130, 629–33.

Nikolopoulos, T. P., Archbold, S., & O'Donoghue, G. M. (2006). Does cause of deafness influence outcome after cochlear implantation in children? *Pediatrics* 118, 1350–56.

Nikolopoulos, T. P., Dyar, D., Archbold, S., & O'Donoghue, G. M. (2004). Development of spoken language grammar following cochlear implantation in prelingually deaf children. *Archives of Otolaryngology: Head and Neck Surgery* 130, 629–33.

Nittrouer, S. (2002). From ear to cortex: A perspective on what clinicians need to understand about speech perception and language processing. *Language, Speech, and Hearing Services in Schools* 33, 237–52.

Nittrouer, S. & Thuente Burton, L. (2003). The role of early language experience in the development of speech perception and language processing abilities in children with hearing loss. *The Volta Review* 103, 5–37.

Oller, D. K. (1980). The emergence of the sounds of speech in infancy. In G. Yeni-Komshian, J. Kavanagh, & C. Ferguson (eds.), *Child phonology, Vol. 1: Production* (pp. 93–112). New York: Academic Press.

Oller, D. K. (1991). Similarities and differences in vocalizations of deaf and hearing infants. In J. Miller (ed.), *Research on child language disorders: A decade of progress* (pp. 277–84). Austin, TX: Pro-Ed.

Oller, D. K. (2000). *The emergence of the speech capacity.* Mahwah, NJ: Lawrence Erlbaum.

Oller, D. K. (2006). Vocal language development in deaf infants: New challenges. In P. E. Spencer & M. Marschark (eds.), *Advances in the spoken language development of deaf and hard-of-hearing children* (pp. 22–41). New York: Oxford University Press.

Oller, D. K. & Eilers, R. E. (1988). The role of audition in infant babbling. *Child Development* 59, 441–9.

Oller, D. K., Eilers, R. E., Bull, D. H., & Carney, A. E. (1985). Pre-speech vocalizations of a deaf infant: A comparison with normal metaphonological development. *Journal of Speech and Hearing Research* 28, 47–63.

Oller, D. K., Eilers, R. E., Neal, A. R., & Schwartz, H. K. (1999). Precursors to speech in infancy: The prediction of speech and language disorders. *Journal of Communication Disorders* 32, 223–46.

Osberger, M. J. (1992). Speech intelligibility in the hearing impaired: Research and clinical implications. In R. D. Kent (ed.), *Intelligibility in speech disorders* (pp. 233–65). Philadelphia: John Publishing.

Padden, C. (1991). The acquisition of fingerspelling by deaf children. In P. Siple & S. Fischer (eds.), *Theoretical issues in sign language research*, Volume 2 (pp. 191–210). Chicago: University of Chicago.

Padden, C. (2006). Learning to fingerspell twice: Young signing children's acquisition of fingerspelling. In B. Schick, Marschark, & P. E. Spencer (eds.), *Advances in the sign language development of deaf children* (pp. 189–291). New York: Oxford Press.

Palmer, C. (1998). Quantification of the ecobehavioral impact of a soundfield loudspeaker system in elementary classrooms. *Journal of Speech, Language, and Hearing Research* 41, 819–33.

Paul, P. V. (1997). Reading for students with hearing impairments: Research review and implications. *The Volta Review* 99, 73–98.

Paul, P. V. (2000). *Literacy and deafness: The development of reading, writing, and literate thought*. Boston: Allyn and Bacon.

Peng, S.-C., Tomblin, J. B., Spencer, L. J., & Hurtig, R. R. (2007). Imitative production of rising speech intonation in pediatric cochlear implant recipients. *Journal of Speech, Language, and Hearing Research* 50, 1210–27.

Perez-Pereira, M. & Castro, J. (1992). Pragmatic functions of blind and sighted children's language: A twin case study. *First Language* 12, 17–37.

Perez-Pereira, M. & Conti-Ramsden, G. (2001). The use of directives in verbal interactions between blind children and their mothers. *Journal of Visual Impairment and Blindness* 96, 133–49.

Perfect, M. (2001). Examining communicative behaviors in a 3-year-old boy who is blind. *Journal of Visual Impairments and Blindness* 95, 353–65.

Perier, O., Charlier, B., Hage, C., & Alegria, J. (1988). Evaluation of the effects of prolonged cued speech practice upon the reception of spoken language. In I. G. Taylor (ed.), *The education of the deaf: Current perspectives* (Vol. 1) (pp. 47–59). London: Croom Helm.

Petitto, L. & Marentette, P. (1991). Babbling in the manual mode: Evidence from the ontogeny of language. *Science* 251, 1493–96.

Pipp-Siegel, S. (1998). Touch and emotional availability in hearing and deaf or hard of hearing toddlers and their hearing mothers. *The Volta Review* 100, 238–50.

Pipp-Siegel, S., Sedey, A. L., & Yoshinaga-Itano, C. (2002). Predictors of parental stress of mothers of young children with hearing loss. *Journal of Deaf Studies and Deaf Education* 8, 133–45.

Preisler, G., Tvingstedt, A.-L., & Ahlstrom, M. (2005). Interviews with deaf children about their experiences using cochlear implants. *American Annals of the Deaf* 150, 260–7.

Pressman, L. J. (1998). A comparison of the links between emotional availability and language gain in young children with and without hearing loss. *The Volta Review* 100, 251–78.

Prezbindowski, A. K., Adamson, L. B., & Lederberg, A. R. (1998). Joint attention of deaf and hearing 22-month-old children and their hearing mothers. *Journal of Applied Developmental Psychology* 19, 377–87.

Pring, L. & Dewart, H. (1998). Social cognition in children with visual impairments. *Journal of Visual Impairment and Blindness* 92, 754–69.

Ramsay, C. & Padden, C. (1998). Reading ability in signing deaf children. *Topics in Language Disorders* 18 (4), 30–46.

Reed, C. M. & Delhorne, L. A. (1995). A study of the tactual recognition of sign language. *Journal of Speech and Hearing Research* 38, 477–89.

Reed, C. M., Delhorne, L. A., Durlach, N. I., & Fischer, S. D. (1990). A study of the tactual and visual reception of finger-spelling. *Journal of Speech and Hearing Research* 33, 786–97.

Reed, C. M., Durlach, N. I., Braida, L. D., & Schultz, M. C. (1982). Analytic study of the Tadoma method: Identification of consonant and vowels by an experienced Tadoma user. *Journal of Speech and Hearing Research* 25, 108–16.

Richburg, C. M. & Goldberg, L. R. (2005). Teachers' perceptions about minimal hearing loss: A role for educational audiologists. *Communication Disorders Quarterly* 27, 4–19.

Robbins, A. M., Svirsky, M., & Kirk, K. I. (1997). Children with implants can speak, but can they communicate? *Archives of Otolaryngology – Head and Neck Surgery* 117, 155–60.

Rodriguez, M. S. & Lara, E. T. (1996). Dyadic interactions between deaf children and their communication partners. *American Annals of the Deaf* 141, 245–51.

Rosel, J., Caballer, A., Jara, P., & Oliver, J. C. (2005). Verbalism in the narrative language of children who are blind and sighted. *Journal of Visual Impairments and Blindness* 99, 413–25.

Santana Hernandez, R., Torres Monreal, S., & Garcia Orza, J. (2003). The role of cued speech in the development of Spanish prepositions. *American Annals of the Deaf* 148, 323–32.

Schirmer, B. R. (2000). *Language and literacy development in children who are deaf.* Boston: Allyn and Bacon.

Sikora, D. & Plapinger, D. (1994). Using standardized psychometric tests to identify learning disabilities in students with hearing impairments. *Journal of Learning Disabilities* 27, 352–9.

Silberman, R. (1981). A comparison of visual functioning in hearing impaired and normally hearing children. *The Volta Review* 82, 10–18.

Spencer, L., Tomblin, J. B., & Gantz, B. J. (1997). Reading skills in children with multichannel cochlear-implant experience. *The Volta Review* 99, 193–202.

Spencer, P. E. (2000). Looking without listening: Is audition a prerequisite for normal development of visual attention during infancy. *Journal of Deaf Studies and Deaf Education* 5, 291–302.

Spencer, P. E. (2004). Individual differences in language performance after cochlear implantation at one to three years of age: Child, family, and linguistic factors. *Journal of Deaf Studies and Deaf Education* 9, 395–412.

Spencer, P. E., Bodner-Johnson, B., & Gutfreund, M. (1992). Interacting with infants with a hearing loss: What we can learn from others who are deaf? *Journal of Early Intervention* 16, 64–78.

Spencer, P. & Lederberg, A. (1997). Different modes, different models: Communication and language of young deaf children and their mothers. In L. Adamson & M. Romski (eds.), *Communication and language acquisition: Discoveries from atypical development* (pp. 205–17). Baltimore: Paul H. Brookes.

Spencer, P. E., Swisher, M. V., & Waxman, R. (2004). Visual attention: Maturation and specialization. In K. Meadows-Orlans, P. Spencer, & L. Koester (eds.), *The world of deaf infants* (pp. 168–88). New York: Oxford University Press.

Stark, R. E. (1972). Some features of the vocalizations of young deaf children. In J. F. Bosma (ed.), *Third symposium on oral sensations and perceptions: The mouth of the infant* (pp. 431–41). Springfield, IL: Charles C. Thomas.

Stark, R. E. (1980). Stages of speech development in the first year of life. In G. Y. Komshian, J. Kavanagh, & C. Ferguson (eds.), *Child phonology: Vol. 1: Production* (pp. 73–90). New York: Academic Press.

Stark, R. E. (1983). Phonatory development in young normally hearing and hearing-impaired children. In I. Hochberg, H. Levett, & M. J. Osberger (eds.), *Speech of the hearing-impaired: Research, training, and personnel preparation* (pp. 297–312). Baltimore, MD: University Park Press.

Steinberg, A., Bain, L., Li, Y., Delgado, G., & Ruperto, V. (2003). Decisions Hispanic families make after the identification of deafness. *Journal of Deaf Studies and Deaf Education* 8, 291–314.

Stewart, D. A. & Kluwin, T. N. (2001). *Teaching deaf and hard of hearing students: Content, strategies, and curriculum.* Boston: Allyn and Bacon.

Stoel-Gammon, C. & Otomo, K. (1986). Babbling development of hearing impaired and normally hearing subjects. *Journal of Speech and Hearing Disorders* 51, 33–41.

Stone, P. (1988). *Blueprint for developing conversational competence: A planning/ instruction model with detailed scenarios.* Washington, DC: Alexander Graham Bell Association.

Sugarman-Bell, S. (1978). Some organizational aspects of pre-verbal communication. In I. Markova (ed.), *The social context of language* (pp. 49–66). Chichester, UK: Wiley.

Tharpe, A. M. & Bess, F. H. (1991). Identification management of children with minimal hearing loss. *International Journal of Pediatric Otorhinolaryngology* 21, 41–50.

Thoutenhoofd, E. (2006). Cochlear implanted pupils in Scottish schools: 4-year school attainment data (2000–2004). *Journal of Deaf Studies and Deaf Education* 11, 171–88.

Toe, D., Beattie, R., & Barr, M. (2007). The development of pragmatic skills in children who are severely and profoundly deaf. *Deafness and Education International* 9, 101–17.

Torres, S., Moreno-Torres, I., & Santana, R. (2006). Quantitative and qualitative evaluation of linguistic input support to a prelingually deaf child with cued speech: A case study. *Journal of Deaf Studies and Deaf Education* 11, 438–48.

Tuncer, A. T. & Altunay, B. (2006). The effect of a summarization-based cumulative retelling strategy on listening comprehension of college students with visual impairments. *Journal of Visual Impairments and Blindness* 100, 353–65.

Tur-Kaspa, H. & Dromi, E. (1998). Spoken and written language assessment of orally trained children with hearing loss: Syntactic structures and deviations. *The Volta Review* 100, 186–202.

Tye-Murray, N. (1994). *Let's converse: A how-to guide to develop and expand conversational skills of children and teenagers who are hearing impaired.* Washington, DC: Alexander Graham Bell Association.

Tyler, R. S., Fryauf-Bertschy, H., Kelsay, D., Gantz, B., Woodworth, G., & Parkinson, A. (1997). Speech perception by prelingually deaf children using cochlear implants. *Otolaryngology – Head and Neck Surgery* 117, 180–7.

Vermeulen, A. M., van Bon, W., Schreuder, R., Knoors, H., & Snik, A. (2007). Reading comprehension of deaf children with cochlear implants. *Journal of Deaf Studies and Deaf Education* 12, 283–302.

Vieu, A., Mondain, M., Blanchard, K. et al. (1998). Influence of communication mode on speech intelligibility and syntactic structure of sentences in profoundly hearing impaired French children implanted between 5 and 9 years of age. *International Journal of Pediatric Otorhinolaryngology* 44, 15–22.

Von Hapsburg, D. & Davis, B. (2006). Auditory sensitivity and the prelinguistic vocalizations of early-amplified infants. *Journal of Speech, Language, and Hearing Research* 49, 809–22.

Von Hapsburg, D., Davis, B., & MacNeilage, P. F. (2008). Frame dominance in infants with hearing loss. *Journal of Speech, Language, and Hearing Research* 51, 306–20.

Waxman, R. & Spencer, P. (1997). What mothers do to support infant visual attention: Sensitivities to age and hearing status. *Journal of Deaf Studies and Deaf Education* 2, 104–14.

Wheeler, A., Archbold, S., Gregory, S., & Skipp, A. (2007). Cochlear implants: The young people's perspective. *Journal of Deaf Studies and Deaf Education* 12, 303–16.

Wilcox, S. (1992). *The phonetics of fingerspelling*. Philadelphia: J. Benjamins.

Wood, B. & Wood, H. (1997). Communicating with children who are deaf: Pitfalls and possibilities. *Language, Speech, and Hearing Services in Schools* 28, 348–54.

Yoshinaga-Itano, C. (2003a). Early intervention after universal neonatal hearing screening: Impact on outcomes. *Mental Retardation and Developmental Disabilities Research Reviews* 9, 252–66.

Yoshinaga-Itano, C. (2003b). From screening to early identification and intervention: Discovering predictors to successful outcomes for children with significant hearing loss. *Journal of Deaf Studies and Deaf Education* 8, 11–30.

Yoshinaga-Itano, C. (2006). Early identification, communication modality, and the development of speech and spoken language skills. In P. E. Spencer & M. Marschark (eds.), *Advances in the spoken language development of deaf and hard of hearing children* (pp. 298–327). New York: Oxford University Press.

Yoshinaga-Itano, C. & Sedey, A. L. (1992). Learning to communicate: Babies with hearing impairments make their needs known. *The Volta Review* 95, 107–29.

Yoshinaga-Itano, C. & Sedey, A. L. (1998). Language of early- and late-identified children with hearing loss. *Pediatrics* 102, 521–9.

Yoshinaga-Itano, C., Sedey, A.V., Coulter, D. K., & Mehl, A. (1998). Language of early- and later-identified children with hearing loss. *Pediatrics* 102, 1161–71.

Zabel, H. & Tabor, M. (1993). Effects of classroom amplification on spelling performance in elementary school children. *Educational Audiology Monograph* 3, 5–9.

Zaidman-Zait, A. (2007). Parenting a child with a cochlear implant: A critical incident study. *Journal of Deaf Studies and Deaf Education* 12, 221–41.

Zaidman-Zait, A. & Dromi, E. (2007). Analogous and distinctive patterns of prelinguistic communication in toddlers with and without hearing loss. *Journal of Speech, Language, and Hearing Research* 50, 1166–80.

Zaidman-Zait, A. & Young, R. A. (2007). Parental involvement in the habilitation process following children's cochlear implantation: An action theory. *Journal of Deaf Studies and Deaf Education* 13, 39–60.

4 Intelligibility Impairments

MEGAN HODGE AND TARA WHITEHILL

1 Introduction

Intelligibility, or how understandable one's speech is to another, is a functional indicator of oral communication competence. It reflects a talker's ability to convert language to a physical signal (speech) and a listener's ability to perceive and decode this signal to recover the meaning of the talker's message. Speech (articulation, vocal quality, loudness, resonance, and prosody) and language (semantics, morphosyntax, discourse coherence) variables influence a talker's ability to make speech understandable to others. As discussed by Müller (2002), intelligibility is a multifaceted, complex, and dynamic process when considered within the context of real-life communicative interactions. Linguistic and paralinguistic characteristics of the spoken message, contextual factors, knowledge and expectations of conversational partners, their online processing abilities and skill in recognizing and repairing communication breakdowns contribute to whether mutual understanding is achieved. Concepts and issues addressed in this chapter that are central to intelligibility in speech-language pathology are: (1) how broadly or narrowly it is defined, (2) how it is measured, (3) how intelligibility measures are used, and (4) how intelligibility can be increased. The chapter closes with a brief description of current directions in intelligibility measurement and research.

2 Definitions and Related Terms

The concept of intelligibility originated in the study of transmission channels for speech signals (e.g., lecture rooms, telephone lines) and reflected the adequacy of a communication system or the ability of people to communicate in environments of various noise levels. Intelligibility was expressed as a percentage of words, sentences, or phonemes (consonants and vowels) identified by a well-defined listener group and produced by an experienced talker. Audio recordings of a talker's productions of standard word or sentence lists were prepared and played to listeners who identified what words they heard, without knowledge of the intended utterances. These recordings permitted comparisons among different communication systems using exactly the same speech material. High fidelity recordings were required so that recording quality did not add another source of variability to measurement. Talker, spoken message, and listener variables were well controlled and the quality of the acoustic transmission system was evaluated. These same concepts and principles were applied subsequently to persons with speech disorders (Kent et al., 1989) or to those who speak a non-native language (Munro & Derwing, 1995), but here the objective is to control transmission system variables as well as listener, message, and environmental variables in order to evaluate the adequacy of the speech signal produced by the talker. Specifying and controlling these variables are challenges that need to be addressed when defining and measuring intelligibility of persons with spoken language impairments because talkers communicate typically with a range of listeners about a range of topics in a variety of communicative contexts and environments.

2.1   Comprehensibility and acceptability

Terms related to intelligibility in the speech-language pathology literature include "comprehensibility" and "acceptability." Yorkston, Strand, and Kennedy (1996) contrasted their definition of intelligibility (degree to which the listener understands the sound signal produced by the talker) with the concept of comprehensibility (degree to which the listener understands utterances produced by the talker in a communication context). Comprehensibility reflects the condition where the talker is speaking in a natural communicative context and the listener uses every source of information available to understand the message. While intelligibility and comprehensibility are both influenced by factors affecting the predictability of the message, the familiarity of the listener, the listener's motivation to understand the talker's message, and the noise level of the communication environment, comprehensibility is further influenced by a talker's paralinguistic cues (e.g., facial expression, gestures), supplementary cues such as the first letter of the word (Hanson, Yorkston & Beukelman, 2004), situational cues, and strategies that the talker and listener use to manage mutual understanding within the context of their ongoing interaction. The concept of comprehensibility is very useful in intervention planning for persons with reduced speech intelligibility. It provides a framework to identify non-speech factors that can be enhanced to increase a person's communicative effectiveness (Müller, 2002; Yorkston, Strand, & Kennedy, 1996), including the attitudes and behaviors of the listener. However, the multiple factors that contribute to comprehensibility are difficult to control and create even greater challenges for reliable, valid, and sensitive measurement than intelligibility. Measures of communication effectiveness provide one means to estimate comprehensibility. These typically take the form of rating scales with descriptors (Eadie et al., 2006). Ideally, these measures would capture perceptions of the talker and listener about the degree to which they achieve mutual understanding (Müller, 2002).

Acceptability is a less well understood and less common measure of speech function than intelligibility. Definitions of acceptability range from subjective impressions of the pleasingness of speech to the potential for a person to experience social, educational, or vocational problems because of speech (Lang, Starr, & Moller, 1992). Whitehill (2002) found that over 20 percent of studies interchanged the terms "intelligibility" and "acceptability" in her critical review of the literature on intelligibility and cleft palate. Although it is often confused with intelligibility, evidence suggests that acceptability and intelligibility are not the same entity, at least for some populations of speakers. Whitehill and Chun (2002) reported a significant positive correlation of 0.61 between intelligibility scores (measured by a multiple-choice task employing phonetic contrasts) and acceptability (measured using a 7-point equal appearing interval scale or EAI) in speakers with cleft palate. They also examined the relationships of articulation scores (percentage of single words transcribed correctly) and nasality ratings (7-point EAI scale) to intelligibility scores and acceptability ratings. While significant correlations were found between the articulation scores and both intelligibility (r = 0.77) and acceptability (r = 0.56), only the correlation between nasality and acceptability was significant (r = 0.78). Whitehill, Ciocca, and Yiu (2004) investigated the extent to which aspects of voice, resonance, and prosody contributed to listener judgments of acceptability in Cantonese speakers with dysarthria. While monopitch, mono-loudness, and pitch deviations correlated strongly with measures of acceptability and intelligibility, strained-strangled voice quality contributed significantly more to the variance in acceptability than could be accounted for by sentence intelligibility alone. These results suggest that resonance and laryngeal quality ratings may distinguish intelligibility from acceptability for certain types of speech disorders. However, the lack of a standard definition of acceptability and knowledge of what differentiates it from intelligibility make it difficult to interpret and apply measures of acceptability to judge spoken communicative competence. This chapter focuses on intelligibility, acknowledging that while it is an essential feature of spoken communication, it alone does not determine a person's communicative competence or the psychosocial impact of the speech signal on a listener in everyday situations.

3   Intelligibility Measurement

Measures of intelligibility provide an index of the cumulative impact that mechanism impairments and error patterns have on an individual's speech and are used typically to provide an index of the severity of a speech disorder (Gordon-Brannan & Hodson, 2000; Yorkston et al., 1999). As observed by Kent et al. (1989), an intelligibility measure is not absolute. It should be selected based on the purpose for which it is to be used and considered relative to the conditions under which it is measured. The same talker may get different intelligibility scores depending on the method of measurement. Variables to consider when selecting a measure of intelligibility include characteristics of the talker, nature of the speaking task, characteristics of the listeners, nature of the judging task, and characteristics of the recording and listening environment.

3.1   Talker characteristics and speaking task

An intelligibility measure needs to be appropriate for the expressive language capabilities of the talker. If the language level of the stimulus material is above that of the talker (e.g., a preschooler or older individual with a language delay or disorder), the validity of the measure is compromised. Similarly, if the message content is to be read aloud, the reading level of the material needs to be appropriate for the talker's reading ability. The length of the stimulus material also needs to be appropriate for the severity of the talker's disorder. For example, talkers with severe speech disorders as a result of neurological impairment may be able to produce single words but not longer utterances, and may fatigue easily (Kent et al., 1989).

Imitation (word and sentence), reading, and spontaneous speech tasks have been used to obtain samples of speech for intelligibility judgments. Spontaneous speaking tasks are considered to have the highest face validity because they reflect the talker's self-generated language. However, these lack control of language and phonetic content across samples. Conversely, imitative word or sentence tasks can be controlled for linguistic and phonetic content but have less face validity. The Children's Speech Intelligibility Measure (Wilcox & Morris, 1999) and the CID Picture SPINE (Monsen, Moog, & Geers, 1988) are examples of measures that use imitation to elicit single word productions. The Beginners' Intelligibility Test (Osberger et al., 1994) uses objects, pictures, and a spoken model to elicit sentence productions ranging from two to six words. Gordon-Brannan and Hodson (2000) reported correlations of 0.79 between word identification scores from a 100-word conversation sample and a word imitation task (Children's Speech Intelligibility Measure) and 0.85 between word identification scores from a 100-word conversation sample and sentence imitation task for 4-year-old children who ranged in severity of speech delay.

For talkers with adequate reading ability, oral reading tasks provide a compromise between spontaneous and imitative speech samples. The Assessment of Intelligibility of Dysarthric Speech (Yorkston & Beukelman, 1981) provides single word and sentence tasks, controlled for linguistic context, which can be read or imitated after a model. The sentence items range from five to 15 words and can be timed to provide measures of speaking rate. Monsen (1983) created an intelligibility measure that has sets of sentences differing in phonetic and linguistic complexity. These range from Set 1, which contains monosyllabic and spondee words with no clusters and simple syntax, to Set 4, which contains monosyllable and disyllable words and more complex sentence structure (e.g., passives, embedded clauses).

3.2   Listener characteristics

Listeners' hearing status, speech perception abilities, memory, and engagement influence their performance when judging a talker's speech intelligibility. Their ability to predict distorted or missing information in the speech sample also affects their judgments. Therefore their knowledge of the language, familiarity with the talker's speech patterns and message content, and number of times they listen to all or parts of the sample to be judged need to be controlled to make valid comparisons of their scores with other listeners for the same task. Markham and Hazan (2004) assessed speech intelligibility with typical talkers and listeners. They found that when three words were presented after a precursor sentence spoken by the same person (e.g., "and the next three words are: cat, dog, horse"), higher word intelligibility scores were obtained than when just presented with a single word. Hustad and Cahill (2003) compared speech intelligibility scores for adults with mild to severe dysarthria secondary to cerebral palsy when listeners were presented with sentences spoken by the same talker for 50 consecutive minutes. They found higher intelligibility scores for the last quarter of the words (mean = 66 percent) when compared to the first quarter (mean = 55 percent). When McNaughton et al. (1994) presented children and adults with words from speech synthesizers, they found that over five sessions, both children and adults improved their word identification scores. This improvement was 17.7 percent and 14.3 percent for one device, and 20.85 percent and 23.35 percent for another device for children and adults respectively. A possible explanation for these results is that as listeners become more familiar with the individual talker's voice, they are better able to perceive the acoustic cues in the speech signal, resulting in higher speech intelligibility scores.

Many studies of intelligibility have used college students in speech-language pathology as listeners because of convenience of recruitment. However, "everyday listeners" (Klasner & Yorkston, 2005) are more representative of unfamiliar listeners that a talker will encounter in daily communication situations and may be preferred, depending on the purpose of the measure. The roles that listeners' speech perception and online cognitive processing contribute to understanding speech are receiving greater recognition and study in the clinical intelligibility literature (e.g., Liss et al., 2002).

3.3   Judging task

Rating scales and word and phoneme identification tasks have been used to measure intelligibility. More recent studies have also investigated the amount of effort perceived by listeners when judging the intelligibility of talkers with speech disorders. Descriptions and examples of these measurement approaches follow.

3.3.1   Scaling   Rating scales provide a means to quantify listeners' subjective impressions of a talker's intelligibility. They include equal-appearing interval and descriptive scales. The *Speech Intelligibility Rating Scale* (Allen, Nikolopoulos, Dyar, & O'Donoghue, 2001) is an example of a published five-point scale for children with hearing impairments. A rating of "5" corresponds to "Connected speech is intelligible to all listeners. Child is understood easily in everyday contexts," and a rating of "1" corresponds to "Connected speech is unintelligible; primary mode of communication may be manual." Listeners are experienced with the type of speech being judged and panels of listeners are used to increase the stability of the score. The ratings are made by speech-language pathologists, based on a child's spontaneous speech rated in a familiar (home or school) environment. While rating scales provide a quick way to measure intelligibility, their reliability and sensitivity are lower than for word identification tasks, especially for talkers with speech intelligibility in the mid-range. Samar and Metz (1988) compared rating scales to methods where the listener writes down what was perceived word by word to measure the intelligibility of adults with hearing impairment. They reported that 95 percent of talkers who were assigned a rating of 3 on a scale with half-steps from 1 to 5 had actual word identification scores between 25 percent and 90 percent. Samar and Metz observed that voice and prosody characteristics may also influence ratings of intelligibility when interval scales are used (i.e., the same number of words may be identifiable for two talkers but one may be rated lower on an interval scale if voice quality or prosody is atypical). Therefore, listeners may have difficulty focusing only on intelligibility when other abnormal speech variables are present, with the result that scaled ratings of intelligibility are more vulnerable to interference from these variables than word identification tasks.

Schiavetti (1992) argued that if a scaling method is used to measure intelligibility, direct magnitude estimation (DME) is preferable to interval scaling because it does not assume that intelligibility is linear in nature. Investigators who have used DME to measure intelligibility typically instruct listeners to rate the intelligibility of a talker by comparing the speech sample against a "standard" stimulus using a ratio. For example, listeners hear a speech sample from the standard talker, are given a number that corresponds to that talker (or asked to assign a number on their own), then hear speech spoken by the "test" talker. Then they rate the target talker compared to the standard talker. For example, if the standard talker was assigned the number 100 and the target talker is judged to be half as intelligible, the target talker is rated as 50. A major shortcoming is that ratings obtained from DME appear to depend greatly on the intelligibility of the standard talker (Weismer & Laures, 2002).

3.3.2   Word and phoneme identification   Word identification tasks require more time than scaling methods for intelligibility measurement. However, they have the advantage of greater reliability and sensitivity (Whitehill, 2002). Word identification tasks can be performed by orthographic transcription, where the listener writes out each word perceived in a talker's utterances (i.e., open-set task), or by selection of words spoken from a limited set of choices (i.e., closed-set task). Note that identification tasks differ from articulation tests. In the latter, a trained professional judges the talker's productions of known word and sound targets against internal models of adult-like productions. In the former, listeners identify the word or sound perceived without knowledge of the intended utterance.

Closed-set identification tasks yield inflated scores relative to open-set tasks because of the limited response options but are influenced less by listener experience, familiarity with the test items and by language, prosody, and contextual factors. Some closed-set tasks, such as those described by Boothroyd (1985), Hodge and

Gotzke (2007), Kent et al. (1989), Monsen (1981), and Yorkston, Beukelman, and Hakel (1996) are constructed so that word choices differ by one phonetic contrast (e.g., chin, tin, sin, fin, pin, shin, thin). These provide a means to measure how well a talker can make selected sound targets identifiable in words that are members of real word minimal pairs, to a listener who does not know which word the talker is intending to say. For selected populations, identification tasks have been used for isolated phoneme productions. Fletcher, Dagenais, and Critz-Crosby (1991a, 1991b) described such tasks for isolated vowels and consonants produced by talkers with profound hearing impairment. LaRivere, Seilo, and Dimmick (1975) asked speakers with a glossectomy to produce CVC (consonant–vowel–consonant) nonsense syllables for a vowel identification task. The error patterns obtained from these tasks can guide speech-language pathologists in choosing sounds to target in treatment to increase intelligibility.

In word identification methods such as the Assessment of Intelligibility of Dysarthric Speech and the Children's Speech Intelligibility Measure, the number of words identified correctly serves as the intelligibility score and is measured by the match between the words intended in the talker's utterances and the listener's responses. This requires that a "key" of the talker's intended utterances be available to compare with the listener's responses. Note that if word identification tasks are used to obtain intelligibility scores from spontaneously generated speech samples, a disadvantage is that a transcript of the sample needs to be prepared to create a "key" to use to score the listener's responses. This is time consuming and difficult if the talker has a significant intelligibility deficit. The number of words identified correctly out of the total number of words spoken yields the intelligibility score, expressed typically as a percentage. An example of a variation on this approach was described by Monsen (1983), who assigned each word in a sentence a percentage in accordance with its frequency of occurrence, as opposed to each word contributing equally to the score.

Studies that are more recent have attempted to quantify listeners' perceived mental effort when performing word identification tasks (Cote-Reschny, 2007; Preminger & Van Tasell, 1995; Whitehill & Wong, 2006). There is agreement that response time and listening effort increase as intelligibility decreases (i.e., listeners need more time and exert greater mental effort to understand speech of talkers with more severe intelligibility impairments). Findings from these studies provide quantitative information to help persons with speech disorders realize that when their words are not clear, listeners need extra time to understand, and to help their communicative partners realize that increased mental effort and time are needed when listening to talkers with more severe intelligibility deficits.

3.4   Characteristics of the recording and listening environment

In most cases, intelligibility judgments are made from audio recordings. Good-quality recording equipment used in a quiet environment is essential to obtain a high-fidelity recording of the talker's speech signal. Historically, quiet environments that are free from distractions have also been recommended for listener judging because background noise can influence the intelligibility scores obtained. For example, Rogers, Dalby, & Nishi (2004) reported that listeners with normal hearing were 95 percent correct in identifying content words in sentences spoken by native speakers of English at + 10 dB SNR but only 30 percent correct at − 5 dB SNR using multi-talker babble as the background noise. However, noise distracters have been included in recent clinical studies to simulate more typical communication environments and provide more sensitive measures of talkers with mild intelligibility deficits. For example, Adams et al. (2008) examined the effect of multi-talker background noise on speech-to-noise levels and conversational speech intelligibility in individuals with hypophonia due to Parkinson's disease (PD). Twenty-five participants with PD and 15 normal control participants were engaged in conversation while they experienced no noise and three levels (60, 65, and 70 dB) of multi-talker background noise. As noise level increased there was a significant decrease in the PD participants' speech-to-noise levels and transcribed conversational speech intelligibility scores, suggesting that speech-to-noise level and conversational intelligibility in individuals with hypophonia and PD are more sensitive to background noise than in healthy controls.

While most current clinical measurement tools for speech intelligibility provide listeners with access to the talker's acoustic signal alone, researchers have also been interested in the effect of providing listeners with visual information on intelligibility scores. Monsen (1983) found that when listeners were asked to identify words spoken by talkers with a hearing impairment, word identification scores were 14 percent higher when the listener both saw the face and heard the speech sample of the talker than when listeners were only able to hear the speech sample. Keintz, Bunton, and Hoit (2007) studied eight subjects with PD and found that intelligibility scores were significantly higher in the auditory-visual than auditory-only condition only for the three subjects with the lowest intelligibility scores. Hustad, Dardis, and McCourt (2007) examined the effect of visual information and linguistic class (open versus closed) on the intelligibility scores of seven adults with cerebral palsy. They found a significant effect of word class (higher scores for closed than open class) in auditory-only and auditory-visual conditions (no interaction) for six of seven subjects. Scores in the auditory-visual condition were significantly higher than in the auditory-only condition for only three subjects, but, unlike the findings of Keintz et al., these three subjects' scores were in the moderate range of severity. These varied results suggest that one cannot assume that providing visual information will significantly enhance the speech intelligibility of a person with a speech disorder; rather it appears that at the very least, type and severity of speech disorder need to be considered.

4 Use of Intelligibility Measures

In the field of speech-language pathology, intelligibility first gained widespread use as a measure of severity of speech disorder and outcome for persons who are deaf or hard of hearing. Intelligibility measures developed for this population have provided models to apply to persons with other conditions affecting speech (e.g., speech sound disorders of unknown origin, dysarthria, cleft palate, cancer of the vocal tract). In addition to a role in determining the severity of a person's speech disorder and its impact on spoken communication, intelligibility measures have been used to help determine if – and what type of – intervention is needed, and to evaluate the effectiveness of specific interventions, quantify speech outcomes for persons with different types of speech disorders, and understand the basis of intelligibility deficits.

4.1   Examples of uses of intelligibility measures

4.1.1   Determining the need for intervention   There is consensus that by age 48 months most children are 100 percent intelligible to their communication partners in natural communication contexts, and to unfamiliar listeners who write down the words they perceive the child to say, based on audio recordings of the child's conversation with an adult (Weiss, 1982). Gordon-Brannan and Hodson (2000) recommended that speech-language intervention is indicated for 4-year-old children with speech intelligibility scores of 66 percent or less, based on orthographic transcription by unfamiliar adults of an audio recording of 100 contiguous words of the child's conversational speech. Hodson (2004) suggested that children between 48 and 66 months of age, who are receiving speech therapy, be dismissed when unfamiliar listeners can understand at least 90 percent of words in a 100-word conversational sample. In addition, percentages for phonological deviations must be below 40 percent (except liquids, which must be below 90 percent). Hodson noted that children sometimes require additional treatment later for residual articulation errors.

4.1.2   Determining the nature of intervention   Monsen (1981) reported that when speech intelligibility scores of persons who are deaf or hard of hearing were less than 60 percent, listeners classified speech as "unintelligible"; scores between 60 percent and 70 percent were classified as "difficult to understand." For persons with intelligibility deficits of this severity, use of some type of augmentative system and explicit training of the person with the speech disorder and his/her communicative partners to prevent and repair communication breakdown appear warranted to ensure that the individual has a functional means to communicate in daily roles. This principle has also been applied to progressive disorders such as amyotrophic lateral sclerosis where intelligibility measures have been used to index rate of disease progression and guide decision making about use of augmentative communication approaches (Yorkston et al., 1999).

4.1.3   Determining effectiveness of specific interventions and quantifying speech outcomes in different speech disorders   Yorkston et al. (1999) also described multiple examples of how intelligibility measures can be used to assess the effect of different intervention approaches for persons with dysarthria including palatal lifts, intensive voice therapy, and rate control procedures. Dowden (1997) described use of the Index of Augmented Speech Comprehensibility in Children to determine how supplementary cues (semantic and first letter) influenced listeners' identification of words spoken by children with severe dysarthria. Chin, Tsai, and Gao (2003) reported the intelligibility scores of children with normal hearing and those with cochlear implants on the Beginner's Intelligibility Test at yearly intervals from 3 to 7 years of age and older. At 3 years of age, the children with cochlear implants had a median intelligibility score of 4 percent, but by age 7 years this had increased to 76 percent, which was similar to that of the 3-year-old children with normal hearing. Intelligibility has also been used as an outcome measure in speakers with cleft palate. Historical debates about the ideal timing and surgical approach for primary surgical closure of the palate are still not resolved, but intelligibility is regarded as an important outcome measure in this debate. Speech understandability and speech acceptability were included as two of the outcome measures in a recent proposal for universal reporting parameters for individuals born with cleft palate (Henningsson et al., 2008).

4.1.4 Understanding intelligibility deficits   Kent et al. (1989) described a single word, closed-set minimal contrast approach to measure intelligibility and to determine which phonetic contrasts contribute to reductions in intelligibility in persons with dysarthria. These authors observed that intelligibility prediction is complex because it is a joint product of the acoustic signal, linguistic redundancy of the message, and contextual information. However, they hypothesized that if all other contributors are controlled (i.e., redundancy and context), then it should be possible to predict speech intelligibility from characteristics of the speech signal itself. In theory, speech therapy intervention could then target those contrasts most likely to lead to improvements in intelligibility. Identifying acoustic correlates of intelligibility can help determine what characteristics of speech result in an utterance being unintelligible and provide insights about changes in physical characteristics that may increase the intelligibility of the utterance. The relationships between acoustic characteristics of vowels and measures of speech intelligibility have been studied most frequently and several investigators have found these to be significant (e.g., Higgins & Hodge, 2002).

Whitehill and Chau (2004) designed a minimal contrast-based intelligibility test for Cantonese-speaking children with cleft palate. They modified their previous test that had been designed for Cantonese speakers with dysarthria to incorporate contrasts known to be vulnerable in speakers with cleft palate. The most problematic contrasts, based on listener choices, were place of articulation of stops and nasals (e.g., alveolar versus velar nasal) and manner of articulation (stop versus fricative and stop versus affricate). Single-word intelligibility could be predicted with 91 percent accuracy using three phonetic contrasts. This study was limited by its inability to capture error patterns that could not be characterized phonemically. Hodge and Gotzke (2007) employed a similar method in their intelligibility probe for English-speaking children with cleft palate. Their measure included open (orthographic transcription) and closed-set (multiple-choice) tasks with the addition of a binary clarity rating ("clear" or "distorted") to the closed-set task to capture non-phonemic errors.

5 Improving Speech Intelligibility

Factors that influence speech intelligibility measurement (i.e., those related to the talker, message, environment, and the listener) can be exploited as strategies to increase speech intelligibility. For the talker, a first step is to use predictable sentence structure and grammar and maintain "clear speech." Instructions given to talkers about how to use clear speech include "speak as clearly as possible, as if trying to communicate in a noisy environment," "enunciate consonants more carefully and with greater (vocal) effort," and telling the person to not slur the words together (Picheny, Durlach, & Braida, 1985, 1986). When compared with conversational speech, characteristics of clear speech include greater intensity and more precise articulation by releasing the stops in words and making vowels more distinct from each other (Picheny, Durlach, & Braida, 1986). The expectation is that in attempting to increase the clarity of the spoken message, the talker will increase his or her effort, which will increase loudness and articulatory precision and improve the voice quality of the speech signal produced. It may also serve to reduce speaking rate, which is an effective strategy to increase intelligibility in some speech disorders (Yorkston et al., 1999).

Hanson, Yorkston, and Beukelman (2004) reviewed the published evidence for using speech supplementation techniques (e.g., alphabet cues, illustrative gestures, semantic cues) with dysarthria. These additional cues, beyond those in the acoustic speech signal, may help listeners to predict and decode the message more easily. Hanson et al. concluded that: (1) these strategies may be useful for speakers with severe or profound dysarthria, regardless of medical diagnosis or dysarthria type; (2) the best candidates exhibit dysarthria that interferes with communication function in natural settings, have adequate pragmatic and cognitive skills and sufficient motor function to generate the cues; (3) selection of supplementation type must be individualized as each type has unique advantages and disadvantages; (4) strategies are best when the gains are sufficiently large to move speakers into a functional range of intelligibility; (5) some strategies also improve speech production, especially when rate reduction is an appropriate target for intervention; and (6) listeners play a critical role in ensuring the successful use of supplementary strategies and therefore listener education and training are important elements of the intervention.

Due to the chronic nature of many speech intelligibility deficits, factors beyond those related to the talker need to be considered to maximize communication success. These include altering the communication environment and listener behavior. The former can be accomplished by ensuring that the environment is ideal for spoken communication (e.g., being in a quiet place with a high signal-to-noise ratio and few interfering distractions; moving closer together). Listener behavior can be altered in several ways. For example listeners could be trained to: (1) attend more closely to the talker, especially to words that they have difficulty under-standing (e.g., open-class words); (2) remind talkers to use behaviors that increase speech intelligibility (e.g., use clear speech techniques) and comprehensibility (e.g., reminding talkers to give the listener hints, or cues, about what they are talking about); and (3) use explicit comprehension monitoring strategies to get feedback about their interpretation of the talker's message. Listeners could also be familiarized with the speech of the talker through auditory training. Both talkers and listeners need to recognize potential situations where communication may be difficult and know about strategies that reduce communication breakdowns and associated frustration. For example, repeating the message, revising what was said, or increasing the loudness and precision of the acoustic signal may help a talker to increase speech intelligibility after a spoken communication breakdown. Repeating the message and adding supplemental cues may also help the listener to predict and decode the message more easily. These strategies all increase the amount of information about the message that is available to the listener.

6   Current Directions in Intelligibility Measurement and Research

Over the past three decades, interest in intelligibility in speech-language patho-logy has resulted in the development of scaling and word identification measures for children and adults, more frequent reporting of intelligibility measures in investigations of persons with speech-language impairments, and systematic examination of factors that enhance or decrease the intelligibility of persons with speech disorders. Examples of factors that will influence use of intelligibility measures in the future include:

1   Recognition that while intelligibility measures are related to a person's com-municative effectiveness, they do not measure this directly and so cannot predict with certainty how successfully a person can communicate in everyday interactions. Development of reliable, valid, and sensitive measures of com-municative effectiveness is in progress (e.g., Eadie et al., 2006).

2   A shift from focusing primarily on the talker to studying listeners' speech perception behaviors and strategies when identifying degraded speech signals. The influence of cognitive psychology on knowledge of factors that affect lexical decision making and of studies that have tested hypotheses about listeners' performance based on speech perception theories (e.g., Liss et al., 2002) demonstrate that listeners are an important variable to be exploited in understanding and increasing a talker's intelligibility potential. Clinical studies are needed that explore instructional techniques, their effectiveness for training listeners to make use of any and all information when communicating with persons with speech disorders, and how these techniques vary depending on the type and severity of speech disorder (Hustad, Dardis, & McCourt, 2007).

3   The availability of digital recording technology and remote access to talkers and listeners via the internet. These have the potential to increase the efficiency and power of intelligibility measurement. Computer technology is being incorporated into intelligibility measurement in several ways. The Sentence Intelligibility Measure software (Yorkston, Beukelman, & Hakel, 1996) generates, administers and scores the sentence format of the Assessment of Intelligibility of Dysarthric Speech, currently the most widely used intelligibility measure in speech-language pathology. While the software does not include a utility for recording the talker's utterances to the computer or playing these back to listeners, external audio recording and editing software can run concurrently to record and play .wav files of the recordings. The Speech Intelligibility Probe for Children with Cleft Palate (Hodge & Gotzke, 2007) is a software program that an examiner uses to generate, administer, record, and play back recordings to listeners for open- and closed-set identification tasks. The software includes a sound server that records and saves each utterance produced by the child and plays these back in the judging software. Listeners type their response on a monitor. The software saves the responses for each item to a separate computer file and provides an initial score based on the match between the target word and the listener's response for each item. This provides a time-efficient way to obtain and play back recordings but does not solve the problem of finding listeners. Ziegler and Zierdt (2008) described a web-based version of the Munich Intelligibility Profile (MVP-Online), which uses a multiple-choice word recognition format and a phonetically balanced list of target words. Sophisticated randomization techniques and a large database of words and carrier phrases are used to reduce listeners' ability to predict the target words. The client is examined online, the recorded speech samples are transmitted to a server, and the recordings are evaluated by a panel of listeners. Listeners are recruited, trained, and perform the judgment task remotely via a website within a specified time-frame. An operating team coordinates communication between clients and listeners, scores the MVP protocol, and provides the results to the client.

The availability of software to make digital recordings of talkers at multiple sites that can be accessed remotely for judging makes it more feasible to obtain standard intelligibility measures from large numbers of talkers with speech disorders for studies of treatment effectiveness and long-term outcomes. An alternative to using human listeners that is being explored is to apply automatic speech recognition approaches to generate intelligibility measures (e.g., Schuster et al., 2006). If this becomes feasible, the time and expense involved in using human listeners will be eliminated. This has the advantage of increasing the likelihood that word identification measures of intelligibility are used in clinical settings. However, knowing how to interpret the scores obtained relative to how successfully a talker and listener can achieve mutual understanding in an interaction remains a challenge.

The ability to successfully convey a message to another is a fundamental human need and right. Intelligibility has become established as an important severity indicator for disordered speech. With its increasing use as an outcome measure, it is essential that our methods for evaluating intelligibility are valid, reliable, and responsive; that there is a sensitive understanding of the variables that influence it; and that the search continues for factors that both reduce and that most effectively improve intelligibility.

REFERENCES

Adams, S. G., Dykstra, A., Jenkins, M., & Jog, M. (2008). Speech-to-noise levels and conversational intelligibility in hypophonia and Parkinson's disease. *Journal of Medical Speech-Language Pathology* 16, 165–72.

Allen, C., Nikolopoulos, T., Dyar, D., & O'Donoghue, G. (2001). Reliability of a rating scale for measuring speech intelligibility after pediatric cochlear implantation. *Otology and Neurology* 22, 631–3.

Boothroyd, A. (1985). Evaluation of speech production of the hearing impaired: Some benefits of forced-choice testing. *Journal of Speech and Hearing Research* 28, 185–96.

Chin, S. B., Tsai, P. L., & Gao, S. (2003). Connected speech intelligibility of children with cochlear implants and children with normal hearing. *American Journal of Speech-Language Pathology* 12, 440–51.

Cote-Reschny, K. (2007). Effects of talker severity and repeated presentations on listener judgments of the speech intelligibility of young children with dysarthria. Unpublished masters thesis, University of Alberta, Edmonton, AB.

Dowden P. (1997). Augmentative and alternative decision-making for children with severely unintelligible speech. *AAC: Alternative and Augmentative Communication* 13, 48–58.

Eadie T. L., Yorkston, K. M., Klasner, E. R., Dudgeon, B. J., Deitz, J. C., Baylor, C. R., Miller, R. M., & Amtmann, D. (2006). Measuring communicative participation:

A review of self-report instruments in speech-language pathology. *American Journal of Speech-Language Pathology* 15, 307–20.

Fletcher, S. G., Dagenais, P. A., & Critz-Crosby, P. (1991a). Teaching consonants to profoundly hearing-impaired speakers using palatometry. *Journal of Speech and Hearing Research* 34, 929–42.

Fletcher, S. G., Dagenais, P. A., & Critz-Crosby, P. (1991b). Teaching vowels to profoundly hearing-impaired speakers using glossometry. *Journal of Speech and Hearing Research* 34, 943–56.

Gordon-Brannan, M. & Hodson, B. W. (2000). Intelligibility/severity measurements of prekindergarten children's speech. *American Journal of Speech-Language Pathology* 9, 141–50.

Hanson, E., Yorkston, K., & Beukelman, D. (2004). Speech supplementation techniques for dysarthria: A systematic review. *Journal of Medical Speech-Language Pathology* 12 (2), ix–xxix.

Henningsson, G., Kuehn, D., Sell, D., Sweeney, T., Trost-Cardamone, J., & Whitehill, T. (2008). Universal parameters for reporting speech outcomes in individuals with cleft palate. *Cleft Palate-Craniofacial Journal* 45, 1–17.

Higgins, C. & Hodge, M. (2002). Vowel area and intelligibility in children with and without dysarthria. *Journal of Medical Speech-Language Pathology* 10, 271–7.

Hodge, M. & Gotzke, C. L. (2007). Preliminary results of an intelligibility measure for English-speaking children with cleft palate. *Cleft Palate-Craniofacial Journal* 44, 163–74.

Hodson, B. W. (2004). *Hodson Assessment of Phonological Patterns*, 3rd ed. Austin, TX: Pro-Ed.

Hustad, K. C. & Cahill, M. A. (2003). Effects of presentation mode and repeated presentation on intelligibility of dysarthric speech. *American Journal of Speech-Language Pathology* 12, 198–208.

Hustad, K. C., Dardis, C. M., & McCourt, K. A. (2007). Effects of visual information on intelligibility of open and closed class words in predictable sentences produced by speakers with dysarthria. *Clinical Linguistics & Phonetics* 21 (5), 353–67.

Keintz, C. K., Bunton, K., & Hoit, J. D. (2007). Influence of visual information on the intelligibility of dysarthric speech. *American Journal of Speech-Language Pathology* 16, 222–34.

Kent, R. D., Weismer, G., Kent, J. F., & Rosenbek, J. C. (1989). Toward phonetic intelligibility testing in dysarthria. *Journal of Speech and Hearing Disorders* 54, 482–99.

Klasner, E. L. & Yorkston, K. M. (2005). Speech intelligibility in ALS and HD dysarthria: The everyday listener's perspective. *Journal of Medical Speech-Language Pathology* 13, 127–39.

Lang, B. K., Starr, C. D., & Moller, K. (1992). Effects of pubertal changes on the speech of persons with cleft palate. *Cleft Palate-Craniofacial Journal* 29 (3), 268–70.

LaRivere, C., Seilo, M. T., & Dimmick, K. C. (1975). Report on the speech intelligibility of a glossectomee: Perceptual and acoustic observations. *Folia Phoniatrica* 27, 201–14.

Liss, J. M., Spitzer, S. M., Caviness, J. N., & Adler, C. (2002). The effects of familiarization on intelligibility and lexical segmentation in hypokinetic and ataxic dysarthria. *Journal of the Acoustical Society of America* 112 (6), 3022–30.

Markham, D. & Hazan, V. (2004). The effect of talker- and listener-related factors on intelligibility for a real-word, open-set perception test. *Journal of Speech, Language, and Hearing Research* 47, 725–37.

McNaughton, D., Fallon, K., Tod, J., Weiner, F., & Neisworth, J. (1994). Effect of repeated listening experiences on the intelligibility of synthesized speech. *Augmentative and Alternative Communication* 10, 161–8.

Monsen, R. B. (1981). A usable test for the speech intelligibility of deaf talkers. *American Annals of the Deaf* 126, 845–52.

Monsen, R. B. (1983). The oral speech intelligibility of hearing-impaired talkers. *Journal of Speech and Hearing Disorders* 48, 286–96.

Monsen, R., Moog, J. S., & Geers, A. E. (1988). *CID Picture SPINE (SPeech INtelligibility Evaluation)*. St. Louis: Central Institute for the Deaf.

Müller, N. (2002). Intelligibility and negotiated meaning in interaction. *Clinical Linguistics and Phonetics* 17, 317–24.

Munro, M. J. & Derwing, T. M. (1995). Foreign accent, comprehensibility, and intelligibility in the speech of second language learners. *Language Learning* 45, 73–97.

Osberger, M. J., Robbins, A. M., Todd, S. L., & Riley, A. I. (1994). Speech intelligibility of children with cochlear implants. *Volta Review* 96, 169–80.

Picheny, M. A., Durlach, N. I., & Braida, L. D. (1985). Speaking clearly for the hard of hearing: I. intelligibility differences between clear and conversational speech. *Journal of Speech & Hearing Research* 28, 96–103.

Picheny, M. A., Durlach, N. I., & Braida, L. D. (1986). Speaking clearly for the hard of hearing: II. acoustic characteristics of clear and conversational speech. *Journal of Speech & Hearing Research* 29, 434–45.

Preminger, J. W. & Van Tasell, D. J. (1995). Quantifying the relation between speech quality and speech intelligibility. *Journal of Speech and Hearing Research* 38, 714–25.

Rogers, C. L., Dalby, J., & Nishi, K. (2004). Effects of noise and proficiency on intelligibility of Chinese-accented English. *Language and Speech* 47, 139–54.

Samar, V. J. & Metz, D. E. (1988). Criterion validity of speech intelligibility rating-scale procedures for the hearing-impaired population. *Journal of Speech and Hearing Research* 31, 307–16.

Schiavetti, N. (1992). Scaling procedures for the measurement of speech intelligibility. In R. D. Kent (ed.), *Intelligibility in Speech Disorders* (pp. 233–64). Philadelphia: John Benjamins Publishing Company.

Schuster, M., Maier, A., Haderlein, T., Nkenke, E., Wohlleben, U., Rosanowski, F., Eysholdt, U., & Nöth, E. (2006). Evaluation of speech intelligibility for children with cleft lip and palate by means of automatic speech recognition. *International Journal of Pediatric Otorhinology* 70, 1741–7.

Weismer, G. & Laures, J. (2002). Direct magnitude estimation of speech intelligibility: Effects of a chosen standard. *Journal of Speech, Language, Hearing Research* 45, 421–33.

Weiss, C. (1982). *Weiss Intelligibility Test*. Tigard, OR: CC Publications.

Whitehill, T. L. (2002). Assessing intelligibility in speakers with cleft palate: A critical review of the literature. *Cleft Palate-Craniofacial Journal* 39, 50–8.

Whitehill, T. L. & Chau, C. H.-F. (2004). Single-word intelligibility in speakers with repaired cleft palate. *Clinical Linguistics & Phonetics* 18, 341–55.

Whitehill, T. & Chun, J. C. (2002). Intelligibility and acceptability in speakers with cleft palate. In F. Windsor, M. L. Kelly, & N. Hewlett (eds.), *Investigations in clinical phonetics and linguistics* (pp. 405–15). Mahwah, NJ: Lawrence Erlbaum Associates, Inc.

Whitehill, T., Ciocca, V., & Yiu, E. M. (2004). Perceptual and acoustic predictors of intelligibility and acceptability in Cantonese speakers with dysarthria. *Journal of Medical Speech-Language Pathology* 12, 229–33.

Whitehill, T. L. & Wong, C. C.-Y. (2006). Contributing factors to listener effort for dysarthric speech. *Journal of Medical Speech-Language Pathology* 14, 335–41.

Wilcox, K. & Morris, S. (1999). *Children's Speech Intelligibility Measure*. Toronto: The Psychological Corporation, Harcourt Brace & Company.

Yorkston, K. M. & Beukelman, D. R. (1981). *Assessment of Intelligibility of Dysarthric Speech*. Austin, TX: Pro-Ed, Inc.

Yorkston, K., Beukelman, D., & Hakel, M. (1996). *Phoneme identification task for Windows*. Lincoln, NE: Communication Disorders Software.

Yorkston, K. M., Beukelman, D. R., Strand, E. A., & Bell, K. R. (1999). *Management of motor speech disorders in children and adults*. Austin, TX: Pro-Ed, Inc.

Yorkston, K., Strand, E., & Kennedy, M. (1996). Comprehensibility of dysarthric speech: Implications for assessment and treatment planning. *American Journal of Speech-Language Pathology* 5, 55–66.

Ziegler, W. & Zierdt, A. (2008). Web-based clinical assessment of intelligibility in dysarthria: MVP-Online. Paper presented at the 14th Biennial Conference on Motor Speech: Motor Speech Disorders and Speech Motor Control, Monterey, CA (March, 2008).

5 Genetic Syndromes and Communication Disorders

VESNA STOJANOVIK

1 Introduction

A syndrome is defined as the presence of multiple anomalies in the same individual with all of those anomalies having a single cause. So far over 300 different genetic syndromes with possible communicative disorder components have been identified (Shprintzen, 1997). For over 30 years (Adler, 1976) attention has been devoted to the impact of genetic syndromes on the communicative abilities of children. However, when compared with other medical and behavioral components, the focus on communication disorders and syndromes is still under-represented in the research literature (Van Borsel, 2004).

In 1981 when Sparks and Millard published their review article in the *Journal of Communication Disorders*, their focus was on 16 syndromes and the potential impact on speech and language abilities, but the foci (and the list) continued to grow. In 1982, Siedel-Sadewitz and Shprintzen produced a summary of anatomical and functional characteristics of 105 syndromes that might involve speech or language problems. Jung (1989) and Shprintzen (1997) later published books on the genetic syndromes and communicative disorders, with Shprintzen compiling information on 334 syndromes in a "limited" list. Whether the focus is on individual syndromes (e.g., Akefeldt, Akefeldt, & Gilberg, 1997; Branson, 1981; Brock, 2007; Sudhapter & Belser, 2001) or on the deviant patterns of communication across numerous syndromes (e.g., Rice, Warren, & Betz, 2005; Van Borsel, 2004; Van Borsel & Tetnowski, 2007), more data are currently being compiled on this topic. In this chapter, the reasons for studying genetic syndromes in communicative disorders will be discussed, followed by a discussion of general patterns of concomitance in genetic syndromes and then a focus on several syndromes.

2 Why Study Genetic Syndromes?

Populations affected by genetic syndromes have been studied for different reasons. One strong motivation is to gain knowledge about the behavioral manifestations

The Handbook of Language and Speech Disorders, First Edition. Edited by Jack S. Damico, Nicole Müller, and Martin J. Ball. © 2013 Blackwell Publishing Ltd except for editorial material and organization © 2013 Jack S. Damico, Nicole Müller, Martin J. Ball. Published 2013 by Blackwell Publishing Ltd.

of a specific genetic abnormality, with a view to having a better understanding of the condition and informing diagnosis and remediation. Originating with Adler (1976) and carrying on through the emphasis placed on service delivery to these syndromes in the clinical field (e.g., Branson, 1981; Hodapp & Fedler, 1999; Laws & Bishop, 2003, 2004; Philofsky, Fidler, & Hepburn, 2007; Sparks & Millard, 1981), understanding the impact, the needs, and how to provide intervention has been the primary focus. Another reason for studying genetic syndromes, however, is the potential contribution to theoretical debates on the role of general cognitive mechanisms for language acquisition. According to Marcus and Rabagliati (2006), developmental disorders provide a naturalistic way of testing the relation between the biological (and psychological) basis of language and the biological (and psychological) basis of other cognitive or neural systems. Theories of language acquisition have often been informed by evidence from atypical populations, particularly those that show marked dissociations between their verbal and non-verbal abilities (Curtiss, 1977; Lenneberg, 1967; Yamada, 1990). For example, the publication of Fodor's (1983) *Modularity of Mind* had a profound impact on the study of language. It proposed that many of the processes involved in language comprehension are undertaken by special brain systems termed *modules*, which have a number of different functions such as informational encapsulation, domain specificity, and a dedicated neural location (innateness). According to this view, the modular system observed in the adult end state is also present in the infant start state. One of the challenges to this view has been that modules are not specified innately from the outset (Karmiloff-Smith, 1994) and that the brain becomes modularized in the process of development under the influence of the environment (neuroconstructivism). Although it is widely acknowledged that the adult brain is a modular system and different brain regions are highly specialized for specific functions, which has been supported by evidence from adult neuropsychological studies (Siegal, Varley, & Want, 2001; Varley & Siegal, 2000), these studies do not show that particular brain regions are specialized for certain cognitive functions, such as language, from birth.

A related issue, pertinent to this debate, is whether cognitive development in individuals with genetic syndromes follows a developmental trajectory that mirrors the one seen in typical development, or whether, due to the genetic abnormality, the developmental trajectory may be atypical. If we assume the innate modularity view, then we would predict that language and cognitive development in populations with genetic disorders follow a developmental trajectory that mirrors the one seen in typical development (Pinker 1999), although one or more components of this system may be anomalous. If we assume the alternative view, neuroconstructivism (Karmiloff-Smith, 1998), then we would predict that a genetic abnormality inevitably affects the developmental pathway, such that development proceeds along an atypical trajectory.

Genetic syndromes have had a prominent role in this debate. As previously discussed, despite several decades of intensive research, a meta-analysis study (Van Borsel, 2004), which investigated 299 different syndromes, concluded that communication disorders in genetic syndromes is still an under-researched area. Although it is well established that many syndromes are associated with communication disorders, there is still a large number of disorders for which there is no information available. The six best-known genetic syndromes as far as language is concerned are: Williams syndrome, Down syndrome, Fragile-X syndrome, Prader–Willi syndrome, cri-du-chat syndrome, and Noonan syndrome (Rondal, 2001). After discussing some general trends noted in the genetic syndromes that exhibit communicative disorders, this chapter will focus on the three most relevant syndromes for this handbook.

3 Genetic Syndromes and Communicative Disorders

3.1 Documented general patterns

In his meta-analysis of the 299 genetic syndromes documented by Shprintzen (1997) that were "compatible with life," John van Borsel noted several emerging trends when considering various speech disorders (i.e., voice and resonance disorders). First, he noted that the disorders of voice and resonance in genetic syndromes are not typically isolated problems. Of the syndromes studied, approximately 61 percent (182/299) were associated with a cognitive impairment, 56 percent (166/299) were associated with hearing problems, and facial or palate clefting was present in over one-third of the syndromes (101/299). When those syndromes with voice and resonance problems were tallied, more than 90 percent of the syndromes with voice disorders also exhibited a cognitive and/or a hearing problem and 93 percent of the syndromes with resonance disorders similarly exhibited cognitive, hearing, or clefting problems. Since it is possible that some of these speech problems are reflections of cognitive and/or hearing problems, it is also likely that those syndromes associated with language problems are due to cognitive and/or hearing concomitants. Given that intact auditory and cognitive capacity are necessary for normal oral language development (e.g., Bishop & Mogford, 1988; Jung, 1989; Rice, 1996; Rice, Warren & Betz, 2005), it would not be surprising to note high co-occurrence of language with cognitive and/or hearing problems as well in genetic syndromes.

The second trend noted by Van Borsel was that the high frequency of co-occurrence of speech and language disorders with cognitive and/or hearing problems may constitute a problem with the study of genotype–phenotype correlations in communication and language. Due to the pervasive impact of the cognitive and/or hearing problems, specific descriptions of the genetic correlations for the speech and language problems can become blurred so that rich descriptions of the clinical features and natural history of speech and language problems in separate syndromes is not easily documented.

Finally, Van Borsel noted that analysis of the occurrence of voice and resonance disorders according to etiological category seems to suggest that distinct causal mechanisms within the genetic syndromes are not a major factor in determining the presence of voice and resonance disorders. Van Borsel and Tetnowski (2007) found that this was also the case with the occurrence of fluency disorders in genetic syndromes and, by extension, the same appears likely for language problems as well.

3.2   *Language and communication in Williams syndrome (WS)*

Williams Syndrome (WS) is a rare genetic disorder which is typically found in 1 in 20,000–50,000 live births (Greenberg, 1990), although recent research has reported incidence of 1 in 7,500 (Stromme, Bjornstad, & Ramstad, 2002). It occurs due to a deletion of approximately 25 genes on chromosome 7. The deletion includes the gene ELN, which codes for the protein elastin (Lowery et al., 1995). WS is characterized by physical abnormalities, heart and renal problems, failure to thrive in infancy, a characteristic face morphology known as "elfin" face, and mild to moderate learning difficulties. The WS neuro-cognitive profile is often described as uneven. This is due to the fact that individuals with WS have moderate to severe learning difficulties, profound impairments in planning, problem solving and spatial cognition in the face of relative strengths in social cognition, linguistic abilities, face processing, and auditory rote memory (Mervis et al., 1999).

Early studies investigating language in WS reported "intact" language with regard to morphosyntactic abilities. Pioneering work by Bellugi and colleagues argued that despite severe cognitive impairments, individuals with WS have superior syntactic abilities (Bellugi et al., 1988; Bellugi et al., 1992; Bellugi, Wong, & Jernigan, 1994). Bellugi and colleagues were the first to suggest that individuals with WS offered evidence that there are clear dissociations between language and other cognitive abilities in the human cognitive system. A number of recent reports have also indicated that individuals with WS show enhanced grammatical ability compared with lexical ability, and better performance in grammar over lexical semantics (Clahsen & Almazan, 1998, 2001; Clahsen & Temple, 2003; Ring & Clahsen, 2005). These studies have argued that WS offers evidence for dissociations within the linguistic system (internal modularity) into a computational component (concerned with rule-governed operations involved in passive constructions, formation of past tense in English, binding) and a lexical component (vocabulary store). In their studies, Clahsen and colleagues showed that individuals with WS perform better with regular grammatical inflections compared to irregular, which involved retrieving items from the lexicon. The regular/ irregular inflection issue has attracted a lot of interest and debate because of the theoretical implications. A number of studies have shown that individuals with WS perform better on regular inflections than on irregular ones (Bromberg et al., 1995; Clahsen, Ring, & Temple, 2004; Pléh, Lukács, & Racsmány, 2003). Studies have also reported that individuals with WS may be significantly impaired on irregular inflections compared to controls but not on regular inflections (Clahsen & Almazan, 1998; Penke & Krause, 2004; Zukowski, 2004). However, no study to date has reported that individuals with WS outperform mental-age controls, either on regular or irregular inflection. Furthermore, the results of studies that have employed a larger number of participants (such as Thomas et al., 2001) show no interaction between group and regularity. As pointed out by Brock (2007), all the studies which have investigated the performance of individuals with WS on regular versus irregular inflections suffer from "ceiling" effects, in that most of the participants in all the studies perform at ceiling on regular inflection, which makes it impossible for any group differences on irregular inflection to be found.

A large body of research has provided evidence for impaired morphosyntactic abilities in individuals with WS (Joffe & Varlokosta, 2007; Karmiloff-Smith et al., 1998; Karmiloff-Smith et al., 2003; Mervis & Klein-Tasman, 2000; Stojanovik, Perkins, & Howard, 2001; 2004; Thomas et al., 2001; Volterra et al., 2003). Some of these studies show that not only do the individuals with WS not have superior language abilities, but also that their language abilities may be on a par with that of children with diagnosed language impairments. For example, Stojanovik et al. (2004) compared the performance of a group of participants with WS and a group of participants with Specific Language Impairment (SLI) on a range of receptive and expressive standardized verbal measures, including measures of morphosyntax, and found similar performance across the two groups on all the measures. The children with WS were completely indistinguishable on measures of morphosyntax from children with clinically diagnosed language impairment.

Most recently, Joffe and Varlocosta (2007) found that participants with WS and Down syndrome (DS) performed similarly on standardized measures of grammatical ability, as well as on experimental tasks that tapped comprehension of passives, and production and comprehension of wh-questions. Participants with DS performed significantly more poorly than both the WS group and typically developing (TD) controls on the repetition of wh-questions. Both the WS and DS cohorts performed significantly more poorly on most of the syntactic tasks compared to the younger TD controls.

Studies have also shown that the onset of language acquisition in WS in the early stages is delayed (Paterson et al., 1999; Semel & Rosner, 2003; Stojanovik & James, 2006). Studies of infants and toddlers with WS are few, and, although informative, show inconsistencies: there is evidence for an asynchronous relationship due to poorer language than cognitive abilities (Stojanovik & James, 2006), but also due to stronger language than cognitive abilities (Mervis & Bertrand, 1997). Early language acquisition in WS is an under-researched area and more longitudinal studies are needed in order to find out how language is acquired in WS and to examine the relationship between language and other cognitive abilities.

Despite a large body of research into the morphosyntactic abilities of people with WS, there have been fewer studies investigating actual communication skills in this population. There have been reports that good social communication skills are a "hallmark" of the syndrome (Jones et al., 2000). Mervis, Klein-Tasman, and Mastin (2001), using the Vineland Adaptive Behavior Scales (VABS; Sparrow, Balla, & Chichetti, 1984), reported that communication in WS is a relative strength. In particular, Jones et al. (2000) argued that superior social-communication skills distinguish this population from populations with other developmental disorders, such as Down syndrome (DS) and autism. In a series of tasks, Jones et al. (2000) reported that children with WS include a higher number of inferences about the affective state and motivation of story characters in comparison to typically developing children and children with DS. In the same study, individuals with WS provided a greater number of descriptions of affective states and evaluative comments during an interview task, and were more likely to ask questions of the interviewer. This was interpreted as showing that individuals with WS are "hypersocial."

There have also been clinical and parental reports, as well as a number of research studies, which have shown that individuals with WS have problems with establishing friendships and have social difficulties, such as disinhibition and social isolation (Davies, Udwin, & Howlin, 1998).

Some studies have shown that individuals with WS are not sensitive to the needs of the conversational partner (Udwin & Yule, 1991). Further, Stojanovik, Perkins and Howard (2001) reported a high level of conversational inadequacy in a pilot study of a group of children with WS, in which participants with WS were found to have a tendency to provide insufficient information for the conversational partner. Laws and Bishop (2004) reported pragmatic language impairment and social deficits in a group of older children and young adults with WS, using the Children's Communication Checklist (Bishop, 1998). The checklist ratings showed pragmatic language deficits, evident from inappropriate initiations of conversation, and use of stereotyped conversation. Furthermore, Stojanovik (2006) reported that children with WS have difficulties with exchange structure and responding appropriately to the interlocutor's requests for information and clarification. They also had significant difficulties with interpreting meaning and providing enough information for the conversational partner.

Most recently, Lacroix, Bernicot, and Reilly (2007) investigated the abilities of children with WS to interact for the purpose of attaining a goal. The task required the mother and the child to collaborate and negotiate in order to produce a drawing on the computer, on the basis of a drawing model. The authors reported that during this collaborative conversation task, the children and adolescents with WS (similarly to those with DS) produced fewer utterances than the typically developing participants and played a weak role in the conversation compared to their mother. However, they readily expressed their psychological states (like younger children of the same mental age). Also, the children and adolescents with WS responded to maternal directives less often than all other groups.

Heterogeneity in WS has also been reported. It has been suggested by Jarrold, Baddeley, and Hewes (1998) and by Pezzini et al. (1999) that there are individual differences in the WS profile overall, though linguistic variation in WS has not been described in detail. In the Pezzini et al. study, only measures of vocabulary were considered as measures of language. Stojanovik, Perkins, and Howard (2006) showed that there was a lot of variability in the verbal profiles of five children with WS. The scores on a number of standardized language measures ranged from between 2 to 3 standard deviations below the mean for some participants to well above average for other participants. However, the participants who scored highest on the language assessments had the highest mental ages. In a much larger study involving 31 individuals with WS, Porter and Coltheart (2005) reported substantial cognitive variability within individuals and they even suggested that there may be several different subgroups depending on the profile of strengths and weaknesses they show.

In summary, although it is evident that research on WS has moved substantially from the initial claims that these children have 'intact' language abilities despite severe cognitive deficits, the emerging picture is much less clear and the question of the contribution of atypical populations, such as individuals with WS to which constraints guide typical language acquisition, is more open to debate than ever before.

3.3   *Language and communication in Down syndrome*

Down syndrome (DS) is a genetic disorder caused by abnormalities on chromosome 21. It affects about 1 in 1,000 live births (McGrowter & Marshall, 1990). DS is characterized by mild to moderate learning difficulties and delayed language abilities. A lot can be learnt about language in individuals with DS by reading reports on individuals with WS because people with DS are often included as a comparison group. This is because individuals with WS and those with DS have similar non-verbal abilities but often different language profiles (Bellugi et al., 2000; Bellugi, Wong, & Jernigan, 1994; Jarrold, Baddeley, & Hewes, 1998; Reilly, Klima, & Bellugi, 1990).

Similar to the profile of individuals with WS, the profile of individuals with DS is also often characterized as "uneven" with weaknesses in auditory short-term memory relative to visual short-term memory and other aspects of cognition (Chapman, 2003) and with strengths in their social functioning abilities (Kasari & Bauminger, 1998). Language acquisition is a challenge for people with DS, although vocabulary level tends to be less impaired than grammatical abilities (Chapman, Schwartz, & Kay-Raining Bird, 1991; Miller, 1996). Many children with DS do not acquire their first words before the age of 2 (Rondal, 2001); however, early lexical development generally shows a positive linear relationship with mental age (Rondal & Edwards, 1997). Individual variation has been reported. Miller (1999) studied 43 children with DS using the McArthur Child Development Inventory and found that 65 percent of the children scored below their mental age on vocabulary and only 35 percent of the children had vocabulary ranges which were consistent with their mental age.

Compared to typically developing individuals matched for mental age, children and adults with DS often have receptive vocabulary deficits (Jarrold, Baddeley, & Phillips, 2002), although studies have also shown some children with DS have similar expressive and receptive vocabulary to typically developing children of the same mental age (Laws & Bishop, 2003). General language performance tends to be lower than expected from their general level of cognitive development (Chapman & Hesketh, 2000; Fowler, Gelman, & Gleitman, 1994; Perovic, 2001,

2002; Vicari, Caselli, & Tonucci, 2000). Exceptionally, language abilities may in some cases be higher than other cognitive abilities (Rondal, 1994). In a study that compared language development in infants with WS and those with DS, Singer-Harris et al. (1997) reported that children with DS were much more likely to use gesture compared to children with WS.

With regard to morphosyntactic abilities, Eadie et al. (2002) compared the accuracy of marking finiteness in spontaneous speech. Children with DS were compared to children with SLI. The study found that the profiles of the groups of children were similar, suggesting that grammatical abilities in children with DS are comparable to those of children with known language impairments.

It is interesting to note, however, that people with DS are very keen to engage in conversation and to keep the conversation going; however, they often lack the appropriate language skills to do so (Rondal, 2001). Two studies described in Abbeduto and Murphy (2004) point to some strengths and weaknesses in the DS communication profile. For example, in a barrier task, individuals with DS were less likely than typically developing individuals matched for mental age and individuals with Fragile-X syndrome to provide listeners with referential frames which help the listener's comprehension. Also they were less likely than mental-age-matched peers to signal non-comprehension, suggesting that perhaps they are unable to monitor their own comprehension, which can seriously disrupt the conversational interaction. On the other hand, individuals with DS were found to be appreciative of shared knowledge in conversation and they made appropriate shifts from indefinite descriptions (such as "a house") to definite descriptions (such as "the house"). In a task which required the participants to describe a novel shape to their interlocutor, the individuals with DS were found to be very consistent when describing the same shape every time it occurred, suggesting awareness of the listener's informational needs compared to individuals with Fragile X-syndrome.

In summary, research studies so far point to the fact that children with DS generally have expressive language difficulties which are often lower than what would be expected of their mental age and with different strengths and weaknesses across their cognitive profile.

3.4   Language and communication in Fragile-X syndrome (FXS)

FXS is the most prevalent form of heritable mental retardation (Rice, Warren, & Betz, 2005). It results from a single gene mutation (FMR1) on the X chromosome at Xq27.3 (Brown, 2002). It occurs in 1 in 4,000 males and in 1 in 8,000 females (Crawford, Acuna, & Sherman, 2001) and it is associated with various nervous system anomalies. The gene mutation is X-linked and therefore, in general, females are less affected than males and most studies on language and communication in FXS have included male participants.

Most research on language and communicative abilities in FXS has focused on affected males. Similarly to DS and WS, the behavioral phenotype of the individuals with FXS is characterized by cognitive strengths and weaknesses. Thus they are reported to have poor auditory short-term memory (Freund & Reiss, 1991) and difficulties with directing and sustaining attention (Mazzocco, Pennington, & Hagerman, 1993), but relatively good long-term memory (Freund & Reiss, 1991) and a preserved ability to distinguish between the self's representations of the world and those of other people (Garner, Callias, & Turk, 1999). Autistic-like behaviors are also common in FXS and affect between 10 and 40 percent of the FXS population (Demark, Feldman, & Holden, 2003).

The speech and language abilities of male individuals with FXS have been reported to be atypical. In comparison to the breadth of studies on the language and communication of individuals with WS and DS, there are fewer reports on the language and communication abilities in individuals with FXS. Bailey et al. (2004) found that, similarly to children with WS, children with FXS show a verbal advantage compared to visuo-spatial tasks, although acquisition of speech and language is initially delayed (Cornish, Munir, & Cross, 2001), but the delay is in line with non-verbal cognitive delays (Abbeduto & Murphy, 2004). Expressive language skills have been found to develop more slowly than receptive skills (Roberts, Mirret, & Burchinal, 2001).

Similarly to children with DS, children with FXS also have speech difficulties which can often make their speech unintelligible (Spinelli et al., 1995) due to hypotonia that involves the oro-facial musculature. With regards to social interaction abilities, a number of difficulties have been reported. For example, males with FXS often use tangential language in conversations. Specifically, they have a tendency to ask off-topic questions, give inadequate response or comments that do not follow the conversational thread, and they often reintroduce their favorite topics over and over again (i.e., perseverative language) (Sudhalter & Belser, 2001; Sudhalter et al., 1990) or repeat sounds, words or utterances within a conversational turn (Belser & Sudhalter, 2001). This has been attributed to their inability to control arousal and, as a result, they are prone to long periods of sustained hyperarousal, especially during social interactions (Cornish, Sudhalter, & Turk, 2004). Abbeduto and Murphy (2004) also studied the pragmatic abilities of children with FXS using a barrier task (as mentioned above in the section on DS). The individuals with FXS were able to appropriately switch from indefinite to definite object descriptions during conversation and were able to provide referential frames for the listeners. However, deficits were found in these individuals' ability to consistently describe the same shapes each time the shape was presented and signal non-comprehension in conversations.

4 Conclusions

The summaries of the studies reported in this chapter with regard to language and communication abilities for three different genetic syndromes clearly show that, in each of the populations, there are different areas of strengths and weaknesses within their language and communication profiles. What has also emerged is that there is no systematic evidence from the three disorders for clear dissociations between different cognitive skills, largely due to heterogeneity within each of the syndromes. This should not be discouraging further research, by any means. It is very important that inquiry into language and communication impairments in genetic syndromes continues if we are to understand the effects of genes on development. As pointed out by Rice, Warren, and Betz (2005), although we have a lot of information with regard to individual diagnostic profiles of different syndromes, there are few comparative studies, and therefore there is much need for systematic comparisons across disorders if we are to fully understand what is common across conditions so that we can clarify the nature of language impairments. One way forward would definitely be longitudinal studies detailing how language is acquired in the context of cognitive development and how development of language and communication skills proceeds and interacts with other cognitive abilities in different disorders. In order to inform theories of language acquisition and address more directly the debate with regard to the neural specialization of different modules from birth, it is crucial to examine language and cognitive abilities from as near to the infant start-state as possible.

REFERENCES

Abbeduto, L. & Murphy, M. M. (2004). Language, social cognition, maladaptive behaviour, and communication in Down syndrome and fragile X syndrome. In M. L. Rice and S. F. Warren (eds.), *Developmental language disorders: From phenotype to aetiologies*. Mahwah, NJ: Lawrence Erlbaum Associates.

Adler, S. (1976). The influence of genetic syndromes upon oral communication skills. *Journal of Speech and Hearing Disorders* 41, 136–7.

Akefeldt, A., Akefeldt, B., & Gilberg, C. (1997). Voice, speech and language characteristics of children with Prader–Willi syndrome. *Journal of Intellectual Disability Research* 41, 302–11.

Akefeldt, A., Gilberg, C., & Larson, C. (1991). Prader–Willi syndrome in a Swedish rural country; epidemiological aspects. *Developmental Medicine and Child Neurology* 33, 715–21.

Bailey, D. B., Roberts, J. E., Hooper, S. R., Hatton, D. D., Mirrett, P. L., & Schaaf, J. M. (2004). Research on fragile X syndrome and autism: implications for the study of genes, environments, and developmental language disorders. In M. Rice and S. Warren (eds.), *Developmental language disorders: From phenotypes to etiologies* (pp. 121–50). Mahwah, NJ: Lawrence Erlbaum Associates.

Bellugi, U., Marks, S., Bihrle, A., & Sabo, H. (1988). Dissociation between language and cognitive functions in Williams Syndrome. In D. Bishop and K. Mogford (eds.), *Language development in exceptional circumstances* (pp. 177–89). London: Churchill Livingstone.

Bellugi, U., Bihrle, A., Neville, H., & Doherty, S. (1992). Language, cognition and brain organization in a neurodevelopmental disorder. In M. Gunnar and C. Nelson (eds.), *Developmental behavioral neuroscience: The Minnesota symposium* (pp. 201–32). Hillsdale, NJ: Lawrence Erlbaum Associates.

Bellugi, U., Wong, P., & Jernigan, T. L. (1994). Williams syndrome: An unusual neuropsychological profile. In S. H. Broman and J. Grafman (eds.), *Atypical cognitive deficits in developmental disorders: Implications for brain function* (pp. 23–56). Hillsdale, NJ: Lawrence Erlbaum Associates.

Bellugi, U., Linchtenberger, L., Lai, Z., & St. George, M. (2000). The neurocognitive profile of Williams Syndrome: A complex pattern of strengths and weaknesses. *Journal of Cognitive Neuroscience* 12 (supplement), 7–29.

Belser, R. C. & Sudhalter, V. (2001). Conversational characteristics of children with fragile X-syndrome: repetitive speech. *American Journal of Mental Retardation* 106, 28–38.

Bishop, D. (1998). Development of the Children's Communication Checklist (CCC): a method for assessing the qualitative aspects of communicative impairment in children. *Journal of Child Psychology and Psychiatry* 39, 879–91.

Bishop, D. & Mogford, K. (eds.) (1988). *Language development in exceptional circumstances*. Hove, UK: Psychology Press.

Branson, C. (1981). Speech and language characteristics of children with Prader–Willi syndrome. In V. A. Holm, S. Sulzbacher, & P. L. Pipes (eds.), *The Prader–Willi syndrome* (pp. 179–83). Baltimore, MD: University Park Press.

Brock, J. (2007). Language abilities in Williams syndrome: a critical review. *Developmental Psychopathology* 19, 97–127.

Bromberg, H., Ullman, M., Marcus, G., Kelly, K., & Coppola, M. (1994). A dissociation of memory and grammar: evidence from Williams syndrome. Paper presented at the Eighteenth Annual Boston University Conference on Language Development.

Bromberg, H. S., Ullman, M., Marcus, G., Kelly, K. B., & Levine, K. (1995). A dissociation of lexical memory and grammar in Williams syndrome: Evidence from inflectional morphology. *Genetic Counseling*, special issue, 6, 166–7.

Brown, W. T. (2002). The molecular biology of the fragile X mutation. In R. J. Hagerman & P. J. Hagerman (eds.), *Fragile X syndrome: Diagnosis, treatment and research* (pp. 110–35). Baltimore, MD: Johns Hopkins University Press.

Chapman, R. S. (2003). Language and communication in individuals with Down syndrome. In L. Abbeduto (ed.), *International Review of Research into Mental Retardation* 27, 1–34.

Chapman, R. S. & Hesketh, L. J. (2000). Behavioural phenotype of individuals with Down syndrome. *Mental Retardation and Developmental Disabilities Research Reviews* 6, 84–95.

Chapman, R. S., Schwartz, S. E., & Kay-Raining Bird, E. (1991). Language skills of children and adolescents with Down syndrome; I. Comprehension. *Journal of Speech, Language and Hearing Research* 34, 1106–20.

Clahsen, H. & Almazan, M. (1998). Syntax and morphology in Williams syndrome. *Cognition* 68, 167–98.

Clahsen, H. & Almazan, M. (2001). Compounding and inflection in language impairment: Evidence from Williams syndrome (SLI). *Lingua* 111, 729–57.

Clahsen, H. & Temple, C. (2003). Words and rules in children with Williams syndrome. In Y. Levy & J. Schaeffer (eds.), *Language competence across populations* (pp. 23–352). Mahwah, NJ: Erlbaum Press.

Clahsen, H., Ring, M., & Temple, C. (2004). Lexical and morphological skills in English-speaking children with Williams syndrome. In S. Bartke and J. Siegmüller (eds.), *Williams syndrome across languages* (pp. 221–44). Amsterdam/Philadelphia: John Benjamins.

Cornish, K. M., Munir, F., & Cross, G. (2001). Differential impact of the FMR-1 full mutation on memory and attention functioning: a neuropsychological perspective. *Journal of Cognitive Neuroscience* 13, 144–50.

Cornish, K. M., Sudhalter, V., & Turk, J. (2004). Attention and language in fragile X. *Mental Retardation and Developmental Disabilities Research Reviews* 10, 11–16.

Crawford, D. C., Acuna, J. M., & Sherman, S. L. (2001). FMR1 and the fragile X syndrome: Human genome epidemiology review. *Genetics in Medicine* 3, 359–71.

Curtiss, S. (1977). *Genie: A psycholinguistic study of a modern-day "Wild-child".* New York: Academic Press.

Davies, M., Udwin, O., & Howlin, O. (1998). Adults with Williams syndrome. Preliminary study of social, emotional and behavioural difficulties. *British Journal of Psychiatry* 172, 273–6.

Demark, J. L., Feldman, M. A., & Holden, J. J. A. (2003). Behavioural relationship between autism and Fragile-X syndrome. *American Journal of Medical Genetics* 108, 359–71.

Downey, D. A. & Knutson, C. L. (1995). Speech and language issues. In L. R. Greenswag & R. C. Alexander (eds.), *Management of Prader–Willi syndrome* (pp. 142–55). New York: Springer-Verlag.

Eadie, P. A., Fey, M. E., Douglas, M. E., & Parsons, C. L. (2002). Profiles of grammatical morphology and sentence imitation in children with specific impairment and Down syndrome. *Journal of Speech, Language and Hearing Research* 45, 720–32.

Fodor, J. A. (1983). *The modularity of mind.* Cambridge, MA: MIT Press.

Fowler, A., Gelman, R., & Gleitman, L. (1994). The course of language learning in children with Down syndrome. In H. Tager-Flusberg (ed.), *Constraints on language acquisition: Studies of atypical children* (pp. 91–140). Hillsdale, NJ: Lawrence Erlbaum Associates.

Freund, L. S. & Reiss, A. L. (1991). Cognitive profiles associated with fragile-X syndrome in males and females. *American Journal of Medical Genetics* 38, 542–57.

Garner, C., Callias, M., & Turk, J. (1999). Executive function and theory of mind performance in boys with fragile-X syndrome. *Journal of Intellectual Disability Research* 43, 466–74.

Greenberg, F. (1990). Introduction. *American Journal of Medical Genetics* 6 (supplement), 85–8.

Hodapp, R. M. & Fidler, D. J. (1999). Special education and genetics: Connections for the 21st century. *Journal of Special Education* 33 (4), 130–7.

Jarrold, C., Baddeley, A. D., & Hewes, A. K. (1998). Verbal and non-verbal abilities in the Williams Syndrome phenotype: evidence for diverging developmental trajectories. *Journal of Child Psychology and Psychiatry* 39 (4), 511–23.

Jarrold, C., Baddeley, A., & Phillips, C. (2002). Verbal short-term memory deficits in Down syndrome: a problem of memory, audition or speech? *Journal of Speech, Language and Hearing Research* 45, 531–44.

Joffe, V. L. & Varlokosta, S. (2007). Patterns of syntactic development n children with Williams syndrome and Down syndrome: Evidence from passives and Wh-questions. *Clinical Linguistics and Phonetics* 21 (9), 705–27.

Joffe, V. L. & Varlokosta, S. (2007). Language abilities in William Syndrome: Exploring comprehension, production and repetition. *Advances in Speech-Language Pathology* 9, 1–3.

Jones, W., Bellugi, U., Lai, Z., Chiles, M., Reilly, J., Lincoln, A., & Adophs, R. (2000). Hypersociability in Williams syndrome. *Journal of Cognitive Neuroscience* 12, 30–46.

Jung, J. H. (1989). *Genetic syndromes in communicative disorders.* Austin, TX: Pro-Ed.

Karmiloff-Smith, A. (1994). *Beyond modularity: a developmental perspective on cognitive science*. Cambridge, MA: MIT Press.

Karmiloff-Smith, A. (1998). Development itself is the key to understanding developmental disorders. *Trends in Cognitive Science* 2 (10), 389–98.

Karmiloff-Smith, A., Tyler, L. K., Voice, K., Sims, K., Udwin, O., Howlin, P., & Davies, M. (1998). Lingustic dissociations in Williams syndrome: evaluating receptive syntax in on-line and off-line tasks. *Neuropsychologia* 36, 343–51.

Karmiloff-Smith, A., Brown, J. H., Grice, S., & Peterson, S. (2003). Dethroning the myth: Cognitive dissociations and innate modularity in Williams syndrome. *Developmental Neuropsychology* 23, 227–42.

Kasari, C. & Bauminger, N. (1998). Social and emotional development in children with mental retardation. In J. A. Burack., R. M. Hodapp., & E. Ziegler (eds.), *Handbook of mental retardation and development* (pp. 411–33). New York: Cambridge University Press

Lacroix, A., Bernicot, J., & Reilly, J. (2007) Narration and collaborative conversation in French-speaking children with Williams syndrome. *Journal of Neurolinguistics* 20 (6), 445–61.

Laws, G. & Bishop, D. (2003). A comparison of language abilities in adolescents with Down syndrome and children with specific language impairment. *Journal of Speech, Language and Hearing Research* 46, 1324–39.

Laws, G. & Bishop, D. (2004). Pragmatic language impairment and social deficits in Williams syndrome: A comparison with Down's syndrome and specific language impairment. *International Journal of Language and Communication Disorders* 39 (1), 45–64.

Lenneberg, E. H. (1967). *Biological foundations of language*. New York: John Wiley Sons.

Lowery, M. C., Morris, C. A., Ewart, A., Brothman, L. J., Zhu, X. L., Leonard, C. O., Carey, J. C., Keating, M., & Brothman, A. R. (1995). Strong correlation of elastin deletions, detected by FISH, with Williams syndrome. *American Journal of Human Genetics* 57, 49–53.

Marcus, G. & Rabagliati, H. (2006). What developmental disorders can tell us about the nature and origins of language? *Nature Neuroscience* 9 (10), 1226–9.

Mazzoco, M. M., Pennington, B., & Hagerman, R. J. (1993). The neurocognitive phenotype of female carriers of fragile X or Turner syndrome and their sisters. *Journal of Autism and Developmental Disorders* 28, 509–17.

McGrowter, C. W. & Marshall, B. (1990). Recent trends in incidence, morbidity, and survival in Down's syndrome. *Journal of Mental Deficiency Research* 34, 49–57.

Mervis, C. & Bertrand, J. (1997). Developmental relations between cognition and language: evidence from Williams syndrome. In L. B. Adamson and M. A. Romsky (eds.), *Communication and language acquisition: discoveries from atypical development* (pp. 75–160). Baltimore, MD: Paul Brookes.

Mervis, C. B., Morris, C. A., Bertrand, J., & Robinson, B. F. (1999). William syndrome: Findings from an integrated programme of research. In H. Tager-Flusberg (ed.), *Neurodevelopmental disorders: Contributions to a new framework from cognitive neuroscience* (pp. 65–110). Cambridge, MA: MIT Press.

Mervis, C. B. & Klein-Tasman, B. P. (2000). Williams syndrome: Cognition, personality, and adaptive behaviour. *Mental Retardation and Developmental Disabilities Research Reviews* 6, 148–58.

Mervis, C. B., Klein-Tasman, B. P., & Mastin, M. E. (2001). Adaptive behaviour of 4-through 8-year old children with Williams syndrome. *American Journal of Mental Retardation* 106, 82–93.

Miller, J. (1996). The search for the phenotype of disordered language performance. In M. L. Rice (ed.), *Towards a genetics of language* (pp. 297–314). Mahwah, NJ: Lawrence Erlbaum Associates.

Miller, J. F. (1999). Profiles of language development in children with Down syndrome. In L. Nadel (ed.), *The psychobiology of Down syndrome* (pp. 167–98). Cambridge, MA: MIT Press.

Paterson, S. J., Girelli, J. H., Gsodl, M. K., Johnson, M. H., & Karmiloff-Smith, A. (1999). Cognitive modularity and genetic disorders. *Science* 286, 2355–8.

Penke, M. & Krause, M. (2004). Regular and irregular inflectional morphology in German Williams syndrome. In S. Bartke & J. Siegmüller (eds.), *Williams syndrome across languages*. Amsterdam: John Benjamins.

Perovic, A. (2001). Binding principles in Down syndrome. UCL *Working Papers in Linguistics* 13, 425–45.

Perovic, A. (2002). Language in Down syndrome: Delay of principle A effect? *Durham Working Papers in Linguistics* 8, 97–110.

Pezzini, G., Vicari, S., Volterra, V., Milani, L., & Ossella, M. T. (1999). Children with Williams Syndrome: Is there a single neuropsychological profile? *Developmental Neuropsychology* 15, 141–55.

Philofsky, A., Fidler, D. J., & Hepburn, S. (2007). Pragmatic language profiles of school-age children with autism spectrum disorders and Williams syndrome. *American Journal of Speech-Language Pathology* 16, 368–80.

Pinker, S. (1999). *Words and rules*. London: Weidenfeld and Nicolson.

Pléh, Cs., Lukács A., & Racsmány, M. (2003). Morphological patterns in Hungarian children with Williams syndrome and the rule debates. *Brain and Language* 86, 377–83.

Porter, M. A. & Coltheart, M. (2005). Cognitive heterogeneity in Williams syndrome. *Developmental Neuropsychology* 27 (2), 275–306.

Reilly, J., Klima, E. S., & Bellugi, U. (1990). Once more with feeling: affect and language in atypical populations. *Development and Psychopathology* 2, 367–91.

Rice, M. L. (ed.) (1996). *Towards a genetics of language* (pp. 297–314). Mahwah, NJ: Lawrence Erlbaum.

Rice, M., Warren, S., & Betz, S. K. (2005). Language symptoms of developmental language disorders: An overview of autism, Down syndrome, fragile X, specific language impairment, and Williams syndrome. *Applied Psycholinguistics* 26, 7–27.

Ring, M. & Clahsen, H. (2005). Distinct patterns of language impairment in Down's syndrome and Williams syndrome: The case of syntactic chains. *Journal of Neurolinguistics* 18, 479–501.

Roberts, J. E., Mirret, P. L., & Burchinal, M. (2001). Receptive and expressive communication development of young males with Fragile X syndrome. *American Journal of Mental Retardation* 106, 216–30.

Rondal, J. (1994). Exceptional language development in mental retardation: the relative autonomy of language as a cognitive system. In H. Tager-Flusberg (ed.), *Constraints on language acquisition: Studies of atypical children* (pp. 155–74). Hillsdale, NJ: Lawrence Erlbaum Associates.

Rondal, J. (2001). Language in mental retardation: Individual and syndromic differences and neurogenetic variation. *Swiss Journal of Psychology* 60, 161–78.

Rondal, J. & Edwards, S. (1997). *Language in mental retardation*. London: Whurr Publishers.

Semel, E. & Rosner, S. (2003) *Understanding Williams syndrome: Behavioural patterns and interventions*. Mahwah, NJ: Lawrence Erlbaum.

Shprintzen, R. J. (1997). *Genetics, syndromes and communication disorders*. San Diego: Singular.

Siedel-Sadewitz, V. & Shprintzen, R. J. (1982). The relationship of communication disorders to syndrome identification. *Journal of Speech and Hearing Disorders* 47, 338–54.

Siegel, M., Varley, R., & Want, S. C. (2001). Mind over grammar: reasoning in aphasia and development. *Trends in Cognitive Sciences* 5 (7), 296–301.

Singer-Harris, N. G., Bellugi, U., Bates, E., Jones, W., & Rossen, M. (1997). Contrasting profiles of language development in children with Williams and Down syndromes. *Developmental Neuropsychology* 13, 345–70.

Sparks, S. N. & Millard, S. (1981). Speech and language characteristics of genetic syndromes. *Journal of Communication Disorders* 14, 411–19.

Sparrow, S. S., Balla, D., & Cichetti, D. (1984). *Vineland adaptive behaviour scales*. Circle Pines, MN: American Guidance Service.

Spinelli, M., Rocha, A., Giacheti, C., & Richieri-Costa, A. (1995). Word finding difficulties, verbal paraphasias, and verbal dyspraxia in ten individuals with fragile X syndrome. *American Journal of Medical Genetics* 60, 39–43.

Stojanovik, V. (2006) Social interaction deficits in Williams syndrome. *Journal of Neurolinguistics* 19, 157–73.

Stojanovik, V. & James, D. (2006). A short-term longitudinal study of a child with Williams syndrome. *International Journal of Language and Communication Disorders* 41 (2), 213–23.

Stojanovik, V., Perkins, M., & Howard, S. (2001). Language and conversational abilities in Williams syndrome: How good is good? *International Journal of Language and Communication Disorders* 36 (supplement), 234–40.

Stojanovik, V., Perkins, M., & Howard, S. (2004). Williams syndrome and specific language impairment do not support claims for developmental double associations and innate modularity. *Journal of Neurolinguistics* 17, 403–24.

Stojanovik, V., Perkins, M., & Howard, S. (2006). Linguistic heterogeneity in Williams syndrome. *Clinical Linguistics and Phonetics* 20, 7–8, 547–52 .

Stromme, P., Bjornstad, P. G., & Ramstad, K. (2002). Prevalence estimation of Williams syndrome. *Journal of Child Neurology* 17, 269–71.

Sudhalter, V. & Belser, R. C. (2001). Conversational characteristics of children with fragile X. *American Journal of Medical Genetics* 64, 340–5.

Sudhalter, V., Cohen, I. L., Silverman, W., et al. (1990). Conversational analyses of males and females with fragile X, Down syndrome and autism: A comparison of the emergence of deviant language. *American Journal of Mental Retardation* 94, 431–42.

Thomas, M. S. C., Grant, J., Barham, Z., Gsödl, M., Laing, E., Lakusta, L., Tyler, L. K., Grice, S., Paterson, S., & Karmiloff-Smith, A. (2001). Past tense formation in Williams syndrome. *Language and Cognitive Processes* 16, 143–76.

Udwin, O. & Yule, W. (1991). A cognitive and behavioural phenotype in Williams Syndrome. *Journal of Clinical and Experimental Neuropsychology* 32, 129–41.

Van Borsel, J. (2004). Voice and resonance disorders in genetic syndromes: A meta analysis. *Folia Phoniatrica et Logopaedica* 56, 83–92.

Van Borsel, J. & Tetnowski, J. A. (2007). Fluency disorders in genetic syndromes. *Journal of Fluency Disorders* 32, 279–96.

Varley, R. & Siegal, M. (2000). Evidence for cognition without grammar from causal reasoning and "theory of mind" in an agrammatic aphasic patient. *Current Biology* 10, 723–6.

Vicari, S., Caselli, M., & Tonucci, F. (2000). Asynchrony of lexical and morpho-syntactic development in children with Down syndrome. *Neuropsychologia 24*, 138–49.

Volterra, V., Caselli, M. C., Capirci, O., Tonucci, F., & Vicari, S. (2003). Early linguistic abilities of Italian children with Williams syndrome. *Developmental Neuropsychology 23*, 33–58.

Yamada, J. E. (1990). *Laura – a case for the modularity of language.* Cambridge, MA: MIT Press.

Zukowski, A. (2004). Investigating knowledge of complex syntax: Insights from experimental studies of Williams syndrome. In M. Rice and S. Warren (eds.), *Developmental language disorders: From phenotypes to etiologies.* Mahwah: NJ: Lawrence Erlbaum Associates.

6 Principles of Assessment and Intervention

BONNIE BRINTON AND MARTIN FUJIKI

1 Introduction

Elizabeth, a brand new master's degree in hand, reports for work in a facility within the public school system. Her work context is fairly unique: she is assigned to a classroom where preschool and early elementary schoolchildren with a variety of disabilities are placed for several months in order to allow school personnel to determine the most appropriate placements. Elizabeth is a member of a diagnostic team responsible for this assessment. At the same time she also provides language services within the classroom.

Elizabeth looks around her on the first day of class. Four-year-old Mickey smiles eagerly. He is non-verbal and has had numerous health problems with frequent periods of hospitalization. Four-year-old Jimmy sits on the floor manipulating a book and reciting a radio commercial verbatim. Three-year-old Gary walks around and around in a circle flapping his fingers and vocalizing, "Zzzzzzz." Seven-year-old Alberto and 5-year-old Miguel sit quietly by the window. They have just arrived from Mexico and are evidently not accustomed to hearing English. Seven-year-old Juan and Jose wrestle one another fighting over a toy car; and 5-year-old Lisa stares blankly at the ceiling, manipulating a piece of soft cloth. Some of these children have been followed for special services in the school system; others have been identified through a "child find" program.

Elizabeth gulps. She seriously doubts that her training has prepared her to meet the needs of this varied group. "What now?" she wonders. "Where do I start?" "What can I do for these children?"

Elizabeth might well feel overwhelmed. Assessment and intervention are challenging endeavors that demand a high level of problem-solving ability, technical knowledge, insight, perspective taking, and interpersonal skill. Elizabeth thinks that her relative inexperience will limit her effectiveness. That may be true for a while, but it is also the case that even long experience will not render the task of evaluating and treating children with communication disorders easy or formulaic. Each child she sees will be unique in some way and will require an individualized approach. Clinical practice in speech-language pathology is never routine.

The Handbook of Language and Speech Disorders, First Edition. Edited by Jack S. Damico, Nicole Müller, and Martin J. Ball. © 2013 Blackwell Publishing Ltd except for editorial material and organization © 2013 Jack S. Damico, Nicole Müller, Martin J. Ball. Published 2013 by Blackwell Publishing Ltd.

Providing clinical services is a high-stakes proposition. The procedures and tasks Elizabeth employs in treatment will almost certainly have an influence on each child's development and will likely extend to the child's family, classroom, and community. There is no neutral ground in actual practice – no clinical Switzerland. The children in Elizabeth's classroom will learn things in treatment – even if it is just that they never want to come back. There is no question that educational programs have impact. The question is, what kind of impact will Elizabeth's interventions have, and will that impact be one she would intend?

Elizabeth wonders where to start in trying to meet the needs of her varied group. Perhaps the first thing she should do is to consider the purpose of intervention. What is she ultimately trying to do for each child? Once she has a clear vision of long-range goals, Elizabeth must then ponder how best to achieve those goals. Throughout this process Elizabeth will be part of a team charged with determining the direction that special services and regular education will take. The team has a lot to learn about each child and important conclusions to draw. Elizabeth's contribution to this team will be critical. She will contribute a vital piece to the diagnostic puzzle. Unlike jigsaw puzzles, pieces in a diagnostic puzzle may overlap and blend together. The information Elizabeth brings to the table will overlap with psychological, behavioral, and academic assessments. Only through teamwork will a coherent picture of each child emerge, and only through teamwork can the most effective intervention programs be implemented.

The questions that Elizabeth must answer are far-reaching and not always easily addressed, even by experienced clinicians. In considering these issues, we have identified the following general treatment principles, which have guided our own clinical practice. We have developed some of these ideas from the research literature in speech-language pathology and related disciplines such as psychology, linguistics, education, and special education. We have learned from others, from our own investigation, and from clinical experience. We have also benefited greatly from the experience of the master clinicians whom we have observed and worked with through the years. We believe the way to begin the clinical process is to consider what one ultimately hopes to achieve in intervention.

2   Principles of Assessment and Intervention

2.1   *Begin with the end in mind*

Like Elizabeth, one of our first clinical positions was in a preschool for children with special needs. Our caseload contained individuals with a variety of abilities and challenges, and our job was to address the communication needs of each child. The children were very young, and most of them were just beginning their relationship with the educational system. It was easy to be optimistic about their future – most had at least 12 years of formal education and special services ahead of them. It seemed appropriate to plan for their immediate needs and to rely on the natural course of development to "kick in" and maximize their growth in the future.

A decade or so later, we found ourselves working with adults with developmental disabilities. This population had received special services for many years and represented the end result of intervention combined with maturation. We had the opportunity to evaluate many aspects of these individuals' language and behavioral functioning. We observed how their skills impacted their educational, vocational, and social opportunities. Although many of these men and women were relatively high functioning in terms of language and intellectual ability, they demonstrated a wide range of adjustment within their living situations. It became dramatically evident how much their social communication contributed to their independence, their interpersonal relationships, and their overall quality of life. It should be noted that the term "social communication" extends to the entire range of verbal and non-verbal behaviors that individuals use to communicate as they participate in social interactions (Adams, 2005; Timler, Olswang, & Coggins, 2005).

Working with these mature individuals caused us to reflect back on the pre-school children we worked with years before. Some of the behaviors and skills that we thought were important at the time did not seem nearly as compelling as other behaviors that were more important to communication. We asked ourselves, if we were able to do it over again, what would we do differently? The answer was clear: we would take a broader view. We would look farther ahead. We would try to visualize where we would like each child to be not just at the next annual review meeting, but years later. We would think in terms of each individual's future independence and quality of life, and we would select every treatment target and task to help the child move in that direction. To quote Stephen R. Covey (1989), we would "begin with the end in mind."

In order to begin with the end in mind, one must have some idea of what that end should look like. In thinking about the ultimate outcome of intervention, it is helpful to consider Fey's (1986) description of two contrasting views of disability and treatment. From a neutralist perspective, the focus is on the discrepancy between the child's ability and the typical development standard. From the normativist perspective, the central consideration is quality of life.[1] How does the individual's impairment impact the ability to make friends, to hold a job, to learn to read – basically to do things that are fulfilling and satisfying?

The *International Classification of Functioning, Disability and Health* (ICF) (WHO, 2001) operationalizes a normativist perspective. As Westby (2007) reports, "The intent of the ICF framework is to determine how the person's quality of life can be enhanced by optimizing communication" (p. 266). The ICF provides a system that includes assessment of a child's activity or execution of activities. It also considers a child's participation or involvement in life events. As Westby explains, language impairment (LI) may restrict an individual's activity, "which in turn may limit the life situations in which children can or will participate" (pp. 267–8). The extent to which an individual can participate in life events is a major factor in quality of life.

To us, the primary purpose of speech and language intervention is to improve communication in a way that enhances an individual's ability and/or opportunities to participate fully in the life events that are most important to that person's quality of life. We would also contend that the most important life events are

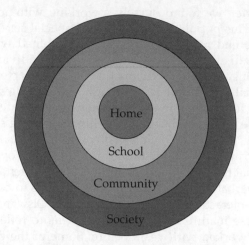

Figure 6.1   Concentric circles of influence that impact quality of life.

those that help establish and maintain interpersonal relationships (Hundeide, 2004). The concentric circles in Figure 6.1 represent this notion.

The primary context for many life events is the home setting, and the most important relationships that communication must support are those among family members. The next most important context for most children and adolescents is the classroom or school. In the school culture, relationships between a child and peers and the child and teachers and other professionals are vital to the individual's development in many domains. In addition, language and communication within the school setting are critical to gain access to knowledge and academic success. Next, the individual's ability to communicate within the community context affects vocational and avocational pursuits as well as the ability to function independently. Lastly, even though the personal relationships may not be as close, the ability to communicate within a wider societal context will be important as an individual's social world expands.

Finally, in beginning with the end in mind, we must take care not to predict limitations. Development may take a number of paths, complete with twists and turns. Forming a rigid opinion of an individual's potential can be detrimental to the point of being self-fulfilling. Beginning with the end in mind means that we keep desired long-term outcomes in view when planning current objectives and procedures. For example, in working with a child with marked language delays, we envision the interactional skills that child might need to establish relationships as an adult. We keep ultimate outcomes in mind even working with adults, although we may not have the luxury of planning for an extended period of time in treatment. For an adult with aphasia, for instance, we would envision what behaviors and support would allow that individual to interact most positively with family and friends.

Once we know where we want to go in intervention, we can then begin to consider how to get there. To do this effectively, we must have a strong understanding of our starting point. This idea highlights the importance of a good assessment of the individual's strengths and limitations, which leads us to the second principle.

2.2 Good intervention requires good assessment

We have recently been introduced to the wonders of a global positioning system (GPS). We enter the address of our desired destination into this device, and the GPS provides a map and detailed verbal directions as we drive. It works like a charm – except when it loses the satellite connection that informs it of our current position. When this happens, it can't give us any information at all – even though it knows exactly where we want to go. If the GPS doesn't know where we are currently, it cannot plot our route.

Like a road trip, the intervention process is a journey, and knowing where one would like to end up is essential. But in order to plot a reasonable path toward a desired destination, one has to know where one is at any moment. This claim may seem like an exercise in the obvious, but we feel it deserves more consideration than it is often allotted. When clinical resources are stretched, it can be tempting to launch intervention programs quickly, based on a fairly cursory understanding of the individual's current level of functioning. This will rarely result in an optimal use of clinical resources because the nature of the problem may not be clearly understood (an exception being if the intervention takes the form of dynamic assessment, which is discussed later). Negotiating a clinical path is very much like a GPS in that the route needs to be constantly monitored and frequently adjusted along the way to accommodate obstacles and breakthroughs. As the level of functioning changes, the clinical route must be adjusted accordingly. It is our experience that resources devoted to initial diagnostic work are well spent. It is important to use the best available instruments and procedures to provide an accurate snapshot of an individual's communicative strengths and challenges.

Fortunately, there are many tools available to assess an individual's communication. These include checklists and rating scales, direct observation, informal probes, and standardized tests. Each of these tools, used within the limits for which it was designed, can make an important contribution to assessment. Some of these instruments are best used to identify individuals who are in need of more in-depth testing. Others can provide evidence to qualify an individual for intervention. Still other tools can provide a detailed look at an individual's strengths and limitations. Few tools can be used effectively for all of these purposes. This point can be illustrated by considering rating scales. A well-designed rating scale can help the clinician organize critical behaviors and provide access to valuable impressions from those who know the child well. At the same time, however, rating scales do not sample actual behavior, but perceptions of behavior. They are also subject to various sources of error, such as rater bias and temporal variability (Merrell, 2003). Given these strengths and limitations, rating scales can provide an indication that there is a problem that needs attention. On the other hand, they often do not provide a specific indication of level of function, and thus have limited value in determining what to work on in intervention.

One of the most important goals of assessment is to identify intervention targets. These targets should be selected because they represent progress toward the desired endpoint – much like landmarks along the way on a trip. To select appropriate targets, the clinician needs diagnostic tools and procedures that can inform treatment. As indicated above, not all assessment tools provide information that can be used to specify treatment targets. Perhaps the most frequently misused tools in this respect are norm-referenced standardized tests (e. g., McCauley, 2001; McCauley & Swisher, 1984; Plante & Vance, 1994). There are a number of reasons why normal-referenced tests cannot effectively be used to identify treatment targets. McCauley and Swisher (1984) list several of these reasons, including the fact that these instruments do not comprehensively examine behaviors or levels of development. Those behaviors and levels that are examined are probed by a relatively small number of items in a limited number of contexts.

Keep in mind that the above-stated issues may not be problematic when standardized tests are used for the purpose for which they were designed, which is to separate typical from atypical performance. The difficulty arises when performance on test items is taken as providing a representative picture of an individual's communicative strengths and limitations. To understand why this is the case, consider that test developers place a premium on behaviors that separate groups of children (e.g., an item that consistently distinguishes 5-year-olds from 6-year-olds). Behaviors that can be used to separate groups of individuals may not necessarily be representative of a language domain (McCauley, 2001). Additionally, they may not be critical to communication. For example, consider items from the Peabody Picture Vocabulary Test-III (Dunn & Dunn, 1997). Starting at age 4;0 years, the first five words tested are "digging," "cow," "drum," "feather," and "painting." These are not necessarily the five most important words for a 4;0-year-old child to know, nor would they be particularly good targets for an older child who had a limited vocabulary. These words were most likely included because they were effective at separating age groups rather than because they were developmentally or functionally important. In order to recognize words that might be most important for an individual child to acquire, one would need to consider the child's current productive and receptive vocabulary in communicative settings as well as the words that are most important to communication within those settings. This might best be accomplished using informal assessment procedures such as direct observation, interviews with caregivers and teachers, and individualized probes.

By stressing the importance of careful initial assessments, we do not wish to imply that the evaluation process is static. The initial assessment provides a snapshot – a picture of the individual at one point in time. What we really need is a continual video picture. Assessment should be an ongoing process that continues after intervention has been initiated. Dynamic assessment paradigms, which recognize that the individual being assessed is an active learner in a meaningful context, can be highly useful. These methods, which combine aspects of assessment and intervention, can be used not only to identify targets but also to describe the strategies and support needed to maximize learning (Merritt & Culatta, 1998).

To use our road trip analogy, one needs to be constantly aware of where the individual is, even as the position changes. Sometimes, change can be dramatic enough to force us to rethink our destination and re-plot our route. For example, a number of years ago, we worked with Laura, an adult with intellectual disabilities. We evaluated Laura's communication and concluded that her productive language consisted of a small vocabulary with a few two-word combinations. She had been virtually non-verbal in the supported work setting she attended every day for several years, and she seemed isolated and lonely. We set a long-term goal to establish some peer interaction. We initiated treatment on a trial basis and included Laura in a small group where we worked on conversation. The following exchange occurred a few weeks later:

CLINICIAN: What did you do last night?
LAURA: We have cake last night. Daddy eat cake. Mommy eat cake. I no eat cake.
CLINICIAN: You had cake last night? Daddy ate cake? Mommy ate cake? But *you* did not have any cake? Why not?
LAURA: Fattening.

We were absolutely stunned by the sophistication Laura demonstrated in this exchange. Her supervisors were subsequently shocked – and not altogether pleased – when she began talking and joking with her co-workers in her supported work setting. Obviously, we needed to adjust our planned clinical destination for Laura as well as our route. Although most cases will not require such dramatic reconceptualization, many will require frequent adjustment along the route, as individual needs change and become more clearly defined.

Once the clinician knows what the ultimate goal is and has a good understanding of the individual's strengths and limitations, it is then possible to formulate what might be the best way of achieving the objectives leading to that goal. The next two points address related aspects of this issue. The first considers how one might gather and organize resources so they can be effectively used in intervention. The second concerns the level and contexts at which intervention is conducted.

2.3 Focus on what is most important to achieve your goals

In intervention, as in life, resources are almost always limited. Although an individual may have many important needs, it will rarely be possible to address all of them effectively. It is critical, therefore, to decide what behaviors are the most important to achieve the long-term goal and then to focus energy on those targets. Borrowing again from Stephen R. Covey, we might say, "Put first things first" (Covey, 1989).

When working with an individual exhibiting a complex disability, it is easy to develop a long list of needs, spreading intervention time and resources across many objectives. Although this may be most likely to happen when there is involvement in several developmental systems, it is also an issue for individuals who have what might be considered as milder impairments. For example, it would not be unusual for a 7-year-old child with language-learning impairment to exhibit delays in syntactic, phonological, and semantic development. The same child might also have problems in social interactions involving pragmatic skills or more general social communication behaviors. Additionally, this child would most likely have difficulty with literacy skills. As Elizabeth might have asked in our case example, where do we start?

In determining what is most important to address in intervention, we pose two primary questions. First, what is the child ready to learn, and second, what behaviors would enhance communication the most (Brinton & Fujiki, 1994)? Considering what the individual is ready to learn seems most relevant when working with children, but aspects of readiness may affect more mature individuals as well (e.g., Barrlett, Armstrong, & Roberts, 2005; Legg et al., 2005). In thinking about what someone might be ready to learn, the clinician should consider cognitive, linguistic, and social development. Given the child's development in each of these areas, where is the child ready to go next? What are appropriate targets? It is important to select targets that are likely to be within the individual's reach within a reasonable amount of time. It should be cautioned that developmental sequences documented for groups of children might not exactly describe the developmental pattern of an individual child. Even more importantly, behaviors that develop earlier in a developmental sequence may or may not be prerequisite to behaviors that appear later. It is important to understand the developmental or readiness level of each individual to the extent that we can predict their capacity for growth in specific domains and behaviors.

There is at least one additional factor to think about when determining what an individual might be ready to learn: motivational factors or self-efficacy may affect readiness for change. Targeting a behavior that is developmentally appropriate but of little perceived or functional value to the individual is likely to present an exercise in frustration for all involved. Sometimes, however, guiding an individual to invest in a treatment target he had not previously appreciated can be an important part of the clinical process. For example, encouraging an aggressive child to adopt more cooperative social goals might be foundational to facilitating targets such as positive verbal interactions with peers (Brinton & Fujiki, in press). It may take some effort, however, to guide the child to value and desire cooperative behavior.

Considering what would enhance communication the most helps focus attention on the behaviors that might contribute to the individual's ability to communicate within important contexts. When approaching a new case in treatment, we ask, "If I could change one thing to improve this person's ability to communicate, what would it be?" Sometimes the answer seems obvious to the point of triviality – for instance, a non-verbal child's communication would be most improved if she could talk, or an adult with aphasia might improve most dramatically if he could retrieve words efficiently. But, more thoughtful consideration will yield insight into behaviors that are at the heart of communication for an individual within their social, academic, or vocational world. For example, the communication of a child with autism spectrum disorder (ASD) might improve the most if she could request help to meet basic needs; the communication of an adolescent might improve the most if he could engage in conversational exchanges with peers. The point is, it is helpful to consider what kinds of change would make the most difference for an individual in the current context.

Answers to the two questions, "What is an individual ready to learn?" and "What would improve communication the most?" must be considered simultaneously. Putting first things first demands that the answers to these two questions be balanced. As Nelson writes, the question becomes, "What needs to change if life is to improve for this person?," considered along with the question, "What can be changed?" (Nelson, 1998, p. 8). There may be behaviors that are developmentally appropriate that would make a minimal difference to the child's ability to communicate more effectively. In turn, the behavior that would improve communication the most may be something the individual is in no way ready to learn. It is important to focus on those behaviors and skills an individual might be able to learn that would enhance communication the most. Identifying the best combination of developmentally feasible and communicatively effective behaviors to target in treatment will help ensure the best use of valuable clinical resources. This is important because, as noted above, every minute of intervention is critical. Even though the young children with whom we work may receive years of intervention in the future, it is unlikely that there will be time to do all that needs to be done. In addition, even if clinical resources were endless, most children and many adults have a finite capacity to work at intervention tasks within a given timeframe. Likewise, their families only have so much time and energy to invest in supporting intervention. To have the greatest impact, it is important to prioritize goals by putting first things first.

2.4   Aim for authenticity: Focus on functional communication

As indicated previously, it is important to identify treatment targets that are both developmentally appropriate and critical to communication. There is an additional, associated issue, however, that demands consideration in planning and implementing intervention. That issue has to do with the nature of both the behaviors we select to target in intervention and the context in which that intervention is conducted. We believe that it is important to work on authentic communication behaviors in authentic communication contexts.

As noted previously, children with language impairment often have a variety of problems, including difficulty with syntax, limited vocabulary, and poor pragmatic skills. Intervention targets within any of these aspects of language could reasonably be justified. For example, if the clinician believes that lexical items, morphological features, and sentence structure are building blocks for more complex communicative behaviors, intervention might focus on selected syntactical forms or vocabulary items. This kind of approach can be straightforward because of the relative ease in identifying, probing, and observing the targeted behaviors. Traditional intervention methods to teach such behaviors often focus on modeling, imitation, and intensive drill in stimulus–response–reinforcement formats. Targeted forms may be isolated from other aspects of language and taught in situations that bear little resemblance to the natural contexts in which they are actually used (Owens, 2004).

Although such methods can produce learning, generalization to contexts outside of the clinical setting is often a problem. Illustrative of this point is intervention with individuals with ASD. It has repeatedly been found that behaviors taught using operant procedures with discrete trial formats often fail to generalize beyond the contexts in which they were trained. Sometimes, it is even more concerning when these behaviors *do* generalize. For example, a child with ASD who has been working on naming colors in intervention may insist on naming the color of every object he sees during conversation. This will hinder, rather than help, communication. In recognition of this problem, more recent behavioral approaches (e.g., enhanced milieu teaching) have incorporated naturalistic contexts to achieve better generalization (Prizant, Wetherby, & Rydell, 2000).

The isolated structural behaviors and many of the tasks we use to elicit these behaviors often lack authenticity. That is, they may not reflect real-life communication as it occurs in actual interactions. Authentic language behaviors are those that occur when individuals communicate because they need to convey meaning or want to interact with other people (see Damico, Secord, & Wiig, 1992, for elaboration on the concept of authenticity). For example, writing down a list of vocabulary words may have an academic purpose, at least from the perspective of a teacher. But little self-motivated communication is involved on the part of the student, and the behavior itself does not constitute an authentic communicative event. In contrast, passing written notes in class entails a personal contact and an active exchange of information. Note passing is compelling enough for students that generations of teachers have been unable to extinguish the activity. In passing notes, students are often highly motivated to use their language and literacy skills to convey very specific messages. Texting in class may serve as a technologically enhanced form of note passing. Passing notes represents an authentic communicative event, even if it annoys teachers. Fortunately, authentic communicative behaviors need not be outside the prescribed rules of a classroom context, or any other context. Authentic communicative behaviors are simply those that are employed in real communicative situations.

In choosing treatment goals and objectives, we aim for authenticity by intervening at the most holistic language level possible in the most naturalistic context available. For an elementary school age child, this might mean working on specific types of discourse, even though the child may have difficulties at the structural level. For example, intervention might target conversation within a collaborative group or the ability to give a report in class, even if the child has problems with basic language formulation.

Focusing on authenticity helps the clinician avoid what Nelson (1998) refers to as the "forest and the trees" problem. Clinicians can become so focused on treating a specific behavior that they lose sight of how that behavior might fit with the overall goal that the individual is working toward. It also avoids what Damico (1988) has referred to as the "fragmentation fallacy" – the notion that language can be separated into discrete behaviors for assessment and intervention purposes. Isolating specific language behavior in therapy ignores the fact that individual aspects of syntax, semantics, phonology, and pragmatics always occur in interaction with each other. They might be artificially separated for academic study, but in actual communication they rarely occur in isolation.

In suggesting that intervention take place in the most authentic context possible, we favor a sociocultural perspective (see Stone, 2004). This view of language intervention recognizes that language exists to communicate meaning and that communicative exchanges take place in a context that will influence meaning. Emphasis is placed on active participation on the part of the learner (Norris & Damico, 1990). It also recognizes the importance of both social interaction and the communicative partner to the intervention process (Simmons-Mackie & Damico, 2007). At the same time, we concede that there may be occasions when the clinician judges that a child needs to focus on specific skills or abilities. This occurs when discourse cannot move forward without specific behaviors or skills in place. For example, a child giving a report on sharks in class may need to learn specific vocabulary items to express the desired content. A child who monopolizes the floor in conversation may need to work on turn exchange in order to support a targeted goal in peer interaction. Thus, working at the discourse level does not preclude working on more specific language behaviors. In fact, a simultaneous focus on holistic and structural levels may be found in several contemporary intervention programs that address higher-level discourse or literacy skills while also focusing attention on more specific skills (e.g., Gillam & Ukrainetz, 2006; Justice & Kaderavek, 2004). We conceptualize a somewhat similar approach where we identify targets, employ tasks that are as authentic as possible, and then "drill down" to focus on more specific behaviors as needed (e.g., Brinton & Fujiki, 1994; Culatta, 1994; Weaver, 1996). Even when we need to drill down, we try to make the activities used to facilitate these behaviors as communicative as possible.

There are several advantages of working at the most authentic intervention level possible. Perhaps the major advantage is that skills are more likely to generalize to real-world contexts. In some cases, the behavior targeted in treatment may be a real-world event, such as exchanging ideas in cooperative learning activities. If the child demonstrates a target behavior, the child has achieved a level of generalization. For example, in working with an adolescent with language impairment, we targeted responding to the bids of peers in conversation. We facilitated responding in real interactions such as car pool conversations. When the young man made gains in these "scaffolded" interactions, he had participated in a real-life conversation. Gains then began to generalize to other peer conversations.

A second advantage of working at the most authentic level possible is the likelihood that learning will take place at lower levels of behavior without direct instruction (Wells, 2001). In our own clinical experience, we have found that learning from the bottom (specific) to the top (general) does not often occur spontaneously. Many of us have had the experience of facilitating a structure such as "is verbing" with a child only to find that he remains reticent in conversations with peers. In contrast, learning from the top to the bottom may occur without extra treatment. Participating in actual communicative events may well result in improved performance on specific structural skills, even if those skills have not been specifically targeted. To illustrate: there is little chance that progress on specific structural skills will spontaneously result in better storytelling skills, but learning how to tell a story may well result in better syntactic skills (Norris & Damico, 1990).

Another advantage of working at the most authentic communication level possible is that it is likely to be more motivating than working on isolated behaviors. More holistic methods such as narrative approaches designed to enhance language (e.g., Culatta, 1994) allow clinicians to engage children in meaningful activities. Children and adults have real ideas that they want to communicate in the course of the interaction, and they are likely to invest in treatment activities that enhance their ability to share those ideas. If they feel that treatment objectives and approaches enhance their functioning in authentic contexts that are important to them, they will be motivated to work hard to improve. This can be particularly important for individuals who have received special services for an extended period of time. Authentic treatment targets and approaches help individuals understand that intervention might actually make their lives better.

To this point, we have focused on what goals to highlight, how to best use resources, and what contexts to use in intervention. All of these factors address important aspects of intervention for individuals with communication problems. These factors cross diagnostic categories. In the next section we consider some of the limitations of clinical categories and labels.

2.5   *Disorders without borders*

Many years ago, we took a class that required that we identify the diagnostic category of several speakers based on short speech samples. One of us experienced a minor academic triumph when our professor applauded our ability to recognize the impairment categories represented by these samples even though we had no clinical experience. We were particularly proud that we identified the category of "cleft palate" from listening to a short sample of hypernasal speech. We were hopeful that we were on our way to learning to spot individuals as having cleft palate based on the speech pattern we had learned to recognize. We did not anticipate at the time, however, that in subsequent clinical practice, we would hear similar speech patterns from speakers with a variety of etiologies including a recent tonsillectomy, a brain tumor, and hearing loss. The notion of "cleft palate" as a diagnostic category had limited relevance when we were faced with these cases. Although hypernasality is associated with cleft palate speech, as a symptom it is not limited to this category – in essence, the symptom has no categorical border.

In the course of practice, one encounters individuals of all ages who have a wide variety of strengths and challenges. It is tempting to think about these people in terms of the commonalities of their impairment, to group them based on perceived similarities in behavior and dispositions. This categorical perspective is part of the culture of intervention and is ingrained in service providers from the time we begin our training. As students, we take classes with titles such as *aphasia, language impairment, motor speech disorders, fluency,* or *intellectual disabilities.* As professionals, we may use these same labels to identify our interests and areas of specialty. Because a categorical approach is so integral to our thinking, it is important to consider how this perspective influences practice.

It may be helpful to begin with some positives. Categories provide a relatively straightforward way of organizing and summarizing what is known about particular groups of individuals. In addition, it is frequently necessary for an individual to be categorized or labeled in some way in order to receive speech and language services (Paul, 2001). Although categories may provide a general guide to etiology and behavior, they do have some important limitations.

One problem with category labels is that they can take on a life of their own and can influence expectations and perceptions of behavior. In other words, if we think an individual fits within a categorical designation, we may perceive behaviors associated with that category whether the behaviors are there or not. We are reminded of a young adult with a diagnosis of behavioral disorders who was followed through the mental health system. Evaluation of his performance and behavior indicated that he had a low IQ. His low general functioning seemed to fit much better within the category of intellectual disability. On one occasion, he attempted to hug a woman he met at a social function. Since he was considered to have a behavioral disorder, he was charged with sexual assault and incarcerated. If he had been identified as having intellectual disability, his behavior would have been considered as problematic but not criminal, and he would have received special services. In this case, the categorical diagnosis affected the way his behaviors were perceived and addressed in a very dramatic way.

Another serious problem is that category labels do not predict the nature of impairment at a specific enough level to dictate intervention goals (Lahey, 1988). Even children of similar ages who have similar scores on standardized testing may not present similar behaviors in actual communication; children with the same diagnostic label often have highly variable profiles of communicative strengths and limitations.

In considering the variability of individuals within a category, we are reminded of six first-grade children we worked with in a research study. They were all categorized as having specific language impairment (SLI). In addition to being placed in the same classroom, these children were relatively close in age, had non-verbal IQ scores in the typical range, and received speech and language intervention services on a pull-out basis. Despite these similarities, each child had a unique profile of speech and language problems, and each child needed a unique set of language objectives in treatment. Further, the differences between children did not end with their language profiles. When we identified them for our study based on accepted categorical boundaries of SLI, we did not anticipate that each child would also have a unique profile of social strengths and limitations that had a notable impact on their functioning. One of these children was the most hated and feared child in the classroom. She was physically larger that most of her peers and displayed both aggressive and withdrawn behaviors. Another child was among the most popular children in the classroom and was well accepted by most of the other children. The four remaining children also displayed unique combinations of withdrawn, aggressive, and sociable behavior in addition to their impaired communication skills (Brinton et al., 2000). Clearly, the label that they shared could not sum up these individuals.

The truth is, the nature of impairment is variable and dynamic, and categories become fluid (Perkins, 2007). As an example, let us consider ASD and SLI. The language difficulties of children with ASD are often characterized as being pragmatic in nature, whereas the problems of children with SLI are often thought to involve language form and content. Recent study has suggested, however, that some children with ASD demonstrate the same types of structural language problems observed in children with SLI (Kjelgaard & Tager-Flusberg, 2001). At the same time, it has been reported that children with SLI can show pragmatic problems that do not appear to be linked to their structural limitations (Bishop et al., 2000; Brinton, Fujiki, & Powell, 1997). It has also been argued that there is a third group of children, referred to as having pragmatic language impairment (originally referred to as semantic pragmatic deficit syndrome). These children have poor pragmatic skills in the face of relatively good structural language abilities (see Chapter 12). Although such a description could also be applied to some high-functioning children with autism, most children with pragmatic language impairment do not meet all the diagnostic criteria for autism (Bishop & Norbury, 2002).

The fuzziness of the boundaries between ASD and SLI has led some to propose a continuum between the two disorders (Bishop, 2003). It is important to note that this continuum is not intended to suggest regular progression from one state to another in the way that red moves gradually to purple to blue on a color continuum. Rather, it is a general way of indicating that disorders have no borders and we can expect considerable overlap between categories.

It is important to think about the way that we characterize the individuals with whom we work. We need systematic ways to help us organize what we know about each person we treat and to use that information to make the best intervention decisions possible. Categories may describe general trends, but they also suggest borders between category designations that may not exist. Systems such as the ICF may help us focus on the strengths and needs of an individual rather than on a diagnostic category and thus may be more helpful in making clinical decisions. In affirming that disorders have no borders, we are simply stating that we should consider each individual's assessment and treatment needs without filtering our impressions through the lens of a category label or any preconceived ideas of how that individual will function. The popularity of category designations and category labels tend to change with time. The fact that each individual requires intervention geared to specific needs does not.

2.6   *Time and effort: We are in this for the long haul*

A number of years ago, a father brought his 5-year-old daughter to our clinic for a speech and language evaluation. The little girl showed clear evidence of language impairment, including difficulty with language formulation. As we were explaining the assessment results to her father, we mentioned that the child produced immature pronoun structures including "Her go home," and "Me eat candy." The father indicated that he had recently explained to his daughter that a subjective pronoun should be used as the subject in a sentence, and an objective pronoun as an object. He seemed puzzled that even after his careful explanation, his child still made the same errors.

Several years later, we gave a class lecture on using action scripts to facilitate social communication. Within a few days, a student in the class came to talk with us. She explained that she had a daughter with language problems that were often manifest in social interaction. Following our lecture, she and her husband had gathered their children together and had carefully taught them a car pool script, including getting in the minivan, greeting the driver, chatting with the other children in the van, and thanking the driver when they were dropped off. The student reported that all her other children picked up the script quickly and demonstrated the targeted behaviors in the car pool the next day. Why, she questioned, did the daughter with language problems fail to "get it?"

In each of these cases, we could only think, "If only it were so easy!" It takes considerable time and effort to treat most communication impairments effectively. We all understand that language learning is a very laborious process for children with language impairment. It is easy to underestimate, however, just how much more exposure and experience children with language impairment need in comparison to typical language learners. For example, typically developing children may be able to use a new lexical item after hearing it once in a salient context, but a child with language impairment may require many more exposures to recognize the word, and still more to produce it appropriately.

Communication disorders are often chronic in nature and affect an individual's life over the course of years. Developmental language impairment is a prime example as it is both persistent and pervasive. As the child develops, the nature of the impairment may shift, and different symptoms emerge at different ages and in different contexts. The underlying disorder, however, is likely to remain and to impact both academic and social development (Ahlsèn, 2008; Bashir, Wiig, & Abrams, 1987). To illustrate the persistence of LI, consider the work of Conti Ramsden and her colleagues who followed a group of 242 children originally diagnosed with SLI at age 7. When 200 of these children were reassessed at age 11, only 23 received standardized test scores within the typical range. Of these 23, 7 still had some difficulty with pragmatics, thus leaving only 16 who showed no evidence of communicative problems (Conti Ramsden et al., 2001).

It is generally recognized that individuals with more severe disabilities require intervention over an extended period of time. There is less consensus, at least in practice, regarding the intensity of that intervention. We agree with Gillam and

Ukrainetz (2006) who suggest that a major problem with language intervention delivered in school settings is that it is not intense enough. These authors point out that most school therapy is delivered in 30-minute sessions, twice a week to groups as large as eight students. Most individuals with communication problems need more concentrated time to acquire new understanding and practice new skills.

A recent intervention study conducted by Gillam and colleagues provides some intriguing data that indirectly address the effect of intensity of intervention. Gillam et al. (2008) compared four language intervention methods: (a) Fast ForWord language, a program of computer games designed to enhance language skills; (b) academic enrichment, involving computer games designed to improve skills but not specifically focused on language; (c) literature-based language intervention delivered by a speech-language pathologist; and (d) computer-assisted language intervention, consisting of a collection of commercially available programs designed to enhance language skills. All of the procedures were administered in sessions 1 hour 40 minutes long, 5 days a week, for 6 weeks. When delivered at this same level of intensity, the programs all produced similar gains. In that the study was not designed to examine the effect of intensity per se on intervention, we cannot conclude that intensity alone effected the change. Further, intensity of intervention is a complex issue with numerous factors to be considered (Warren, Fey, & Yoder, 2007). Nonetheless, the results are intriguing and suggest the need for further consideration of the importance of intensity in language intervention.

How much intervention is necessary to make a difference? How intense should intervention be, and how long should it go on? These questions are difficult to answer since it is impossible to predict how much intervention an individual will need in order to make meaningful gains. Intense intervention (frequent treatment sessions lasting more than a half hour) is often advisable, but issues of practicality complicate matters. As indicated previously, clinical resources are almost always limited, and speech-language pathologists commonly lament the fact that they are spread so thinly that they cannot provide minimal services, let alone intense intervention. In thinking about how long a person with language impairment stays in treatment, we do not want to assume that an individual will never adequately overcome or compensate for a communication disorder. Nevertheless, in our experience in working with children with language impairment, it has proved realistic to think ahead in terms of *years* of treatment rather than weeks or months (Brinton, Fujiki, & Robinson, 2005). Unfortunately, limited clinical resources often mitigate against keeping individuals in a special service system over an extended period of time.

In the final analysis, decisions about how intense intervention should be and how long it should go on must be made on an individual basis. In order to make such decisions, it is necessary to observe an individual's development carefully and regularly. It is important to determine appropriate indicators of change and to recognize and document increments of progress. This will help us adjust treatment as an individual's needs change. It is safe to anticipate, however, that brief sessions once or twice a week will be only a drop in the bucket. We cannot conclude that intervention is not effective based on a lack of change resulting from such minimal involvement. It will take considerable time and effort to assist individuals to acquire new communicative behaviors and to help them manage or work around the communicative challenges that occur with development and changing life contexts.

The bottom line is: Most of the people we work with need intense intervention over an extended period of time. Yet, we rarely have the resources to provide the level of treatment necessary to effect meaningful change, and we too often see only minimal progress. This nasty reality can breed discouragement among professionals and sap the morale of our clients and students. It is necessary to think creatively and to work cooperatively to combat this clinical dilemma. We cannot overemphasize the importance of working with parents, caregivers, teachers, other professionals, family members, friends, and the clients themselves in facilitating communication.

As speech-language pathologists, we may not be able to provide intervention that is as intense and extensive as necessary, but we may well be able to work with others to help choreograph a variety of supportive contexts and learning activities that will facilitate, support, and reinforce important communicative behaviors. As response to intervention initiatives are more fully implemented in school settings, there will be an increased need to work cohesively with members of the educational team (Sampson Graner, Faggella-Luby, & Fritschmann, 2005).

Often, many facilitating resources are available if we can just muster and coordinate them effectively. It seems unwise to expend any of these resources on fragmented or isolated endeavors. It is critical to establish intervention goals and implement approaches that will yield the most functionality in the most important life contexts (home, school, community, and society). Teamwork is essential to design a unified plan to assist growth in a way that improves an individual's quality of life. Even with a coordinated effort, however, we have to realize that the disabilities we deal with are persistent, pervasive, and formidable. We are in this process for the long haul.

3   A Final Word

Let's return to Elizabeth, our overwhelmed beginning clinician. If we were to advise her, we would assure her that her anxiety is understandable and reflects an appropriate respect for the importance of the work that lies before her. Assessment and intervention are high-stakes propositions. Because we are involved in intervention every day over an extended period of time, we may forget this, and our practice may become routine. When we have conducted a mediocre therapy session, we do not receive immediate feedback. Children do not walk out of the treatment room and die because therapy was mediocre or ineffective. In a very real sense, however, the consequences of our assessment and intervention are real and have lifelong implications for the individuals with whom we work.

We would also counsel Elizabeth that as she continues to work with individuals with communication problems, it is guaranteed that the available tests, approaches, and clinical materials will change and rise and wane in popularity. Hopefully Elizabeth's response to these changes will reflect her increased experience, enhanced ability to problem solve, and developing clinical judgment.

Elizabeth's effectiveness as a speech-language pathologist will depend, in part, on her ability to learn from the clients she serves and her awareness of advances in clinical research. It will be critical, however, for her to adopt, refine, and act according to thoughtful clinical principles. If Elizabeth practices according to sound principles, the work that she does will contribute to an improved quality of life for the individuals she serves.

NOTE

1   For an extended discussion on normativism and neutralism and their influence on conceptualizations of learning disability the reader is referred to Tomblin (2006).

REFERENCES

Adams, C. (2005). Social communication intervention for school-age children: Rationale and description. *Seminars in Speech and Language* 26, 181–8.

Ahlsèn, E. (2008). Conversational implicature and communication impairment. In M. J. Ball, M. R. Perkins, N. Müller, & S. Howard (eds.), *Handbook of clinical linguistics* (pp. 32–8). Oxford: Blackwell.

Barrlett, S. C., Armstrong, E., & Roberts, J. (2005). Linguistic resources of individuals with Asperger syndrome. *Clinical Linguistics and Phonetics* 19, 203–14.

Bashir, A., Wiig, E. H., & Abrams, J. C. (1987). Language disorders in childhood and adolescence: Implications for learning and socialization. *Pediatric Annals* 16, 145–56.

Bishop, D. V. M. (2003). Autism and specific language impairment: Categorical distinction or continuum? *Novartis Foundation Symposium* 251, 213–34.

Bishop, D. V. M., Chan, J., Adams, C., Hartley, J., & Weir, F. (2000). Conversational responsiveness in specific language impairment: Evidence of disproportionate pragmatic difficulties in a subset of children. *Development and Psychopathology* 12, 177–99.

Bishop, D. V. M. & Norbury, C. F. (2002). Exploring the borderlands of autistic disorder and specific language impairment: A study using standardized diagnostic instruments. *Journal of Child Psychology and Psychiatry and Allied Disciplines* 43, 917–29.

Brinton, B. & Fujiki, M. (1994). Ways to teach conversation. In J. Duchan, L. E. Hewitt, & R. M. Sonnenmeier (eds.), *Pragmatics: From theory to practice* (pp. 59–71). Englewood Cliffs, NJ: Prentice Hall.

Brinton, B. & Fujiki, M. (in press). "The social stuff is everything:" How social differences in development impact treatment for children with language impairment. In A. Weiss (ed.), *Therapeutic change in communication disorders: Borrowing from developmental knowledge of individual differences.* New York: Psychology Press.

Brinton, B., Fujiki, M., & Powell, J. M. (1997). The ability of children with language impairment to manipulate topic in a structured task. *Language, Speech and Hearing Services in Schools* 28, 3–11.

Brinton, B., Fujiki, M., & Robinson, L. (2005). Life on a tricycle: A case study of language impairment from 4 to 19. *Topics in Language Disorders* 25, 338–52.

Brinton, B., Fujiki, M., Montague, E. C., & Hanton, J. L. (2000). Children with language impairment in cooperative work groups: A pilot study. *Language, Speech, and Hearing Services in Schools* 31, 252–64.

Conti-Ramsden, G., Botting, N., Simkin, Z., & Knox, E. (2001). Follow-up of children attending infant language units: Outcomes at 11 years of age. *International Journal of Language and Communication Disorders* 36, 207–19.

Covey, S. R. (1989). *The seven habits of highly effective people.* New York: Fireside.

Culatta, B. (1994). Representational play and story enactments: Formats for language intervention. In J. F. Duchan, L. E. Hewitt, & R. M. Sonnenmeier (eds.), *Pragmatics: From theory to practice* (pp. 105–19). Englewood Cliffs, NJ: Prentice Hall.

Damico, J. S. (1988). The lack of efficacy in language therapy: A case study. *Language, Speech, and Hearing Services in Schools* 19, 85–94.

Damico, J. S., Secord, W. A., & Wiig, E. H. (1992). Descriptive language assessment at school: Characteristics and design. In W. A. Secord (ed.), *Best practices in school speech-language pathology* (pp. 1–8). San Antonio, TX: Psychological Corporation.

Dunn, L. M. & Dunn, L. M. (1997). *Peabody Picture Vocabulary Test-III.* Circle Pines, MN: American Guidance Service.

Fey, M. E. (1986). *Language intervention with young children.* San Diego: College Hill Press.

Gillam, R. B., Frome Loeb, D., Hoffman, L. M., Bohman, T., Champlin, C. A., Thibodeau, L., Widen, J., Brandel, J., & Friel-Patti, S. (2008). The efficacy of Fast ForWord language intervention in school-age children with language impairment: A randomized controlled trial. *Journal of Speech, Language, and Hearing Research* 51, 97–119.

Gillam, R. B. & Ukrainetz, T. A. (2006). Language intervention through literature-based units. In T. A. Ukrainetz (ed.), *Contextualized language intervention: Scaffolding PreK-12 literacy achievement* (pp. 59–94). Eau Claire, WI: Thinking Publications.

Hundeide, K. (2004). A new identity, a new lifestyle. In A. Perrer-Clermont, C. Pontecorvo, L. Resnick, & B. Burge (eds.), *Joining society. Social interaction and learning in adolescence and youth* (pp. 86–108). Cambridge: Cambridge University Press.

Justice, L. & Kaderavek, J. N. (2004). Embedded-explicit emergent literacy intervention I: Background and description of approach. *Language, Speech, and Hearing Services in Schools* 35, 201–11.

Kjelgaard, M. & Tager-Flusberg, H. (2001). An investigation of language impairment in autism: Implications for genetic subgroups. *Language and Cognitive Processes* 16 (2/3), 287–308.

Lahey, M. (1988). *Language disorders and language development.* New York: Macmillan.

Legg, C., Penn, C., Temlett, J., & Sonnenberg, B. (2005). Language skills of adolescents with Tourette Syndrome. *Clinical Linguistics and Phonetics* 19, 15–33.

McCauley, R. J. (2001). *Assessment of language disorders in children*. Mahwah, NJ: Lawrence Erlbaum Associates.

McCauley, R. J. & Swisher, L. (1984). Use and misuse of norm-referenced tests in clinical assessment: A hypothetical case. *Journal of Speech and Hearing Disorders* 49, 338–48.

Merrell, K. W. (2003). *Behavioral, social, and emotional assessment of children and adolescents*, 2nd ed. Mahwah, NJ: Lawrence Erlbaum Associates.

Merritt, D. D. & Culatta, B. (1998). Dynamic assessment, language processes, and curricular content. In D. D. Merritt & B. Culatta (eds.), *Language intervention in the classroom* (pp. 99–142). San Diego: Singular Publishing Group.

Nelson, N. W. (1998). *Childhood language disorders in context: Infancy through adolescence*, 2nd ed. Boston: Allyn and Bacon.

Norris, J. A. & Damico, J. S. (1990). Whole language in theory and practice: Implications for language intervention. *Language, Speech, and Hearing Services in Schools* 21, 212–20.

Owens, R. E. (2004). *Language disorders*, 4th ed. Boston: Allyn & Bacon.

Paul, R. (2001). *Language disorders: From infancy through adolescence*, 2nd ed. St. Louis: Mosby.

Perkins, M. R. (2007). *Pragmatic impairment*. Cambridge: Cambridge University Press.

Plante, E. & Vance, R. (1994). Selection of preschool language tests: A data-based approach. *American Journal of Speech-Language Pathology* 4, 70–6.

Prizant, B. M., Wetherby, A. M., & Rydell, P. (2000). Communication intervention issues for young children with autism spectrum disorders. In A. M. Wetherby & B. M. Prizant (eds.), *Autism spectrum disorders: A transactional developmental perspective* (pp. 193–224). Baltimore, MD: Paul H. Brookes.

Sampson Graner, P., Faggella-Luby, M. N., & Fritschmann, N. S. (2005). An overview of responsiveness to intervention: What practitioners ought to know. *Topics in Language Disorders* 25, 93–105.

Simmons-Mackie, N. N. & Damico, J. S. (2007). Access and social inclusion in aphasia: Interactional principles and applications. *Aphasiology* 21, 81–97.

Stone, A. (2004). Contemporary approaches to the study of language and literacy development: A call for the integration of perspectives. In C. A. Stone, E. R. Silliman, B. J. Ehren, & K. Apel (eds.), *Handbook of language and literacy: Development and disorders* (pp. 3–24). New York: Guilford Press.

Timler, G. R., Olswang, L. B., & Coggins, T. E. (2005). Social communication interventions for preschoolers: Targeting peer interactions during peer group entry and cooperative play. *Seminars in Speech and Language* 26, 170–80.

Tomblin, B. J. (2006). A normativist account of language-base learning disability. *Learning Disabilities Research & Practice* 21, 8–18.

Warren, S. F., Fey, M. E., & Yoder, P. J. (2007). Differential treatment intensity research: A missing link to creating optimally effective communication interventions. *Mental Retardation and Developmental Disabilities Research Reviews* 13, 70–7.

Weaver, C. (1996). Teaching grammar in the context of writing. *English Journal* 85, (November), 15–24.

Wells, G. (2001). The case for dialogic inquiry. In G. Wells (ed.), *Action, talk & text. Learning and teaching through inquiry* (pp. 171–94). New York: Teachers College Press.

Westby, C. (2007). Application of the ICF in children with language impairments. *Seminars in Speech and Language* 28, 265–72.

World Health Organization. (2001). *International classification of functioning, disability and health*. Geneva, Switzerland: WHO.

Part II Language Disorders

7 Autism Spectrum Disorders: The State of the Art

JOHN MUMA AND STEVEN CLOUD

1 Introduction

With recent developments in the field of communication disorders, the disorder category known as autism spectrum disorders (ASD) has been expanded and this expansion has been accompanied by a number of questions regarding this disorder. For example, the estimates of the incidence of children with ASD have increased greatly and this has led to debates in the literature and the popular media (e.g., Baker, 2008; Fombonne, 2003; Gernsbacher, Dawson, & Goldsmith, 2005). Similarly, with greater awareness, there is more attention placed on how assessment and treatment of ASD is handled in the rehabilitative disciplines. Basically, these issues may be viewed from different perspectives that greatly influence our understanding of ASD and whether our actions with regard to ASD are linked to real evidence or to artifacts biased by our orientations to the field of autism.

1.1 Incidence: Real evidence or artifacts

A primary example of greater awareness – and confusion – regarding ASD arises from the question, "What is the incidence of autism spectrum disorders (ASD)?" Reported estimates of incidence vary greatly, with the more recent estimates much higher than in the past. The question of what accounts for such large recent estimates can be converted into several others. Are there truly more individuals with ASD than previously? Does the increased incidence merely reflect an increased awareness of these problems? Are professionals more inclined to use the term ASD in a loose, non-disciplined way thereby inflating the reports of these problems? Does the increased incidence of ASD reflect the money allocated to identify and study autism spectrum disorders? Each of these questions may have some degree of relevance. But it is important to remember that the answers to each of these questions and how they impact on the question of changing incidence also depend on whether the data employed and their interpretations are defensible. One thing should be remembered: estimates of data or indefensible interpretations of data sets do not always equate with evidence.

The Handbook of Language and Speech Disorders, First Edition. Edited by Jack S. Damico, Nicole Müller, and Martin J. Ball. © 2013 Blackwell Publishing Ltd except for editorial material and organization © 2013 Jack S. Damico, Nicole Müller, Martin J. Ball. Published 2013 by Blackwell Publishing Ltd.

A study by Pinborough-Zimmerman et al. (2007) indicated that over the previous 30 years, the estimates of ASD incidence in Utah have increased dramatically. Even so, they found that 6.3 percent of 8-year-old children evidenced communication disorders. The ratio of boys to girls is 8:1. Of these children, 3.7 percent were considered to have ASD. While this may be solid evidence as far as it can be appropriately extended (but see Chapter 1), the question arises as to whether the incidence rate for Utah should be generalized across the nation and whether the 8-year level is representative of other age levels. In a recent discussion of similar reports of increase in California, Gernsbacher, Dawson, and Goldsmith (2005) demonstrated that estimates made based upon selected types of data without considering all the evidence may be misleading.

1.2   An enigma

Autism spectrum disorders are something of an enigma. One reason for this may be the views that we hold for this disorder category. There are two basic underlying views of ASD: one based upon behaviorism and the other based upon constructionism (cognitive socializatic). While many ASD specialists claim that these views blend into a unified perspective, a consideration of the underlying aspects of these views reveals that they are incompatible. Further, these views often influence the types of data reported and how these data are interpreted. In this regard, while much of this literature is based on empirical evidence, rational evidence is obviously lacking.

A cursory review of the impact of these two underlying views of ASD is instructive and reveals a number of relevant points. First, while behaviorism and constructionism (cognitive socialization) are richly evident in the literature, there is a remarkable lack of appreciation as to why these different philosophical views are incongruent. The result is a clinical orientation that is often based on impressionism sponsored by procedures rather than substantive issues. Specifically, procedures pertaining to positive and negative reinforcement, cuing, and timeout are involved.

Second, partly due to this confusion regarding the two underlying views, there are only a few general understandings of ASD. Even then, there is disagreement regarding the true nature of autism and related disorders in a "spectrum" of symptoms. The shift from considering autism as a clinical entity to an array of closely related clinical problems under the realm of ASD may have been a step toward elegance on the one hand and a step toward rationalization to appease alternative accounts on the other. The result is that the definitions of ASD, and related disorders, are slippery and open to a variety of interpretations.

Third, there appear to be two, possibly three, major orientations that have arguably different perspectives on the nature of ASD, assessment, and intervention. These orientations are all the more perplexing because they use some of the same terms with very different underlying meanings. Notable in this regard are the terms "communication," "language," "cognition," "learning," "linguistic mapping," "functional," and "scientific or scholarly."

Fourth, while these orientations agree in general that ASD is a constitutional impairment and that the relevant behavioral manifestations typically show up at about 2 to 3 years of age (Wetherby, Prizant, & Hutchinson, 1998; Woods & Wetherby, 2003), given the lack of a definitive perspective, such behavioral symptoms are suggestive rather than definitive. Indeed, this aspect of the literature on ASD needs to be more firmly enunciated.

These points lead to a situation in which both assessment and intervention evidence for ASD is very much impressionistically driven by those who have biases for each of the orientations, and so while there appears to be a large assessment and intervention literature on ASD, much of the evidence is impressionistic, provisional, and equivocal. Accordingly, the literature on ASD needs to be critically reviewed toward upgrading. Meanwhile, the assessment and treatment of ASD appears to be more of an art than a science.

The purpose of this chapter is to cite specific instances in which it would be desirable to upgrade this literature and to create a better understanding of ASD. Toward this end, the discussion section reflects these questions. First, focusing on points of agreement, there will be a brief section characterizing some of the general characteristics of autism. Next, the importance of a theoretical orientation will be discussed followed by specifics of the two primary orientations to ASD and a discussion of a hybrid of the two. These discussions will weave in ways that each orientation influences the perception and service delivery to ASD. The next section will address some of the substantive issues that must be considered once one gains an awareness of the theoretical orientations. At the end of this chapter, some very brief case reports are presented to underscore several of the issues raised herein.

2   General Understandings of ASD

The autism spectrum disorders generally include five pervasive developmental disorders of childhood: autistic disorder, Rett's disorder, childhood disintegrative disorder, pervasive developmental disorder-NOS (PDD-NOS), and Asperger's disorder (DSM-IV, 1994). The general consensus about the nature of ASD is that these disorders encompass three major problem areas: social interaction, communication, and aversive behaviors. While each of the disorders are somewhat different with regard to the severity and manifestation of these three problems areas, each of the five disorders do exhibit some level of difficulties in each one. Basically, all three areas act within a symbolic and social context to implicate social dysfunction.

2.1   Social interaction

Regarding social interaction, individuals with problems in this area are essentially "disconnected" from others. These children typically do not strive to interact with others. In a sense, they attempt to "go it alone." But, unfortunately for children who evidence ASD, humans are inherently social, so attempts to "go it alone" are contrary to the way that humans function. While it may sound like the act of "going it alone" is a volitional act, in ASD such ventures are more likely to be a default reaction rather a than volitional response because there is increasing evidence that individuals with ASD have atypical neurophysiology and genetics (Lauritsen & Ewald, 2001; Pericak-Vance, 2003). Thus, these children may be operating with a flawed central nervous system that somehow prevents, or limits, social interaction.

There are two interesting ramifications of "going it alone." The first is that parents of children with ASD often find themselves resorting to caregiving activities that are stripped of fruitful social interactions. That is, parents may dress and feed their children, but they leave much of the child's world barren of social interaction. This circumstance evolves unconsciously over an extended period of time. Parents want and encourage social interaction from infancy. However, over time, and with minimal responses from the infant, the reduction of social interaction emerges because it is simply more efficient to dress and feed with less and less social interaction sustained only by parents. We have seen many children with ASD where the parental role was reduced down to basic caregiving with marginal social interaction initiated by parents.

The second ramification involves the responsiveness of children with ASD to concerted efforts for social interaction. Apparently, when concerted efforts are made to fight the tendency for interactional reduction and more social interaction is provided, these children pass a threshold of some kind whereby they become more responsive to social interactions than they were previously. A misconception about these children is that they need individual intervention because they cannot deal with social interaction. Yet, we have routinely included children with ASD in groups of other children with speech and language problems. Furthermore, we have had their parents maintain logs of notes pertaining to new social experiences. These logs have rejuvenated parental interests in social interactions and documented their effects. We have seen surprisingly good results. Nearly all of the individuals with ASD evidenced noticeable improvements in social interaction as a consequence of participating in group clinical activities and parental logs.

2.2   Communication

Communication difficulties with children with ASD typically focus on those children who are old enough that we note that there are some difficulties with their anticipated verbal language acquisition, that is, that they are developmentally delayed or that their verbal productions are unexpectedly different. Obviously, communication difficulties due to ASD are hard to identify in preverbal children since the precursors to language are limited. It has been reported that children eventually identified as ASD typically attempt little, if any, babbling in the first year but more research is needed in this area. Similarly, it has been suggested that colic might be used as an indication of difficulty in pre-verbal children. This is due to the report from Brazelton (1991) that colic is the product of excessive stimulation during the previous day: that is, the infant's premature central nervous system is unable to fully process the stimulation of the previous day. Then, colic occurs that night to release the cognitive tension from the stimulation. Inasmuch as infants with ASD may lack processing, it is likely that these children do not become "over-stimulated." Therefore, they are likely to have few, if any, periods of colic. On the other hand, these infants may be easily over-stimulated. In such cases, infants with ASD may evidence a great deal of colic. Obviously, in this area there is also a need for more research.

In the most severe forms of ASD (autistic disorder, PDD-NOS), there is little or no indication of pre-verbal intent and early pre-verbal/gestural systems of communication fail to develop at 12–15 months. With Rett's disorder and child-hood disintegrative disorder there may be initial development pre-verbally and even up to words of sentences but then there is regression to a pre-verbal level. Individuals identified with Asperger's disorder typically don't exhibit significant linguistic or cognitive delays until after 3 years of age . . . but the more social aspects of communication that mark this condition are harder to identify until that time period.

Regarding children with ASD who are verbal, their development is mixed and often significantly delayed – especially for all but Asperger's disorder. With regard to some of the unique aspects of verbal communication in ASD, several issues arise. First, many of these children employ echolalia – often for communicative purposes (Local & Wootton, 1995; Prizant, 1983). However, the fact that some of these children engage in echolalia is evidence that they have achieved some measure of grammar; yet, they have major communication difficulties. Second, when variegated echolalia occurs, there is evidence of abilities, albeit latent, to generate new constructions. Third, when perseveration occurs, it raises the question about an individual's cognitive abilities to know what to say when topics and contexts change. Fourth, reliance on stereotypical utterances usually wedded to particular routines raises the question as to whether true communication is taking place. Fifth, these children usually have much difficulty with pragmatic skills such as greetings, topic initiation, topic sharing, topic development, deictic reference, three types of anaphora (loading, competition, vacancy), pre-closing, and closing. Sixth, another area of difficulty related to pragmatic skills is role taking. Children are likely to have difficulties understanding the perspectives of others. Seventh, the literature on theory of mind (ToM) indicated that these children evidence difficulties in this arena. Three dimensions of ToM are of special interest: disclosing one's own feelings to others, perceiving the feelings of others, and sharing experiences or objects with others. Interestingly, we have seen a few of these children who evidence social indifference to others carrying out "protectionistic" stances with younger children and pets.

2.3 Aversive behaviors

A large and varied array of aversive behaviors is observed with ASD. The fol-lowing is surely a partial list of such behaviors: body rocking, body spinning, stomping, head banging, hand and/or arm flailing, twitching, cyclic behavior, lining up or stacking items, putting items in containers, yelling or squealing, undressing, throwing food, inspecting objects and mechanisms, adherence to certain routines, and so on. Needless to say, each child may evidence his/her unique set of such behaviors.

It is our experience in dealing with a large number of these individuals over many years that aversive behaviors begin to wane, or even to drop out, as a function of increased social interaction, especially in one's home. Said differently, it appears that these behaviors serve as "self-stimulation" in the absence of other stimulation.

Within a clinical context, we never used reinforcement when dealing with aversive behaviors; rather, we focused on each child's intentions to participate. One telling observation that an aversive behavior is about to be dropped occurs when a child pauses after the behavior and looks to the other participant (not necessarily the clinician) to see what response that person may have. If that person attended to the communicative intent rather than the aversive behavior, the aversive behavior would eventually be dropped. Thus, intent replaced reinforcement as a viable intervention principle.

3   Rational Evidence: Lacking

Rational evidence when dealing with ASD incorporates one's philosophical views and the theoretical perspectives that underwrite an understanding of the nature of ASD. These views and perspectives define appropriate assessments and interventions for children with ASD. The value of rational evidence is that it provides disciplined views and perspectives toward achieving scholarly understandings. By incorporating philosophical views one can examine underlying assumptions and propositions for establishing coherence in understanding and practice.

3.1   *The philosophical views and theoretical perspectives*

With coherent views, a particular philosophy obtains credibility (Searle, 1992) and this credible philosophical view results in a theoretical perspective that establishes disciplined understandings, explanations, and predictions (Kaplan, 1964; Kerlinger, 1973). Scholarly fields strive to deal with theoretical perspectives in order to be oriented on disciplined perspectives. For example, the 1983 ASHA Training Standards (Rees & Snope, 1983), Resolution II-B, stated that in order to overcome technicianship and to encourage clinicianship, all coursework should be theory-based.

Because theories provide disciplined understandings, they establish appropriate clinical services. Professionals who do not understand the functions of theories are inclined to say, "Don't give me the theories, I want practical 'hands-on' directives." Such thinking is counterproductive because it invites impressionism and capriciousness which undermine the credibility of a profession.

Theoretical perspectives are derived primarily from philosophical views. Furthermore, theories obtain credibility when they acquire descriptive and explanatory adequacies. Descriptive adequacy is obtained for theories of cognition and language when they meet the following criteria: they are complete, formal, simple, and non-contradictory (Tunkis, 1963). A theory is complete when it accounts for the full arena of phenomena rather than selected aspects. It is formal when it can be enunciated in terms of rules. It is simple when the set of rules are the most parsimonious. It is non-contradictory when one aspect of a theory does not contradict another aspect.

Explanatory adequacy for a theory is achieved either by developmental evidence or mental processing evidence. When a theory successfully explains or predicts acquisition, it has achieved explanatory adequacy. Also, when a theory explains or predicts mental processing, it has achieved explanatory adequacy. Perera (1994) identified five theories of language acquisition that have achieved acceptable levels of descriptive and explanatory adequacies. Accordingly, they were regarded as the five most influential theories of language acquisition over the previous 25 years; they continue to be the most influential theories. The five theories were:

- Government and binding theory (Chomsky, 1968, 1982) with the sister theories known as learnability theories (Hyams, 1986; Lightfoot, 1989; Pinker, 1984, 1988, 1989), which were derived from Chomsky's theories. Chomsky's theories provide disciplined understandings of mental processing, whereas the learnability theories account for language acquisition.
- Bootstrapping theories (Bruner, 1981; Gleitman, 1994; Pinker, 1987) are based on the premise that verbal skills in one aspect of language provide a context for learning other aspects. One context that is available to an individual can "bootstrap" or assist in learning other aspects of language. For example, the "double-whammy" occurs when a child has the requisite knowledge of a referent and the referent becomes named (Gleitman, 1994; Muma, 1998). This dubbing ceremony (Bruner, 1981; Stalnaker, 1972) functions in word acquisition.
- Relevance theory (Sperber & Wilson, 1986) identified intent as the "irreducible nucleus" of language acquisition (Bruner, 1986; Nelson, 1985, 1996; Searle, 1992) and the distinctions between explicit and implicit content of messages as they are derived from an individual's knowledge of the world (Lakoff, 1987), possible worlds (Bruner, 1986), and situated mind (Nelson, 1996). Explicit content is the basic ideas entailed in a message, whereas implicit content is knowledge of the world that allows explicit content to be meaningful.
- Modularity theory (Fodor, 1983) posits mental functions underlying language acquisition with respect to whether these functions arise from encapsulated aspects of the cortex or not. This theory is used to account for differentiated mental skills in development and in brain injury.
- The parallel distributed processing theory (McClelland & Rummelhart, 1986) accounts for the ability to parallel process information. Parallel processing occurs when an individual can hold some aspects of information in abeyance while processing other aspects of information. For example, in constructing relative clauses, it is necessary to hold the relative clause information in abeyance until it is useful to "apply" it to a sentence construction.

There are two important observations about this list of the most influential theories of language acquisition. First, reinforcement theory did not make the list. This is most likely because it does not provide a viable account of language acquisition (Bowerman, 1994; Cazden, 1988; Chomsky, 1968; Macken, 1987; Mandler, 1983; Pinker, 1988; Searle, 1992). This inadequacy is particularly noted with regard to the importance of acquired forms being applied over time and space and the maintenance of what is learned and/or acquired over time. Interestingly, advocates of reinforcement often report that intervention lacked generalization (carry-over) and/or maintenance. Bopp, Brown, and Mirenda (2004) made the following summary comment for 15 studies: "fewer than half included assessment of generalization of new communicative behavior and only two provided data related to maintenance of outcomes over time" (p. 13). Thus, many studies did not attempt to assess generalization or maintenance. These are two reasons, among others, why reinforcement is not endorsed by major language acquisition scholars.

The second observation regarding these five influential theories is that modality theory (Osgood, 1957) was not on this list. This theory holds that there are crucial differences between the expressive and receptive language modalities and between oral and written modalities. However, Clark and Clark (1977) showed that the modality aspects of information processing become purged early, and the essential processing underlying language occurs with symbolization (Macken, 1987), representation (Mandler, 1983), and the coin-of-the-realm (Muma, 1998). Nelson (1996) indicated that the "interesting activity takes place" in the central processor irrespective of modalities (p. 4). Perhaps it should be noted that the foremost scholars of language acquisition and use do not endorse the modality theory (e.g., Bloom, Brown, Bruner, Cazden, Gleitman, Grice, Pinker, Searle, Sperber, Wilson).

4   The Impact of the Different Theoretical Perspectives

The literature on ASD is obviously oriented on two, possibly three, different perspectives of practice governed by different and incompatible philosophical views with their attendant theoretical perspectives underwriting this literature. One perspective is based on behaviorism, characterized by a reliance on reinforcement theory (Kashinath, Woods, & Goldstein, 2006; McDuffie, Yoder, & Stone, 2005; Yoder & Stone, 2006; Yoder & Warren, 2002). Another perspective is based on constructionism, characterized by an orientation on natural communicative contexts and on developmental perspectives (Prizant, 1999; Prizant & Wetherby, 1998). Finally, Diehl (2003) claimed that "functional communication training and positive behavioral support have effectively blended these two points of view" (p. 178). Thus, a third perspective is presumably a mixture of the first two, with functional communication training and positive behavioral support (FCT/PBS). Each of these perspectives will be described below.

4.1   *Behaviorism*

Behaviorism (Skinner, 1957) is a philosophical view that is very different from the other primary orientation, constructionism. Advocates of behaviorism contend that individuals are passive learners waiting to be taught. They hold that behavior must be observable, or tangible, in order to manipulate it by positive or negative reinforcement and cueing. One telling limitation of behaviorism is that it denies the existence of mental states. Searle wrote, "The absurdity of behaviorism lies in the fact that it denies the existence of any mental states" (1992, p. 35).

While the neo-behaviorists retort that they use verbal reinforcement such as "I'm proud of you," and they suggest some kind of mental state, according to Skinner such utterances fall outside of the purview of behaviorism. Neo-behaviorists also contend that they deal with intent (Meline, 2006). Yet, their accounts of intent essentially deal with elicitation not intentionality. Their intentions in this regard are very limited, and they do not fit with the construc-tionists' views of the nature and role of intentions in cognitive and language development (Sperber & Wilson, 1986).

Based upon their orientation to learning as a non-strategic and non-mentalistic approach whereby learning is based on principles of stimulus and response, behaviorists focus on how consequent events function as the products of positive and negative reinforcement and cueing (Bopp, Brown, & Mirenda, 2004; Kashinath, Woods, & Goldstein, 2006; McDuffie, Yoder, & Stone, 2005; Yoder & Stone, 2006). To demonstrate these operations in ASD, they often rely on studies with only a few participants who may not represent the population of children with ASD because of the heterogeneous nature of this population. Further, their evidence is derived from very small samples of behaviors. For example, Dawson et al. (1990) and McArthur and Adamson (1996) studied 10-minute interactions; Kasari et al. (1990) studied 8-minute interactions. Studies in this arena tend to present baseline tables for interpretation, which results in impressionism.

Behaviorists strive to explain the effects of reinforcement and cueing toward increasing, or decreasing, the occurrence of targeted behaviors and generalization and maintenance of these behaviors. In a sense, behaviorists are interested in performance changes rather than learning. Performance changes are usually indexed by frequencies (sometimes converted into percentages). For example, Yoder and Stone (2006) stated that, "increasing the frequency of intentional com-munication could increase the frequency with which children with ASD will receive linguistic mapping of their communicative messages, which may in turn facilitate their language acquisition" (p. 699).

Interestingly, evidence of intervention effectiveness is largely equivocal for the behaviorist studies dealing with ASD. First, the targeted areas for language acquisition are marginal – of little consequence for achieving communicative competence. Second, the targeted areas for language acquisition typically are not based on a child's intentions but rather on elicitation. Third, the evidence of generalization is usually only of limited success. Fourth, in a behaviorist approach, the evidence of presumed learning is based upon frequencies of behavior.

However, frequencies of behavior merely index the notion of "habit strength" rather than learning.

Brown (1973) and Cazden (1988) indicated that frequencies of behavior do not correlate with language acquisition. Rather than focus on frequencies, if true learning occurred in language acquisition, it would be evidenced by lexical variation (Brown, 1973), by progress in acquisition sequences (Brown, 1973), by alternative language learning strategies (Goldfield & Snow, 2001), and/or by active language learning loci (Muma, 1986, 1998; Muma & Cloud, 2008). Fifth, evidence of maintenance is sparse. Furthermore, the most comprehensive examination of behaviorist approaches has shown that the results are either short-term or suspect (Kohn, 1993). Sixth, the foremost scholars of language acquisition do not regard behaviorism in general, and reinforcement in particular, as offering viable accounts of language acquisition (Bowerman, 1994; Bruner, 1978, 1986; Cazden, 1988; Nelson, 1985; Pinker, 1988; Searle, 1992).

Regarding the province of learning, behaviorism once again varies from constructivism (Muma, 1978). Behaviorists regard a child as a passive learner waiting to be taught. The province of learning is vested with the teacher/clinician who decides the content, sequencing, pacing, and reinforcement/cueing aspects of intervention.

4.2   Constructivism

The other theoretical orientation is based upon constructivism (Searle, 1992). Constructionism is the view that human beings are active processors of information toward constructing each individual's mental states such as knowledge of the world (Lakoff, 1987), possible worlds (Bruner, 1986), or situated minds (Nelson, 1996). One's possible worlds constitute the cognitive bases for thinking and communicating. Thus, it is necessary for individuals to have dynamic and ever-expanding experiential, social, and emotional bases to construct possible worlds. This understanding of the construction of one's world provides constructionists with a very different view of functionalism than the one advocated by neo-behaviorists. They are interested in how cognitive and communicative functions develop in a social nexus. The main cognitive functions are representation (Karmiloff-Smith, 1992; Macken, 1987; Mandler, 1983) and mediation (Nelson, 1996). The main communicative functions are intent (Bruner, 1986; Nelson, 1996; Searle, 1992), explicit content (Sperber & Wilson, 1986), and implicit content (Sperber & Wilson, 1986). Furthermore, intent has emerged as the "irreducible nucleus of language" (Bruner, 1986; Nelson, 1996; Searle, 1992).

Given these orientating facts about constructivism, the behaviorist orientation does not appear as well suited to a rationale for the development of language or communication. In this regard, Nelson (1996) indicated that language acquisition is success-driven. Thus, it is not so much frequency, but the effects that each communicative event has on intent that counts. Furthermore, Brown (1973) indicated that frequency is not as potent as varied communicative efforts when they work as intended. Sperber and Wilson (1986) showed that messages are made to make communicative intent recognizable.

The naturalistic, or developmental, approach (Prizant, 1999; Wetherby, Prizant, & Hutchinson, 1998; Wetherby & Prutting, 1984; Woods & Wetherby, 2003) also was called the psycholinguistic approach (Long, 2005). Perhaps it would be more prudent to regard this approach as a "cognitive socialization" approach in keeping with the underlying philosophical view of constructionism with its attendant acquisition theories.

Much of the underlying literature emanates from Roger Brown and his colleagues at Harvard University. As early as 1956, Brown held that language acquisition is "a process of cognitive socialization" (p. 247). The literature over the past five decades has substantiated the fact that language acquisition, and cognitive acquisition for that matter, is a process of cognitive socialization.

Mandler (1979) indicated that cognitive development occurs in a social nexus. Rogoff (1990) provided a comprehensive account of cognitive development in a social nexus. Brown (1973, 1986) has explicated the cognitive socialization perspective over the previous five decades. Perhaps the finest flower of the cognitive socialization approach was Nelson's (1996) book. Clinical applications of the cognitive socialization approach are available (Muma, 1978, 1986, 1998; Muma & Cloud, 2008; Muma & Teller, 2003).

As discussed previously, this cognitive socialization approach – that has arisen from constructivism – is oriented on the five most influential theories of language that were identified by Perera (1994). The two key issues for relevance theory are the centrality of intent and the distinctions between explicit and implicit content. The key premise for bootstrapping theories is that an individual's competence in one aspect of language provides a context for learning other aspects. The key issue for learnability theory is that the formal aspects of language are innately available and acquired spontaneously as a function of actual communicative interaction.

Advocates of the cognitive socialization approach hold that a child is an active processor of information. Therefore, the province of learning is with the child. Accordingly, content, sequencing, pacing, and intent are derived from what a child does with language in actual social commerce from representative samples. Thus, a child's performance in actual social commerce informs clinicians how a child is actively learning. The key information for ascertaining what a child knows and does in actual social commerce is that child's repertoire of skills (Ninio et al., 1994), progress in acquisition sequences (Brown, 1973; Greenfield & Smith, 1976), alternative language acquisition strategies (Goldfield & Snow, 2001), and active language learning loci (Muma, 1978, 1986, 1998; Muma & Cloud, 2008).

There are major differences between behaviorist and cognitive socialization approaches. Table 7.1 summarizes these differences.

4.3   A hybrid of behaviorism and constructivism

Finally, the third perspective is the hybrid, what Diehl (2003) claimed was a mixture of the orientations to behaviorism and constructivism. The primary features of this orientation were the linkage of functional communication training and positive behavioral support (FCT/PBS). In making this claim, Diehl (2003) asserted

Table 7.1   Differences between behavioristic and cognitive socialization approaches

	Behavioristic approaches	*Cognitive socialization*
Philosophical views:	Behaviorism	Constructionism
Functionalism:	Consequent events	Cognitive functions; representation and mediation; communicative functions: intent, explicit and implicit content
Theoretical perspectives:	Reinforcement	Relevance theory; bootstrapping theory; learnability theory
Province of learning:	Teacher/clinician: content, sequence, pacing, reinforcement, frequency	Child: content, sequence, pacing, intent, variation
Targets:	Tangibles; generalization and relations; maintenance	Early intentions, semantic functions grammatical repertoires, acquisition sequences, alternative language acquisition strategies, active language learning loci

that, "these applied sciences, developed from applied behavior analysis…" (p. 178). However, the constructivist approach advocated by Prizant, Wetherby, and others was not developed from applied behavior analysis. It was developed by the language acquisition literature which, in turn, was derived from constructionism and theories of generative grammar (Chomsky, 1968, 1982) and by relevance theory with the centrality of communicative intent (Bruner, 1986; Nelson, 1985, 1996; Searle, 1992; Sperber & Wilson, 1986).

To assume that the FCT/PBS effectively blends behaviorism and constructionism is a major mistake wrought with misused terms and conflicting underlying assumptions (Searle, 1992). Scholars in the philosophy of language and cognition have cautioned against mixing two philosophies with conflicting underlying assumptions. Maratsos (1989) wrote, "Mixed descriptions…are accepted uncomfortably and under what could be described as empirical and theoretical duress" (p. 110). Johnston (1983) stated, "When we advocate the use of 'reinforcing consequent events' to affect 'abstract rule formation,' we are not combining the best of two worlds. We are building a theory that can't work" (p. 55). Macken (1987) indicated that symbolic rule acquisition underlying language development cannot be achieved by the use of reinforcement but rather by the ability to abstract (Mandler, 1983). Anglin (1977) and Bruner (1973) indicated that both cognitive and language development are driven by the ability to abstract, or to represent, which is the ability to abstract by going beyond the information given. Such cognitive abilities are outside of the purview of behaviorism. Moreover, they are success-driven in the sense that they spontaneously establish a coherent grammatical system (Nelson, 1996) motivated by intent (Bruner, 1986; Nelson, 1985, 1996; Searle, 1992) and emerging from a social nexus (Mandler, 1983; Rogoff, 1990).

Another major problem for asserting that behaviorism and constructionism should be combined is that the underlying concepts and terminology are abused. For example, citing Bates (1979), Yoder and Stone (2006) indicated that communicative intent is a prerequisite for speech development and that children with ASD are deficient in dealing with communicative intent. They held that communicative intent is learned by establishing joint references for objects which capitalizes on non-verbal behavior already available to most children with ASD. While their motivation is desirable, their notions of communicative intent come up short in appreciating its role. Such behaviorists' activities are based on elicitation rather than intention. Furthermore, the behaviorists do not strive to ascertain an individual's use of the seven early intentions (Halliday, 1975). The foremost language acquisition scholars (Bloom et al., 1988; Brown, 1973, 1986; Bruner, 1981, 1986; Cazden, 1988; Greenfield, 1980; Grice, 1975; Nelson, 1985, 1996; Searle, 1992; Sperber & Wilson, 1986) have established intent as the irreducible nucleus of communication (Bruner, 1986, p. 17). Ninio et al. (1994) wrote, "Describing speaker's repertoires of communicative intents and rules for expressing those intents is crucial to any complete description of the language capacity" (p. 157). Sperber and Wilson (1986) indicated that the primary purpose of coding a message (verbally or non-verbally) is to make intentions recognizable. Bruner (1986) underscored the importance of communicative intent by stating, "Meaning is not 'what' but 'what for'" (p. 157).

Yoder and Stone (2006) wanted to utilize non-verbal behaviors that were already used by children with ASD. They believed that these non-verbal behaviors evidence "performatives" such as the communicative point (Bates, 1979; Bruner, 1981), displayed references (Muma, 1986, 1998), and sounds to indicate specific referents. While they focused on joint reference, which pertains to communicative intent, they did not realize the developmental sequence of semantic functions and relations launched by performatives and motivated by communicative intent (Greenfield & Smith, 1976).

Yoder and Stone (2006) also used the term "linguistic mapping," which is tangential to how that term is used in the word acquisition literature. For them, linguistic mapping is evidenced when a child hands a picture of a referent to an adult who requested it. Yet, in the language acquisition literature, mapping, or "fast mapping," is evidenced when a child has an experiential base that pertains to a new label. Under such conditions, a child "fast maps" or has a rudimentary understanding of the label because the basic underlying concept is at hand. Vygotsky (1962) described what is currently called "fast mapping" as spontaneous learning in contrast to scientific learning of words.

Finally, Ventor, Lord, and Schopler (1992) defined "useful speech" as "at least 5 communicative words used daily." Yoder and Stone (2006) stated, "it is clear that useful speech has come to mean speech that is frequent, communicative, nonimitative, and referential" (p. 698). Interestingly, they do not distinguish between pre-grammatical and grammatical in considering useful speech.

For pre-grammatical children, the language acquisition literature has indicated that it is necessary to ascertain a child's progress in the acquisition of semantic functions and relations beginning with performatives (Greenfield & Smith, 1976), seven early communicative intentions (Halliday, 1975), cognitive precursors (object permanence, causality, deferred imitation, means-ends) (Bates, 1979), and rudimentary symbolic play (Nicholich 1975).

Once a child has achieved varied subject–verb–object constructions, a child has become grammatical (Bloom, 1973; Brown, 1973). With grammatical children, it becomes necessary to ascertain each child's repertoires of grammatical, phonological, and pragmatic skills (Ninio et al., 1994), progress in acquisition sequences (Brown, 1973), alternative language acquisition strategies (Goldfield & Snow, 2001), and active language learning loci (Muma, 1978, 1986, 1998).

5   Early Behavior Manifestations

The National Research Council (NRC) (2001) endorsed the naturalistic behavior or developmental approach for understanding and treating children with ASD. Woods and Wetherby (2003) stated, "the NRC (2001) concluded that at this point in time, a naturalistic behavioral or developmental method appears to be the most effective to address the core social and communication skills of children with ASD" (p. 185).

The crucial issues for an endorsement of this type are the nature of a naturalistic or developmental method and the "core" social and communication skills that are targeted. The nature of this kind of approach is discussed below. The point of interest here is the early core of social and communication skills.

ASD researchers have selected some early aspects of social communicative skills, but they have missed some other crucial skills (Wetherby, Prizant, & Hutchinson, 1998; Wetherby & Prutting, 1984; Woods & Wetherby, 2003). While the importance of "joint reference" is recognized as a social issue in this literature, it misses how joint reference plays a role in the emergence of semantic functions and relations toward establishing grammatical skills (Greenfield & Smith, 1976) and in establishing primary and secondary intersubjectivity (Sugarman, 1984).

Greenfield and Smith (1976) showed that pre-linguistic children begin with performatives and then proceed to develop language in the following sequence: indicatives (conventional and unconventional labeling), volition (superimposed prosody), agent (instigator of action), action (proto-locative, intransitive, transitive, state), object (animate, inanimate), locative (including possessive), dative (indirect object), and modification (adjectives, relative clauses, adverbs). There are three kinds of performatives: joint reference established by a communicative point, displayed reference such as holding a toy up for all to see, and sounds to identify the referent (e.g., motor noise for car).

Obviously, the ASD literature would be enhanced by conducting an assessment of semantic functions and relations for pre-grammatical children. There are three issues for this assessment: identifying which semantic functions and relations are used by a child, identifying which combinations of semantic relations are used by a child, and ascertaining a child's progress in the acquisition sequence for these semantic functions and relations.

Greenfield and Smith (1976) showed that when a child can do varied subject–verb–object (SVO) constructions, varied datives, or varied modifications, that child has become a grammatical child. At this stage, a pre-grammatical assessment is unnecessary. A grammatical assessment is needed for grammatical children. Such assessments should address repertoires for basic SVO systems (Ninio et al., 1994), progress in acquisition sequences (Brown, 1973), alternative language learning strategies (Goldfield & Snow, 2001), and active language learning loci (Muma, 1986, 1998; Muma & Cloud, 2008).

Sugarman (1984) pointed out that young babies first establish primary inter-subjectivity (PI) followed by secondary intersubjectivity (SI). PI occurs when an infant becomes aware, and seeks, interaction with another person, usually the infant's mother who is called the security base. A very good indicator of PI occurs when an infant is nursing, or immediately after nursing. The infant spends much time contentedly watching the mother's face. Possibly ASD children may not engage in this type of activity.

Early signs of ASD include a lack of smiling and little, if any, babbling. Discrepancy learning theorists have shown that smiling as early as 3 months of age is the most predictive overt behavior of information processing, and EEG peaking is the most predictive covert response (Kagan, 1970, 1971; Kagan & Lewis, 1965). Thus, the lack of smiling by infants with ASD is likely to mean that these infants are not processing available information. It is for this reason that such infants are likely to evidence little, if any, colic. As for babbling, it may be useful to ascertain if infants do reduplicated and/or variegated babbling (Menn & Stoel-Gammon, 2005).

Infants typically engage in vocal play as a form of dialogue. They will produce a stream of vocal play and then pause with the expectation that another person will take part and also produce a stream of vocalization. It may be that children with ASD do not take part in reciprocal vocal play.

SI occurs when an infant is not only aware of another person in an interaction but also aware of a joint referent. In this situation, a young child engages in producing performatives and indicatives. This is the circumstance in which mothers frequently engage in the dubbing ceremony (Bruner, 1981; Stalnaker, 1972), the combined active awareness of the linguistic context and the referential context (Gleitman, 1994), or the "double whammy" (Muma, 1986, 1998). In these contexts, a mother provides the names of objects into which the child is actively attending. Furthermore, as a child acts on a toy, the child engages in enactive processing (Bruner, 1964).

Once a child learns the name of a referent, the referential principle comes into play. This principle is that one word has many referents and one referent has many words (Brown, 1958). For example, the word "ball" can refer to many different balls; and one ball (referent) can be named many different ways. Therefore, an important assessment question for children with ASD is: Can the child evidence the referential principle for his/her words?

There are a few dimensions of early word learning that are missed, or ignored, in this literature. Specifically, children typically learn the functional aspects of a referent before they learn the static attributes (Nelson, 1974). For example, children learn what can be done with a ball before they attend to its color, size, and shape. Strangely, preschool programs often teach color, size, and shape as stand-alone entities. Yet, children typically learn about these features as secondary attributes of objects, and the primary attributes are the objects' functions.

Another aspect of early word learning is the occurrence of over-extensions and under-extensions. Over-extensions occur when a child uses a term that "goes beyond" the adult use of a term. For example, a child may say, "Doggy" while pointing to a cow. An under-extension occurs when a child does not allow a word to be used as an adult would use the term. For example, a child's mother might point to a German Shepherd and say, "Look at the pretty dog." Then her child, who has a little fluffy dog that he/she calls "Doggy," will say, "No, doggy. Fluffy, my doggy."

The ASD researchers have ignored, or missed, the literature on attachment theory (Ainsworth, 1969, 1972, 1973, 1974; Ainsworth et al., 1978; Bowlby, 1969, 1973; Emde, 1989; Haynes & Pinzola, 1998; Howes & Hamilton, 1992; Lamb et al., 1985; Lewis & Brooks, 1975; Ragozin, 1980). This literature is exceedingly important for really understanding the asocial behaviors of children with ASD.

Attachment theory addresses three main issues that explain how preschool children handle their emotions in an interpersonal context. The issues are attachment, separation anxiety, and stranger anxiety.

Infants and young children may show attachment in many different ways. For example, a child may climb onto his/her mother's lap, lean into her, hold onto her, lean against her legs as she is sitting, "calibrate" to his/her mother's feelings, etc. Separation anxiety occurs when a child is separated from his/her mother. Most young children will protest during impending separation, but they recover very quickly after their mother leaves. Most young children also need ready access to their "security base" (usually the mother) in order to function without separation anxiety. Stranger anxiety occurs when a young child interacts with a stranger. Most young children seek attachment to their security bases when dealing with strangers. They "calibrate" emotionally to how their mother reacts to a stranger. When they feel comfortable, the children will release from the security base and remain released.

Although children with ASD are typically detached, they sometimes choose special people with whom to interact. Some of these children have emotional tirades when encountering strangers. Thus, the literature on attachment theory could provide an index of the degree to which children with ASD evidence socio-emotional disconnections.

6 A Shift in Perspectives

A shift in intervention approaches has occurred recently. There is an interest in providing alternative configurations of intervention for children with ASD. Previously, intervention followed the "pull-out" approach, or special education classes specifically tailored for children with ASD. However, because of an interest in ecologically validity (Bronfenbrenner, 1979), intervention was reconfigured not only to include parental participation, but also to utilize a child's home as the site of intervention.

The ecological orientation is more compatible with the natural developmental approach (e.g., Prizant, Wetherby) than the behaviorist approach (e.g., Yoder, Warren) because it is focused on communicative intent rather than elicitation. Furthermore, spontaneous performance in a child's home is more inferentially palatable than performances on contrived tasks (tests).

6.1 *Dependent variables*

The dependent variables for substantiating the effects of an ecological orientation to intervention either have changed, or should change as a function of the shift toward ecological validity. Previously, frequencies (Goldstein,) or intensity (Woods & Wetherby, 2003) provided evidence of presumed intervention effectiveness. Yet, such evidence pertains more to habit strength than to learning something new.

Discrepancy learning theorists (Kagan, 1970, 1971; Kagan & Lewis, 1965) showed that variation promotes learning. In accordance with this theory, Brown (1973) wrote that lexical variation and progress in acquisition sequences provide the most appropriate evidence of grammatical acquisition. Thus, it is possible that the most appropriate evidence of language intervention for children with ASD is lexical variation as evidenced by expanding repertoires (semantic, syntactic, phonological, and pragmatic systems) and progress in acquisition sequences (pre-grammatical children: semantic functions and relations; grammatical children: grammatical and pragmatic systems).

Relying on frequency data has three major problems. First, frequencies pertain to performances rather than to new learning. Second, frequency data are often converted into percentages inappropriately. When the data exceed 100 instances, the use of percentages is appropriate. However, when the instances are less than 100, the conversion to percentage inflates the data. For example, if a child has 5 of 20 correct performances, the conversion to percentage (25 percent) inflates the data by a factor of 4, thereby creating an illusion. Third, when frequency data are plotted as "baseline" changes, the result is open to any interpretation. This creates impressionism. For example, the various "baseline" graphs in Kashinath, Woods, and Goldstein (2006) are open to any interpretation including possible generalizations about the effectiveness of intervention.

The use of multiple baselines in intervention studies is a tricky business. On the one hand, these baselines may reveal dimensions of effectiveness that may have been missed. On the other hand, these baselines are vulnerable to spurious findings. That is, the more variables that are included in multiple baselines the greater the likelihood that false findings will occur. This is where replications play an important role. If comparable results are obtained in replications of multiple baselines, the new results verify the previous results. However, if a replication does not provide comparable results, the initial results and the results of the replication are suspect.

Interestingly, researchers of various multiple baseline studies of children with ASD generalize about intervention effectiveness prematurely. Such generalizations are premature because they typically deal with a very small number of participants. Under such conditions, the chances are high that the results are unduly affected by one or a few individuals who may not be representative of the ASD population. Because the ASD population is heterogeneous, the likelihood of spurious results from studies of a few individuals is high. Second, multiple baselines are inherently vulnerable to spurious findings just by chance.

Bates and MacWhinney (1987) provided two basic assessment and intervention principles: expansion and replacement. The expansion principle is that as a child learns, available repertoires expand accordingly. Therefore, the assessment principle is to ascertain each child's repertoire for basic skills. The intervention principle is to expand various targeted repertoires. The replacement principle is that old skills become replaced by new skills as a child progresses in acquisition sequences. The assessment principle is to ascertain each child's progress in acquisition sequences. The intervention principle is to facilitate a child's acquisition of skills by following such sequences.

The communicative pay-off principle (Muma, 1986, 1998) is also promising. Recognizing intent as the "irreducible nucleus" of both cognitive and language acquisition (Bruner, 1986; Nelson, 1996; Searle, 1992), clinicians should recognize communicative intents by children with ASD and respond appropriately to those intents. By doing so, children begin to realize that their communications "work as intended." It is our experience with communicative payoff (Muma, 1981, 1986, 1998; Muma & Cloud, 2008) that there are two major responses. First, children talk more because they become re-energized to use language when it works as intended. Second, and more importantly, they attempt to do new things with communication, which is in keeping with the replacement principle. Yoder and Warren (2002) described a similar intervention approach under the acronym of RPMT.

Nelson (1986) showed that a child's daily routines provide a subculture for learning about the world and for language acquisition. Thus, daily routines provide ready intervention contexts not only for learning language and pragmatic skills but also for other skills (cognitive, social, emotional). The study by Kashinath, Woods, and Goldstein (2006) dealt with a child's daily routines.

7 Needed Substantive Issues

Given the aforementioned substantive issues, perhaps it is useful to summarize them in Table 7.2, which lists issues that should be studied in ASD to advance

Table 7.2   Additional issues that should be considered in studying ASD

1. Centrality of intent rather than elicitation.
2. Early infancy: colic.
3. Infancy: Vocal play with dialogue.
4. Attachment theory: babies study their mothers' faces during or after nursing.
5. Word development: children first learn functions of objects followed by static variables.
6. Word development: dubbing ceremony – double whammy.
7. Word development: over- and under-extensions.
8. Referential principle for word knowledge.
9. Daily routines: subcultures.
10. Lexical variation rather than frequency.
11. Performatives including joint reference.
12. Primary and secondary intersubjectivity.
13. Pre-grammatical children: semantic functions and relations; seven early intentions; cognitive precursors.
14. Grammatical children: repertoires; progress in acquisition sequences; strategies of learning; and active language learning loci.
15. Targeted "language" behaviors are so limited, or marginal, that they should not be regarded as language. Rather, they are selected aspects of a language.
16. Questionable multiple baselines.
17. Studies of a few participants.
18. Data displays invite impressionism.

the field accordingly. Some of these issues may be useful for the early identification of children with ASD. Specifically, items 2, 3, 4, 11, and 12 offer the potentials of achieving early identification of children with ASD.

8   A Few Brief Case Examples

8.1   "Clinic day?"

There was one higher functioning individual with ASD who had been in a behavior modification program for several years. He was in a group of four other children who were focused on speech and language, but they were not autistic. Communicative pay-off was the focus of his intervention. His response to intervention was remarkable. He evidenced joy and increased confidence when we responded to his spontaneous intentional efforts to communicate. He was so responsive that his mother said he drove her crazy asking, "Clinic day?" all the time because he wanted to come to the clinic.

8.2   "All wrong"

We had a child with ASD in a group of several young children who were not ASD. We focused on peer interactions and choices for activities and partners in the activities. This child tended to follow a girl in the group. Whatever she did, he would do (not necessarily with her). Over a number of sessions, he became increasingly willing to spontaneously engage others in activities, especially the girl. His mother was thrilled with his socio-emotional progress. She asked if his teacher could come to observe (he was in a small class of children with ASD). We consented.

His teacher came to an intervention session, and within seconds, she announced that the therapy was "all wrong. He needs a structured program where he must follow directions and be compliant." She agreed that he had made progress in socio-emotional conduct, but she insisted that he needed structure and compliance. In other words, she wanted to control him. We were allowing him to make decisions, and his decisions were fostering new socio-emotional behavior. The teacher told his mother that if she didn't take him out of our program, the school would no longer include him in special education. That was the last that we saw of him.

8.3   "Autistic-like behavior"

The school speech-language pathologist suspected that this girl was autistic. The practice in that state was to send a child suspected of being autistic to an assessment program with the child's mother for one week. The girl and her mother went to the assessment program. They received a lengthy assessment report (about 20 pages) that contained many observations of her behavior over the week. The conclusion was that this girl evidenced "autistic-like behaviors."

Her mother was devastated. She brought her daughter to our clinic. We saw her for one semester. We disagreed with the assessment report, determining that she was reticent. She was reluctant to engage in social behavior. However, when she did participate, her behavior was not unusual. We used the SMILE (Muma & Cloud, 2008) procedure and the communicative pay-off procedure (Muma, 1986, 1998). In relatively short order, she engaged in social activities spontaneously.

We informed her mother that she was reticent but not autistic. Her mother was relieved. She carried out a series of social activities in their home, and her child did fine. We wrote to the state assessment committee and documented many social activities in which she had participated to substantiate the point that she was not autistic.

8.4   Lethal label

We saw a boy whom the school speech-language pathologist and special education director labeled autistic. After a year in our clinic, this boy was doing very well in interpersonal relationships in a variety of situations. We informed his mother that he was not autistic and that there was no need to continue therapy. She was elated. We wrote a clinical report to that effect. His school SLP refused to accept our view, and she insisted that he remain in the special education classroom for children with ASD. To this day (several years later), this SLP will not speak to the authors. Even so, this child is now doing very well in the regular classroom.

REFERENCES

Ainsworth, M. (1969). Object relations, dependency, and attachment: A theoretical view of the mother–child relationship. *Child Development* 40, 969–1025.

Ainsworth, M. (1972). Attachment and dependency: A comparison. In J. Gewirtz (ed.), Attachment and dependency (pp. 97–137). Washington, DC: Winston.

Ainsworth, M. (1973). The development of infant–mother attachment. In B. Caldwell & H. Ricciuti (eds.), *Review of child development research*, Vol. 3 (pp. 1–94). Chicago, IL: University of Chicago Press.

Ainsworth, M. (1974). Infant–mother attachment and social development: Socialization as a product of reciprocal responsiveness to signals. In M. Edwards (ed.), *The integration of the child into the social world*. Cambridge: Cambridge University Press.

Ainsworth, M., Blehar, M., Waters, E., & Wall, S. (1978). *Patterns of attachment: A psychological of the strange situation*. Hillsdale, NJ: Erlbaum.

American Psychological Association (1974). *Standards for educational and psychological tests*. Washington, DC: American Psychological Association.

American Psychiatric Association (1994). *DSM-IV. Diagnostic and Statistical Manual of Mental Disorders*, 4th ed. Washington, DC: American Psychiatric Association.

Anglin, J. (1977). *Word, object, and concept development*. New York: Norton.

Baker, J. (2008). Mercury, vaccines, and autism. *American Journal of Public Health* 98 (2), 244–54.

Bates, E. (1979). *The emergence of symbols*. New York: Academic Press.

Bates, E. & MacWhinney, B. (1987). Competition, variation, and language learning. In B. MacWhinney (ed.), *Mechanisms of language acquisition* (pp. 157–94). Hillsdale, NJ: Lawrence Erlbaum.

Bloom, L. (1973). *One word at a time*. The Hague: Mouton.

Bloom, L., Beckwith, R., Capatides, J., & Hafitz, J. (1988). Expression through affect and words in the transition from infancy to language. In P. Baltes, D. Featherman, & R. Lerner (eds.), *Life-span development and behavior*, Vol. 8 (pp. 99–127). Hillsdale, NJ: Erlbaum.

Bopp, K., Brown, K., & Mirenda, P. (2004). Speech-language pathologists' roles in the delivery of positive behavior support for individuals with developmental disabilities. *American Journal of Speech-Language Pathology* 13, 5–19.

Bowerman, M. (1994). Learning a semantic system. What role do cognitive predispositions play? In P. Bloom (ed.), *Language acquisition: Core readings* (pp. 329–63). Cambridge, MA: MIT Press.

Bowlby, J. (1969). *Attachment and loss: Vol. I. Attachment*. New York: Basic Books.

Bowlby, J. (1973). *Attachment and loss: Vol. II. Separation*. New York: Basic Books.

Brazelton, T. (1991). *Touchpoints*, Vol. 2. New York: Good Times.

Bronfenbrenner, U. (1979). *The ecology of human development*. Cambridge, MA: Harvard University Press.

Brown, R. (1956). Language and categories: Appendix. In J. Bruner, J. Goodnow, & G. Austin (eds.), *A study of thinking* (pp. 247–312). New York: Wiley.

Brown, R. (1958). *Words and things*. New York: Free Press.

Brown, R. (1973). *A first language: The early stages*. Cambridge, MA: Harvard University Press.

Brown, R. (1986). *Social psychology*, 2nd ed. New York: Free Press.

Bruner, J. S. (1964). The course of cognitive growth. *American Psychologist* 19, 1–15.

Bruner, J. (1973). *Beyond the information given*. New York: Norton.

Bruner, J. (1978). Foreword. In A. Lock (ed.), *Action, gesture, symbol* (pp. vii–viii). New York: Academic Press.

Bruner, J. (1981). The social context of language acquisition. *Language & Communication* 1, 155–78.

Bruner, J. (1986). *Actual minds, possible worlds*. Cambridge, MA: Harvard University.

Cazden, C. (1988). Environmental assistance revisited: Variation and functional equivalence. In F. Kessel (ed.), *The development of language and language researchers* (pp. 281–98). Hillsdale, NJ: Erlbaum.

Chomsky, N. (1968). *Language and mind*. New York: Harcourt, Brace, & Jovanovich.

Chomsky, N. (1982). *Lectures on government and binding*. New York: Foris.

Clark, H. & Clark, E. (1977). *Psychology and language*. New York: Harcourt, Brace, & Jovanovich.

Dawson, G., Hill, D., Spencer, A., Galpert, L., & Watson, L. (1990). Affective exchanges between young autistic children and their mothers. *Journal of Abnormal Child Psychology* 18, 335–45.

Diehl, S. (2003). Autism spectrum disorder: The context of speech-language pathologist intervention. *Language, Speech, and Hearing Services in Schools* 34, 177–9.

DSM-IV. (1994). *Diagnostic and statistical manual of mental disorders*, 4th ed. Washington, DC: American Psychiatric Association.

Emde, R. (1989). The infant's relationship experience: Developmental and affective aspects. In A. Sameroff & R. Emde (eds.), *Relationship disturbances in early childhood* (pp. 33–51). New York: Basic Books.

Fodor, J. (1983). *The modularity of the mind: An essay on faculty psychology*. Cambridge, MA: MIT Press.

Fombonne, E. (2003). Epidemiological surveys of autism and other pervasive developmental disorders: An update. *Journal of Autism and Developmental Disorders* 33, 365–82.

Gernsbacher, M. A., Dawson, M., & Goldsmith, H. H. (2005). Three reasons not to believe in an autism epidemic. *Current Directions in Psychological Science* 14 (2), 55–8.

Gleitman, L. (1994). The structural sources of verb meanings. In P. Bloom (ed.), *Language acquisition: Core readings* (pp. 174–221). Cambridge, MA: MIT Press.

Goldfield, B. & Snow, C. (2001). Individual differences: Implications for the study of language acquisition. In J. Gleason (ed.), *The development of language* (pp. 315–46). Boston: Allyn & Bacon.

Greenfield, P. (1980). Going beyond information theory to explain early word choice: A reply to Roy Pea. *Journal of Child Language* 7, 217–21.

Greenfield, P. & Smith, J. (1976). *Communication and the beginnings of language*. New York: Academic Press.

Grice, H. (1975). Logic and conversation. In P. Cole & J. Morgan (eds.), *Syntax and semantics: Vol. 3, Speech acts* (pp. 41–58). New York: Seminar Press.

Halliday, M. (1975). Learning how to mean. In E. Lenneberg & E. Lenneberg (eds.), *Foundations of language development: A multidisciplinary approach* (pp. 239–66). New York: Academic Press.

Haynes, W. & Pindzola, R. (1998). *Diagnosis and evaluation in speech pathology*, 5th ed. Boston: Allyn & Bacon.

Howes, C. & Hamilton, C. (1992). Children's relationships with caregivers: Mothers and child care teachers. *Child Development* 63, 859–66.

Hyams, N. (1986). *Language acquisition and the theory of parameters*. Dordrecht, Holland: Reidel.

Johnston, J. (1983). Discussion: Part I: What is language intervention? The role of theory. In J. Miller, D. Yoder, & R. Schiefelbusch (eds.), *Contemporary issues in language intervention* (ASHA Reports No. 12, pp. 52–60). Rockville, MD: ASHA.

Kagan, J. (1970). The determinants of attention in the infant. *American Scientist* 56, 298–306.

Kagan, J. (1971). *Change and continuity in infancy*. New York: Wiley.

Kagan, J. & Lewis, M. (1965). Studies of attention in the human infant. *Merrill-Palmer Quarterly* 11, 95–127.

Kaplan, A. (1964). *The conduct of inquiry: Methodology for behavioral science*. San Francisco, CA: Chandler.

Karmiloff-Smith, A. (1992). *Beyond modularity*. Cambridge, MA: MIT Press.

Kasari, C., Sigman, M., Munday, P., & Yirmiya, N. (1990). Affective sharing in the context of joint attention. *Journal of Autism and Developmental Disorders* 20, 87–100.

Kashinath, S., Woods, J., & Goldstein, H. (2006). Enhancing generalized teaching strategy use in daily routines by parents of children with autism. *Journal of Speech, Language, and Hearing Research* 49, 466–85.

Kerlinger, F. (1973). *Foundations of behavioral research*, 2nd ed. New York: Holt, Rinehart, & Winston.

Kohn, A. (1993). *Punished by rewards*. Boston: Houghton & Mifflin.

Lakoff, G. (1987). *Women, fire, and dangerous things: What categories reveal about the mind*. Chicago: University of Chicago Press.

Lamb, M., Thompson, R., Gardner, W., & Charnov, E. (1985). *Infant–mother attachment: The origins and developmental significance of individual differences in strange situation behavior*. Hillsdale, NJ: Erlbaum.

Lauritsen, M. & Ewald, H. (2001). The genetics of autism. *Acta Psychiatrica Scandinavica* 103, 411–27.

Lewis, M. & Brooks, J. (1975). Infants' social perception: A constructionist view. In L. Cohen & P. Salapatek (eds.), *Infant perception: From sensation to cognition: Perception of space, speech, and sound*, Vol. 2. New York: Academic.

Lightfoot, D. (1989). The child's trigger experience: Degree-O learnability. *Behavioral and Brain Sciences* 12, 321–75.

Local, J. & Wootton, A. (1995). Interactional and phonetic aspects of immediate echolalia in autism: A case study. *Clinical Linguistics and Phonetics* 9 (2), 155–84.

Long, S. (2005). Language and children with autism. In V. Reed (ed.), *Children with language disorders*, 3rd ed. Boston: Allyn & Bacon.

Macken, M. (1987). Representation, rules, and overgeneralization in phonology. In B. MacWhinney (ed.), *Mechanisms of language acquisition* (pp. 367–97). Hillsdale, NJ: Erlbaum.

Mandler, J. (1979). Commentary: A trilogy on dialogue. In M. Bornstein & W. Kessen (eds.), *Psychological development from infancy* (pp. 373–82). Hillsdale, NJ: Erlbaum.

Mandler, J. (1983). Representation. In P. Mussen (series ed.), J. Flavell, & E. Markman (eds.), *Handbook of child psychology: Vol. 3, Cognitive development*, 4th ed. (pp. 420–94). New York: Wiley.

Maratsos, M. (1989). Innateness and plasticity in language acquisition. In M. Rice & R. Schiefelbusch (eds.), The teachability of language (pp. 121–52). Hillsdale, NJ: Erlbaum.

McArthur, D. & Adamson, L. (1996). Joint attention in preverbal children: Autism and developmental language disorders. *Journal of Autism and Developmental Disorders* 26, 481–96.

McClelland, J. & Rummelhart, D. (1986). *Parallel distributed processing*, Vol. 2. Cambridge, MA: Bradford.

McDuffie, A., Yoder, P., & Stone, W. (2005). Prelinguistic predictors of vocabulary in young children with autism spectrum disorders. *Journal of Speech and Hearing Research* 48, 1080–97.

Meline, K. (2006). *Research in communication sciences and disorders*. Upper Saddle River, NJ: Prentice Hall.

Muma, J. (1978). *Language handbook*. Englewood Cliffs, NJ: Prentice Hall.

Muma, J. (1981). *Language primer*. Lubbock, TX: Natural Child.

Muma, J. (1986). *Language acquisition: A functionalistic perspective*. Austin, TX: Pro-Ed.

Muma, J. (1998). *Effective speech-language pathology: A cognitive socialization approach*. Mahwah, NJ: Erlbaum.

Muma, J. & Cloud, S. (2008). *Advancing communication disorders: 60 basic issues*. Hattiesburg, MS: Natural Child Publisher.

Muma, J. & Teller, H. (2003). *Proactive deaf education: Cognitive socialization*. Hillsboro, OR: Butte Publications.

National Research Council. (2001). *Educating children with autism*. Washington, DC: National Academy Press.

Nelson, K. (1974). Concept, word, and sentence: Interrelations in acquisition and development. *Psychological Review* 81, 267–85.

Nelson, K. (1985). *Making sense: The acquisition of shared meaning*. New York: Academic Press.

Nelson, K. (1986). *Event knowledge: Structure and function in development*. Hillsdale, NJ: Erlbaum.

Nelson, K. (1996). *Language in cognitive development*. New York: Cambridge University.

Nicholich, L. (1975). *A longitudinal study of representational play in relation to spontaneous imitation and development of multiword utterances*. (Final Report). Washington, DC: National Institute of Education.

Ninio, A., Snow, C., Pan, B., & Rollins, P. (1994). Classifying communicative acts in children's interactions. *Journal of Communicative Disorders* 27, 157–87.

Osgood, C. (1957). *Motivational dynamics of language behavior. Nebraska Symposium on Motivation*. Lincoln, NB: University of Nebraska Press.

Perera, K. (1994). Editorial: Child language research: Building on the past, looking to the future. *Journal of Child Language* 21, 1–7.

Pericak-Vance, M. (2003). The genetics of autistic disorder. In R. Plomin, C. DeFries, I. Craig, & P. McGuffin (eds.), *Behavioral genetics in the postgenomic era* (pp. 267–88). Washington, DC: APA Books.

Pinborough-Zimmerman, J., Satterfield, R., Miller, J., Hossain, S., & McMahon, W. (2007). Communication disorders: Prevalence and comorbid intellectual disability, autism, and emotional/behavioral disorders. *American Journal of Speech-Language Disorders* 16, 359–67.

Pinker, S. (1984). *Language learnability and language development*. Cambridge, MA: Harvard University Press.

Pinker, S. (1987). The bootstrapping problem in language acquisition. In B. MacWhinney (ed.), *Mechanisms of language acquisition*. Hillsdale, NJ: Erlbaum.

Pinker, S. (1988). Learnability theory and the acquisition of a first language. In F. Kessel (ed.), *The development of language and language researchers* (pp. 97–120). Hillsdale, NJ: Erlbaum.

Pinker, S. (1989). *Learnability and cognition*. Cambridge, MA: MIT Press.

Prizant, B. M. (1983). Language acquisition and communicative behavior in autism: Toward an understanding of the "whole" of it. *Journal of Speech and Hearing Disorders* 48, 296–307.

Prizant, B. (1999). Contemporary issues in intervention for autism spectrum disorders: A commentary. *Journal of the Association for Persons with Severe Handicaps* 24, 199–208.

Prizant, B. & Wetherby, A. (1998). Communication and language assessment for young children. *Infants and Young Children* 5, 20–34.

Ragozin, A. S. (1980). Attachment behavior of day-care children – naturalistic and laboratory observations. *Child Development* 51, 409–15.

Rees, N. & Snope, J. (1983). National conference on undergraduate, graduate, and continuing education. *ASHA* 25, 49–59.

Rogoff, B. (1990). *Apprenticeship in thinking: Cognitive development in social context*. New York: Oxford University Press.

Searle, J. (1992). *The rediscovery of the mind*. Cambridge, MA: MIT Press.

Skinner, B. (1957). *Verbal behavior*. New York: Appleton-Century-Crofts.

Sperber, D. & Wilson, D. (1986). *Relevance: Communication and cognition*. Cambridge, MA: Harvard University Press.

Stalnaker, R. (1972). Pragmatics. In D. Davidson & G. Harman (eds.), *Semantics of natural language*, 2nd ed. Boston, MA: Reidel.

Sugarman, S. (1984). The development of preverbal communication. In R. Schiefelbusch & J. Pickar (eds.), The acquisition of communicative competence (pp. 23–67). Baltimore, MD: University Park Press.

Tunkis, G. (1963). Linguistic theory in the transformational approach. *Lingua* 16, 384–96.

Ventor, A., Lord, C., & Schopler, E. (1992). AQ follow-up study of high functioning autistic children. *Journal of Child Psychology and Psychiatry* 33, 489–507.

Vygotsky, L. (1962). *Thought and language*. Cambridge, MA: MIT Press.

Wetherby, A., Prizant, B., & Hutchinson, T. A. (1998). Communicative, social/affective, and symbolic profiles of young children with autism and pervasive developmental disorders. *American Journal of Speech-Language Pathology* 7, 79–91.

Wetherby, A. & Prutting, C. (1984). Profiles of communicative and cognitive-social abilities in autistic children. *Journal of Speech and Hearing Research* 27, 364–77.

Woods, J. & Wetherby, A. (2003). Early identification of and intervention for infants and toddlers who are at risk for autism spectrum disorder. *Language, Speech, and Hearing Services in Schools* 34, 180–93.

Yoder, P. & Stone, W. (2006). A randomized comparison of the effect of two prelinguistic communication interventions on the acquisition of spoken communication in preschoolers with ASD. *Journal of Speech, Language, and Hearing Research* 49, 698–711.

Yoder, P. & Warren, S. (2002). Effects of prelinguistic milieu teaching and parent responsivity education on dyads involving children with intellectual disabilities. *Journal of Speech, Language, and Hearing Research* 45, 1158–74.

8 Delayed Language Development in Preschool Children

DEBORAH WEISS AND RHEA PAUL

1 Introduction

Delays in the acquisition of language are the most common presenting problem in preschool children referred for clinical evaluations (Drillion & Drummond, 1983). Rescorla (1989) found that 15 percent of middle-class 2-year-olds failed to achieve expected language milestones, and the rates of delay were even higher in children from less privileged backgrounds. Rates of language delay at school age, on the other hand, are reported to be 7–8 percent (Nippold, 2004). This fact, in conjunction with longitudinal studies of preschoolers who present with language delays (Paul, 1996; Rescorla, 2002, 2005; Whitehurst & Fischel, 1994), suggests that the many preschoolers with delayed language development move within the normal range in terms of their oral language skills by the time they reach school age, although they may retain subtle deficits in higher-level language and literacy skills (Snowling et al., 2001; Snowling & Bishop, 2000; Weismer & Evans, 2002). For these reasons, many researchers and clinicians (e.g., Paul, 2000; Rescorla & Lee, 2001; Whitehurst & Fischel, 1994) argue that the label "language impaired" or "specific language impairment" should be reserved for children who retain significant deficits in language acquisition after the age of 4, at which age research suggests deficits are more likely to be chronic (Bishop & Edmunson, 1987; see also Chapter 9, this volume).

This chapter will describe the language development and departures from typical acquisition in preschool children who show delays in their language learning. Although the term "specific language impairment" (SLI) is the label that is now generally accepted for referring to children with language deficits not associated with any other disability, the present chapter will reserve this term to refer to children beyond preschool age who demonstrate significant, chronic deficits in their production, use, and understanding of language. To describe the population of preschool children with slower-than-normal growth of speech and language skills in the absence of other identified disabilities, we will employ the term "delayed language development" (DLD) in order to suggest a distinction between this possibly transient condition and the more chronic, established deficits that characterize SLI in school-aged children.

For both preschoolers with DLD and school-aged children who retain SLI, a basic condition of the diagnostic label is its definition by exclusion (Benton, 1959). That is, both children with DLD and those with SLI evidence problems with language that cannot be explained by intellectual disability, hearing impairment, autism, emotional disturbance, neglect, or neurological damage. Their difficulty in the ability to produce and understand language appears relatively isolated, with other aspects of development proceeding in a more-or-less typical fashion. This chapter presents a discussion of current research findings on the linguistic characteristics of children with DLD under the age of 5. Assessment and intervention with this population, as well as indicators of prognosis will be addressed. Unless otherwise noted, this discussion focuses on monolingual English speakers.

2   Linguistic Characteristics of Children with DLD

Children with DLD exhibit communication patterns that are similar to those of children at comparable levels of language development, as indexed by MLU (mean length of utterance). However, although their language development is more accurately described as delayed than deviant, it is often asynchronous; that is, some developmental features may be more delayed than others (Leonard, 1991). Although discussion of cognitive, psychological, perceptual, and social issues related to this population is beyond the scope of this chapter, these are important correlates of language development and should be considered in assessment and treatment. For our purposes in this chapter, we will describe what is known about the language of children who present with circumscribed delays in communication development during the preschool period.

2.1   *Speech sounds*

Many preschoolers are referred to a speech-language pathologist (SLP) primarily because their speech contains frequent articulation errors or because they are hard to understand. Yet these children often demonstrate difficulties in the areas of syntax, morphology and semantics, as well (Paul & Shriberg, 1982; Ruscello, St. Louis, & Mason, 1991; Shriberg & Kwiatkowski, 1994). Shriberg and Austin (1998) reported a co-occurrence rate of speech and language delay of approximately 40 percent in the preschool years. In some cases, it may be difficult to distinguish speech from language problems. Children who demonstrate inaccurate sound production may have difficulty producing some morphological inflections that are marked by sounds that are difficult for them to pronounce, such as /s/. In any case, it is advisable for children with suspected speech problems to have a complete language assessment as well.

Paul and Jennings (1992) found that children with DLD acquire consonants and syllable shapes in the same order as typically developing children, but at a slower rate. Although sound acquisition and phonological simplification processes in children with DLD are similar to those of peers, consonant sound repertoire is smaller, and children with DLD take longer to acquire CVC syllables and multisyllabic productions (Paul & Jennings, 1992; Rescorla & Ratner, 1996; Roberts et al., 1998). Although children with DLD and those with typical development (TD) show similar patterns in changing sounds (Leonard, 1997), there is a greater frequency of deletion of word-initial weak syllables, (e.g., *'cation* for *vacation*) and prevocalic voicing, (*doe* for *toe*) in DLD. Unusual errors, such as substitution of liquids for glides, (/l/ for /w/), which are not seen in typical development, may also appear (Leonard & Leonard, 1985).

There is a close relationship between the development of sounds and words. Young children who produce few sounds also tend to produce few words (Stoel-Gammon, 2002). Children with DLD acquire words more readily when the words begin with consonants that they are already producing correctly in other words (Leonard et al., 1982), a pattern that is seen in typically developing toddlers, as well (Schwartz & Leonard, 1982).

2.2   Word meaning

Use of early semantic relations in young children with DLD appears to be similar to that of language-matched peers (Leonard, 1989). Early lexical development in children with DLD has a slower pace, however. Average age for use of first word in DLD is 23 months, compared to 12 months in children with TD (Trauner et al., 1995). Children with DLD have an expressive vocabulary of about 20 words by the age of 2 years, compared to more than 300 words among typically developing peers (Paul, 1996; Rescorla & Alley, 2001; Rescorla, Mirak, & Singh, 2000; Rescorla, Roberts & Dahlsgaard, 1997). They also talk and communicate less often (Rescorla & Lee, 2001). By age 3 to 4, there is typically some resolution of the vocabulary deficit (Paul, 1996; Rescorla, Mirak, & Singh, 2000); however, children with DLD have been found, in quick, incidental learning tasks, to be less able than peers with TD to learn new words rapidly or completely (Alt, Plante, & Creusere, 2004; Dollaghan, 1987; Kiernan & Gray, 1998; Rice, Buhr, & Oetting, 1992; Weismer & Evans, 2002). Overall, children with DLD require more repetitions to comprehend a new word and more opportunities to use a word before adding it to their productive lexicon (Gray, 2003). Children with DLD may also demonstrate what appear to be word-finding difficulties, but this may result from the fact that the children simply do not have the words in their repertoire. Regardless of its source, this difficulty is sometimes accompanied by the use of vague words, such as "thingie" and "stuff," as well as dysfluencies, characterized by hesitations, fillers, pauses, and repetitions (Hedge & Maul, 2006). Nelson (1998) reported a persistence of under-extension and over-extension in word use beyond the typical age of 3 years in children with DLD.

Children with DLD typically learn words in similar order to that seen in TD (Hedge & Maul, 2006), but they have greater difficulty acquiring verbs with specific meanings, such as *build* and *dig*, as opposed to *make* (Olswang, Rodriguez, &

Timler; 1998). Two-word combinations appear at around 36 months in DLD, compared to 18 to 24 months in TD (Trauner et al., 1995). Typically developing children also learn quickly to extend the variety of two-word utterances to include combinations indicating *possession* as in, "My baby," *disappearance*, "Baby gone," and *rejection*, "No baby," whereas children with DLD retain the exclusive noun + verb combination for a longer period of time (Hedge & Maul, 2006).

2.3 Syntax

Children with DLD appear to acquire syntactic rules in the same order as typical children do, but it takes them a longer time (Rescorla & Lee, 2001; Rescorla & Roberts, 2002). The first noticeable delay in syntax acquisition is evident with the failure to combine words spontaneously at 18 to 24 months (Paul, 1996; Rescorla, Roberts, & Dahlsgaard, 1997; Rescorla, Mirak, & Singh, 2000; Rescorla & Roberts, 2002). This lag in syntactic development continues, according to follow-up studies (Rescorla, Mirak, & Singh, 2000; Rescorla & Mirren, 1998), although approximately half the children with slow expressive language development as toddlers show syntactic skills within the normal range by 4 years of age (Paul, 1993). Children with DLD demonstrate a higher rate of ungrammatical sentences and make more errors for longer periods of time (Rescorla & Lee, 2001; Rescorla & Roberts, 2002). Sentences tend to be shorter and less varied and complex, limiting the communication repertoire. There is difficulty producing a variety of sentence types, such as passive sentences and questions, as well as a tendency to omit function words such as the determiners *a* and *the*, or the conjunction *and* (Hedge & Maul, 2006). Hadley and Short (2005) reported that children who fail to develop a diverse verb lexicon or to produce frequent and diverse simple sentences by age 3 are at risk for long-term delay.

2.4 Morphology

Morpheme acquisition, including regular and irregular plurals and their allomorphic variations, possessive *'s*, regular and irregular tense inflections, present progressive *–ing*, auxiliary forms, third-person singular forms, and copula *be* verbs, is particularly difficult for children with DLD (Leonard, 1997). Even when compared to younger children at the same language level, children with DLD have difficulty with morphemes that complicate the phonological structure of the output word, such as plural *s* that turns *cat* into a word with a final cluster, *cats* (Cleave & Rice, 1997; Leonard, 1989). Morphological deficiency is considered to be a likely clinical marker of SLI at school age (Leonard, Miller, & Gerber, 1999), and failure to demonstrate the onset of tense marking by 3 years of age has been proposed as a danger signal for chronic delay in preschoolers, as well (Hadley & Short, 2005). Possible causes of these deficiencies include specific grammatical disability (Gopnik & Crago, 1991; Rice & Wexler, 1996), deficits in phonological and working memory (Gathercole & Baddeley, 1990), particular aspects of auditory processing (Tallal et al., 1996), or more general processing difficulties (Bishop, 1997; Leonard, 1997) (see also Chapter 9, this volume).

2.5   *Pragmatics*

2.5.1   Conversation   There is a general consensus that conversational deficits in children with DLD are in the mild range, that pragmatic skills are generally better than skills in language form and that they are secondary to the primary difficulties in morphosyntax (Rice, Warren, & Betz, 2005), a characteristic that differentiates this population from children with autism spectrum disorders (Caparulo & Cohen, 1983). However, Paul and Shiffer (1991), Pharr, Ratner, and Rescorla (2000), and Rescorla and Mirren (1998) showed that late-talking toddlers generally demonstrate lower rates of communication, vocalization, initiation, and joint attention, even non-verbally, than their typical peers. Further, Marton, Abramoff, and Rosenzweig (2005) reported significant deficits in social knowledge, and, in a review of studies of pragmatic language skills, Leonard (1997) found many contradictions in the areas that have been researched.

Some studies have demonstrated age-appropriate skills in turn taking, conversation initiation, requesting clarification, and providing revisions among children with DLD and SLI (Craig & Evans, 1993; Fey & Leonard, 1984; Gallagher & Darnton, 1978; Griffin, 1979; Van Kleeck & Frankel, 1981). Other studies, however, have reported conversational deficits, indicating reluctance or difficulty in the initiation of conversations and the use of such devices as shouting or interrupting in order to gain attention prior to beginning a conversation (Fey, 1986; Lucas, 1980; Paul, 1991).

Rescorla and Lee (2001) found level of interaction to be similar to that of younger language-matched children, although children with DLD were less interactive than age-matched peers. Paul and Shiffer (1991) also found fewer joint attention interactions with caregivers. There is also a preference for initiating conversations with language-matched children (Fey, Leonard, & Wilcox, 1981) or adults (Rice, Sell, & Hadley, 1991) rather than with age-matched peers, the opposite of the tendency seen in typically developing children, as well as a tendency not to respond reliably when peers initiate interactions (Hadley & Rice, 1991). Peer-group conversational interactions are also difficult for children with DLD (Brinton et al., 1997; Craig, 1993). Another area of deficit for some of these children is the appropriate use of prosody (Wells & Peppé, 2003).

Hedge and Maul (2006) point out that the contradictions in the literature on pragmatics in DLD may be due to methodological differences between the various studies. They suggest that since there is some question about the degree to which pragmatic deficits exist in children with DLD, each child should receive an assessment of pragmatic abilities as part of the clinical or educational evaluation.

2.5.2   Narratives   There are some significant differences in the narratives of children with DLD when compared to those of same-age peers. Some of these differences include a lack of maturity, based on Applebee's (1978) narrative stages, and a reduced quantity of information included (Paul, 1996; Paul & Smith, 1993).

These findings are not surprising, given the limited vocabulary and difficulty with syntax and morphology demonstrated by these children. Narratives are more difficult to produce than dialogue, in which some of the burden is shared by the conversational partner. Competency in the narrative form is an important component of academic success, however, because early signs of difficulty with narratives have been shown to predict later academic performance (Bishop & Edmundson, 1987; Feagans & Applebaum, 1986).

3   Screening and Assessment of Language in Children with DLD

Some children with DLD will be identified some time after their second birthday. Adults may be concerned that the child does not seem to hear or has failed to start talking or to move past single words. Others may be identified at age 3–4 because their speech is hard to understand or because the child is not producing age-appropriate sentences. We will examine the assessment process separately for each of these two typical points of referral, the first in the emerging language phase, and the second in the developing language period. We will also distinguish between two aspects of evaluation: *screening*, which can be used by pediatricians or preschool teachers to determine which children are at risk for disorder, and *assessment*, in which more in-depth testing and behavioral observation are used to describe the range of the child's communication difficulties.

3.1   Emerging language stage

3.1.1   Screening   A first step in the assessment process is often the completion of a screening in order to make a general determination about whether further evaluation for a communication disorder is needed. Because vocabulary delay is often the first sign of DLD in toddlers, parent report measures that focus primarily on vocabulary size have been developed. The MacArthur–Bates Communicative Development Inventories (CDIs) (Fenson et al., 2006) has been shown in a variety of studies to be effective in identifying toddlers with low-language skills (e.g., Girolametto et al., 2001; Heilmann et al., 2005; Lyytinen, Eklund, & Lyytinen, 2003; Weismer & Evans, 2002) and to be valid for both English- and Spanish-speaking toddlers (Marchman & Martinez-Sussman, 2002), as has the Language Development Survey (LDS; Rescorla, 1989) (Klee, Pearce, & Carson, 2000; Rescorla & Achenbach, 2002; Rescorla & Alley, 2001).

3.1.2   Assessment   An otherwise typically developing child of 18 to 36 months who fails to begin talking, who talks very little, or who fails a language screening may be evidencing delay; however, many of these very young children will spontaneously "catch up" with their peers. Whitehurst and Fischel (1994) and Paul (1996, 1997) propose that highest priority for intervention be given to young children with slow language development who also present with an accumulation of risk factors, including cognitive deficits, hearing impairments or chronic middle ear disease, social or pre-verbal communicative problems, dysfunctional families, risks associated with their birth histories, or family history of language and reading problems (Bishop et al., 2003; Lyytinen et al., 2001). For this reason, an in-depth assessment makes sense for toddlers with DLD in order to evaluate their level of risk for chronic delay. Paul (2007) suggests the following areas for assessment in children with DLD at this phase.

3.1.2.1 Play and gesture assessment   Gestures are highly related to language in early development in children with TD (Bates & Dick, 2002; Goldin-Meadow & Butcher, 2003) and DLD (Capone & McGregor, 2004). Play assessment provides a non-linguistic comparison against which to gauge a child's linguistic performance and adds insight into aspects of the child's conceptual and imaginative abilities. This can help to determine the activities, materials, and contexts that will be most appropriate to encourage learning and conceptual referent. Play is also is the most natural context for language learning. Knowing the level of play behavior that the child is able to use can help the clinician structure play sessions that will maximize the child's participation and opportunities for learning.

Although there is a long history of debate about the relationship between language and cognitive skills (Johnston, 1994; Johnston & Schery, 1976), and there is a close relationship between language and cognitive development in TD (Goodwyn, Acredolo, & Brown, 2000), this relationship is more complicated for children with language delays (Krassowski & Plante, 1997; Rice, Warren, & Betz, 2005). For this reason, current practice guidelines advocate using play and gesture assessment only in the ways discussed above and not as a way of determining "prerequisite" skills for eligibility for language intervention (ASHA, 2007).

A variety of methods is available for assessing level of play skills in children at the 18- to 36-month developmental level, including the Communication and Symbolic Behavior Scales-Developmental Profile (CSBS-DP; Wetherby & Prizant, 2003) which has been shown to be reliable and valid for identifying children with developmental delays in the emerging language period (Wetherby et al., 2002). Another tool is Carpenter's Play Scale (Carpenter, 1987), which is designed to assess symbolic behavior in non-verbal children, and is appropriate both for non-speaking toddlers and for older children in the emerging-language stage. McCune (1995) and Casby (2003) provide methods of analyzing play behavior using standard sets of toys. Using hierarchical criteria, the child's current and emerging levels of symbolic behavior can be determined by comparing skills observed to the sequence of typical development.

3.1.2.2 Pre-verbal communication   It is important to determine whether children with little speech are exhibiting other forms of communication. Some options to assess communication include parent report instruments such the MacArthur–Bates Communicative Development Inventories (CDIs) (Fenson et al., 2006) or the Vineland Adaptive Behavior Scales-2 (Sparrow, Cicchetti, & Balla, 2006). Direct observational measures include The Communication and Symbolic Behavior Scales-Developmental Profile (Wetherby & Prizant, 2003), which provides normative data for the 8- to 24-month developmental range and can be used with children as old as 6 years. It is valid with children from culturally different backgrounds, as well (Roberts et al., 1997).

Additional assessments include the Preschool Functional Communication Inventory (Olswang, 1996), Interdisciplinary Clinical Assessment of Young Children with Developmental Disabilities (Guralnick, 2000), Alternative Approaches to Assessing Young Children (Losardo & Notari-Syverson, 2001), and the Assessment, Evaluation, and Programming System for Infants and Children (Bricker, Capt, & Pretti-Frontczak, 2002). These provide dynamic, criterion-referenced procedures that use developmentally appropriate approaches and provide measures of pre-verbal expression of communicative intention.

Communication assessment can also be accomplished through the use of informal methods that examine communicative functioning in several domains independently. This strategy, advocated by Crais and Roberts (1991) and Paul (2007), integrates assessment and intervention activities from which a communication profile is derived and allows more direct, less formal clinician/child interaction as well as ultimately more detailed intervention planning in areas such as non-verbal communication, expressive language, receptive language, and phonology. Paul (2005) provided a worksheet for recording observations on the frequency, form, and functional range of early communication intentions observed during an unstructured play interaction. This appears in Table 8.1.

3.1.2.3 Comprehension   Deficits in understanding language predict a poorer prognosis for children with DLD. In addition, parents often overestimate children's comprehension skills (Coggins, 1998; Miller & Paul, 1995; Paul, 2000), so the direct assessment of comprehension is necessary.

Parent checklists designed to assess receptive vocabulary, such as the *CDI*, are less reliable than those assessing expressive skills at the emerging language level (Dale, 1991; Thal et al., 1999), although they can give some impression of receptive language performance. The Communication and Social Behavioral Scales-DP (Wetherby & Prizant, 2003) provides a scale for assessing single-word vocabulary that shows good predictive validity in children under 24 months of age (Wetherby et al., 2002). The Peabody Picture Vocabulary Test – Revised (PPVT-IV) (Dunn & Dunn, 2006) is a standardized test that can be effective for assessing receptive vocabulary for children functioning over the age of 24 months who can respond to a standard picture pointing task. General scales, such as the Receptive-Expressive Emergent Language Scale (3rd edition, Bzoch, League, & Brown, 2003) and the Sequenced Inventory of Communicative Development (Hedrick, Prather, & Tobin, 1995) look at a range of responses to both verbal and non-verbal auditory stimuli. Although these are useful for assessing listening skills, it is often helpful to have more specific information about how children process word combinations and sentences. Miller and Paul (1995) provide a broad range of comprehension assessment activities for accomplishing this task.

Table 8.1 Worksheet for recording observation of pre-verbal communicative behavior in an unstructured play sample

Means of communication	Function of communication								
	Request objects	Request actions	Protest	Comment/ joint attention	Show/ share	Respond to name	Respond to question	Request information
Gaze to person								
3-point gaze*								
Conventional gesture								
Unconventional gesture								
Typical vocalization								
Unusual vocalization								
Echo								
Spontaneous speech								

*child looks at object, at person, then back at object; or at person, at object, then back at person.
Based on Paul (2005).

3.1.2.4 Expressive vocabulary We have already mentioned several parent report forms that can be used to assess expressive vocabulary size. The CSBS-DP also includes a word scale that provides norm-referenced information for comparing a child's frequency of spontaneous production of words in a semi-structured play setting with that of typically developing children up to 24 months of age.

3.1.2.5 Phonological skills Due to the strong relationship between lexical and phonetic inventories and the high co-morbidity of speech problems with language delays, assessing phonological production in children with emerging language is useful as both a prognostic indicator and as an aid in choosing words to be included in the child's first lexicon. As Schwartz and Leonard (1982) have shown, children are more likely to add words to their productive lexicons if the words contain consonants already in their phonetic repertoire.

A first step in phonological assessment can involve the compilation of a consonant inventory (Shriberg & Kwiatkowski, 1980). While listening to a live or recorded vocalization sample, each consonant used at least once in the sample is transcribed. This inventory can be used to select words for therapy that begin with the inventoried consonants or as an index of severity of phonological delay. The CSBS-DP also provides a norm-referenced scale for comparing the range of speech sounds produced by a child with DLD in a semi-structured play setting with that of typically developing children up to 24 months of age (for a more in-depth discussion of phonological and articulation impairments, see Chapter 15, this volume).

3.1.2.6 Parent/caregiver–child interaction and the assessment process Research has indicated that parental input is generally well matched to the language level of children with SLI (Leonard, 1989) and DLD (Paul & Elwood, 1991), although there are some subtle differences in input to children with DLD compared with input to typically developing children (Vigil, Hodges, & Klee, 2005). Some of the language behaviors that have been found to be different between parent/caregiver–child interactions with children with DLD include use of more directive language (commands), more frequent use of recast sentences in response to children's initiations, and faster speed of response, which can discourage a child from coming up with his or her own responses. Instruments such as The Infant-Toddler Family Assessment Instrument (Apfel & Provence, 2001) are helpful in assessing parent/caregiver communication.

Although a causal connection between these behaviors and language delay has not been established, they can serve as maintaining factors, and the child can benefit from their modification. This should be done, however, in a manner that avoids any appearance of blaming the parent for the child's communication problem. It is also important to be sensitive to cultural differences in communication styles. Parents from all cultures do not talk to toddlers in the same manner as middle-class contemporary American parents (Garrett, 2002; Rodriques & Olswang, 2003; Westby, 1998). A large number of studies (summarized by Law, Garrett, & Nye, 2004) have shown that parents can be trained to modify their language input to children with DLD and that this has positive effects on development.

Table 8.2   Risk of long-term delay in toddlers at 30–35 months

Speech risks	Language risks	Non-language risks
Limited pre-linguistic vocalizations and babbling as infant	Small vocabulary; few verbs	Lack of symbolic play
Limited phonetic inventory	Six-month delay in language comprehension	Play is mostly grouping or exploring
Limited syllable structures	Large comprehension-production gap	Few gestures used to communicate
Greater consistency in sound errors	Few spontaneous verbal imitations	Reduced rate of communication
Fewer than 50% consonants correct	Reliance on direct modeling and prompting in imitation	Few conversational initiations
Atypical errors	Changes in the number of unique syntactic types when MLU is between 1.0 and 2.0 (Hadley, 1999)	Behavior problems

Adapted from Olswang, Rodriguez, and Timler (1998) and Williams and Elbert (2003).

When a toddler with slow language development shows significant risk factors, intervention is clearly warranted in order to minimize the effects of these factors on the language acquisition. Olswang, Rodriguez, and Timler (1998) provided guidelines for using these assessment data to make decisions about which toddlers demonstrate such risks. These appear in Table 8.2.

3.2   Developing language stage

3.2.1   Screening   Many standardized instruments are commercially available for screening purposes with preschool populations. A sampling of these is presented in Table 8.3. Less formal measures, such as checklists and questionnaires, can also be used for this purpose. Examples include the General Language Screen (Stott et al., 2002), a parent report screening measure for 3-year-olds that has been shown in British studies to demonstrate high reliability, validity, and reasonable accuracy; and Restrepo's (1998) parent questionnaire. Typical questions from these measures might include: *For his/her age, is your child hard to understand? For his/her age, does your child have trouble pronouncing words? Does your child make mistakes in sentences when speaking more than just a little? Is it difficult for your child to tell you what s/he did during the day? Does your child enjoy listening to simple stories?*

Table 8.3 A sample of language screening tools at the developing language level

Test (name, author[s], date, publisher)	Age range	Areas assessed
Bankson Language Screening Test – 2nd edition. Bankson, N. W. (1977). Baltimore, MD: University Park Press	4–7 yr	Receptive and expressive: semantics, morphology; syntax; auditory and visual perception
Denver II Frankenburg, W. K., et al. (1990). Denver, CO: Denver Developmental Materials	2 wk–6 yr	Language, expressive-receptive vocabulary, concepts, personal-social, fine and gross motor
Early Screening Profiles (ESP) Harrison, P., Kaufman, A., Kaufman, N., Bruininks, R., Rynders, J., Ilmers, S., Sparrow, S., & Cicchetti D. (1990). Circle Pines, MN: American Guidance Service	2–6;11 yr	Profiles cognitive, language, self-help and social, motor; surveys articulation, home health behavior
Fluharty Preschool Speech and Language Screening Test – 2nd edition. Fluharty, N. B. (2000). Circle Pines, MN: AGS Publishing	3–6;11 yr	Articulation, receptive and expressive language, composite language
Joliet 3-Minute Speech and Language Screen (Revised) Kinzler, M. C., & Johnson, C. C. (1993). San Antonio, TX: Harcourt Assessment	K, 2nd, and 5th grades	Expressive syntax, receptive vocabulary, articulation, voice and fluency
Kindergarten Language Screening Test – 2nd edition (KLST-2) Gauthier, S., & Madison, C. (1998). Austin, TX: Pro-Ed	3;6–6;11 yr	School readiness

Adapted from Paul (2007).

3.2.2   Assessment

3.2.2.1   Standardized tests   There is a large number of standardized tests available for this age group. Although results of standardized testing with older preschool children are more easily obtained and reliable than in the emerging language phase, it is important not to rely strictly on standardized tests in order to assess children with possible DLD. As with younger children, parent/caregiver–child interactions should be considered. In addition, the assessment of language use and understanding in naturalistic contexts, such as play and conversation, are also important pieces of information. Some examples of standardized tests that can be used at the developing language level appear in Table 8.4.

3.2.2.2   Phonology assessment   Due to the high co-morbidity of speech problems and DLD, phonological assessment should be a consideration with this population. A sense of general intelligibility can be ascertained simply by talking with the child for 5 to 10 minutes (Paul, 2007). Morris, Wilcox and Schooling (1995) suggest using the Preschool Speech Intelligibility Measure, in which children repeat a list of words that are recorded and subsequently judged by listeners. If the sample is judged to be difficult to understand, an articulation test or test of phonological disorder can be used to follow up. As described for children in the emerging language stage, a phonetic inventory can be completed in order to judge severity and plan therapy.

3.2.2.3   Syntax and morphology   Given the difficulty that many children with DLD have with syntax and morphology, these areas should be assessed very carefully, taking into account those morphemes known to be problematic. Within this age group, children's use of complex sentences and verb-tense grammatical markings will be especially relevant. Testing should be done for expressive and receptive modalities. Paul (2007) suggests beginning receptive testing with a standardized test of receptive syntax and morphology, followed by criterion-referenced measures to further explore weak areas exposed through standardized testing. Children who perform poorly on the criterion-referenced measures should be tested using a more contextualized format.

Language-sample analysis, which is especially well suited for the assessment of expressive syntax and morphology, provides important information about spontaneous language production, once it has been established that there is a language delay. There are numerous analyses that can be completed by utilizing the language sample, including mean length of utterance (MLU) (Brown, 1973), Developmental Sentence Analysis (Lee, 1974), the Index of Productive Syntax (Scarborough, 1990), and Miller's (1981) Assigning Structural Stage Procedure.

3.2.2.4   Vocabulary assessment   Paul (2007) recommends focusing on lexical comprehension during assessment, and on production during treatment. This follows a strategy recommended by Lahey (1988), which is based upon the knowledge that in the developing language stage, children's understanding of individual words may not include full comprehension by adult standards, and children may

Table 8.4 Examples of standardized tests for assessment at the developing language level

Test	Age range	Areas assessed
Batelle Developmental Inventory – 2nd edition Newborg, J., Stock, J. R., & Wnek, L. (2004). Chicago, IL: Riverside Publishing	Birth–8 yr	Speech and language, social/ emotional, cognitive, motoric skills, learning, and hearing
Boehm 3 – Preschool Boehm, A. E. (2001). San Antonio, TX: Harcourt Assessment	3–5;11 yr	Receptive concepts: space, time, quantity
Clinical Evaluation of Language Fundamentals – Preschool, 2nd ed. (CELF-Preschool) Wiig, E. H., Secord, W., & Semel, E. (2004). San Antonio, TX: Harcourt Assessment	3–6 yr	Concepts, syntax, semantics, morphology
Expressive One-Word Picture Vocabulary Test – 2000 edition Brownell, R., (ed.) (2000). Novato, CA: Academic Therapy	2–18 yr	Expressive vocabulary
Expressive Vocabulary Test Williams, K. T. (1997). Circle Pines, MN: AGS	2;6–adult	Naming, synonyms
Peabody Picture Vocabulary Test – 4th edition (PPVT-4) Dunn, L., & Dunn, L. (2006). Circle Pines, MN: American Guidance Service	2;6 yr–adult	Receptive vocabulary
Preschool Language Scale – 4 (PLS-4) Zimmerman, I. L., Steiner, V., & Pond, R. (2002). San Antonio, TX: Harcourt Assessment	Birth–6;11 yr	Language precursors; expressive and receptive semantics, syntax, morphology, integrative thinking, auditory comprehension

Table 8.4 (Cont'd)

Test	Age range	Areas assessed
Sequenced Inventory of Communication Development – Revised (SICD-R) Hedrick, D. L., Prather, E. M., & Tobin, A. R. (1984). Seattle, WA: University of Washington Press	4 mo–4 yr	Receptive language (speech and sound awareness and understanding); expressive language (imitating, initiating, responding)
Structured Photographic Expressive Language Test 3 (SPELT-3) Dawson, J., Eyer, J., & Stout, C. (2003). DeKalb, IL: Janelle Publications	4–9;11 yr	Syntax and morphology
Test for Auditory Comprehension of Language (TACL03) Carrow-Woolfolk, E. (1999). Austin, TX: Pro-Ed	3–9;11 yr	Receptive language: word classes and relations, grammatical morphemes, elaborated sentence constructions
Test of Early Language Development – 3rd edition (TELD-3) Hresko, W. P., Redi, K., & Hammill, D. D. (1999). Austin, TX: Pro-Ed	2;7–11 yr	Receptive and expressive syntax and semantics
Test of Language Development – 3: Primary (TOLD-3:P) Newcomer, P. L., & Hammill, D. D. (1997). Austin, TX: Pro-Ed	4–8;11 yr	Receptive and expressive semantics and syntax
Test of Pragmatic Language (TOPL) Phelps-Terasaki, D., & Phelps-Gunn, T. (1992). Austin, TX: Pro-Ed	5–13;11 yr	Comprehensive assessment of student's abilities to use pragmatic language effectively

Adapted from Paul (2007).

produce a word even with limited knowledge of its meaning. A measure like the Peabody Picture Vocabulary Test – IV (Dunn & Dunn, 2006) can be used for this purpose. Criterion-referenced methods can then be used to look more closely at word classes that are important in the child's communicative environment. Although for most children with DLD expressive vocabulary is broadly within the normal range by age 3 or 4, deficits remain for some children, particularly in the areas of confrontation naming, word finding, and the development of abstract words. Because of this, particular attention should be paid to these areas when designing criterion-referenced measures.

3.2.2.5   Pragmatics assessment   This is one area in which standardized tests are less useful. It is tempting to neglect this area, especially given widespread conceptions that language form is the primary area of deficit, with relative sparing of pragmatic skills. But, as was discussed earlier, research suggests difficulties in initiating and maintaining conversations and a reduced level of interaction, especially with age-matched peers. It is important to observe children in a variety of settings in order to determine their level of comfort and success in varied interactions. Several checklists and observational schemes are available in the literature for structuring this assessment (Chapman, 1981; Craighead, 1984; Girolametto, 1997; Shipley & McAfee, 2004).

3.2.2.6   Literacy development   There is a strong relationship between oral language development and the acquisition of literacy (Snow, 1983, 1999), although, as we have discussed, some special kinds of language experiences are necessary to optimize readiness for reading (Snow, Burns & Griffin,1998). Children with both speech and language delays are at higher than usual risk for difficulties in learning to read (Bishop & Snowling, 2004; Rvachew et al., 2003; Snowling & Bishop, 2000). They have, however, been shown to benefit from explicit instruction in pre-literacy skills (Gillon, 2000). For this reason, children with speech and language delays should be considered candidates for this kind of training, especially when there is a family history of reading difficulties (Pennington et al., 1991).

4   Intervention for Children with DLD

4.1   Emerging language

Based on the results of the evaluation, toddlers with DLD who show a significant accumulation of risk factors may be deemed eligible for early intervention services. These services will generally focus on the following areas identified as affected by the assessment: the development of functional and symbolic play and gesture; the use of intentional communicative behavior; language comprehension; and production of sounds, words, and word combinations. Brief suggestions for procedures and contexts for intervention in each of these areas will be presented.

4.1.1 Developing play and gesture   For a child who is not yet demonstrating age-appropriate use of objects or symbolic play and gestures, it may be necessary to establish a more basic foundation in reciprocity and anticipatory sets (see Paul, 2007). For children who already show reciprocal behavior (such as turn taking in back-and-forth babbling games), functional and symbolic behaviors, such as early conventional and symbolic play and deictic gestures (pointing and showing), can be encouraged. The clinician can use a direct or consultative approach, modeling or showing a parent/caregiver how to model the early forms of conventional and symbolic play and giving the child opportunities to imitate them. Adding an accompaniment of simple language will also promote receptive language development. Scripts with familiar routines can then be utilized to facilitate more advanced play behaviors, such as pretending to give a doll a bath, feed it a meal, take it to the store, and so on. Deictic and representational gestures can be modeled in a similar way.

4.1.2 Intentional communicative behaviors   If a child demonstrates low rates of communication overall, and the overriding goal is to increase the frequency of any kind of intentionality, any form of behavior conveying intention should be accepted. If there is no clear sign of communication, Prizant (1991) suggests treating any behavior as communicative, and responding accordingly, thus shaping the behavior into communication.

One way to target increasing the frequency of intentional communication is through the use of *pre-linguistic milieu teaching* (PMT) (Warren & Yoder, 1998; Yoder & Warren, 1998). This method follows the basic principles of arranging the environment to elicit child communication, following the child's lead, embedding instruction in ongoing interaction, focusing on target behaviors, and using prompts and reinforcement to elicit and maintain communicative behaviors. An important component of this approach is to provide a lengthy amount of time, i.e. 15 seconds, for the client to respond. This method is especially effective with parents/caregivers who are already quite responsive to their children's communicative attempts. A good deal of research (summarized in Warren et al., 2006) supports the efficacy of this approach. Other methods for increasing frequency of communication include *prompt-free approaches* (Mirenda & Santogrossi, 1985), and the Picture-Exchange Communication System (Bondy & Frost, 1998).

If the range of intentional functions is limited, therapy should address eliciting both proto-imperative and proto-declarative functions. Warren and Yoder (1998) suggest establishing social routines, then having the adult withhold a turn and look expectantly at the child or provide a verbal prompt, such as "What do you want?" to encourage the child's production. To encourage proto-declaratives, novel events or objects can be introduced to the child to encourage comments or routines can be sabotaged with silly or unusual events. These kinds of activities can help children learn how to direct other people's attention to topics on which they are focused. Approaches such as PMT are often used to accomplish these goals.

For children who demonstrate frequent use of a range of proto-imperative and proto-declarative functions but use only gestures, the goal is to increase the maturity of the mode of communication by eliciting vocalizations, and then conventional words. Whitehurst et al. (1988) suggested withholding responses until the child produces some vocalization that contains consonants to help move the child in the direction of speech. Following this, closer approximations to the conventional word can be required. Approaches based on behaviorist principles for eliciting first words have also appeared in the literature (MacDonald & Carroll, 1992; Tsiouri & Greer, 2003).

4.1.3 Developing receptive language   Indirect language stimulation (ILS) is a form of structured input-based intervention that is especially appropriate for clients in the 18- to 36-month developmental range, providing opportunities for children to observe how language maps non-linguistic context onto words. In this approach, adults follow the child's lead by imitating the child's actions, sounds, and words and provide language that matches the child's actions and intentions. The child chooses the topic, activity, or material and the adult comments on the child's focus of interest. The techniques used in ILS are listed in Table 8.5. Adults are encouraged to provide super-normal levels of these facilitative stimuli. A large body of research (summarized by Girolametto & Weitzman, 2006) has shown this method to be effective in increasing language skill at this developmental level, whether it is delivered by clinicians or by trained parents, teachers or caregivers.

4.1.4 Increasing phonological skills   The primary goal of phonological intervention in the earliest stages of language development is enlargement of the child's consonant inventory and range of syllable shapes. For the child with fewer than 50 expressive vocabulary words, this can take place in the context of back-and-forth babbling games. Initially, the clinician imitates the child's vocalizations. After establishing a back-and-forth imitation pattern, a new consonant is introduced and produced for the child to imitate. Any new consonant which the child produces, even if it is not the one modeled by the clinician, should be rewarded. Kuhl and Meltzoff (1996) showed that this method was effective in expanding babbling in TD infants.

4.1.5 Developing a first lexicon   An important consideration for first lexicon vocabulary is choosing words that are functional and fulfill a broad range of communicative purposes (Owens, 2004). Children should be taught words that can be used to accomplish their social goals. MacDonald (1989) suggested that words be chosen that encode ideas and interests that children already have, identified through analysis of play behavior. If, for example, a child demonstrates driving cars during the play assessment, car would be a first word to consider.

Another consideration is the phonological shape and composition of the words to be taught. A choice of words with one-syllable CV or CVC shapes based on the child's consonant inventory would be appropriate. Later, as new sounds enter the inventory by means of phonological work, new words containing those sounds can be added.

Table 8.5   Techniques used in indirect language stimulation

ILS technique	Example
Self-talk	Child plays with a car; adult parallel plays and narrates own actions. "I'm driving; I'm driving the car!"
Parallel talk	Child plays with a car; adult parallel plays and comments on child action. "You're driving; You're driving the car!"
Imitation	Child plays with a car and making "vroom" noises; adult imitates child's actions and sounds; adds words. "I'm driving; Vroom! It goes fast!"
Expansion	Child makes a single word or short remark; adult uses it to make a complete sentence expressing the same thought. Child: "Go!" Adult: "Your car can go! Go, go! I see it go!"
Extension	Child makes a simple remark; adult additional meaning Child: "Go!" Adult: "Yes, it goes fast!"
Build-ups and break-downs	Child makes a simple remark; adult expands it, then restates it in phrase-sized pieces Child: "Go!" Adult: "Look at it go! It goes fast. It goes. It's going fast. I see you making it go fast! Go fast!"
Recasts	Expansions that give the conversational turn back to the child to obligate a response. Child: "Go!" Adult: "It is going, isn't it?"

Adapted from Paul (2007).

ILS is often advocated to increase word knowledge and production (Lahey, 1988; Owens, 2004). Weismer (2000) suggested *script therapy*, in which the clinician and child engage in a verbal routine or ritualized pattern of actions involving words targeted for the child's early lexicon. Whitehurst et al. (1991) proposed a program based on scripts using picture books intended to be used by parents for stimulating the early stages of language development in DLD. Lederer (2001) showed that an approach referred to as *focused stimulation*, in which parents were trained to provide multiple, structured presentations of specific words in a play context, was also effective in increasing overall and target vocabulary acquisition.

4.1.6   Developing word combinations   Children's first word combinations are used to talk about the semantic relations they already encode with single words

(Bloom & Lahey, 1978). They should be encouraged to talk about these typical early semantic relations when first two-word combinations are being trained.

Frome-Loeb and Armstrong (2001) showed that ILS techniques aimed at increasing word combinations were effective in eliciting longer utterances from toddlers with language delays. Whitehurst et al.'s program (1991) includes an extension designed to be used by parents to elicit two-word utterances. Milieu teaching, using the same techniques as PMT, but requiring words from the child to attain goals, has also been shown to increase frequency of communication, use of vocabulary and word combinations in clients with a variety of disabilities (Warren, Yoder, & Leew, 2002; Wilcox and Shannon, 1998). Focused stimulation (Bunce, 1995; Kouri, 2005; Wilcox & Shannon, 1998) and behaviorist-based approaches (Leonard, 1975; MacDonald et al., 1974) are other techniques that have demonstrated efficacy in eliciting both early words and word combinations.

4.1.7 Pre-literacy development   The emerging language period is a time during which typically developing toddlers acquire important experiences with books and print (Dodici, Draper, & Peterson, 2003). Rosenquest (2002) and Scheffel and Ingrisano (2000) described ways to use storybooks in working with toddlers and their families in order to build early language and literacy skills. Parents can be taught routine interactive reading strategies, such as pointing out connections between pictures and text, stopping to let children fill in elements after they have heard a story several times, using exaggerated intonation and stress to highlight important elements in the text, developing play activities around the themes from the book, and relating the stories to children's own day-to-day activities. In addition, encouraging parents to read children's books that contain rhymes and to use rhyming games and songs in daily interactions contributes to the development of phonological awareness (Bradley & Bryant, 1983), which in turn provides a basis for decoding and reading (Blachman, 1994).

4.2   Developing language

As we have seen, the primary areas of communication deficit seen in children with DLD in this phase include speech sounds, syntax, and morphology. Delays in the acquisition of vocabulary, play and pragmatics, and pre-literacy skills may also be seen.

4.2.1 Intervention for speech sounds   Goals in this area include expanding the phonetic and phonological repertoire, decreasing the number of speech sound substitutions and deletions, and increasing intelligibility. Approaches typically make use of play-based activities that provide modeling and practice of speech sounds and words, as well as more drill-like exercises in which multiple repetitions of sounds and words are practiced. Research suggests that the most effective way to improve speech production is to work directly on the articulation of sounds and words, rather than doing exercises of the articulators that do not include speech (Lof, 2003).

4.2.2 Syntax and morphology Connell and Stone (1992) showed that children with specific language impairment were more likely to learn to produce new grammatical morphemes if they were required to imitate them during instruction rather than if modeling alone were used. But there has been a long-running debate on whether elicited imitation activities or child-centered approaches such as ILS and focused stimulation are more effective. Kouri (2005) reported that approaches using both elicited imitation ("Say, shoes") and focused stimulation, in which children listened to multiple models of target forms during play interactions without being required to imitate, were equally effective. At this time, there are no clear guidelines that assist in matching the best technique to a particular child, and both elicited imitation and less clinician-directed approaches have all demonstrated success in increasing syntactic and morphological production.

4.2.3 Vocabulary Targets for vocabulary training for preschoolers with DLD should include both functional words that will assist in interaction and daily living skills – such as names for clothing, food, and utensils – as well as vocabulary related to academic development, such as colors, numbers, and letters. However, since it is known that children with DLD tend to have restricted verb vocabularies, verbs that encode specific actions, such as *walk, run, hop*, and *skip*, are also appropriate. Descriptive terms, including opposite pairs, such as *thick/thin, wide/narrow*, will also allow more mature expression. Methods for teaching vocabulary can include indirect language stimulation and focused stimulation in settings where materials foster the use of target vocabulary, as well as script therapy and literature-based scripts chosen to exemplify the use of target words.

4.2.4 Play and pragmatics Play is often a context for intervention in this period, and pragmatic skills at this level are often being developed and challenged in the context of peer play. A goal of incorporating play in intervention is to encourage the child to use the language being learned to organize pretend play, solve problems, and explore interactions. For these reasons, peers are often included in the play and pragmatic activities designed for children with DLD. A large body of literature (summarized in Goldstein, Kaczmarek, & English, 2002) has demonstrated that children with a range of disabilities benefit from interactions with trained peers to facilitate play and social interaction. Several programs are available in the literature to guide the provision of peer-mediated programs, including *Buddy Time* (English et al., 1997), *Play, Plan, Report* (Craig-Unkefer & Kaiser, 2003), and *Peer Group Entry* (Beilinson & Olswang, 2003).

4.2.5 Pre-literacy development As has been discussed, many preschoolers with speech and language problems go on to have difficulty learning to read and write (Stothard et al., 1998). For this reason, any child with DLD should be considered at risk for literacy problems and should be provided with preventive intervention in this area. Kaderavek and Justice (2004) outlined the major goals of pre-literacy development for these children. They are listed in Table 8.6.

Table 8.6 Major goals of preventive pre-literacy intervention for preschoolers with DLD

Domain	Instructional goals
Phonological awareness	Recognize and produce rhymes
	Segment sentence into words
	Identify words with same beginning, ending sound
	Segment words into syllables
	Segment words into phonemes; count phonemes in words
	Synthesize words from component phonemes
Print concepts	Orientation of books, left–right progression of print
	Understanding metalinguistic terms (*word, letter, sound*)
	Understand that print is speech written down
Alphabet knowledge	Sing alphabet song
	Recognize own name in print
	Recognize letters in environmental print
	Sort upper and lower case letters
	Write own name
	Name all letters, upper and lower case
	Understand letters stand for sounds
	Associated sounds with appropriate letters
Narrative and literate language	Listen to stories, answer questions
	Retell stories with temporal and causal connections
	Retell stories including talk about goals and plans
	Use mental (*think*) and linguistic (*say*) verbs in story retells

Based on Kaderavek and Justice (2004).

Kaderavek and Justice reviewed literature that shows that explicit instruction in each of these four areas embedded in daily preschool activities has positive effects on children's readiness to read. Additionally, Gillon (2002) showed that individual instruction, particularly in the area of phonological awareness, was also effective in improving literacy outcomes for children with DLD.

5 Conclusions

Developmental language delays are characterized by slow acquisition of communication skills during the preschool period, in the absence of other significant developmental disorders. In at least 50 percent of cases the delays are transient, so that oral language development appears normal by school age, although subtle deficits that can affect academic achievement may persist. Initially, delays appear in the acquisition of vocabulary and speech sounds during the second year of life. Later, vocabulary tends to improve more quickly than other areas and deficits in syntax and morphology become more prominent. Although many children with DLD are good communicators, some manifest problems in the area of pragmatic use of language and the development of play skills, particularly with peers. They are also at higher than usual risk for reading disabilities.

Assessment of this population begins with standard screening measures to identify children at risk. For children under the age of 3, these typically involve parent checklists that focus primarily on vocabulary. Screening for children over the age of 3 examines a wider range of skills. More in-depth assessment of children who fail screening measures will involve some standardized testing, but will also include informal measures of speech intelligibility, use and understanding of pre-academic vocabulary, and ability to engage in symbolic and pretend play. Assessment at this level also requires the observation of the use of language in a natural setting and the analysis of forms and functions that appear in spontaneous speech samples.

Intervention for preschool children can take a range of forms, including highly structured activities based on principles of behaviorism, more child-centered activities in which adults follow the child's lead, and activities that fall between these extremes. For toddlers, intervention focuses on increasing the frequency and function of communicative acts and the use of words and word combinations. For children over the age of 3, syntax and morphology, along with articulation, are often the primary goals of an intervention program. However, it is also important to devote attention to the acquisition of pre-academic vocabulary, the enhancement of play and social communication with peers, and the development of pre-literacy skills including phonological awareness, print and alphabet knowledge, and narrative and literate language.

REFERENCES

Alt, M., Plante, E., & Creusere, M. (2004). Semantic features in fast-mapping: Performance of preschoolers with specific language impairment versus preschoolers with normal language. *Journal of Speech, Language, and Hearing Research* 47, 407–20.

American Speech-Language and Hearing Association (2007). *Roles and responsibilities of speech-language pathologists serving infants and toddlers*. Rockville, MD: Author.

Apfel, H. & Provence, S. (2001). *Infant-toddler and family instrument*. Baltimore, MD: Paul H. Brookes.

Applebee, A. (1978). *The child's concept of a story: Ages 2 to 17*. Chicago, IL: University of Chicago Press.

Bates, E. & Dick, F. (2002). Language, gesture and the developing brain. *Developmental Psychobiology* 40, 293–310.

Beilinson, J. & Olswang, L. (2003). Facilitating peer group entry in kindergartners with impairments in social communication. *Language, Speech and Hearing Services in Schools* 34, 154–66.

Benton, A. (1959). Aphasia in children. *Education* 79, 408–12.

Bishop, D. (1997). *Uncommon understanding: Development and disorders of language comprehension in children.* East Sussex, UK: Psychology Press Limited.

Bishop, D. & Edmundson, A. (1987). Language-impaired 4-year-olds: Distinguishing transient from persistent impairment. *Journal of Speech and Hearing Disorders* 52, 156–73.

Bishop, D., Price, T., Dale, P., & Plomin, R. (2003). Outcomes of early language delay: II. Etiology of transient and persistent language difficulties. *Journal of Speech, Language, and Hearing Research* 46, 561–75.

Bishop, D. & Snowling, M. J. (2004). Developmental dyslexia and specific language impairment: Same or different? *Psychological Bulletin* 130 (6), 858–86.

Blachman, B. (1994). What we have learned from longitudinal studies of phonological processing and reading, and some unanswered questions. *Journal of Learning Disabilities* 27, 287–91.

Bloom, L. & Lahey, M. (1978). *Language development and language disorders.* New York: Wiley.

Bondy, A. & Frost, L. (1998). The picture exchange communication system. *Seminars in Speech and Language* 19, 373–89.

Bradley, L. & Bryant, P. (1983). Categorizing sounds and learning to read – a causal connection. *Nature* 30, 419–21.

Bricker, D., Capt, B., & Pretti-Frontczak, K. (2002). *Test for birth to three years and three to six years: Assessment, evaluation and programming system for infants and children,* 2nd ed. Baltimore, MD: Paul H. Brookes.

Brinton, B., Fujiki, M., Spencer, J. C., & Robinson, L. A. (1997). The ability of children with specific language impairment to access and participate in ongoing interaction. *Journal of Speech, Language, and Hearing Research* 40, 1011–25.

Brown, R. (1973). *A first language. The early stages.* Cambridge, MA: Harvard University Press.

Bunce, B. (1995). *Building a language-focused curriculum for the pre-school classroom: A planning guide* (vol. II). Baltimore, MD: Paul H. Brookes.

Bzoch, K., League, R., & Brown, V. (2003). *The receptive expressive emergent language test,* 3rd ed. Austin, TX: Pro-Ed.

Caparulo, B. & Cohen, D. (1983). Developmental language studies in the neuropsychiatric disorders of children. In K. E. Nelson (ed.). *Children's language 4* (pp. 423–63). Hillsdale, NJ: Erlbaum.

Capone, N. & McGregor, K. (2004). Gesture development: A review for clinical and research practices. *Journal of Speech, Language, and Hearing Research* 47, 173–87.

Carpenter, R. (1987). Play scale. In L. Olswang, C. Stoel-Gammon, T. Coggins, & R. Carpenter (eds.), *Assessing prelinguistic and early behaviors in developmentally young children* (pp. 44–77). Seattle, WA: University of Washington Press.

Casby, M. (2003). Developmental assessment of play: A model for early intervention. *Communication Disorders Quarterly* 24, 175–83.

Chapman, R. (1981). Exploring children's communicative intents. In J. Miller (ed.), *Assessing language production in children* (pp. 111–38). Baltimore, MD: University Park Press.

Cleave, P. & Rice, M. (1997). An examination of the morpheme BE in children with specific language impairment. *Journal of Speech, Language, and Hearing Research* 40, 480–92.

Coggins, T. (1998). Clinical assessment of emerging language: How to gather evidence and make informed decisions. In A. M. Wetherby, S. F. Warren, & J. Reichle (eds.), *Transitions in prelinguistic communication* (pp. 233–59). Baltimore, MD: Paul H. Brookes.

Connell, P. & Stone, C. (1992). Morpheme learning of children with specific language impairment under controlled instructional conditions. *Journal of Speech and Hearing Research* 34, 1329–38.

Craig, H. (1993). Social skills of children with specific language impairment. *Language, Speech, and Hearing Services in Schools* 24, 206–15.

Craig, H. & Evans, J. (1993). Pragmatics and SLI: Within-group variations in discourse behaviors. *Journal of Speech and Hearing Research* 36, 777–89.

Craig-Unkefer, L. & Kaiser, A. (2003). Increasing peer-directed social-communication skills of children enrolled in Head Start. *Journal of Early Intervention* 25, 229–47.

Craighead, N. (1984). Strategies for evaluating and targeting pragmatic behaviors in young children. *Seminars in Speech and Language* 5, 241–52.

Crais, E. & Roberts, J. (1991). Decision making in assessment and early intervention planning. *Language, Speech, and Hearing Services in Schools* 22, 19–30.

Dale, P. (1991). The validity of a parent report measure of vocabulary and syntax at 24 months. *Journal of Speech and Hearing Research* 34, 565–71.

Dodici, B., Draper, D., & Peterson, C. (2003). Early parent–child interactions and early literacy development. *Topics in Early Childhood Special Education* 23, 124–36.

Dollagan, C. (1987). Fast mapping in normal and language-impaired children. *Journal of Speech and Hearing Disorders* 52, 218–22.

Drillion, E. & Drummond, M. (1983). *Developmental screening and the child with special needs*. London: Heinemann.

Dunn, L. & Dunn, L. (2006). *Peabody picture vocabulary test, IV*. Circle Pines, MN: American Guidance Service.

English, K., Goldstein, H., Shafer, K., & Kaczmarek, L. (1997). Promoting interactions among preschoolers with and without disabilities: Effects of a buddy system skills training program. *Exceptional Children* 63, 229–43.

Feagans, L. & Applebaum, M. (1986). Validation of language subtypes in learning disabled children. *Journal of Educational Psychology* 78, 358–64.

Fenson, L., Marchman, V., Thal, D., Dale, P., Reznick, S., & Bates, E. (2006). *MacArthur–Bates Communicative Development Inventories (CDIs)*, 2nd ed. Baltimore, MD: Paul H. Brookes.

Fey, M. (1986). *Language intervention with young children*. San Diego, CA: College-Hill Press.

Fey, M. & Leonard, L. (1984). Partner age as a variable in the conversational performance of specifically language-impaired children. *Journal of Speech and Hearing Research* 27, 413–23.

Fey, M., Leonard, L., & Wilcox, K. (1981). Speech-style modifications of language-impaired children. *Journal of Speech and Hearing Disorders* 46, 91–7.

Frome-Loeb, D., & Armstrong, N. (2001). Case studies on the efficacy of expansions and subject–verb–object models in early language intervention. *Child Language Teaching and Therapy* 17, 35–53.

Gallagher, T. & Darnton, B. (1978). Conversational aspects of the speech of language-disordered children: Revision behaviors. *Journal of Speech and Hearing Research* 21, 118–35.

Garrett, J. (2002). Supporting multicultural, multilingual families. *Child Care Information Exchange* 147, 42–4.

Gathercole, S. & Baddeley, A. (1990). Phonological memory deficits in language-disordered children: Is there a causal connection? *Journal of Memory and Language* 29, 336–60.

Gillon, G. (2000). The efficacy of phonological awareness intervention for children with spoken language impairment. *Language, Speech and Hearing Services in Schools* 31, 126–41.

Gillon, G. (2002). Follow-up study investigating the benefits of phonological awareness intervention of children with spoken language impairment. *International Journal of Language and Communication Disorders* 37, 381–400.

Girolametto, L. (1997). Development of a parent report measure for profiling the conversational skills of preschool children. *American Journal of Speech-Language Pathology* 6, 25–33.

Girolametto, L. & Weitzman, E. (2006). It takes two to talk: The Hanen Program for parents. In R. McCauley & M. Fey (eds.), *Treatment of language disorders in children* (pp. 77–101). Baltimore, MD: Paul H. Brookes.

Girolametto, L., Wiigs, M., Smyth, R., Weitzman, E., & Pearce, P. (2001). Children with a history of expressive vocabulary delay: Outcomes at 5 years of age. *American Journal of Speech-Language Pathology* 10, 358–69.

Goldin-Meadow, S. & Butcher, C. (2003). Pointing toward two-word speech in young children. In K. Sotaro (ed.), *Pointing: Where language, culture and cognition meet* (pp. 85–107). Mahwah, NJ: Erlbaum.

Goldstein, H., Kaczmarek, L., & English, K. (eds.). (2002). *Promoting social communication: Children with developmental disabilities from birth to adolescence.* Baltimore, MD: Paul H. Brookes.

Goodwyn, S., Acredolo, L., & Brown, C. (2000). Impact of symbolic gesturing on early language development. *Journal of Nonverbal Behavior* 24, 81–103.

Gopnik, M. & Crago, M. (1991). Familial aggregation of developmental language disorder. *Cognition* 39, 1–50.

Gray, S. (2003). Word-learning by preschoolers with specific language impairment: What predicts success. *Journal of Speech, Language, and Hearing Research* 46, 56–67.

Griffin, S. (1979). "Requests for clarification made by normal and language impaired children."

Unpublished master's thesis, Emerson College.

Guralnick, M. (2000). *Interdisciplinary clinical assessment of young children with developmental disabilities.* Baltimore, MD: Paul H. Brookes.

Hadley, P. (1999). Validating a rate-based measure of early grammatical ability: Unique syntactic types. *American Journal of Speech-Language Pathology* 8, 261–72.

Hadley, P. & Rice, M. (1991). Conversational responsiveness of speech- and language-impaired preschoolers, *Journal of Speech and Hearing research* 34, 1308–17.

Hadley, P. & Short, H. (2005). The onset of tense marking in children at-risk for specific language impairment. *Journal of Speech, Language, and Hearing Research* 48, 1344–62.

Hedge, M. & Maul, C. (2006). *Language disorders in children: An evidence-based approach to assessment and treatment.* Boston, New York, San Francisco: Pearson.

Hedrick, D., Prather, E., & Tobin, A. (1995). *Sequenced inventory of communication development, Revised.* Los Angeles, CA: Western Psychological Services.

Heilmann, J., Weismer, S., Evans, J., & Hollar, C. (2005). Utility of the MacArthur–Bates Communicative Development Inventory in identifying language abilities of late-talking and typically developing toddlers. *American Journal of Speech-Language Pathology* 14, 40–51.

Johnston, J. (1994). Cognitive abilities of children with language impairment. In R. Watkins & M. Rice (eds.), *Specific language impairments in children* (vol. 4, pp. 107–21). Baltimore, MD: Paul H. Brookes.

Johnston, J. & Schery, T. (1976). The use of grammatical morphemes by children with communication disorders. In D. M. Morehead & A. E. Morehead (eds.), *Normal and deficient child language.* Baltimore, MD: University Park Press.

Kaderavek, J. & Justice, L. (2004).
Embedded-explicit emergent literacy
intervention II: Goal selection and
implementation in the early childhood
classroom. *Language, Speech, and Hearing
Services in Schools* 35, 212–28.

Kiernan, B. & Gray, S. (1998). Word
learning in a supported-learning context
by preschool children with specific
language impairment. *Journal of Speech,
Language, and Hearing Research* 40, 75–82.

Klee, T., Pearce, K., & Carson, D. K. (2000).
Improving the positive predictive value
of screening for developmental language
disorder. *Journal of Speech, Language, and
Hearing Research* 43, 821–33.

Kouri, T. (2005). Lexical training through
modeling and elicitation procedures
with late talkers who have specific
language impairment and
developmental delays. *Journal of Speech,
Language, and Hearing Research* 48,
157–72.

Krassowski, E. & Plante, E. (1997).
IQ variability in children with SLI:
Implications for use of cognitive
referencing in determining SLI. *Journal
of Communication Disorders* 30, 1–9.

Kuhl, P. & Meltzoff, A. (1996). Infant
vocalizations in response to speech:
Vocal imitation and developmental
change. *Journal of the Acoustical Society of
America* 100, 2425–38.

Lahey, M. (1988). *Language disorders and
language development*. New York:
Macmillan.

Law, J., Garrett, Z., & Nye, C. (2004). The
efficacy of treatment for children with
developmental speech and language
delay/disorder: A meta-analysis. *Journal
of Speech, Language, and Hearing Research*
47, 924–43.

Lederer, S. (2001). Efficacy of parent–child
language group intervention for
late-talking toddlers. *Infant-Toddler
Intervention* 11, 223–35.

Lee, L. (1974). *Developmental sentence
analysis*. Evanston, IL: Northwestern
University Press.

Leonard, L. (1975). Modeling as a clinical
procedure in language training.
*Language, Speech, and Hearing Services in
the Schools* 6, 72–85.

Leonard, L. (1989). Language learnability
and specific language impairment in
children. *Applied Psycholinguistics* 10,
179–202.

Leonard, L. (1991). Specific language
impairment as a clinical category.
*Language, Speech, and Hearing Services in
Schools* 22, 66–8.

Leonard, L. (1997). *Children with specific
language impairment*. Cambridge, MA:
MIT Press.

Leonard, L. & Leonard, J. (1985). The
contribution of phonetic context to an
unusual phonological pattern: a case
study. *Language, Speech, and Hearing
Services in Schools* 16, 110–18.

Leonard, L., Miller, C., & Gerber, E. (1999).
Grammatical morphology and the
lexicon in children with specific
language impairment. *Journal of Speech,
Language, and Hearing Research* 42,
678–89.

Leonard, L., Schwartz, R., Chapman, K.,
Rowan, L., Prelock, P., Terrel, B., Weiss,
A., & Messick, C. (1982). Early lexical
acquisition in children with specific
language impairment. *Journal of Speech
and Hearing Research* 25, 554–64.

Lof, G. L. (2003). Oral motor exercises
and treatment outcomes. *Perspectives
on Language Learning and Education* 10,
7–11.

Losardo, A. & Notari-Syverson, A. (2001).
*Alternative approaches to assessing young
children*. Baltimore, MD: Paul H.
Brookes.

Lucas, E. (1980). *Semantic and pragmatic
language disorders: Assessment and
remediation*. Rockville, MD: Aspen.

Lyytinen, P., Eklund, K., & Lyytinen, H.
(2003). The play and language behavior
of mothers with and without dyslexia
and its association to their toddlers'
language development. *Journal of
Learning Disabilities* 36, 74–86.

Lyytinen, P., Poikkeus, A., Laakso, M., Eklund, K., & Lyytinen, H. (2001). Language development and symbolic play in children with and without familial risk for dyslexia. *Journal of Speech, Language, and Hearing Research* 44, 873–85.

MacDonald, J. (1989). *Becoming partners with children: From play to conversation.* San Antonio, TX: Special Press.

MacDonald, J., Blott, J., Gordon, K., Spiegel, B., & Hartmann, M. (1974). An experimental parent-assisted treatment program for preschool language-delayed children. *Journal of Speech and Hearing Disorders* 39, 395–415.

MacDonald, J. & Carroll, J. (1992). A social partnership model for assessing early communication development: An intervention model for preconversational children. *Language, Speech, and Hearing Services in Schools* 23, 113–24.

Marchman, V. & Martinez-Sussmann, C. (2002). Concurrent validity of caregiver/ parent report measures of language for children who are learning both English and Spanish. *Journal of Speech, Language, and Hearing Research* 45, 983–97.

Marton, K., Abramoff, B., & Rosenzweig, S. (2005). Social cognition and language in children with specific language impairment (SLI). *Journal of Communication Disorders* 38, 143–62.

McCune, L. (1995). A normative study of representational play at the transition to language. *Developmental Psychology* 31, 200–11.

Miller, J. (1981). *Assessing language production in children.* Boston, MA: Allyn & Bacon.

Miller, J. & Paul, R. (1995). *The clinical assessment of language comprehension.* Baltimore, MD: Paul H. Brookes.

Mirenda, P. & Santogrossi, J. (1985). A prompt-free strategy to teach pictorial communication system use. *Augmentative and Alternative Communication* 1, 143–50.

Morris, S., Wilcox, K., & Schooling, T. (1995). The preschool speech intelligibility measure. *American Journal of Speech-Language Pathology* 4, 22–8.

Nelson, N. (1998). *Childhood language disorders in context: Infancy through adolescence,* 2nd ed. New York: Macmillan.

Nippold, M. (2004). Language disorders in school-age children: Aspects of assessment. In R. Kent (ed.) *Encyclopedia of Communication Disorders* (pp. 324–6). Cambridge, MA: MIT Press.

Olswang, L. (1996). *Preschool functional communication inventory.* Seattle, WA: University of Washington Speech and Hearing Clinic.

Olswang, L., Rodriguez, B., & Timler, G. (1998). Recommending intervention for toddlers with specific language learning difficulties: We may not have all the answers, but we know a lot. *American Journal of Speech-Language Pathology* 7, 23–32.

Owens, R. (2004). *Language disorders: A functional approach to assessment and intervention,* 4th ed. Boston, MA: Allyn & Bacon.

Paul, R. (1991). Profiles of toddlers with slow expressive language development. *Topics in Language Disorders* 11, 1–13.

Paul, R. (1993). Patterns of development in late talkers: Preschool years. *Journal of Childhood Communication Disorders* 15, 7–14.

Paul, R. (1996). Clinical implications of the natural history of slow expressive language development. *American Journal of Speech-Language Pathology* 5, 5–21.

Paul, R. (1997). Understanding language delay: A response to van Kleeck, Gillam, and Davis. *American Journal of Speech–Language Pathology* 6, 41–9.

Paul, R. (2000). Understanding the whole of it: Comprehension assessment. *Seminars in Speech and Language* 21, 10–17.

Paul, R. (2005). Assessing communication in autism spectrum disorders. In F. Volkmar, A. Klin, R. Paul, & D. Cohen (eds.), *Handbook of autism and pervasive developmental disorders*, 3rd ed. (vol. II, pp. 799–816). New York: Wiley & Sons.

Paul, R. (2007). *Language disorders from infancy through adolescence: Assessment and intervention*, 3rd ed. St. Louis: Mosby.

Paul, R. & Elwood, T. (1991). Maternal linguistic input to toddlers with slow expressive language development. *Journal of Speech and Hearing Research* 34, 982–8.

Paul, R. & Jennings, P. (1992). Phonological behavior in toddlers with slow expressive language development. *Journal of Speech and Hearing Research* 35, 99–107.

Paul, R. & Shiffer, M. (1991). Communicative initiations in normal and late-talking toddlers. *Applied Psycholinguistics* 12, 419–31.

Paul, R. & Shriberg, L. (1982). Associations between phonology and syntax in speech-delayed children, *Journal of Speech and Hearing Research* 25, 536–47.

Paul, R. & Smith, (1993). Narrative skills in 4-year-olds with normal, impaired, and late-developing language. *Journal of Speech and Hearing Research* 36, 592–8.

Pennington, B., Gilger, J, Pauls, D., Smith, S. A., Smith, S. D., & DeFries, J. (1991). Evidence for major gene transmission of developmental dyslexia. *Journal of American Medical Association* 266, 1527–34.

Pharr, A., Ratner, N., & Rescorla, L. (2000). Syllable structure development of toddlers with expressive specific language impairment. *Applied Psycholinguistics* 21, 429–49.

Prizant, B. (1991). *Early intervention: Focus on communication assessment and enhancement*. Workshop presented in Beaverton, OR.

Rescorla, L. (1989). The Language Development Survey: A screening tool for delayed language in toddlers. *Journal of Speech and Hearing Disorders* 54, 587–99.

Rescorla, L. (2002). Language and reading outcomes to age 9 in late-talking toddlers. *Journal of Speech, Language, and Hearing Research* 45, 360–71.

Rescorla, L. (2005). Age 13 language and reading outcomes in late-talking toddlers. *Journal of Speech, Language, and Hearing Research* 48, 459–72.

Rescorla, L. & Achenbach, T. (2002). Use of the Language Development Survey in a national probability sample of children from 18 to 35 months old. *Journal of Speech, Language, and Hearing Research* 45, 1092–4388.

Rescorla, L. & Alley, A. (2001). Validation of the Language Development Survey: A parent report tool for identifying language delay in toddlers. *Journal of Speech, Language, and Hearing Research* 44, 34–45.

Rescorla, L. & Lee, E. (2001). Language impairment in young children. In T. Layton, E. Crais, & L. Watson (eds.), *Handbook of early language impairments in children: nature* (pp. 11–55). Albany, NY: Delmar.

Rescorla, L., Mirak, J., & Singh, L. (2000). Vocabulary growth in late talkers: Lexical development from 2;0 to 3;0. *Journal of Child Language* 27, 293–311.

Rescorla, L. & Mirren, L. (1998). Communicative intent in late-talking toddlers. *Applied Psycholinguistics* 19, 393–411.

Rescorla, L. & Ratner, N. B. (1996). Phonetic profiles of toddlers with severe expressive language impairments (SLI–E). *Journal of Speech and Hearing Research* 39, 153–65.

Rescorla, L. & Roberts, J. (2002). Nominal versus verbal morpheme use in late talkers at ages 3 and 4. *Journal of Speech, Language, and Hearing Research* 45, 1219–32.

Rescorla, L., Roberts, J., & Dahlsgaard, K. (1997). Late talkers at 2: Outcome at age 3. *Journal of Speech and Hearing Research* 40, 556–66.

Restrepo, M. (1998). Identification of predominantly Spanish-speaking children with language impairment. *Journal of Speech, Language, and Hearing Research* 41, 1398–411.

Rice, M., Buhr, J. C., & Oetting, J. (1992). Speech-language impaired children's quick incidental learning of words: The effect of a pause. *Journal of Speech and Hearing Research* 35, 1040–48.

Rice, M., Sell, M., & Hadley, P. (1991). Social interactions of speech, and language-impaired children. *Journal of Speech and Hearing Research* 34, 1299–307.

Rice, M., Warren, S., & Betz, S. (2005). Language symptoms of developmental language disorders: An overview of autism, Down syndrome, fragile X, specific language impairment, and Williams syndrome. *Applied Psycholinguistics* 26, 7–27.

Rice, M. & Wexler, K. (1996). Toward tense as a clinical marker of specific language impairment in English-speaking children, *Journal of Speech and Hearing Research* 39, 1239–57.

Roberts, J., Medley, L., Swartzfager, J., & Neebe, E. (1997). Assessing the communication of African-American one-year-olds using the communication and symbolic behavior scales. *American Journal of Speech-Language Pathology* 6, 59–65.

Roberts, J., Rescorla, L., Giroux, J., & Stevens, L. (1998). Phonological skills of children with specific expressive language impairments: Outcome at age 3. *Journal of Speech, Language, and Hearing Research* 41, 374–85.

Rodriguez, B. & Olswang, B. (2003). Mexican-American and Anglo-American mothers' beliefs and values about child rearing, education and language impairment. *American Journal of Speech-Language Pathology* 12, 452–62.

Rosenquest, B. (2002). Literacy-based planning and pedagogy that supports toddler language development. *Early Childhood Education Journal* 29, 241–9.

Ruscello, D., St. Louis, K., & Mason, M. (1991). School-aged children with phonologic disorders: Coexistence with other speech/language disorders. *Journal of Speech and Hearing Research* 34, 236–42.

Rvachew, S., Ohberg, A., Grawburg, M., & Heyding, J. (2003). Phonological awareness and phonemic perception in 4-year-old children with delayed expressive phonology skills. *American Journal of Speech-Language Pathology* 12, 463–71.

Scarborough, H. (1990). Index of productive syntax. *Applied Psycholinguistics* 11, 1–22.

Scheffel, D. & Ingrisano, D. (2000). Linguistic emphasis in maternal speech to preschool language learners with language impairments: An acoustical perspective. *Infant-Toddler Intervention: The Transdisciplinary Journal* 10, 127–35.

Schwartz, R. & Leonard, L. (1982). Do children pick and choose? Phonological selection and avoidance in early lexical acquisition. *Journal of Child Language* 9, 319–36.

Shipley, K. & McAfee, J. (2004). *Assessment in speech-language pathology: A resource manual*, 3rd ed. Clifton Park, NY: Thomson Delman Learning.

Shriberg, L. & Austin, D. (1998). Comorbidity of speech-language disorder: Implications for a phenotype marker for speech delay. In R. Paul (ed.), *Exploring the speech-language connection*. Baltimore, MD: Paul H. Brookes.

Shriberg, L. & Kwiatkowski, J. (1980). *Natural process analysis: A procedure for phonological analysis of continuous speech samples*. New York: John Wiley & Sons.

Shriberg, L. & Kwiatkowski, J. (1994). Developmental phonological disorders, I: A clinical profile. *Journal of Speech and Hearing Research* 37, 1100–26.

Snow, C. (1983). Literacy and language: Relationships during the preschool years. *Harvard Educational Review* 53, 165–89.

Snow, C. (1999). Facilitating language development promotes literacy learning. In L. Eldering & P. Leseman (eds.), *Effective early intervention: Cross-cultural perspectives* (pp. 141–61). New York: Falmer.

Snow, C., Burns, S., & Griffin, P. (1998). *Preventing reading difficulties in young children*. Washington, DC: National Academy Press.

Snowling, M. & Bishop, D. (2000). Is preschool language impairment a risk factor for dyslexia in adolescence? *Journal of Child Psychology and Psychiatry* 41, 587–600.

Snowling, M., Adams, J., Bishop, D., & Stothard, S. (2001). Educational attainments of school leavers with a preschool history of speech-language impairments. *International Journal of Language and Communication Disorders* 36, 173–83.

Sparrow, S., Cichetti, D., & Balla, D. (2006). *Vineland Adaptive Behavior Scales-2*. Circle Pines, MN: Pearson.

Stoel-Gammon, C. (2002). Intervocalic consonants in the speech of typically developing children: Emergence and early use. *Clinical Linguistics & Phonetics* 16, 155–68.

Stothard, S., Snowling, M., Bishop, D., Chipchase, B., & Kaplan, C. (1998). Language-impaired preschoolers: A follow-up into adolescence. *Journal of Speech, Language, and Hearing Research* 41, 407–18.

Stott, D., Merricks, M., Bolton, P., & Goodyer, I. (2002). Screening for speech and language disorders: The reliability, validity and accuracy of the General Language Screen. *International Journal of Language and Communication Disorders* 37, 133–50.

Tallal, P., Miller, S., Bedi, G., Byman, G., Wang, X., Nagarajan, S., Schreiner, C.,

Jenkins, W., & Merzenich, M. (1996). Language comprehension in language learning impaired children improved with acoustically modified speech. *Science* 271, 81–4.

Thal, D., O'Hanlon, L., Clemmons, M., & Fralin, L. (1999). Validity of a parent report measure of vocabulary and syntax for preschool children with language impairment. *Journal of Speech, Language, and Hearing Research* 42, 482–96.

Trauner, D., Wulfeck, B., Tallal, P., & Hesselink, J. (1995). *Neurologic and MRI profiles of language impaired children: Technical Report CND-9513*. San Diego: Center for Research in Language, University of California.

Tsiouri, I. & Greer, R. (2003). Inducing vocal verbal behavior in children with severe language delays through rapid motor imitation responding. *Journal of Behavioral Education* 12, 185–206.

Van Kleeck, A. & Frankel, T. (1981). Discourse devices used by language disordered children: A preliminary investigation. *Journal of Speech and Hearing Disorders* 46, 250–7.

Vigil, D., Hodges, J., & Klee, T. (2005). Quantity and quality of parental language input to late-talking toddlers during play. *Child Language Teaching and Therapy* 21, 107–23.

Warren, S., Bredin-Oja, S., Fairchild, M., Finestack, L., Fey, M., & Brady, N. (2006). Responsivity education/ Prelinguistic milieu teaching. In R. McCauley & M. Fey (eds.), *Treatment of language disorders in children* (pp. 47–75). Baltimore, MD: Paul H. Brookes.

Warren, S. & Yoder, D. (1998). Facilitating the transition from preintentional to intentional communication. In A. Wetherby, S. Warren, & J. Reichle (eds.), *Transitions in prelinguistic communication* (pp. 365–84). Baltimore, MD: Paul H. Brookes.

Warren, S., Yoder, P., & Leew, S. (2002). Promoting social-communicative development in infants and toddlers. In H. Goldstein & L. Kaczmarek (eds.), *Promoting social communication: Children with developmental disabilities from birth to adolescence* (pp. 121–49). Baltimore, MD: Paul H. Brookes.

Weismer, S. (2000). Intervention for children with developmental language delay. In D. Bishop & L. Leonard (eds.), *Speech and language impairments in children: Causes, characteristics, intervention and outcome* (pp. 157–76). New York: Psychology Press.

Weismer, S. & Evans, J. (2002). The role of processing limitations in early identification of specific language impairment. *Topics in Language Disorders* 22, 15–29.

Wells, W. & Peppé, S. (2003). Intonation abilities of children with speech and language impairments. *Journal of Speech, Language, and Hearing Research* 46, 5–20.

Westby, C. (1998). Social-emotional bases of communication development. In W. Haynes & B. Shulman (eds.), *Communication development: Foundations, processes, and clinical applications* (pp. 165–204). Baltimore, MD: Williams & Wilkins.

Wetherby, A., Allen, L., Cleary, J., Kublin, K., & Goldstein, H. (2002). Validity and reliability of the Communication and Symbolic Behavior Scales Developmental Profile with very young children. *Journal of Speech, Language, and Hearing Research* 45, 1202–18.

Wetherby, A. & Prizant, B. (2003). *Communication and symbolic behavior scales – Developmental profile.* Baltimore, MD: Paul H. Brookes.

Whitehurst, G., Falco, F., Lonigan, C., Fischel, J., DeBaryshe, B., Valdez-Menchaea, M., & Caulfield, M. (1988). Accelerating language development through picture-book reading. *Developmental Psychology* 24, 552–8.

Whitehurst, G. & Fischel, J. (1994). Early developmental language delay: What, if anything, should the clinician do about it? *Journal of Child Psychology and Psychiatry* 35, 613–48.

Whitehurst, G., Fischel, J., Lonigan, C., Valdez-Menchaca, M., Arnold, D., & Smith, M. (1991). Treatment of early expressive language delay: If, when, and how. *Topics in Language Disorders* 11, 55–68.

Wilcox, M. J. & Shannon, M. S. (1998). Facilitating the transition from prelinguistic to linguistic communication. In A. M. Wetherby, S. F. Warren, & J. Reichle (eds.), *Transitions in prelinguistic communication* (pp. 385–416). Baltimore, MD: Paul H. Brookes.

Williams, A. & Elbert, M. (2003). A prospective longitudinal study of phonological development in late talkers. *Language, Speech and Hearing Services in Schools* 34, 138–54.

Yoder, P., & Warren, S. (1998). Maternal responsivity predicts the prelinguistic communication intervention that facilitates generalized intentional communication. *Journal of Speech, Language, and Hearing Research* 41, 1207–19.

9 Specific Language Impairment

SANDRA L. GILLAM AND
ALAN G. KAMHI

1 Introduction

The acquisition of language is one of the most important milestones in early childhood. Most children seem to acquire language effortlessly, giving little conscious attention to the rules that govern language structure and use. Language is much more than a means to communicate. It plays an important role in problem solving, thinking, and building and maintaining relationships. Because language provides the foundation for learning to read, it also has a significant impact on academic learning and success in school (Catts et al., 2005). For some children, however, language is not easily acquired. Children who have difficulty learning language have been variously referred to as having a language disorder, language impairment, language delay, or specific language impairment (SLI). Because SLI is the term most commonly used in the research literature, we will focus on this group of children throughout this chapter, though we will also discuss children with language disorders who do not meet the criteria for SLI. After discussing ways in which children with SLI have been defined and identified, we consider how they have been classified and subtyped. We will then discuss prognosis and intervention outcomes. The chapter ends with a discussion of some prevailing views on the causes of SLI and directions for future research.

2 Defining and Identifying Children with SLI

SLI refers to a condition in which children experience significant language learning difficulties in the absence of substantial cognitive, hearing, oral-motor, emotional, or environmental deficits (Leonard, 1998; Tomblin et al., 1997). Morphosyntax, the use of morphemes that mark tense and agreement, is a particular area of weakness for children with SLI (Bedore & Leonard, 1998). SLI occurs in approximately 7.4 percent of the kindergarten population with a slightly higher prevalence rate for boys (8 percent) than girls (6 percent) (Tomblin et al., 1997).

The Handbook of Language and Speech Disorders, First Edition. Edited by Jack S. Damico, Nicole Müller, and Martin J. Ball. © 2013 Blackwell Publishing Ltd except for editorial material and organization © 2013 Jack S. Damico, Nicole Müller, Martin J. Ball. Published 2013 by Blackwell Publishing Ltd.

Researchers have traditionally defined children with SLI using a combination of exclusionary and inclusionary criteria. Typically excluded are children with mental deficiency, hearing loss, severe emotional disturbance, and frank neurological deficits. Sometimes researchers also exclude children whose language problems are the result of sociocultural or environmental factors. Children with severe phonological impairments are also excluded, but the specific criterion varies. In some cases, children whose speech delays are more severe (6 months or more) than their language difficulties are excluded (Aram, Morris, & Hall, 1993) whereas in others, children are only excluded if their speech errors affect performance in the study. For example, in studies involving grammatical morphology, children must be able to produce final /s/ and /t/ (Goffman & Leonard, 2000; Leonard et al., 2006). Excluding children with phonological impairments may be too restrictive, however, because so many children with SLI also have phonological impairments (Haskill & Tyler, 2007).

The principal inclusionary criterion for SLI is performance within the normal range on a measure of non-verbal intelligence. Most investigators define "typical performance" as within one standard deviation (SD) of the mean (i.e., non-verbal IQ must be above 85). Some investigators allow non-verbal IQ to be as low as 70 to allow for measurement error, whereas others (e.g., Plante, 1998) use 75 as the cut-off point in order to clearly differentiate children with SLI from those with significant intellectual disabilities (IQ < 68–70). Typical measures of non-verbal intelligence include the Leiter International Performance Scale (Roid & Miller 1997), The Columbia Mental Maturity Scale (*CMMS*; Burgemeister, Blum, & Lorge, 1972), The Test of Nonverbal Intelligence – 3 (TONI-3; Brown, Sherbenou, & Johnsen, 1988), and the performance (non-verbal) subtests of the Wechsler Preschool and Primary Scales on Intelligence (WIPSI) or WISC (Wechsler, 1967, 1974). The Universal Nonverbal Intelligence Test (UNIT; Bracken & McCallum, 2006) is a more recent non-verbal intelligence test with good psychometric properties that has become a popular tool in the research literature.

Tomblin, Records, and Zhang (1996) attempted to standardize the criteria used for diagnosing SLI in a prospective study of more than 7,000 kindergarten (age 5 years) children in the USA. The diagnostic sensitivity for SLI was found to be best when two or more composite scores of language modality (comprehension and production) or domain (vocabulary, grammar, narration) were -1.2 standard deviations below the mean. Children also had to meet the usual exclusionary criteria and perform within normal age limits on a measure of non-verbal intelligence. Using these criteria, 7.4 percent of the kindergarten children met the criteria for SLI.

Unfortunately, the exclusionary and inclusionary criteria used by researchers to define SLI may not be used by practitioners to identify children with language impairments. For example, clinicians would rarely administer a measure of non-verbal intelligence to determine eligibility for services because they may not feel the assessment of intelligence is within their scope of practice. They also may see no compelling reason to administer a measure of non-verbal IQ because they know that cognitive referencing should not be used to determine eligibility for language intervention services. As Cole and his colleagues have shown, the use of cognitive referencing is consistent with a unidirectional view regarding the relationship between language and cognition (i.e., cognitive abilities determine language abilities) (Cole et al., 1995). This is an overly simplistic view of the relationship between cognition and language that results in the denial of services to children with language problems who will benefit from such services. For example, Cole, Dale, and Mills (1992) have shown that mental age had little influence on the impact of language therapy for children with language disorders. There is some evidence, however, that cognitive abilities may be linked to learning tense markers. Rice et al. (2004) found that children who met the criteria for SLI show faster growth trajectories in learning to mark tense than children with language disorders who did not perform within normal age limits on a measure of non-verbal intelligence.

The most common way clinicians determine eligibility for services is to obtain an omnibus measure of language skills by administering a norm-referenced, standardized test such as the Test of Language Development (TOLD; Newcomer & Hammill, 1988) or the Comprehensive Evaluation of Language Fundamentals-4 (CELF-4; Semel, Wiig & Secord, 2004). In most cases a child who performs <1 SD of the mean would be eligible for services, although the specific criteria vary according to the clinical setting. The use of norm-referenced tests to determine service eligibility is, of course, not without problems. Because these tests primarily assess vocabulary and grammar, children who have social-pragmatic language difficulties might be missed. Another problem with standardized tests is that they do not provide information about children's specific intervention needs. Children with language problems do not present with identical profiles of language abilities, which means that clinicians must use other types of assessments to determine the specific aspects of language that need to be targeted in therapy.

Questions have also been raised about the appropriateness of using standardized tests that use normative samples to identify children with language disorders. For example, it has been argued that when a child performs 1–2 standard deviations below the mean on a test that uses a normative sample that includes only typically developing children, the score would fall within the low normal range, which is not necessarily disordered (Ukrainetz McFadden, 1996). Alternatively, Peña, Spaulding, and Plante (2006) have argued that including children with impairments in the normative sample would yield more accurate means and standards deviations that would reflect the entire population of children.

3   Subtyping and Classification of Children with Language Disorders

Despite the problems with standardized tests, most practicing clinicians appear to have little difficulty identifying children with language disorders. The clinically identified children with language disorders are much more heterogeneous than the research-defined children with SLI. In a now classic study, Stark and Tallal (1981) wondered how prevalent SLI was in a clinical population of children with language disorders. Speech-language pathologists (SLPs) were asked to identify children on their caseloads between the ages of 4;0 and 8;5 who demonstrated language impairments, but who did not demonstrate significant deficits in hearing, intellectual, social, or emotional functioning. A total of 132 children were given a series of assessments measuring hearing, intellectual status, emotional/behavioral, neurological, and oral/motor functioning, and reading level. Half of these children performed below 85 on a measure of non-verbal intelligence. To be considered language disordered, receptive language age had to be at least 6 months below their chronological age or non-verbal mental age and expressive language age had to be at least 12 months below chronological age or non-verbal mental age. Thirty-three additional children did not meet these language criteria, meaning that only about 25 percent of the clinically identified children with language disorders met the research criteria for SLI. Clinically identified children with language disorders obviously encompass a much broader range of co-occurring deficits (particularly cognitive ones) than SLI.

There have been many subsequent attempts to differentiate and subtype the population of children with language disorders. Tomblin, Records, and Zhang (1996) used two different methods to identify subgroups of SLI: a cut-off score and cut-off plus discrepancy criteria. With the cut-off criterion, performance on a composite measure of expressive or receptive language had to be at least 1.25 standard deviations below the mean. Using this criterion, 35 percent of the children had expressive problems, 28 percent receptive problems, and 35 percent both expressive and receptive problems. When discrepancy criteria were added to the cut-off criterion, only 10.7 percent were categorized as SLI-E (expressive < receptive) and 6.5 percent as SLI-R (receptive < expressive). The vast majority of children (80.6 percent) did not have a discrepancy between expressive and receptive language. These data indicate that children with SLI, as currently defined, are a heterogeneous group of children with varying degrees of expressive and receptive language problems. As such, some of these children's problems are probably not limited to language and many will have language problems that are very similar to children who have lower non-verbal IQs.

Using yet a different approach, a British group of researchers, Conti-Ramsden, Crutchley, and Botting (1997, 1999), questioned the stability of subtypes over time. They identified 242 children with speech and language impairment at age 7. The children were administered a battery of speech and language measures that assessed grammar, word reading, story retelling, phonology, and expressive vocabulary. Six distinct subgroups were identified and are shown in Table 9.1. Cluster 1 (lexical-syntactic) is the closest to SLI. Cluster 2 is a language-reading group. There were two speech subgroups, one speech-language group, and one semantic pragmatic group.

The children were retested at age 8. While the subgroups were shown to remain stable over time, 45 percent of children (90/201) moved from one cluster to another as their specific strengths and weaknesses changed over time. For example, children may have fallen into cluster 5 at age 7, demonstrated improvement in their phonological abilities, and then fit into cluster 1 at age 8. Thus, while the

Table 9.1   Conti-Ramsden, Crutchley, and Botting's (1997) subgroup classification of children with language impairment.

	Comprehension of grammar	Word reading	Retelling a story	Phonology	Expressive vocabulary
Cluster 1 (lexical-syntactic)	x	x	x		
Cluster 2 (language-reading)		x			
Cluster 3 (verbal dyspraxia)	x	x	x	x	
Cluster 4 (phonological programming)		x		x	x
Cluster 5 (phonological-syntactic)	x	x	x	x	x
Cluster 6 (semantic-pragmatic)	x		x		

x denotes a problem in that specific domain performance at <40th percentile

clusters or categories remained stable over time, children's membership in a cluster was variable.

The last study we will consider questioned whether younger children with SLI could be reliably subgrouped using taxometric analysis procedures (Dollaghan, 2004). A total of 620 3- and 4-year-old children were administered measures of cognition, vocabulary, articulation, and non-word repetition. Spontaneous language samples were also obtained. There were four possible variables that were considered as category markers: vocabulary (PPVT-R; Dunn & Dunn, 1981), mean length of utterance (MLU), number of different words (NDW), and the number of words reported on the Language Development Survey (LDS; Rescorla, 1989). None of these markers were found to identify distinct subgroups of young children. In short, there were no distinct subgroups of language impairment in preschool children with SLI.

4   Implications of Subtyping Research for Clinical Practice

As summarized in the previous section, children with language disorders can be classified based on their cognitive abilities, language abilities, and co-occurring deficits. Although one might expect that children with low cognitive abilities would have poorer outcomes than children with SLI, studies have shown that this is not necessarily the case (Cole, Dale, & Mills, 1992; Cole et al., 1995). Children with lower cognitive abilities have been shown to make the same gains in language as children with higher cognitive skills.

As a general rule, one might also expect that children with co-occurring disorders might have poorer outcomes than children with SLI. For example, many children with language impairments have co-occurring speech delays, as Conti-Ramsden and her colleagues have shown. Given the morphosyntactic problems exhibited by these children, it is not surprising to find studies that have examined the relationship between phonological and morphosyntactic skills in this population. In a recent study, Haskill and Tyler (2007) compared the use of finite and non-finite morphemes in 23 children with deficits in language (LI) to 40 children with deficits in phonology and language (PLI). Children in the PLI group were further subdivided on the basis of final consonant and cluster use. There were 29 children who rarely demonstrated final consonant deletion or final cluster reduction (PLI/FCD-) and 11 children who did (PLI/FCD+). The findings were straightforward: The LI group had higher levels of finite and non-finite morpheme production than both of the PLI groups. These data clearly show that children with co-occurring disorders have more severe language impairments than children who just have a language delay. Typically, the more severe the impairment, the less amenable it is to intervention. The next section summarizes research studies that have examined the long-term stability of SLI and reviews intervention outcomes for children with differing patterns of impairment.

5   Long-term Stability and General Outcomes for SLI

A number of studies have shown that language impairment is an enduring condition that begins in early childhood and may persist into adolescence and adulthood (Clegg et al., 2004; Records, Tomblin, & Freese, 1992; Stothard et al., 1998; Tomblin et al., 2003). In an early study, Records et al. (1992) compared perceptions of the quality of life for 29 young adults (ages 17–25) who had been identified as SLI in early elementary school with age-matched typically developing individuals. Participants were asked to rate themselves on a number of variables including marital status, independent living, social life, and happiness. The participants were also administered a series of language, literacy, and cognitive measures.

Participants with SLI performed significantly more poorly on all measures of language, literacy, and cognition compared to age-matched peers; however, they did not perceive their lives differently. The two groups had similar ratings of personal happiness and satisfaction with life (job, family, living situation). While participants with SLI were found to be more likely to be working rather than attending post-high school education, there were no differences with regard to income between the two groups (at least in their mid-twenties). One must remember, however, that the age-matched group was more likely to be working part time and going to school. Thus, the participants with SLI were earning full-time what the controls were earning part-time. After college or trade school, the control group will likely earn much more than the SLI group.

A more recent study by Clegg et al. (2005) reported on the long-term cognitive and psychosocial ramifications of SLI for 17 adult males (30 years of age) diagnosed with severe delays in receptive and/or expressive language disorder during childhood (ages 4–9). Non-verbal IQ averaged 92.1 at 30 years of age. These individuals were compared to (1) typically developing siblings (male or female sibling within 5 years of age); (2) adults matched for age, gender, and performance IQ; and (3) a subsample of men matched for childhood performance IQ and parental social class. Everyone was administered measures of cognition, language, literacy, memory, phonological processing, theory of mind, psychosocial functioning, and social adaptation.

Significant language impairment was shown to persist into adulthood for the cohort of men with DLD. These men also demonstrated significantly poorer cognitive (verbal and performance), literacy, and theory of mind skills than comparison groups. The most disturbing data reported in this study dealt with employment, independent living, and relationship issues. Although all of the men with language impairments exited school by age 16, only 10 were employed, all in unskilled and manual labor positions. All had experienced unemployment, dismissal, and many were dependent on family and friends for their well-being. Half of the participants reported having minimal relationships with persons outside of their families because of continued problems in social adaptation.

A larger study with a more heterogeneous group of speech-language disorders was conducted in England by Stothard and her colleagues (Stothard et al., 1998). Seventy-one adolescents with a history of speech-language impairment were given a series of language and literacy assessments when they were 15 years old. The group was divided according to non-verbal IQ, and children whose non-verbal IQs were within the average range were defined as SLI. Adolescents with SLI were further subdivided based on whether or not their language impairment had resolved or persisted into adolescence. Adolescents with general language delay and persistent SLI performed significantly more poorly on measures of spoken language and literacy than typically developing children. Interestingly, while children with "resolved" SLI performed similarly to children developing typically on measures of spoken language, they continued to demonstrate difficulties on measures of literacy that affected their academic success in later years.

In the largest study to date, Tomblin et al. (2003) examined the stability of language status and group membership of 196 children with primary language disorder (PLD) over the course of 4 years in elementary school (8–10 years of age). A total of 54 percent of children diagnosed with PLD in kindergarten continued to qualify as PLD two years later. Four years after their initial diagnosis, 52 percent of children initially diagnosed as PLD continued to meet criteria for language impairment.

Recall from our earlier discussion that children in this study with PLD were subdivided into SLI and NLI groups on the basis of non-verbal IQ (>87 SLI; <87

NLI) to examine long-term prognosis/stability of group membership. When children were evaluated 2 and 4 years later, the risk for continued language impairment was greater for children in the NLI group than the SLI group (75 percent to 44 percent respectively).

Patterns of stability according to language domain (receptive only, expressive only, mixed receptive–expressive) were also examined. Children with receptive only impairments or expressive only impairments were found to demonstrate a higher rate of progress over a 2-year and 4-year follow-up period than children who demonstrated impairments in both receptive and expressive language domains. Most research that has examined intervention outcomes for children with mixed receptive–expressive language impairments has found this to be true (Bishop, Adams, & Rosen, 2006; Boyle et al., 2007; Law, Garrett & Nye, 2004; Tomblin & Zhang, 2006). However, other studies suggest that children with mixed or receptive only impairments may respond as well to intervention as children with expressive only impairments (Cohen et al., 2005; Gillam et al., 2008). The next section presents a brief overview of representative studies that have shown negative and positive outcomes for children with expressive, receptive, or mixed receptive–expressive impairments.

6 Intervention Outcomes

There have been several recent studies that have examined intervention outcomes in children with language impairments. In a large-scale randomized controlled trial conducted in England, Boyle et al. (2007) examined the effects of indirect and individual therapy versus group therapy for children with language impairment. A total of 124 children between the ages of 6 and 11 participated in the study and were included on the basis of their performance on the CELF-3 UK (Semel, Wiig, & Secord, 2000) (-1.25 SD below the mean on receptive and/or expressive language scales). Children were randomly assigned to one of five groups. Children in groups 1 and 2 received therapy from a speech-language pathologist and children in groups 3 and 4 from a trained speech aide. Children in groups 1 and 3 received individual therapy, and children in groups 2 and 4 received group therapy. Children in group 5 received speech and language therapy from their community-based speech-language pathologist. Thus, group 5 served as a standard practice control group. Each group contained between 31 and 34 children. All of the children demonstrated significant problems in expressive language at the outset of the study. About 75 percent of children demonstrated problems in expressive language with receptive language scores above the 10th percentile for their chronological age while the remaining participants demonstrated significant delays in both expressive and receptive language.

Children in the control group received about eight sessions of treatment from community-based providers while children in the experimental groups received about 38 sessions of treatment over the course of the academic year. All of the children in the experimental group performed significantly better at post-test and follow-up on the CELF-3 UK when compared to children in the control group; Cohen's effect sizes ranged from .26 to .47. The different interventions were shown to be equally effective.

Logistic regressions were conducted to examine profiles of children who made progress versus those who did not. Half (49 percent) of the children made significant improvements on the CELF-3 UK receptive language scale, and 46 percent made significant improvements on the expressive language scale. Girls were three times more likely to make progress in receptive language than boys. Children with mixed receptive–expressive difficulties were some six times more likely to progress in their receptive language scores compared with those with specific expressive language impairment.

There were no significant differences in post-test performance between children with receptive delay and those in the control group. Non-verbal cognitive ability was not found to mediate progress in intervention.

Several studies have examined the efficacy of programs like Fast ForWord in ameliorating language impairments in children. Cohen et al. (2005), for example, conducted a randomized controlled trial that examined the effects of Fast ForWord-Language (FFW-L; Scientific Learning Corporation, 1998) on improving language abilities in 77 children (age range 6–10, M = 7) with severe mixed receptive–expressive and expressive language impairments. To be included in the study, children had to perform -1.25 SD below the mean on the receptive and expressive subtests of the CELF-3 UK and have a non-verbal IQ above 80 on the British Ability Scales: 2nd Edition (BAS II; Elliot, Smith, & McCulloch, 1996) or Raven's Coloured Progressive Matrices (Raven, Court, & Raven, 1995). Children with a hearing loss, speech or fluency disorders were excluded from the study. Children were randomly assigned to one of three groups who received (a) home intervention with FFW-L, (b) home intervention with commercially available language and reading computer games that did not contain modified speech, and (c) no additional intervention. All of the children continued to receive speech-language intervention services through their schools. Children participated in 9 weeks of therapy with FFW-L. The findings were quite straightforward. All of the children made significant improvements on the CELF-3 UK regardless of group assignment, indicating that the home intervention and FFW-L intervention provided no additional benefits. The unusually small gains from pre- to post-test and to 6 months follow-up did not indicate that interventions resulted in clinically significant improvement in language abilities.

In a similar study, Bishop, Adams, and Rosen (2006) randomly assigned children with receptive language impairments between the ages of 8 and 13 years of age to one of three conditions to determine whether computerized grammatical training programs would result in improved grammatical comprehension. Some children (n = 512) were asked to respond to reversible sentences containing pauses before critical phrases and others (n = 512) to the same sentences containing acoustically modified speech that amplified or extended intensity and durational elements in sentences to make them more salient, a similar approach to that used in FFW-L (Scientific Learning Corporation, 1998). A total of 59 children were assigned to an untrained control group. Children in all groups (including the untrained group) performed similarly on post-measures of grammatical under-standing. That is, children with receptive language impairments did not appear to benefit from either computer training program.

In a more recent study, Gillam and colleagues (Gillam et al., 2008) also examined the efficacy of FFW-L in improving language abilities. A total of 216 elementary school-aged (6–9 years) children with specific language impairment were randomly assigned to four treatment conditions: (1) Fast ForWord; (2) computer-assisted language intervention (CALI); (3) non-specific computer games (Academic Enrich-ment; AE); and (4) individual language intervention (ILI). Children participated in intervention activities for 1 hour and 40 minutes per day, 5 days per week for a total of 6 weeks. Children in all four groups were found to improve significantly on the Comprehensive Assessment of Spoken Language (CASL, Carrow-Woolfolk, 1999). Effect sizes, analyses of standard error of measurement, and normalization percentages supported the clinical significance of the language improvements for children in all four groups.

A follow-up study (Gillam, Loeb, & Hoffman, in preparation) compared children with receptive only, expressive only, and mixed receptive–expressive language impairment. As in the previous study, all of the treatments improved children's language from pre- to post-testing on the CASL [(F (1, 200) = 41.89, p < .001, eta 2 = .173]. The nature of the language impairment had no impact on treatment effectiveness. A follow-up logistic regression analysis was performed to compare the performance of children with expressive only, receptive only, and mixed receptive–expressive impairment on specific subtest scores obtained on the CASL. Only one subtest differentiated the groups, the syntax construction task. On this measure, children with expressive impairments were 1.8 times more likely to make significant improvements than children with receptive language impairments.

These studies present somewhat mixed findings with regard to intervention outcomes for children with SLI. Part of the reason for this is that researchers often measure outcome using omnibus measures of language performance rather than specific measures of language performance. For example, the expressive language composite on the CELF-4 is a combination of scores taken from various subtests measuring component skill areas. Component skill areas are more specific measures of language performance and include tasks such as the word structure subtest, which requires children to use past tense, plurals, and possessives in closed sentence formats using picture and verbal prompts. We suspect that com-posite language measures are less sensitive to improvements in specific areas of language. Two recent studies that focus on improving specific aspects of language, grammatical morphology, and verb argument structure support this impression.

In the first study, Leonard and colleagues (Leonard et al., 2006) investigated the use of focused stimulation in facilitating the use of third-person singular –s and auxiliary *is*, *are*, *was* for 25 children with SLI. The children ranged in age from 3;0 to 4;4 (M = 3;5) at the beginning of the study. Children were assigned to either a treatment condition focused on third-person singular (n = 15) or a treatment condition focused on auxiliary *is*, *are*, *was* (n = 10). Each treatment condition involved two activities: (1) the clinician read a story while acting out the events using toys and props, and (2) the clinician provided conversational recasts of the child's utterances during play. Intervention took place over a 12-week period, two times daily, twice per week. Not surprisingly, the intervention was found to improve children's use of the target forms. The discussion focused on the role that maturational processes play in the progress children make in intervention.

In the second study, Ebbels, van der Lely, and Dockrell (2007) investigated two theoretically motivated interventions aimed at improving verb argument structure in 27 school age (11–16 years of age) children who met the criteria for SLI. Children were randomly assigned to one of three groups: Group 1 received syntactic–semantic therapy using shapes, colors, and coding schemes aimed at highlighting different parts of speech and/or morphology. Group 2 received semantic therapy that focused solely on semantic aspects of verbs. The experimenter was careful to highlight only semantic and not syntactic information by using gerunds to introduce verbs (e.g., This is pouring). Group 3 served as the control group. They received intervention that focused on the ability to formulate inferences during text comprehension. Children participated in three assessment sessions: one prior to beginning intervention, one after participating in intervention, and one follow-up session 3 months after participating in the intervention. As in the previous study, the intervention was effective. The two intervention groups used significantly more verb argument structures than the control group. These gains were maintained at follow-up testing 3 months later.

In summarizing the research on intervention outcomes, several findings are clear. Intervention that targets specific aspects of language is generally effective. Clinicians can take comfort in findings that common treatment approaches like focused stimulation and conversational recasts are effective interventions. Less comforting, however, is the difficulty untangling the effects of intervention from the maturational gains that may occur without treatment (Leonard et al., 2007). Also less comforting are studies showing that long-term outcomes are not always positive for individuals with language impairment. Subtle and not-so-subtle language problems often persist into adulthood, and in many cases these difficulties impact career choices, income levels, and social-personal relationships. In the final section, we consider the underlying causes of the initial difficulty in learning language and the likelihood that these causes do not disappear with age.

7　Causal Explanations for SLI

There are two broad categories of causal explanations for SLI: linguistic and processing accounts. Linguistic accounts typically focus on the difficulty children with SLI have in learning grammatical morphology. The most popular linguistic account, extended optional infinitive (EOI), was proposed by Wexler (1994). Wexler found developmental evidence that English-speaking children progress through a stage of language acquisition in which the marking of tense in main clauses is not obligatory. Inconsistent marking of tense is thus a typical stage in the English acquisition process. The problem for children with SLI is that they do not move through the optional infinitive stage as quickly as typically developing children. Evidence for this account comes from studies that have shown that English-speaking children with SLI use morphemes that are unrelated to tense (e.g., regular plural –s; –ing) with much higher accuracy than morphemes that are related to tense (Rice & Wexler, 1996).

There are several other linguistic accounts of SLI: an implicit grammatical rule deficit (Gopnik, 1990; see Leonard, 1998), the missing agreement account (Clahsen, 1989), and the computational grammatical complexity account (CGC; Marshall & van der Lely, 2007). The CGC proposes that some children demonstrate a specific form of SLI called grammatical-SLI. For these children, SLI is caused by deficits in "computational grammatical systems" including the phonological system, and this affects their ability to produce, for example, regular past tense forms. Proponents of this explanation report that as compared to typically developing children, children with G-SLI have difficulty in producing inflected forms, particularly those that end in consonant clusters (Marshall & van der Lely, 2007).

An absence or reduction in the use of grammatical morphemes can also be explained by processing limitations. Since morphemes are brief in duration and must be perceived and processed quickly in the context of running speech, processing accounts propose that general and/or specific limitations in information processing may explain the problems that children with SLI experience in learning the morphology of the language (Gathercole & Baddeley, 1990; Kail, 1994; Montgomery, 1995).

If children have difficulty processing incoming information quickly and efficiently, it will affect their ability to detect and process inflectional morphemes or make judgments about grammaticality (Wulfeck & Bates, 1995). Typically, tasks that measure speed of processing are used to support processing accounts of SLI, the assumption being that processing speed will determine how much information can be processed during a given amount of time. There is considerable evidence to suggest that children with SLI demonstrate slowed response times on a variety of tasks (Leonard et al., 2007; Miller et al., 2001). Some have argued that processing efficiency is the problem rather than processing speed (Gillam, Cowan, & Day, 1995). The processing efficiency viewpoint is supported by studies that show that children with SLI take longer to complete more difficult tasks than easier ones. Research has also shown that children with SLI consistently demonstrate limitations in working memory capacity (Mainela-Arnold & Evans, 2005; Montgomery, 2000), particularly when the information requires phonological processing (Montgomery, 2004; Montgomery & Windsor, 2007).

A recent study by Leonard and colleagues (Leonard et al., 2007) examined the relationship between processing speed and working memory and attempted to determine whether these measures could account for the language impairment itself. Two hundred and four 14-year-olds participated in the study. All of the adolescents were administered a battery of processing speed and working memory tasks and a comprehensive language test battery. When speed and working memory were considered together they were shown to account for 62 percent of the variance in children's composite language scores, with verbal working memory making the largest contribution. It was not possible from this study to determine whether or not problems in processing merely limit children's abilities to demonstrate the linguistic knowledge they have, or if these problems themselves cause linguistic deficits.

The most parsimonious explanation of language learning difficulties in children with SLI is that these difficulties are caused by some combination of both linguistic and processing deficiencies. Working memory limitations seem compatible with linguistic accounts because sorting out the rules for tense and agreement place more interpretation demands on listening than conceptually easier aspects of language. The exact relationship between linguistic and processing explanations is complicated by cross-linguistic differences in children with SLI. For example, there is currently no explanation for the significantly higher percentage of accurate tense usage in Swedish SLI than in English SLI (Leonard, 2004).

8   Summary and Conclusions

This chapter has provided an overview of some central issues about one of the most common developmental disorders: SLI. Although researchers have been investigating SLI for about 40 years, the specific criteria for defining and identifying the disorder continue to be questioned. Most researchers use a measure of non-verbal intelligence to ensure that children do not have significant cognitive impairments. In contrast, most clinicians do not administer a cognitive measure. The result of these different identification procedures is that the research-defined population of SLI is more restricted and homogeneous than the clinical population of children with developmental language disorders. Fortunately, the children with lower cognitive abilities tend not to have poorer outcomes than children with higher cognitive abilities. Unfortunately, language impairment for many children can be an enduring condition that persists into adolescence and adulthood. One study we discussed (Clegg et al., 2005) found that many individuals with a history of SLI had experienced unemployment and were often dependent on family and friends for their well-being.

The less than positive long-term outcomes are contrasted by a number of studies showing the efficacy of language intervention, particularly with targeted interventions on specific areas of language (e.g., Leonard et al., 2006). The inconsistencies between short- and long-term outcomes no doubt reflects changes in the manifestation of the language disorders with age and the impact the disorder has on academic performance and social-interpersonal skills.

In the final section of the chapter, we considered some of the possible causes of language learning problems. The most current views on causation implicate both linguistic and processing deficiencies. Unlike some other disorders where understanding causation might lead to prevention (e.g., reading disability), knowing the cause of SLI may have little impact on the nature of treatment or treatment outcome. Early intervention may speed the acquisition of language and reduce the risk of subsequent academic and social problems, but even the best remediation efforts may not be able to completely eliminate the lifelong consequences associated with SLI (although some young children with SLI do not have subsequent academic and social problems). The challenge for all of us is to continue to learn as much as we can about the disorder, its prognosis and manifestations, and do as much as possible to improve the outcomes for individuals whose language impairment persists through adolescence and adulthood.

REFERENCES

Aram, D., Morris, R., & Hall, N. (1993). Clinical and research congruence in identifying children with specific language impairment. *Journal of Speech and Hearing Research* 36, 580–91.

Bedore, L. & Leonard, L. (1998). Specific language impairment and grammatical morphology: A discriminant function analysis. *Journal of Speech, Language, and Hearing Research* 41, 1185–92.

Bishop, D., Adams, C., & Rosen, S. (2006). Resistance of grammatical impairment to computerized comprehension training in children with specific and non-specific language impairments. *International Journal of Language and Communication Disorders* 41, 19–40.

Boyle, J., McCartney, E., Forbes, J., & O'Hare, A. (2007). A randomized controlled trial and economic evaluation of direct versus indirect and individual versus group modes of speech and language therapy for children with primary language impairment. *Health Technology Assessment* 25, 1–155.

Bracken, B. & McCallum, S. (2006). *Universal Nonverbal Intelligence Test*. Rolling Meadows, IL: Riverside Publishing.

Brown, L., Sherbenou, R. J., & Johnsen, S. K. (1988). *Test of Nonverbal Intelligence*, 2nd ed. Austin, TX: Pro-Ed.

Burgemeister, B., Blum, L., & Lorge, I. (1972). *Columbia Mental Maturity Scale*, ed. 3. New York: Psychological Corporation.

Carrow-Woolfolk, E. (1999). *Comprehensive Assessment of Spoken Language*. Circle Pines, MN: American Guidance Systems.

Catts, H., Adlof, S., Hogan, T., & Ellis Weismer, S. (2005). Are specific language impairment and dyslexia distinct disorders? *Journal of Speech, Hearing, and Language Research* 48, 1378–96.

Clahsen, H. (1989). The grammatical characterization of developmental dysphasia. *Linguistics* 27, 897–920.

Clegg, J., Hollis, C., Mawhood, L., & Rutter, M. (2005). Developmental language disorders – a follow-up in later adult life. Cognitive, language and psychosocial outcomes. *Journal of Child Psychology and Psychiatry* 46 (2), 128–49.

Cohen, W., Hodson, A., O'Hare, A., Boyle, J., Durrani, T., McCartney, E., Mattey, M., Naftalin, L., & Watson, J. (2005). Effects of computer-based intervention through acoustically modified speech (Fast ForWord) in severe mixed receptive–expressive language impairment: Outcomes from a randomized controlled trial. *Journal of Speech, Language and Hearing Research* 48, 715–29.

Cole, K., Dale, P., & Mills, P. (1992). Stability of the intelligence quotient–language quotient relation: Is discrepancy modeling based on a myth? *American Journal on Mental Retardation* 97 (2), 131–43.

Cole, K., Schwartz, I., Notari, A., Dale, P., & Mills, P. (1995). Examination of the stability of two measures of defining specific language impairment. *Applied Psycholinguistics* 16, 103–23.

Conti-Ramsden, G., Crutchley, A., & Botting, N. (1997). The extent to which psychometric tests differentiate subgroups of children with SLI. *Journal of Speech, Language, and Hearing Research* 40, 765–77.

Conti-Ramsden, G., Crutchley, A., & Botting, N. (1999). Classification of children with specific language impairment: Longitudinal considerations. *Journal of Speech, Language, and Hearing Research* 42, 1195–204.

Dollaghan, C. (2004). Taxometric analysis of specific language impairment in 3- and 4-year-old children. *Journal of Speech, Language, and Hearing Research* 47, 464–75.

Dunn, L. & Dunn, L. (1981). *Peabody Picture VocabularyTest – Revised*. Circle Pines, MN: American Guidance Service.

Ebbels, S., van der Lely, H., & Dockrell, J. (2007). Intervention for verb argument structure in children with persistent SLI: A randomized controlled trial. *Journal of Speech, Language, and Hearing Research* 50, 1330–49.

Elliot, C., Smith, P., & McCulloch, K. (1996). *British Ability Scales-II*. Windsor, UK: NFER-Nelson.

Gathercole, S. & Baddeley, A. (1990). Phonological memory deficits in language disordered children: is there a causal connection? *Journal of Memory and Language* 29, 336–60.

Gillam, R., Cowan, N., & Day, L. (1995). Sequential memory in children with and without language impairment. *Journal of Speech and Hearing Research* 38, 393–402.

Gillam, R., Loeb, D., Hoffman, L., Bohman, T., Champlin, C., Thibodeau, L., Widen, Brandl, L., & Friel-Patti, S. (2008). The efficacy of Fast ForWord language intervention in school-age children with language impairment: A randomized clinical trial. *Journal of Speech, Language, and Hearing Research* 51, 97–119.

Gillam, R., Loeb, D., & Hoffman, L. (in preparation). Language outcomes from a national clinical trial: Subtype analyses. To be submitted to *Journal of Speech, Language, and Hearing Research*.

Goffman, L. & Leonard, J. (2000). Growth of language skills in preschool children with specific language impairment: Implications for assessment and intervention. *American Journal of Speech Language Pathology* 9, 151–61.

Goldman, R. & Fristoe, M. (1986). *Goldman–Fristoe Test of Articulation*. Circle Pines, MN: American Guidance Association.

Gopnik, M. (1990). Feature-blind grammar and dysphasia. *Nature* 344, 715.

Haskill, A. & Tyler, A. (2007). A comparison of linguistic profiles in subgroups of children with specific language impairment. *American Journal of Speech Language Pathology* 16, 209–21.

Kail, R. (1994). A method of studying the generalized slowing hypothesis in children with specific language impairment. *Journal of Speech and Hearing Research* 37, 418–21.

Law, J., Garrett, Z., & Nye, C. (2004). The efficacy of treatment for children with developmental speech and language delay/disorder: A meta-analysis. *Journal of Speech, Language, and Hearing Research* 47, 924–943.

Leonard, L. (1998). *Children with specific language impairment*. Cambridge, MA: MIT Press.

Leonard, L. (2004). Specific Language Impairment in children: A comparison of English and Swedish. *Language Acquisition* 12, 219–46.

Leonard, L., Camarata, S., Pawtowska, M., Brown, B., & Camarata, M. (2006). Tense and agreement morphemes in the speech of children with specific language impairment during intervention: Phase 2. *Journal of Speech, Language, and Hearing Research* 49, 749–70.

Leonard, L., Ellis Weismer, S., Miller, C., Francis, D., Tomblin, J., & Kail, R. (2007). Speed of processing, working memory, and language impairment in children. *Journal of Speech, Language, and Hearing Research* 50, 408–28.

Mainela-Arnold, E. & Evans, J. (2005). Beyond capacity limitations: Determinants of word recall performance on verbal working memory span tasks in children with SLI. *Journal of Speech, Language, and Hearing Research* 48, 897–909.

Marshall, C. & van der Lely, H. (2007). The impact of phonological complexity on past tense inflection in children with grammatical-SLI. *Advances in Speech Language Pathology* 9, 191–203.

Miller, C., Kail, R., Leonard, L., & Tomblin, B. (2001). Speed of processing in children with specific language impairment. *Journal of Speech, Language, and Hearing Research* 44, 416–33.

Montgomery, J. (1995). Examination of phonological working memory in specifically language-impaired children. *Applied Psycholinguistics* 16, 355–78.

Montgomery, J. (2000). Verbal working memory and sentence comprehension in children with specific language impairment. *Journal of Speech, Language, and Hearing Research* 43, 293–308.

Montgomery, J. (2004). Sentence comprehension in children with specific language impairment: effects of input rate and phonological working memory. *International Journal of Language and Communication Disorders* 39, 115–33.

Montgomery, J. (2005). Effects of input rate and age on the real-time language processing of children with specific language impairment. *International Journal of Language and Communication Disorders* 1, 177–88.

Montgomery, J. & Windsor, J. (2007). Examining the language performances of children with and without specific language impairment: Contributions of phonological short-term memory and speed of processing. *Journal of Speech, Language, and Hearing Research* 50, 778–97.

Newcomer, P. & Hammill, D. (1988; 1997). *Test of Language Development-Primary-3.* Austin, TX: Pro-Ed.

Peña, E., Spaulding, T., & Plante, E. (2006). The composition of normative groups and diagnostic decision making: Shooting ourselves in the foot. *American Journal of Speech-Language Pathology* 15, 247–54.

Plante, E. (1998). Criteria for SLI: The Stark and Tallal legacy and beyond. *Journal of Speech, Language, and Hearing Research* 41, 951–7.

Raven, J., Court, J., & Raven, J. (1995). *Coloured progressive matrices.* Oxford, UK: Oxford Psychologists Press.

Records, N., Tomblin, B., & Freese, P. (1992). The quality of life of young adults with histories of specific language impairment. *American Journal of Speech Language Pathology* 2, 44–53.

Rescorla, L. (1989). The language development survey: A screening tool for delayed language in toddlers. *Journal of Speech and Hearing Disorders* 54, 587–99.

Rice, M., Tomblin, B., Hoffman, L., Richman, W., & Marquis, J. (2004). Grammatical tense deficits in children with SLI and nonspecific language impairment: Relationships with nonverbal IQ over time. *Journal of Speech, Language, and Hearing Research* 47, 816–34.

Rice, M. & Wexler, K. (1996). Toward tense as a clinical marker of specific language impairment in English-speaking children. *Journal of Speech and Hearing Research* 39, 1239–57.

Roid G. & Miller, L. (1997). *The Leiter International Performance Scale – Revised.* Lansing, MI: Psychological Assessment Resources.

Scientific Learning Corporation. (1998). *Fast ForWord–Language* [Computer software]. Berkeley, CA: Author.

Semel, E., Wiig, E., & Secord, W. (2000). *Clinical Evaluation of Language Fundamentals UK – Third edition.* San Antonio, TX: The Psychological Corporation.

Semel, E., Wiig, E., & Secord, W. (2004). *Clinical Evaluation of Language Fundamentals – Fourth Edition.* San Antonio, TX: The Psychological Corporation.

Stark, R. & Tallal, P. (1981). Selection of children with specific language deficits. *Journal of Speech and Hearing Disorders* 46, 114–22.

Stothard, S., Snowling, M., Bishop, D., Chipchase, B., & Kaplan, C. (1998). Language impaired preschoolers: A follow-up into adolescence. *Journal of Speech, Language, and Hearing Research* 41, 407–18.

Tomblin, B., Records, N., & Zhang, X. (1996). A system for the diagnosis of specific language impairment in kindergarten children. *Journal of Speech and Hearing Research* 39, 1284–94.

Tomblin, B., Records, N., Buckwalter, P., Zhang, X., Smith, E., & O'Brien, M. (1997). Prevalence of specific language impairment in kindergarten children. *Journal of Speech, Language, and Hearing Research* 40, 1245–60.

Tomblin, B. & Zhang, X. (2006). The dimensionality of language ability in school-age children. *Journal of Speech, Language, and Hearing Research* 49, 1193–208.

Tomblin, B., Zhang, X., Buckwalter, P., & O'Brien, M. (2003). The stability of primary language disorder: Four years after kindergarten diagnosis. *Journal of Speech, Language, and Hearing Research* 46, 1283–96.

Ukrainetz McFadden, T. (1996). Creating language impairments in typically achieving children: The pitfalls of normal normative sampling. *Language, Speech and Hearing Services in Schools* 27, 3–9.

Wechsler, D. (1967). *Wechsler preschool and primary scale of intelligence.* New York: Psychological Corp.

Wechsler, D. (1974). *Wechsler intelligence scale for children – revised.* New York: Psychological Corp.

Wexler, K. (1994). Optional infinitives, head movement, and the economy of derivations. In D. Lightfoot & N. Hornstein (eds.), *Verb Movement* (pp. 305–50). Cambridge: Cambridge University Press.

Wulfeck, B. & Bates, E. (1995). *Grammatical sensitivity in children with language impairment.* Technical Report CND-9512. Center for Research in Language, University of California at San Diego.

10 Pragmatic Impairment

MICHAEL R. PERKINS

1 Introduction

Pragmatic impairment[1] is a term used in connection with individuals who experience difficulties with language use. Rather than referring to a straightforward, unitary disorder, this single label is in fact an umbrella term applied to a wide range of disparate phenomena with no single underlying cause. Indeed, although included in the section on Language Disorders, this chapter would have been equally at home in the section on Cognitive and Intellectual Disorders since pragmatic impairment is most commonly linked to cognitive or neurological dysfunction. However, the consequences of such dysfunction for communication between individuals inevitably bring into play a wide range of other phenomena – including language, speech, gesture, eye contact, hearing, and vision, to name but a few – which can, in turn, reciprocally implicate cognitive processing. In addition, non-cognitive deficits – for example in grammar, motor control, or auditory processing – can also contribute to pragmatic impairment in their own right.

The mapping out of such complex interactions is no easy task, and in fact has been largely glossed over through the tendency to focus only on specific manifestations of pragmatic impairment (e.g., problems with inference and appropriateness during conversation) in a narrow range of communication disorders (e.g., right hemisphere damage (RHD), traumatic brain injury (TBI), and autism). I will first of all consider why this should be the case by examining the slipperiness of the concept of pragmatics, followed by a brief review of the way pragmatic impairment has been studied and assessed over the last few decades. I will then take a more detailed look at the various conditions that underlie pragmatic impairment, and the role played by compensatory adaptation.

The Handbook of Language and Speech Disorders, First Edition. Edited by Jack S. Damico, Nicole Müller, and Martin J. Ball. © 2013 Blackwell Publishing Ltd except for editorial material and organization © 2013 Jack S. Damico, Nicole Müller, Martin J. Ball. Published 2013 by Blackwell Publishing Ltd.

2   Approaches to Pragmatic Impairment

2.1   *Pragmatics*

Pragmatics is a branch of linguistics which focuses primarily on the way in which language is used by actual speakers in real-life situations, rather than on its formal properties, which can be considered independently of speakers and hearers. For example, the made-up sentence "I've forgotten my umbrella" can be analyzed in terms of its grammar, vocabulary, and phonology without the need to specify any actual context of use. If, on the other hand, we witness this sentence being uttered by a specific individual on a unique occasion, we are naturally drawn to factors such as what other utterances and events (if any) precede and follow it, why the speaker chose this particular form of words, who the utterance is addressed to, its intended – and actual – effect on the addressee and other incidental hearers, where and when it was uttered, the speaker's facial expression, body posture and any accompanying gestures, the extent to which the utterance reflects or manifests a particular set of sociocultural parameters, and so on. However, although the grammatical, semantic, and phonological form of utterances may be studied independently of context, it is still crucial to pragmatic considerations such as why an utterance with these particular formal properties was chosen rather than any other of the infinite range of possible contenders ("I've forgotten it," "The umbrella completely slipped my mind," and "Damn!," to name but three). It also follows that anyone who has problems with grammar, phonology, or semantics will also have a concomitant pragmatic problem to the extent that their ability to produce or comprehend the requisite range of contextually appropriate utterances is limited.

Although the primary focus of *linguistic* pragmatics is on the use of language, pragmatics was originally more broadly conceived as being to do with the communicative use of all "signs," not just linguistic ones (Morris, 1938), and this wider semiotic interpretation is particularly evident in the field of speech and language pathology where the use of non-linguistic signaling systems such as gesture and facial expression is commonly seen as a means of compensating pragmatically for language deficits – for example, in aphasia (e.g., Davis & Wilcox, 1985; Dronkers, Ludy, & Redfern, 1998). The definition of pragmatics I will use in this chapter, therefore, is "the use of linguistic and nonlinguistic capacities for communicative purposes" (cf. Perkins, 2007, p. 10).

2.2   *Pragmatic impairment*

The acknowledgment and identification of the condition(s) known as pragmatic impairment dates from the late 1970s and early 1980s (e.g., Gallagher & Prutting, 1983; Rees, 1978), and was triggered by work in the emerging field of theoretical pragmatics by the philosophers Austin, Grice, and Searle. Particularly influential were Speech Act Theory (Austin, 1962; Searle, 1969), which focused on the communicative functions of speakers' utterances and their effect on others, and Grice's Co-operative Principle (Grice, 1975), which specified how we are able to work out the non-literal meanings (or "implicatures") of utterances by taking for granted that all speakers follow a common set of conversational "maxims" (say what you believe to be true, don't say more or less than you have to, be relevant, be clear). Relevance Theory (Sperber & Wilson, 1995), a more recent cognitively based theory of pragmatics which focuses on the counterbalancing of inferential processing effort and "contextual effects," has likewise been taken on board by some speech and language pathologists. A second major influence on the characterization of pragmatic impairment was the separate field of Discourse Analysis, particularly the work of Halliday and Hasan (1976), which identified a range of means by which a sequence of utterances – particularly in narrative – was able to form a coherent whole over and above its individual constituent sentences. In more recent years, the analytical method known as Conversation Analysis has been increasingly influential in clinical pragmatics by emphasizing the joint contribution of both interlocutors, not merely that of the person with the impairment. (For recent overviews of each of these areas and their clinical relevance, see Ahlsén, 2008; Leinonen & Ryder, 2008; Müller, Guendouzi, & Wilson, 2008; and Wilkinson, 2008.)

Because of this variety of historical influences, there is no one agreed definition of pragmatic impairment beyond the rather vague "problems with language use," and the single term is therefore not overly helpful as a diagnostic category. A bewildering array of different behaviors have been described as symptoms of pragmatic impairment – for example, and to name but a few: saying too little or too much; overuse of certain phrases; failure to initiate conversation; over-literalness; repetitiveness; problems with inference, topic maintenance, lexical retrieval, fluency, humor, figurative language, intonation, facial expression, tense use, eye gaze, intelligibility, event sequencing, physical proximity, politeness, and so forth.

Faced with this, the most common practice both in clinical work and research is to characterize pragmatic impairment in terms of performance on one of many available evaluation instruments. Some of these profile performance across a wide range of communicative behaviors, not unlike those listed in the previous paragraph (e.g., Penn, 1985; Prutting & Kirchner, 1983). Others target specific aspects of pragmatics such as turn taking and topic management (Perkins, Whitworth, & Lesser, 1997) or "cohesion" (Armstrong, 1991), or features specific to a particular communicative disorder such as RHD (Bryan, 1989) or TBI (Douglas, O'Flaherty, & Snow, 2000). Yet others are built around concepts taken directly from a particular theory of pragmatics such as Speech Act Theory (Bara, Bosco, & Bucciarelli, 1999) or Conversational Implicature (Damico, 1985). Finer assessment-based distinctions are possible, such as the diagnostic category of "pragmatic language impairment" (PLI) which may or may not coexist with autism (Bishop, 2003). It must not be forgotten, though, that such characterizations and sub-categorizations of pragmatic impairment are no more than artifacts of the particular evaluation measure used, and do not necessarily identify some independent, pre-existing, discrete condition that was merely waiting to be discovered. This important point is often overlooked, as is evident in the widespread assumption that pragmatic impairment is a distinct, relatively clear-cut and easily identified pathology. Unfortunately, the reality is far more complex.

In the rest of the chapter I will attempt to map out this complex reality as follows. Firstly I will outline the range of underlying deficits that contribute to behaviors commonly described as, or seen as symptoms of, pragmatic impairment. These deficits can be expressed in neurological, cognitive, linguistic, or sensorimotor terms as the *intra*personal capacities of individuals. They are pragmatic in so far as they impact on interaction *between* individuals who are communicating with each other, and this *inter*personal dimension brings into play various phenomena – such as turn taking and topic transition during conversation – which can only be fully understood as properties of pair or group activity, rather than in purely individual terms. A further important feature of pragmatic impairment is the way in which both individuals and groups adapt to, or compensate for, specific problems. So, for example, a conversation may be disrupted at a particular point by an attempt to resolve a word-finding difficulty either through self-cueing or through cueing by an interlocutor. Thus although the behaviors that we describe as instances of pragmatic impairment may be triggered by a particular deficit within an individual, they are typically the eventual outcome of a complex chain of events played out both intra- and interpersonally. Another way of putting this is to describe pragmatics as "emergent" – i.e., a complex entity that derives from interactions between entities at "lower" levels (Perkins, 2005, 2008).

3   Factors Which Contribute to Pragmatic Impairment

3.1   *Neurological deficits*

Given the range of behaviors seen as instances of pragmatic impairment, it is hardly surprising that no single area of cerebral activity is uniquely implicated (Stemmer, 2008a). Instead, researchers in what has come to be known as "neuro-pragmatics" typically focus on the neural substrates of particular pathological conditions commonly associated with pragmatically atypical behavior such as damage to the right hemisphere, and TBI in which the frontal lobes are most commonly affected. Various pragmatically relevant cognitive functions have been linked to specific areas of the brain such as prefrontal cortex (cognitive control, memory for source of information, metamemory judgment, and the processing of novelty), orbitofrontal cortex (emotional and social control), right frontal lobe (awareness of others' – and one's own – mental states and retrieval of episodic memory), left frontal lobe (memory encoding), and ventromedial frontal lobe (social reasoning and empathy) (Stemmer, 2008b). Despite this knowledge being largely derived from lesion studies, we are still very much in the dark about the neurological specifics since much of the research carried out (and particularly on RHD) has tended not to be overly precise about site of lesion. If anything, we know even less about the neurology of developmental disorders which result in pragmatic impairment, though Dapretto et al. (2006) suggest that in children with autism there is a malfunction of "mirror neurons" – a class of neurons in the medial prefrontal cortex which enable us to replicate behaviors we observe being performed by others – and this has been linked to impaired ability to represent the mental states of others. Work in neuropragmatics has so far focused almost exclusively on the neural substrates of cognitive dysfunction, but for the neurology of the full range of pragmatic impairments to be properly understood, it will also be necessary to identify how these are networked with linguistic and sensorimotor processing.

3.2 Cognitive deficits

As noted earlier, pragmatic impairment has been most commonly linked to underlying problems with cognition – i.e., the capacity for thought and reasoning. For convenience, a representative range of cognitive deficits and their pragmatic consequences are grouped somewhat arbitrarily under five headings. For more extensive and in-depth coverage, see Perkins (2007, chapter 5).

3.2.1 Inference Inferential reasoning – the drawing of conclusions from available evidence – is the cognitive function most extensively involved in pragmatics. Essentially a computational process, its success is also dependent on the quality of its input data. Thus, a blind person might be unable to infer that "Wonderful!" – uttered with a grimace – is actually intended ironically to mean anything but wonderful. Individuals with RHD, on the other hand, sometimes ignore such evidence even when it is readily accessible. Bihrle et al. (1986) found that adults with right hemisphere damage were less adept than adults with left hemisphere damage at identifying the correct joke punchlines from a set of four, and in fact sometimes preferred humorous non sequiturs that were unrelated to the subject matter of the joke. In addition to irony and humor, problems with inferential reasoning have also been shown to affect understanding of sarcasm, lies, ambiguity, emotion, and indirect replies and requests (Bissett & Novak, 1995; Holtgraves, 1999; McDonald, 1999; Molloy, Brownell, & Gardner, 1990; Tompkins et al., 2001). Transcript 1 illustrates the inferential difficulties of a 6-year-old child with autism spectrum disorder (ASD) who is playing a word guessing game with an adult.

Transcript 1
ADULT: this is something to help you travel . to go places on . and it's got wheels
CHILD: car
ADULT: and it's got a seat to sit on . and it's got a handlebar . and only one person can ride on it
CHILD: wheelchair
ADULT: and . it's got pedals . it's got two wheels and pedals and a seat and a handlebar and one person can ride it
CHILD: a wheelchair
(From Perkins, 2007, pp. 75–6)

It is not clear, however, whether the child has a problem with the inferential process itself or with some aspect of the input – for example, the fact that the information is only provided verbally.

3.2.2   Theory of mind   Theory of mind (ToM) – also known as "mindreading" and "mentalizing" – is a term used to refer to our ability to attribute mental states such as beliefs, desires, and intentions to others, and ToM difficulties are commonly seen as a core deficit underlying pragmatic impairment in autism (Baron-Cohen, 1995). ToM ability is typically assessed by a "false-belief" task – for example, if Tim sees Amy put a coin in her pocket, but doesn't see her subsequently take it out, we assume that Tim still believes the coin to be in Amy's pocket. Many individuals with autism would wrongly attribute knowledge of the coin's genuine whereabouts to Tim, despite knowing he didn't see it being moved. Views of ToM vary from those who regard it as a discrete mental "module" (Wilson, 2005) to those who regard it as a by-product of "weak central coherence" (Frith, 2003) or the inability to engage socially with others (Hobson & Bishop, 2003). Some support for this latter view comes from the finding that young children whose ability to interact socially is restricted because of impaired hearing or vision also appear to have problems passing ToM tests (Hobson & Bishop, 2003; Peterson & Siegal, 2000), as do some adults with TBI and RHD (Bibby & McDonald, 2005; Champagne, Desautels, & Joanette, 2003). Impaired ToM is commonly linked to pragmatic problems such as being unable to identify speakers' intentions when they are not linguistically explicit, as in the interpretation of indirect speech acts, the detection of irony and sarcasm, and the disambiguation of ambiguous utterances. For example, Transcript 2 shows a typical misreading of speaker intention by a child with ASD.

Transcript 2
ADULT: Would you say that the boy looked ill?
CHILD: The boy looked ill
(From Bishop & Adams, 1989, p. 249)

3.2.3   Executive function   Another type of mental processing frequently cited as being centrally involved in pragmatic competence is "executive function" (EF), a shorthand term for a related set of higher cognitive processes including planning, control, inhibition, monitoring, abstraction, problem solving, decision making, and multi-tasking. Executive dysfunction (ED) has been proposed as an alternative to ToM as the primary cognitive deficit in autism (Russell, 1997), but is more commonly associated with the pragmatic impairments found in conditions such as TBI, dementia, schizophrenia, and attention-deficit/hyperactivity disorder (ADHD) (Hashimoto et al., 2004; McDonald, Togher, & Code, 1999; Morrison-Stewart et al., 1992; Tannock & Schachar, 1996). For example, inattention, hyperactivity, and impulsiveness in ADHD have been associated with pragmatically disruptive behaviors such as excessive volubility, problems with turn taking and topic management, and using language inappropriately tailored to listener needs and specific contexts (Tannock & Schachar, 1996).

3.2.4   Memory   Memory in its various manifestations – whether it be short-, medium-, or long-term – also plays a key role in pragmatic processing, with working memory in particular being directly implicated in EF (Baddeley, 2003). Restrictions in the amount of linguistic material one is able to retain in short-term memory can impair sentence processing both in production and comprehension, which can subsequently disrupt conversational interaction. For example, Almor et al. (1999) found that excessive use of pronouns with no obvious referent by individuals with Alzheimer's disease was linked to problems with working memory, rather than being directly attributable to a semantic deficit. Losing track of what has already been covered in a conversation (what some have referred to as "medium-term memory") can lead to odd shifts in topic. Wilson, Baddeley, and Kapur (1995) report a case of severe amnesia in which the inability to recall recent events meant that the speaker returned again and again to topics already discussed minutes before. Perkins, Body, and Parker (1995) describe the case of a man with TBI whose poor verbal and non-verbal recall similarly led him to loop back continually to previously covered topics, but who also showed "topic drift" over much shorter time spans, as seen in Transcript 3.

> Transcript 3
> I have got faults and . my biggest fault is . I do enjoy sport . it's something that I've always done . I've done it all my life . I've nothing but respect for my mother and father and . my sister . and basically sir . I've only come to this conclusion this last two months . and . as far as I'm concerned . my sister doesn't exist (From Perkins et al., 1995, p. 305)

3.2.5   Emotion   Another area of mental processing commonly linked to pragmatic impairment is that of emotion or affect. Most frequently described is the inability to accurately "read" the emotions of others, as found in people with autism who have particular difficulty, for example, in interpreting facial expression and prosody (Baron-Cohen, 1991) and in people with schizophrenia who find it difficult to identify information which is emotionally salient (Phillips et al., 2003). This can make it difficult to identify communicative intent, particularly when the speaker's affective state is at odds with the literal meaning of what is being said, as can occur in the communication of irony, sarcasm, humor, and teasing. Problems with the expression of emotion can likewise cause pragmatic problems – for example the inability of people with bipolar disorder to inhibit inappropriate emotions (Murphy et al., 1999) and the flat affect found in some individuals suffering from depression (Scherer, 1986), Parkinson's disease (Möbes et al., 2008) or schizophrenia (Cohen & Docherty, 2004).

3.3   *Linguistic deficits*

As noted earlier, there is more to pragmatics than just cognition. When interacting with others, even if we have a full appreciation of the context, the mental and emotional states of the participants and what is communicatively appropriate at any given moment, we are not going to be successful unless we also have the necessary ability to produce and understand *language* across its full range of complexity and subtlety. It's all very well knowing that in some circumstances an individual may be identified merely by saying "she" while in others we need to be more explicit by saying something like "the short, dark-haired girl in the corner," but unless we have in addition the necessary syntactic and lexical ability – in this case, the ability to produce and/or understand a complex noun phrase – we are not going to get very far. Pragmatics is as much about *language* use as it is about language *use*. In this section I will briefly outline the pragmatic impact of a selective range of linguistic deficits. (For a more extensive account, see Perkins, 2007, chapter 6.)

3.3.1   Syntax and morphology   Any limitation in syntactic or morphological knowledge and processing capacity will (a) reduce the morphosyntactic choices available for fitting structure to context, and (b) impose an extra processing burden on one's interlocutor.

> Transcript 4
> and er . two weeks . my stroke . Saturday . Saturday tea time . me chips for me . fish for me

Transcript 4 shows a brief extract from a conversation involving a man with aphasia. Although one might hazard a number of guesses at the meaning he intended to convey (e.g., "on the Saturday two weeks before I had my stroke I bought some fish and chips for my tea"), his morphosyntactic problems (e.g., various obligatory clause and phrase elements are omitted and variation in pro-nominal case marking (I/me) is absent) mean that there is insufficient information encoded for us to be sure, and the hearer is thus faced with an ultimately impossible inferential reconstruction task. His linguistic limitations also mean he is unlikely to be able to vary the syntax of his utterances very much to fit different contexts (e.g., "What happened?: My mother and I bought ourselves fish and chips" vs. "Who did you buy them for? We bought them for ourselves" vs. "Did you buy them? Yes, we did").

3.3.2   Semantics   Problems with semantics, and with lexical selection in particular, are often seen as part and parcel of pragmatic impairment. In fact, for a number of years "semantic-pragmatic disorder," a term originally coined by Rapin and Allen (1983), was commonly used to refer to a range of communicative problems found in ASD, though it has now generally been supplanted by "pragmatic language impairment" (Bishop, 2000). Idiosyncratic vocabulary use in autism – of which it is a defining feature (World Health Organization, 2004) – includes neologisms (as italicized in Transcript 5, taken from a letter written by an adult with autism), and anomalous lexico-grammatical constructions as in Transcript 6 (spoken by an adult with autism):

Transcript 5
Later on we got to King's Cross, we *vamperated* the train, then we *consailed* the King's Cross underground
(From Werth, Perkins, & Boucher, 2001, p. 116)

Transcript 6
Tell me is it the sunset do?
(From Perkins et al., 2006, p. 802)

Perkins et al. (2006) report instances of adults with autism apparently using words appropriately, and then asking what they mean, which suggests that their lexical use may not reflect conceptual understanding.

Word-finding problems in conditions such as aphasia can also be pragmatically disruptive when they result in prolonged attempts at self-repair and circumlocution, as in Transcript 7, where an adult with anomic aphasia is trying to retrieve the word "watch."

Transcript 7
it's er - [*sighs*] what I put on my hair on . er not my hair . er - [*tuts*] put it right er . [*sighs*] dear dear dear get it . I'll get it in a minute [*looks at watch and shakes his head*] it's not going through . it's not getting it . it's not that one . it's easy that one . it's dead easy that is

3.3.3 Discourse Discourse overlaps with pragmatics to the extent that it focuses on linguistic context, though it differs by highlighting in particular the way in which extended sequences of language mesh together. For example, part of the context of any given utterance is the language that precedes and follows it, and there are various mechanisms available for indicating how various elements in both local and extended sequences are linked. "Cohesive" devices such as anaphora, ellipsis, information structure, and "discourse markers" (e.g., words like "so" and "therefore") provide a means of doing this linguistically, whereas the ordering of elements in stories and other narrative genres, for example, provides a non-linguistic means of achieving "coherence." People with poor linguistic ability – e.g., resulting from aphasia or specific language impairment (SLI) – also tend to be poor at cohesion (Chapman, Highley, & Thompson, 1998; Miranda, McCabe, & Bliss, 1998), whereas the discourse production problems of individuals with RHD, TBI, and Alzheimer's disease are typically linked to problems with social cognition, inference, and memory (Body & Perkins, 2004; Brownell & Martino, 1998; Chapman et al., 1998). Atypical handling of the structure of conversational interaction has been identified in children and adults with ASD (e.g., Dobbinson, Perkins, & Boucher, 1998; Radford & Tarplee, 2000).

3.3.4 Phonology As with other areas of linguistic disability, problems with producing or perceiving phonological distinctions incur a concomitant pragmatic cost. For example, if one's attempts at producing "sit," "sick," "stick," and "tick" all result in the identical sound sequence [tɪk], in order to work out which word is intended any interlocutor will need to rely on contextual inferences to a far greater extent than usual. However, it is problems with non-segmental phonology, or prosody – e.g., intonation, stress, pitch, and loudness – that are most commonly linked to pragmatics. People with autism, for example, typically have difficulty in identifying emotional correlates of others' prosody, and may also manifest unusual prosodic patterns in their speech output including overly monotonous or exaggerated intonation contours and atypical accent placement (McCann et al., 2007).

3.4   *Sensorimotor deficits*

Although not often mentioned in discussions of pragmatics, problems with sensory and motor processing can also, at least indirectly, lead to behaviors which have clear pragmatic consequences. For example, problems with visual or auditory processing, which are necessary for identifying facial expression and voice quality respectively, can contribute to failure to detect sarcasm and irony. As noted above, children who are either deaf or blind are delayed in acquiring the ability to pass ToM tests, and Hobson and Bishop (2003) report interesting parallels in the communicative behaviors of blind and autistic children such as limited engagement in social interaction and infrequent comment on the world around them. Likewise, the communication of individuals with limitations in motor output processing resulting from conditions such as cerebral palsy and Parkinson's disease can be compromised across a range of functions including articulation, prosody, facial expression, and limb movement with concomitant restriction on the expression of meaning though speech and gesture and conveying emotion and mental attitudes toward meaning content (McNamara & Durso, 2003). Also, some non-vocal children with cerebral palsy have been reported as being unable to pass first-order ToM tasks (Dahlgren, Sandberg, & Hjelmquist, 2003).

4   Compensatory Adaptation and Pragmatic Impairment

While useful for identifying factors which contribute to pragmatic impairment, the deficit-based perspective of sections 3.2 to 3.4 provides only a partial and in some ways inaccurate picture. Firstly, the link between a specific deficit – be it cognitive, linguistic, or sensorimotor – and a subsequent communicative behavior is often tenuous to say the least. In reality, there is extensive adaptation to specific deficits by individuals. Secondly, pragmatics is inherently interpersonal, the outcome of joint engagement between two or more interactants which cannot be entirely reduced to the distinct capacities of individuals, and there is evidence that some of the pragmatic impairments we interpret as resulting from underlying intrapersonal deficits may in fact be the by-products of interpersonal activity.

4.1   *Intrapersonal adaptation*

Although it may be convenient for research and assessment purposes to target a particular skill or behavior in isolation, this is ecologically suspect since in reality extensive interactions exist between different cognitive, linguistic, and sensorimotor processes. Even the specification of entities such as EF and the mental lexicon as discrete systems between which interactions may take place is somewhat simplistic since their specification is inevitably a function of the analytical procedure used. To take just one example, various mental processes covered by the term EF have also been described in terms of ToM, central coherence, inference, and memory (Martin & McDonald, 2003). To follow up just one of these, some have argued that ToM is a developmental prerequisite of EF (Ozonoff, Pennington, & Rogers, 1991), while others have argued that the direction of causality is in fact the other way round (Fine, Lumsden, & Blair, 2001). ToM has also been strongly linked to linguistic ability, with some arguing that a ToM deficit has a negative effect on language performance (Tager-Flusberg, 1997) whereas others claim that it is the linguistic task demands of ToM tests themselves which prevent some children from demonstrating their true level of ToM ability (Miller, 2004). Furthermore, the discrete status, coherence and even reality of underlying deficits commonly cited as being responsible for pragmatic impairment and to which individuals may be considered to adapt – e.g., impaired theory of mind, weak central coherence, executive dysfunction – have been questioned by some researchers who argue that they are no more than descriptive artifacts derived from the very behaviors they purport to explain (Muskett, 2008).

What this suggests, then, is that not only should we be extremely cautious in linking pragmatically anomalous behaviors directly to a single underlying deficit, but that mapping out interactions and adaptations between underlying systems and processes is itself far from straightforward, given that the very nature of the entities involved in the interactions is not fully understood. In the case of developmental communication disorders, it has been argued by Karmiloff-Smith (1998) that a deficit in one area of the child's cognitive-linguistic system will invariably affect the system as a whole such that a normal developmental trajectory for initially unaffected areas cannot be assumed. A further complicating factor is that underlying compensatory adaptations are not only difficult to predict purely on the basis of test results and behavioral observation, but may even be counterintuitive (Thomas, 2005).

Despite these methodological and conceptual constraints on our ability to characterize compensatory adaptations implicated in pragmatic impairment, the evidence that we do have suggests that they are both pervasive and extensive. As exemplified above in the relationship between ToM and language, a wide range of trade-offs have been identified both between and within our cognitive, linguistic, and sensorimotor systems. One-way, two-way, and multiple interactions have been observed between phonetics, phonology, morphology, syntax, discourse, inference, ToM, EF, memory, emotion, attitude, gesture, eye gaze, hearing, and vision (for a comprehensive account, see Perkins, 2007).

As an illustration of this, Perkins (2007) presents a case study of a child whose pragmatic impairment could be characterized both in terms of pragmatic theory (e.g., breaking Grice's maxims of quantity, relevance, and manner) and performance on various pragmatic profiles (e.g., lack of coherence, referential problems, word-finding difficulty, use of repetitions, stereotypes and circumlocutions, dysfluency and extensive pausing, problems with topic introduction and maintenance). Rather than being the direct consequence of any one particular deficit, his pragmatic problems were traced back to multiple sources involving complex compensatory adaptations. For example, difficulties with auditory verbal memory caused problems with remembering both what he and others had already said, and this was compounded by poor auditory selective attention, making it hard for him to process what others were saying when there was background noise. Possibly as a result of this, he experienced significant cognitive and linguistic processing problems. Despite having a good vocabulary and being capable of producing complex syntax, he found it difficult to coordinate the two, and syntactic complexity was often achieved at the expense of lexical simplicity, and vice versa. He frequently experienced severe word-finding difficulties, found it hard to keep track of the topic, and was often dysfluent. A notable consistent feature of his performance was his variability: his apparent limited multi-tasking ability meant that optimum performance in any one area had to be offset by reducing resources to others. This brief summary gives no more than a flavor of the complex adaptations evidenced, but the important point to make is that this is not an atypical case. His developmental profile between the ages of 2 and 9 merely showed a child consistently lagging approximately 2 years behind his peers (as shown by standard speech and language assessments), experiencing difficulties in conversation, and finding it hard to keep up at school. It was only his variable performance observed by parents and teachers that gave any hint of the complex compensatory adaptations that lay beyond the reach of standard tests.

One corollary of this is that some pragmatic deficits as identified by language assessments do not necessarily imply global pragmatic incompetence. As pointed out in section 2.2 above, an extremely wide variety of "pragmatic" communication problems is targeted by an equally wide range of evaluation instruments, and performing badly on a particular pragmatics test does not mean that one is necessarily pragmatically impaired across the board. Schegloff (2003), for example, describes the case of a "split brain" patient with a diagnosis of pragmatic impairment following formal testing who nonetheless demonstrated great skill in turn taking and sequence organization during the interaction with the tester. Nevertheless, there is a common tendency to apply a single label such as "pragmatic impairment" fairly indiscriminately to describe the behaviors such tests identify, despite their heterogeneity.

4.2 *Interpersonal adaptation*

An important dimension not highlighted in the preceding section is that all communication is a form of social action in which two or more individuals are reciprocally engaged in a mutual endeavor. It is this joint activity which constitutes the domain of pragmatics, and the various cognitive, linguistic, and sensorimotor processes covered above can only be considered as pragmatic to the extent that they are motivated by this joint interpersonal agenda. There are two main aspects which I will cover here: firstly, the fact that intrapersonal difficulties can sometimes be resolved interpersonally, and secondly, that some apparently pragmatically anomalous behaviors are not the direct result of an intrapersonal deficit but in fact arise indirectly out of attempts to compensate for and resolve the communicative challenges caused by the deficit. In other words, they may be seen as an interpersonal success story rather than an intrapersonal problem.

4.2.1   Interpersonal resolution of intrapersonal problems   To view the individual as the sole locus of pragmatic impairment ignores the fact that interactions involving individuals with some kind of communicative problem may actually be entirely successful in terms of mutual understanding, achievement of intended communicative goals, speaker satisfaction and many other criteria. This is not to suggest that they are indistinguishable from comparable interactions between healthy individuals – for example, they may be experienced as more effortful by the participants or appear "atypical" in various ways to observers. Nevertheless, it is quite common for such dyads to jointly overcome the pragmatic effects of an individual's specific difficulties. For example, there are various ways in which lexical retrieval problems may be resolved as a joint activity. In Transcript 8, Ed, who is unable to retrieve the word "x-ray," engages his interlocutors in a joint word-search exercise in which they suggest likely contenders, which he either rejects or accepts.

Transcript 8
MG   Then they realized, then they put you in the hospital.
M   Uh huh
Ed   Yeah but then they did uh (1.2) the uh (1.9) uh what do you call it (2.1) the uh-
M   MRI?
Ed   No
M   Angioplasty?
Ed   No
MG   EEG?
Ed   No (1.5) The irr, no (tsk, tsk) srays, what do you call it? (1.0)
M   An x-ray?
Ed   X-ray.
(From Oelschlaeger & Damico, 2000, p. 213)

In Transcript 9, Lucy, a 4-year-old girl with SLI who is describing a picture of a swimming pool scene, facilitates the retrieval of the word "swimming" by her interlocutor by miming the action itself.

Transcript 9
ADULT: why are they wet?
LUCY: been in water
ADULT: they have
LUCY: [*moves her arms gesturing swimming*]
ADULT: they've been swimming in that water haven't they?

In both of these cases, an individual's lexical retrieval difficulty has been resolved in different ways at an interpersonal level. In conversation, the word-finding problems of an individual become a joint problem requiring a joint solution.

The success of interpersonal compensation for an individual's communicative problems is not guaranteed, however, and depends to a large extent on the seriousness of the problem and the skill and resourcefulness of the people involved. Body and Parker (2005) describe a case of topic repetitiveness in a man with TBI which was actually aggravated by his wife's use of clarification requests and backchannel behaviors which, in typical conversation, are generally regarded as facilitative. Their study also highlights the fact that despite its being the manifestation of an underlying cognitive deficit, repetitiveness in conversation is inherently interpersonal – or, as they put it, "people are not repetitive on their own" (Body & Parker, 2005, p. 383).

4.2.2   Anomalous behaviors as a pragmatic achievement   Neither of the compensatory behaviors described in the previous section is particularly unusual – we all occasionally elicit help from others when we can't remember a particular word, and we also use gesture to a greater or lesser extent when we communicate. It is not uncommon, however, for compensatory adaptations to take a far more unusual form to the extent that they are sometimes seen as primary deficits or symptoms in their own right. In recent years, the use of Conversation Analysis to analyze interactions involving people with communication problems has revealed that in some cases such apparently anomalous behaviors are in fact manifestations of interpersonally adaptive behavior which is acknowledged as such – though not necessarily consciously – by interlocutors. Damico and Nelson (2005) describe the systematic use of a high piercing creaking sound and an unusual pointing-like gesture by a boy with autism for communicative purposes – viz., roughly as an expression of discomfort and a request for a new activity or shift in location respectively. At least, this was the way in which the child's interlocutor appeared to treat the behaviors judging from what happened in the ensuing interaction. Damico and Nelson interpreted these behaviors as compensatory adaptations to underlying linguistic limitations which are motivated by, and played out in, the interpersonal domain. Echolalia by people with autism has likewise been shown to be used for jointly acknowledged communicative purposes (Dobbinson, Perkins, & Boucher, 2003; Local & Wootton, 1995), as has the use of neologisms, stereotyped phrases, repetition, gesture, and posture by people with aphasia (Simmons-Mackie & Damico, 1996).

5   Concluding Comments

There are four key points to highlight from this chapter.

1   *Pragmatic impairment is not a unitary phenomenon.* Despite the common use of labels such as pragmatic impairment/disorder/disability, what they refer to can vary tremendously from occasion to occasion. Behaviors as disparate as excessive volubility, inaccurate use of tense, dysfluency, and failing to detect irony have all been described as instances of pragmatic impairment. When using the term we should always be careful to specify exactly which aspect we mean. Furthermore, it should not be assumed that a diagnosis of pragmatic impairment made using one test will equate to one made using another.

2   *Pragmatic impairment has disparate and multiple causes.* Two instances of what might appear to be the same type of pragmatically anomalous behavior may have quite different underlying causes. For example, a contextually inappropriate response to a request could result from a failure to infer what the speaker intended to convey, a syntactic or lexical processing problem, poor auditory memory, a short attention span, or some combination of these.

3   *Pragmatic impairment involves compensatory adaptation.* The assumption that any given instance of pragmatic impairment is the direct consequence of some discrete underlying deficit is almost always simplistic. Compensatory adaptation invariably takes place both within the individual – e.g., compensating for a syntactic or lexical processing problem by using referentially opaque pronouns instead of more fully specified noun phrases – and between individuals – e.g., using simplified syntax, gesture, and visual clues when talking to someone with poor comprehension.

4   *Pragmatic impairment is emergent.* In short, pragmatic impairment is emergent – i.e., it is best described not as, or in terms of, a specific underlying deficit, but as, and in terms of, the way in which interactions between cognitive, linguistic and/or sensorimotor difficulties play out in dyadic or group interaction.

NOTE

1   I am using the term "impairment" in a broader, more generic sense than that originally proposed by the World Health Organization (World Health Organization, 1980), and will use "impairment," "disorder," and "disability" interchangeably. This is not uncommon practice, and in addition recognizes that pragmatic impairment, as conceived here and elsewhere (e.g. Perkins, 2007, 2008), is not exclusively sited within the individual.

REFERENCES

Ahlsén, E. (2008). Conversational implicature and communication impairment. In M. J. Ball, M. R. Perkins, N. Müller, & S. Howard (eds.), *Handbook of clinical linguistics* (pp. 32–8). Oxford: Blackwell.

Almor, A., Kempler, D., MacDonald, M. C., Andersen, E. S., & Tyler, L. K. (1999). Why do Alzheimer patients have difficulty with pronouns? Working memory, semantics, and reference in comprehension and production in Alzheimer's disease. *Brain and Language* 67, 202–27.

Armstrong, E. M. (1991). The potential of cohesion analysis in the analysis and treatment of aphasic discourse. *Clinical Linguistics and Phonetics* 5 (1), 39–51.

Austin, J. L. (1962). *How to do things with words*. Oxford: Clarendon Press.

Baddeley, A. (2003). Working memory and language: an overview. *Journal of Communication Disorders* 36, 189–208.

Bara, B. G., Bosco, F. M., & Bucciarelli, M. (1999). Developmental pragmatics in normal and abnormal children. *Brain and Language* 68, 507–28.

Baron-Cohen, S. (1991). Do people with autism understand what causes emotion? *Child Development* 62, 385–95.

Baron-Cohen, S. (1995). *Mindblindness: An essay on autism and theory of mind*. Cambridge, MA: MIT Press.

Bibby, H. & McDonald, S. (2005). Theory of mind after traumatic brain injury. *Neuropsychologia* 43, 99–114.

Bihrle, A. M., Brownell, H. H., Powelson, J. A., & Gardner, H. (1986). Comprehension of humorous and non-humorous materials by left and right brain-damaged patients. *Brain and Cognition* 5, 399–411.

Bishop, D. V. M. (2000). Pragmatic language impairment: a correlate of SLI, a distinct subgroup, or part of the autistic continuum? In D. V. M. Bishop & L. B. Leonard (eds.), *Speech and language impairments in children: Causes, characteristics, intervention and outcome* (pp. 99–113). Hove, UK: Psychology Press.

Bishop, D. V. M. (2003). *The children's communication checklist, version 2 (CCC-2)*. London: Psychological Corporation.

Bishop, D. V. M. & Adams, C. (1989). Conversational characteristics of children with semantic-pragmatic disorder. II: What features lead to a judgement of inappropriacy? *British Journal of Disorders of Communication* 24, 241–63.

Bissett, J. D. & Novak, A. M. (1995). Drawing inferences from emotional situations: Left versus right hemisphere deficit. *Clinical Aphasiology* 23, 217–25.

Body, R. & Parker, M. (2005). Topic repetitiveness after traumatic brain injury: an emergent, jointly managed behaviour. *Clinical Linguistics and Phonetics* 19, 379–92.

Body, R. & Perkins, M. R. (2004). Validation of linguistic analyses in narrative discourse after traumatic brain injury. *Brain Injury* 18 (7), 707–24.

Brownell, H. & Martino, G. (1998). Deficits in inference and social cognition: the effects of right hemisphere brain damage on discourse. In M. Beeman & C. Chiarello (eds.), *Right hemisphere language comprehension: Perspectives from cognitive neuroscience* (pp. 309–28). Mahwah, NJ: Erlbaum.

Bryan, K. L. (1989). *The right hemisphere language battery*. Kibworth: Far Communications.

Champagne, M., Desautels, M.-C., & Joanette, Y. (2003). Accounting for the pragmatic deficit in RHD individuals:

A multiple case study. *Brain and Language* 87, 210–11.

Chapman, S. B., Highley, A. P., & Thompson, J. L. (1998). Discourse in fluent aphasia and Alzheimer's disease: linguistic and pragmatic considerations. *Journal of Neurolinguistics* 11, 55–78.

Cohen, A. S. & Docherty, N. M. (2004). Affective reactivity of speech and emotional experience in patients with schizophrenia. *Schizophrenia Research* 69 (1), 7–14.

Dahlgren, S., Sandberg, A. D., & Hjelmquist, E. (2003). The non-specificity of theory of mind deficits: evidence from children with communicative disabilities. *European Journal of Cognitive Psychology* 15 (1), 129–55.

Damico, J. S. (1985). Clinical discourse analysis: A functional approach to language assessment. In C. S. Simon (ed.), *Communication Skills and Classroom Success* (pp. 165–204). Basingstoke, UK: Taylor and Francis.

Damico, J. S. & Nelson, R. L. (2005). Interpreting problematic behavior: systematic compensatory adaptations as emergent phenomena in autism. *Clinical Linguistics and Phonetics* 19, 405–17.

Dapretto, M., Davies, M. S., Pfeifer, J. H., Scott, A. A., Sigman, M., Brookheimer, S. Y., & Iacoboni, M. (2006). Understanding emotions in others: mirror neuron dysfunction in children with autism spectrum disorders. *Nature Neuroscience* 9, 28–30.

Davis, G. A. & Wilcox, M. J. (1985). *Adult aphasia rehabilitation: Applied pragmatics.* San Diego: College Hill Press.

Dobbinson, S., Perkins, M. R., & Boucher, J. (1998). Structural patterns in conversations with a woman who has autism. *Journal of Communication Disorders* 31, 113–34.

Dobbinson, S., Perkins, M. R., & Boucher, J. (2003). The interactional significance of formulas in adult autistic language.

Clinical Linguistics and Phonetics 17, 299–307.

Douglas, J., O'Flaherty, C. A., & Snow, P. (2000). Measuring perception of communicative ability: the development and evaluation of the La Trobe communication questionnaire. *Aphasiology* 14, 251–68.

Dronkers, N. F., Ludy, C. A., & Redfern, B. B. (1998). Pragmatics in the absence of verbal language: descriptions of a severe aphasic and a language-deprived adult. *Journal of Neurolinguistics* 11, 179–90.

Fine, C., Lumsden, J., & Blair, R. J. R. (2001). Dissociation between "theory of mind" and executive functions in a patient with early left amygdala damage. *Brain* 124, 287–98.

Frith, U. (2003). *Autism: Explaining the enigma*, 2nd ed. Oxford: Blackwell.

Gallagher, T. & Prutting, C. A. (eds.) (1983). *Pragmatic assessment and intervention issues in language.* San Diego: College Hill Press.

Grice, H. P. (1975). Logic and conversation. In F. Cole & J. L. Morgan (eds.), *Syntax and semantics 3: Speech acts* (pp. 41–58). New York: Academic Press.

Halliday, M. A. K. & Hasan, R. (1976). *Cohesion in English.* London: Longman.

Hashimoto, R., Meguro, K., Yamaguchi, S., Ishizaki, J., Ishii, H., Meguro, M., & Sekita, Y. (2004). Executive dysfunction can explain word-list learning disability in very mild Alzheimer's disease: the Tajiri Project. *Psychiatry and Clinical Neurosciences* 58, 54–60.

Hobson, R. P. & Bishop, M. (2003). The pathogenesis of autism: insights from congenital blindness. *Philosophical Transactions of the Royal Society* (Series B358), 335–44.

Holtgraves, T. (1999). Comprehending indirect replies: when and how are their conveyed meanings activated? *Journal of Memory and Language* 41, 519–40.

Karmiloff-Smith, A. (1998). Development itself is the key to understanding developmental disorders. *Trends in Cognitive Sciences* 2, 389–98.

Leinonen, E. & Ryder, N. (2008). Relevance theory and communication disorders. In M. J. Ball, M. R. Perkins, N. Müller, & S. Howard (eds.), *Handbook of clinical linguistics* (pp. 49–60). Oxford: Blackwell.

Local, J. & Wootton, T. (1995). Interactional and phonetic aspects of immediate echolalia in autism: a case study. *Clinical Linguistics and Phonetics* 9, 155–84.

Martin, I. & McDonald, S. (2003). Weak coherence, no theory of mind, or executive dysfunction? Solving the puzzle of pragmatic language disorders. *Brain and Language* 85, 451–66.

McCann, J., Peppé, S., Gibbon, F. E., O'Hare, A., & Rutherford, M. (2007). Receptive and expressive prosodic ability in children with high-functioning autism. *Journal of Speech Language and Hearing Research* 50, 1015–28.

McDonald, S. (1999). Exploring the process of inference generation in sarcasm: A review of normal and clinical studies. *Brain and Language* 68, 486–506.

McDonald, S., Togher, L., & Code, C. (1999). The nature of traumatic brain injury: basic features and neuropsychological consequences. In S. McDonald, L. Togher, & C. Code (eds.), *Communication disorders following traumatic brain injury* (pp. 19–54). Hove, UK: Psychology Press.

McNamara, P. & Durso, R. (2003). Pragmatic communication skills in patients with Parkinson's disease. *Brain and Language* 84, 414–23.

Miller, C. A. (2004). False belief and sentence complement performance in children with specific language impairment. *International Journal of Language and Communication Disorders* 39, 191–213.

Miranda, A. E., McCabe, A., & Bliss, L. S. (1998). Jumping around and leaving things out: a profile of the narrative abilities of children with specific

language impairment. *Applied Psycholinguistics* 19, 647–67.

Möbes, J., Joppich, G., Stiebritz, F., Dengler, R., & Schröder, C. (2008). Emotional speech in Parkinson's disease. *Movement Disorders* 23, 824–9.

Molloy, R., Brownell, H. H., & Gardner, H. (1990). Discourse comprehension by right-hemisphere stroke patients: deficits of prediction and revision. In Y. Joanette & H. H. Brownell (Eds.), *Discourse ability and brain damage: Theoretical and empirical perspectives* (pp. 113–30). New York: Springer-Verlag.

Morris, C. W. (1938). Foundations of the theory of signs. In O. Neurath, R. Carnap, & C. Morris (eds.), *International encyclopedia of unified science* (pp. 77–138). Chicago: University of Chicago Press.

Morrison-Stewart, S. L., Williamson, P. C., Corning, W. C., Kutcher, S. P., Snow, W. G., & Merskey, H. (1992). Frontal and non-frontal lobe neuropsychological test performance and clinical symptomatology in schizophrenia. *Psychological medicine* 22, 353–9.

Müller, N., Guendouzi, J. A., & Wilson, B. (2008). Discourse analysis and communication impairment. In M. J. Ball, M. R. Perkins, N. Müller, & S. Howard (eds.), *Handbook of clinical linguistics* (pp. 3–31). Oxford: Blackwell.

Murphy, F. C., Sahakian, B. J., Rubinsztein, J. S., Michale, A., Rogers, R. D., Robbins, T. W., & Paykel, E. S. (1999). Emotional bias and inhibitory control processes in mania and depression. *Psychological Medicine* 29, 1307–21.

Muskett, T. (2008). Autism, symptomology and interaction: A discursive psychology project. Unpublished PhD thesis, University of Sheffield, UK.

Oelschlaeger, M. L. & Damico, J. S. (2000). Partnership in conversation: A study of word search strategies. *Journal of Communication Disorders* 33, 205–25.

Ozonoff, S., Pennington, B. F., & Rogers, S. J. (1991). Executive function deficits in high functioning autistic individuals: relationship to theory of mind. *Journal of Child Psychology and Psychiatry* 32, 1081–106.

Penn, C. (1985). The profile of communicative appropriateness. *The South African Journal of Communication Disorders* 32, 18–23.

Perkins, L., Whitworth, A., & Lesser, R. (1997). *Conversation analysis profile for people with cognitive impairments (CAPPCI)*. London: Whurr.

Perkins, M. R. (ed.) (2005). *Clinical pragmatics: An emergentist perspective* (Special Issue of *Clinical Linguistics and Phonetics* 19). New York: Taylor and Francis.

Perkins, M. R. (2007). *Pragmatic impairment*. Cambridge: Cambridge University Press.

Perkins, M. R. (2008). Pragmatic impairment as an emergent phenomenon. In M. J. Ball, M. R. Perkins, N. Müller, & S. Howard (eds.), *Handbook of clinical linguistics* (pp. 79–91). Oxford: Blackwell.

Perkins, M. R., Body, R., & Parker, M. (1995). Closed head injury: assessment and remediation of topic bias and repetitiveness. In M. R. Perkins & S. J. Howard (eds.), *Case studies in clinical linguistics* (pp. 293–320). London: Whurr.

Perkins, M. R., Dobbinson, S., Boucher, J., Bol, S., & Bloom, P. (2006). Lexical knowledge and lexical use in autism. *Journal of Autism and Developmental Disorders* 36, 795–805.

Peterson, C. C. & Siegal, M. (2000). Insights into theory of mind from deafness and autism. *Mind and Language* 15, 123–45.

Phillips, M. L., Drevets, W. C., Rauch, S. L., & Lane, R. (2003). Neurobiology of emotion perception II: implications for major psychiatric disorders. *Biological Psychiatry* 54, 515–28.

Prutting, C. A. & Kirchner, D. M. (1983). Applied pragmatics. In T. M. Gallagher & C. A. Prutting (eds.), *Pragmatic assessment and intervention issues in language* (pp. 29–64). San Diego: College Hill Press.

Radford, J. & Tarplee, C. (2000). The management of conversational topic by a ten year old child with pragmatic difficulties. *Clinical Linguistics and Phonetics* 14, 387–403.

Rapin, I. & Allen, D. A. (1983). Developmental language disorders: Nosologic considerations. In U. Kirk (ed.), *Neuropsychology of language, reading, and spelling* (pp. 155–84). New York: Academic Press.

Rees, N. S. (1978). Pragmatics of language: Applications to normal and disordered language development. In R. L. Schiefelbusch (ed.), *Bases of language intervention* (pp. 191–268). Baltimore, MD: University Park Press.

Russell, J. (ed.) (1997). *Autism as an executive disorder*. Oxford: Oxford University Press.

Schegloff, E. A. (2003). Conversation Analysis and communication disorders. In C. Goodwin (ed.), *Conversation and brain damage* (pp. 21–55). New York: Oxford University Press.

Scherer, K. R. (1986). Vocal affect expression: a review and a model for future research. *Psychological Bulletin* 99, 143–65.

Searle, J. R. (1969). *Speech acts*. Cambridge: Cambridge University Press.

Simmons-Mackie, N. & Damico, J. (1996). The contribution of discourse markers to communicative competence in aphasia. *American Journal of Speech-Language Pathology* 5, 37–43.

Sperber, D. & Wilson, D. (1995). *Relevance: Communication and cognition*, 2nd ed. Oxford: Blackwell.

Stemmer, B. (2008a). Neuropragmatics: disorders and neural systems. In B. Stemmer & H. Whitaker (eds.),

Handbook of the neuroscience of language (pp. 175–87). Amsterdam: Elsevier.

Stemmer, B. (2008b). Neuropragmatics. In M. J. Ball, M. R. Perkins, N. Müller, & S. Howard (eds.), *Handbook of clinical linguistics* (pp. 61–78). Oxford: Blackwell.

Tager-Flusberg, H. (1997). Language acquisition and theory of mind: contributions from the study of autism. In L. B. Adamson & M. A. Romski (eds.), *Communication and language acquisition: Discoveries from atypical development* (pp. 135–60). Baltimore, MD: Paul H. Brookes.

Tannock, R. & Schachar, R. (1996). Executive dysfunction as an underlying mechanism of behavior and language problems in attention deficit hyperactivity disorder. In J. Beitchman, N. Cohen, M. Konstantareas, & R. Tannock (eds.), *Language, learning and behavior disorders: Developmental, biological and clinical perspectives* (pp. 128–55). Cambridge: Cambridge University Press.

Thomas, M. S. C. (2005). Characterising compensation. *Cortex* 41, 434–42.

Tompkins, C. A., Lehman-Blake, M. T., Baumgaertner, A., & Fassbinder, W. (2001). Mechanisms of discourse comprehension impairment after right hemisphere brain damage: suppression in inferential ambiguity resolution. *Journal of Speech, Language, and Hearing Research* 44, 400–15.

Werth, A., Perkins, M., & Boucher, J. (2001). "Here's the Weavery looming up": verbal humour in a woman with high-functioning autism. *Autism* 5, 111–25.

Wilkinson, R. (2008). Conversation analysis and communication disorders. In M. J. Ball, M. R. Perkins, N. Müller, & S. Howard (eds.), *Handbook of clinical linguistics* (pp. 92–106). Oxford: Blackwell.

Wilson, B. A., Baddeley, A. D., & Kapur, N. (1995). Dense amnesia in a professional musician following herpes simplex virus encephalitis. *Journal of Clinical Experimental Neuropsychology* 17, 668–81.

Wilson, D. (2005). New directions for research on pragmatics and modularity. *Lingua* 115, 1129–46.

World Health Organization. (1980). *International classification of impairments, disabilities and handicaps*. Geneva: WHO.

World Health Organization. (2004). *The ICD-10 classification of mental and behavioural disorders: Clinical descriptions and diagnostic guidelines*. Geneva: WHO.

11 Learning Disabilities

ROBERT REID AND LAURA JACOBSON

1 Introduction

Learning Disabilities (LD) is the largest category of disability. Around half of students who receive special education services are identified as LD. In the USA, the prevalence of LD in school-based populations is around 5 percent. However, as we will discuss later, because of problems with identification methods, this figure should be viewed with caution. LD is conceptualized as unexpected difficulty with one or more academic areas that occur among children of normal intelligence who have had adequate opportunity for learning and who do not have social disadvantages (e.g., not native English speakers) or behavior or emotional problems. LD occurs along a continuum, which is to say that children with LD represent the lower tail of the distribution. Additionally, learning problems may vary in severity across children. LD is *not* the result of developmental lag, and children do not "outgrow" LD, but rather, problems are lifelong. This is a significant concern, because on the whole outcomes for individuals with LD are not good; for instance, under-employment and unemployment are common. However, individuals with LD can develop strategies that can enable them to better compensate for problems, and today it is not uncommon for individuals with LD to successfully complete college or other advanced training. Among school-based samples, more males than females are identified as LD. This may be the result of referral bias (i.e., males are more likely to exhibit externalizing behavior problems than females). LD may also exist along with other co-morbid conditions (e.g., conduct disorder), and attention-deficit/hyperactivity disorder (ADHD) is common among children with LD.

2 History

The inception of LD as a field was in 1977 when it was recognized as a disability by the Education for All Handicapped Children Act. However, descriptions of students with what we today would call LD go back over a century, and the foundations of the field of LD go back to research conducted in the late nineteenth and early twentieth centuries. The earliest studies focused on the effects of brain injury. For example, in the late nineteenth century, Gall worked with patients who had sustained brain injuries and lost their ability to express themselves verbally, though they did not appear to have lost any other intellectual functioning. He determined that the brain contains separate areas that control specific functions. Another pioneering researcher, Paul Broca, furthered the knowledge of localized brain function (Hallahan & Mock, 2003). By performing autopsies on patients known to have brain injuries, Broca was able to locate an area of the brain – now known as Broca's area – critical to speech functions. This early work established the belief that specific types of cognitive impairment (e.g., loss of certain speech functions, dyslexia) can be caused by damage to a specific area of the brain (Torgesen, 2004; see also Code, this volume, on the history of aphasia research).

In the early twentieth century, Goldstein worked with soldiers who had received head injuries during World War I. He demonstrated that brain injury could affect many areas of performance, including perception, cognition, and behavior (Hammill, 1993; Kavale & Forness, 2003). Strauss and Werner expanded Goldstein's research line (Kavale & Forness, 2003). They focused on perceptual and attention problems of children with mental retardation who were also believed to be brain damaged. Strauss and Werner originated many of the tenets on which the field of LD is based. These include: (1) individual differences in learning should be understood by examining the different ways that children approach learning tasks; (2) educational procedures should be tailored to patterns of processing strengths and weaknesses in the individual child; and (3) children with deficient learning processes might be helped to learn normally if those processes were strengthened (Torgesen, 2004). These tenets have been the foundation for much of the research in the field, though there were numerous problems with Strauss and Werner's original samples and research methods. Samuel Orton, another foundational researcher, brought the notion of language deficits into the field of LD (Hallahan & Mock, 2003). Orton sought to explain the existence of language disorders in children with no known brain injury, but whose characteristics were similar to those of adults with known injuries. He theorized that language problems in children were rooted in a lack of dominance by a single hemisphere of the brain (Hallahan & Mock, 2003). He also developed remedial programs for students.

The term "learning disability" was coined by Samuel Kirk in 1963 at a meeting of a parent group. The term LD itself was important as it provided a label for a group of students who were *not* mentally retarded but who had marked difficulties in learning. During this time, the field of LD was guided by two fundamental assumptions that still guide much of the field (Torgesen, 1986), namely (1) that LD is caused by limitations or deficiencies in basic psychological processes that are required for academic success, but not effectively measured by standard intelligence tests; and (2) that these limitations are naturally occurring in the brain's substrata, or caused by accident or disease. With varying success, these ideas have served as the foundation of the field's research and theory for nearly 40 years.

In the early years after the field's emergence, "process theories" dominated the research landscape. Process approaches were based on the idea that a variety of cognitive processes were required to work together efficiently to allow effective learning (Kavale & Forness, 2003). These processes included the areas of visual perception, visual-motor development, and psycholinguistic training. Researchers such as Cruickshank, Kirk, Getman, Myklebust (see for example Kavale & Forness, 2003) and others promoted training students in these basic processes with the belief that by remediating deficits in them students would be better able to learn academic skills. These theories were the focus of heated debate through the 1970s and into the 1980s. Instructional approaches based on process approaches ultimately proved to be ineffective.

At present, three paradigms are predominant in the field of LD: neuropsychological, information processing, and applied behavior analysis (Lyon et al., 2006). From the perspective of the neuropsychological paradigm, researchers look at how the systems of the brain support or are related to intellectual functioning. This paradigm conceptualizes poor academic performance of individuals with LD as rooted in a malfunction in certain areas of the brain. Researchers within this paradigm focus on organization and intactness of various brain systems. The information-processing paradigm focuses on how the mind represents and manipulates information. Along with information processing, metacognitive theory, which focuses on higher order cognition (i.e., "thinking about thinking") and instructional approaches based on strategy instruction, became very influential. The behavior modification or task-analytic approach, in contrast, does not deal with internal cognitive process at all. Instead, learning is "explained in terms of the environmental consequences that follow it or the stimulus conditions that precede it" (Torgesen, 1986, p. 401). A hybrid approach, cognitive-behavior modification that combines aspects of applied behavior analysis along with informational processing theory also became influential (Kavale & Forness, 2003).

3 Definition

Although the field of learning disabilities is over 30 years old, professionals still disagree on how LD should be defined. In part this is due to the number of professional groups involved in the study and treatment of students with LD (e.g., educational, medical, psychological), and in part to disagreement over what areas should be covered in the definition. This wide array of professional groups and areas of concern has led to the creation of definitions with foci on different aspects of LD. The current federal definition of learning disabilities has changed little since it was originally created in 1977. According to the Individuals with Disabilities Education Improvement Act (IDEA) (2004) a learning disability is:

> a disorder in one or more of the basic psychological processes involved in understanding or in using language, spoken or written, that may manifest itself in an imperfect ability to listen, think, speak, read, write, spell, or do mathematical calculations,

including conditions such as perceptual disabilities, brain injury, minimal brain dysfunction, dyslexia, and developmental aphasia. The term does not include students who have learning disabilities which are primarily the result of visual, hearing, or motor disabilities, of mental retardation, of emotional disturbance, or of environmental, cultural, or economic disadvantage. (34 Code of Federal Regulations §300.7(c)(10))

This definition has components in three main areas: process, manifestation, and exclusion. The process component suggests that the cause of learning problems is rooted in the cognitive processes of individuals with LD (Mercer et al., 1996). The manifestation refers to the outward expression of the disability (i.e., academic areas affected). The federal definition describes these as "an imperfect ability to listen, think, speak, read, write, spell, or do mathematical calculations." Finally, exclusionary language is used to explain what a learning disability is not. Specifically, a learning disability cannot be a result of sensory, motor, emotional disabilities, mental retardation, or environmental, cultural, or economic disadvantages. However, these conditions may coexist with learning disabilities.

3.1   Problems with the LD definition

The importance of a strong definition cannot be underestimated. Definitions affect both research and practice. Unfortunately, the federal definition has been a source of controversy since its creation. One of the most common criticisms of the definition is that it is primarily one of exclusion. That is, the definition stipulates what LD is *not* but does not adequately define *what LD is*. Lipka and Siegle (2006) note four common exclusionary components seen in LD definitions: (1) LD is not a result of an inadequate education; (2) LD is not caused by sensory deficits; (3) LD is not caused by serious neurological disorders that may interfere with learning; and (4) LD is not caused by major social and/or emotional difficulties. They argue that these exclusions have not been systematically identified and are not substantiated by research, significantly reducing the validity and usefulness of the constructs. While these exclusionary factors were needed originally for reasons of funding and legislation, the exclusionary criteria inherent in the definition continue to be a major source of controversy.

Other criticisms have focused on accurately describing the nature of students with LD. For example, a 1987 criticism noted that the federal definition: (1) does not clearly indicate that learning disabilities are a heterogeneous group of disorders; (2) fails to acknowledge that learning disabilities persist into adulthood; and (3) does not specifically state that individuals with LD process information in a fundamentally different fashion (Interagency Committee on Learning Disabilities, 1987). Another common criticism of the definition is that it provides little guidance in how students with LD should be identified. Moats and Lyon (1993) described the definition as an "impotent" tool with little use in providing guidelines and criteria for the identification of students with LD and distinguishing these students from those with other disabilities.

In terms of practical impact the lack of a sound operational definition for the identification of students with LD is the most serious problem. An operational definition provides a concrete set of criteria for defining a variable or condition (e.g., LD) with objectivity (Babie, 2001). Current federal guidelines operationally define LD in terms of a discrepancy between actual achievement and perceived potential for learning. Unfortunately, under federal regulations no specific formulas, assessment tools, or numerical values are provided to define exactly what constitutes a significant discrepancy (Lyon, 1996), and, as we will discuss in the next section, there are technical and conceptual problems that have led the field to explore alternative avenues of identification of students with LD.

For educators, an operational definition provides a consistent set of procedures and standards that can be used to identify children with LD. For researchers, an operational definition ensures that the same population is studied, which allows researchers to replicate and generalize research findings (Swanson, 1991). Lyon et al. (2006) suggest that the current federal operational definition is too ambiguous and vague to provide guidance to educators and researchers. The lack of precision in the definition causes ambiguity, resulting in a wide variety of definitional interpretations (Kavale & Forness, 2003; Kavale, Forness, & Lorsbach, 1991). This in turn has caused problems in both research and practice. By using different operational definitions, LD research may be of limited use because it may not generalize across the greater population of individuals with LD. It may be impossible to replicate studies because the sample used in the original study cannot be duplicated. Problems of practice occur when states operationalize LD differently which in turn leads to students who would qualify for services as LD in one state but not another. Thus a child could be "cured" of LD simply by crossing a state line.

4 Identification of Learning Disabilities

Until recently, students were identified as LD primarily on the basis of a discrepancy between IQ and achievement. The roots of discrepancy methods can be traced to 1965 when Barbara Bateman proposed a definition of LD that focused on the "educationally significant discrepancy between . . . estimated potential and actual level of performance " (1965, p. 220). Though criticized from the beginning, the discrepancy concept was widely adopted, particularly by school systems. In 1977, as a response to the lack of specificity in the federal definition, the US Office of Education issued regulations to clarify the identification of individuals with learning disabilities. These regulations provided no specific formulas, assessment tools, or numerical values to assess discrepancy (Lyon, 1996), but included serious achievement-ability discrepancy, in the absence of other conditions, as a major component of LD (Meyer, 2000).

A discrepancy is most often operationalized as a significant difference between aptitude and achievement, as measured by IQ and achievement test scores (Fletcher et al., 2004). However, there has been a wide variety of discrepancy formulas proposed as a means of identifying students with LD. These formulas have included (a) grade-level deviations that compare expected grade levels to actual grade level scores; (b) expectancy formulas that include a combination of IQ, chronological age, mental age, years in school, and grade age; (c) standard score methods that use a direct comparison of intellectual ability and academic achievement using instruments with common metrics; and (d) regression methods in which errors in measurement of IQ and achievement are accounted for (Mellard, Deshler, & Barth, 2004). Regression methods use a student's IQ to predict his or her expected achievement score. This score is then compared to the actual achievement score. A significant difference between the two is considered a significant discrepancy (McDermott et al., 2006).

The discrepancy approach has been the most commonly used method to identify students with LD in the schools (Reschly & Hosp, 2004) and until recently was a part of the identification procedure in nearly every state (Francis et al., 2005). The use of the discrepancy criterion is efficient and convenient for schools (Kavale & Forness, 2000). However, as we will discuss in a later section, schools and researchers are increasingly moving away from discrepancy approaches and the model is coming under ever increasing criticism because of several inherent problems.

The first problem lies with the use of IQ tests. There are several problems inherent in the use of IQ scores. IQ is not an effective predictor of reading potential (Aaron, 1997). For students with LD, IQ tests have not been found to accurately predict achievement potential in reading or mathematics. Other variables such as level of parental education or the child's socioeconomic status can be equally effective predictors of student performance (Fletcher et al., 2004). IQ tests do not tap the cognitive process involved in learning. For example, phonological awareness is widely considered a critical prerequisite skill for reading acquisition and a core deficit for students with dyslexia, yet none of the subtests of the standard IQ tests deal with it. IQ tests generally deal with reasoning skills and learned knowledge; however, the specific, underlying cognitive deficits of students with LD "are only minimally correlated with measures of global intelligence" (Meyer, 2000, p. 320). Additionally, failure to adjust for the correlation between IQ and achievement tests leads to over-identification of LD for students with high IQs and under-identification of LD with lower IQs (Francis, Fletcher, & Shaywitz, 1996).

The second problem is that, in practice, the discrepancy model has also been unable to consistently distinguish between those who have LD and those who do not (Fletcher et al., 1994; Stanovich, 1991). Part of the problem lies in the use of specific cut-points for identification purposes. Cut-points are basically arbitrary. In order for cut-points to be valid, naturally occurring breakpoints should be used. However, natural breaks do not occur, or are not apparent (Fletcher, Denton, & Francis, 2005). Measurement error also poses a problem for discrepancy approaches, especially for those students whose scores are close to cut-points. Because a student's scores on a measure will vary from one administration to the next, small fluctuations could mean the child could be identified on one testing but not the next. Thus, measurement errors associated with the model make it unable to identify a unique set of under-achievers (Fletcher, Denton, & Francis, 2005). An additional problem is that discrepancy approaches cannot consistently differentiate between groups identified as having LD and those deemed low achievers. Stuebing et al. (2002) found no significant difference between LD and low achieving groups in areas closely related to reading. Other studies have been unable to distinguish subgroups of students who are LD versus low achievers based on IQ-achievement discrepancy, and in fact recent studies have found that poor readers with and without discrepancies show similar performance on reading-related tasks (Fuchs et al., 2003).

The third problem is the relationship between reading and the "Matthew effect" (Stanovich, 1986) (a biblical reference associated with the concept of the rich getting richer and the poor getting poorer). Children who are good readers tend to read voraciously. As a result, they are able to increase their vocabulary, comprehension of the world, and their global understanding, allowing them better access to the environment around them. Because IQ tests generally assess learned information and reasoning skills, this knowledge and understanding gained through reading is reflected in higher IQ scores. Conversely, poor readers tend not to read widely and thus do not develop their knowledge and understanding. Because of these gaps in understanding, those students with poor reading skills may have depressed IQ scores, thus reducing the discrepancy between their IQ and achievement, leading to under-identification of these students (Dombrowski, Kamphaus, & Reynolds, 2004). Fuchs and colleagues (2003) suggested that Matthew effects can lead to an under-identification of students from low-income families, leading to an apparent class bias.

The fourth problem is practical in nature. The discrepancy approach has been termed a "wait to fail model" by critics. Using discrepancy criteria, the student has to demonstrate a "severe discrepancy" between achievement and ability. This makes early identification difficult or impossible since most children do not demonstrate a severe discrepancy in the early grades. The necessary discrepancy may not be evident until grade three or later, by which time students may have fallen significantly behind their peers (Dombrowski et al., 2004). This delay in the provision of services is a concern because of the potential impact on the child's ability to make sufficient progress to close the gap between their own progress and that of their peers. It also makes remediation more difficult because of the degree of the deficit.

Fifth, discrepancy may be more directly related to under-achievement than LD. Under-achievement indicates the possibility that a learning disability is present (Kavale, Holdnack, & Mostert, 2005); however, while under-achievement is a characteristic of LD it is not the sole criterion of LD (Kavale & Forness, 2003). For any given individual, low achievement could be as rooted in socioeconomic status, lack of exposure to effective instruction, or English as a second language, as the presence of a learning disability (Kavale & Forness, 2003). Therefore, the assumption that the presence of a discrepancy equates to a child having a LD is not necessarily reliable or valid (Francis et al., 2005). Simply because a student meets the discrepancy criteria does not mean that the child has a central nervous dysfunction or other psychological process disorder, which is a requirement of the current LD definition (Fletcher et al., 2004).

Ironically, in practice the failings of discrepancy methods may be of little practical import, because in practice the established guidelines and formulas are commonly ignored. Instead, the identification process is often driven by the desire to provide students with special education services. Assessment data, LD definitions or guidelines formally adopted by a school district are often seen as being of secondary importance in the decision-making process (Holdnack & Weiss, 2006; Mellard, Deshler, & Bart, 2004; Scruggs & Mastropieri, 2002). Thus, in practice, the primary eligibility criterion for LD can become a need for services, not the presence of a LD, and, under these conditions, the category of LD becomes a "catch all" category where whether the student does or does not have LD is moot (Kavale & Forness, 2003).

4.1   *Response to intervention*

While the discrepancy identification method continues to be widely used, alternative identification methods have been proposed. IDEA 2004 does not require states to take into account a severe discrepancy between ability and achievement. States may use processes of identification that include a student's response to scientific, research-based interventions. Response-to-instruction (RTI) is the most widely acknowledged alternative procedure to date. The most recent legislation does not require that RTI be used, but does suggest that it may be used as a part of the evaluation procedures.

The RTI model is a tiered, intervention-based approach. While there a few variations, the basic structure is as follows:

Tier 1: Class-wide intervention and universal assessment
- All students receive high-quality instruction; all students are given screening assessments, with regular progress monitoring.
- Those who do not meet benchmarks are then eligible for services provided in Tier 2.

Tier 2: Targeted interventions
- A school-based team selects individualized interventions for those students who did not make sufficient progress in Tier 1; OR a standard treatment is administered to all Tier 2 students.
- Progress is monitored regularly.
- Students whose progress is satisfactory return to Tier 1.
- Students who do not make adequate progress go to Tier 3.

Tier 3: Intensive, individual interventions
- More intensive interventions or special education services.

The RTI model moves the emphasis away from traditional testing procedures, using instead a lack of responsiveness as an indicator of underachievement (Mellard, Deshler, & Bart, 2004). The benefits of an intervention-based model cannot be ignored. The universal, ongoing assessment of students and provision of intervention without extensive eligibility requirements eliminates the need to "wait to fail" (Fletcher et al., 2004). RTI shifts the focus onto the provision of effective instruction, rather than meeting eligibility criteria. RTI also has the potential to reduce the numbers of children requiring special education evaluations and improve the learning of students whose difficulties are environmentally, linguistically, or culturally based (Holdnack & Weiss, 2006). In theory, RTI ensures that a student will not be identified as having a disability because of a lack of instruction, ensuring that this requirement on the LD definition is met (Fletcher et al., 2004).

There are two major approaches to RTI. The first is known as the problem-solving model, which is similar to the student-assistance-team model. Solutions to learning problems are found by evaluating a student's responsiveness through a four-staged process. This includes problem identification, problem analysis, plan implementation, and problem evaluation. The model involves a consultant, teacher, and student in the problem-solving process (Fuchs et al., 2003). The second RTI model is the standard-protocol approach. This model requires that a single empirically validated treatment be used for all children with similar problems (e.g., reading). The benefits of the standard-protocol approach include ease in training due to the single intervention, increased understanding of what needs to be implemented, and ease in the assessment of fidelity. Proponents of the model believe it results in more consistent instructional delivery, and is more likely to facilitate quality instruction (Fuchs et al., 2003).

Few argue that RTI should not be a component of LD evaluation, since its usefulness is obvious. There are, however, a number of concerns. First, there is concern that RTI will simply be substituted in place of the discrepancy model. The latest IDEA regulations state clearly that the use of RTI is to be a part of an evaluation process, not the process itself (Willis & Dumont, 2006). Additionally, IDEA requires a comprehensive evaluation in order to identify a child as having a disability, and the brief screenings proposed by proponents of RTI may not be in line with this requirement (Holdnack & Weiss, 2006). Concerns about the construct of LD also arise (Holdnack & Weiss, 2006). The RTI model does not appear to provide evidence of "a basic disorder in one or more psychological processes." If RTI is the only means by which a LD determination is based, this component of the definition is ignored and the construct of LD is being altered (Ofiesh, 2006; Reschly, 2005). This could result in LD being a category of students with mixed characteristics, who for any variety of reasons failed to respond (Ofiesh, 2006).

Finally, the time, money, training, and expertise required to effectively implement an RTI model is a concern. Teachers must be trained to conduct assessments and provided with the time to perform these assessments. Staff must be available to provide the required interventions, and have the necessary training to do so effectively. Data collection methods must be clear to all those involved in the process. Interventions must be timed to allow students to remain in their classes without missing necessary content, and money must be available for teacher training. In summary, RTI is resource intensive. In a time when budgets are already strained it remains to be seen how feasible RTI will be in practice.

The efficacy of RTI is still being established; however, RTI does appear promising. Evidence suggests that RTI can improve outcomes for at-risk students (Speece, Case, & Molloy, 2003; Vellutino et al., 2006) and that RTI is a valid method for identification of LD (Vaughn, Linan-Thompson, & Hickman, 2003). Still, RTI remains a matter of some controversy (Fuchs et al., 2003). Supporters want RTI to replace the discrepancy model immediately, whereas others see RTI as a potentially potent strategy that takes time and needs to be done carefully to ensure the program is useful, able to be maintained, and successfully avoids the pitfalls of the current model. Finally, others see RTI as simply a more complex version of the pre-referral process, which has already been found difficult to implement.

5   Types of Learning Disabilities

Students with LD are highly heterogeneous. LD is not typically a problem that crosses all academic areas; rather, LD tends to be domain specific. That is, learning problems occur in specific academic areas. Although these types of LD are distinct and separable, some children may have a LD in more than one area. Table 11.1 shows the types of LD that are empirically supported. Three of the types involve reading, one is specific to math, one combines math and reading, and one centers on difficulty in written expression. The research base for different types varies considerably. For example, the most common type of LD, "the reading – word level" type (also termed dyslexia) has a considerable research base. In contrast, there has been relatively little research on the "reading – comprehension" group, which tends to occur in older children; however there is good evidence that skill at word reading can be dissociated from comprehension skills (Oakhill, Cain, & Bryant, 2003). Math disabilities are not yet well understood, although there is emerging evidence that working memory deficits are closely associated with this type (e.g., Fuchs et al., 2006; Swanson, & Beebe-Frankenberger, 2004; Swanson & Sachs-Lee, 2001). Written expression groups suffer from a lack of a clear operational definition that addresses all areas of written language (Berninger, 2004). There is a clear need for research in this area, as many children with LD have difficulty with some form of written language.

6   Factors Underlying Learning Disabilities

Researchers have searched for the cause(s) of learning disabilities for decades. The search has been difficult for a number of reasons: (a) students with LD are a highly heterogeneous group; (b) a number of environmental or social factors can result in learning problems (e.g., brain damage, exposure to environmental toxins, hunger,

Table 11.1 Types of learning disability

Subtype	Description
Reading – word level	• Difficulty with accuracy and fluency of decoding. • Associated with poor phonological processing, rapid naming abilities, and verbal short-term memory deficits. • Occurs along a continuum (i.e., in degrees). • Profound impact on reading ability because it impacts foundational reading abilities.
Reading – comprehension	• Problems with language comprehension and inferencing ability, integration of textual information, and abstraction. • May have more deficits in vocabulary and understanding syntax. • Difficulties with working memory. • Phonological skills, short-term memory, and verbatim recall not usually impacted. • Problems parallel those of listening comprehension.
Reading – fluency	• "Rate deficit group." • No decoding problems. • Comprehension problems due to inability to rapidly process information.
Math	• Normal reading/spelling. • Difficulty with learning, representing, and retrieving math facts. • Difficulties in learning and using problem-solving strategies required for calculations.
Reading and math	• Memory-based deficit. • Potentially related to working memory and long-term memory access.
Written expression	• Difficulty with spelling. • Impaired motor development impacting handwriting. • Difficulty with expression/text generation.

Sources: Fletcher et al. (2002); Fletcher, Morris, and Lyon (2003); Lyon, Fletcher, and Barnes (2003).

lack of exposure to effective instruction); (c) co-morbidity with other conditions (e.g., ADHD); and (d) until fairly recently it has been difficult to pinpoint the cognitive processes that result in learning problems. Although research has not yet fully unraveled the problem of LD, some cognitive processes that are related to the learning problems of students with LD have now been firmly established.

6.1   Memory

Memory is fundamental to learning. It is difficult to conceive of a learning task that would not entail storing or retrieving information from memory. Modern memory researchers use an information processing approach to memory that utilizes three components: short-term memory (STM), working memory (WM), and long-term memory (LTM) (Baddeley & Logie, 1999). There is evidence to suggest that students with LD have problems in some or all of these areas.

6.1.1   Short-term memory   STM serves as temporary storage for information, which can be maintained in STM for a short period of time only. Unless it is rehearsed (i.e., repeated) or processed it will be lost. Compared to controls, children with LD perform more poorly on STM tasks that involve verbal information (O'Shaughnessy & Swanson, 1998); however, differences were small for non-verbal information (e.g., shapes). The fact that STM problems are greater for verbal content suggests that STM deficits may be implicated in reading problems.

6.1.2   Working memory   WM is that portion of memory used for temporarily storing and processing information. Although there is some overlap between WM and STM, they are seen as distinct entities. WM has been associated with difficulties in a number of academic areas including word recognition, comprehension, mathematics, and writing. The most influential model of working memory explains it as consisting of three components (Baddeley & Logie, 1999). Two components – the phonological loop and the visuo-spatial sketchpad – are conceived as subsystems (or "slave systems") that are responsible for short-term maintenance of information. The phonological loop stores auditory information and prevents its decay by continuously rehearsing its contents. There is persuasive evidence that students with LD in the area of reading have deficits in their phonological loop. This is likely the reason that students with LD exhibit STM deficits with verbal material. The phonological loop has also been associated with math difficulties (Holmes & Adams, 2006). The visuo-spatial sketchpad stores visual and spatial information. It allows for constructing and manipulating visual images. Whether students with LD exhibit a visuo-spatial deficit is unclear.

The third component – the central executive – functions as a sort of orchestral conductor. It coordinates and controls the functions of the slave systems. The central executive also coordinates various cognitive processes. There are three broad areas of control: monitoring and updating information in WM, inhibiting irrelevant responses/suppressing irrelevant information, and shifting between mental sets (Miyake et al., 2000). Students with LD exhibit deficits in monitoring and updating, and suppression of irrelevant information; they also have difficulties with tasks that require both information storage and processing (Swanson, 2005).

6.1.3   Long-term memory   LTM involves long-term storage and retrieval of information. There is good evidence that children with LD have difficulty with LTM storage and retrieval and that these difficulties are a major factor in LTM differences between students with LD and controls (Swanson & Sachs-Lee, 2001). In part LTM problems can be linked to less efficient strategies. It is also possible that students with LD have systemic difficulties in acquisition of new information and remembering everyday information (McNamara & Wong, 2003).

6.2 *Phonological processing*

Phonological processing, the ability to discern, process, and manipulate the sounds of spoken language, is fundamental to successful reading. To read successfully, children must be able to rapidly associate letters with the sounds they represent and then translate these sounds into the word they represent. There is now persuasive evidence that deficits in phonological processing are the core problems that result in dyslexia (i.e., reading disabilities) for many students (Shaywitz & Shaywitz, 2003). Sophisticated new imaging techniques have demonstrated that compared to fluent readers children with dyslexia activate different areas of the brain during reading tasks. Children with dyslexia literally process printed words differently than fluent readers. Moreover, the problem is chronic and does not represent a developmental lag that may be outgrown. Even though these children may improve their reading skills, they will still be deficient compared to peers. There is now compelling evidence that there is a strong genetic basis to reading disabilities (see Raskind, 2001 for a review). There is also evidence that effective instruction can facilitate neural development (Shaywitz & Shaywitz, 2003).

6.3 *Metacognition*

Metacognition refers to knowledge about and regulation of one's cognitive processes (Flavell, 1976); current conceptions of metacognition also include motivational beliefs and affect. Students with well-developed metacognitive skills tend to be better learners and are adept at analyzing the nature of a task, choosing an effective strategy, monitoring progress, and maintaining focus on a task. Affective or emotional components are also important. After repeated failure experiences, students with LD may develop the belief that they lack the ability to perform academic tasks, and simply avoid them. Not surprisingly, students with LD tend to have metacognitive deficits. Research has shown that metacognitive and motivational variables are strong predictors of LD (Sideridis et al., 2006).

7 Contemporary Treatment Models

Early treatment approaches to LD centered on medical models that focused on the underlying biological bases for LD, and psychoeducational models that focused on children's ability to perceive visual and auditory information. Neither of these approaches proved successful. In contrast, behavioral approaches, which did not consider causal factors and instead focused on direct instruction of skills using carefully sequenced curricula, were notably effective. Currently there are four influential treatment models: Cognitive, Cognitive-behavioral, Task-analytic, and Neuropsychological. These models are all to some degree derived from those of previous eras; however, many have evolved considerably in terms of effectiveness. Note that although we discuss the models separately, there is considerable overlap in some cases, and some components (e.g., direct teaching of skills) are used in multiple models.

7.1   Cognitive

Cognitive models have evolved from the psychoeducational models of previous eras and have their roots in cognitive and developmental psychology (Lyon, et. al., 2006). Modern cognitive approaches focus on specific information-processing skills such as long-term and working memory, higher-order cognitive processes such as metacognition, and specific skills such as phonological awareness. Cognitive models promote instruction aimed at deliberate effort and strategic learning. Instructional emphases fall in three main areas: (1) increasing awareness of task demands, (2) teaching strategies to aid in task completion, and (3) monitoring progress (Lyon & Moats, 1988). Procedures include instruction in strategic use of existing academic skills to aid in the acquisition, manipulation, storage, retrieval, and expression of information (Lyon et al., 2006). Effective development and use of strategies is especially important for children with LD as it is well documented that these students often fail to develop or deploy effective appropriate strategies for academic tasks (Torgeson, 1987). Many of the current strategy instruction methods are largely derived from cognitive models.

7.2   Cognitive-behavioral

The cognitive-behavioral model weaves together the behavioral ideas of contingent reinforcement's influence on behavior and the influence of affective and cognitive states on behavior. The concept of "reciprocal-determinism" is at the core of cognitive-behavioral approaches. Reciprocal-determinism holds that thoughts and feelings, behavior, and environmental events interact and affect one another. This recognition of "covert behavior" (i.e., unobservable mental processes) is a major departure from strict behavioral approaches. From this perspective, students are active collaborators in learning, and learn to monitor their behavior and direct their thinking to accomplish academic tasks. Autonomous performance is a major goal of this approach. One of the strengths of the cognitive-behavioral approach is that it addresses affective, cognitive, and behavioral aspects of LD. The cognitive-behavioral approach has been a very successful model. Interventions such as self-instruction (Meichenbaum, 1977), Self-Regulated Strategy Development (Graham & Harris, 2003), and the Learning Strategies Curriculum (Schumaker, Deshler, & McKnight, 2002) all are derived from the cognitive-behavioral model.

7.3   Task-analytic

The task-analytic model is derived from behavioral approaches and focuses on a student's actions and the instructional environment. In contrast to other approaches, this model does not consider causal factors or underlying cognitions. Instead, it focuses on carefully sequenced curricula and on a fine-grained analysis of the instructional interaction between teacher and student. Instructional programs based on the task-analytic model are highly structured. They require that a specific objective be identified and operationalized, followed by the creation of a detailed, sequenced list of steps required to perform the task. Each of the steps is then taught directly. Task-analytic approaches require teachers to provide considerable structure, and in some cases actually script instructional sequences. This has been a source of criticism; however, research clearly demonstrates the effectiveness of this approach. Programs based on this model have been especially effective at teaching beginning reading skills. One of the best-known examples is Direct Instruction (Adams & Carnine, 2003).

7.4   *Neuropsychological*

Neuropsychological models have roots in both medical and psychoeducational theories. These approaches stress the role of neurobiological factors in learning. These approaches have received tremendous attention, due in part to the advancements in neurosciences and the proliferation of new imaging techniques that allow for analysis of the brain as it actually performs tasks. From this perspective, LD is due to specific problems in information processing. This approach places emphasis on remediation. Based on these ideas, instruction is geared to avoid dysfunctional areas, targeting only those believed to be efficient. A major concern is that there is little evidence that interventions based on this model are effective (Lyon et al., 2006).

8   Treatment

Effective intervention is obviously an area of significant of concern for those involved in the education of students with LD. Historically, there have been numerous instructional approaches that claimed to improve the learning of students with learning problems. Unfortunately, many have proved ineffective. In part this can be traced to the fact that treatments were based on erroneous models of LD (e.g., the psychoeducational). In part it is due to the fact that students with LD are heterogeneous and thus it is unlikely that there is a single treatment that will be effective for all. Research, however, suggests that there are two main treatment approaches that promote learning success for students with LD: direct instruction and strategy instruction (Swanson, 1999). Research shows that for acquisition of decoding skills, direct instruction models are extremely effective for students with LD, as effect sizes (ES) exceeded .80, which indicates significant improvement (Swanson, 2001). Research also indicates that models combining strategy instruction with direct instruction positively influence student performance in a number of academic areas (e.g., reading comprehension, composition, problem solving) (Graham & Harris, 2003; Swanson, 1999). When compared to other models, combined models (direct instruction with strategy instruction) had ES estimates above .80, which is evidence of large effects (Swanson, 1999).

Reading is the most common area of learning difficulty for students with learning disabilities. For reading it is possible to define specific instructional components associated with successful interventions. Swanson (1999) examined the outcomes of interventions on reading comprehension and word recognition. He found nine instructional components that moderated treatment effectiveness. Six of these were associated with reading comprehension. They are:

- Directed response/questioning: Socratic dialogue between teacher and student, directed questioning by the teacher, or questioning by the students as directed by the instructor.
- Control of the difficulty of processing demands of the task: short activities wherein task difficulty is carefully controlled, and simplified demonstrations. For example, activities may be sequenced from easy to difficult, controlled for level of difficulty, or teacher assistance may be gradually faded as the student becomes more proficient.
- Elaboration: providing additional explanation or repetitions of steps, concepts or procedures.
- Modeling: teacher demonstrations of steps or processes needed to enable students to perform a task.
- Small group instruction: instruction in small groups that includes frequent verbal interaction among group members and/or the teacher.
- Strategy cues: reminders to use strategies, teacher verbalization of problem solving, use of "think alouds", and explanation of the benefits of using a strategy.

For acquisition of word recognition skills, direct instruction approaches have demonstrated effectiveness for children with LD. The three components that most influenced treatment effectiveness were:

- Sequencing: breaking down a task, short activities, using step-by-step prompts, or systematically fading cues, difficulty level of task is matched to student.
- Segmentations: breaking a skill or task into its component parts, which are then systematically taught.
- Advanced organizers: directing students to examine previously learned material, providing learning objectives prior to beginning instruction and directing children to particular information.

9 Summary

The field of LD is one of stark contradictions. Over the past 30 years researchers have made great strides in furthering our understanding of the nature of LD. For at least some children with LD, we now have a solid understanding of the nature of their learning problems. Yet the definition of LD still poses a problem for many researchers, and the lack of an empirically supported definition makes even basic prevalence estimates problematic. There have also been tremendous advances in effective means of treatment thanks in part to the recent emphases on interventions that have demonstrated efficacy. Yet, the extent to which many data-based interventions are implemented in the schools is spotty at best, and long-term outcomes for students with LD continue to be a concern. The response-to-instruction model has the potential to fundamentally change our approach to LD, and the field appears to be on the cusp of significant changes in identification processes. Yet RTI could also fundamentally alter our conceptualization of LD or even render the LD construct moot. In summary, despite significant progress in many areas, there are still many intractable problems facing the field.

REFERENCES

Aaron, P. G. (1997). The impending demise of discrepancy formula. *Review of Educational Research* 67 (4), 461–502.

Adams, G. & Carnine, D. (2003). Direct instruction. In H. L. Swanson, K. R. Harris and S. Graham (eds.), *Handbook of learning disabilities* (pp. 403–16). New York: The Guilford Press.

Babie, E. (2001). *The practice of social research*, 9th ed. Belmont, CA: Wadsworth/Thomson Learning.

Baddeley, A. D. & Logie, R. H. (1999). Working memory: The multiple component model. In A. Miyake and P. Shah (eds.), *Models of working memory: Mechanisms of active maintenance and executive control* (pp. 28–61). New York: Cambridge University Press.

Bateman, B. (1965). An educational view of a diagnostic approach to learning disorders. In J. Hellmuth (ed.), *Learning disorders* (vol. 1) (pp. 219–39). Seattle: Special Child Publications.

Berninger, V. W. (2004). Understanding the "graphia" in developmental dysgraphia: A developmental neuropsychological perspective for disorders in producing written language. In D. Dewey and D. Tupper (eds.), *Developmental motor disorders: A neuropsychological perspective* (pp. 328–50). New York: Guilford.

Dombrowski, S. C., Kamphaus, R. W., & Reynolds, C. R. (2004). After the demise of the discrepancy: Proposed learning disabilities diagnostic criteria.

Professional Psychology: Research and Practice 35 (4), 364–72.

Flavell, J. H. (1976). Metacognitive aspects of problem solving. In L. Resnick (ed.), *The nature of intelligence* (pp. 231–6). Hillsdale, NJ: Erlbaum.

Fletcher, J. M., Coulter, W. A., Reschly, D. J., & Vaughn, S. (2004). Alternative approaches to the definition and identification of learning disabilities: Some questions and answers. *Annals of Dyslexia* 54 (2), 304–31.

Fletcher, J. M., Denton, C., & Francis, D. J. (2005). Validity of alternative approaches for the identification of learning disabilities: Operationalizing unexpected underachievement. *Journal of Learning Disabilities* 38 (6), 545–52.

Fletcher, J. M., Lyon, G. R., Barnes, M. A., Stuebing, K. K., Francis, D. J., Olson, R., Shaywitz, S. E., & Shaywitz, B. S. (2002). Classification of learning disabilities: An evidence-based evaluation. In R. Bradley, L. Danielson, & D. P. Hallahan (eds.), *Identification of learning disabilities: Research to practice* (pp. 185–250). Mahwah, NJ: Lawrence Erlbaum Associates.

Fletcher, J. M., Morris, R. D., & Lyon, G. R. (2003). Classification and definition of learning disabilities: An integrative perspective. In H. L. Swanson, K. R. Harris, & S. Graham (eds.), *Handbook of learning disabilities* (pp. 30–56). New York: Guilford Press.

Fletcher, J. M., Shaywitz, S. E., Shankweiler, D. P., Katz, L., Liberman, I. Y., Stuebing, K. K., Francis, D. J., Fowler, A., & Shaywitz, B. A. (1994). Cognitive profiles of reading disability: Comparisons of discrepancy and low achievement definitions. *Journal of Educational Psychology* 85, 1–18.

Francis, D. J., Fletcher, J. M., Stuebing, K. K., Lyon, G. R., Shaywitz, B. A., & Shaywitz, S. E. (2005). Psychometric approaches to the Identification of LD: IQ and achievement scores are not sufficient. *Journal of Learning Disabilities* 38 (2), 98–108.

Francis, D. J., Fletcher, J. M., & Shaywitz, B. A. (1996). Defining learning and language disabilities: Conceptual and psychometric issues with the use of IQ tests. *Language, Speech, and Hearing Services in Schools* 27, 132–43.

Fuchs, L. S., Fuchs, D., Compton, D. L., Powell, S. R., Seethaler, P. M., Capizzi, A. M., Schatschneider, C., & Fletcher, J. M. (2006). The cognitive correlates of third-grade skill in arithmetic, algorithmic computation, and arithmetic word problems. *Journal of Educational Psychology* 98 (1), 29–43.

Fuchs, D., Mock, D. R., Morgan, P. L., & Young, C. L. (2003). Responsiveness-to intervention: Definitions, evidence, and implication for the learning disabilities construct. *Learning Disabilities Research & Practice* 18 (3), 157–71.

Graham, S. & Harris, K. R. (2003). Students with learning disabilities and the process of writing: A meta-analysis of SRSD studies. In H. L. Swanson, K. R. Harris, & S. Graham (eds.), *Handbook of learning disabilities* (pp. 323–44). New York: Guilford Press.

Hallahan, D. P. & Mock, D. R. (2003). A brief history of the field of learning disabilities. In H. L. Swanson, K. R. Harris, & S. Graham (eds.), *Handbook of learning disabilities*. New York: Guilford Press.

Hammill, D. D. (1993). A brief look at the learning disabilities movement in the United States. *Journal of Learning Disabilities* 26 (5), 295–310.

Holdnack, J. A. & Weiss, L. G. (2006). Idea (2004). Anticipated implication for clinical practice-integrating assessment and intervention. *Psychology in the Schools* 43 (8), 871–82.

Holmes, J. & Adams, J. W. (2006). Working memory and children's mathematical skills: Implications for mathematical development and mathematics curricula. *Educational Psychology* 26 (3), 339–66.

Individuals with Disabilities Education Improvement Act of 2004, 20 U.S.C. §1415(k).

Interagency Committee on Learning Disabilities. (1987). Learning disabilities: A report to the U.S. Congress. Bethesda, MD: National Institutes of Health.

Kavale, K. A. & Forness, S. R. (2000). What definitions of learning disabilities say and don't say: A critical analysis. *Journal of Learning Disabilities* 33 (3), 239–56.

Kavale, K. A. & Forness, S. R. (2003). Learning disability as a discipline. In H. L. Swanson, K. R. Harris, & S. Graham (eds.), *Handbook of learning disabilities* (pp. 76–93). New York: Guilford Press.

Kavale, K. A., Forness, S. R., & Lorsbach, T. C. (1991). Definition for definitions of learning disabilities. *Learning Disability Quarterly* 14 (4), 257–66.

Kavale, K. A., Holdnack, J. A., & Mostert, M. P. (2005). Responsiveness to intervention and the identification of specific learning disability: A critique and alternative proposal. *Learning Disability Quarterly* 28 (1), 2–16.

Lipka, O. & Siegel, L. S. (2006). Learning disabilities. In D. A. M. Wolfe & J. Eric (eds.), *Behavioral and emotional disorders in adolescents: Nature, assessment, and treatment* (pp. 410–43). New York: Guilford Publications.

Lyon, G. R. (1996). Learning disabilities. *The Future of Children* 6 (1), 54–76.

Lyon, G. R., Fletcher, J. M., & Barnes, M. A. (2003). Learning disabilities. In E. J. Mash & R. Barkley (eds.), *Child psychopathology*. New York: Guilford Press.

Lyon, G. R., Fletcher, J. M., Fuchs, L. S., & Chhabra, V. (2006). Learning disabilities. In E. J. Mash (ed.), *Treatment of childhood disorders* (vol. 3) (pp. 512–91). New York: Guilford Press.

Lyon, G. R. & Moats, L. C. (1988). Critical issues in the instruction of the learning disabled. *Journal of Consulting and Clinical Psychology* 56 (3), 830–5.

McDermott, P. A., Goldberg, M. M., Watkins, M.W., Stanley, J. L., & Glutting, J. J. (2006). A nationwide epidemiologic modeling study of learning disabilities: Risk, protection, and unintended impact. *Journal of Learning Disabilities* 39 (3), 230–51.

McNamara, J. & Wong, B. (2003). Memory for everyday information in students with learning disabilities. *Journal of Learning Disabilities* 36 (5), 394–406.

Meichenbaum, D. (1977). *Cognitive behavior modification: An integrative approach*. New York: Springer.

Mellard, D. F., Deshler, D. D., & Bart, A. (2004). LD identification: It's not simply a matter of building a better mousetrap. *Learning Disability Quarterly* 27 (4), 229–42.

Mercer, C. D., Jordan, L., Allsopp, D. H., & Mercer, A. R. (1996). Learning disabilities definitions and criteria used by state education departments. *Learning Disability Quarterly* 19 (4), 217–32.

Meyer, M. S. (2000). The ability–achievement discrepancy: Does it contribute to an understanding of learning disabilities? *Educational Psychology Review* 12, 315–37.

Miyake, A., Friedman, N. P., Emerson, M. J., Witzki, A., & Howerter, A. (2000). The unity and diversity of executive functions and their contributions to complex "frontal lobe" tasks: A latent variable analysis. *Cognitive Psychology* 41, 49–100.

Moats, L. C. & Lyon, G. R. (1993). Learning disabilities in the United States: Advocacy, science and the future of the field. *Journal of Learning Disabilities* 26 (5), 282–94.

O'Shaughnessy, T. & Swanson, H. L. (1998). Do immediate memory deficits in students with learning disabilities in reading and writing reflect a developmental lag or deficit? A selective meta-analysis of the literature. *Learning Disability Quarterly* 21 (2), 123–48.

Oakhill, J. V., Cain, K., & Bryant, P. E. (2003). The dissociation of word reading and text comprehension: Evidence from component skills. *Language and Cognitive Processes* 18 (4), 443–68.

Ofiesh, N. (2006). Response to intervention and the identification of specific learning disabilities: Why we need comprehensive evaluations as part of the process. *Psychology in the Schools* 43 (8), 883–8.

Raskind, W. (2001). Current understanding of the genetic basis of reading and spelling disability. *Learning Disability Quarterly* 24 (3), 141–57.

Reschly, D. J. (2005). Learning disabilities identification. *Journal of Learning Disabilities* 38 (6), 510–15.

Reschly, D. J. & Hosp, J. L. (2004). State SLD identification policies and practices. *Learning Disability Quarterly* 27 (4), 197–213.

Schumaker, J. B., Deschler, D., & McKnight, P. (2002). Ensuring success in the secondary general education curriculum through the use of teaching routines. In M. Shinn, H. Walker, & G. Stoner (eds.), *Interventions for academic and behavior problems II: Prevention and remedial approaches* (pp. 791–823). Bethesda, MD: National Association of School Psychologists.

Scruggs, T. E. & Mastropieri, M. A. (2002). On babies and bathwater: Addressing the problems of identification of learning disabilities. *Learning Disability Quarterly* 25 (3), 155–68.

Shaywitz, S. E. & Shaywitz, B. A. (2003). Dyslexia (specific reading disability). *Biological Psychiatry* 57 (11), 1301–9.

Sideridis, G., Morgan, P., Botsas, G., Padeliadu, S., & Fuchs, D. (2006).

Predicting LD on the basis of motivation, metacognition, and psychopathology: An ROC analysis. *Journal of Learning Disabilities* 39 (3), 215–29.

Speece, D. L., Case, L. P., & Molloy, D. E. (2003). Responsiveness to general education instruction as the first gate to learning disabilities identification. *Learning Disabilities Research & Practice* 18 (3), 147–56.

Stanovich, K. E. (1986). Matthew effects in reading: Some consequences of individual differences in acquisition of literacy. *Reading Research Quarterly* 21 (4), 360–402.

Stanovich, K. E. (1991). Discrepancy definitions of reading disability: Has intelligence led us astray? *Reading Research Quarterly* 26 (1), 7–29.

Stuebing, K. K., Fletcher, J. M., LeDoux, J. M., Lyon, G. R., Shaywitz, S. E., & Shaywitz, B. A. (2002). Validity of IQ-discrepancy classifications of reading disabilities: A meta-analysis. *American Educational Research Journal* 39 (2), 469–518.

Swanson, H. L. (1991). Operational definitions and learning disabilities: An overview. *Learning Disability Quarterly* 14 (4), 242–54.

Swanson, H. L. (1999). Reading research for students with LD: A meta-analysis of intervention outcomes. *Journal of Learning Disabilities* 32 (6), 504–32.

Swanson, H. L. (2001). Research on interventions for adolescents with learning disabilities: A meta-analysis of outcomes related to higher-order processing. *The Elementary School Journal* 101, 331–48.

Swanson, H. L. (2005). Working memory, intelligence and learning disabilities. In O. Wilhelm & R. Engle (eds.), *Handbook of understanding and measuring intelligence* (pp. 409–29). Thousand Oaks, CA: Sage.

Swanson, H. L. & Beebe-Frankenberger, M. (2004). The relationship between working memory and mathematical problem solving in children at risk and not at risk for serious math difficulties. *Journal of Educational Psychology* 96, 471–93.

Swanson, H. L. & Hoskyn, M. (2001). Instructing adolescents with learning disabilities: A component and composite analysis. *Learning Disabilities Research & Practice* 16 (2), 109–19.

Swanson, H. L. & Sachs-Lee, C. (2001). Mathematical problem solving and working memory in children with learning disabilities: Both executive and phonological processes are important. *Journal of Experimental Child Psychology* 79 (3), 294–321.

Torgesen, J. K. (1986). Learning disabilities theory: Its current state and future prospects. *Journal of Learning Disabilities* 19 (7), 399–408.

Torgeson, J. K. (1987). Thinking about the future by distinguishing between those that have answers and those that do not. In S. Vaughn & C. Bos (eds.), *Issues and future directions for research in learning disabilities* (pp. 55–64). San Diego, CA: College Hill Press.

Torgesen, J. K. (2004). Learning disabilities: A historical and conceptual overview. In *Learning About Learning Disabilities* (vol. 3) (pp. 3–40). San Diego: Elsevier Academic Press.

Vaughn, S., Linan-Thompson, S., & Hickman, P. (2003). Response to instruction as a means of identifying students with reading/learning disabilities. *Exceptional Children* 69 (4), 391–409.

Vellutino, F. R., Scanlon, D. M., Small, S., & Fanuele, D. P. (2006). Response to intervention as a vehicle for distinguishing between children with and without reading disabilities: Evidence for the role of kindergarten and first-grade interventions. *Journal of Learning Disabilities* 39 (2), 157–69.

Willis, J. O. & Dumont, R. (2006). And never the twain shall meet: Can response to intervention and cognitive assessment be reconciled? *Psychology in the Schools* 43 (8), 901–8.

12 Reading and Reading Impairments

JACK S. DAMICO AND RYAN NELSON

1 Introduction

Within the discipline of speech-language pathology, there is an increasing interest in reading and reading impairment as an area of concentration. This trend is recognizable from the professional policy statements that define the roles and responsibilities for clinicians (e.g., American Speech-Language-Hearing Association, 2001) and from the increased research and intervention publications available regarding literacy service delivery across age ranges and disability types (e.g., Beeson & Henry, 2008; Catts et al., 2002; Catts & Kamhi, 2004; Connor & Zwolan, 2004; Gillon, 2002; Iacono & Cupples, 2004; Lynch et al., in press; Mody & Silliman, 2008; Norris & Hoffman, 2002). As more societal (Gee, 2000; Goody, 1986; Ong, 1982) and educational (Cazden et al., 1996; "No Child Left Behind Act of 2001 (H.R.1)," 2002; Strauss, 2005) attention is given to literacy, it has become a more important issue for the practicing clinician.

The discipline's interest in reading, however, is not necessarily matched by the clinicians' knowledge or perceived competence regarding reading and reading impairments. A nationwide survey found that the majority of practicing speech-language pathologists surveyed indicated that they were not well trained regarding literacy issues and did not have confidence in their abilities to address literacy/reading as a clinical responsibility (Nelson & Damico, 2002). This lack of knowledge and confidence regarding reading is problematic but not surprising. Historically, speech-language pathology evolved with an initial focus on speech and only incorporated an emphasis on language much later in the development of the discipline (Damico, 1993; Duchan, 2008). It is only within the last decade that speech-language pathologists have focused on literacy as a clinical issue. Consequently, the discipline is less informed about literacy/reading than is desirable (Nelson & Damico, 2002), especially since language arts is a complex area fraught with debate.

Literacy theory and instruction is often controversial. Over the past several decades there have been suggestions of the "great debate" in language arts (Chall, 1983), the "reading wars" (Goodman, 1998; Lemann, 1997) regarding literacy education, and there has been a recognition of the role that politics plays in literacy research, policy, and pedagogy (e.g., Allington & Woodside-Jiron, 1999; Berliner, 1997; Davenport & Jones, 2005; Strauss, 2003). Numerous publications critique the ways that research and practice have been influenced by preconceptions based upon ideology (Allington, 2002; Coles, 2003; Garan, 2005) and there have been frequent disagreements across various perspectives within the field (e.g., Coles, 2003; Garan, 2005; Lyon, 1999; Moats, 2000; Richards, 1980; Shanahan, 2004; Stanovich, 1988; Strauss, 2001). The lack of clinician competence, whether real or perceived, linked with the controversies in the literacy field, has resulted in difficulty in determining the best course(s) of action when addressing reading as clinical practice.

The purpose of this chapter is to provide the researcher and practicing clinician with an overview of the primary issues related to reading and reading impairments. This includes a discussion of the conceptualizations of literacy as social practice and as a personal skill, a review of how definitions of reading and reading impairment (dyslexia) have evolved, how these definitions are dependent on contrastive views of how humans learn, and how these views influence aspects of research and service delivery in reading. Given the clinical nature of this handbook, the chapter will also discuss a clinically relevant resolution to some of these controversies by exploiting the advantages of clinical intervention and using these advantages to advance meaningfulness and functionality in the process of acquiring and using literacy/reading.

2   Conceptualizations of Literacy

When considering literacy and its impact, it is prudent to focus on literacy at two different levels. The first level is societal: literacy as it is employed and impacts on the social lives of people in modern bureaucratic societies (Goody, 1986; Ong, 1982) – what Olson and Torrance (2001a) referred to as *social practice*. The second level involves the individual: literacy as it is employed by individuals during reading and writing within particular social and institutional contexts (Scribner & Cole, 1981; Street, 1995) – what Olson and Torrance (2001a) referred to as *personal skill*. The first of these two levels, social practice, is primarily concerned with the implications of literacy for society, while the second level, personal skill, is interested in the implications of literacy on the mind and psychological issues. Since this is a clinically oriented chapter, the main emphasis will be placed upon reading as a personal skill; however, a brief discussion of the impact of literacy/reading as social practice is relevant, especially as it relates to our goals and aspirations in the educational context.

3   Literacy as Social Practice

When conceptualizing literacy as social practice, the group rather than the individual is the focus, and any interest in the individual is more as a societal agent than a person. This conception is considered analysis at a *macro* level, and this work is placed under the purview of sociologists, philosophers, and educational reformers (Sloane, 2005). At this level the roles that reading and writing play in the establishment of social processes like education, government, and jurisprudence are considered along with how literacy influences the evolution of institutions like science, literature, and religion. Olson (1994) suggests that literacy is analyzed to determine how "Our modern conception of the world and our modern conception of ourselves are, we may say, by-products of the invention of a world on paper" (p. 282). The impact of literacy on societal development has been the major focus at this level and it has been referred to as the *causal* conception of literacy (Olson & Torrance, 2001a). However, other varied roles of literacy within cultural contexts have also been examined. In addition to the role of literacy in social development, Olson and Torrance have described six other issues of particular interest, including the evolution of the scripts employed by various literacy systems across different cultures; how literacy is influenced by some functional structures in different cultures (e.g., law, science, and religion); the close and necessary interaction between oral and written modes in various cultures; the creation of a particular orientation to language through a textual strategy honed by literacy experience (i.e., meta-linguistics, meta-discourse); and the role of literacy in creating, or at least sustaining, a dichotomy of folk versus bureaucratic knowledge, superstition versus science, and myth versus history. For our purposes the history of literacy and what it means to be literate is the most relevant issue that we must consider when focusing on literacy as social practice.

3.1   A limited history of reading

When the history of reading is detailed as social practice, it is typically oriented to the development of societal literacy in Western Europe and the United States since reading is often linked to the rise of the modern Western scholarly tradition and to the Enlightenment (but see Almond & Coleman, 1960; Freire & Macedo, 1987; Olson & Torrance, 2001b; Triebel, 1997). In this vein, historical investigation primarily focuses on how reading evolved and influenced society, the ruling elite, the general public, and mass media (Olson & Torrance, 2001a). From this perspective, a review of the history of reading awareness suggests that there have been a number of changes over time regarding reading issues and the definition of what it means to be literate (Triebel, 1997).

In discussing his historical research, Triebel (2001) posits that the societal transformation toward literacy in Europe was a protracted one. Literacy originated in scattered areas at different times and remained localized for centuries before spreading out to permeate large populations. It is interesting to note that these original centers of literacy were varied in terms of locations, occupations, and functions. Triebel describes scribes, administrators, and bookkeepers in ancient Mesopotamia, civil servants in European courts and seats of government, priests and monks in churches, monasteries, and schools, scholars in academies and universities, and merchants and artisans in developing cities as the progenitors of literacy in these pockets of opportunity and maintenance. While in the thirteenth century most priests could read and write, Triebel (2001) estimates that far fewer of any other class or occupation could do the same. He estimated that in the population of Middle Europe at around 1770, no more than 15 percent of the male population above 6 years of age could read. While this figure did steadily increase, 60 years later estimates indicated only a 40 percent literacy rate. Triebel estimates that literacy use among males was approximately 90 percent at the turn of the twentieth century.

In their analysis of the history of literacy awareness in the Western tradition, Resnick and Resnick (1977) discussed three major historical models for reading and reading development before the twentieth century that could be employed to explain the literacy transformations: the Protestant/religious, the elite/technical, and the civic/national models. During the Protestant/religious model of historical experience, approximately 1540 to 1800, Protestant communities intended to develop sufficient literacy in their members so that they could come into personal contact with the Bible and the Christian message. Focusing primarily on males in the community, literacy rates increased dramatically during this period in areas where literacy change was documented (e.g., New England, Scotland, Sweden). However, these mass-literacy efforts were intended to develop reading mastery over a very limited set of prescribed texts as opposed to a generalized reading capacity (Resnick & Resnick, 1977). During the elite/technical model, approximately 1400 to 1850, schools were established for the sons of the ruling elite or for sons of the aristocracy, the bourgeoisie, and a few recognized individuals from the lower classes who exhibited exceptional ability. Operated primarily by religious orders, these schools provided sufficient literacy and education necessary for successful careers in civil and military public service. Finally, the civil/national schooling model, starting approximately 1880, focused on mass education of males and females, broadened the set of texts, and encouraged a focus on citizenship through literacy. However, while some of these students did develop literacy sufficient to engage in critical and inferential reading (as in the elite schools), the vast numbers of students were not expected to employ literacy to acquire new information but only to become fluent oral readers (Resnick & Resnick, 1977).

From this cursory description, it can be noted that the societal purposes for literacy influenced how reading and writing were perceived and how literacy spread from the elite to the masses. The transformation to greater literacy was also mirrored in the materials employed for mass communication during these time periods. While Johannes Gutenberg invented the printing press around 1440, the books and documents that soon became available were primarily intended for the educated elite. It is true that many more individuals had access to literature and to information over the next several centuries due to printing; however, these resources and the skills to benefit from them were still limited to less than 20 percent of the population until the end of the eighteenth century. Analysis of the materials used for large-scale religious, political, educational, and occupational purposes during these time periods revealed that many of the materials were still dominated by pictures or depictions of spectacular events. Many tracts were little more than illustrated fliers that often had little or no text in the forms of captions or notes; this was true until late into the nineteenth century.

3.2 What it means to be literate

Hidden within the evolution of literacy in the Western tradition was the corresponding idea of what it meant to be literate. That is, when could one be considered to have the skills necessary to meet societal requirements for being a reader and/or writer? From a societal orientation this is important since educational policy, curricular design, and pedagogical practice are often dependent on one's desired end point. Analysis of the history of literacy revealed that as society changed its standards and expectations regarding literacy, the conception of adequate literacy and the definition of being literate also changed (Resnick & Resnick, 1977). The terms "literacy," "literate," and "illiterate" are social constructs and not set categories. Consequently, these definitions changed over time and across various social contexts. Early in the sixteenth century, for example, writing one's name was the standard for literacy even if one was not able to read the document being signed. Within the Protestant/religious model, reading/reciting a simple well-known Bible passage aloud was sufficient while later, in the civil/national schooling period, reading a simple well-known set of texts aloud would enable a citizen to pass a literacy test. In such situations, there might be few illiterates and virtually no "reading deficits" in society.

With more relevance to our current understandings, reading defined as a process by which meaning is extracted from something written or printed on a page has fairly recent origins (Wolf, 1977). Newman and Beverstock (1990) investigated various definitions of literacy over historical periods and found that the conception of being literate changed from very basic skills (i.e., the ability to sign one's name), through the ability to read and write, to attainment of fourth grade reading level. Currently, there is another change regarding the criterion for becoming literate. Society is moving the definition of literacy toward the ability to read new material and glean new information from that material. Further, since the 1950s we have expected that this standard of literacy be extended beyond the socioeconomic elite to all participants in public education (Bracey, 2004). While the extension of reading adequacy is not a problem, there has not been a corresponding change in the pedagogies employed in literacy education – this has created a problem. Our current reading levels appear unacceptable because we have changed the criterion for adequate levels of reading without sufficient pedagogical support. While this issue will be discussed later in this chapter, it is important to realize that the conception of *literate* is a social construct and, as a social construct, this label is often just a mirror of the prevailing ideologies that are in vogue at any given time (Baynham, 1995).

4 Literacy as Personal Skill

More relevant to this chapter is the conceptualization of literacy at the second level, literacy as personal skill (Olson & Torrance, 2001a). Attention to this level places the individual and the social context at the center of the discussion and strives to determine how literacy produces psychological change and social action within those individuals who acquire and use literacy. This is the level of the *instrumental* conception of literacy wherein the focus is on what people do and can do with literacy (Olson & Torrance, 2001a). Regarding earlier reference to the controversies in literacy (section 1), these issues typically occur when considering literacy at the individual level and as a personal skill. While there are a number of topics that may be discussed at this level, we will focus primarily on reading and three topics will be highlighted: conceptions of human learning, models of reading, and definitions of dyslexia and reading impairment.

4.1   *Conceptions of human learning*

Whether focusing on reading or other skills, our understanding of how human learning occurs is foundational. This conceptualization influences many other decisions we make with regard to psychological and educational issues. Over the twentieth century, two conceptions of human learning have dominated much of the psychological and social sciences, and they have influenced our expectations and interpretations of human performance, our approaches to research, the way conditions and processes are defined, and how psychology, education, and other human-oriented disciplines interacted with subjects, clients, and pupils. These two major theoretical perspectives are *behaviorism* and *cognitivism*.

4.1.1   Behaviorism   The first theoretical perspective is behaviorism. Based upon the work of John B. Watson (1913, 1930), this perspective approached learning by focusing on behaviors rather than mental states or unconscious processes (Robinson, 1995). Watson was oriented to learning as a subject of inquiry in psychology and he developed his version of behaviorism to focus on this important topic. He stated:

> Psychology as the behaviorist views it is a purely experimental branch of natural science. Its theoretical goal is the prediction and control of behavior. Introspection forms no essential part of its methods, nor is the scientific value of its data dependent upon the readiness with which they lend themselves to interpretation in terms of consciousness. The behaviorist, in his efforts to get a unitary scheme of animal response, recognizes no dividing line between man and brute. (1913, p. 158)

Within this quote several of his stated points became a common set of beliefs for the early behaviorists. First, they denied any intrinsic life to the mind and did not believe that the mind should be an object of study in psychology. Second, they were objectivists in that they believed that the only real data is that which can be directly observed. Third, they were experimentalists, believing that all psychological constructs should be defined operationally and subjected to rigid control through experimental research. Fourth, they were quite willing to employ animal models rather than focus on human behavior. Their reasoning was that since the underlying tenets of learning involved contextual variables, behaviors, and consequences, learning would essentially be the same for any species (Mills, 1988).

Behaviorism allowed Watson (1930) to change the focus of psychology from the consciousness (a concept he deemed subjective and ambiguous) to behavior (a preferred focus on the overt and empirical), and the methods of investigation from introspective analysis to experimentation. Watson eventually turned to classical conditioning as his way to accomplish these goals. He predicted and then confirmed through experimental research the existence of conditioned responses in infants, proposed the conditioned reflex as the unit of habit, and formulated an operant concept of learning (Rilling, 2000).

Watson's work on the mechanisms of learning, however, was not experimentally confirmed nor was it theoretically sound. When his behaviorism became untenable, Tolman (1932) and Skinner (1938) were able to modify his ideas into acceptable formulations; under the neobehaviorist label they created an approach to the study of animal and human behavior that became the *Zeitgeist* of mid-twentieth-century American psychology and education (Amsel, 1989; Shuell, 1986). While some changes occurred, the neobehavioral perspective still held to positivism and materialism, gave top priority to prediction and control, adhered to operationalism, and was obsessed by quantification (Danziger, 1990; Mills, 1998). Importantly, based upon experimental work with a very narrow range of animal species, neo-behaviorists focused on relatively simple forms of learning to advance their ideas (Mills, 1998). For example, when experimenting with human learning, memoriza-tion was often the focused experimental objective, and more complex human skills like comprehension were ignored (Burger, 1972; Shuell, 1986). By the middle of the twentieth century, Skinner's theory of operant conditioning (Skinner, 1938, 1968), which maintains that human behavior can be fostered by reinforcing selected actions, was the dominant perspective in human learning theory.

This perspective gave rise to important overall conceptions regarding learning in the educational context (Shuell, 1986; Smith, 1998). Writing on the impact of behaviorism in education, Smith (1998) contrasts the behavioral orientation – what he termed the "official theory of learning" – with a more social orientation that he termed the "classic view of learning." Several of the contrasts he discusses highlight the principles of the behaviorist learning paradigm. For example, this "official theory" includes the tendency to package learning into sets of separate skills so that there may be a fragmentation of complexity into smaller sets of component units that could be taught. It naturally follows then that learning, based upon operant principles, is often made efficient through repetitive drill and exercises; that the focus is on the behaviors one can observe rather than the underlying concepts or strategies that give rise to these behaviors (see "Cognitivism" below); that these behaviors are increased through principles of reinforcement rather than functional impact (like increased comprehensibility); that once indi-vidual behaviors and component skills are learned they can then be combined to create a functional whole; that learning is an individual activity that tends to require hard work or great effort; and that the measure of progress is through the quantification of the behaviors that make up the learning tasks.

While behaviorism, sustained within animal models of simplistic learning, flourished in many disciplines (and still has current advocates in education), the behaviorist (particularly Skinnerian) paradigm became problematic when more complex forms of learning and human traits like language and mind were targeted. Around the end of the 1950s and throughout the next 20 years, the behaviorist paradigm was increasingly criticized. Noam Chomsky (1959) wrote a powerful negative critique of Skinner's *Verbal Behavior* (1957) that reduced behaviorism's influence in language learning. Other critiques from the anthropological (e.g., Burger, 1972; Henry, 1960; Jones, 1972), psychological (e.g., Amsel, 1989; Gergen, 1985; Mills, 1988; Shuell, 1986; White, 1970; Zuriff, 1985), and philosophical (e.g., Blanshard, 1965; McGill, 1966; Mills, 1998; Smith, 1986) disciplines reduced the influence of behaviorism overall. As these critiques and the problems with more behaviorist practices in human learning appeared (e.g., Bruner, 1960, 1961, 1983, 1985; Searle, 1969; Shore, 1996; Wittrock, 1974), the behaviorist perspective was replaced with other perspectives, most notably, a constructivist perspective termed *cognitivism*.

4.1.2 Cognitivism Unlike behaviorism, the cognitive orientation posits the existence of internalized mental structure(s) that enable the individual to process, reconstruct, organize, and understand his/her physical, social, and biological worlds, thereby giving rise to learning. In effect, the focus was on the underlying structures from which the behavioral manifestations emerge rather than the behaviors themselves. One's mental structure(s) acts as a mediator that interprets the world relative to the individual's current conceptual system. Further, through experience with the environment (i.e., learning), the individual progressively constructs a more elaborate conceptual system to better understand and act upon the world; a system that also becomes progressively more similar to the internalized concepts of those individuals with which the child shares perceptual, epistemological, cultural, and social experiences. Two of the early advocates for this cognitive conception of learning, Jean Piaget (1968, 1970) and Lev Vygotsky (1978, 1981), tended to refer to the nature of the internal mental structure differently (internalized logic and semiotic, respectively) but much of their formulations and their primary principles in constructing what became cognitivism were quite similar (Grobecker, 1996; Pass, 2004).

It has been suggested that the term "cognitivism" comes from the work of Piaget. Throughout his research career, he sought to understand how children construct their conceptions of the world by employing internal cognitive structures and processes (e.g., Piaget, 1968, 1970). Consequently, knowledge structures were discussed as various mental activities within cognitive processing modes such as perception, memory, and organization, and these knowledge structures were the focus of development and learning. They became important for (at least) two reasons. First, they helped give rise to the orientation toward various cognitive abilities and processes that are a hallmark of cognitivism. Second, the focus on knowledge, not behavior, was a crucial break from behaviorism. As suggested by Stevenson, if it is knowledge that one learns, "then behavior must be the result of learning, rather than that which itself is learned" (Stevenson, 1983, p. 214). These shifts weaken the concept of behaviorism.

In discussing the influence of cognition on learning theory, Langley and Simon (1981) have provided a definition of learning from the cognitive perspective. They define learning as "any process that modifies a system so as to improve, more or less irreversibly, its subsequent performance of the same task or of tasks drawn from the same population" (p. 367). This definition emphasizes mental processes and knowledge structures (i.e., "system") rather than the behaviors themselves. Of course, the mental processes and structures are inferred based upon the patterns of behaviors, but it is exactly this focus that separates behaviorism from cognitivism. Shuell (1986) suggests that learning theory as filtered through cognitivism involves at least five different concerns or foci. First, this perspective views learning as an active and constructive process dependent primarily on the mental activities of the learner. In this regard, metacognitive processes like planning are employed to privilege certain kinds of stimuli and learning objectives and then to organize the material being learned. The result of this active processing and mental construction are responses appropriate to the learning context and the construction and employment of various learning strategies. Second, learning involves higher-level processes. These cognitive and metacognitive processes involve regulation, organization, and predictive implementation of the various activities involved in learning and an awareness of what one "does and does not know about the material being learned and the processes involved in learning it" (Shuell, 1986, p. 416). Third, learning involves reliance on cumulative and prior knowledge and on the strategies previously developed to identify, organize, and integrate knowledge. Fourth, due to the third focus, cognitive learning theory is especially concerned with the way knowledge is represented and organized in memory. This creates a significant break from behaviorism in that the emphasis is on the understanding and organization of internal knowledge structures rather than on the behavioral indices of learning. Fifth, Shuell suggests that the cognitivist perspective on learning has a concern for analyzing the learning tasks and the results of learning in terms of the cognitive processes that are involved.

Shuell (1986) discusses several differences between behaviorism and cognitivism that relate directly to human learning. Primarily, while both traditions agree that environmental factors and factors internal to the learner contribute to learning through some sort of interplay, the nature, scope and power of the "internal factors," the degree of influence between the learner versus the environment, what is learned (behaviors versus structured knowledge) and the factors that influence the learning process (reinforcement versus developed strategies for operating on the environment – including obtaining feedback) are very different within these two perspectives. Rather than focus on stimulus and response, cognitivism focuses on the thought processes and the mental activities that mediate the relationship between stimulus and response.

4.2 Models of reading

Based upon the two conceptions of human learning, the language arts literature has focused on reading from two distinct perspectives. The first, a *skills-based model*, is oriented to a behaviorist interpretation of human functioning and focuses primarily on component skills, knowledge, and attitudes that constitute a particular conception of reading. Within this model, reading is seen as a secondary skill based upon oral language coding, and the foci are the skills that enable the translation of the visual modality into oral language and the linkages between the component skills. Advocates of this model view proficient reading primarily as identification of words automatically and fluently (e.g., Adams, 1990; Apel & Swank, 1999; Lyon, 1999; Stanovich, 1991). This perspective has as its target what is termed "conventional literacy" (Whitehurst & Lonigan, 1998). The second perspective is based upon cognitive interpretations of human learning and is oriented to a process of active construction of meaning through a set of strategies that enable the linkage of one's background knowledge of language and the world to create comprehensibility (e.g., Goodman, 1967; Goodman & Goodman, 1994; Goodman, Watson, & Burke, 1996; Meek, 1982; Smith, 1977; Smith, 2004; Weaver, 1990, 1998). This perspective has been termed the "naturalistic" or *"meaning-based"* approach to reading.

4.2.1 The skills-based model   The skills-based model employs a behaviorist approach to linguistics (Bloomfield, 1939) and learning theory that results in a view of reading as a straightforward process of decoding and encoding visual text through one's oral language system. This is necessary because reading is viewed as a secondary language system that employs systematically and explicitly taught component skills (e.g., phonemic awareness, phonics, fluency) to create readers and writers (Bloomfield & Barnhart, 1961; Moats, 1996).

One of the early proponents of the skills-based model was Jeanne Chall. In her book *Learning to read: The great debate* (Chall, 1967), she advocated a fragmented and behavioral model of individual reading competence that focused on five successive stages in reading development. These stages – decoding, confirmation and fluency, reading to learn, multiple viewpoints, and construction and judgment – were intended to describe the process of reading development and learning from a child's pre-literate period of development through college age or adulthood. Within these stages one can see the principles of the skills-based model of reading in which the individual skills or components are emphasized rather than the process of constructing meaning. For example, at the initial stage (decoding) the focus is on the relationship between the letters and sounds, how the alphabetic principle is learned and applied, and how the learner becomes aware of the relationship between sound–symbol correspondences so that he/she can begin to apply this knowledge to the text. Chall emphasized the role of separate knowledge systems and application skills like phonemic awareness and phonics as important precursors to the higher stages. At this stage (and the pre-literate stage) the focus of the learners (4–8 years of age) is on visual code and not meaning during the reading process. The object is to sufficiently learn the code so a direct translation to oral language can eventually occur.

The second stage, confirmation and fluency, builds upon the component skills learned and applied in the earlier stages. The focus is on practice to gain efficiency and fluency, and, as the decoding skills improve, greater efficiency and accuracy in word recognition occurs. Although there is a discussion directed toward giving attention to both the code and meaning, in practice the focus is still on decoding and single word recognition. These first two stages are primarily emphasized until the third or fourth grade, and then the other three stages – reading to learn (around 9 years old), developing multiple viewpoints (around 14–19 years of age), and construction and judgment (college age or older) – are emphasized.

Two points regarding the skills-based model that warrant further discussion involve the conception of reading as a secondary language system and the place that meaning and comprehension play in the model itself. Throughout the literature on the skills-based model there is the suggestion that reading is a secondary language system and that comprehension and meaning construction is typically based upon the process of intermodal transfer through the oral language system (e.g., Adams, 1990; Catts, 1996; Chall, 1967; Critchley, 1970; Foorman et al., 1997; Gillon, 2000; Orton, 1937; Whitehurst & Lonigan, 1998). Mattingly (1972), citing Liberman, even suggested that reading is "parasitic" on spoken language (p. 145). Within this perspective, the primary skill is the ability to decipher printed symbols based upon the individual's success in establishing phonetic or sound representations of those symbols. Within communicative disorders this view is also represented. For example, Catts (1996) advanced this view by stating that, "If dyslexia were only a reading disability, it would imply that humans are somehow biologically predisposed to read and write and that in some individuals this predisposition is disrupted. Such a proposal is highly unlikely" (p. 15).

This tendency to create modules or components of language skills that may be considered primary and secondary to one another is characteristic of the influence of behaviorism evident beginning with the work of the American structural linguist Leonard Bloomfield (1939), and is quite different from the current constructivist conception of oral and visual language as emergent manifestations of a deeper level of semiotic and/or symbolic functioning that views these emergent properties as generally equivalent (e.g., Bruner, 1990; Damico, 2003; Halliday, 1993; Holtgraves, 2002; Iran-Nejad, 1995; O'Connell & Kowal, 2003; Perkins, 1998; Vygotsky, 1978). Within the constructivist orientation, one semiotic and/or symbolic system (e.g., oral language, gestural language, literacy) is as primary and capable of abstract representation as any other. All, however, are conceptualized as cultural tools that have been created through sociocultural necessity and preferences (e.g., Bruner, 1991; Halliday, 1978; Olson, 1996; Ong, 1982; Tomasello, 1999, 2003; Vygotsky, 1978, 1981; Wells, 1994). It is at the level of cultural need and construction that one system may gain primacy over another in a particular temporal and/or spatial context. This does not mean, however, that there are biological dispositions, except in non-interesting ways (e.g., employment of different modalities across two symbolic systems). The modular perspective, though not supported in recent constructivist theoretical formulations, not only provides the impetus for reading as a secondary system, thereby lending credence to a perceived need to engage in intermodal transfer; it also enables orientation to discrete components or skills like phonemic awareness, phonics, and fluency so that these are not seen as emergent dimensions of a synergistic language system but, rather, as separate components to be discretely and explicitly taught. Such an orientation is not consistent with the other model of reading nor is it supported by current constructivist ideas in language arts (e.g., Cambourne, 1988; Damico et al., in review; Geekie, Cambourne, & Fitzsimmons, 1999; Goodman, 1994; Meek, 1982; Oldfather & Dahl, 1994; Smith, 2004; Wells, 1990).

The second issue that warrants further discussion is the place of meaning and comprehension in this skill-based model of reading. Chall (1967) and others (e.g., Adams, 1990, 1991; Adams & Bruck, 1993; Catts et al., 1999; Foorman et al., 1997; Kamhi & Catts, 1986; Rasinski & Padak, 2001; Stanovich et al., 1985; Whitehurst & Lonigan, 1998) have all suggested that in addition to the component skills like phonemic awareness and phonics, there should be an emphasis on meaning. However, within each of these recommendations, the early and significant aspects of reading acquisition and pedagogy focus on the component skills so that there is greater facility to create an intermodal transfer. Consequently, the focus on meaning and attention to it comes too little and too late. Whitehurst and Lonigan (1998) are illustrative even when talking about the importance of the semantic and grammatical systems. First, their primary focus here is on sounds and words. They state that the initial variable is vocabulary, and reading is defined as a "process of translating visual codes into meaningful language. In the earliest stages, reading in an alphabetic system involves decoding letters into corresponding sounds and linking those sounds to single words." (p. 849). When these authors state that "a child's semantic and syntactic abilities assume greater importance later in the sequence of learning to read, when the child is reading for meaning, than early in the sequence, when the child is learning to sound out single words" (p. 850), they are actually emphasizing component skills to the reduction of initial attention on meaning. Even though these writers state that reading is a process motivated by the extraction of meaning, the way that they conceptualize this makes all the difference. Implementation reveals the behaviorist approach with the idea of translation of single words rather than the whole of the linguistic system. This is not synergistic nor is it guided by meaning. Rather, meaning construction based on translation of visual symbols into oral vocabulary is the goal.

4.2.1.1   The component skills approach to teaching   For the purposes of this chapter, the most important application of the skills-based model involves the methods and approaches for teaching and intervention in reading. Consistent with the behaviorist agenda discussed by Smith (1998), Shuell (1986), and Mills (1998), the skills-based model tends to break the process of reading (and writing) into separate components that may be arranged according to some perceived developmental order and then explicitly taught in a decontextualized manner. This teaching and learning is often expected to be effortful and to require diligence on the part of both the teacher and the learner. This is variously referred to as the "component skills approach," the "phonics approach," or the "bottom-up approach."

This component skills approach is the outgrowth of the conception of reading and writing as a set of discrete skills that can be applied incrementally to work toward eventual comprehension. Based upon largely atheoretical experimental studies, component skills reading instruction isolates reading from other language processes, decontextualizes this phenomenon, and focuses on how to read words accurately as the object of instruction. Consequently, the experimental research has tended to focus on building a word-identification technology (Goodman, 1994). It is this focus that has led current reading intervention to spend far too much time on the precursor skills of phonemic awareness, phonics, and/or reading and rehearsing single words to the detriment of authentic reading and writing for beginners in reading.

One of the most influential classroom documents used to advance this component skills approach, *Teaching our children to read: The role of skills in a comprehensive reading program* (Honig, 1996), emphasized phonics and word research and pedagogy, misinterpreted the work of several literacy theorists (Goodman and Smith), and created the following implications for classroom instruction: (1) phonics and word knowledge are prerequisites to successful reading; (2) each grade level has specific skill components that should be taught; and (3) one should use decodable texts for teaching phonics and use other, predictable texts for motivating children, teaching the concept of a word, and teaching other concepts of print. For example, acquiring basic phonemic awareness in kindergarten, being able to decode simple CVC words and non-words, followed by CCVC combinations and long vowels in the first grade, and reading and understanding reduced textbooks by the beginning of the second grade were considered important benchmarks. Within this book there was also a call for a balanced reading program that included time for both separate, explicit skill instruction and language-rich literature instruction. However, the early emphasis was on the component skills themselves both in the pedagogy and in the selection of the materials for reading.

This conception of reading instruction with its focus on explicitly drilled and trained component skills provides a view of the reader as a passive agent that simply responds to the stimuli and consequences provided. In this sense the text, since it contains the visual symbols that need to be translated into oral language, controls the reader in terms of understanding. The familiar distinction between a skills-based model as having meaning *residing in the text* as opposed to the meaning-based model which posits meaning *residing in the reader* highlights this reader passivity (Goodman, 1994; Smith, 2004).

The result of this conception of reading from a behavioral skills-based perspective, with its component skills approach to reading instruction, has been aggressively advocated over the past 8 years with "No Child Left Behind" (2001; Allington, 2002; Strauss, 2005). By linking psychological behaviorism and its operant conditioning with a behaviorist approach to linguistics (Bloomfield, 1939; Fries, 1963), reading education became focused on teaching the sounds of letters and then single words, and programs like *Success for All* and *Open Court* were marketed. Since these programs are based upon the experimental word-identification technology and its precursors, the component skills approach was further established (Strauss, 2005). Just as with the approach itself, these programs (and others) were based upon a separation of the various linguistic elements into discrete categories (phonology, morphology, syntax, semantics) and patterned drills and exercises became the methodology to establish learning.

This application greatly impacts the speech-language pathologist, who often chooses some version of the component skills approach and places a focus on the training of the phonological system (e.g., phonemic awareness) as a precursor to the development of other literacy skills (e.g., Beeson & Henry, 2008; Catts, 1996; Catts & Kamhi, 2004; Foorman et al., 1997; Gillon, 2000, 2002; Iacono & Cupples, 2004; Moats, 1996). While there have been numerous claims regarding the validity of such an approach to intervention, especially with special populations, the focus on phonological/phonemic awareness and its justification as an efficacious approach to reading intervention has not been well documented in the literature. The studies on which the claims rest are often poorly conceived and/or biased toward the behaviorist orientation in which there is little or no focus on meaning and an underlying assumption that one must first learn the component skills before reading can occur. The reader is directed to the work of numerous researchers (e.g., Camilli & Wolfe, 2004; Coles, 2000, 2003; Garan, 2001, 2002; Krashen, 2001a, 2001b, 2001c, 2002a, 2002b, 2003a, 2003b, 2004; Strauss, 2003; Troia, 1999) for further information on the limits of phonological/phonemic awareness in reading education and intervention.

4.2.2   The meaning-based model   With the development of cognitivism, the approaches to reading took on a particular focus very different from the behaviorist model of reading. While the goal is still to make sense of written language, this was not a process of intermodal transfer. Rather, reading is viewed as a primary constructive process that is parallel to oral language in that the development of reading, especially prior to schooling, is a socially constructed process (e.g., Clark, 1976; Cochran-Smith, 1984; Ferreiro & Teberosky, 1979; Geekie, Cambroune, & Fitzsimmons, 1999; Wells, 1986). The parallelism is reflective of the fact that reading acquisition also involves a similar social interaction; the same kinds of mediating events and access to the same kinds of meaningful components described by Bruner (1983) in the acquisition of oral language are employed. This means that the child acquiring reading is recurrently exposed to authentic reading skills successfully modeled by proficient readers/writers. For his/her part, the child, when ready, has an opportunity to attempt the authentic reading skills him/herself with the mediation and corrective feedback of the more capable reader/writer. So, for example, during the period of emerging reading, a child and his/her caregiver may pick up a book together and engage in the social act of reading. When this occurs, there is an underlying (and meaningful) social interaction that is employed so that the caregiver collaborates with the child to construct meaning from print. In engaging in this social framework, the caregiver can assist the child's internalization of what the author was trying to say by reading, discussing, questioning, and inviting the child to participate, and by responding to the child's questions and other contributions. Clearly, it is through such socialized literacy activities that the child eventually acquires authentic reading and writing skills (Cambourne, 1988; Clay, 1998; Clay, 1991; Meek, 1982; Teale & Sulzby, 1986). That is, the social acts of reading and writing provide many of the conditions necessary for literacy acquisition and learning discussed by Cambourne (1988): the child may be exposed to excellent models of reading and writing; the child is exposed to the specific behaviors that are employed in reading and/or writing; the child can observe and internalize the functionality and meaningfulness of this social act; the child will have the chance to practice and perform; and the child will be able to observe and recognize the joys of reading – all through social modeling by individuals important to the child. As with all other forms of meaning making, reading acquisition is social, natural, and continual. It takes place within a recurrent and meaningful context through social interactions with people the child identifies with and, within any such reading encounter, the individuals and their personal relationships are at the heart of the process (Smith, 1998, 2003).

Given the orientation to this developmental constructivism and to the acquisition and use of internalized structures and strategies (Piaget, 1968; 1970), the reading process is strategic wherein visual input from the page is juxtaposed with the reader's background information to construct meaning within the text (Smith, 2004). This constructive process has been described as a "psycholinguistics guessing game" (Goodman, 1967). Within this model, all of the internalized processes occur quickly and primarily at a subconscious level, allowing for a reader's focus to remain on comprehension (Goodman, 1996). The key is not the code on the page or the development of component skills. Rather, the focus is on meaning. At all times and at all stages of the process of reading, meaning is both the objective and it is the context within which the reader strives toward comprehension. The reader creates understanding of the text within his/her conceptualization and while doing this, he/she is constantly guided by the expectation that the text is meaningful and that this meaning can be accessed.

One representative of this more meaning-based orientation is the transactional sociopsycholinguistic (TSP) model (Goodman, 1994) which emphasizes that reading is accomplished when an individual uses all aspects of his/her knowledge system, environment, and culture to help construct meaning out of print. During this meaning-focused approach the reader constructs an internalized representation through transactions with the targeted text, and the reader's schemata are also transformed in the process of transacting with text through the general strategies of assimilation and accommodation (Piaget, 1970). With any specific written text, however, the individual also employs strategies that have been developed to advance the thrust of meaningfulness onto texts of all forms. Such strategies include sampling just enough of the text to confirm or disconfirm the inferences and predictions they are simultaneously implementing based on the particular text being read, their background experience of the world, and their knowledge about how language works. Importantly, this model has numerous clinical and pedagogical implications and applications that have served the language arts community well during reading instruction and intervention (Calkins, 2001; Damico, Nelson, & Bryan, 2005; Smith, 1977; Weaver, 1990).

4.2.2.1   The meaning-based approach to teaching   Based upon the development of the meaning-based model of reading, several relevant approaches to reading teaching and intervention have emerged. While it is not quite correct to consider these as merely techniques or approaches, given the fact that many aspects of the learning process must be altered if the tenets of cognitivism are to be followed, these terms will be employed as a practical facet of the meaning-based model. Variously described as the "whole-language approach," "naturalistic approach," the "apprenticeship approach," the "constructivist approach," or the "top-down approach" to reading intervention, the meaning-based approach is consistent with the cognitivist and constructivist model: proficient reading is conceptualized as a matter of "orchestrating various reading strategies to construct meaning" (Weaver, 1998, p. 293), and each literacy activity involves authentic reading with a focus on meaning rather than accuracy (e.g., Allington, 2001; Allington et al., 1986; Calkins, 2001; Routman, 1994; Waterland, 1985; Weaver, 1990). Consequently, rather than attending to letters, words, or sounds within drills and decontextualized exercises, the focus is on the collaborative reading of meaningful material with the stress on the story narrative and the message within the text.

Consistent with the cognitivism perspective, Cambourne (1988) has drawn our attention to the conditions under which students learn best. These "conditions for engagement to learn literacy" address important considerations from the material to be used in learning, the actions of the learner, and the actions of the mediator. In a constructivist model, all three of these elements must be present and working. While the Cambourne conditions are not always explicitly discussed in the meaning-based approaches to teaching reading, they are often directly or indirectly employed. The first condition involves the extent to which the individual is *immersed* in text of all kinds. If the process of learning to read is a transactional one (Goodman, 1994), then there must be plenty of material from which to draw meaning and significance. Further, these materials need to cover the scope of the different styles and genres that the individual may encounter as a reader. Second, there must be many *demonstrations* of how authentic written texts are constructed and used. Without these two initial conditions, there is not enough authentic experiential input for acquisition/learning to occur.

Throughout the exposure and experience with text, the individual learner must recognize that he/she is capable of becoming a proficient reader and writer, and this recognition, in a social context, most frequently arises from the expectations that others have for the individual. As Cambourne (1988) stated, the *expectations of significant others* are powerful determiners of performance. These expectations alone, however, are not sufficient. The individual learner, as an active participant in the acquisition process, must also take *responsibility* for his/her own decisions about how, when, and what bits to learn in any learning task. Further, the learner needs time and opportunity to *use, employ, and practice* their developing reading in functional, realistic, and authentic ways if he/she is to progress in proficiency. These three conditions – expectations, responsibility, and use – all conspire within the rich context provided by immersion in material and demonstrations to create the process by which the individual learner progresses in reading proficiency. However, the progression also requires assistance from others. In addition to setting the conditions and providing demonstrations, the individual needs the more proficient readers to mediate for them. Indeed, this is essential in a constructivist format. The internalized knowledge and the developing strategies employed as the individual becomes a reader must be progressively acquired and honed, and this process occurs when the learner practices in an authentic reading context with meaningful material and where a more proficient reader accepts *approximations* and provides frequent and consistent *feedback* in context when such feedback and instruction are needed. When these conditions are met, then the final condition of *engagement* occurs. This happens when the individual learner believes that he/she is a potential "doer," and that acquisition of these powerful meaning-making skills will further opportunity and life experiences – that is, there is a functional pay-off.

Within the meaning-based approaches, these conditions are typically met through a particular instructional format. Routman (1994) discusses this format as a balanced reading program, and if it is employed, authentic and mediated reading opportunities that cover Cambourne's conditions for engagement typically occur. The format is one of consistent and repeated exposure to meaningful material by engaging in actual reading and writing activities that are strategically manipulated as the individual becomes more proficient. As a beginner, the individual is exposed to literacy and strong demonstrations through *reading and writing aloud* activities. Once the individual learner receives sufficient mediated experience with meaningful literature and the literacy processes from the continual models that being read to and demonstrations of writing provide, then the individual receives more exposure, more opportunity to read and write him/herself, and more targeted and appropriate feedback when needed during *shared reading* and *shared writing* activities. These activities are at the core of working with struggling readers and writers in that they enable the child to engage in progressively independent reading while being monitored by a more proficient reader and writer who mediates the literacy process when needed (Damico, 2006). Similarly, as the individual learner progresses, the other instructional/acquisitional formats are employed (*guided reading* and *guided writing*, *independent reading* and *independent writing*). For a full description of these formats and the ways to strategically weave the formats together to assist in building a meaning-based approach to reading instruction, see the work of Waterland (1985), Routman (1988; 1994; 2003), Weaver (1990), Goodman, Watson, and Burke (1996), and Lynch et al. (in press). Based upon the principles of cognitivism and social constructivism, the meaning-based approach to reading has proven to be effective for various types of struggling readers including those with reading impairments (e.g., Dahl & Freppon, 1995; Damico, 1991, 2006; Damico & Damico, 1993; Freppon & McIntrye, 1999; Kasten, 1998; Lynch et al., in press; Weaver, 1998).

4.3 Dyslexia

Within the focus on literacy as a personal skill, specific attention has been given to the issues of acquisition/learning of reading skills in average and struggling readers and writers. From the beginnings of the twentieth century there has been an awareness that some individuals exhibit extreme difficulty in learning to read (e.g., Hinshelwood, 1917; Huey, 1908; Morgan, 1896). Orton (1925, 1937) used the term "dyslexia" when discussing this condition and his use of the term has continued to be applied with a few alterations so that an individual with dyslexia can be distinguished from struggling readers. Critchley's definition (1970) of dyslexia as a disability in learning to read despite adequate intelligence, sufficient instruction, and sociocultural emphasis and opportunity is still the primary definition used in the field (Catts, 1996; Weaver, 1998; Whitehurst & Lonigan, 1998).

In his review of the conceptualizations of dyslexia, Vellutino (1977) described three primary alternative explanations of dyslexia. The traditional conceptualization is that dyslexia is primarily due to visual system deficits, what Orton referred to as the perceptual-deficit hypothesis (1937). This conceptualization focuses primarily on visual organization or visual memory problems (Bender, 1957; Young & Lindsley, 1971), and it is from this orientation that the familiar signs that so worry parents, such as perceiving *d* as *b*, *was* as *saw*, and letter reversals in writing, have been implicated as symptoms of possible dyslexia. Close scrutiny of the predictions made by this hypothesis, however, shows that they do not hold up to empirical evidence (e.g., Liberman et al., 1971; Smith, 2006; Vellutino, 1977; Vellutino et al., 1975).

The second conceptualization is that dyslexia is due to neurological problems less visual and more intersensory integrative in nature. Based upon the work of Birch (e.g., Birch & Belmont, 1965), data were presented suggesting significant problems with the integration of visual and auditory input such that there was a difficulty focusing on the sound–symbol associations. Again, however, the data for this conceptualization was found to be scant. The supportive studies themselves were poorly designed so that other variables (e.g., memory, experience, age) could not be ruled out, and in better-controlled studies the results were equivocal at best (Vellutino, 1977).

The third view of dyslexia focused on various aspects of verbal/linguistic processing, and this conceptualization of dyslexia has had the strongest extended support. Based on the assumption that there might be a speech production or language basis for dyslexia, several researchers investigated the relationship between verbal processing of various kinds and struggling readers (e.g., Lyle, 1970; Mattingly, 1972; Perfetti & Hogaboam, 1975; Savin, 1972). While this work typically focused on phonologic deficiencies, other variables were considered as well. In her research on subtypes of dyslexia, Boder (1973) has presented some of the primary data in support of the verbal processing thesis. Employing methods that focus on reading isolated words and focusing on strategies for word decoding as her measures, she has suggested three subtypes of dyslexia. The largest group that her research revealed (69 percent of subjects) was comprised of individuals who lacked word-analysis skills and compensated by attempting to employ a more global visual processing strategy to identify words. The remainder of her subjects either exhibited visual memory problems (9 percent) or a combination of poor linguistic analytic skills and visual memory problems. Other researchers (Elbro, 1991; Goswami & Bryant, 1990; Vellutino & Denckla, 1991) have continued to stress the role of the phonological system in dyslexia, and recently this has focused primarily upon the component skill of phonemic awareness (e.g., Catts, 1991; Mody & Silliman, 2008; Stackhouse, 1997).

As with the models of reading and the approaches to reading instruction, however, one's conception of human learning also influences how dyslexia is conceived. As with any diagnostic category or label (see Chapter 1), "dyslexia" is a constructed term. Monaghan (1980) found that a number of definitions for dyslexia have been employed and that they are always reflective of the current social conditions and "received knowledge" of the time. Boder's (1973) definition, for example, employed a heavy reliance on standardized tests and strategies for reading isolated words and for word decoding rather than authentic reading and writing. This tendency for the social construction of disability and handicapping labels has also been documented in the area of learning disabilities (Coles, 1987). Consequently, we should not simply reify labels such as "literacy" and "dyslexia." Rather, as suggested by Street (1995), the conception of literacy should not be dichotomous (have/have not), but it should be viewed along a continuum that attempts to account for the complexity of this symbolic and social process.

From the meaning-based model, for example, Weaver (1998) has proposed a reconceptualization of dyslexia that is consistent with the perspective of reading as constructing meaning. Her research and that of others (e.g., Brown, Goodman, & Marek, 1996; Davenport, 2002; Goodman, Watson, & Burke, 1987, 1996; Nelson, Damico, & Smith, 2008; Rhodes & Shanklin, 1990), based upon descriptive studies involving miscue analysis, suggests that rather than viewing dyslexia from a deficit perspective involving various components of reading, particularly the phonological aspects, dyslexia can be conceived as "the ineffective use and/or coordination of strategies for constructing meaning" (1998, p. 320). This reconceptualization will enable a more proactive pedagogy, enable a greater focus on meaning-based intervention, and not allow unsupported deficit models (such as the traditional definition of dyslexia) to reduce expectations for overcoming the reading difficulties (Coles, 1987; Fink, 1995/1996; Weaver, 1998).

5 Solutions and Conclusions

This chapter has reviewed the vast area of reading and reading impairments in terms of the issues in the field pertinent to the practicing speech-language pathologist. Importantly, the focus was primarily on how one's conception of human learning orients one's model of reading and subsequent service delivery (Smith, 1998). With behaviorism losing validity across the psychological and social sciences and cognitivism on the ascendency, it is reasonable to move toward the more meaning-based model of reading and its associated approaches to intervention and descriptions of impairment.

For the speech-language pathologist this may be especially relevant. As experts in language impairment, we do recognize the importance of meaning making and the crucial aspects of the context in helping an individual, impaired or normal, in constructing meaning in all of the various meaning-making manifestations (e.g., speaking, reading, memory, cognition). Further, we recognize that individuals with deficits can gain access to meaningfulness and contextualization by means of appropriate and effective mediation by their clinicians and significant others (e.g., Allington, 2001; Bruner, 1981; Damico & Damico, 1993; Damico, Nelson, & Bryan, 2005; Halliday, 1978; Norris, 1988; Routman, 1998; Vygotsky, 1978; Wells, 1990). By employing a meaning-based model of reading we can exploit the very capacities that should assist individuals with exceptionalities (see Chapter 6). Since our case loads and our foci are oriented to smaller numbers of students and to the crucial strengths and weaknesses of our clients and students, individualized attention and careful mediation during authentic reading and writing are both possible and warranted.

This proposed solution may appear to favor the meaning-based approach to a greater extent than it does the component skills approach to intervention. Such is the case. However, if the clinician determines that there are difficulties with some aspects of the linguistic system that should be addressed, this is often best accomplished in more holistic and contextualized ways that are consistent with the meaning-based approach to reading. Consequently, we should transcend our controversies by recognizing that the targets of our service delivery (i.e., what is missing in the abilities of the impaired and what we should focus on) are less controversial than how we approach these targets. Regardless of our orientation we all recognize that struggling readers are missing some of the strategies necessary to construct meaning. With careful description of the individual's authentic reading we can determine which of the various strategies are problematic and we can move to strengthen or compensate for them. The approaches employed to strengthen or compensate, however, should be consistent with the orientation that best assists our clientele.

While researchers and clinicians in speech-language pathology focus on literacy in the research lab, classroom, or therapy suite, it is necessary to take a broader perspective if we are to gain a sufficient understanding of this field of study. Given the influence of literacy on our society, we should strive to provide the most timely and defensible service delivery possible. This chapter has attempted to provide the necessary overview as a context for further learning. Hopefully, the acquired learning will enhance our service delivery to our clients.

REFERENCES

Adams, M. (1990). *Beginning to read: Thinking and learning about print.* Cambridge, MA: MIT Press.

Adams, M. (1991). Why not phonics and whole language? In W. Ellis (ed.), *All language and the creation of literacy* (pp. 40–52). Baltimore, MD: Orton Dyslexia society.

Adams, M. J. & Bruck, M. (1993). Word recognition: the interface of educational policies and scientific research. *Reading and Writing: An Interdisciplinary Journal* 5, 113–39.

Allington, R. (2001). *What really matters for struggling readers. Designing research-based programs.* Portsmouth, NH: Heinemann.

Allington, R. L. (2002). *Big brother and the national reading curriculum. How ideology trumped evidence*. Portsmouth, NH: Heinemann.

Allington, R., Stuetzel, H., Shake, M., & Lamarche, S. (1986). What is remedial reading? A descriptive study. *Reading Research and Instruction* 26 (1), 15–30.

Allington, R. L. & Woodside-Jiron, H. (1999). The politics of literacy teaching: How "research" shaped educational policy. *Educational Researcher* 28 (8), 4–13.

Almond, G. A. & Coleman, J. S. (eds.) (1960). *The politics of developing areas*. Princeton, NJ: Princeton University Press.

American Speech-Language-Hearing Association. (2001). Roles and responsibilities of speech-language pathologists with respect to reading and writing in children and adolescents. *ASHA* 21 (Suppl.), 17–27.

Amsel, A. (1989). *Behaviorism, neobehaviorism, and cognitivism in learning theory: Historical and contemporary perspectives*. Hillsdale, NJ: Lawrence Erlbaum Associates.

Apel, K. & Swank, L. (1999). Second chances: Improving decoding skills in the older student. *Language, Speech, and Hearing Services in Schools* 30, 231–42.

Baynham, M. (1995). *Literacy practices: Investigating literacy in social context*. London: Longman.

Beeson, P. M. & Henry, M. L. (2008). Comprehension and production of written words. In R. Chapey (ed.), *Language intervention strategies in aphasia and related neurogenic communication disorders*, 5th ed. (pp. 654–88). Baltimore, MD: Lippincott, Williams & Wilkins.

Bender, L. A. (1957). Specific reading disability as a maturational lag. *Bulletin of the Orton Society* 7, 9–18.

Berliner, D. C. (1997). Educational psychology meets the Christian Right: Differing views of children, schooling, teaching, and learning. *Teachers College Record* 98, 381–416.

Birch, H. G. & Belmont, L. (1965). Auditory-visual integration in normal and retarded readers. *American Journal of Orthopsychiatry* 34, 852–61.

Blanshard, B. (1965). Critical reflections on behaviorism. *Proceedings of the American Philosophical Society* 109 (1), 22–8.

Bloomfield, L. (1939). *Linguistic aspects of science*. Chicago: University of Chicago Press.

Bloomfield, L. & Barnhart, C. L. (1961). *Let's read. A linguistic approach*. Detroit, MI: Wayne State University Press.

Boder, E. (1973). Developmental dyslexia: A diagnostic approach based on three atypical reading-spelling patterns. *Developmental Medicine and Child Neurology* 15, 663–87.

Bracey, G. W. (2004). *Setting the record straight. Response to misconceptions about public education in the U.S.*, 2nd ed. Portsmouth, NH: Heinemann.

Brown, J., Goodman, K. S., & Marek, A. M. (1996). *Studies in miscue analysis: An annotated bibliography*. Newark, DE: International Reading Association.

Bruner, J. S. (1960). *The process of education*. Cambridge, MA: Harvard University Press.

Bruner, J. S. (1961). The act of discovery. *Harvard Educational Review* 31, 21–32.

Bruner, J. S. (1981). The social context of language acquisition. *Language and Communication* 1, 155–78.

Bruner, J. S. (1983). *Child's talk. Learning to use language*. New York: W. W. Norton & Company.

Bruner, J. S. (1985). Models of the learner. *Educational Researcher* 14 (6), 5–8.

Bruner, J. S. (1990). *Acts of meaning*. Cambridge, MA: Harvard University Press.

Bruner, J. S. (1991). The narrative construction of reality. *Critical Inquiry* 18 (Autumn), 1–21.

Burger, H. G. (1972). Behavior modification and operant psychology:

An anthropological critique. *American Educational Research Journal 9*, 343–60.

Calkins, L. M. (2001). *The art of teaching reading*. New York: Longman.

Cambourne, B. (1988). *The whole story. Natural learning and the acquisition of literacy in the classroom*. Auckland, NZ: Ashton Scholastic.

Camilli, G. & Wolfe, P. (2004). Research on reading: A cautionary tale. *Educational Leadership* 61 (March), 26–9.

Catts, H. (1991). Facilitating phonological awareness: Role of SLP. *Language, Speech, and Hearing Services in Schools* 22, 196–203.

Catts, H. (1996). Defining dyslexia as a developmental language disorder. *Topics in Language Disorders* 16, 14–29.

Catts, H., Fey, M., Tomblin, B., & Zhang, X. (2002). A longitudinal investigation of reading outcomes in children with language impairments. *Journal of Speech, Language, and Hearing Research* 45, 1142–57.

Catts, H., Fey, M., Zhang, X., & Tomblin, J. (1999). Language basis of reading and reading disabilities. *Scientific Studies of Reading* 4, 331–61.

Catts, H. W. & Kamhi, A. G. (2004). *Language and reading disabilities*, 2nd ed. Boston, MA: Allyn & Bacon, Inc.

Cazden, C., Cope, B., Fairclough, N., Gee, J. P., Kalantzis, M., Kress, G., et al. (1996). A pedagogy of multiliteracies: Designing social futures. *Harvard Educational Review* 66, 60–92.

Chall, J. (1967). *Learning to read: The great debate*. New York: McGraw-Hill.

Chall, J. (1983). *Learning to read: The great debate* (updated). New York: McGraw-Hill.

Chomsky, N. (1959). Critique of Skinner, Burrhus, *Verbal behavior* 1957. *Language* 35, 26–58.

Clark, M. M. (1976). *Young fluent readers*. London: Heinemann.

Clay, M. (1998). *By different paths to common outcomes*. York, ME: Stenhouse Publishers.

Clay, M. M. (1991). *Becoming literate. The construction of inner control*. Portsmouth, NH: Heinemann.

Cochran-Smith, M. (1984). *The making of a reader*. Norwood, NJ: Ablex.

Coles, G. (1987). *The learning mystique: A critical look at "learning disabilities."* New York: Pantheon.

Coles, G. (2000). *Misreading reading. The bad science that hurts children*. Portsmouth, NH: Heinemann.

Coles, G. (2003). *Reading the naked truth. Literacy, legislation, and lies*. Portsmouth, NH: Heinemann.

Connor, C. & Zwolan, T. (2004). Examining multiple sources of influence on reading comprehension of skills of children who use cochlear implants. *Journal of Speech, Language, and Hearing Research* 47, 509–26.

Critchley, M. (1970). *The dyslexic child*. London: Heinemann Medical Books.

Dahl, K. & Freppon, P. A. (1995). A comparison of inner-city children's interpretations of reading and writing in the early grades in skills-based and whole language classrooms. *Reading Research Quarterly* 30, 50–74.

Damico, J. S. (1991). *Whole language for special needs students*. Chicago: Riverside Publishing.

Damico, J. S. (1993). Synergy in applied linguistics: theoretical and pedagogical implications. In F. R. Eckman (ed.), *Confluence. Linguistics, L2 acquisition and speech pathology* (pp. 195–212). Philadelphia: John Benjamins Publishing Company.

Damico, J. S. (2003). The role of theory in clinical practice: Reflections on model building. *Advances in Speech Language Pathology* 5 (1), 57–60.

Damico, J. S. (2006). *Shared reading for the exceptional child*. Portland, OR: National CEU.

Damico, J. S. & Damico, S. K. (1993). Mapping a course over different roads: Language teaching with special populations. In J. J. W. Oller (ed.),

Methods that work: A smorgasbord of language teaching ideas, 2nd ed. (pp. 320–31). New York: Newbury House.

Damico, J. S., Damico, H. L., Lynch, K. E., Nelson, R. L., & Doody, M. P. (in review). Reading fluency as an emergent dimension during authentic literacy *Reading Research Quarterly*.

Damico, J. S., Nelson, R. L., & Bryan, L. (2005). Literacy as a sociocultural process for clinical purposes. In M. Ball (ed.), *Clinical sociolinguistics* (pp. 242–9). Oxford: Blackwell Publishers.

Danziger, K. (1990). *Constructing the subject: Historical origins of psychological research*. Cambridge: Cambridge University Press.

Davenport, D. & Jones, J. M. (2005). The politics of literacy. *Policy Review* (April & May), 45–57.

Davenport, M. R. (2002). *Miscues not mistakes. Reading assessment in the classroom*. Portsmouth, NH: Heinemann.

Duchan, J. (2008). Getting here: A short history of speech pathology in America: http://www.acsu.buffalo.edu/~duchan/1975-2000.html.

Elbro, C. (1991). Dyslexics and normal beginning readers read by different strategies: A comparison of strategy distributions in dyslexic and normal readers. *International Journal of Applied Linguistics* 1, 19–37.

Ferreiro, E. & Teberosky, A. (1979). *Literacy before schooling*. Portsmouth, NH: Heinemann.

Fink, R. P. (1995/1996). Successful dyslexics: A constructivist study of passionate interest reading. *Journal of Adolescent and Adult Literacy* 39 (4), 268–80.

Foorman, B. R., Francis, D. J., Shaywitz, S. E., Shaywitz, B. A., & Fletcher, J. M. (1997). The case for early reading intervention. In B. Blachman (ed.), *Foundations of reading acquisition and dyslexia: Implications for early*

intervention (pp. 243–64). Mahwah, NJ: Lawrence Erlbaum Associates.

Freire, P. & Macedo, D. (1987). *Literacy: Reading the word and the world*. South Hadley, MA: Bergin and Garvey.

Freppon, P. A. & McIntrye, E. (1999). A comparison of young children learning to read in different instructional settings. *The Journal of Educational Research* 92, 206–17.

Fries, C. C. (1963). *Linguistics and reading*. New York: Holt, Rinehart & Winston.

Garan, E. M. (2001). Beyond the smoke and mirrors: A critique of the National Reading Panel report on phonics. *Phi Delta Kappan* 82 (March), 500–6.

Garan, E. M. (2002). *Resisting reading mandates: How to triumph with the truth*. Portsmouth, NH: Heinemann.

Garan, E. M. (2005). Murder your darlings: A scientific response to "The voice of evidence in reading research." *Phi Delta Kappan* 86 (February), 438–43.

Gee, J. P. (2000). The new literacy studies: From "socially situated" to the work of the social. In D. Barton, M. Hamilton, & R. Ivanic (eds.), *Situated literacies: Reading and writing in context* (pp. 180–96). London: Routledge.

Geekie, P., Cambourne, B., & Fitzsimmons, P. (1999). *Understanding literacy development*. Stoke-on-Trent, UK: Trentham Books.

Gergen, K. J. (1985). The social constructivist movement in modern psychology. *American Psychologist* 40, 266–73.

Gillon, G. (2000). The efficacy of phonological awareness intervention for children with spoken language impairment. *Language, Speech, and Hearing Services in Schools* 31, 126–41.

Gillon, G. (2002). Follow-up study investigating benefits of phonological awareness intervention for children with spoken language impairment. *International Journal of Language and Communication Disorders* 37, 381–400.

Goodman, K. S. (1967). Reading: A psycholinguistic guessing game. *Journal of the Reading Specialist* 6 (4), 126–35.

Goodman, K. S. (1994). Reading, writing, and written texts: A transactional sociopsycholinguistic view. In R. B. Ruddell, M. R. Ruddell, & H. Singer (eds.), *Theoretical models and processes of reading*, 4th ed. (pp. 1093–130). Newark, DE: International Reading Association.

Goodman, K. S. (1996). *On reading. A common-sense look at the nature of language and the science of reading.* Portsmouth, NH: Heinemann.

Goodman, K. S. (1998). *In defense of good teaching: What teachers need to know about the reading wars.* York, ME: Stenhouse.

Goodman, Y. M. & Goodman, K. S. (1994). To err is human: Learning about language processes by analyzing miscues. In R. B. Ruddell, M. R. Ruddell, & H. Singer (eds.), *Theoretical models and processes of reading.* Newark, DE: International Reading Association.

Goodman, Y. M., Watson, D. J., & Burke, C. L. (1987). *Reading miscue analysis: Alternative procedures.* New York: Robert C. Owens Publishers.

Goodman, Y. M., Watson, D. J., & Burke, C. L. (1996). *Reading strategies: Focus on comprehension*: Richard C. Owen.

Goody, J. (1986). *The logic of writing and the organization of society.* Cambridge: Cambridge University Press.

Goswami, U. & Bryant, P. (1990). *Phonological skills and learning to read.* Hove, UK: Lawrence Erlbaum.

Grobecker, B. (1996). Reconstructing the paradigm of learning disabilities: A holistic/constructivist interpretation. *Learning Disability Quarterly* 19 (Summer), 179–200.

Halliday, M. A. K. (1978). *Language as social semiotic: The social interpretation of language and meaning.* London: Arnold.

Halliday, M. A. K. (1993). Towards a language-based theory of learning. *Linguistics and Education* 5, 93–116.

Henry, J. (1960). A cross-cultural outline of education. *Current Anthropology* 1, 267–305.

Hinshelwood, J. (1917). *Congenital word-blindness.* London: Lewis.

Holtgraves, T. M. (2002). *Language as social action.* Mahwah, NJ: Lawrence Erlbaum Associates.

Honig, W. (1996). *Teaching our children to read: The role of skills in a comprehensive reading program.* Thousand Oaks, CA: Corwin Press.

Huey, B. (1908). *The psychology and pedagogy of reading.* New York: The Macmillan Company.

Iacono, T. & Cupples, L. (2004). Assessment of phonemic awareness and word reading skills of people with complex communication needs. *Journal of Speech, Language, and Hearing Research* 47, 437–49.

Iran-Nejad, A. (1995). Constructivism as substitute for memorization in learning: Meaning is created by learner. *Education* 116, 16–31.

Jones, J. A. (1972). Operant psychology and the study of culture. *Current Anthropology* 12, 171–89.

Kamhi, A. & Catts, H. (1986). Toward an understanding of developmental language and reading disorders. *Journal of Speech and Hearing Disorders* 51, 337–47.

Kasten, W. (1998). One learner, two paradigms: A case study of a special education student in a multiage primary classroom. *Reading & Writing Quarterly* 14, 335–54.

Krashen, S. D. (2001a). Does phonemic awareness training affect reading comprehension? *Perceptual and Motor Skills* 93, 356–8.

Krashen, S. D. (2001b). Low PA can read OK. *Practically Primary* 6 (3), 17–20.

Krashen, S. D. (2001c). More smoke and mirrors: A critique of the National

Reading Panel Report on fluency. *Phi Delta Kappan* 82 (October), 119–23.

Krashen, S. D. (2002a). The NRP comparison of whole language and phonics: Ignoring the crucial variable in reading. *Talking Points* 13 (3), 22–8.

Krashen, S. D. (2002b). Phonemic awareness training necessary? *Reading Research Quarterly* 37 (2), 128.

Krashen, S. D. (2003a). False claims about phonemic awareness, phonics, skills vs whole language, and recreational reading. *NoChildLeft.com* 1, 1–18.

Krashen, S. D. (2003b). The unbearable coolness of phonemic awareness. *Language Magazine* 2 (8), 13–18.

Krashen, S. D. (2004). *The power of reading. Insights from the research.* Portsmouth, NH: Heinemann.

Langley, P. & Simon, H. A. (1981). The central role of learning in cognition. In J. R. Anderson (ed.), *Cognitive skills and their acquisition* (pp. 361–80). Hillsdale, NJ: Lawrence Erlbaum Associates.

Lemann, N. (1997). The reading wars. *Atlantic Monthly* (November).

Liberman, I. Y., Shankweiler, D., Orlando, C., Harris, K. S., & Berti, F. B. (1971). Letter confusion and reversals of sequence in the beginning reader: Implications for Orton's theory of developmental dyslexia. *Cortex* 7, 127–42.

Lyle, J. G. (1970). Certain antenatal, perinatal, and developmental variables and reading retardation in middle class boys. *Child Development* 41, 481–91.

Lynch, K. E., Damico, J. S., Damico, H. L., Tetnowski, J., & Tetnowski, J. (in press). Reading skills in an individual with aphasia: The usefulness of meaning based clinical applications. *Asian-Pacific Journal of Speech, Language, and Hearing.*

Lyon, G. R. (1999). In celebration of science in the study of reading development, reading difficulties, and reading instruction: The NICHD

Perspective. *Issues in Education: Contributions from Educational Psychology* 5, 85–115.

Mattingly, I. G. (1972). Reading, the linguistic process, and linguistic awareness. In J. F. Kavanagh & I. G. Mattingly (eds.), *Language by ear and by eye: The relationships between speech and reading* (pp. 133–48). Cambridge, MA: MIT Press.

McGill, V. J. (1966). Behaviorism and phenomenology. *Philosophy and Phenomenological Research* 26, 578–88.

Meek, M. (1982). *Learning to read.* London: Bodley Head.

Mills, J. A. (1988). An assessment of Skinner's theory of animal behavior. *Journal for the Theory of Social Behavior* 18, 197–218.

Mills, J. A. (1998). *Control: A history of behavioral psychology.* New York: New York University Press.

Moats, L. (1996). *Teaching reading is rocket science.* New York: American Federation of Teachers.

Moats, L. (2000). *Whole language lives on: The illusion of "balanced" reading instruction.* New York: Thomas B. Fordham Foundation.

Mody, M. & Silliman, E. R. (eds.) (2008). *Brain, behavior and learning in language and reading disorders.* New York: Guilford Press.

Monaghan, E. (1980). A history of the syndrome of dyslexia with implications for its treatment. In C. McCullough (ed.), *Inchworm, inchworm: Persistent problems in reading education* (pp. 87–101). Newark, DE: International Reading Association.

Morgan, W. P. (1896). A case of congenital word-blindness. *British Medical Journal* 11, 378.

Nelson, R. & Damico, J. S. (2002). Literacy knowledge: Surveying speech language pathologists' literacy theory and practice, *Annual meeting of the American Speech-Language and Hearing Association.* Atlanta, GA.

Nelson, R. L., Damico, J. S., & Smith, S. K. (2008). Applying eye movement miscue analysis to the reading patterns of children with language impairment. *Clinical Linguistics & Phonetics* 22 (4), 293–303.

Newman, A. P. & Beverstock, C. (1990). *Adult literacy: Contexts and challenges.* Newark, DE: International Reading Association.

No Child Left Behind Act of 2001 (H.R.1). (2002). Washington, DC: 107th Congress.

Norris, J. A. (1988). Using communicative reading strategies to enhance reading strategies. *The Reading Teacher* 47, 668–73.

Norris, J. & Hoffman, P. (2002). Phonemic awareness: A complex developmental process. *Topics in Language Disorders* 22 (2), 1–34.

O'Connell, D. C. & Kowal, S. (2003). Psycholinguistics: A half century of monologism. *American Journal of Psychology* 116, 191–212.

Oldfather, P. & Dahl, K. (1994). Toward a social constructivist reconceptualization of intrinsic motivation for literacy learning. *Journal of Reading Behavior* 26, 139–58.

Olson, D. R. (1994). *The world on paper: The conceptual and cognitive implications of writing and reading.* Cambridge: Cambridge University Press.

Olson, D. R. (1996). Towards a psychology of literacy: On the relations between speech and writing. *Cognition* 60, 83–104.

Olson, D. R. & Torrance, N. (2001a). Conceptualizing literacy as a personal skill and as a social practice. In D. R. Olson & N. Torrance (eds.), *The making of literate societies* (pp. 3–18). Oxford: Blackwell Publishers.

Olson, D. R. & Torrance, N. (eds.). (2001b). *The making of literate societies.* Oxford: Blackwell Publishers.

Ong, W. (1982). *Orality and literacy: The technologizing of the word.* London: Methuen.

Orton, S. (1925). "Word-blindness" in school children. *Archives of Neurology and Psychiatry* 14, 581–615.

Orton, S. (1937). *Reading, writing and speech problems in children.* London: Chapman and Hall.

Pass, S. (2004). *Parallel paths to constructivism: Jean Piaget and Lev Vygotsky.* New York: Informational Age Publishers Inc.

Perfetti, C. A. & Hogaboam, T. (1975). The relationship between single word decoding and reading comprehension skill. *Journal of Educational Psychology* 1975 (67), 461–9.

Perkins, M. R. (1998). Is pragmatics epiphenomenal?: Evidence from communication disorders. *Journal of Pragmatics* 29, 291–311.

Piaget, J. (1968). *Structuralism.* New York: Harper & Row.

Piaget, J. (1970). *Genetic epistemology.* New York: W. W. Norton & Company.

Rasinski, T. V. & Padak, N. D. (2001). *From phonics to fluency. Effective teaching of decoding and reading fluency in the elementary school.* New York: Longman.

Resnick, D. P. & Resnick, L. B. (1977). The nature of literacy: An historical exploration. *Harvard Educational Review* 47, 370–85.

Rhodes, L. K. & Shanklin, N. L. (1990). Miscue analysis in the classroom. *Reading Teacher* 44, 252–4.

Richards, I. A. (1980). Learning to read: The great debate by Jeanne Chall. In M. Wolf, M. K. McQuillan, & E. Radwin (eds.), *Thought & language/ language & reading* (pp. 631–7). Cambridge, MA: Harvard Educational Review.

Rilling, M. (2000). How the challenge of explaining learning influenced the origins and development of John B. Watson's behaviorism. *American Journal of Psychology* 113, 275–301.

Robinson, D. N. (1995). *An intellectual history of psychology*, 3rd ed. Madison, WI: University of Wisconsin Press.

Routman, R. (1988). *Transitions: From literature to literacy*. Portsmouth, NH: Heinemann.

Routman, R. (1994). *Invitations: Changing as teachers and learners K-12*. Portsmouth, NH: Heinemann

Routman, R. (2003). *Reading essentials. The specifics you need to teach reading well*. Portsmouth, NH: Heinemann.

Routman, R. B. A. (1998). How do I actually teach reading now that I am using literature? In C. Weaver (ed.), *Practicing what we know: Informed reading instruction* (pp. 175–83). Urbana, IL: National Council of Teachers of English.

Savin, H. B. (1972). What the child knows about speech when he starts to read. In J. F. Kavanagh & I. G. Mattingly (eds.), *Language by ear and by eye: the relationships between speech and reading* (pp. 319–26). Cambridge, MA: MIT Press.

Scribner, S. & Cole, M. (1981). *The psychology of literacy*. Cambridge, MA: Harvard University Press.

Searle, J. (1969). *Speech acts: An essay in the philosophy of language*. Cambridge: Cambridge University Press.

Shanahan, T. (2004). Critiques of the National Reading Panel report: Their implications for research, policy, and practice. In P. McCardle & V. Chhabra (eds.), *The voice of evidence in reading research* (pp. 235–65). Baltimore, MD: Paul H. Brookes.

Shore, B. (1996). *Culture in mind: Cognition, culture, and the problem of meaning*. New York: Oxford University Press.

Shuell, T. J. (1986). Cognitive conceptions of learning. *Review of Educational Research* 56, 411–36.

Skinner, B. F. (1938). *The behavior of organisms*. New York: Appleton-Century-Crofts.

Skinner, B. F. (1968). *The technology of teaching*. New York: Appleton-Century-Crofts.

Sloane, F. C. (2005). The scaling of reading interventions: Building multilevel insight. *Reading Research Quarterly* 40, 361–6.

Smith, F. (1977). Making sense of reading – and of reading instruction. *Harvard Educational Review* 47 (3), 386–95.

Smith, F. (1998). *The book of learning and forgetting*. New York: Teachers College Press.

Smith, F. (2003). *Unspeakable acts. Unnatural practices. Flaws and fallacies in "scientific" reading instruction*. Portsmouth, NH: Heinemann.

Smith, F. (2004). *Understanding Reading. A psycholinguistic analysis of reading and learning to read*, 6th ed. Mahwah, NJ: Lawrence Erlbaum Associates.

Smith, F. (2006). *Reading without nonsense*, 4th ed. New York: Teachers College Press.

Smith, L. D. (1986). *Behaviorism and logical positivism. A reassessment of the alliance*. Stanford, CA: Stanford University Press.

Stackhouse, J. (1997). Phonological awareness: Connecting speech and literacy problems. In B. Hodson & M. L. Edwards (eds.), *Perspectives in applied phonology* (pp. 157–98). Gaithersburg, MD: Aspen Publications.

Stanovich, K. E. (1988). Science and learning disabilities. *Journal of Learning Disabilities* 21 (4), 210–14.

Stanovich, K. E. (1991). Word recognition: changing perspectives. In R. Barr, M. L. Kamil, P. B. Mosenthal, & P. D. Pearson (eds.), *Handbook of reading research* (Vol. 2) (pp. 418–52). New York: Longman.

Stanovich, K. E., Nathan, R. G., West, R. F., & Vala-Rossi, M. (1985). Children's word recognition in context: Spreading activation, expectancy, and modularity. *Child Development* 56 (6), 1418–28.

Stevenson, H. (1983). How children learn – the quest for a theory. In P. H. Mussen (ed.), *Handbook of child psychology: Vol. 1 History, theory and methods*, 4th ed. (pp. 213–36). New York: Wiley.

Strauss, S. L. (2001). An open letter to Reid Lyon. *Educational Researcher* 30 (June/July), 26–33.

Strauss, S. L. (2003). Challenging the NICHD reading research agenda. *Phi Delta Kappan* 84, 38–42.

Strauss, S. L. (2005). Operation no child left behind. In B. Altwerger (ed.), *Reading for profit. How the bottom line leaves kids behind* (pp. 33–49). Portsmouth, NH: Heinemann.

Street, B. (1995). *Social literacies: Critical approaches to literacy in development, ethnography, and education*. London: Longman.

Teale, W. H. & Sulzby, E. (eds.) (1986). *Emergent literacy: Writing and reading*. Norwood, NJ: Ablex.

Tolman, E. C. (1932). *Purposive behavior in animals and men*. New York: Appleton-Century-Crofts.

Tomasello, M. (1999). *The cultural origins of human cognition*. Cambridge, MA: Harvard University Press.

Tomasello, M. (2003). *Constructing a language. A usage-based theory of language acquisition*. Cambridge, MA: Harvard University Press.

Triebel, A. (1997). *Cognitive and societal development and literacy*. Bonn: German Foundation for International Development.

Triebel, A. (2001). The roles of literacy practices in the activities and institutions of developed and developing countries. In D. R. Olson & N. Torrance (eds.), *The making of literate societies* (pp. 19–53). Oxford: Blackwell Publishers.

Troia, G. A. (1999). Phonological awareness intervention research: A critical review of experimental methodology. *Reading Research Quarterly* 34 (1), 28–52.

Vellutino, F. R. (1977). Alternative conceptualizations of dyslexia: Evidence in support of a verbal-deficit hypothesis. *Harvard Educational Review* 47, 334–54.

Vellutino, F. R. & Denckla, M. B. (1991). Cognitive and neuropsychological foundations of word identification in poor and normally developing readers. In R. Barr, M. L. Kamil, P. B. Mosenthal, & P. D. Pearson (eds.), *Handbook in reading research* (Vol. 2) (pp. 571–608).

Vellutino, F. R., Smith, H., Steger, J. A., & Kaman, M. (1975). Reading disability: Age differences and the perceptual deficit hypothesis. *Child Development* 46, 487–93.

Vygotsky, L. S. (1978). *Mind in society: The development of higher psychological processes*. Cambridge, MA: Harvard University Press.

Vygotsky, L. S. (1981). The genesis of higher mental functions. In J. V. Wertsch (ed.), *The concept of activity in Soviet psychology* (pp. 144–88). Armonk, NY: Sharpe.

Waterland, L. (1985). *Read with me: An apprenticeship approach to reading*. Stroud, UK: The Thimble press.

Watson, J. B. (1913). Psychology as a behaviorist sees it. *Psychological Review* 20, 158–77.

Watson, J. B. (1930). *Behaviorism*, revised ed. New York: W. W. Norton.

Weaver, C. (1990). *Understanding whole language: From principles to practice*. Portsmouth, NH: Heinemann.

Weaver, C. (1998). Reconceptualizing reading and dyslexia. In C. Weaver (ed.), *Practicing what we know. Informed reading instruction* (pp. 292–324). Urbana, IL: National Council of Teachers of English.

Wells, G. (1986). *The meaning makers. Children learning language and using language to learn*. Portsmouth, NH: Heinemann.

Wells, G. (1990). Talk about text: Where literacy is learned and taught. *Curriculum Inquiry* 20, 369–405.

Wells, G. (1994). The complementary contributions of Halliday and Vygotsky to a "language-based theory of learning." *Linguistics and Education* 6, 41–90.

White, S. H. (1970). The learning theory tradition and child psychology. In P. H. Mussen (ed.), *Carmichael's manual of child psychology*, 3rd ed. (Vol. 1) (pp. 657–701). New York: John Wiley.

Whitehurst, G. J. & Lonigan, C. J. (1998). Child development and emergent literacy. *Child Development* 69, 848–72.

Wittrock, M. C. (1974). Learning as a generative process. *Educational Psychologist* 11, 87–95.

Wolf, T. (1977). Reading reconsidered. *Harvard Educational Review* 47, 411–29.

Young, F. A. & Lindsley, D. B. (1971). *Early experience and visual information processing in perceptual and reading disorders*. Washington, DC: National Academy of Sciences.

Zuriff, G. E. (1985). *Behaviorism: A conceptual reconstruction*. New York: Columbia University Press.

13 Substance Abuse and Childhood Language Disorders

TRUMAN E. COGGINS AND JOHN C. THORNE

1 Introduction

A large and growing body of descriptive and experimental research underscores the harmful effects of substance abuse during pregnancy. Arguably, the two prenatal exposures with the highest profiles and societal costs are alcohol and cocaine. Disabilities associated with prenatal alcohol exposure have an estimated occurrence rate of 2 to 6 per thousand live births (Center for Disease Control and Prevention, 2007) and approach the latest estimated prevalence of autism spectrum disorders (Carmichael-Olson et al., 2007). Morrow and her colleagues (2006) found that by the time they reach school, children with prenatal cocaine exposure have a 2.8 times greater risk of a learning impairment or neurodevelopmental disability than their non-cocaine-exposed peers. The complexities of fetal development coupled with the timing, quantity, and frequency of these prenatal exposures produces a spectrum of debilitating effects in prenatal and postnatal development.

Children whose mothers consume alcohol or cocaine during pregnancy often present complex clinical profiles. To be sure, prenatal alcohol exposure (PAE) is a known teratogen that has a broad range of variable effects (Mattson & Riley, 1998; Streissguth et al., 1996) on brain structure (from gross structural abnormalities to subtle neurochemical alterations) and/or function (cognitive and behavioral limitations), leading to cognitive and social deficits (Kodituwakku, 2007; Riley & McGee, 2005). A decade of research examining prenatal cocaine exposure (PCE) suggests that this drug may also lead to neurobiological and social impairments (Cone-Wesson, 2005; Delaney-Black et al., 2000). Moreover, it should come as no surprise that hazardous prenatal substance exposures often occur in the context of adverse environmental influences where dysfunctional adults create or permit erratic social experiences. Given these structural and functional compromises, and frequently reported antagonistic environmental conditions, it is not surprising to learn that by the time they enroll in school, children with PAE or PCE stand at considerable risk for peer-related behavioral problems, processing deficits, and learning difficulties.

One performance limitation shared by many children with PAE and PCE is their difficulty in using language effectively for social communicative purposes. Because youngsters with limited social communication lack pivotal resources for resolving challenges encountered during daily encounters with their families, teachers, and peers, speech-language pathologists are likely to be recruited to provide support services for these vulnerable children. Therefore, the purpose of this chapter is to provide the interested reader with an empirically based perspective for understanding and treating the challenging behaviors associated with children born to, or living with, adults who abuse alcohol and/or cocaine. Toward this end, we first explore the influences of prenatal alcohol and cocaine exposure on language functioning. Next, we review influential environmental factors that exacerbate the consequences of PAE and PCE. We conclude our review by presenting three multifaceted interventions that are currently being field-tested with these clinically complex children.

1.1   Prenatal alcohol exposure

The term "Fetal Alcohol Spectrum Disorders" (FASD) is applied to the full range of disability profiles associated with prenatal alcohol exposure (Astley, 2004; Bertrand, Floyd, & Weber, 2005). Based on data from the Seattle Longitudinal Prospective Study on Alcohol and Pregnancy (Streissguth et al., 1981), Sampson and his colleagues (1997) estimated that the occurrence of fetal alcohol syndrome (FAS) in the general US population is approximately 3 per thousand births. The incidence of FASD (i.e., the full range of disabilities in children with a history of fetal alcohol exposure) is considerably higher, with an estimated rate of nearly 9 per thousand births.

FAS was the first of the alcohol spectrum profile to be recognized (Jones & Smith, 1973) and is diagnosed based on growth deficiency, central nervous system (CNS) impairment, and a unique cluster of facial anomalies in the context of documented prenatal alcohol exposure (Astley, 2004; Astley & Clarren, 1996; Bertrand, Floyd, & Weber, 2005; Chudley et al., 2002; Clarren et al., 2000). The facial features associated with FAS are highly specific to prenatal alcohol exposure, but are *not* a particularly sensitive marker of that exposure and are not associated with all FASD. Rather, it is the child's developing brain that is most sensitive to teratogenic effects of prenatal alcohol exposure and CNS impairments are the most important sequelae of exposure (Cortese et al., 2006; Guerri, 2002; Streissguth & O'Malley, 2000).

Researchers have identified an abundant number of CNS structures negatively impacted by prenatal alcohol exposure. These brain structures include the corpus callosum, cerebellum (e.g., Bookstein et al., 2006), basal ganglia (e.g., Riley, McGee, & Sowell, 2004), and hippocampus (e.g., Autti-Ramo et al., 2002). Both diffuse and regional hypoplasia of white and gray matter have also been reported (McGee & Riley, 2006) with white matter more severely affected (Archibald et al., 2001; Fagerlund et al., 2006; Riley, McGee, & Sowell, 2004). The results of several recent investigations have also led several research teams to postulate a link between structural CNS deficits and cognitive-behavioral impairments (Astley & Clarren, 2001; Cortese et al., 2006; Mattson & Riley, 1998; Thomas et al., 1998).

Children with FASD present complicated profiles. Their overall intellectual abilities are often reported to be within the normal range (Kerns et al., 1997). Still, they often show problems learning from experience, attending to and following directions, and understanding logical consequences (Carmichael-Olson, Morse, & Huffine, 1998). They are frequently unfocused and impulsive (Lee, Mattson, & Riley, 2004; Mattson, Calarco, & Lang, 2006), have decided deficits processing complex information, and have recurring difficulties adapting to school activities and peers (Coles et al., 1997; Kleinfeld & Wescott, 1993; Mattson & Riley, 1998; Streissguth, 1997). It is, therefore, not particularly surprising to find that many school-age children with histories of significant prenatal alcohol exposure have also been diagnosed as having a learning disability and/or an attention-deficit/ hyperactivity disorder (Mattson, Calarco, & Lang, 2006).

The social and behavioral problems often associated with FASD become more pronounced during the school years and coincide with problems in adaptive behavior and secondary disabilities (Streissguth, 1977). This phenomenon likely reflects the increased demands associated with the school years that move increasingly from the acquisition of basic abilities toward the fluent integration and application of those skills to real-time social and academic problems. These effects of PAE have been shown to persist into early adulthood, limiting success in careers and independent living (Spohr, Willms, & Steinhausen, 2007).

Language and communication deficits have frequently been reported in this clinical population. However, to date, most of the existing data have been gathered with standardized language measures that utilize discrete responses at the sentence level or below (Burd et al., 2003; Church & Kaltenbach, 1997; Cone-Wesson, 2005; Greenbaum et al., 2002; Greene et al., 1990; Kodituwakku, 2007; Kvigne et al., 2004; Sowell et al., 2001; Streissguth et al., 1994). These measures are largely ineffective in identifying impairments or compromises at higher levels of language complexity (Martin & McDonald, 2003), often required during unscripted social communicative interactions (Coggins et al., 2003; Kelly, Day, & Streissguth, 2000; Kodituwakku, 2007; O'Leary, 2004; Olson et al., 1997; Riley & McGee, 2005; Whaley, O'Connor, & Gunderson, 2001).

Of particular interest for speech-language pathologists is the impressive number of alcohol-exposed youngsters who exhibit social problems during conversations (Coggins et al., 2003; Hamilton, 1981; Olswang, Coggins, & Timler, 2001; Spohr, Willms, & Steinhausen, 1993; Thomas et al., 1998; Timler, Olswang, & Coggins, 2005). Interestingly, the majority of these youngsters do not typically have debilitating conduct disorders or serious social-emotional problems if they have experienced supportive environments and appropriate expectations (Streissguth, 1997).

What sets these children apart from their school-age peers is their difficulty providing sufficient information to their communicative partners. They appear to lack pivotal communicative abilities necessary for more sophisticated social tasks such as entering peer groups, resolving conflicts, negotiating compromises, and maintaining friendships. While interdisciplinary assessment teams are becoming increasingly effective in diagnosing the spectrum of disabilities associated with FASD (Astley, 2004; Clarren et al., 2000), few professionals have the necessary knowledge or evidence for treating children with these social communication problems (Adams et al., 2005; Adams et al., 2006).

1.2 Prenatal cocaine exposure

Cocaine is a psychoactive agent that crosses the placenta and "has the potential for teratogenicity" (Bandstra et al., 2002). The influence of prenatal cocaine exposure on development has been a persistent concern for the past two and a half decades (see Cone-Wesson, 2005 for an informative and comprehensive review). Although a spectrum of prenatal effects have been described (Morrow et al., 2006), it is not at all clear that children with PCE demonstrate persistent cognitive and behavioral impairments. In fact, based on their meta-analysis Frank and colleagues (2001) have concluded that, in isolation, cocaine does not appear to have a deleterious effect on general cognitive development.

While PCE may not result in general cognitive deficits, more subtle deficits in learning and executive function have been hypothesized. For example, Singer and colleagues (2004) reported on the long-term cognitive outcomes of children with PCE. This research team used the Wechsler Preschool and Primary Scales of Intelligence – Revised (Wechsler, 1974) to compare the overall cognitive abilities of 190 PCE preschool children with 186 of their non-cocaine-exposed peers. The children who participated in the Singer et al. (2004) study included 4-year-old children who had been enrolled in a prospective longitudinal research investigation since their births. The researchers noted that a majority of birth mothers in both groups were women with low socioeconomic status.

A linear regression model was used to analyze the results and adjust for confounding variables. The results revealed no significant effects of PCE on overall (full-scale) IQ, verbal IQ, or performance IQ, a finding consonant with the outcome of Frank and colleagues summarized above. However, PCE was associated with an increased risk for *specific* cognitive deficits (e.g., arithmetic, visual-spatial skills) at 4 years of age. Morrow et al. (2006) found similar results in 7-year-old children with PCE, and Linares et al. (2006) saw increased rates of oppositional defiant disorder and attention-deficit/hyperactivity disorder (ADHD) among 6-year-old children with PCE (see also Bada et al., 2007).

Prenatal cocaine exposure places children at clear risk for language delays. At this point in time, the preponderance of evidence supporting the notion that PCE is a risk marker for disruptions in language have centered on the first few years of life. For example, Malakoff and colleagues (1999) studied the productive language abilities of 46 urban children with PCE and 28 non-PCE peers at their second birthdays. This research team obtained spontaneous language samples during low-structured, mother–child interactions that were generally 4.5–6.5 minutes in length. The results revealed that cocaine-exposed toddlers produced significantly shorter and less complex utterances, with girls typically showing more complex language than boys. Malakoff's research team interpreted the findings as support of their hypothesis that the impact of prenatal and postnatal environments associated with PCE puts children at risk for language delays "over and above that of poverty and its associated environmental stressors" (p. 173).

Malakoff, Mayes, and Schottenfeld (1994) examined language development in 21 preschoolers, ranging in age from 29 to 70 months. All of the children were living with cocaine-dependent caregivers, and 60 percent had been exposed to cocaine *in utero*. The findings indicated that all but three of the children had some degree of language delay. The severity of the impairment, however, was not related to prenatal cocaine exposure, suggesting that any central nervous system effects associated with PCE are less significant to the child's language development than the characteristics of the caregiving environment.

Singer and colleagues (2001) examined the association between level of fetal cocaine exposure and emerging language. The research team administered the Preschool Language Scale – 3 (Zimmerman, Steiner, & Pond, 1992) to 265 infants at 12 months who had been exposed to "heavier amounts" (n = 66), "lighter amounts" (n = 68), or "no amount" (n = 131) of prenatal cocaine. The results revealed that the infants who had experienced heavier cocaine exposure had poorer auditory comprehension scores than the non-exposed controls. Infants with heavier exposures also performed more poorly than infants with lighter-exposure histories and were more likely to be classified as mildly delayed. Interestingly, Singer's research team did not find a relationship between language outcomes and environmental caregiving.

Bandstra et al. (2002) found an association between PCE and deficits in total language functioning in 443 (236 cocaine-exposed and 207 non-cocaine-exposed) children who completed language testing at ages 3, 5, and 7, statistically controlling for potentially confounding influences assessed at birth and follow-up visits (D = −0.17; 95 percent CI = −0.32, −0.03; P = .019). "The link from prenatal cocaine exposure to later language deficits does not appear to be mediated by cocaine-associated deficits in birth weight, length or head circumference. Overall, the evidence tends to support an inference of a stable cocaine-specific effect on indicators of language functioning during early childhood through age 7 years" (Bandstra et al., 2002, p. 306).

Delaney-Black and her colleagues (2000) are one of the few research teams who have examined language behavior in older children with PCE. The results of their prospective cohort study suggest that cocaine exposure in combination with prenatal cigarette exposure may have negative impact on conversational discourse in school-age children. The researchers gathered 15-minute language samples from 186 school-bound youngsters (i.e., 6;0 years of age) with PCE and 272 of their peers who were non-PCE. The samples were collected during a low-structured interaction while each child interacted with an examiner in a clinical setting around figures and toys. The researchers were particularly interested in the child's lexical diversity (as measured by type-token ratios) and complex syntax during conversation.

The results revealed a clear subset of children with PCE who exhibited "low language abilities." For purposes of this study, a child with "low language" was one who had a type-token ratio less than .42 and fewer than 97 word types in their 15-minute language sample. Interestingly, increased exposure to cocaine during pregnancy and prenatal cigarette exposure were predictors of which children were more likely to have "low language."

1.3   Environmental risk

An important area of behavioral teratology research is exploring the effect that maternal abuse of alcohol and illicit drugs exerts on child development. The primary thrust of these research investigations has largely been on the timing and quantity of prenatal exposures and identifying child behaviors that are sensitive to their effect (Hans, 2002). Relatively little evidence has accumulated, however, with respect to how these children's postnatal environment impacts their growth and development. This informational void is unfortunate since there is ample evidence to show that substance abusing adults often live in worlds that are disruptive and prone to violence; often provide poorer-quality care; and often engage in social interactions that are less sensitive and responsive to their children. In fact, the quality of a child's postnatal environment is a powerful and positive protective factor in ameliorating the negative effects of prenatal cocaine exposure (Singer et al., 2004) and prenatal alcohol exposure (Streissguth et al., 2004).

The findings of Streissguth and colleagues (1996) and Willis and Silovsky (1998) have made clear the links between alcohol abuse and violence against others. Hans (2002) has also summarized the results of several follow-up studies of children with documented histories of illicit prenatal drug exposure that reveal a "3- to 12-fold increase in rates of documented child maltreatment" (p. 330). As a result, children who live with dysfunctional adults stand at considerable risk for neuro-biological, psycho-physiological, and/or psychological deficits (Cicchetti, 2004; Coster et al., 1989; Kaufman et al., 2000; McFadyen & Kitson, 1996). The collective results from a series of prospective experimental investigations have also revealed that children with prenatal drug exposure are far more likely to experience multiple home placements than their non-drug-exposed peers (Wasserman & Leventhal, 1993)

Lohmann and Tomasello (2003) have found that early language experiences have a decided influence on children's underlying social cognitive behaviors. Social cognition is concerned with how people conceptualize and think about their social world – the people they observe, the relations between people, and the groups in which they participate. Cicchetti and colleagues (Cicchetti et al., 2003; Eigsti & Cicchetti, 2004) have demonstrated that children with histories of maltreatment have distinct limitations in a "quintessential human characteristic" (p. 1067): namely, their ability to interpret and predict the knowledge, intentions, and beliefs of other people. Thus, maladaptive social-interactive experiences, which often co-occur for children compromised by prenatal alcohol and/or cocaine exposure, are potent risk factors for theory of mind deficits.

Eigsti and Cicchetti (2004) have argued that the social-emotional difficulties experienced by maltreated children "may be mediated or exacerbated by the

observed language and communicative deficits" (p. 99). Based on their comparative review, Kelly, Day, and Streissguth (2000) concluded that prenatal exposure
can alter the course of social communication. Thus, children with FASD may be
particularly vulnerable to social communicative deficits as a result of both the
teratogenic effects of prenatal alcohol exposure and the erratic and atypical social
interactive experiences associated with a maltreating environment.

Not surprisingly, adverse environmental factors have also been implicated in
the social communicative deficits of children with prenatal cocaine exposure.
Mentis and Lundgren (1995) gathered and analyzed spontaneous language
samples from five toddlers (mean age: 2;4 years), exposed prenatally to cocaine,
while each interacted in a low-structured interaction with an examiner. In clear
contrast to their five non-exposed control peers, the data revealed that all five of
the PCE toddlers exhibited significant compromises when they tried to use
their language to share information with their respective listener. Because these
qualitative differences in language use occurred in the presence of adverse
environmental conditions (e.g., family disruptions, poverty, caregiver drug abuse),
Mentis and Lundgren (1995) maintain that communicative deficits are best
understood in the context of each child's social milieu.

Until recently, studies examining the effect of prenatal exposures on development have minimized the role of environment. Investigators have typically viewed
a child's postnatal environment as a confounding variable best controlled using
sophisticated research designs rather than from a dynamic perspective where
"development is determined by a system of many interdependent factors" (Hans,
2002, p. 334). New interactionist models, on the other hand, highlight the synergistic interplay of the child and the environment across the course of development
(Chapman, 2007), and "emphasize[s] the ongoing nature of influences between
organism, behavior, care giving environment, and societal context" (Johnson, 2007,
p. 279).

The significance of these interactions is particularly apparent in the profiles of
children exposed to alcohol and cocaine during pregnancy. While substance abuse
during pregnancy places a child at high risk for developmental compromises, a
caregiver's continued involvement with drugs disrupts the predictability and
responsiveness of the environment. Further, since members of the larger community may expect that children exposed to drugs will perform poorly, developmental opportunities may be further diminished. In short, in order to understand
the full impact of the prenatal drug exposures, it is imperative to consider how
postnatal factors operate to shape development over time, through interactions
between the developing child and the environment.

2   Intervention

There is widespread agreement that children with PAE and PCE benefit from
specialized curricula. Nevertheless, many of these vulnerable children go unrec-
ognized and/or are misdiagnosed because of the lack of probable evidence of

significant central nervous system dysfunction as revealed with standardized, norm-referenced tests. As a result, Watson and Westby (2003) report that these youngsters often do not receive important environmental accommodations in their classrooms or support services they merit since professionals are lacking fundamental knowledge about the nature of this challenging clinical population as well as about what to do to meet their perplexing and multifaceted needs.

What can be gleaned from the literature with respect to treating children with harmful prenatal exposures who exhibit intricate and diffuse neurological compromise? We attempt to provide a beginning answer to this striking question by reviewing recent interventions from three complementary perspectives. The interventions represent three approaches for treating children with complex cognitive and behavioral profiles who have documented histories of drug exposure during pregnancy. Each intervention addresses the remarkable difficulty children with PAE and PCE have in learning and generalizing new behaviors during the school year, particularly interpersonal behaviors that are essential for effective learning and satisfying social relationships.

The first intervention reflects a special educator's approach to learning and performance. The program is designed for teachers who provide daily classroom instruction for the special needs of children with FASD (Clarren, 2004). The second approach is a cognitive-based intervention that a group of clinical researchers are using to teach children how to learn through self-observation and self-regulation (Kalberg & Buckley, 2007). The final intervention reveals how a school-based speech-language pathologist has attempted to teach children the skills they need to become competent communicators in everyday social situations (Timler, Olswang, & Coggins, 2005).

We have adopted McCauley and Fey's (McCauley & Fey, 2006) evidence-based taxonomy to evaluative the three interventions. This clinical decision-making approach admonishes pre-service and in-service professionals to consider three indispensable, interrelated factors in determining the potential value of any intervention. First, serious consideration must be afforded the theoretical basis underlying intervention: in essence, why should the treatment work with this particular child? Second, and arguably most important, what empirical evidence is available that justifies a significant investment of a clinician's "time, resources and hope" in administering treatment (p. 547)? Third, how does a clinician actually implement the intervention (i.e., what are the key components of the approach)? In the following sections, we consider the clinical viability of three contemporary interventions for children with prenatal alcohol and cocaine exposure using these evaluative criteria.

2.1 Teaching students with FSAD: Building strengths, creating hope (Clarren, 2004)

2.1.1 Theoretical basis Students with FASD present a range of complex learning disabilities, behavioral difficulties, and problems expressing and understanding language. Clarren (2004) stresses that many underlying compromises are linked to central nervous system dysfunction "caused by prenatal alcohol exposure" (p. 16). These neurological compromises are manifest in cognitive functioning, self-regulation, and language, particularly the type of language needed for social awareness. At the same time, Clarren acknowledges that other adverse prenatal and postnatal factors could certainly influence brain development. Thus, she implores professionals to be mindful of family factors (e.g., changes in caregivers, caregivers who continue to abuse drugs) when addressing the needs of children at school. Still, the theoretical assumptions underlying the content and structure of *Treating strategies for students with FASD* are muted. Clarren does not provide a well-developed explanation for the nature of outcomes that serve as targets for her intervention.

2.1.2   Key components   *Teaching strategies for students with FASD* is a curriculum to assist professionals in "thinking about and understanding the complex learning and behavioral issues associated with FASD" (Clarren, 2004, p. 15). The curriculum is built on eight underlying components that educators have reported are effective when intervening with children whose neurological impairments are linked to prenatal exposure to harmful agents. The first program component makes clear that different levels and patterns of prenatal alcohol exposure lead to variable neurological impairments that are reflected in atypical ways of learning.

This intervention outlines a series of practical compensatory strategies to support learning and performance. Clarren provides environmental supports that allow the child to compensate for neurological limitations that may be standing in the way of learning new behaviors and skills. These supports, accommodating the child's limitations in self-regulatory skills, planning, and inferencing, include strategies to structure the physical learning environment and develop effective routines.

2.1.3   Empirical basis   Clarren's approach reflects a clear commitment to clinical research. Still, the bases for much of this program appear to be personal testimonies and clinical endorsements from master clinicians. While unsatisfied with the current state of affairs, Clarren maintains that until there are evidence-based treatments upon which to inform treatment decisions, professionals working with this population will need to "rely on the best practices identified by educators and parents" (p. 27).

2.2   Cognitive control therapy

2.2.1   Theoretical basis   School-age children with FASD have diminished capacities to process or integrate complex information (Coggins et al., 2003; Kodituwakku, 2007). This core processing deficit has immediate relevance for speech-language pathologists attempting to teach more sophisticated language structures (e.g., embedded sentences) as well as classroom teachers who are charged with creating stimulating learning environments.

Cognitive control therapy (CCT) is built on a developmental-interaction model where a set of cognitive mechanisms or controls develop in concert with changes in a child's personality and demands of the environment (Santostefano, 1985). The goal of CCT is to get children to reflect on their knowledge about what they know and to use that developing knowledge to facilitate their own learning style and learning challenges. CCT is a "progressive skill building intervention" (Kalberg & Buckley, 2007, p. 283) designed for children and adolescents with cognitive dysfunctions.

From birth, children have access to a set of cognitive controls. The presumed function of these internal controls is to integrate information from the environment with the child's internal experiences (i.e., emotions, motives) to meet the demands of specific situational challenges. By the time children begin school, they have successfully integrated cognitive, affective, and personality variables into higher-order mental processes that provide children with the knowledge they need in deciding whether a strategy is effective in learning new information or resolving new social dilemmas.

2.2.2   Key components   The essence of CCT is the successful interplay between internal processes and the external environment. If children's underlying mental processes are compromised, it is remarkably difficult to integrate perceptions with their ideas, affect, and personality (Santostefano, 1985). From the CCT perspective, children with short attention spans, with difficulty organizing and sticking with tasks, and/or coping with the demands of a changing environment are seen as individuals with dysfunctional cognitive controls.

The key constituent elements of CCT intervention are five developmental cognitive processes that control learning and a child's adaptation to the environment (Santostefano, 1985). By the end of the preschool years, cognitive controls are sufficiently differentiated and interdependent for efficient learning to occur. A description of each control, presented in developmental order, is presented below:

- *Body ego-tempo*: the manner in which an individual uses symbols to represent and mentally regulate body movements.
- *Focal attention*: the manner in which an individual scans a field of information.
- *Field articulation*: the manner in which an individual attends selectively to some stimuli while ignoring others.
- *Leveling-sharpening*: the manner in which an individual compares images of past information with perceptions of present information.
- *Equivalence range*: the manner in which an individual categorizes and conceptualizes information.

2.2.3   Empirical basis   A research team has begun to explore the efficacy of cognitive control therapy (CCT) with school-age children in South Africa exposed prenatally to alcohol, living with substance abusing caregivers, in adverse environment (as reported in Riley et al., 2003). The primary goal of this ambitious study was to assess whether this skill-building intervention would improve children's understanding of their learning difficulties and behavioral challenges. A selected sample of 10 first grade youngsters, with presumed fetal alcohol syndrome (FAS), were randomly assigned to either a control group (n = 5; mean age 8;6 years) or the CCT intervention group (n = 5; mean age 8;4 years).

CCT intervention was delivered to the five experimental subjects one hour each week for 10 months by therapists experienced in this metacognitive approach. The five control subjects (matched for age, language, SES, grade and school setting) participated in the established first-grade curriculum for 10 months. The cognitive control strategies and neuropsychological functioning of children in both groups were assessed before and after intervention. The preliminary findings in this pre-test/post-test feasibility study revealed no statistically significant between-group differences on any of the outcome measures. To be fair, the primary goal of a feasibility study is not to establish statistical significance but rather to determine the clinical viability of an untested intervention and whether further investigation is warranted. On this point, the authors maintain that "qualitative improvements were noted by the therapists in the children's self-sufficiency, motivation, cooperation, self-confidence and emotionality" (Riley et al., 2003, p. 366). While this approach is not yet fully validated, Kalberg and Buckley (2007) maintain that CCT intervention "is showing promising results" (p. 2830).

2.3   Social communication intervention

2.3.1   Theoretical basis   Children with PAE and PCE have documented difficulties providing sufficient information to their partners during conversations and oral narratives (Coggins, Friet, & Morgan, 1998; Hamilton, 1981; Thorne et al., 2007). These limitations appear to be the result of an array of subtle, but strong, compromises in language, social cognition, and higher-order executive functions (Coggins, Timler, & Olswang, 2007). Maladaptive social experiences, which often co-occur with substance abuse, also negatively impact the social language behaviors children must develop to predict and explain people's behavior (Cicchetti, 2004; Cicchetti et al., 2003). Thus, children with PAE and PCE are subject to multiple risk factors that limit the kind of social savvy they need to perform adequately in socially demanding situations.

Failing to account for another person's perspective, intentions, or feelings have led some to speculate that children with prenatal substance abuse, and/or those living in adverse environments, may have a constellation of limitations that give rise to theory of mind deficits (Cicchetti, 2004; Coggins, 1997; Kodituwakku et al., 1997). Theory of mind is the ability to reason about mental states of other people, such as their thoughts, beliefs, and desires. Deficits in theory of mind have far-reaching consequences for appropriate social interactions.

Timler, Olswang, and Coggins (2005) have designed a multidimensional treatment to teach children with prenatal alcohol exposure the skills they need to be competent communicators in social situations. The social communication intervention (SCI) program takes into account both the behaviors and skills that clinicians need to teach as well as the environmental support children need to be competent communicators.

2.3.2   Key components   The SCI treatment is built on a multidimensional framework. The intervention focuses on the linguistic skills that support theory of mind and the social cognitive skills that purport to teach children what to do and say when confronted with social dilemmas. The ability to establish and maintain meaningful interpersonal relationships is a pivotal developmental achievement (Gresham, Sugai, & Horner, 2001).

The SCI blends three intervention components in teaching these interrelated skills to school-age youngsters. The components include: (1) role-playing techniques to assist children in assuming the perspectives of others; (2) a checklist to guide children through a routine for resolving social dilemmas; and (3) the direct modeling of socially appropriate responses by a clinician. The checklist, presented in Figure 13.1, is designed to be used to increase the use of socially appropriate strategies in resolving a social dilemma successfully.

2.3.3   Empirical basis   The research supporting the effectiveness of the SCI for children with PAE is encouraging but preliminary. Timler and colleagues (2005) have reported the results of an initial feasibility case study in a peer-reviewed journal. A feasibility study determines whether an untested intervention is clinically viable and merits further programmatic investigation supporting claims of treatment effectiveness.

The participant was a 9;8-year-old girl with PAE who presented with a complex cognitive and behavioral profile. The intervention was conducted over 6 weeks, with 2 weeks of individual treatment (i.e., two 1-hour weekly sessions) and 4 weeks of group treatment (i.e., three 2-hour weekly sessions with two school-age peers). The data that were gathered monitored the girl's responses to a set of checklist questions. The checklist was designed to elicit mental state verbs (e.g., What does he *know*?), social cognitive strategies for obtaining a social goal (e.g., What are all the things you could do?), and appropriate consequences for an action (e.g., What is the *best* thing for you to do?). Treatment data revealed that the checklist was effective in increasing the number of strategies the participant used for obtaining a social goal and promoting mental state verb production. While further study is clearly needed, the feasibility of this intervention is promising for clinicians who have caseloads that include youngsters with diverse clinical profiles and social communication difficulties.

In summary, teaching essential social and communicative skills is a key component of the above interventions. Two of the interventions provide a clear theoretical rationale as to why a professional would want to use the approach in treating children who have prenatal alcohol and/or cocaine exposures (i.e., cognitive control therapy, social communication intervention). Unfortunately, at this point in time, only one of the interventions has provided quantitative data supporting the value of the treatment for children with absent or impaired social behaviors (social communication intervention). To be sure, these feasibility studies

Card 1
STOP, LOOK, & LISTEN

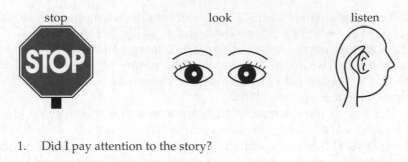

stop   look   listen

1. Did I pay attention to the story?

    _____ YES! _____ NO, I need help!

2. What do I know?

3. How do I know this?

think

Card 2
SEEING AND HEARING LEADS TO
THINKING AND KNOWING!

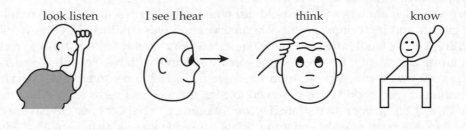

look listen   I see I hear   think   know

1. Did I pay attention to what others saw and heard?

    _____ YES! _____ NO, I need help!

friend

2. What does everyone else think or know
    about the story?

3. How do they know this?

Figure 13.1   A four-card checklist to increase the use of children's socially appropriate strategies in resolving a social dilemma. Reprinted with permission from Timler, from: "'Do I know what I need to do?' A social communication intervention for children with complex clinical profiles," by G. R. Timler, L. B. Olswang, and T. E. Coggins. *Language, Speech, and Hearing services in Schools* 36 (1), 73–85. Copyright 2005 by American Speech-Language-Hearing Association. All rights reserved.

Card 3
PLAN AND TAKE ACTION!

binoculars map calendar

1. Do I know what I need to do?

choose

_____ YES! _____ NO, I need help!

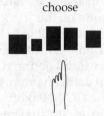

2. What do you think I could do?

3. What do I think is the BEST choice?

4. why do I believe this is the BEST choice?

Card 4
EVALUATE THE CONSEQUENCES!

1. What do I think happened?

2. How do I know this?

3. What do others think happened?

4. Why do they think this?

5. Did it turn out the way I believed it would?

YES! NO!

Make
another
choice!

congratulations

Figure 13.1 *Cont'd*

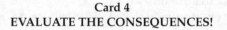
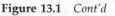

do not address the contribution of individual treatment components or the optimal time to administer the intervention. Thus, while each intervention appears capable of accomplishing meaningful change with children who have documented prenatal exposures to alcohol and/or cocaine, they remain largely untested and therefore should be considered cautiously at this formative stage of development.

3   Conclusion

Substance abuse during pregnancy remains a divisive societal problem. Policy makers, researchers, educators, and families continue to struggle to understand the motivations of those individuals who abuse alcohol and drugs and the implications of their abuse, particularly with respect to children who are in their care.

The results of this review reveal that children with PAE and PCE may be particularly susceptible to language and social communicative deficits as a result of the harmful prenatal exposures they experience. Moreover, many of these children have also endured dysfunctional postnatal social interactions that further complicate and constrain the course of their development (Coggins, Timler, & Olswang, 2007; Malakoff et al., 1999). These coexisting conditions frequently conspire to create the perfect storm to disrupt developmental, psychosocial, and/or communicative functions. The unacceptably high prevalence rate of pre- and postnatal substance abuse highlights the need for continued and coordinated efforts at prevention and treatment.

Neurobiological and environmental risks contribute to multiple deficits in children. Interventions with this clinical population have, therefore, endorsed comprehensive treatment models that simultaneously address deficits in language, social cognition, attention/memory, and executive function. Clinicians who must treat these complex children should seriously consider more integrative tasks in their assessments and treatments that mimic the demands of everyday social interactions. This challenge is formidable as there are few evidence-based treatment data to guide clinical decision making.

REFERENCES

Adams, C., Baxendale, J., Lloyd, J., & Aldred, C. (2005). Pragmatic language impairment: case studies of social and pragmatic language therapy. *Child Language Teaching and Therapy* 21 (3) (October 1), 227–50.

Adams, C. V., Lloyd, J., Aldred, C., & Baxendale, J. (2006). Exploring the effects of communication intervention for developmental pragmatic language impairments: A signal-generation study. *International Journal of Language & Communication Disorders* 41 (1), 41–65.

Archibald, S. L., Fennema-Notestine, C., Gamst, A., Riley, E. P., Mattson, S. N., & Jernigan, T. L. (2001). Brain dysmorphology in individuals with severe prenatal alcohol exposure. *Developmental Medicine and Child Neurology* 43 (3) (March), 148–54.

Astley, S. J. (2004). *Diagnostic guide for fetal alcohol spectrum disorders: The four-digit diagnostic code*, 3rd ed. Seattle: FAS Diagnostic and Prevention Network, University of Washington, electronic version available from http://fasdpn.org.

Astley, S. J. & Clarren, S. K. (1996). A case definition and photographic screening tool for the facial phenotype of fetal alcohol syndrome. *Journal of Pediatrics* 129 (1) (July), 33–41.

Astley, S. J. & Clarren, S. K. (2001). Measuring the facial phenotype of individuals with prenatal alcohol exposure: Correlations with brain dysfunction. *Alcohol & Alcoholism* 36 (2), 147–59.

Autti-Ramo, I., Autti, T., Korkman, M., Kettunen, S., Salonen, O., & Valanne, L. (2002). MRI findings in children with school problems who had been exposed prenatally to alcohol. *Developmental Medicine & Child Neurology* 44 (2) (February), 98–106.

Bada, H. S., Das, A., Bauer, C. R., Shankaran, S., Lester, B., LaGasse, L., Hammond, J., Wright, L. L., & Higgins, R. (2007). Impact of prenatal cocaine exposure on child behavior problems through school age. *Pediatrics* 119 (2) (February 1), 348–59.

Bandstra, E. S., Morrow, C. E., Vogel, A. L., Fifer, R. C., Ofir, A. Y., Dausa, A. T., Xue, L., & Anthon, J. C. (2002). Longitudinal influence of prenatal cocaine exposure on child language functioning. *Neurotoxicology and Teratology* 24 (3) (May–June), 297–308.

Bertrand, J., Floyd, L. L., & Weber, M. K. (2005). Guidelines for identifying and referring persons with fetal alcohol syndrome. *Morbidity and Mortality Weekly Report: Recommendations and Reports* 54:RR-11 (October 28), 1–14.

Bookstein, F. L., Streissguth, A. P., Connor, P. D., & Sampson, P. D. (2006). Damage to the human cerebellum from prenatal alcohol exposure: The anatomy of a simple biometrical explanation. *Anatomical Record. Part B, New Anatomist* 289B:5 (September 5), 195–209.

Burd, L., Cotsonas-Hassler, T. M., Martsolf, J. T., & Kerbeshian, J. (2003). Recognition and management of fetal alcohol syndrome. *Neurotoxicology and Teratology* 25 (6), 681–8.

Carmichael-Olson, H., Morse, B. A., & Huffine, C. (1998). Development and psychopathology: fetal alcohol syndrome and related conditions. *Seminars in Clinical Neuropsychiatry* 3, 262–84.

Carmichael-Olson, H., Jirikowic, T., Kartin, D., & Astley, S. (2007). Responding to the challenge of early intervention for fetal alcohol spectrum disorders. *Infants and Young Children* 20, 172–89.

Centers for Disease Control and Prevention (2007). Retrieved June 10, 2008, from http://www.cdc.gov/ncbddd/fas/default.htm

Chapman, R. (2007). Children's language learning: An interactionist perspective. In R. Paul (ed.), *Language disorders from a developmental perspective* (pp. 1–54). Mahwah, NJ: Lawrence Erlbaum Associates.

Chudley, A., Conry, J., Cook, J., Loock, C., Rosales, T., & LeBlanc, N. Public Health Agency of Canada's National Advisory Committee on Fetal Alcohol Spectrum (2002). Canadian Pediatric Society Statement. (CPS): Fetal Alcohol Syndrome Fetal alcohol spectrum disorder: Canadian guidelines for diagnosis. *Pediatric Child Health* 7, 161–74.

Church, M. W. & Kaltenbach, J. A. (1997). Hearing, speech, language, and vestibular disorders in the fetal alcohol syndrome: A literature review. *Alcoholism, Clinical and Experimental Research* 21 (3) (May), 495–512.

Cicchetti, D. (2004). An odyssey of discovery: Lessons learned through three decades of research on child maltreatment. *American Psychologist* 58, 731–41.

Cicchetti, D., Rogosch, F. A., Maughan, A., Toth, S. L., & Bruce, J. (2003). False belief understanding in maltreated children. *Development and Psychopathology* 15 (4), 1067–91.

Clarren, S. (2004). *Teaching strategies for students with fetal alcohol spectrum disorder.* Alberta Learning available at http://www.education.gov.ab.ca/k_12/curriculum/bySubject/healthpls/fas.pdf.

Clarren, S., H. Carmichael Olson, H., Clarren, S. K., & Astley, S. J. (2000). A child with fetal alcohol syndrome. In M. Guralnick (ed.), *Interdisciplinary clinical assessment of young children with developmental disabilities* (pp. 307–26). Baltimore, MD: Paul H. Brookes.

Coggins, T. E. (1997). Assessment of language and social communication in fetal alcohol syndrome. Paper presented at the Prevention and Management – Fetal Alcohol Syndrome & Prenatal Substance Abuse Conference of the Colorado Fetal Alcohol and Substance Abuse Coalition, Breckenridge, CO (July).

Coggins, T. E., Friet, T., & Morgan, T. (1998). Analysing narrative productions in older school-age children and adolescents with fetal alcohol syndrome: An experimental tool for clinical applications. *Clinical Linguistics & Phonetics* 12, 221–36.

Coggins, T. E., Olswang, L. B., Carmichael-Olsen, H., & Timler, G. (2003). On becoming socially competent communicators: The challenge for children with fetal alcohol exposure. *International Review of Research in Mental Retardation* 27, 121–50.

Coggins, T. E., Timler, G. R., & Olswang, L. B. (2007). A state of double jeopardy: impact of prenatal alcohol exposure and adverse environments on the social communicative abilities of school-age children with fetal alcohol spectrum disorder. *Lang Speech Hear Serv Sch* 38 (2) (April), 117–27.

Coles, C. D., Platzman, K. A., Raskind-Hood, C. L., Brown, R. T., Falek, A., & Smith, I. E. (1997). A comparison of children affected by prenatal alcohol exposure and attention deficit, hyperactivity disorder. *Alcoholism: Clinical and Experimental Research* 21 (1), 150–61.

Cone-Wesson, B. (2005). Prenatal alcohol and cocaine exposure: Influences on cognition, speech, language, and hearing. *Journal of Communication Disorders* 38 (4), 279–302.

Cortese, B. M., Moore, G. J., Bailey, B. A., Jacobson, S. W., Delaney-Black, V., & Hannigan, J. H. (2006). Magnetic resonance and spectroscopic imaging in prenatal alcohol-exposed children: Preliminary findings in the caudate nucleus. *Neurotoxicology and Teratology* 28 (5), 597–606.

Coster, W., Gersten, M., Beeghly, M., & Cicchetti, D. (1989). Communicative functioning in maltreated toddlers. *Developmental Psychopathology* 25, 1020–9.

Delaney-Black, V., Covington, C., Templin, T., Kershaw, T., Nordstrom-Klee, B., Ager, J., Clark, N., Surendran, A., Martier, S., & Sokol, R. J. (2000). Expressive language development of children exposed to cocaine prenatally: Literature review and report of a prospective cohort study. *Journal of Communication Disorders* 33 (6), 463–81.

Eigsti, I. M. & Cicchetti, D. (2004). The impact of child maltreatment on expressive syntax at 60 months. *Developmental Science* 7, 88–102.

Fagerlund, A., Heikkinen, S., Autti-Ramo, I., Korkman, M., Timonen, M., Kuusi, T., Riley, E. P., & Lundbom, N. (2006). Brain metabolic alterations in adolescents and young adults with Fetal Alcohol Spectrum Disorders. *Alcoholism: Clinical and Experimental Research* 30 (12), 2097–104.

Frank, D. A., Augustyn, M., Knight, W. G., Pell, T., & Zuckerman, B. (2001). Growth, development, and behavior in early childhood following prenatal cocaine exposure: a systematic review. *JAMA* 285 (12) (March 28), 1613–25.

Greenbaum, R., Nulman, I., Rovet, J., & Koren, G. (2002). The Toronto experience in diagnosing alcohol-related neurodevelopmental disorder: a unique profile of deficits and assets. *The Canadian Journal of Clinical Pharmacology* 9 (4) (Winter), 215–25.

Greene, T., Emhart, C. B., Martier, S., Sokol, R., & Ager, J. (1990). Prenatal alcohol exposure and language development. *Alcoholism: Clinical and Experimental Research* 14 (6), 937–45.

Gresham, F. M., Sugai, G., & Horner, R. H. (2001). Interpreting outcomes of social skills training for students with high-incidence disabilities. *Exceptional Children* 67 (3) (Spring), 331–44.

Guerri, C. (2002). Mechanisms involved in central nervous system dysfunctions induced by prenatal ethanol exposure. *Neurotoxicity Research* 4 (4), 327–35.

Hamilton, M. (1981). Linguistic abilities of children with fetal alcohol syndrome. Unpublished doctoral dissertation, University of Washington.

Hans, S. L. (2002). Studies of prenatal exposure to drugs: focusing on parental care of children. *Neurotoxicology and Teratology* 24 (3) (May–June), 329–37.

Johnson, H. (2007). The development of communicative competence. In R. Paul (ed.), *Language disorders from a developmental perspective* (pp. 277–98). Mahwah, NJ: Lawerence Erlbaum Associates.

Jones, K. & Smith, D. (1973). Recognition of the fetal alcohol syndrome in early infancy. *Lancet* 2, 999–1001.

Kalberg, W. O. & Buckley, D. (2007). FASD: What types of intervention and rehabilitation are useful? *Neuroscience & Biobehavioral Reviews* 31 (2), 278–85.

Kaufman, J., Plotsky, P. M., Nemeroff, C. B., & Charney, D. S. (2000). Effects of early adverse experiences on brain structure and function: clinical implications. *Biological Psychiatry* 48 (8), 778–90.

Kelly, S. J., Day, N., & Streissguth, A. P. (2000). Effects of prenatal alcohol exposure on social behavior in humans and other species. *Neurotoxicology and Teratology* 22 (2) (Mar–April), 143–9.

Kerns, K. A., Don, A., Mateer, C. A., & Streissguth, A. P. (1997). Cognitive deficits in nonretarded adults with fetal alcohol syndrome. *Journal of Learning Disabilities* 30 (6) (November–December), 685–93.

Kleinfeld, J. & Wescott, S. (eds.) (1993). *Fantastic Antone succeeds!: Experiences in educating children with fetal alcohol syndrome*. Fairbanks, AK: University of Alaska Press.

Kodituwakku, P. W. (2007). Defining the behavioral phenotype in children with fetal alcohol spectrum disorders: A review. *Neuroscience & Biobehavioral Reviews* 31 (2), 192–201.

Kodituwakku, P. W., May, P., Ballinger, L., Harris, M., Aese, J., & Aragon, A. (1997). Executive control functioning and theory of mind in children prenatally exposed to alcohol. Paper presented at the Prevention and Management – Fetal Alcohol Syndrome & Prenatal Substance Abuse Conference of the Colorado Fetal Alcohol and Substance Abuse Coalition, Breckenridge, CO (July).

Kvigne, V. L., Leonardson, G. R., Neff-Smith, M., Brock, E., Borzelleca, J., & Welty, T. K. (2004). Characteristics of children who have full or incomplete fetal alcohol syndrome. *Journal of Pediatrics* 145 (5) (November), 635–40.

Lee, K. T., Mattson, S. N., & Riley, E. P. (2004). Classifying children with heavy prenatal alcohol exposure using measures of attention. *Journal of the International Neuropsychological Society* 10 (2) (March), 271–7.

Linares, T. J., Singer, L. T., Kirchner, H. L., Short, E. J., Min, M. O., Hussey, P., & Minnes, S. (2006). Mental health outcomes of cocaine-exposed children at

6 years of age. *Journal of Pediatric Psychology* 31 (1) (January 1), 85–97.

Lohmann, H. & Tomasello, M. (2003). The role of language in the development of false belief understanding: A training study. *Child Development* 74, 1130–44.

Malakoff, M. E., Mayes, L. C., & Schottenfeld, R. (1994). Language abilities of preschool-age children living with cocaine-using mothers. *American Journal on Addictions* 3 (4), 346–54.

Malakoff, M. E., Mayes, L. C., Schottenfeld, R., & Howell, S. (1999). Language production in 24-month-old inner-city children of cocaine-and-other-drug-using mothers. *Journal of Applied Developmental Psychology* 20 (1), 159–80.

Martin, I. & McDonald, S. (2003). Weak coherence, no theory of mind, or executive dysfunction? Solving the puzzle of pragmatic language disorders. *Brain and Language* 85 (3), 451–66.

Mattson, S. N., Calarco, K. E., & Lang, A. R. (2006). Focused and shifting attention in children with heavy prenatal alcohol exposure. *Neuropsychology* 20 (3) (May), 361–9.

Mattson, S. N. & Riley, E. P. (1998). A review of the neurobehavioral deficits in children with fetal alcohol syndrome or prenatal exposure to alcohol. *Alcoholism-Clinical and Experimental Research* 22 (2) (April), 279–94.

McCauley, R. & Fey, M. E. (eds.) (2006). *Treatment of language disorders in children.* Baltimore, MD: Brookes Publishing.

McFadyen, R. & Kitson, W. (1996). Language comprehension and expression among adolescents who have experienced childhood physical abuse. *Journal of Child Psychology, Psychiatry & Allied Disciplines* 37, 551–62.

McGee, C. L. & Riley, E. P. (2006). Brain imaging and fetal alcohol spectrum disorders. *Annali dell'Istituto Superiore di Sanità* 42 (1), 46–52.

Mentis, M. & Lundgren, K. (1995). Effects of prenatal exposure to cocaine and associated risk factors on language development. *Journal of Speech and Hearing Research* 38 (6) (December 1), 1303–18.

Morrow, C. E., Culbertson, J. L., Accornero, V. H., Xue, L., Anthony, J. C., & Bandstra, E. S. (2006). Learning disabilities and intellectual functioning in school-aged children with prenatal cocaine exposure. *Developmental Neuropsychology* 30 (3), 905–31.

O'Leary, C. M. (2004). Fetal alcohol syndrome: diagnosis, epidemiology, and developmental outcomes. *Journal of Paediatrics and Child Health* 40 (1–2) (January–February), 2–7.

Olson, H. C., Streissguth, A. P., Sampson, P. D., Barr, H. M., Bookstein, F. L., & Thiede, K. (1997). Association of prenatal alcohol exposure with behavioral and learning problems in early adolescence. *Journal of the American Academy of Child and Adolescent Psychiatry* 36 (9) (September), 1187–94.

Olswang, L. B., Coggins, T. E., & Timler, G. R. (2001). Outcome measures for school-age children with social communication problems. *Topics in Language Disorders: Alternative Measures for Evaluating Treatment Outcomes* 22 (1), 50–73.

Riley, E. P., Mattson, S. N., Li, T.-K., Jacobson, S. W., Coles, C. D., Kodituwakku, P. W., Adnams, C. M., & Korkman, M. I. (2003). Neurobehavioral consequences of prenatal alcohol exposure: An international perspective. *Alcoholism: Clinical and Experimental Research* 27 (2), 362–73.

Riley, E. P. & McGee, C. L. (2005). Fetal alcohol spectrum disorders: an overview with emphasis on changes in brain and behavior. *Experimental Biology and Medicine (Maywood, N.J.)* 230 (6) (June), 357–65.

Riley, E. P., McGee, C. L., & Sowell, E. R. (2004). Teratogenic effects of alcohol: a decade of brain imaging. *American Journal of Medical Genetics Part C:*

Seminars in Medical Genetics 127 (1) (May 15), 35–41.

Sampson, P. D., Streissguth, A. P., Bookstein, F. L., Little, R. E., Clarren, S. K., Dehaene, P., Hanson, J. W., & Graham, Jr., J. M. (1997). Incidence of fetal alcohol syndrome and prevalence of alcohol-related neurodevelopmental disorder. *Teratology* 56 (5) (November), 317–26.

Santostefano, S. (1985). *Cognitive control therapy with children and adolescents.* New York: Pergamon Press.

Singer, L. T., Arendt, R., Minnes, S., Salvator, A., Siegel, A. C., & Lewis, B. A. (2001). Developing language skills of cocaine-exposed infants. *Pediatrics* 107 (5) (May), 1057–64.

Singer, L. T., Minnes, S., Short, E., Arendt, R., Farkas, K., Lewis, B., Klein, N., Russ, S., Min, M. O., & Kirchner, H. L. (2004). Cognitive outcomes of preschool children with prenatal cocaine exposure. *JAMA* 291 (20) (May 26), 2448–56.

Sowell, E. R., Mattson, S. N., Thompson, P. M., Jernigan, T. L., Riley, E. P., & Toga, A. W. (2001). Mapping callosal morphology and cognitive correlates: Effects of heavy prenatal alcohol exposure. *Neurology* 57 (2) (July 24), 235–44.

Spohr, H. L., Willms, J., & Steinhausen, H. C. (2007). Fetal alcohol spectrum disorders in young adulthood. *Journal of Pediatrics* 150 (2) (February), 175–9, 79 e1.

Spohr, H. L., Willms, J., & Steinhausen H. C. (1993). Prenatal alcohol exposure and long-term developmental consequences. *The Lancet* 341 (8850), 907–10.

Streissguth, A. P. (1977). Maternal drinking and the outcome of pregnancy: implications for child mental health. *American Journal of Orthopsychiatry* 47 (3) (July), 422–31.

Streissguth, A. P. (1997). *Fetal alcohol syndrome: A guide for families and communities.* Baltimore, MD: Paul H. Brookes.

Streissguth, A., Martin, D., Martin, J., & Barr, H. (1981). The Seattle longitudinal prospective study on alcohol and pregnancy. *Neurobehavioral Toxicology and Teratology* 3, 223–33.

Streissguth, A. P., Barr, H. M., Kogan, J., & Bookstein, F. L. (1996). Understanding the occurrence of secondary disabilities in clients with fetal alcohol syndrome and fetal alcohol effects: Final report. Seattle, WA: University of Washington.

Streissguth, A. P., Barr, H. M., Olson, H. C., Sampson, P. D., Bookstein, F. L., & Burgess, D. M. (1994). Drinking during pregnancy decreases word attack and arithmetic scores on standardized tests: adolescent data from a population-based prospective study. *Alcoholism, Clinical and Experimental Research* 18 (2) (April), 248–54.

Streissguth, A. P., Bookstein, F. L., Barr, H. M., Sampson, P. D., O'Malley, K., & Young, J. K. (2004). Risk factors for adverse life outcomes in fetal alcohol syndrome and fetal alcohol effects. *Journal of Developmental and Behavioral Pediatrics* 25 (4) (August), 228–38.

Streissguth, A. P. & O'Malley, K. (2000). Neuropsychiatric implications and long-term consequences of fetal alcohol spectrum disorders. *Seminars in Clinical Neuropsychiatry* 5 (3) (July), 177–90.

Thomas, S. E., Kelly, S. J., Mattson, S. N., & Riley, E. P. (1998). Comparison of social abilities of children with fetal alcohol syndrome to those of children with similar IQ scores and normal controls. *Alcoholism: Clinical and Experimental Research* 22 (2), 528–33.

Thorne, J. C., Coggins, T. E., Carmichael-Olsen, H., & Astley, S. J. (2007). Exploring the utility of narrative analysis in diagnostic decision-making: Picture-bound reference, elaboration, and Fetal Alcohol Spectrum Disorders. *Journal of Speech, Language, and Hearing Research* 50 (2), 459–74.

Timler, G. R., Olswang, L. B., &. Coggins, T. E (2005). "Do I know what I need to do?" A social communication intervention for children with complex clinical profiles. *Language, Speech, and Hearing Services in Schools* 36 (1) (January), 73–85.

Wasserman, D. R. & Leventhal, J. M. (1993). Maltreatment of children born to cocaine-dependent mothers. *American Journal of Diseases of Children* 147 (12) (December 1), 1324–8.

Watson, S. M. R. & Westby, C. E. (2003). Strategies for addressing the executive function impairments of students prenatally exposed to alcohol and other drugs. *Communication Disorders Quarterly* 24 (4) (Summer), 194–204.

Wechsler, D. (1974). *Manual for the Wechsler Intelligence Scale for Children – Revised.* San Antonio, TX: The Psychological Corporation.

Whaley, S. E., O'Connor, M. J., & Gunderson, B. (2001). Comparison of the adaptive functioning of children prenatally exposed to alcohol to a nonexposed clinical sample. *Alcoholism: Clinical and Experimental Research* 25 (7), 1018–24.

Willis, D. & Silovsky, J. (1998). Prevention of violence at the societal level. In P. Trickett & C. Schellenach (eds.), *Violence against children in the family and the community* (pp. 401–16). Washington, DC: American Psychological Association.

Zimmerman, I. L., Steiner, V. G., & Pond, R. E. (1992). *Preschool Language Scale*, 3rd ed. San Antonio, TX: The Psychological Corporation.

14 Aphasia

CHRIS CODE

1 What Is Aphasia?

The history of aphasia is one of disagreement and controversy, and any attempt at a universally acceptable definition of aphasia is fraught with danger. Nevertheless, an overview chapter on aphasia, such as this one, needs to make an attempt at some kind of definition. *Aphasia* is the term most workers in the field would use to describe impairments of the *use* of language, the expression and comprehension of language in any modality – whether through speech, writing, or linguistic signing – and is caused by some acquired form of damage to the brain. So, aphasia is not an impairment of articulation (*dysarthria*) or of voice (*aphonia*) (see also Chapters 16 and 20, this volume).

One view is that the term "aphasia" should be reserved for the observed impairments or symptoms of language use caused by damage to the left hemisphere that can be described in terms of the core domains of a standard *componential* model of language covering the domains of semantics (word and sentence meaning), syntax (grammatical structure), morphology (word structure), and phonology (sound structure). The model, the basic units of which are words, phonemes, syllables, morphemes, and their *combinatory* features (syntactic, morphological, and phonological combination), provides an account of many of the features of aphasia accompanying brain damage. The model is less satisfactory when dealing with *discourse* and everyday *conversation*, which can also be impaired, particularly following traumatic head injury and right brain damage, and these conditions are dealt with elsewhere in this handbook (see Chapters 24 and 25, this volume). This definition of aphasia, then, excludes some complex language impairments arising from damage to the right hemisphere such as problems with using verbal jokes, understanding inferences and metaphors, using pragmatic aspects of language concerned with the behavioral context of language use, and prosody – the meaning carried by stress, rhythm, intonation, and emotional tone (see Chapter 10, this volume).

The term "aphasia" is also commonly used with the language impairments that develop in a range of dementias and other progressive conditions. The term also

The Handbook of Language and Speech Disorders, First Edition. Edited by Jack S. Damico, Nicole Müller, and Martin J. Ball. © 2013 Blackwell Publishing Ltd except for editorial material and organization © 2013 Jack S. Damico, Nicole Müller, Martin J. Ball. Published 2013 by Blackwell Publishing Ltd.

includes what is most often called *apraxia of speech*, sometimes called *motor aphasia* or *aphemia*: impairments in the fluent production of speech arising from damage to the mechanisms controlling the planning and programming of speech before articulation is attempted. In apraxia of speech, therefore, there is no muscular paralysis or incoordination and therefore apraxic impairments to motor speech are not caused by dysarthria (see Chapters 16 and 17, this volume.)

2   The Incidence and Prevalence of Aphasia

The exact incidence and prevalence of aphasia is unknown, in part because of the variety of conditions that have been or can be labeled *aphasia*: how often aphasia occurs and how many people will have aphasia depends on what we say aphasia is. For example, if we include the communication problems that result from traumatic brain injury (TBI), progressive aphasia, and dementia and right hemisphere damage, incidence and prevalence go up. While aphasia can occur as a result of head injury (MacDonald, Togher, & Code, 1999) and dementia (Au, Albert, & Obler, 1988) incidence and prevalence of aphasia in these populations is even more difficult to determine than in the stroke population. In the case of aphasia following stroke, the most common cause, many stroke survivors do not enter hospital, some will never even see a physician and, even if they do, records may not be kept or contributed to surveys of incidence or prevalence.

A range of studies have estimated incidence and prevalence of aphasia following stroke, but they have used different methodologies and different criteria to determine presence of aphasia in people with stroke, and aphasia incidence or prevalence is often estimated based on the incidence and prevalence of stroke. Most studies have used stroke banks and surveys that are assumed to underestimate incidence and prevalence of stroke and of aphasia, and estimates of incidence vary; some variability is noted in different parts of the world.

Incidence of stroke varies across the world, and Sudlow and Warlow (1997) compared data from 11 studies of stroke incidence in Europe, Russia, Australasia, and the United States, comprising approximately 3.5 million person-years and 5,575 stroke incidents. Age- and sex-standardized annual incidence rates for participants aged 45–84 years were similar in most places (between approximately 300 per 100,000 and 500 per 100,000) but were significantly lower in Dijon in France (238 per 100,000), and higher in Novosibirsk in Russia (627 per 100,000). Brust and colleagues estimated that approximately 20 percent of those who have had an acute stroke will have aphasia (Brust et al., 1976). Similarly, Hier et al. (1994) examined the Stroke Data Bank in the USA and found a prevalence of aphasia of 20.95 percent. The cumulative estimated prevalence of disabled stroke survivors in the USA in the 1990s was 3 million (Bronner, Kanter, & Manson, 1995). If 20 percent of these are aphasic, the prevalence of aphasia subsequent to stroke would be 600,000. An estimate of incidence and prevalence is provided by the American National Aphasia Association (Klein, 1995), who suggest that the incidence is about 83,000 in the USA and a prevalence of one million people with some degree of aphasia. This is a convenient and emotive figure, but it could be higher. With a population of 250 million, this makes the incidence 0.03 percent and the prevalence 0.4 percent. In the United Kingdom the incidence is estimated to be two in 1,000 (0.2 percent) of the population (approximately 55 million) (Langton Hewer, 1997; Warlow, 1998) but it is estimated that only 85 percent of strokes are admitted to hospital. So the incidence of 110,000 first strokes for the United Kingdom population is based on strokes admitted to hospital (Ebrahim & Redfern, 1999) and will therefore be an underestimate. The Bristol Stroke Study in the UK examined survival from stroke and found that approximately 30 percent of patients die within the first few weeks, 30 percent recover completely and about 40 percent have chronic disability, including aphasia (Langton Hewer, 1997).

Fuh et al. (1996) conducted a more direct door-to-door survey in rural Taiwan of residents of 50 years or older, and conducted a standard neurological examination. They found 96 cases of stroke in a population of 5,061 (prevalence of 2.45 percent). This figure is higher than most estimates for stroke, and indicates a significant hidden population in the community. However, in the Copenhagen Stroke Study (Pederson et al., 1995), incidence of aphasia in 881 acute stroke patients on admission to hospital was 38 percent. But this study used a very basic three-part rating scale of aphasia, which may not be reliable.

The incidence of aphasia in stroke at acute stages is higher than at chronic stages, reflecting the spontaneous recovery of aphasia for some. Kertesz (1979) found that from 93 aphasic patients assessed on the Western Aphasia Battery (WAB; Kertesz, 1982) at 1 month post-onset, up to 20 percent made "almost complete recoveries" by 12 months. Given that the WAB is recognized as being poor at detecting milder forms of aphasia, this 20 percent is likely to be an overestimate of recovery. The figure of 38 percent of stroke patients with aphasia on hospital admission found by Pedersen et al. reduced to 18 percent on discharge from hospital – nearer the 20 percent figure commonly quoted for prevalence of aphasia above.

If communication impairments subsequent to TBI are called aphasic, incidence and prevalence escalate markedly. Incidence of head injury annually in the USA is approximately 200 per 100,000 (Annegers et al., 1980). Approximately one-third of those who sustain a closed head injury are reported to be aphasic (Luzzatti et al., 1989; Sarno, Buonaguro, & Levita, 1986).

If we consider communication impairments in people with dementia as aphasia, incidence and prevalence of aphasia again increase. Dementia affects 10 percent of the population over 65 years of age and as many as 50 percent of those over 85 years of age. According to the UK Alzheimer's Society, there were approximately 700,000 persons with dementia in the UK in 2007, and the number is expected to increase to a million by 2025. It is estimated that the proportion of persons with dementia doubles for every five-year age interval, and that one-third of those aged 95 and over have dementia (Alzheimer's Society, 2007). Dementia results in a significant communication deficit (Au, Albert, & Obler, 1988), and significant language impairments are detectable, even in the early stages of dementia (e.g., Code & Lodge, 1987). Little research has been conducted into the incidence and prevalence of primary progressive aphasia, in which language becomes progressively impaired while other cognitive processes remain relatively intact.

Therefore, while we do not have the figures, we can infer that the prevalence of aphasia in the community is probably increasing, based on the knowledge that while the incidence of stroke may be stable or reducing a little in the Western world because of healthier lifestyles (although levels of obesity are rising), survival of stroke is increasing, and people are living longer. More people survive to become chronically disabled, including having aphasia.

3   Some History

Aphasia has probably existed since humans began to use language, but the first records we have noting speech and communication problems following head injury come from ancient Egyptian writings from between 3000 to 2200 years BC. The foundations for modern aphasiology are usually considered to have been the mid-1800s, and have even been pinpointed to 1861, when Pierre Paul Broca (1824–80) studied the impairments of language and speech of the aphasic man Leborgne, and described the nature of his brain damage to a packed meeting of the Anthropological Society of Paris on April 18, 1861. This single event is considered by many to be the most important step in the beginnings of modern aphasiology, and indeed of modern neuropsychology (Tesak & Code, 2008). Broca was interested, as many in those days, in asking whether particular cognitive functions, in this case speech and language, had localized representation in the brain, as had been claimed by Franz Josef Gall (1764–1828), an idea that was supported by the most influential physician in Paris at that time, Jean-Baptiste Bouillaud (1796–1881). Leborgne's impairments were predominantly in the production and expression of language, and, according to Broca's examination, comprehension and gesture were mostly intact. Broca emphasized that he had described an impairment in motor speech production which was not due to paralysis or muscular incoordination, and he called the condition *aphemia*, from the Greek, "I speak." He also claimed that the main area of damage, the third frontal convolution, was the site of "the faculty of articulated language" (Broca, 1861). The term "aphemia" soon lost favor: Armand Trousseau (1801–67) introduced the term "aphasia" in 1864, to Broca's disappointment, as he felt that aphemia emphasized the essential impairment to "motor speech."

The young German physician Carl Wernicke published his highly influential book *Der Aphasische Symptomencomplex: Eine psychologische Studie auf anatomischer Basis* (The symptom-complex of aphasia: A psychological study on an anatomical basis) in 1874 (translations in Eggert, 1977) and developed a model that included Broca's *aphemia* and Broca's Area, but added other aphasia types, including a sensory form of aphasia, subsequently called "Wernicke's aphasia," resulting from damage to the posterior superior convolutions of the temporal lobe in the posterior brain. This form of aphasia contrasted clearly with the non-fluent aphemia that Broca had described. It included severe auditory comprehension difficulties, but with normal articulated speech, and fluent production of inappropriate words and speech sounds. Wernicke's model was developed further by Ludwig Lichtheim (1845–1928), who published just one paper on aphasia in a long career. The model also included conduction aphasia, transcortical aphasias (motor and sensory), and pure aphasic syndromes. The paper, and the model that it developed, had a massive impact and was published in English translation in the then new journal *Brain* in 1885, the same year it appeared in German. An early version of what is known as the Wernicke–Lichtheim model is shown in Figure 14.1.

Interest in localization and terminology waned between the world wars, and it was the American neurologist Norman Geschwind who reintroduced a version of the classic model to the English-speaking world in the 1960s (Geschwind, 1965). This version is sometimes called the Wernicke–Lichtheim–Geschwind model. The model dominated aphasiology for many years, but in the latter part of the twentieth century aphasiologists became influenced by developments in neuro-linguistics, cognitive neuropsychology, and cognitive neuroscience, and a new paradigm emerged based on a more theoretically motivated psycholinguistic model developed through detailed single-case investigations using psycholinguistically controlled tests. Inspired by the mental "faculties" suggested by Gall, an information processing model developed which saw language, and other cognitive functions, organized into autonomous and encapsulated "modules" with connections between modules. Aphasic impairments were interpreted in terms of damage to these modules or the connections between modules. An early version of the cognitive neuropsychological model is reproduced in Figure 14.2. This model had a significant impact on clinical aphasiology, especially the design of tests for aphasia.

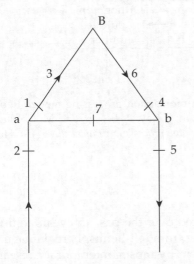

B:	concept center
a:	sound image center
b:	motor center
1	cortical sensory aphasia
2	subcortical sensory aphasia
3	transcortical sensory aphasia
4	cortical motor aphasia
5	subcortical motor aphasia
6	transcortical motor aphasia
7	conduction aphasia

Figure 14.1 The Wernicke–Lichtheim model. Reprinted with permission from Psychology Press Ltd, from: J. Tesak and C. Code (2008). *Milestones in the history of aphasia: Theories and Protagonists* (p. 91). Hove, UK: Psychology Press.

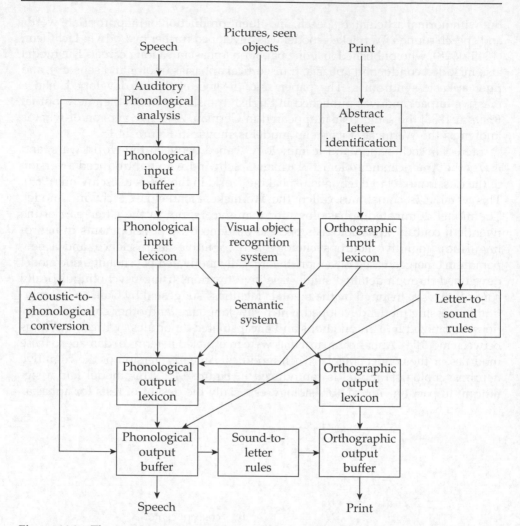

Figure 14.2   The cognitive neuropsychological information-processing model. Reprinted with permission from Psychology Press Ltd, from: J. Kay, R. Lesser, and M. Coltheart (1992). *PALPA: Psycholinguistic assessment of language processing in aphasia* (p. 15). Hove, UK: Lawrence Erlbaum Associates.

4   The Features of Aphasia

The array of terms that have been introduced over the past 150 years to describe the symptoms or features of aphasia arising from left hemisphere damage could fill a dictionary. Despite the acknowledgment by most contemporary researchers and clinicians that the "types" of aphasia that make up the Wernicke–Lichtheim– Geschwind classification have little value for either research or clinical work, the classification remains with us. Several of the most popular aphasia batteries (e.g., The Boston Diagnostic Aphasia Examination – BDAE, Goodglass & Kaplan, 1972; the

Western Aphasia Battery – WAB, Kertesz, 1982; and other tests derived from these batteries) still classify aphasic speakers into types on the basis of their performance on the tests (Katz et al., 2000), and variations of the classical scheme are still emerging (Ardila, in press). Below we will sketch the main features of aphasia.

An aphasic condition is said to be *fluent* or *non-fluent*. Aphasia is non-fluent if speech is hesitant and slow with many pauses and a lack of articulatory precision and prosody in speech. Some speakers are significantly non-fluent with severe apraxia of speech. The fluency distinction, which originated with Wernicke (Tesak & Code, 2008), is widely used. The classic aphasia types traditionally arising from left hemisphere damage that were initially developed in the late 1800s by Wernicke, Broca, and Lichtheim are most often grouped according to whether they are fluent or non-fluent forms of aphasia. The fluency dimension is closely linked to anatomy: fluent forms of aphasia are said to arise from a lesion posterior to the central Rolandic fissure and non-fluent forms from lesions anterior to the Rolandic fissure. It has been suggested that classification of aphasia need go no further than this basic fluency distinction, and there has been a steady condemnation of classification at least since Weisenburg and McBride (1935). Still others attempt to upgrade and modernize the classical types (Ardila, in press). A range of features or aphasic symptoms is associated with this basic fluent–non-fluent division.

Perhaps the most common feature of aphasia is a word-finding problem, or *anomia*, but the term "anomia" can have several meanings. It can refer to *a type of aphasia*, or it can be used to refer to a symptom that can occur in many types of aphasia. It is particularly common and describes a problem with retrieving or accessing common words like the names of things, actions, and events. Such naming or word-finding impairments are usually referred to as examples of *anomia*. But a failure to name an object might arise because the individual does not recognize the object, or does recognize it but cannot recall the word from lexical memory, or because they cannot initiate or program the necessary actions to utter a word they do recall. So there appear to be several forms of naming impairment producing different symptoms and apparently arising as a result to damage to different brain-language components or connections.

Semantic paraphasias, where a speaker incorrectly produces a word that is semantically related to the intended word, like saying "table" for "chair," are also considered to result from an underlying problem accessing the correct word from the lexicon. Semantic paraphasia is sometimes called *verbal* paraphasia, although a verbal paraphasia is not necessarily a semantic paraphasia if it is not semantically related to the intended word. Where an individual produces incorrect speech sounds and appears to have difficulties with accessing or retrieving the appropriate phonemes for a planned utterance, the result is called *phonemic paraphasia*, or sometimes *literal* paraphasia; an example is where instead of "cat," the speaker produces "pat." Phonemic paraphasias can also result in verbal paraphasias, where the utterance is an existing word ("sat" for "cat"), often called *formal* paraphasias. Paraphasias are considered to occur in fluent aphasias. If an aphasic speaker produces many paraphasic substitutions in their speech, then the severely impaired result, which may be mostly unintelligible, is described as *jargon* or *jargonaphasia*.

Speakers who produce phonemic paraphasia and/or jargon can be highly *fluent*, with few signs of hesitation or articulatory difficulty.

Agrammatism is a feature of non-fluent aphasia and is used to describe impairments in the use of syntax: it can disrupt a number of syntactic processes. Agrammatism has a variable presentation (e.g., Webster, Franklin, & Howard, 2004), and a variety of impairments emerge in different languages. In English, there may be a lack or nearly complete absence of grammatical function words in contrast to content words, omission of auxiliary verbs, impaired inflection of verbs and tense marking, impaired syntactic comprehension and thematic argument structure, considered to reflect a problem mapping meaning from semantics to syntax, called thematic role assignment. Some see agrammatism as a central syntactic disorder (for review see Caplan, 1987; cf. Grodzinsky, 2000; DeBleser, Bayer, & Luzzatti, 1996; Perlman Lorch, 1989), but agrammatism is unlikely to be a unitary syntactic disorder. A range of underlying impairments have been proposed, including impaired working memory, verb and other lexical access deficits, argument assignment impairments, adaptation to impaired mechanisms, economy of effort, among others (see Perlman Lorch, 1989, for review). The form of agrammatism can evolve with recovery over time, changing the pattern of syntactic deficit from severe to milder forms (e.g., Guasti & Luzzatti, 2002) with features at later stages more likely reflecting adaptation and compensation. A motor element to agrammatism has been claimed or implied by a number of theories (e.g., Goodglass, 1976; Isserlin, 1922; Lenneberg, 1975), providing some support for theories suggesting a motor-gestural basis to syntax (e.g., Armstrong, Stokoe, & Wilcox, 1994).

Berndt and Caramazza (1980) attempted to redefine Broca's aphasia in terms of a combined, but dissociable, disorder with a distinct syntactic parsing impairment and a separate articulatory deficit. Their suggestion is that the non-fluent output characteristic of the syndrome and the problems with sentence comprehension are accounted for in terms of impairment by a "combination of two primary deficits and the operation of compensatory mechanisms that are employed in an attempt to establish communication despite existing deficits" (p. 271). The primary deficits "involve the syntactic parsing system with resulting agrammatism . . . [and] . . . severe impairment of the physiological mechanism responsible for the articulation of speech. These two deficits are theoretically and practically separate and, in principle, need not occur together" (p. 271). This account, however, does not go far enough for many who find it hard to think of a non-fluent agrammatic speaker who does not have some apraxia of speech. Agrammatism in English is often realized as a *telegraphic* or *telegrammic* style of speech, because speech is reminiscent of a telegram where there is a cost for every word used: in telegraphic speech function words are omitted, but the speaker retains the content words, the meaning-carrying words in the sentence. Agrammatism can occur in writing also.

Alexia/dyslexia and *agraphia/dysgraphia* or reading and writing impairments (see also Damico, this volume) are common and varied in aphasia, affecting single-word and connected sentence processing; a wide range of types have been described. *Repetition impairments* are also common in aphasia, where the speaker has particular problems in repeating the speech of others. While this may seem to present few problems in everyday communication, it can have a significant impact, and has important diagnostic and theoretical implications. Repetition impairment may also occur as a result of a number of problems, for instance, apraxia of speech, but where it dominates in the context of an otherwise fluent pattern of speech, the diagnosis of *conduction aphasia* is often made. Speakers with conduction aphasia are said to have specific problems with repetition because the route from their posterior speech reception system to their anterior speech production system is damaged. *Speech automatisms* and *stereotypies*, sometimes called *recurrent* or *recurring utterances*, are common in aphasic speech and can account for the majority of some severely aphasic speakers' utterances. Two different forms have been described: lexical, made up of real words, and non-lexical, where the utterance is commonly made up of repeated consonant–vowel combinations. Various examples of the lexical type include expletives, sentence stems, "yes" and "no," family names, high frequency and automatic expressions. Non-lexical types are simply repeated non-meaningful syllables such as "ta, ta." Speech automatism can occur in non-fluent aphasia and fluently produced stereotypies in fluent aphasia. *Comprehension impairments*, or impairments in understanding speech, are common for aphasic people and can occur for sentence meaning, single word meaning, and in reading.

There have been many attempts to show patterns and dissociations in the symptoms of aphasia and to identify types of aphasia within some classification or other (see Ardila, in press, for review). Many contemporary researchers and clinicians prefer not to use aphasia classifications at all, but to describe the impairments they observe in objective terms without reference to a classification system. It is hard to argue against this approach: all classifications have theoretical implications, but some basic groupings can help provide a basis for understanding. As indicated above, two major types of aphasia distinguished by the fluency dimension are Broca's aphasia, the major form of non-fluent aphasia, which is sometimes described as an *expressive* or *motor* aphasia, and Wernicke's aphasia, the archetypical fluent aphasia, a *receptive* or *sensory* aphasia. Broca's aphasia can be mild with some mild articulatory problems, word-finding difficulties, and mild agrammatism, or severe with prominent apraxia of speech, speech automatisms, and severe agrammatism. In milder forms, comprehension may be well preserved. Wernicke's aphasia, in contrast, can include significant fluently produced paraphasias and significant comprehension difficulties with jargon characterizing more severe forms.

However, aphasia does not occur in glorious isolation very often, and there are cognitive impairments that can commonly co-occur with aphasia. Language use, after all, is crucially dependent on other cognitive domains. We depend on action and motor processes (for instance, we have to move our phonoarticulatory mechanism in order to produce speech), memory (we need working memory, for instance, in order to store verbal material for short periods while we are processing it for production or comprehension), and we need perception in order to process visual and auditory information from the environment, as in reading and auditory processing of speech.

People with aphasia also often experience significant negative emotional and psychosocial changes, some of which are related to the nature of their brain damage and some of which are natural reactions to disability and are discussed more fully below. The nature of an individual's aphasic impairment is also significantly determined by what kind of injury they have and where it occurs in the brain. Most aphasia research is conducted with people who have experienced a cerebrovascular accident that affects anterior or posterior brain systems, or both, and subcortical as well as cortical regions. Aphasia is a cross-disciplinary concern; there are a range of ways of looking at language and language breakdown, and the view we take can obscure an alternative view. Speech and language pathologists and therapists, neurologists, cognitive and clinical neuropsychologists, and linguists are engaged in research and clinical work, but it is the speech-language pathologist or therapist who will be the most involved, responsible as they are for the overall assessment and management of people affected by aphasia. Contemporary perspectives of aphasia can be compared in Davis (2000), Hillis (2002), Rapp (2001).

Aphasia is universal, of course, although most of the research base in aphasia has been amassed from work conducted in German, English, and French. But aphasia manifests itself differently in different languages (Menn, Niemi, & Laine, 1996), reflecting the differences inherent in individual languages. This makes comparison of aphasia between languages difficult. An added issue, and one that aphasiologists recognize as increasingly important, is that the majority of the people in the world, including the aphasic people in the world, are bilingual or even multilingual.

Ribot (1881), in support for his theory that recent memories are more vulnerable to loss than earlier ones in aphasic people (Paradis, 1981), suggested that bilingual speakers who are aphasic will recover their native language first. This became known as Ribot's rule. Pitres (1895), in contrast, who conducted the first important work on aphasia in bilingual speakers, stated that the most recently learnt and most familiar language will recover first, and he based this view on detailed review of the research, and an analysis of eight cases. This is known as Pitres's rule (see Paradis, 1983 for translations of relevant papers). Pitres's pioneering work formed the basis for a broader appreciation of the range of recovery patterns that can be observed in bi- and multilingual speakers with aphasia (Paradis, 1981).

5   Recovery

Research has shown that most aphasic people make some recovery from acute stages, but most studies have used *operational* definitions of what recovery is, based on a group's performance on a standardized test battery (Basso, 1992; Code, 2001). Such operational definitions, like change in a total score on a psychometric battery, are used widely, but tell us little about the cognitive and neurological processes underlying recovery. One hypothesis is that recovery is best seen as neural *sparing* and distinguishes between "losses" which simply cannot be recovered, and behavioral deficits which are the result of attempts to shift control to undamaged neural systems. *Real* recovery requires the sparing of the underlying neural tissue. Behavioral *deficits* – the symptoms or features by which we recognize aphasia, for instance – are *compensatory*. Recovery for an individual therefore may occur through a combination of *restitution* of lost cognitive functions or *compensation* for lost functions.

A range of *prognostic factors* have been identified, and significant relationships are often found between demographic variables and outcome, but there is disagreement on the importance of many of them (Basso, 1992; Code, 2001). Such factors as severity of aphasia, aphasia type, site and extent of lesion, presence of dysarthria and bilateral damage, are clearly interrelated and probably interdependent (Code, 1987). There is considerable controversy as to whether some are useful theoretical constructs at all (e.g., type of aphasia, as discussed above). For some, like age, sex, and handedness, there is considerable disagreement between studies regarding their prognostic value (Basso, 1992; de Riesthal & Wertz, 2004).

One approach involves classification into aphasia type, as described above, with each type having a particular prognosis (e.g., Kertesz, 1979). However, between 30 and 70 percent of aphasic speakers are not classifiable (Basso et al., 1985). Many change type with recovery (Kertesz, 1979), and many do not recover in predictable ways. Fundamentally, milder types (conduction, transcortical, anomia) have the best prognosis, and severe types (global, Broca's, Wernicke's) have the least hopeful. However, aphasia type correlates highly with severity, and the argument has been made that it is initial severity that is the crucial variable (Schuell, 1965).

A small number of studies have used statistical approaches to prediction, entailing detailed analysis of test scores. Porch et al. (1980) used multiple regression with scores on the Porch Index of Communicative Abilities (the PICA) (Porch, 1967), and demonstrated that PICA scores at 1 month post-onset could predict an overall PICA score at 3, 6, and 12 months post-onset with correlations ranging from 0.74 to 0.94. Code, Rowley, and Kertesz (1994) trained neural networks to predict recovery for 90 aphasic participants tested at 1 and 12 months post-onset on the WAB (Kertesz, 1979). This study found that it was possible to predict recovery at 12 months to within 4–5 percent from scores at 1 month. However neither clinicians nor people with aphasia are just interested in this kind of "psychometric" recovery, but mainly in the ability to cope, to function, and to adjust, which is what really matters to the person with aphasia and their family: recovery of these aspects of communication disability have hardly been researched at all, although preliminary studies suggest a complex relationship between the severity of aphasia, its recovery and psychological or emotional status (Hemsley & Code, 1996; Kuroda & Kuroda, 2005), and scores on a range of standard aphasia measures fail to predict communication distress in aphasic people (Doyle et al., 2006).

6 Therapy

In this chapter we can only briefly review some issues in the treatment of aphasia and summarize some approaches to treatment. There is clear agreement in the field that treatment aimed at aphasic impairments can result in significant improvement for many aphasic people. At its best, therapy for impairments is tailor-made for the individual and guided by their pattern of impairment, but treatments aimed at shared impairment patterns can also be effective, and intense and extended treatment is most effective. It was thought that treatment had to be delivered during acute stages to be effective, but it is becoming recognized more recently that people with chronic aphasia can also show significant improvements (for review see Bhogal, Teasell, & Speechley, 2003; Davis, 2000; Robey, 1998; Robey et al., 1999; Wertz, 1995).

Bhogal et al. (2003) took the changes in mean scores from the large clinical trials that have been conducted over the years to investigate the outcomes of aphasia therapy after stroke. They also recorded the intensity of therapy in terms of the hours of therapy provided each week and the total hours of therapy. They found that those studies demonstrating a significant treatment effect had provided 8.8 hours of therapy per week for 11.2 weeks, compared to studies that did not find a significant effect of treatment providing only 2 hours per week for 22.9 weeks. Studies with a positive outcome had provided an average total of 98.4 hours of therapy and ineffective studies provided 43.6 hours of therapy. The total number of hours of therapy provided in a week was significantly correlated with greater improvement. The study concluded that intense therapy over a short amount of time can significantly improve outcomes of speech and language.

Treatment for aphasia is generally targeted at language impairments and/or communication disabilities – how the impairments impact on using communication in the aphasic person's everyday interactions with people in their community. Treatment aims either at *restoration* (or *restitution* or *reestablishment*) of lost functions or *compensation* (or *substitution*) for lost functions (Code, 2001). Therapists may employ specific *reorganizational* methods in an attempt to restore or compensate. Therapy utilizes aspects of education, learning theory, counseling, linguistics, neuro- and cognitive psychology. Following Howard and Hatfield (1987), we can classify most approaches into several main approaches, although in practice many clinicians adopt a fairly eclectic approach. Didactic methods aim to re-teach language using traditional and intuitive educational methods from child and foreign-language teaching. Behavioral methods such as repetition, imitation, modeling, prompting, and cuing are routinely used. These are often utilized in hierarchically organized therapy approaches for apraxia of speech and contemporary computer-based methods using systematic behavioral methods (see chapters in Code & Muller, 1989, 1995; and Helm-Estabrooks & Albert, 1991).

Language *stimulation*, a general approach to treatment originating with Wepman and Schuell (Schuell, Jenkins, & Jimenez-Pabon, 1964; Tesak & Code, 2008) is also universally used where functions are considered to be inaccessible, rather than lost. For this approach, language performance is seen to be impaired but language competence has survived. Therapy involves facilitating and stimulating language use. If improvement occurs it is because the aphasic individual facilitates and integrates what he or she already knows, not because they relearn lost vocabulary or syntactic forms. Intense auditory stimulation, requiring maximum response from the speaker and a great deal of repetition, facilitation, and various types of cuing are general features.

Luria's (1970) neuropsychological model is the foundation for an approach to the reorganization of function. On this model, intact functional subsystems can substitute for impaired subsystems. For instance, "articulograms," which use drawings of the lips producing particular combinations of speech sounds, have been developed for severe apraxia of speech. In this way, the speaker uses an intact visual route into the speech production system. A range of other approaches have been developed for the treatment of the apraxia of speech, which is common in non-fluent aphasia (Duffy, 2005; McNeil, 1997).

Approaches exist based on surviving right hemisphere processing; these are mostly reorganizational and aim to compensate for lost functions (Code 1987, 1994). Melodic intonation therapy (Helm-Estabrooks & Albert, 1991), for instance, tries to reestablish some speech in speakers with apraxic problems by reorganization of the speech production process using speech with exaggerated intonation, and there is a range of treatment studies using gesture and drawing (Helm-Estabrooks & Albert, 1991). Group therapy is often considered relevant for the development of everyday functional communication (see chapters in Chapey, 1987, 1994; Code & Muller 1989, 1995; Helm-Estabrooks & Albert, 1991).

Research in cognitive neuropsychology has strongly influenced the development of an hypothesis-driven single-case testing process based on information processing models. The claim is that standardized assessment batteries provide inadequate information on the specific deficits underlying individual impairment, but hypotheses developed by the clinician concerning impairments must be tested using psycholinguistically controlled tests, and such resources have been developed (Kay, Lesser, & Coltheart, 1992). An alternative view is that standardized and reliable tests should provide a baseline against which to measure change (Howard, Swinburn, & Porter, in press; Shallice, 1979). Aphasia test batteries may be best seen as standardized and reliable screening tests providing a basic profile, and can identify areas for more detailed investigation. Howard and Patterson (1990) suggest three strategies for impairment-based therapy inspired by the cognitive neuropsychological model: (1) re-teaching of the missing information, missing rules or procedures based on detailed testing; (2) teaching a different way to do the same task; (3) facilitating the use of impaired access routes. Research suggests that person- and deficit-specific treatment can improve performance in speakers that cannot be accounted for in terms of spontaneous recovery or non-specific effects (Howard & Hatfield, 1987).

7 Psychosocial and Emotional Response to Aphasia

Contemporary approaches based on social models have been developed in more recent times, as therapists have begun to acknowledge the psychosocial implications of aphasia. The aim is to attempt to improve the aphasic person's quality of communicative experience by adjusting the communicative and social environment of the aphasic person through the education and training of those who come into contact most with aphasic people (for instance, family, shop assistants, health professionals). Research shows that recovery and response to treatment are probably significantly influenced by emotional and psychosocial factors (Code & Herrmann, 2003; Hemsley & Code, 1996).

There are three broad factors to consider concerning the emotional and psychosocial effects of brain damage on the individual with aphasia. The *direct* effects of neurological damage on the neurophysical and neurochemical substrate of emotional processing; the *indirect* effects, which we should see as natural reactions to catastrophic personal circumstances; and the preexisting psychological balance, constitution, and ways of coping that an individual can harness.

"Psychosocial" refers to the social context of emotional experience. Most emotions are closely associated with our interactions with others, and this is what produces most of our happiness, sadness, anxiety, and so forth. Psychosocial adjustment to aphasia entails coming to terms with a unique set of life events. Because the aphasia affects others too, it has implications for the individual's whole social network, especially the immediate family (Code & Muller, 1992; Code & Herrmann, 2003; Duchan & Byng, 2004). The *disability* experienced by the aphasic person, rather than the impairment itself, is of particular importance. Studies investigating how psychosocial adjustment to aphasia is perceived have concluded that aphasic people and their families experience considerable stressful changes resulting from professional, social, and familial role changes, reductions in social contact, depression, loneliness, frustration, and aggression. The *value-dimensions* of psychosocial factors in our lives, like health, sexuality, career, creativity, partnership, intelligence, money, family, and so forth are markedly affected for aphasic people and their relatives (Herrmann & Wallesch, 1989).

There has been increased attention to direct emotional conditions recently, as interest in the cerebral representation of emotion and its relationship to language impairment has grown (see Code, 1987; Starkstein & Robinson, 1988, for reviews). Post-stroke depression is significantly correlated with anterior lesions, but does not appear to correlate with aphasia type. However, research also shows that with time since onset there is an increase in the interaction between extent of cognitive and physical impairment and depression (see Code & Herrmann, 2003, for review). But there has been little research that has sought to identify reactive emotional states following brain damage, and to separate them from direct effects. Herrmann, Bartels, and Wallesch (1993) found no differences in overall depression between acute and chronic aphasic groups, but acute speakers showed significantly higher ratings for physical signs of depression and disturbances of cyclic functions (e.g., sleep), generally considered direct effects, and an association between severity of depression and anterior lesions close to the frontal pole. Further, aphasic people with major depression (all acute) shared a common subcortical lesion. This suggests that the symptoms of depression in acute aphasic speakers may be caused more by the direct effects of the damage. At later times post-onset it is a more reactive depression that emerges.

One approach has been to view the depression accompanying aphasia within *the grief model* (Tanner & Gerstenberger, 1988), where individuals grieving for the loss of the ability to communicate move through stages of denial, anger, bargaining, depression, and acceptance. The extent to which aphasic people work through the stages of the model has not been investigated. The psychological processing of denial, bargaining, acceptance are less amenable to more objective forms of measurement, but have been investigated in aphasic persons through interpretive assessments, like personal construct therapy techniques (PCT), by Brumfitt (1985), who argues that the impact of becoming aphasic is seen as an event of such magnitude as to affect the way people construe their core role, and that the grief the aphasic individual feels concerns loss of the essential element of *oneself as a speaker*.

Studies of depression following brain damage have used factors considered symptomatic of depression, like diminished sleep and eating, restlessness and crying. These are the factors included in depression questionnaires, although these symptoms may be caused by physical illness and hospitalization and not directly related to mood state (Starkstein & Robinson, 1988). While the most reliable method of gaining information on the emotional state of people seems to be to ask them how they feel, language impairment plays a special role in the problem of identifying and measuring mood for aphasic individuals. The intersection of language with mood is further problematic because mood manifests itself externally through facial expression, voice quality, rate and amount of speech, gesture and posture, as well as linguistic expression and comprehension, all of which can be affected in impaired mood, and all of which can be affected by neurological damage.

Relatives and friends can assist to verify accuracy but determining mood in an individual with aphasia presents many problems. One approach to tapping inner feelings is to use the non-verbal Visual Analogue Mood Scale (VAMS). Despite its simplicity the VAMS has been shown to be reliable and valid (Folstein & Luria, 1973). The VAMS can be made more meaningful to severely aphasic speakers by substituting schematic faces for words (Stern & Bachman, 1991). Facial expression is the most direct method of communicating emotion and an ability that should be preserved in most aphasic individuals.

Conversation is a feature of interaction that strongly reflects the social function of language use. Conversations do not always serve to exchange transactional information but can be used to share gossip and engage in "social grooming," often consisting of significant amounts of formulaic and non-propositional talk. Conversations follow specific rules, however, and have systematic structure, and conversation analysis (CA), which is a range of methods that identifies and explores these rules and structures, has became increasingly relevant in the observation of aphasic speech behavior. Aspects of conversation that have been examined in most detail are turn taking, conversational repair, and the role of the aphasic person's communication partner (see the special issue of *Aphasiology* devoted to CA edited by Hesketh & Sage, 1999; and Goodwin, 2003).

Although aphasic speakers generally know the rules of turn taking in conversations, their impairments often hinder their attempts to end or take a turn because they may, for instance, produce too long a pause which is misunderstood by the communication partner as a request to take a turn, or the communication partner may interrupt because they are unable to understand the aphasic person (Lesser

& Milroy, 1993). Studies show that the relatives of aphasic speakers often speak *for* them, taking away their opportunity to take over an appropriate speaker role in a conversation.

Conversation repair refers to a variety of behaviors concerned with "trouble" in talk (Lesser & Milroy, 1993). A repair may occur when a conversationalist identifies a problem in their own talk or the other's talk, or because of a failure of understanding, and studies have been conducted on repair in aphasic speakers and their conversational partners, and the extent to which conversation participants are able to solve problems together (Ferguson, 1994; Lesser & Algar, 1995). Conversation analysis considers the "interaction as a result of cooperation between the aphasic and the non-aphasic conversation participants" (Perkins, 1998, p. 77), where the communication partner of the aphasic person makes a significant and essential contribution to the success of a conversation. It has been found that speaking slowly and clearly and using simple sentence structures, while avoiding abrupt changes in topic, and minimizing background noises, can make a significant contribution to the success of the conversational exchange (see Perkins, 2003, for details). Such studies of conversation in aphasia are making an important contribution to compensatory approaches and to the social reintegration of aphasic people into their communities.

With an improved understanding of the social context of communication and its importance to the reintegration of aphasic people to the community, approaches have developed that focus on the communication interaction, rather than the aphasic impairments, and other speakers in the communicative exchange, like relatives, health care professionals, shop keepers, policemen. The aim of an aphasic communicator, after all, is the same as that of a non-aphasic communicator, that is, successful communication. Research indicates that targeting these "conversational partners" who have intact resources, rather than the aphasic person with reduced resources, can make a significant contribution to improved communication (Kagan et al., 2001; Togher et al., 2004).

REFERENCES

Alzheimer's Society (2007). *Dementia UK.* London: Alzheimer's Society. Retrieved May 2009, from www.alzheimers.org.uk

Annegers, J. F., Grabow, J. D., Kurland, L. T., & Laws, E. R. (1980). The incidence, causes, and secular trends of head trauma in Olmsted-County, Minnesota, 1935–1974. *Neurology* 30, 912–19.

Ardila, A. (in press). A proposed reinterpretation and reclassification of the aphasia syndromes. *Aphasiology.*

Armstrong, D. F., Stokoe, W. C., & Wilcox, S. E. (1994). Signs of the origin of syntax. *Current Anthropology* 35, 349–68.

Au, R., Albert, M. L., & Obler, L. K. (1988). The relation of aphasia to dementia. *Aphasiology* 2, 161–73.

Basso, A. (1992). Prognostic factors in aphasia. *Aphasiology* 6, 337–48.

Basso, A., Lecours, A.-R., Moraschini, S., & Vanier, M. (1985). Anatomococlinical correlations of the aphasias as defined through computerized tomography: exceptions. *Brain & Language* 26, 201–9.

Berndt, R. S. & Caramazza, A. (1980). A redefinition of the syndrome of Broca's aphasia: Implications for a neuropsychological model of language. *Applied Psycholinguistics* 1, 225–78.

Bhogal, S. K., Teasell, R., & Speechley, M. (2003). Intensity of aphasia therapy, impact on recovery. *Stroke* 34, 987–93.

Broca, P. (1861). Remarques sur le siège de la faculté du langage articulé, suivies d'une observation d'aphémie (perte de la parole). *Bulletins et memoires de la Société Anatomique de Paris*, XXXVI, 330–57.

Bronner, L. L., Kanter, D. S., & Manson, J. E. (1995). Medical progress – primary prevention of stroke. *New England Journal of Medicine* 333, 1392–1400.

Brumfitt, S. (1985). The use of repertory grids with aphasic people. In N. Beail (ed.), *Repertory grid techniques and personal constructs* (pp. 89–106). London: Croom Helm.

Brust, J. M. M., Shafer, S. Q., Richer, R. W., & Brown, B. (1976). Aphasia in acute strock. *Stroke* 7, 167–74.

Caplan, D. (1987). *Neurolinguistics and linguistic aphasiology*. Cambridge: Cambridge University Press.

Chapey, R. (ed.) (1987). *Language intervention strategies in adult aphasia*, 2nd ed. Baltimore, MD: Williams & Wilkins.

Chapey, R. (ed.) (1994). *Language intervention strategies in adult aphasia*, 3rd ed. Baltimore, MD: Williams & Wilkins.

Code, C. (1987). *Language aphasia and the right hemisphere*. Chichester, UK: Wiley.

Code, C. (1994). The role of the right hemisphere in the treatment of aphasia. In R. Chapey (ed.), *Language intervention strategies in adult aphasia* (pp. 380–6). Baltimore, MD: Williams & Wilkins.

Code, C. (2001). Multifactorial processes in recovery from aphasia: developing the foundations for a multilevelled framework. *Brain & Language* 77, 25–44.

Code, C. & Herrmann, M. (2003). The relevance of emotional and psychosocial factors in aphasia to rehabilitation. *Neuropsychological Rehabilitation* 13, 109–32.

Code, C. & Lodge, B. (1987). Language in dementia of recent referral. *Age & Ageing* 16, 366–72.

Code, C. & Muller, D. J. (eds.) (1989). *Aphasia therapy*. London: Whurr.

Code, C. & Muller, D. J. (1992). *The Code–Muller protocols: Assessing perceptions of psychosocial adjustment to aphasia and related disorders*. London: Whurr.

Code, C. & Muller, D. J. (eds.) (1995). *The treatment of aphasia: From theory to practice*. London: Whurr.

Code, C., Rowley, D. T., & Kertesz, A. (1994). Predicting recovery from aphasia with connectionist networks: preliminary comparisons with multiple regression. *Cortex* 30, 527–32.

Davis, G. A. (2000). *Aphasiology: Disorders and clinical practice*. Needham Heights, MA: Allyn & Bacon.

DeBleser, R., Bayer, J., & Luzzatti, C. (1996). Linguistic theory and morphosyntactic impairments in German and Italian aphasics. *Journal of Neurolinguistics* 9, 175–85.

Doyle, P. J., Matthews, C., Mikolic, J. M., Hula, W., & McNeil, M. R. (2006). Do measures of language impairment predict patient-reported communication difficulty and distress as measured by the *Burdon of Stroke Scales (BOSS)*? *Aphasiology* 20, 349–61.

Duchan, J. F. & Byng, S. (eds.) (2004). *Challenging aphasia therapies: Broadening the discourse and extending the boundaries*. Hove, UK: Psychology Press.

Duffy, J. R. (2005). *Motor speech disorders*, 2nd ed. St. Louis: Elsevier Mosby.

Ebrahim, S. & Redfren, J. (1999). *Stroke care – a matter of chance*. London: The Stroke Association.

Eggert, G. H. (ed.) (1977). *Wernicke's work on aphasia. A sourcebook and review*. The Hague: Mouton Publishers.

Ferguson, A. (1994). The influence of aphasia, familiarity and activity on conversational repair. *Aphasiology* 8, 143–57.

Folstein, M. F. & Luria, R. (1973). Reliability, validity, and clinical application of the visual analogue mood scale. *Psychological Medicine* 3, 479–86.

Fuh, J. L., Wang, S. J., Larson, E. B., & Liu, H. C. (1996). Prevalence of stroke in Kinmen. *Stroke* 27, 1338–41.

Geschwind, N. (1965). Disconnexion syndromes in animals and man. *Brain* 88, 237–94; 585–644.

Goodglass, H. (1976). *Agrammatism*. In H. Whitaker & H. A. Whitaker (eds.), *Studies in neurolinguistics*, vol. 1. New York: Academic Press.

Goodglass, H. & Kaplan, E. (1972). *The assessment of aphasia and related disorders*. Philadelphia: Lea & Febiger.

Goodwin, C. (ed.) (2003). *Conversation and brain damage*. Oxford: Oxford University Press.

Grodzinsky, Y. (2000). The neurology of syntax: language use without Broca's area. *Behavioral and Brain Sciences* 23, 1–21.

Guasti, M. T. & Luzzatti, C. (2002). Syntactic breakdown and recovery of clausal structure in agrammatism. *Brain & Cognition* 48, 385–91.

Helm-Estabrooks, N. & Albert, M. L. (1991). *Manual of aphasia therapy*. Austin, TX: Pro-Ed.

Hemsley, G. & Code, C. (1996). Interactions between recovery in aphasia, emotional and psychosocial factors in subjects with aphasia, their significant others and speech pathologists. *Disability & Rehabilitation* 18, 567–84.

Herrmann, M. & Wallesch, C.-W. (1989). Psychosocial changes and adjustment with chronic and severe non-fluent aphasia. *Aphasiology* 3, 513–26.

Herrmann, M., Bartels, C., & Wallesch, C. W. (1993). Depression in acute and chronic aphasia: Symptoms, pathoanatomical-

clinical correlations and functional implications. *Journal of Neurology, Neurosurgery and Psychiatry* 56, 672–8.

Hesketh, A. & Sage, K. (eds.) (1999). Special issue: Conversation analysis. *Aphasiology* 13, 329–444.

Hier, D. B., Yoon, W. B., Mohr, J. P., Price, T. R., & Wolf, P. A. (1994). Gender and aphasia in the stroke data bank. *Brain and Language* 47, 155–67.

Hillis, A. E. (ed.) (2002). *The handbook of adult language disorders*. New York: Psychology Press.

Howard, D. & Hatfield, F. M. (1987). *Aphasia therapy: Historical and contemporary issues*. London: Lawrence Erlbaum Associates.

Howard, D. & Patterson, K. (1990). Methodological issues in neuropsychological therapy. In X. Seron & G. Deloche (eds.), *Cognitive approaches in neuropsychological rehabilitation* (pp. 39–64). London: Lawrence Erlbaum Associates.

Howard, D., Swinburn, K., & Porter, G. (in press). Putting the CAT out: what the *Comprehensive Aphasia Test* has to offer. *Aphasiology*.

Isserlin, M. (1922). Über Agrammatismus. *Zeitschrift für die gesamte Neurologie und Psychiatrie* 75, 332–410.

Kagan, A., Black, S., Duchan, J., Simmons Mackie, N., & Square, P. (2001). Training volunteers as conversational partners using "Supported Conversation with Adults with Aphasia" (SCA): a controlled trial. *Journal of Speech, Language, and Hearing Research* 44, 624–38.

Katz, R., Hallowell, B., Code, C., Armstrong, E. Roberst, P., Pound, C., & Katz, L. (2000). A multi-national comparison of aphasia management practices. *International Journal of Language & Communication Disorders* 35, 303–14.

Kay, J., Lesser, R., & Coltheart, M. (1992). *Psycholinguistic assessments of language processing in aphasia.* Hove, UK: Lawrence Erlbaum Associates.

Kertesz, A. (1979). *Aphasia and associated disorders.* New York: Grune & Stratton.

Kertesz, A. (1982). *The Western Aphasia Battery.* New York: Grune & Stratton:.

Klein, K. (ed.) (1995). *Aphasia community group manual.* New York: National Aphasia Association.

Kuroda, Y. & Kuroda, R. (2005). The relationship between verbal communication and observed psychological status in aphasia: preliminary findings. *Aphasiology* 19, 849–59.

Langton Hewer, R. (1997). The epidemiology of disabling neurological disorders. In R. Greenwood, M. Barnes, T. McMillan, & C. Ward (eds.), *Neurological rehabilitation* (pp. 3–12). Hove, UK: Psychology Press.

Lenneberg, E. (1975). In search of a dynamic theory of aphasia. In E. Lenneberg & E. Lenneberg (eds.), *Foundations of language development: A multidisciplinary approach*, vol. 2. New York: Academic Press.

Lesser, R. & Algar, L. (1995). Towards combining the cognitive neuropsychological and the pragmatic in aphasia therapy. *Neuropsychological Rehabilitation* 5, 67–92.

Lesser, R. & Milroy, L. (1993). *Linguistics and aphasia: Psycholinguistic and pragmatic aspects of intervention.* London: Longman.

Lichtheim, L. (1885). On aphasia. *Brain* 7, 433–85.

Luria, A. R. (1970). *Traumatic aphasia.* The Hague: Mouton.

Luzzatti, C., Willmes, K., Taricco, M., Colombo, C., & Chiesa, G. (1989). Language disturbances after severe head-injury – do neurological or other associated cognitive disorders influence type, severity and evolution of the verbal impairment? A preliminary report. *Aphasiology* 3, 643–53.

MacDonald, S., Togher, L., & Code, C. (1999). *Communication disorders in traumatic brain injury.* Hove, UK: Psychology Press.

McNeil, M. R. (ed.) (1997). *Clinical management of sensorimotor speech disorders.* New York: Thieme.

Menn, L., Niemi, J., & Laine, M. (eds.) (1996). Special issue: Comparative aphasiology. *Aphasiology* 10, 523–656.

Paradis, M. (1981). Acquired aphasia in bilingual speakers. In M. Taylor Sarno (ed.), *Acquired aphasia*, 3rd ed. (pp. 531–49). San Diego: Academic Press.

Paradis, M. (ed.) (1983). *Readings on aphasia in bilinguals and polyglots.* Montreal: Marcel Didier.

Pedersen, P. M., Jorgensen, H. S., Nakayama, H., Raaschou, H. O., & Olsen, T. S. (1995). Aphasia in acute stroke: Incidence, determinants, and recovery. *Annals of Neurology* 38, 659–66.

Perkins, L. (1998). Die Anwendung der Konversationsanalyse auf Aphasie [The application of conversation analysis to aphasia]. In I. M. Ohlendorf, W. Widdig, & J.-P. Malin (eds.), *Arbeiten mit Texten in der Aphasietherapie. 6. Rhein-Ruhr-Meeting in Bonn [Working with texts in aphasia therapy. 6th Rhine-Ruhr-meeting in Bonn]* (pp. 75–90). Freiburg, Germany: Hochschul Verlag.

Perkins, L. (2003). Negotiating repair in aphasic conversation: Interactional issues. In C. Goodwin (ed.), *Conversation and brain damage* (pp. 147–62). Oxford: Oxford University Press.

Perlman Lorch, M. (1989). Agrammatism and paragrammatism. In C. Code (ed.), *The characteristics of aphasia* (pp. 75–88). Hove, UK: Psychology Press.

Pitres, A. L. (1895). Etude sur l'aphasie chez les polyglottes. *Revue de Medicine* 15, 873–99. (Translated in Paradis, 1983, pp. 26–49.)

Porch, B. E. (1967). *The Porch Index of Communicative Ability.* Palo Alto: Consulting Psychologists Press.

Porch, B. E., Collins, M., Wertz, R. T., & Friden, T. P. (1980). Statistical prediction of change in aphasia. *Journal of Speech & Hearing Research* 23, 312–21.

Rapp, B. (ed.) (2001). *The handbook of cognitive neuropsychology.* New York: Psychology Press.

Ribot, T. (1881). *Les maladies de la mémoire.* Paris: G. Baillère.

de Riesthal, M. & Wertz, R. T. (2004). Prognosis for aphasia: relationship between selected biographical and behavioural variables and outcome and improvement. *Aphasiology* 18, 899–915.

Robey, R. R. (1998). A meta-analysis of clinical outcomes in the treatment of aphasia. *Journal of Speech, Language, and Hearing Research* 41, 172–87.

Robey, R. R., Schultz, M. C., Crawford, A. B., & Sinner, C. A. (1999). Single-subject clinical-outcome research: designs, data, effect sizes, and analyses. *Aphasiology* 13, 445–73.

Sarno, M. T., Buonaguro, A., & Levita, E. (1986). Characteristics of verbal impairment in closed head injury patients. *Archives of Physical Medical and Rehabilitation* 67, 400–5.

Schuell, H. (1965). *The Minnesota Test for the Differential Diagnosis of Aphasia.* Minneapolis: University of Minnesota Press.

Schuell, H. M., Jenkins, J. J., & Jimenez-Pabon, E. (1964). *Aphasia in adults: Diagnosis, prognosis and treatment.* New York: Harper and Row.

Shallice, T. (1979). Case study approach in neuropsychological research. *Journal of Clinical Neuropsychology* 1, 183–211.

Starkstein, S. E. & Robinson, R. G. (1988). Aphasia and depression. *Aphasiology* 2, 1–20.

Stern, R. A. & Bachman, D. L. (1991). Depressive symptoms following stroke. *American Journal of Psychiatry* 148, 351–6.

Sudlow, C. L. M. & Warlow, C. P. (1997). Comparable studies of the incidence of stroke and its pathological types: Results from an international collaboration. *Stroke* 28, 491–9.

Tanner, D. C. & Gerstenberger, D. L. (1988). The grief response in neuropathologies of speech and language. *Aphasiology* 2, 79–84.

Tesak, J. & Code, C. (2008). *Milestones in the history of aphasia.* Hove, UK: Psychology Press.

Togher, L., MacDonald, S., Code, C., & Grant, S. (2004). Training communication partners of people with TBI: a randomized controlled trial. *Aphasiology* 18, 313–35.

Warlow, C. P. (1998). Epidemiology of stroke. *The Lancet* 352, (suppl III), 1–4.

Webster, J., Franklin, S., & Howard, D. (2004). Investigating the sub-processes involved in the production of thematic structure: an analysis of four people with aphasia. *Aphasiology* 18, 47–68.

Weisenburg, T. H. & McBride, K. E. (1935). *Aphasia: a clinical and psychological study.* New York: The Commonwealth Fund.

Wernicke, C. (1874). *Der Aphasische Symptomencomplex. Eine psychologische Studie auf anatomischer Basis.* Breslau: Cohn & Weigert.

Wertz, R. T. (1995). Efficacy. In C. Code & D. J. Muller (eds.), *The treatment of aphasia: From theory to practice.* London: Whurr.

Part III Speech Disorders

15 Children with Speech Sound Disorders

SARA HOWARD

1 Introduction

One thing that is clear about developmental speech disorders is that they form a significant proportion of the communication difficulties encountered by speech-language pathologists (SLPs) working with children (Fox, Dodd, & Howard, 2002). Some developmental speech disorders have an identifiable etiology (e.g., cleft lip and palate, cerebral palsy), but for many children who struggle to produce acceptable or intelligible speech there is no obvious reason for their difficulties. It is this latter category of disorder that we will focus on in this chapter. Even with this limitation, we are still contemplating a field of considerable breadth, both in terms of the types of speech difficulties encountered, and also in terms of the differences of theoretical and clinical approaches to their identification, assessment, and intervention. Crucial to our understanding of the field is the heterogeneity of the speakers and the speech data we might expect to encounter. As Elbert (1997, p. 55) observes: "The key word is individual. The population of children with phonology disorders is not a homogeneous population."

2 Nature

2.1 Prevalence and incidence

Knowing that there is a large number of children with speech sound disorders is one thing; working out actual numbers is another. Making reliable estimates of the prevalence and incidence of developmental speech difficulties is notoriously difficult (Law et al., 2000; McKinnon, McLeod, & Reilly, 2007), with methodological differences related to age, inclusion and exclusion criteria, and approaches to sampling and screening all serving to create significant discrepancies between various epidemiological studies. A systematic review of the literature covering the period 1967 to 1997 (Law et al., 2000), for example, reports prevalence figures

The Handbook of Language and Speech Disorders, First Edition. Edited by Jack S. Damico, Nicole Müller, and Martin J. Ball. © 2013 Blackwell Publishing Ltd except for editorial material and organization © 2013 Jack S. Damico, Nicole Müller, Martin J. Ball. Published 2013 by Blackwell Publishing Ltd.

for children with speech delay ranging from as low as 2.3 percent to an upper figure of 24.6 percent.

Even when we distinguish developmental speech difficulties of unknown origin from other types of difficulties, there is still the issue of co-morbidity (Shriberg, Tomblin, & McSweeny, 1999). Schuele (2004) suggests that over half of all children referred to a speech and language clinic with speech problems also have a language impairment of some kind. This is an important issue, not least because the two groups of children are likely to have different etiologies and prognoses, and children with combined speech and language problems are less likely to have their problems resolve spontaneously with age than children who have a primary speech disorder (Lewis, Freebairn, & Taylor, 2002).

2.2   *Perspectives on developmental speech sound disorders*

It is a reflection of the heterogeneity of the population of children with speech sound disorders that there exist a wide range of theoretical and clinical approaches to them, encompassing numerous classificatory terms and descriptors.

Stackhouse and Wells (1997) outline three main theoretical perspectives – medical, linguistic, and psycholinguistic. The first two of these overlap to a large degree with Shriberg's (1994) use of the terms "etioliogic/clinical inferential" and "descriptive-linguistic" respectively. To these we should now also add the "biopsychosocial" perspective discussed by McLeod (2006). These different perspectives partly reflect a historical timecourse in speech science research, with medical views prevailing throughout the nineteenth century and the first half of the twentieth century, until linguistic approaches began to emerge in the 1960s and 1970s, to be followed by a psycholinguistic perspective from the 1990s onward. This is not to imply that each approach has superseded the previous one: rather in current practice they are seen as complementary, and each continues to be developed and extended in different ways.

The medical perspective on childhood speech difficulties is particularly concerned with matters of diagnosis, etiology, and, to an extent, prognosis. Its primacy for much of the nineteenth and twentieth centuries reflects the fact that many of the earliest influential professionals in the field had a medical background (Weiner, 1986). Speech disorders were originally seen as having a strictly medical and articulatory basis, as summed up, for example, by Holmes (1879, p. 181): "the tongue or lips may be naturally clumsy and awkward in their movements." The medical perspective, however, encountered a problem when it became increasingly clear that a large proportion of children's speech problems could not be linked satisfactorily to a specific cause. In response to this quandary, a new diagnostic distinction was proposed, as described by Travis and Rasmus (1931, p. 196): "On the basis of determined or inferred organic pathology and the lack of such we classify disorders . . . as organic and functional respectively," paving the way for the term "functional articulation disorder" (FAD), which, though now falling into disuse, proved enduringly popular for much of the twentieth century. However, current research within a medical model, which looks at speech difficulties from genetic, neurological, and neurophysiological perspectives, shows significant promise as a means of providing detailed etiological information for many problems currently classified as having unknown origin (Hayiou-Thomas, 2008; Maassen et al., 2006; Lewis et al., 2006).

The second major theoretical perspective on child speech sound disorders, that of linguistics, emerged gradually in the 1960s as researchers began to observe that even atypical sound systems generally displayed their own internal consistency. Thus Applegate (1961, p. 193) speaks of "an autonomous system with well-developed rules," and Haas (1963, p. 240) comments on the subject of his study that "the boy has settled down to a language system of his own." In the light of this growing body of linguistic investigation, by the time of Ingram's landmark publication on phonological disability in children, he was able to remark, "virtually every study that has undertaken a linguistic analysis of a child with a phonological disability has revealed system in the child's speech" (Ingram, 1976, p. 99). Ingram's work, and complementary work by Grunwell in the UK (Grunwell, 1975, 1981), as well as demonstrating systematic phonological behavior in children with atypical speech production, introduced the concept of phonological processes (Stampe, 1969, 1979) as a useful framework for speech assessment and intervention. So influential has process-based phonological analysis been that it is arguably still the most commonly used approach in speech pathology today, despite some significant reservations which have arisen about its clinical application over the intervening period (Miccio & Scarpino, 2008), and despite a range of other phonological theories which have subsequently also made significant contributions to our understanding of phonetic and phonological behavior in atypical speech production, including Optimality Theory (Gierut & Morrisette, 2005), Gestural Phonology (Kent, 1997; van Lieshout & Goldstein, 2008); and a range of non-linear approaches (Ball, 2008; Bernhardt & Stemberger, 1998; Bernhardt & Stoel-Gammon, 1994).

One of the most powerful influences of the linguistic-phonological perspective was a radical shift away from consideration of articulatory and motor factors, to the construal of children's speech difficulties as essentially cognitive in nature, related to problems with the mental organization and selection of appropriate speech sound within a structured system. Howell and Dean (1991, p. 11), for example, echo a widely held view that "most phonologically disordered children appear to have no difficulty in articulating speech sounds." Even so, a number of detailed phonetic investigations were carried out during this period which uncovered subtle articulatory behaviors in children's atypical speech production, operating within various parameters including VOT (voice onset time) and voicing (Maxwell & Weismer, 1982), vowel length (Weismer, Dinnsen, & Elbert, 1981), place of articulation and lingual-palatal contact patterns (Forrest et al., 1994; Gibbon, 1990; Howard, 1994), which suggested the speaker's intention to realize phonological distinctions, however unsuccessfully this was communicated to the listener. Thus, clinical phonetics and phonology began to operate to some extent in two different spheres, one using perceptual analysis to identify largely phoneme-based phonological processes operating to simplify the child's sound system and word structures; the other using a range of instrumental phonetic techniques to identify perceptually inaccessible behaviors which are not necessarily compatible with simple phoneme-based analyses. Both approaches, however, are firmly focused on the description of spoken output and do not make strong claims about the explanations for the observed atypical behaviors.

While medical and linguistic perspectives on developmental speech disorders have existed for many years, the psycholinguistic perspective is a more recent addition to our fund of ways in which to conceptualize and investigate speech difficulties. Where the medical perspective aims to classify speech disorders and the linguistic perspective aims to describe the phonetic and phonological behaviors found in children with atypical speech production, the psycholinguistic perspective, as Stackhouse and Wells (1997) note, aims to explain speech difficulties in terms of the breakdowns in the multiple, interrelated psycholinguistic processes involved in the perception, storage, and production of speech. Evolving from earlier "box-and-arrow" models of speech processing (Hewlett, 1990; Menn & Matthei, 1992), perhaps the most well-known and well-used approach in the field of speech pathology is the psycholinguistic model devised by Stackhouse and Wells (1997), which spans input, representation, and output and can be applied to both speech and writing. From this model Stackhouse and Wells devised a speech processing profile which breaks down the overall process of using spoken (and written) language into a series of discrete skills which can, consequently, be individually assessed by discrete tasks.

Rather than explicitly seeking to identify different subcategories of developmental speech disorder and assign children to these mutually exclusive categories, a psycholinguistic approach emphasizes the heterogeneity of developmental speech difficulties to the extent that each child is seen as an individual, with an individual profile of strengths and weaknesses.

One consequence of a psycholinguistic perspective is that it shifts the focus away from speech output, giving equal attention to the input skills involved in speech processing and to the ways in which these input skills might contribute to the formation of the child's underlying lexical representations. In addition to the traditional evaluation of speech production, auditory perception, and auditory discrimination, the psycholinguistic approach has added a particular focus on metaphonological skills and on the child's awareness of the internal phonological structure of words. Significantly, phonological awareness (PA) may distinguish between different children with similar-sounding speech production. It has been suggested that many children with speech output difficulties may have PA problems (Bird & Bishop, 1992), but also that not all of them will (Hesketh et al., 2000), and that children with underlying problems with PA may require different intervention from those with a relatively discrete speech output problem.

An added advantage of the psycholinguistic approach is that it can offer a unified account of both speech and literacy difficulties, and may be able to identify covert speech processing difficulties in older children who no longer have perceptually atypical speech production, but who may find aspects of reading and writing more challenging than their peers.

Stackhouse and Wells (1997) have also developed a "stage" model of phonological development which permits the application of psycholinguistic analysis to children of different ages and at different stages of speech development. The approach has also been applied to children with persisting speech difficulties (Pascoe, Stackhouse, & Wells, 2006), to connected speech (Pascoe, Stackhouse, & Wells, 2005), and to difficulties with prosody and intonation (Catterall et al., 2006).

It should be stressed that the three perspectives discussed here are complementary and not mutually exclusive. Although historically the linguistic and psycholinguistic perspectives were originally motivated by perceived shortcomings in previous approaches, currently much illuminating work on developmental speech difficulties combines aspects of all three perspectives.

2.3   Classification and subgrouping

Efforts have long been made to subcategorize the population of children with developmental speech sound disorders (see, for example, Blanton, 1916). In recent years, a number of schemes have had significant impact on the field. From a linguistic perspective, phonological process analysis offered the possibility of classifying children's speech output within a developmental framework. Grunwell (1982) thus distinguished between normal development (the presence of phonological processes typical for a child's chronological age) and phonological disability. The latter was further subdivided into "Persisting Normal Processes," where children continue to use the phonological processes more appropriate to a younger child (equivalent to Ingram's (1976) category of "phonological delay"), "Chronological Mismatch," where a child's speech evidences a combination of phonological patterns, some characteristic of early child speech and some reflecting more advanced phonological development, and "Unusual and Idiosyncratic Processes," where children use processes not found in typical speech development (Ingram's (1976) "phonological deviance"). This subclassification corresponds to the broad and clinically influential distinction of phonological delay versus phonological disorder.

More recently, but also using a descriptive-linguistic approach, Dodd and colleagues (Dodd, 1995; Dodd et al., 2006b) have proposed a four-category system: Articulatory Disorder, Phonological Delay, Consistent Phonological Disorder, and Inconsistent Phonological Disorder, encompassing both a developmental perspective (with delay being by far the most common speech difficulty encountered) and also a particular focus on consistency and variability in speech output. Dodd hypothesizes that these categories reflect different underlying speech processing difficulties, and a growing body of research suggests that there is cross-linguistic support for the classificatory system (Fox & Dodd, 2001; Goldstein & Iglesias, 1996; Hua & Dodd, 2000; So & Dodd, 1994; Topbaþ, 2006), and there is also some evidence of differential literacy outcomes for children in the different subgroups (Leitão & Fletcher, 2004).

The other extremely influential classificatory system of recent years has been the SDCS (the Speech Disorders Classification System), the work of Shriberg and colleagues (Shriberg, 1994; Shriberg et al., 1997). Using a combination of information from the medical, linguistic, and psychosocial domains, as well as consideration of the child's age and the developmental trajectory of the disorder, the authors propose that most speech problems can be described as one of a number of subtypes of delay (of known or unknown origin). Further subcategories accommodate different types of residual speech errors in older children (with, it is hypothesized, different etiologies).

3   Assessment

3.1   Sampling

Tyler and Tolbert (2002, p. 219) express a universal challenge in the assessment of children's speech sound problems: "Typically there is a limited amount of time in clinical settings for the examination of children's speech and language skills." With this constrained timeframe being anything from 90 minutes (Tyler & Tolbert, 2002) to 45 (Khan, 2002), speech-language pathologists are under pressure from the outset to make maximally efficient and effective use of every minute, including the time needed to put parents and child at their ease in what may be an unfamiliar and potentially stressful situation. A clear idea of the material and information to be gathered and of the overall aims of the session is an obvious prerequisite. A number of complementary aims may exist for any specific session related to issues of identification, diagnosis, intervention planning, and information sharing.

While the identification of the presence of a speech problem is important in terms of eligibility for therapy, an overall assessment of the severity of the problem and of its likely educational and psychosocial effects may also be necessary at this stage in order to make decisions about prioritization if access to therapy is limited. In addition, Davis (2005, p. 8) reminds us that as well as issues of clinical diagnosis and estimates of severity, our assessment should also include "the larger context of each child's communication profile," which will include family and cultural factors.

Even 90 minutes is not long when we consider the range of issues and information which need to be covered. Whilst the focus, given a referral for some kind of speech problem, will be mainly on speech production and processing, other areas must also be covered. Given the common co-morbidity of speech and language problems, some kind of formal or informal language screening will generally be necessary. Equally, we will not wish to limit our assessment to the production of specific sound segments, but will also want to give at least cursory attention to voice quality and fluency, as well as to prosodic issues (including stress, rhythm, and intonation patterns), and to an evaluation of overall intelligibility. Impressionistic assessment of hearing, together with a brief examination of the structure and function of peripheral vocal tract, may also be included.

Nevertheless, the main focus of the assessment will be on the child's speech output and speech processing abilities and difficulties. The central component of a pediatric speech assessment is typically some sort of standardized or non-standardized test of speech output, based on the elicitation of a set of single words by picture- or object-naming. Where issues of eligibility and access to treatment are involved, it will likely be important that the test chosen is standardized. Many assessments currently exist; McLeod (2007) constitutes a rich source of information about assessments for developmental speech disorders in varieties of English and many other languages.

Selecting a standardized assessment and choosing what further tests to carry out will rest partly on decisions about the number of sounds, words, utterances, and contexts that it is feasible and/or desirable to collect. Published tests vary from those which sample somewhere around 50 words (e.g., the GFTA-3, Goldman & Fristoe, 2000) to those which sample 100–200 (e.g., PACS, Grunwell, 1985). Underlying this variation is a difference in aims in terms of the exhaustiveness of the evaluation and of the practical tension expressed by Khan (2002, p. 253) as "thoroughness against efficiency." Generally, tests with larger numbers of words or items seek to capture either or both a greater number of contexts for individual sounds (e.g., syllable initial, syllable final, word initial, within-word, etc.) and a greater number of tokens of the same word, in order to identify important information about the consistency or variability of the child's speech output (Ingram & Ingram, 2001). It may well be important to assess vowel production as well as consonant production, and to detect any consonant–vowel interactions or constraints operating in the child's system (Bates, Watson, & Scobbie, 2002). It is also frequently recommended that a sample of connected speech is collected for the purposes of evaluating intelligibility, as well as considering issues of prosody, voice quality, and the severity of the problem. Significantly, however, a connected speech sample is also crucial at the segmental level if, as is often observed, there is a perceptible gap between the accuracy or intelligibility of the child's speech in single-word production versus spontaneous speech. For some children unusual phonetic and phonological behaviors at word boundaries have a detrimental effect on their speech output, but such problems cannot be identified if assessment is restricted to consideration of single words (Howard, 2004, 2007; Wells, 1994).

Whereas traditionally the child's speech output has been the primary, and sometimes sole, focus of assessment, nowadays it is increasingly common to consider issues of phonological awareness and of the individual input and output processing skills which contribute to a child's speech production. Stackhouse and Wells (1997) describe a psycholinguistic framework of speech processing skills, together with suggestions for methods of assessment, and Stackhouse et al. (2007) provide an extensive battery of assessment materials for psycholinguistic profiling.

An important issue with regard to collecting a speech sample is how best to record or capture the data. Generally speech-language pathologists combine real-time transcription during the assessment session with an audio or video recording. Live observation obviously provides the highest-quality exposure to the child's speech output, but of course its overriding drawback is its transitory nature. Everything happens only once and is gone forever. And the challenges of making accurate and informative phonetic transcriptions under such conditions, despite this being common clinical practice, are not to be underestimated. Amorosa et al. (1985), for example, argue from experimental evidence that live transcription typically contains many errors and omissions and cannot provide a reliable basis for even the most superficial of phonological analyses of atypical speech data. This is not to say that transcription from audio or video recordings is without its very real challenges (for summaries of the challenges and pitfalls of clinical transcription see Kent, 1996; Howard & Heselwood, 2002), but a recording allows for more considered and more detailed evaluation of the data.

Accurate transcription is important, as Kent and Ball (1997) remind us that any phonological analysis is only as good as the phonetic data upon which it is based. Time constraints often tempt us, understandably, to make broad phonemic tran- scriptions, but more detailed phonetic transcriptions may actually capture clinically significant patterns which, importantly, have phonological implications for the speaker's sound system (Heselwood & Howard, 2002; Howard, 1993). The wide range of symbols provided by the International Phonetic Alphabet (IPA, 2005), the Extensions to the IPA for Disordered Speech (ExtIPA, Duckworth et al.,1990) and the Voice Quality Symbols (VoQS, Ball, Esling, & Dickson, 1995) offer a means of documenting not just consonant production, but also vowel production, con- sonant–vowel interactions, aspects of co-articulation, voice quality, and prosodic features of speech production, including stress, pitch, rate and duration, pauses, and intonation patterns, to provide a much more extensive characterization of the child's speech output.

This may, arguably, be unnecessary for children with more "straightforward" speech delays or minimal misarticulations, but for children with complex and/ or pervasive problems, a detailed phonetic analysis, based on narrow transcrip- tion, may illuminate important issues for consideration in both diagnosis and intervention planning. Furthermore, some speech output difficulties may be erroneously categorized as "straightforward" precisely because a misleadingly simplistic analytic approach has been adopted (Ball, Rahilly, & Tench, 1996; Howard, 1994).

3.2   *Phonetic and phonological assessment*

Children with speech sound problems have speech output which is either not as intelligible or not as acceptable to listeners as typical speech production. This is generally due not only to misarticulations of individual segments, but also, crucially, to a loss of contrastivity between adult phonological targets and perhaps also an unacceptable level of variability and unpredictability in multiple realiza- tions of the same words. A good functional starting point in phonetic and phonological assessment is to ask, as Velleman (2005, p. 23) puts it, "What is not working here?"

Over the past 50 years, clinical phonologists have attempted to answer this question by analyzing speech output data from a variety of theoretical perspec- tives in order to describe the unusual and atypical patterns of sound usage found therein. Traditionally focus was on the realization of individual sound segments (usually consonants) within the phonological domain of the single word. Thus Van Riper and Irwin (1958) introduced the "SODA" taxonomy, classifying children's individual segmental "errors" as Substitutions, Omissions, Distortions, or Additions and although the generative phonological analyses of the 1970s introduced the idea of sound *classes* (based on distinctive feature analysis), the generative approach was still largely focused on consonant matches or mismatches between the target (or "underlying" form) and the child's realization (the surface form), with little attention paid to vowels, prosody, variability, etc. Analysis could also sometimes be both time-consuming and also abstracted to an uncomfortable degree from the actual speech data.

It is unsurprising that natural phonology (Stampe, 1969) and phonological process analysis (Grunwell, 1981; Ingram, 1976) captured the imagination of SLPs in the late 1970s and the 1980s. Here was a theory which could be applied to children's speech data to identify phonological patterns in the speech, rather simply and quickly. By appealing to the notion of universal simplifying phonological processes which applied to the child's word productions in a developmentally transparent way, the SLP could examine both the child's phonological system (how many contrastive segments there were in speech output) and phonological structure (how the child combined segments into words in terms of syllable and word shapes). In addition, it was possible to consider how consistent or variable the child's speech output was. All SLPs are now familiar with the vocabulary of structural processes (e.g., Final Consonant Deletion, Weak Syllable Deletion) and systemic process (e.g., Fronting, Stopping, Gliding), which were seen to affect not just single sounds but sound classes, thereby offering a more economical framework for assessment and intervention. Such has been the popularity of phonological process analysis that 30 years after they were first introduced into the clinical field and despite significant critical appraisal (see, e.g., Miccio & Scarpino, 2008), they arguably remain the most popular framework of assessment and analysis for practicing SLPs and also for much research into developmental speech disorders (see, e.g., work by Dodd and colleagues).

More recently, however, alternative phonological theories have also been applied to atypical developmental speech data, illuminating children's speech difficulties in different ways. Non-linear models have alerted us to the importance of considering words as consisting not just of a linear string of sound segments, but also of phonologically functional units both smaller (e.g., the distinctive feature) and larger (e.g., the metrical foot, the syllable, onsets and rimes) than the segment. If a word is seen as comprising a hierarchy of different-sized phonological units, not only can patterns at any of these levels be captured, but interactions between different levels of organization may also explain seemingly unpredictable output patterns. Bernhardt (1992) and Yavas (1994), for example, provide examples of atypical speech production where apparently random segmental variability across different words proved to be patterned and predictable once segmental realizations were considered in relation to stress patterns and syllable position.

A third influential approach, based on Optimality Theory (OT) (Prince & Smolensky, 1997), explains children's immature and/or atypical outputs within a constraints-based system (Dinnsen & Gierut, 2008). Rather than viewing speech output as the product of phonological rules or processes, OT posits a set of universal constraints which apply to all languages but whose application is ranked differently in different languages, thus accounting for cross-linguistic differences in phonological structures and permissible outputs. Two basic sets of constraints are hypothesized: markedness constraints (which reflect phonological universals) and faithfulness constraints, whose basic premise is that outputs match the input form (i.e., the underlying representation). It can be seen that the two types of constraint are potentially in opposition to each other and this conflict is suggested as an explanation of the differences between adult and child outputs. In adult speech faithfulness constraints outrank markedness constraints; in children's immature and/or atypical speech production, the opposite prevails. Thus an atypical sound system is seen as the produce of an inappropriate ranking of phonological constraints. Phonological assessment within an OT framework consists of establishing a complete ranking of constraints to explain all of an individual child's outputs. In this way, all of the atypical output patterns used by a child can be accounted for within a single, unified analysis, rather than as the product of sets of unrelated rules, representations, or processes. Target- and goal-setting in intervention for an individual child can then be designed to reflect the specific constraints ranking of that child.

A further phonological theory which has existed for some time, but which is only at an early stage of clinical application, is Articulatory Phonology (also sometimes known as Gestural Phonology) (Browman & Goldstein, 1992). Articulatory Phonology (AP) proposes that phonological structures are intimately related to articulatory gestures and to the temporal and spatial properties of speech production. Movements of the lips, tongue, jaw, velum, and vocal folds are seen as being coordinated in time to produce sets of articulatory gestures which form the basis of syllabic units and, thus, of words. In an AP model, phonological impairment is explained as the product of temporal and/or spatial incoordination of the articulatory gestures required to produce specific syllables and words (Kent, 1997; van Lieshout & Goldstein, 2008). In this way, articulatory substance and phonological function are seen as being inextricably connected. To date AP has been more extensively used in the field of acquired speech impairments, but it also has potential for illuminating aspects of developmental speech difficulties. Bahr (2005), for example, has suggested that speech output in children with speech disorders of unknown origin may be at least partially differentiated from the output of children with childhood apraxia of speech by differing patterns in the coordination of speech gestures. Although no clinical assessment protocols exist yet based on AP, it may be that in future it will prove a valuable perspective clinically.

The linguistic perspective is also useful in assessing aspects outside the usual focus on speech sound production in single words, including the phonetic and phonological behaviors encountered in connected speech (Howard, 2007; Howard, Wells, & Local, 2008), the interaction of speech output with other linguistic levels (Crystal, 1987; Raine-Killeen, Howard, & Perkins, 2008), and the impact of socio-phonetic factors such as language variety and accent differences on our assessment of a developmental speech disorder (Docherty & Khattab, 2008; Watts Pappas & Bowen, 2007).

3.2 Psycholinguistic assessment

Using a psycholinguistic approach, the focus of assessment shifts radically from the traditional focus on speech production, to investigate the child's strengths and weaknesses across the whole range of processes which contribute to speech perception, storage, and production. Assessment aims to identify areas of break-down that can be specifically targeted in intervention, and aims to produce a detailed profile of skills and difficulties for each individual child. To achieve this, Stackhouse and Wells (1997) and colleagues (Stackhouse et al., 2007) have compiled a comprehensive set of tasks which tap into the discrete processing skills contained in their psycholinguistic profile. Sutherland and Gillon (2005) also provide a set of tests aimed at providing the SLP with more knowledge about the child's underlying lexical representations. For example, to answer one of the questions on input contained in the profile ("Are the children's phonological representations accurate?"), investigation could proceed by using one or several of a range of Auditory Lexical Decision tasks (e.g., Vance, 1995; Constable, Stackhouse, & Wells, 1997), while the output-related question "Can the child articulate speech sounds without reference to lexical representations?" might be answered by using a Non-Word Repetition task, such as that devised by Vance, Stackhouse, and Wells (2005). One of the most challenging aspects of carrying out psycholinguistically based assessment is selecting or devising the appropriate task to effectively tap a specific skill. Rees (2001, p. 67) notes that a task may be thought of as the combination of specific materials with a specific test procedure together with specific feedback and possibly a specific technique: given this, she cautions us that "Altering any one of these four components, even minimally, can change the psycholinguistic nature of the task."

It may be that for a particular child it is not felt necessary to complete all sections of the profile, although as Ebbels (2000) and Stackhouse et al. (2007) point out, underlying skills and weaknesses cannot necessarily be assumed either from clinical diagnosis or from speech production, and, indeed, a deficit in one area may not necessarily accurately predict a deficit in a related area.

Stackhouse and Wells' Speech Processing Profile has not yet been standardized, but at least some normative data has been gathered for all of the tests (Stackhouse et al., 2007). The profile offers a method of systematically gathering detailed information about a child's strengths and weaknesses which can be used to devise individually tailored intervention and can also be used to assess change following intervention.

4   Intervention

Over recent years it has often been observed that there is an almost bewildering range of approaches to intervention for developmental phonological disorders (Baker, 2006; Ingram, 1997; Kamhi, 2006). Baker (2006, p. 159) offers a list of 22 current approaches, noting this as a "selection," and therefore not an exhaustive catalogue. Given all of these, and given the current lack of plentiful and reliable guidance from evidence-based practice (Dodd, 2007), how do we decide on an effective intervention strategy for an individual child? Two further observations in the literature may be of some assistance. Kamhi (2005) comments on the notable lack of change in the techniques which speech-language pathologists actually use to elicit speech sound production, and Gierut (2001, p. 229) notes that "it may be more informative to focus on *what* is being taught, rather than *how* it is being taught." These observations serve to emphasize the critical importance of selecting appropriate short- and long-term goals and targets, based on careful and informative assessment. But "what is being taught" will also depend on the theoretical perspective adopted (either specific or eclectic) and this is, of course, where differences in intervention principles and procedures emerge, sometimes producing apparently conflicting or contradictory advice. Intervention planning is also, we must not forget, a question of balancing theoretical motivations with more practical constraints. Dodd et al. (2006a) provide seven questions on which to base decisions about intervention, only some of which relate to the individual child and their speech; others concern service delivery, such as group versus individual therapy and involvement in intervention of parents and/or school personnel.

As with assessment, intervention approaches can be usefully divided into those based on phonetic/phonological principles and those with a psycholinguistic orientation. Although there is clearly some overlap between the two, these will be discussed separately.

4.1   *Phonetic and phonological intervention*

Phonetic and phonological approaches to intervention aim at improving speech intelligibility (Dodd & Bradford, 2000) by expanding the child's speech sound inventory and their system of phonological contrasts as expressed in their speech output. Intervention may target sounds and sound classes, syllable shapes and phonotactic structures, or the interaction between segmental and prosodic properties of words. They may work at word level, or aim to establish a basic functional vocabulary for the child. There may be a specific focus on issues of consistency and variability, and effective generalization of sound changes is usually of particular interest no matter which theoretical approach is adopted.

Historically, the "sound-by-sound" articulatory approach which dominated the first half of the twentieth century was followed by a period where strictly phonological approaches held sway and very little attention was paid to the possible motor or articulatory components of developmental speech problems. More recently there has been a greater appreciation of the possibility that articulatory/motor, perceptual, and cognitive-linguistic factors may all contribute to children's speech production problems (Baker, 2006), with a concomitant move toward intervention approaches which reflect this complexity.

The shift of focus to include consideration of phonetic factors has been prompted in part by a greater appreciation of the differences between non-speech oral motor skills and oral motor skills for speech. Whereas there has been a growing recognition that non-speech oral motor practice does not appear to promote change in speech production (Forrest, 2002; Powell, 2008), there has been a parallel awareness that for some children with developmental speech difficulties, their problems may be underpinned to some extent by specific motor constraints (for example, the undifferentiated tongue gestures discussed by Gibbon, 1999). For such children effective intervention may include motor-based work tied to carefully selected segmental targets (Forrest, 2002) and a greater appreciation of the ways in which articulatory and perceptual skills underpin phonological organization and output (Goffman, 2005; Rvachew, 2005). For such children, instrumental intervention techniques, including electropalatography, may prove an appropriate avenue to bringing about speech production changes (Hardcastle & Gibbon, 2005; Ruscello, 1995).

For other researchers, articulatory and motor aspects of speech production are still seen as playing at most a peripheral role in the majority of developmental speech disorders. Dodd and McIntosh (2008), for example, argue from wide-ranging assessment of the motor, perceptual, and cognitive skills of a group of children with developmental speech problems that their major difficulty lies in the mental representation and organization of the sound system and thus truly reflects the title "developmental phonological disorder."

Phonological intervention for developmental speech problems is typically motivated by a specific theoretical perspective. Thus, for example, SLPs working within a natural phonology framework aim for a developmentally motivated suppression of phonological processes evident in the child's sound system (Grunwell, 1982), while SLPs using an OT-based approach would see the problem as one of reordering the set of phonological constraints operating on the child's speech output (Dinnsen & Gierut, 2008), and a non-linear approach might seek to bring about segmental change by working simultaneously on segments and also on non-segmental aspects of phonology, such as stress and rhythm (Bernhardt, 1992).

Underlying these approaches, and motivating decisions about how to structure intervention and where to start, are differing views about how children learn, how phonological development takes place, and how change is best brought about in a child's phonological system. One enduring central belief which influences several current approaches, and has formed a cornerstone of intervention for children's speech difficulties over many years, is that therapy should reflect the well-established fact that typical phonological development is a gradual process and that, although there is individual variation in the exact paths taken by different children, overall there are strong common developmental trends and patterns (Grunwell, 1982; Hodson & Paden, 1991; Ingram, 1976, 1997). From a developmental perspective, intervention should reflect the normal developmental trajectory, choosing sounds and structures to work on which are relatively early to develop and building gradually on the sound structures and contrasts which the child already has. At a segmental level, then, one might aim to introduce a stop-fricative contrast into a child's system before choosing to work on affricates or liquids. In terms of structure, a child with a CV syllable preference might be encouraged first to introduce word final consonants into their phonotactic repertoire, rather than complex clusters. Rvachew and Novak (2001), for example, report greater intervention success targeting earlier-developing sounds than working on sounds that are late to emerge in typical phonological development.

Interestingly, this stands in direct contrast to another influential current approach, developed by Gierut and colleagues and based on Optimality Theory. In what is often termed a "complexity" approach, the aim is "to induce the greatest phonological change or generalization in the child's sound system" (Gierut, 2001, p. 229), and Gierut and her co-researchers believe that this is best achieved by working on more, rather than less, complex (or "marked") sounds. Gierut (2001) notes that this may seem surprising and, indeed, counterintuitive, but argues that a complexity approach produces more extensive change and wider generalization of therapy gains in a child's speech output. Support for this view is found in a study by Tyler and Figurski (1994), who provided contrasting intervention for two children both of whom stopped fricatives and produced the liquid /l/ as a glide. For one child a "developmental" approach focused therapy on suppressing the stopping process, while for the second child a "complexity" approach targeted gliding. While both children acquired the contrasts specifically targeted, the child whose therapy focused on gliding also acquired fricatives, but conversely the child whose therapy targeted stopping did not acquire /l/.

Another intervention approach based on the principle of complexity, but in a rather different way, is the Multiple Oppositions Approach (Williams, 2000). Where traditional therapy based on minimal pairs focuses on a single phonemic contrast using sets of minimally contrastive words (e.g., working on /t/ versus /k/ might use TEA versus KEY, TAR versus CAR, BAT versus BACK, etc.), Williams has developed a procedure which contrasts several target sounds simultaneously as a group, thus targeting multiple collapses of contrast within the phonological system. In this approach KEY may be contrasted with TEA but also with SEA, SHE, PEA, etc. Clearly this approach is best suited to children with more severe speech difficulties which manifest in extreme homonymy in speech output.

Whether intervention is based on developmental or complexity approaches, a further aim, particularly in the case of more severe disorders, is to achieve change in a child's output system which has maximum effect on improving intelligibility. This may be accomplished by obtaining maximum generalization of sound changes (cf. Gierut, 2001; Williams, 2000), but also consideration may be given to the segmental and structural errors which have the greatest negative influence on the listener's ability to comprehend the child's speech. Klein and Flint (2006), for example, compared the effect of different phonological processes on speech intelligibility in developmental speech disorder, concluding that final consonant deletion and stopping were more deleterious than fronting. It might be predicted that a structural process such as final consonant deletion would exert a particularly negative effect, resulting, as it does, in the loss of multiple potential oppositions. Klein and Flint's finding offers support to Velleman (2005), who contends that structural and phonotactic aspects of developmental speech disorders have typically received less attention in the research literature and in the clinical domain than specific segmental contrasts and that they merit more focus in both assessment and intervention.

Stimulability, defined as "a child's ability to immediately modify speech production errors when presented with a model" (Miccio, 2005, p. 163), should also be considered in planning intervention. Research has shown that sounds for which the child is stimulable, even if they are not produced in the child's typical speech output, are likely to emerge eventually without specific intervention (Miccio, Elbert, & Forrest, 1999). Conversely, unstimulable sounds are likely to require specific therapeutic attention (Miccio, Elbert, & Forrest, 1999; Powell, Elbert, & Dinnsen, 1991).

A further important issue in planning intervention for children with speech problems is that of the consistency or variability of their speech output. While it seems clear that some children display significant variability in their realizations of sound segments (Dodd, 1995; Forrest, Elbert, & Dinnsen, 2000; Tyler, Williams, & Lewis, 2006), devising objective measurements that capture variability accurately and reliably is a complex and challenging task (Tyler, Williams, & Lewis, 2006). Variability may be viewed as a good thing, signifying a phonological system in flux and ripe for further change (Grunwell, 1982) or, conversely, as a bad thing, signaling fuzzy and unstable underlying phonological representations which may prove resistant to remediation (Forrest, Elbert, & Dinnsen, 2000). Variability has also been seen as a diagnostic marker for a particular subgroup of children (Dodd, 1995) and as suggesting potentially different outcomes from atypical but consistent sound systems (Dodd, 1995; Forrest, Elbert, & Dinnsen, 2000), although this is not an uncontroversial view (Tyler, Williams, & Lewis, 2006).

A case has also been made that variable sound systems respond best to specific intervention approaches (Dodd & Bradford, 2000; Crosbie, Holm, & Dodd, 2005). This point is significant, as it adds weight to the viewpoint that there is no "one size fits all" intervention for developmental speech problems, and that not only may different children respond better to different intervention approaches (Hesketh et al., 2000), but also that some children may need a variety of approaches presented sequentially over the course of treatment (Dodd & Bradford, 2000). Furthermore, we may need to make careful estimation of the wider context of readiness for therapy, however appropriate we believe intervention to be from a phonological perspective. Kwiatkowski and Shriberg's Capability-Focus perspective (1993) reminds us that while capability to learn (as assessed by cognitive, linguistic, and psychosocial factors) is clearly of extreme importance, the child's ability to focus on therapy (seen as their motivation to change and the support needed to maintain that motivation and energy) also has an effect on progress and outcomes and on the way intervention programs may need to be structured.

In the previous section, on assessment, a case was made for the need to investigate connected speech production more closely and to consider the effects of word juncture behaviors on children's speech intelligibility. In terms of intervention, there has as yet been little work carried out on connected speech with a specific focus on phonetic and phonological behaviors at word boundaries. Pascoe, Stackhouse, and Wells (2005), however, provide an interesting case study of a 6-year-old girl with a severe and persisting speech impairment. Intervention, unusually, focused at different stages on word production in isolation and in connected speech. The authors' conclusions are telling in terms of intervention generalization and speech intelligibility: "It seems that improvement in connected speech was brought about only by specifically addressing connected speech in a carefully structured way" (Pascoe, Stackhouse, & Wells, 2005, p. 214).

4.2 *Psycholinguistic intervention*

Psycholinguistic approaches target any or all aspects of speech processing which, on the basis of a detailed assessment, are thought to be problematic for the child. Thus therapy may aim at improving speech input skills, at establishing or strengthening accurate phonological representations, or at improving the intelligibility of speech production by addressing motor and articulatory aspects of speech processing.

One central question in psycholinguistic intervention is how far working on metaphonological awareness helps speech output and/or literacy skills. Howell and Dean (1991), for example, targeted the suppression of simplifying processes in speech output, such as fronting, stopping, final consonant deletion, etc., by explicitly focusing on phonological awareness, providing the child with information about sound characteristics, similarities and differences. The primary aim in their approach, Metaphon, is to give the child a conceptual framework for sound contrasts, which may be drawn from other domains (e.g., contrasting stops and fricatives as "long" and "short" sounds and comparing them to "long" and "short" objects and pictures). Consequently intervention, particularly in the initial phase, emphasizes speech input rather than requiring the child to produce speech sounds. Howell and Dean (1991) and Dean et al., (1996) provide case studies evaluating the efficacy of Metaphon therapy and showing how improving children's awareness of the contrastive features of speech sounds and sound classes can result in improvements in speech production.

Hesketh et al. (2000) and Gillon (2005) have compared traditional articulation therapy and phonological awareness (PA) therapy for children with developmental speech disorders, coming to somewhat different conclusions from each other. Gillon (2005) reported gains in both speech intelligibility and PA in 3- and 4-year-old children receiving intervention combining traditional phonological approaches and PA work. However, the 4- and 5-year-old children in Hesketh et al.'s study (2000) also received either PA or articulation therapy, but the results were less conclusive and overall the authors concluded that "therapy had an effect on both metaphonological abilities and speech output, but there was no effect of therapy type" (Hesketh et al., 2000, p. 349).

A further contribution of the psycholinguistic approach is to increase SLPs' awareness of the stages of development of phonological awareness and children's likely knowledge of intra-lexical structure at specific ages, which in turn allows for more informed reflection on the psycholinguistic demands of specific intervention tasks for speech, and consideration of how age appropriate these might be even for normally developing children, and thus even more so for children with speech difficulties (Hesketh, Dima, & Nelson, 2007).

5 Conclusion

Throughout this chapter we have noted the heterogeneity of the population of children with speech disorders of no identifiable etiology. This heterogeneity is reflected in the breadth of theoretical and clinical approaches current in the field. Exciting work drawing on linguistic, psycholinguistic, and medical perspectives continues to deepen our understanding of the nature of developmental speech difficulties and of the ways in which they may be most effectively managed by speech-language pathologists. Additionally, this research also informs theoretical linguistics and psychology and can thus enhance our understanding of speech development and speech processing in typical speakers.

REFERENCES

Amorosa, H., von Benda, U., Wagner, E., & Keck, A. (1985). Transcribing detail in the speech of unintelligible children: a comparison of procedures. *British Journal of Disorders of Communication* 20, 281–7.

Applegate, J. (1961). Phonological rules of a subdialect of English. *Word* 17, 186–93.

Bahr, R. (2005). Differential diagnosis of severe speech disorders using speech gestures. *Topics in Language Disorders* 25 (3), 254–65.

Baker, E. (2006). Management of speech impairment in children: The journey so far and the road ahead. *Advances in Speech-Language Pathology* 8 (3), 156–63.

Ball, M. J. (2008). Government phonology and speech impairment. In M. J. Ball, M. R. Perkins, N. Mueller, & S. Howard

(eds.), *The handbook of clinical linguistics* (pp. 452–66). Oxford: Blackwell.

Ball, M. J., Esling, C., & Dickson, G. (1995). The VoQS system for the transcription of voice quality. *Journal of the International Phonetic Association* 25, 61–70.

Ball, M. J., Rahilly, J., & Tench, P. (1996). *The phonetic transcription of disordered speech.* San Diego, CA: Singular.

Bates, S. A. R., Watson, J. M. M., & Scobbie, J. M. (2002). Context-conditioned error patterns in disordered systems. In M. J. Ball & F. E. Gibbon (eds.), *Vowel disorders* (pp. 145–86). New York: Butterworth-Heinemann.

Bernhardt, B. (1992). The application of nonlinear phonological theory to intervention with one phonologically disordered child. *Clinical Linguistics and Phonetics* 6, 283–316.

Bernhardt, B. & Stemberger, J. (1998). *Handbook of phonological development: From a nonlinear constraints-based perspective*. San Diego, CA: Academic Press.

Bernhardt, B. & Stoel-Gammon, C. (1994). Nonlinear phonology: Introduction and clinical application. *Journal of Speech and Hearing Research* 37, 123–43.

Bird, J. B. & Bishop, D. (1992). Perception and awareness of phonemes in phonologically impaired children. *European Journal of Disorders of Communication* 27 (4), 289–311.

Blanton, S. (1916). A survey of speech defects. *Journal of Educational Psychology* 7, 581–92.

Browman, C. & Goldstein, L. (1992). Articulatory phonology: An overview. *Haskins Laboratory Status Report on Speech Research* SR-111/112, 23–42.

Catterall, C., Howard, S., Stojanovik, V., Szczerbinski, M., & Wells, B. (2006). Investigating prosodic ability in Williams syndrome. *Clinical Linguistics and Phonetics* 20 (7–8), 531–8.

Constable, A., Stackhouse, J., & Wells, B. (1997). Developmental word-finding difficulties and phonological processing: The case of the missing handcuffs. *Applied Psycholinguistics* 18, 507–36.

Crosbie, S., Holm, A., & Dodd, B. (2005). Intervention for children with severe speech disorders: a comparison of two approaches. *International Journal of Language and Communication Disorders* 40 (4), 467–91.

Crystal, D. (1987). Towards a bucket theory of language disability: Taking account of interaction between linguistic levels. *Clinical Linguistics and Phonetics* 1, 7–22.

Davis, B. L. (2005). Clinical diagnosis of developmental speech disorders. In A. G. Kamhi & K. E. Pollock (eds.), *Phonological disorders in children* (pp. 3–21). Baltimore, MD: Brookes.

Dean, E., Howell, J., Waters, D., & Reid, J. (1996). Metaphon: A metalinguistic approach to the treatment of phonological disorder in children. *Clinical Linguistics and Phonetics* 12 (2), 127–46.

Dinnsen, D., & Gierut, J. (2008). Optimality theory: A clinical perspective. In M. J. Ball, M. R. Perkins, N. Mueller, & S. Howard (eds.), *The handbook of clinical linguistics* (pp. 439–51). Oxford: Blackwell.

Docherty, G. & Khattab, G. (2008). Sociophonetics. In M. J. Ball, M. R. Perkins, N. Mueller, & S. Howard (eds.), *The handbook of clinical linguistics*. Oxford: Blackwell.

Dodd, B. (1995). *Differential diagnosis and treatment of children with speech disorder*. London: Whurr.

Dodd, B. (2007). Evidence-based practice and speech-language pathology: Strengths, weaknesses, opportunities, and threats. *Folia Phoniatrica & Logopaedica* 59, 118–29.

Dodd, B. & Bradford, A. (2000). A comparison of three therapy methods for children with different types of developmental phonological disorder. *International Journal of Language and Communication Disorders* 35 (2), 189–209.

Dodd, B., Holm, A., Crosbie, S., & McIntosh, B (2006a). A core vocabulary approach for management of inconsistent speech disorders. *Advances in Speech-Language Pathology* 8 (3), 220–30.

Dodd, B., Holm, A., Hua, Z., Crosbie, S., & Broomfield, J. (2006b). English phonology: acquisition and disorder. In H. Zhu & B. Dodd (eds.), *Phonological development and disorders in children*. Clevedon, UK: Multilingual Matters.

Dodd, B. & McIntosh, B. (2008). The input processing, cognitive linguistic and oro-motor skills of children with speech difficulty. *International Journal of Speech-Language Pathology* 10 (3), 169–78.

Duckworth, M., Allen, G., Hardcastle, W., & Ball, M. (1990). Extensions to the

International Phonetic Alphabet for the transcription of atypical speech. *Clinical Linguistics and Phonetics* 4, 273–80.

Ebbels, S. (2000). Psycholinguistic profiling of a hearing-impaired child. *Child Language, Teaching and Therapy* 16 (1), 3–22.

Elbert, M. (1997). From articulation to phonology: the challenge of change. In B. W. Hodson & M. L. Edwards (eds.), *Perspectives in applied phonology*. Gaithersburg, MD: Aspen.

Forrest, K. (2002). Are oral-motor exercises useful in the treatment of phonological/articulatory disorders? *Seminars in Speech and Language* 23 (1), 15–25.

Forrest, K., Elbert, M., & Dinnsen, D. (2000). The effect of substitution patterns on phonological treatment outcomes. *Clinical Linguistics and Phonetics* 14 (7), 519–31.

Forrest, K., Weismer, G., Elbert, M., & Dinnsen, D. (1994). Spectral analysis of target-appropriate /t/ and /k/ produced by phonologically disordered and normally articulating children. *Clinical Linguistics and Phonetics* 8 (4), 267–81.

Fox, A. V. & Dodd, B. (2001). Phonologically disordered German-speaking children. *American Journal of Speech-Language Pathology* 109, 291–307.

Fox, A. V., Dodd, B., & Howard, D. (2002). Risk factors for speech disorders in children. *International Journal of Language and Communication Disorders* 37, 117–31.

Gibbon, F. (1990). Lingual activity in two speech-disordered children's attempts to produce velar and alveolar stop consonants: evidence from electropalatographic (EPG) data. *British Journal of Disorders of Communication* 25, 329–40.

Gibbon, F. (1999). Undifferentiated lingual gestures in children with articulation/phonological disorders. *Journal of Speech, Language, and Hearing Research* 42, 382–97.

Gierut, J. (2001). Complexity in phonological treatment: clinical factors. *Language, Speech and Hearing Services in Schools* 32, 229–41.

Gierut, J. & Morrisette, M. (2005). The clinical significance of Optimality Theory for phonological disorders. *Topics in Language Disorders* 25 (3), 266–80.

Gillon, G. T. (2005). Facilitating phoneme awareness development in 3- and 4-year-old children with speech impairment. *Language, Speech & Hearing Services in Schools* 36, 308–24.

Goffman, L. (2005). Assessment and classification: and integrative model of language and motor contributions to phonological development. In A. Kahmi & K. Pollock (eds.), *Phonological disorders in children* (pp. 51–64). Baltimore, MD: Brookes.

Goldman, R. & Fristoe, M. (2000). *Goldman–Fristoe Test of Articulation – 3*. Circle Pines, MN: American Guidance Service.

Goldstein, B. & Iglesias, A. (1996). Phonological patterns in Puerto-Rican Spanish-speaking children with phonological disorders. *Journal of Communication Disorder* 29, 367–87.

Grunwell, P. (1975). The phonological analysis of articulation disorders. *British Journal of Disorders of Communication* 10 (1), 31–42.

Grunwell, P. (1981). *The nature of phonological disability in children*. London: Academic Press.

Grunwell, P. (1982). *Clinical phonology*, 1st ed. London: Croom Helm.

Grunwell, P. (1985). *Phonological Assessment of Child Speech (PACS)*. Windsor: NFER-Nelson.

Haas, W. (1963). Phonological analysis of a case of dyslalia. *Journal of Speech and Hearing Disorders* 28, 239–46.

Hardcastle, W. J. & Gibbon, F. E. (2005). EPG as a research and clinical tool: 30 years on. In W. J. Hardcastle & J. Mackenzie Back (eds.), *A figure of* speech: a Festschrift for John Laver (pp. 39–60). New York: Lawrence Erlbaum.

Hayiou-Thomas, M. E. (2008). Genetic and environmental influences on early speech, language and literacy development. Journal of Communication Disorders 41, 397–408.

Heselwood, B. C. & Howard, S. J. (2002). The realization of English liquids in impaired speech: A perceptual and instrumental study. In F. Windsor, L. Kelly, & N. Hewlett (eds.), Investigations in clinical linguistics and phonetics (pp. 225–41). New York: Lawrence Erlbaum.

Hesketh, A., Adams, C., Nightingale, C., & Hall, R. (2000). Metaphonological abilities of phonologically disordered children. International Journal of Language and Communication Disorders 20 (4), 483–98.

Hesketh, A., Dima, E., & Nelson, V. (2007). Teaching phoneme awareness to pre-literate children with speech disorder: a randomized controlled trial. International Journal of Language and Communication Disorders 42 (3), 251–71.

Hewlett, N. (1990). Processes of development and production. In P. Grunwell (ed.), Developmental speech disorders: Clinical issues and practical implications. London: Churchill Livingstone.

Hodson, B. W. & Paden, E. (1991). Targeting intelligible speech, 2nd ed. Austin, TX: Pro-Ed.

Holmes, G. (1879). A treatise on vocal physiology and hygiene with especial reference to the cultivation and preservation of the voice. London: J. & A. Churchill.

Howard, S. J. (1993). Articulatory constraints on a phonological system: a case study of cleft palate speech. Clinical Linguistics and Phonetics 7 (4), 299–317.

Howard, S. J. (1994). Spontaneous phonetic reorganisation following articulation therapy: an electropalatographic study. In R. Aulanko & A.-M. Korpijaakko-Huuhka (eds.),

Proceedings of the 3rd Congress of the International Clinical Phonetics and Linguistics Association, 1993, Helsinki (vol. 39) (pp. 67–74). Helsinki: Department of Phonetics, University of Helsinki.

Howard, S. J. (2004). Connected speech processes in developmental speech impairment: observations from an electropalatographic perspective. Clinical Linguistics and Phonetics 18 (6–8), 405–17.

Howard, S. J. (2007). The interplay between articulation and prosody in children with impaired speech: Observations from electropalatographic and perceptual analysis. Advances in Speech-Language Pathology 9 (1), 20–35.

Howard, S. J. & Heselwood, B. C. (2002). Learning and teaching phonetic transcription for clinical purposes. Clinical Linguistics and Phonetics 16, 371–401.

Howard, S. J., Wells, B., & Local, J. (2008). Connected speech. In M. J. Ball, M. R. Perkins, N. Mueller, & S. J. Howard (eds.), The handbook of clinical linguistics. Oxford: Blackwell.

Howell, J. & Dean, E. (1991). Treating phonological disorders in children: Metaphon – theory to practice, 1st ed. Kibworth, UK: Far Communications.

Hua, Z. & Dodd, B. (2000). Development and change in the phonology of Putonghua-speaking children with speech difficulties. Clinical Linguistics and Phonetics 14 (5), 351–68.

Ingram, D. (1976). Phonological disability in Children, 1st ed. New York: Elsevier.

Ingram, D. (1997). The categorisation of phonological impairment. In B. W. Hodson & M. L. Edwards (eds.), Perspectives in applied phonology. Gaithersburg, MD: Aspen.

Ingram, D. & Ingram, K. D. (2001). A whole-word approach to phonological analysis and intervention. Language, Speech and Hearing Services in Schools 32 (4), 271–83.

Kamhi, A. (2005). Summary, reflections and future directions. In A. G. Kamhi & K. E. Pollock (eds.), *Phonological disorders in children* (pp. 211–28). Baltimore, MD: Brookes.

Kamhi, A. (2006). Treatment decisions for children with speech-sound disorders. *Language, Speech and Hearing Services in Schools* 37 (4), 271–9.

Kent, R. D. (1996). Hearing and believing: Some limits to the auditory-perceptual assessment of speech and voice disorders. *American Journal of Speech-Language Pathology* 5 (3), 7–23.

Kent, R. D. (1997). Gestural phonology: Basic concepts and applications in speech-language pathology. In M. J. Ball & R. D. Kent (eds.), *The new phonologies: Developments in clinical linguistics* (pp. 247–68). San Diego, CA: Singular.

Kent, R. D. & Ball, M. J. (1997). Introduction: Phonetics for clinical phonologies. In M. J. Ball & R. D. Kent (eds.), *The new phonologies* (pp. 1–6). San Diego, CA: Singular.

Khan, L. M. (2002). The sixth view: Assessing preschoolers' articulation and phonology from the trenches. *American Journal of Speech-Language Pathology* 11, 250–4.

Klein, E. S. & Flint, C. B. (2006). Measurement of intelligibility in disordered speech. *Language, Speech and Hearing Services in Schools* 37, 191–9.

Kwiatkowski, J. & Shriberg, L. D. (1993). Speech normalization in developmental phonological disorders: A retrospective study of capability-focus theory. *Language, Speech & Hearing Services in Schools* 24, 10–18.

Law, J., Boyle, J., Harris, F., Harkness, A., & Nye, C. (2000). Prevalence and natural history of primary speech and language delay: Findings from a recent systematic review of the literature. *International Journal of Language and Communication Disorders* 35, 165–88.

Leitão, S. & Fletcher, J. (2004). Literacy outcomes for students with speech impairment: long-term follow-up. *International Journal of Language and Communication Disorders* 39 (2), 245–56.

Lewis, B. A., Freebairn, L. A., & Taylor, H. G. (2002). Correlates of spelling abilities in children with early speech sound disorders. *Reading and Writing: An Interdisciplinary Journal* 15, 389–407.

Lewis, B. A., Shriberg, L. D., Freebairn, L. A., Hansen, A. J., Stein, C. M., Taylor, H. G., & Iyengar, S. K. (2006). The genetic bases of speech sound disorders: Evidence from spoken and written language. *Journal of Speech, Language, and Hearing Research* 49 (6), 1294–312.

Maassen, B., Pasman, J., Nijland, L., & Rotteveel, J. (2006). Clinical use of AEVP- and AERP-measures in childhood speech disorders. *Clinical Linguistics and Phonetics* 20 (2/3), 125–34.

Maxwell, E. M. & Weismer, G. (1982). The contribution of phonological, acoustic and perceptual techniques to the characterisation of a misarticulating child's voice contrast for stops. *Applied Psycholinguistics* 3, 29–43.

McKinnon, D. H., McLeod, S., & Reilly, S. (2007). The prevalence of stuttering, voice, and speech-sound disorders in primary school students in Australia. *Language, Speech & Hearing Services in Schools* 38 (1), 5–15.

McLeod, S. (2006). An holistic view of a child with unintelligible speech: Insights from the ICF and ICF-CY. *Advances in Speech-Language Pathology* 8 (3), 293–315.

McLeod, S. (2007). Australian English speech acquisition. In S. McLeod (ed.), *The international guide to speech acquisition* (pp. 241–56). Clifton Park, NY: Thomson Delmar.

Menn, L. & Matthei, E. (1992). The "two-lexicon" account of child phonology: Looking back, looking ahead. In C. Ferguson, L. Menn, & C. Stoel-Gammon (eds.), *Phonological development: Models, research, implications.* Maryland: York Press.

Miccio, A. (2005). A treatment program for enhancing stimulability. In A. Kahmi & K. Pollock (eds.), *Phonological disorders in children* (pp. 163–73). Baltimore, MD: Brookes.

Miccio, A. W., Elbert, M., & Forrest, K. (1999). The relationship between stimulability and phonological acquisition in children with normally developing and disordered phonologies. *American Journal of Speech-Language Pathology* 8, 347–63.

Miccio, A. W. & Scarpino, S. E. (2008). Phonological analysis, phonological processes. In M. J. Ball, M. R. Perkins, N. Mueller, & S. Howard (eds.), *The handbook of clinical linguistics* (pp. 412–22). Oxford: Blackwell.

Pascoe, M., Stackhouse, J., & Wells, B. (2005). Phonological therapy within a psycholinguistic framework: Promoting change in a child with persisting speech difficulties. *International Journal of Language and Communication Disorders* 40 (2), 189–220.

Pascoe, M., Stackhouse, J., & Wells, B. (2006). *Persisting speech difficulties in children*. Chichester, UK: Wiley.

Powell, T. (2008). An integrated evaluation of nonspeech oral motor treatments. *Language, Speech, and Hearing Services in Schools* 39, 422–7.

Powell, T., Elbert, M., & Dinnsen, D. (1991). Stimulability as a factor in the phonological generalization of misarticulating school children. *Journal of Speech and Hearing Research* 34 (6), 1318–28.

Prince, A. & Smolensky, P. (1997). Optimality: From neural networks to universal grammar. *Science* 275, 1604–10.

Raine-Killeen, H., Howard, S., & Perkins, M. R. (2008). Emergence of word juncture in a child with SLI: Evidence of multiple interactions in speech and language development. *The 12th Congress of the International Clinical*

Phonetics and Linguistics Association. Istanbul, Turkey.

Rees, R. (2001). What do tasks really tap? In J. Stackhouse & B. Wells (eds.), *Children's speech and literacy difficulties 2: Identification and intervention.* London: Whurr.

Ruscello, D. (1995). Visual feedback in treatment of residual phonological disorders. *Journal of Communication Disorders* 28, 279–302.

Rvachew, S. (2005). The importance of phonetic factors in phonological intervention. In A. Kahmi & K. Pollock (eds.), *Phonological disorders in children* (pp. 175–87). Baltimore, MD: Brookes.

Rvachew, S. & Novak, M. (2001) The effect of target-selection strategy on phonological learning. *Journal of Speech, Language, and Hearing Research* 44, 610–3.

Schuele, C. M. (2004). The impact of developmental speech and language impairments on the acquisition of literacy skills. *Mental Retardation and Developmental Disabilities Research Reviews* 10, 176–83.

Shriberg, L. (1994). Five types of developmental phonological disorders. *Clinics in Communication Disorders* 4, 38–53.

Shriberg, L. D., Austin, D., Lewis, B. A., McSweeny, J. L., & Wilson, D. (1997). The Speech Disorders Classification System (SDCS): Extensions and lifespan reference data. *Journal of Speech and Hearing Research* 40 (4), 723–40.

Shriberg, L. D., Tomblin, J. B., & McSweeny, J. L. (1999). Prevalence of speech delay in 6-year-old children and comorbidity with language impairment. *Journal of Speech, Language, and Hearing Research* 42 (6), 1461–81.

So, L. & Dodd, B. (1994). Phonolgically-disordered Cantonese-speaking children. *Clinical Linguistics and Phonetics* 8 (3), 235–55.

Stackhouse, J., Vance, M., Pascoe, M., & Wells, B. (2007). *Compendium of auditory and speech tasks.* Chichester, UK: Wiley.

Stackhouse, J. & Wells, B. (1997). *Children's speech and literacy difficulties: A psycholinguistic framework*. London: Whurr.

Stampe, D. (1969). The acquisition of phonetic representation. *Papers from the Fifth Regional Meeting of the Chicago Linguistic Society*, Chicago, Illinois.

Stampe, D. (1979). *A dissertation on natural phonology*. New York: Garland.

Sutherland, D. & Gillon, G. T. (2005). Assessment of phonological representations in children with speech impairment. *Language, Speech & Hearing Services in Schools* 36, 294–307.

Topbaş, S. (2006). Does the speech of Turkish-speaking phonologically disordered children differ from that of children speaking other languages? *Clinical Linguistics and Phonetics* 20 (7–8), 509–22.

Travis, L. & Rasmus, B. (1931). *Speech pathology*. New York: Appleton.

Tyler, A. & Tolbert, L. C. (2002). Speech-language assessment in the clinical setting. *American Journal of Speech-Language Pathology* 11, 215–20.

Tyler, A. A. & Figurski, G. (1994). Phonetic inventory changes after treating distinctions along an implicational hierarchy. *Clinical Linguistics and Phonetics* 8 (2), 91–107.

Tyler, A. A., Williams, M. J., & Lewis, K. E. (2006). Error consistency and the evaluation of treatment outcomes. *Clinical Linguistics and Phonetics* 20 (6), 411–22.

van Lieshout, P. H. H. M., & Goldstein, L. M. (2008). Articulatory phonology and speech impairment. In M. J. Ball, M. R. Perkins, N. Mueller, & S. Howard (eds.), *The handbook of clinical linguistics*. Oxford: Blackwell.

Van Riper, C. & Irwin, J. V. (1958). *Voice and articulation*. Englewood Cliffs, NJ: Prentice Hall.

Vance, M. (1995). Investigating speech processing skills in young children. *Caring to Communicate, Proceedings of the Golden Jubilee Conference of the RCSLT*. London: RCSLT.

Vance, M., Stackhouse, J., & Wells, B. (2005). Speech production skills in children aged 3–7 years. *International Journal of Language and Communication Disorders* 40 (1), 29–48.

Velleman, S. (2005). Perspectives on assessment. In A. G. Kamhi & K. E. Pollock (eds.), *Phonological disorders in children* (pp. 23–33). Baltimore, MD: Brookes.

Watts Pappas, N. & Bowen, C. (2007). Speech acquisition and the family. In S. McLeod (ed.), *The international guide to speech acquisition*. New York: Thomson Delmar.

Weiner, P. S. (1986). The study of childhood language disorders: Nineteenth century perspectives. *Journal of Communication Disorders* 19, 1–47.

Weismer, G., Dinnsen, D., & Elbert, M. (1981). A study of the voicing distinction associated with omitted, word-final stops. *Journal of Speech and Hearing Disorders* 46, 320–7.

Wells, W. (1994). Junction in developmental speech disorder: A case study. *Clinical Linguistics and Phonetics* 8 (1), 1–25.

Williams, A. L. (2000). Multiple oppositions: Case studies of variables in phonological intervention. *American Journal of Speech-Language Pathology* 9, 289–99.

Yavas, M. (1994). Extreme regularity in phonological disorder: A case study. *Clinical Linguistics and Phonetics* 8 (2), 127–39.

16 Dysarthria

HERMANN ACKERMANN, INGO HERTRICH, AND WOLFRAM ZIEGLER

1 The Brain Network of Speech Motor Control in Normal Speakers

1.1 *Functional brain imaging*

Speech production is built upon coordinated and largely automatized sequences of respiratory, laryngeal, and orofacial movement patterns, "programmed" or "planned" as concatenations of "elementary" phonetic gestures. So far, studies of the brain mechanisms subserving articulatory and phonatory functions predominantly had to rely upon the analysis of dysarthric deficits in patients with focal cerebral lesions or neurodegenerative diseases, restricted to defined central-motor subsystems. Depending upon "natural" events, these data, however, are often confounded by individual variation in the severity and/or localization of the respective disorders and, thus, do not always allow for unambiguous conclusions on the neural mechanisms underlying motor aspects of speech production. As an alternative, functional imaging techniques such as positron emission tomography (PET) or functional magnetic resonance imaging (fMRI) provide the opportunity to visualize task-related hemodynamic activation patterns across the whole brain in normal speakers. During the last decade, these techniques have been used to delineate the cerebral network bound to speech production (Ackermann & Riecker, 2009; Ackermann, Riecker, & Wildgruber, 2004). Based upon animal experimentation, an "automatic" increase of regional cerebral blood flow (rCBF) in response to local changes of neural activity had first been suggested in the late nineteenth century (neurovascular coupling). PET engages a radioactive marker of blood flow, making use of the unique positron-emitting decay characteristics of unstable isotopes such as 15O. Following the injection of a small amount of 15O-labeled water, the amount of radioactivity at the level of the cerebral cortex increases in direct proportion to local blood flow. In contrast to PET, fMRI represents a non-invasive procedure, primarily based on the different magnetic resonance properties of oxygenated and desoxygenated blood (= "blood oxygen level

The Handbook of Language and Speech Disorders, First Edition. Edited by Jack S. Damico, Nicole Müller, and Martin J. Ball. © 2013 Blackwell Publishing Ltd except for editorial material and organization © 2013 Jack S. Damico, Nicole Müller, Martin J. Ball. Published 2013 by Blackwell Publishing Ltd.

dependent" (BOLD) effect). Furthermore, the latter technique is superior to PET in terms of spatial resolution, approximating that of anatomical MR imaging.

1.2 *"Minimal cerebral network" bound to speech motor planning and execution*

The first systematic account of the cerebral circuitry underlying speech motor control emerged as a by-product of a PET investigation of lexical aspects of single-word processing (Petersen et al., 1989; for reviews see Ackermann & Ziegler, 2009; Ackermann, Riecker, & Wildgruber, 2004). Besides activation of the supplementary motor area (SMA), located within the medial wall of the frontal lobes, bilateral responses of sensorimotor cortex and anterior-superior portions of the cerebellum could be documented. Unexpectedly, furthermore, an activation spot "buried" in the depth of the lateral sulcus emerged, whereas both Broca's area and the basal ganglia did not show any significant hemodynamic effects. In line with several sporadic observations, a subsequent PET study based upon the repetition of aurally presented nouns (versus stimulus anticipation as baseline condition) was able to assign the intrasylvian response to the anterior insula (Wise et al., 1999).

During the past years, a series of functional imaging studies addressed the cerebral correlates of speech motor control. For example, a recent fMRI investigation considered four tri-syllabic items ("ta-ta-ta" / "ka-ru-ti" / "stra-stra-stra" / "kla-stri-splu"), systematically varied in sequence complexity (the same three versus three different items in a row) and syllabic complexity (CV versus CCCV onset), as test materials (Bohland & Guenther, 2006). The "minimal cerebral network of overt speech production," in terms of the conjunction of hemodynamic activation across the four test materials (versus baseline), was found to encompass the post- and precentral gyrus, encroaching upon the posterior parts of the left inferior frontal convolution, the anterior insula, the superior temporal cortex, SMA, the basal ganglia, thalamic areas, and the superior cerebellar hemispheres of both hemispheres. Significant left-lateralization effects emerged at the level of intrasylvian cortex. By contrast, Broca's area and sensorimotor cortex failed to display comparable side-differences of hemodynamic activation. An increase of stimulus complexity in either dimension yielded, as expected, enhanced activation of at least some components of the "basic speech network."

1.3 *Contribution of the basal ganglia and the cerebellum to the control of syllable rate*

As compared to the production of lexical items or pseudo-words, syllable repetition tasks represent a more direct probe of articulatory performance, avoiding any lexical or syntactic operations. In the absence of acoustic or visual stimulus application, furthermore, elaborated subtraction designs accounting for signal-encoding cognitive processes are not necessary. Oral diadochokinesis, i.e., syllable repetitions performed as fast as possible, has been claimed to provide a sensitive and, within some limits, specific measure of dysarthric deficits while conversational speech rate might still be within the normal range in some speech disorders. For example, a reduced maximum syllable repetition rate could be documented in spastic and ataxic dysarthria. By contrast, subgroups of patients with Parkinson's disease (PD) even may exhibit "speech hastening," i.e., involuntary acceleration of speaking rate.

In order to further elucidate the differential contribution of the various components of the cerebral speech motor network to the control of speaking rate, a fMRI study of our group measured hemodynamic brain activation during syllable repetitions at different rates extending from two to six syllables per second. These utterances had either to be synchronized to an acoustic pacing signal or were

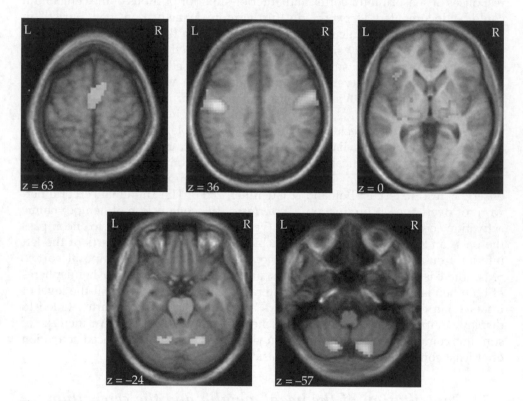

Figure 16.1 Functional imaging of the cerebral network of speech motor control: fMRI during repetitions of the syllable /ta/, synchronized to an external pacing signal (applied via headphones): Hemodynamic main effects calculated across all six frequency conditions (2, 2.5, 3, 4, 5, and 6 Hz) and across all subjects versus baseline (passive listening to the pacing stimuli; z = distance to the intercommisural plane; L = left hemisphere, R = right hemisphere). Significant responses (yellow spots) emerged within SMA, bilateral sensorimotor cortex (SMC), bilateral basal ganglia (BG), left anterior insula (aINS), left inferior frontal gyrus (not shown here), and both cerebellar hemispheres (CERE).

produced in a self-paced manner (Riecker et al., 2005, 2006). In line with other functional imaging studies (e.g., Bohland & Guenther 2006), significant hemodynamic main effects across all repetition rates (versus passive listening to the pacing signals) emerged within SMA, precentral areas, Broca's region, anterior insula, thalamus, basal ganglia, and cerebellum. Dorsolateral frontal and intrasylvian cortex as well as the caudate nucleus showed lateralized responses in favor of the left side whereas the other components displayed a rather bilateral activation pattern (Figure 16.1).

These findings are in good accord with clinical data since dysfunctions of the cerebral structures referred to here may compromise verbal behavior, giving rise to dysarthria, apraxia of speech, or transcortical motor aphasia (see below). SMA, sensorimotor cortex, anterior insula, and cerebellar activation spots showed a positive linear rate/response relationship, i.e., the hemodynamic response increased in parallel with syllable repetition rate. Most noteworthy, hemodynamic activation of the cerebellum was characterized, at either side, by a step-wise increase of the BOLD signal between 3 and 4 Hz (Figure 16.2). In line with the latter finding, preceding acoustic studies had revealed syllable rate not to fall below a value of ca. 3 Hz in patients with ataxic dysarthria both during oral diadochokinesis and sentence production tasks (for reviews see Hertrich & Ackermann 1997, Ackermann & Hertrich 2000, Ackermann, Mathiak, & Ivry, 2004; Ackermann, Mathiak, & Riecker, 2007). Thus, clinical and functional imaging data appear to indicate that the cerebellum "pushes" speaking rate beyond a level of about 3 Hz.

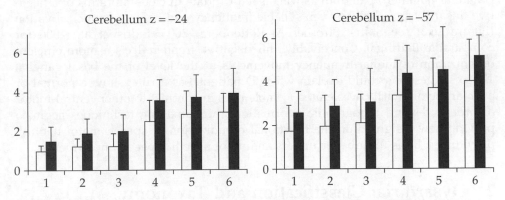

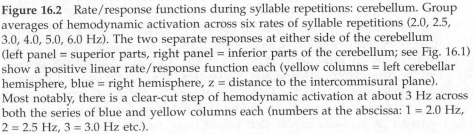

Figure 16.2 Rate/response functions during syllable repetitions: cerebellum. Group averages of hemodynamic activation across six rates of syllable repetitions (2.0, 2.5, 3.0, 4.0, 5.0, 6.0 Hz). The two separate responses at either side of the cerebellum (left panel = superior parts, right panel = inferior parts of the cerebellum; see Fig. 16.1) show a positive linear rate/response function each (yellow columns = left cerebellar hemisphere, blue = right hemisphere, z = distance to the intercommisural plane). Most notably, there is a clear-cut step of hemodynamic activation at about 3 Hz across both the series of blue and yellow columns each (numbers at the abscissa: 1 = 2.0 Hz, 2 = 2.5 Hz, 3 = 3.0 Hz etc.).

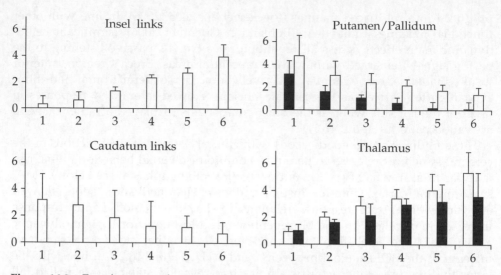

Figure 16.3   Rate/response functions during syllable repetitions: basal ganglia. Most noteworthy, hemodynamic activation declines along with an increase of repetition rate within the basal ganglia (both sides of the putamen/pallidum, left caudate nucleus). For the sake of comparison, the rate/response functions of left anterior insula and thalamus are shown; similar relationships emerged at sensorimotor cortex and SMA.

A different rate/response pattern was observed at the level of the basal ganglia (bilateral putamen/pallidum as well as left caudate nucleus) in terms of a negative linear relationship between syllable frequency and hemodynamic activation (Figure 16.3; see Sidtis, Strother, & Rottenberg, 2003; Sidtis et al., 2006 for comparable findings). Conceivably, this negative trend reflects a more efficient organization of higher-frequency movements at the level of the basal ganglia. These suggestions could explain why PD patients, as a rule, show a normal or even an involuntarily accelerated syllable rate, in contrast to other central-motor disorders. Beyond topographic information, thus, imaging techniques begin to provide new insights into the functional organization of speech motor control, providing a basis for a better understanding of specific speech impairments.

2   Dysarthria: Classification and Taxonomy

In their seminal work on motor speech disorders, Darley, Aronson, and Brown (1975) applied the term *dysarthria* to all abnormalities of spoken language "resulting from disturbances in muscular control over the speech mechanisms due to damage of the central or peripheral nervous system" (Duffy, 2005, p. 5). By definition, thus, the concept of dysarthria does not extend to disrupted articulatory or phonatory functions subsequent to acquired or innate structural anomalies of the vocal tract such as glossectomy or cleft palate (see Chapter 22 in this volume).

Clinical data indicate "muscular control" of vocal tract structures during speech production (motor execution), i.e., the adjustment of "speed, range, and temporal coordination of the respective movements" (Netsell & Rosenbek, 1985), to depend upon primary motor cortex, including its efferent pathways (upper motor neuron), the cranial nerve nuclei (lower motor neuron), the basal ganglia, the thalamus, and the cerebellum (for a recent review see Ackermann & Ziegler, 2009). Since dysarthric deficits result from elementary motor impairments such as paresis of orofacial structures or rigidity of the laryngeal muscles, non-verbal activities of the vocal tract, as a rule, are also impaired. Depending upon their localization and severity, neurological disorders may affect a single segment of the vocal tract only (e.g., velopharyngeal incompetence following damage to the respective lower cranial nerves), or may compromise all functional components of spoken language, i.e., respiration, phonation, articulation, nasal resonance, and even more super-ordinate aspects of speech production such as prosody and fluency.

Motor speech disorders may be categorized along a variety of dimensions such as medical diagnosis, affected neuroanatomical structures, or presumed pathophysiology (Wertz, 1985). As a prerequisite to (eventual) medical or surgical therapy, the underlying disease process, e.g., multiple sclerosis, must be determined. By contrast, the planning of speech therapy, as a rule, depends upon the characterization of the profile of functional deficits. The Mayo Clinic classification of dysarthria types, based upon the work of Darley, Aronson, and Brown (1975), still represents the most widely adopted system in these regards (see Duffy 2005 for a recent review). These authors had performed a systematic auditory-perceptual evaluation of speech production in "model diseases" of the motor system. Altogether, 38 dimensions of speech production were considered for analysis, including various aspects of respiration, phonation, articulation, and prosody (see below). In analogy to pathophysiological concepts within the domain of limb movements, "flaccid," "spastic," "hypokinetic," "hyperkinetic," and "ataxic" syndromes of motor speech deficits could be delineated (Table 16.1).

In its strict sense, the definition of dysarthria encompasses central-motor disorders often referred to as neurogenic dysphonias, such as spasmodic dysphonia or essential voice tremor (see Chapter 20). Furthermore, stuttering-like abnormalities of spoken language as well as compulsive repetitions of mostly utterance-final words or phrases (palilalia) may emerge, especially, in association with hypokinetic dysarthria. Presumably, these clinical phenomena also reflect compromised speech motor control mechanisms (Benke & Butterworth, 2001; Benke et al., 2000). In isolation, e.g., after traumatic brain injury or ischemic cerebral lesions, these abnormalities are, however, labeled (acquired) dysfluencies rather than dysarthric deficits (see Chapter 19).

Acquired apraxia of speech (AOS), sparing basic motor functions such as muscle tone and force development, is, as a rule, not included in the list of dysarthria syndromes (see Chapter 18). This speech disorder encompasses phonological errors, variable distortions of consonants and vowels, and a non-fluent speech flow exhibiting trial-and-error groping behavior. Psycholinguistic studies indicate an impaired capability of AOS patients to "plan" speech movements at the level of

Table 16.1   Auditory-perceptual characteristics of the major dysarthria syndromes

Flaccid dysarthria (lower motor neuron/neuromuscular junction)
Respiration: short expiratory cycles
Phonation: breathy/harsh voice quality, reduced loudness, <u>low pitch</u>
Articulation: imprecise consonants, advanced tongue posture, hypernasality
Prosody: <u>slow rate</u>, monotonous speech

Spastic dysarthria (upper motor neuron)
Respiration: short expiratory cycles
Phonation: <u>strained</u>/harsh <u>voice quality</u>, reduced loudness
Articulation: imprecise consonants, <u>retracted tongue posture</u>, hypernasality
Prosody: <u>slow rate</u>, monotonous speech

Rigid-hypokinetic dysarthria (e.g., Parkinson's disease)
Respiration: short expiratory cycles
Phonation: <u>breathy</u>/harsh voice quality, reduced loudness, <u>high pitch (men)</u>
Articulation: imprecise consonants
Prosody: <u>normal or accelerated rate</u>, monotonous speech

Ataxic dysarthria (especially cerebellar dysfunctions)
Respiration: <u>inadequate respiratory patterns</u>, e.g., audible inspiration
Phonation: fluctuating voice quality (strained/breathy/harsh), <u>fluctuating pitch and loudness</u>
Articulation: predominantly imprecise, eventually "explosive" sound production
Prosody: reduced rate, <u>scanning rhythm</u>

Based on Ziegler et al. (2002). The affected component of the central-motor system is given in parentheses; the most salient features are underlined.

syllable-sized or even larger linguistic units (Ziegler, 2008). Speech motor control is often characterized as a process of two subsequent and hierarchically organized stages, i.e., planning of a sequence of phonetic gestures followed by the specification and execution of single gestures. Based upon this model, AOS roughly refers to the former and dysarthria to the latter level of spoken language. Most often, AOS has been observed to arise from ischemic infarctions within the area of blood supply of the left medial cerebral artery (MCA) and, hence, must be considered a syndrome of the language-dominant hemisphere. However, the more specific neuroanatomic substrate of this constellation, at a finer topographic level than the vascular areas of major cerebral vessels, is still a matter of dispute (see Chapter 17).

Patients suffering from left-sided SMA lesions may exhibit reduced spontaneous verbal behavior, in the absence of any motor deficits of the vocal tract muscles and any deterioration of language functions. This pattern of disrupted acoustic communication has been considered, by some authors, a variant of transcortical motor aphasia (see Ackermann & Ziegler, 2009 for a review). In addition, dysfluent, i.e., stuttering-like speech utterances in terms of sound prolongations and syllable repetitions, as well as a "flat" and monotonous intonation, resembling "motor aprosodia" subsequent to dysfunctions of the basal ganglia, have been observed in subjects with mesiofrontal lesions of the dominant hemisphere. Finally, bilateral damage to mesiofrontal areas, encroaching, presumably, upon the anterior cingulate gyrus (ACG) and its projections to SMA, may give rise to the syndrome of akinetic mutism, characterized by a lack of self-initiated motor activities, including speech production. In consideration of these clinical data, the medial wall of the frontal lobes has been assumed to mediate motivational aspects of verbal motor behavior and to operate as a "starting mechanism of speech" (Botez & Barbeau, 1971). Though this proposed "starting mechanism," presumably, must be considered a component of the speech motor control system, the dysfunctions of verbal communication due to mesiofrontal disorders, as a rule, are not classified as dysarthric deficits.

3 Auditory-Perceptual and Instrumental Analysis of Motor Speech Disorders

3.1 Introduction

Neurological diagnoses do not provide a sufficient basis for treatment planning. Rather, therapeutic interventions must be tailored to each patient according to the profile of deficits across the various subsystems involved in speech production. Non-instrumental speech examination includes client history, inspection of vocal tract structures, clinical evaluation of oral and pharyngeal sensory functions as well as tests of non-speech, speech-like, and citation tasks (Kent, 1997). As a framework for the functional evaluation of speech disorders, Rosenbek and LaPointe (1985) suggested combining a system of "point-places" (respiratory system, larynx, velopharyngeal port, tongue blade, tongue tip, lips, jaw) with a "process model" (articulation, resonance, phonation, respiration, prosody). In addition, a variety of instrumental techniques are available for more detailed analyses of speech motor deficits, yielding objective and quantitative measures of vocal tract functions (for a review see, e.g., Ball & Lowry, 2001). These data allow for a "physiological approach" to treatment, based upon hypotheses about the pathomechanism of the observed dysarthric deficits (Netsell & Rosenbek, 1985).

3.2 Auditory-perceptual evaluation of speech and assessment of intelligibility

Despite major advancements in speech technology, auditory analysis is still the "gold standard" of dysarthria assessment, implicitly providing a comprehensive account of the functionally relevant motor aspects of verbal behavior, including breathing, voice, articulation, and fluency. At comparatively little expense, human listeners are able to integrate observations across large samples of speech and to work out rather detailed profiles of speaking performance. Two basically different approaches can be distinguished: (a) description of the salient features of a patient's spoken language by experienced experts according to established neurophonetic standards; (b) more or less direct evaluation of the intelligibility of a speaker's verbal utterances, the most important functional aspect of speech.

The first approach has been elaborated by Darley, Aronson, and Brown (1975): altogether, 38 perceptual dimensions of dysarthric speech, including audible signs of impaired speech breathing (e.g., "audible inspiration"), phonation (e.g., "voice tremor"), resonance (e.g., "hypernasality"), articulation (e.g., "imprecise consonants"), and prosody (e.g., "reduced stress"), were considered for analysis, and the prominence of each feature represented on a seven-point scale. Later, Kluin et al. (1988) modified this evaluation procedure, focusing on the differentiation of spastic and ataxic dysarthria. Nicola, Ziegler, and Vogel (2004), finally, developed a more economic system, based upon the German language, which encompasses nine perceptual scales conforming to psychometric testing principles. As a major shortcoming of all these assessment systems, listeners often do not agree in their ratings across the different auditory dimensions. Thus, Zyski and Weisiger (1987) found very low overall accuracy rates (19–56 percent) across experienced speech pathologists, using the inventory proposed by Darley et al. (1975) for syndrome classification. Similarly, the method proposed by Nicola et al. (2004) showed only moderate between-listener agreements at the level of single speech samples. However, an acceptable level of inter-rater reliability could be noted, after all 12 speech samples of this test had been combined.

Intelligibility is probably the most important communicative aspect of dysarthric speech motor deficits. Several measurement procedures have been proposed, including auditory-perceptual rating scales, sentence transcriptions, and word identification tasks (see Kent et al., 1989, for a review). For example, the Assessment of Intelligibility of Dysarthric Speech (Yorkston & Beukelman, 1984) is based upon 50 single-word utterances spoken by a dysarthric patient. Each of these items is drawn quasi-randomly from an ensemble of 12 similar-sounding words. Later, a listener is required to identify all 50 spoken words among their 12 phonologically similar competitors. A further part of this test requires listeners to transcribe sentences of different lengths spoken by the patient. A phonetically more balanced word identification test was developed by Kent and colleagues (1989), allowing for the classification of a listener's identification errors in terms of phonetic features. However, the a priori chance rate for correct responses amounts to 25 percent. An alternative approach encompasses computerized target word selection (Ziegler & Zierdt, 2008). Both the dysarthric speech samples and the listener data may be assembled via web applications. This procedure provides a statistically reliable measure of intelligibility, specifying the factors influencing a patient's communication problem.

3.3 Analysis of the acoustic speech signal

Although an indirect approach, acoustic parameters may provide valuable insights into speech motor control processes (for an overview see, e.g., Kent & Read, 2001). One major group of measures refers to the temporal organization of speech output in terms of the duration of intervals between characteristic signal events. For example, voice onset time (VOT), i.e., the time span between release burst of a stop consonant and voicing onset of the following vowel, has been studied in several patient groups (Özsancak et al., 2001). Being perceived in a categorical manner, VOT contributes to the fortis/lenis or voicing contrast of many languages. In terms of articulatory processes, this measure can be considered an "index of subsystem coordination" (Kent et al., 1999), i.e., the temporal adjustment of laryngeal devoicing–voicing gestures and supralaryngeal closing–opening movements involved in the production of the respective (voiceless) consonants, e.g., /p/. Similarly, speech motor disorders may give rise to prolonged or more variable lengths of stop consonant occlusions as well as vowel and fricative sounds, representing information-bearing phonetic parameters in some languages (e.g., Ackermann et al., 1999). Apart from distinctions at the segmental level, durational measurements can also provide quantitative parameters of speech rate and some aspects of speech prosody, e.g., word stress and phrase boundaries (Hird & Kirsner, 1993).

A second group of acoustic parameters derives from spectral characteristics of verbal utterances, providing insights into the filter characteristics of vocal tract geometry. The quality of the sound source, for example, can be addressed by the calculation of the spectral slope, i.e., the steepness of the decline of voiced energy toward higher frequencies. Some cases of hypokinetic dysarthria, for example, may exhibit a loss of higher harmonics in the spectrum as indicated by an increased "soft phonation index" (Kent, Vorperian, & Duffy, 1999). At the segmental level, the formant frequencies, i.e., the eigenfrequencies of the vocal tract, are the most salient acoustic parameters indicating articulatory configurations. As a rule, the first formant indicates tongue height and the second formant refers to the front–back dimension of tongue articulation. Using these two parameters as orthogonal axes of a two-dimensional coordinate system, the vowel space of a language can be displayed. Dysarthric speakers may exhibit an abnormal vowel space (Tjaden et al., 2005; Turner, Tjaden, & Weismer, 1995), for example due to target undershoot, i.e., an articulator such as the tongue fails to reach its adequate target configuration. As concerns consonant production, the initial opening gestures of consonant–vowel (CV) syllables, e.g., /ba/ or /da/, give rise to characteristic formant transitions. These shifts of spectral energy distribution, usually extending across a time interval of ca. 40 ms, provide at the perceptual level information on place of articulation (labial, coronal, dorsal). An abnormal duration or steepness of these acoustic trajectories, thus, may compromise speech intelligibility. Within the domain of dysarthria assessment, the measurement of formant transitions (Weismer et al., 1992) might be used, e.g., as an index of articulatory velocity.

3.4   Kinematic and electromyographic techniques

3.4.1   Overview   A variety of techniques have been developed to directly assess the various speech-related motor activities of the vocal tract. On the one hand, these methods can visualize the entire ensemble of events generating the speech signal; on the other hand, specific parameters can be obtained quantifying the kinematic working characteristics of single subsystems engaged in speech production (see Hertrich & Ackermann, 2007, for further references).

3.4.2   Evaluation of laryngeal functions (vocal fold vibrations)   As a rule, the various dysarthria syndromes compromise the activity of the vocal folds, giving rise to abnormalities of voice quality or pitch control. Apart from high-speed video kinematography, two complementary methods have been introduced so far that allow for the evaluation of the glottal aperture or the contact area between the vocal folds, respectively. Photoglottography (PGG) measures at a high temporal resolution the amount of light passing the glottis whereas electroglottography (EGG) or laryngography register the changes of electric impedance at the level of the glottis in a non-invasive manner.

3.4.3   Imaging of vocal tract structures   Historically, X-ray cineradiographic recordings of speech movements provided spatial and temporal information of articulatory movements. Though this technique is no longer applicable within the domain of the speech sciences, due to considerable radiation exposure, reformatted X-ray films are available at the following website: http://psyc.queensu. ca/~munhallk/05_database.htm. Meanwhile, MRI techniques (see above) allow for the visualization of the entire vocal tract during speech production, providing high-resolution images of vocal tract configurations as well as three-dimensional cine-MRI sequences, based upon stroboscopy-like techniques that reconstruct an articulatory sequence from multiple productions of the same phrase (e.g., Mathiak et al., 2000).

Two-dimensional contours of the surface of the tongue during speech production can be displayed by means of ultrasound techniques. In case of static vocal tract configurations, it is also possible to obtain a 3-D picture of the tongue (see volume 19, issue 6/7 of *Clinical Linguistics and Phonetics* for a review of the state of the art of ultrasound methods in speech research). Furthermore, a more recent procedure combines ultrasound measurements with infrared-emitting diodes (Whalen et al., 2005).

3.5   Movement trajectories of single articulators

Various measurement devices are available for monitoring rapid excursions of single articulators. As a rule, two- or three-dimensional trajectories of single fleshpoints are recorded, e.g., by means of electro-mechanical movement transducers.

If articulatory movements are visible from outside the mouth, optoelectronic methods allow for the registration of reflecting markers or light-emitting diodes attached to the moving structures. Intraoral movement trajectories have been investigated by means of the X-ray microbeam system, a procedure that tracks small gold pellets by detecting a "shadow" in the direction of the X-ray beam (Westbury, 1991). A more convenient alternative is provided by magnetometric methods (Perkell et al., 1992; Schönle et al., 1987): transmitter coils outside the head generate alternating magnetic fields of different carrier frequencies each. In order to track articulatory movements, small transducer coils (size ca. 2 mm) can be attached to moving articulators such as the blade of the tongue or even the velum. The transducer signals, transferred by thin cables to an electronic device, can be transformed into spatial coordinates. The most recent system (AG500; Carstens Medizinelektronik, Göttingen, Germany) can provide five-dimensional coordinates (three locational and two orientational dimensions) at high temporal (200 samples/s) and spatial (0.3 mm; Kaburagi, Wakamiya, & Honda, 2005) accuracy.

3.6 Lingual–palatal contact patterns

Quantitative measures of the tongue–palate contact areas during speech production can be obtained by means of electropalatography (EPG). Subjects must be provided with an acrylic pseudo-palate encompassing a two-dimensional array of electrodes. At those sensors getting into touch with the tongue, a high-frequency carrier signal is modulated. As a consequence, the temporal profile and the spatial extent of palatal contact can be displayed (Hardcastle, Gibbon, & Jones, 1991; McAuliffe & Ward, 2006). Glossometry, an intra-oral optical tracking method measuring the distance of the tongue surface from the palate, can be used to determine the place of constriction of speech sounds such as vowels or approximants, characterized by incomplete closure of the oral cavity. As the most recent development within this domain, optopalatography measures the light reflected by the tongue surface, using optical fibers mounted on a pseudo-palate.

3.7 Electromyographic recordings

Principally, electromyography (EMG), i.e., the registration of the electrical activity of muscles by means of surface skin or intramuscular fine-wire electrodes, may provide more direct information about neural control mechanisms than, for example, kinematic trajectories. Quantitative evaluation of EMG signals, however, faces considerable difficulties, and the obtained quantitative measures, such as burst duration of muscular activity, depend to a considerable degree upon signal processing and display procedures (for a review see Luschei & Finnegan, 1997). As a consequence, these techniques have found so far rather limited application within the area of dysarthria assessment.

4   Dysarthric Deficits in Neurological Disorders

4.1   *Dissociation of speech and non-speech vocal tract motor dysfunctions*

4.1.1   Speech production and swallowing   Most muscles engaged in speech production also contribute to the oral and pharyngeal stages of swallowing. Nonetheless, there is no straightforward relationship between dysarthric deficits and dysphagia in brain lesions or diseases. For example, the syndrome of pure dysarthria, i.e., dysarthria without dysphagia, in stroke patients represents a striking example of a dissociation between speaking and swallowing functions (for a review see Ackermann & Ziegler, 2009). These findings cannot simply reflect enhanced demands on motor coordination during speech production, as compared to mastication or deglutition, since some cerebrovascular disorders also may give rise to the reverse pattern, i.e., dysphagia without dysarthria. At some level, therefore, swallowing functions and speech articulation must be associated with different cerebral networks.

4.1.2   Speech production and facial/vocal expression of emotions   Vocal expression of affective states also provides evidence for a dissociation of speech production and non-verbal vocal tract activities. For example, patients with pseudobulbar palsy may show preserved phonation and unimpaired orofacial movements during spontaneous emotional behavior such as laughter and crying, although voluntary control of the muscles supplied by the lower cranial nerves, including verbal utterances, is severely disrupted or even abolished. These cases indicate an "automatic-voluntary" dissociation between affective vocalizations, on the one hand, and speech-related motor activity, on the other. Conceivably, emotional "bursts" are mediated by a "limbic vocalization system," which has been documented in subhuman primates. Thus, two distinct cerebral pathways appear to act upon the motor nuclei of the lower cranial nerves in humans ("dual-pathway model of acoustic communication," Ackermann & Ziegler, 2009).

4.2   *Disorders of primary motor cortex and its efferent corticobulbar pathways (upper motor neuron)*

Damage to the efferent projections of the face, mouth, and larynx areas of primary motor cortex to the respective brainstem nuclei represents the most frequent pathomechanism of dysarthric deficits in stroke patients. As a rule, unilateral damage to the corticobulbar system yields only mild and transient dysarthric impairments. By and large, articulatory and phonatory functions recover within a time interval of several days to a few weeks (Urban et al., 1999). This time course of speech restitution can be explained by the fact that the brainstem nuclei subserving the innervation of vocal tract muscles receive input from both cerebral hemispheres, with the exception of some functional asymmetries at the level of lower face muscles (Triggs et al., 2005). Transcranial magnetic stimulation studies, indeed, suggest that preexisting uncrossed motor pathways of the intact hemisphere participate in the compensation of dysarthric deficits subsequent to unilateral dysfunctions of the upper motor neurons (Müllbacher, Artner, & Mamoli, 1999; Müllbacher et al., 2001). This model received further support by a recent follow-up fMRI study in a patient with left-hemisphere striato-capsular infarction: the emergence of a mirror-like reversal of hemodynamic activation within motor cortex and cerebellum was found to parallel recovery of speech production (Riecker et al., 2002). Nevertheless, however, a subgroup of patients with unilateral upper motor neuron syndrome may suffer from persistent dysarthria (Duffy & Folger, 1996).

Damage to the left precentral gyrus rostral to the "face area" of primary motor cortex has repeatedly been associated with prominent articulatory disorders referred to as dysarthria, anarthria, aphemia, or apraxia of speech (Terao et al., 2007). These observations have been interpreted as indicating that a specialized higher-order articulo-motor network is localized near the primary motor representation of the tongue and lower face muscles.

Bilateral damage to the upper motor neuron either at the cortical or the subcortical level, e.g., in patients suffering from pseudobulbar palsy, may give rise to the syndrome of spastic dysarthria. This constellation has been reported to encompass slowed articulatory gestures of a reduced amplitude, hypernasality due to insufficient velar elevation, tongue retraction, increased constriction of the pharynx, and hyperadduction of the shortened vocal folds (Ziegler & von Cramon, 1986). In its extreme, anarthria and/or aphonia may develop under these conditions, e.g., the Foix–Chavany–Marie syndrome. In case of a supranuclear localization of the relevant lesion, orofacial, pharyngeal, and laryngeal reflex mechanisms must be preserved, and emotional mimic or vocal behavior remains intact as long as the respective efferent bulbar projections of mesiofrontal areas are spared (see above).

4.3 Disorders of the basal ganglia: Syndromes of hypo- and hyperkinetic dysarthria

4.3.1 Parkinson's disease Parkinson's disease (PD; synonym: idiopathic Parkinsonian syndrome) is primarily characterized by progressive degeneration of dopaminergic pathways, originating within the substantia nigra and projecting, among others, to the basal ganglia. The salient motor signs of this disorder such as akinesia, bradykinesia, hypokinesia, and rigidity are assumed to reflect presynaptic depletion of this neurotransmitter at the level of the striatum. Tracing back to the work of Darley, Aronson, and Brown (1975), basically the same pathomechanisms, acting upon vocal tract muscles, are considered to be engaged in PD dysarthria, giving rise to monopitch, reduced stress, monoloudness, imprecise consonants, inappropriate silences, short rushes of speech, harsh voice quality, (continuous) breathy voice, low pitch, and variable rate (the most to the least salient signs; Duffy, 2005, p. 196; see Table 16.1 above). Hence, these perceived speech motor deficits were lumped together into the syndrome of hypokinetic or rigid dysarthria. During the course of PD, phonatory difficulties seem to precede articulatory impairments arising at the level of the supralaryngeal tract (Logemann et al., 1978). Besides PD, representing the "prototypic" constellation, dysfunctions of the basal ganglia of, for example, vascular, traumatic, or inflammatory origin, also may give rise to this syndrome of articulatory and phonatory abnormalities.

Among all dysarthria types, the motor speech deficits of PD have been most extensively studied by means of instrumental techniques such as acoustic and kinematic analyses (see Duffy, 2005, pp. 206f., for an exhaustive review). These investigations were able to further refine the characteristics of hypokinetic dysarthria. Thus, acoustic measurements revealed, in accordance with the auditory-perceptual features of monopitch and -loudness, a reduced long-term variability of fundamental frequency and speech intensity during sentence productions. As a further example, EGG recordings detected gender differences in voice quality (Hertrich & Ackermann, 1995). Several kinematic studies measured range and velocity of articulatory gestures to determine whether hypometria (undershooting) and bradykinesia (slowness) – well-established abnormalities of upper limb movements in PD – also affect vocal tract structures. So far, discrepant data have been obtained (see Ackermann & Hertrich, 2008 for further references), presumably because the emergence of articulatory undershooting depends upon speaking rate.

In contrast to corticobulbar and cerebellar dysfunctions, PD patients, as a rule, show normal speaking rate, and a subgroup of about 10 percent of these subjects even may exhibit an accelerated speech tempo ("speech hastening"; Adams, 1997). Tracking of lip movements during syllable repetitions suggests this phenomenon reflects the activity of an involuntary pacemaker operating at a frequency of 8 to 9 Hz (Ackermann et al., 1993, 1997). Under these conditions, articulatory undershoot emerges, ending up in unintelligible "numbling" speech. Furthermore, stuttering-like sentence-initial dysfluencies or compulsive repetitions of mostly utterance-final words or phrases (palilalia) have been observed in hypokinetic dysarthria (Benke et al., 2000). Whereas up to 14 percent of PD patients show an "unsteady voice" at perceptual evaluation, "true voice tremor" seems, however, to be an uncommon sign of this disorder (Duffy, 2005).

4.3.2 Huntington's chorea   Besides PD, Huntington's chorea (HC), an autosomal-dominant hereditary disease, represents, within some limits, a further paradigm of a striatal dysfunction. Whereas the degenerative process, at least in earlier stages of the disease, predominantly involves the caudate nucleus and the putamen, other components of the basal ganglia, the thalamus, the cerebellum as well as neocortical areas also will be compromised during further follow-up. The characteristic clinical signs of HC encompass choreatic hyperkinesia, personality changes such as increased irritability, and progressive decline of cognitive functions. Perceptual speech evaluation in these patients revealed, among others, fluctuating pitch and/or loudness, involuntary vocalizations and "overshooting" articulatory gestures, abnormalities assumed to reflect hyperkinetic activity of vocal tract muscles (Duffy, 2005). Acoustic analyses of sentence utterances found increased durational variability in HC patients and in ca. 50 percent of the cases a slowed syllable rate (Hertrich & Ackermann, 1994). Furthermore, kinematic recordings of lip movements during speech production indicate a tendency toward slowed movement execution (Ackermann et al., 1997). The few available instrumental studies do not yet, however, allow for unambiguous inferences on the pathomechanisms of HC speech motor deficits.

4.3.3 Focal damage to the basal ganglia So far, only a few data on the articulatory and phonatory dysfunctions in subjects with focal damage confined to the basal ganglia have been reported. Whereas a patient suffering from an isolated lesion restricted to the left caudate nucleus exhibited severe speech motor deficits, as part of a choreatic syndrome, other studies point at a rather limited contribution of this component of the basal ganglia to speech motor control (see Ackermann & Ziegler, 2009 for a review). By contrast, ischemic lesions of the putamen and the (left) pallidum have been observed to elicit "hypophonic" and "numbling" verbal utterances, closely resembling the syndrome of hypokinetic dysarthria. A similar constellation also has been noted in a case of bilateral ischemic damage to the thalamus (Ackermann, Ziegler, & Petersen, 1993). Presumably, the infarction encroached upon target areas of the pallidal efferent projections, giving rise, thereby, to a disruption of the cortico-striato-thalamo-cortical motor loop.

4.3.4 Dystonias and essential tremor Spasmodic dysphonia, characterized by strained and harsh voice quality, low volume and pitch, vocal tremor, and irregularly distributed stoppages as well as catches of the voice, is now widely recognized as a variant of focal dystonia, acting upon laryngeal muscles (see Chapter 19). Tentatively, therefore, this disorder must be attributed to an impairment of basal ganglia circuitries. The same suggestion applies to voice tremor, being either a component of the syndrome of essential tremor or an isolated sign (essential voice tremor). In more advanced stages, both these disorders may compromise the production of distinct speech sounds. Besides spasmodic dysphonia, Meige syndrome represents another constellation of dystonia, affecting besides the eyelids also the oromandibular system. Although this syndrome seems to be responsive to deep brain stimulation (globus pallidus internus; Ostrem et al., 2007), a recent fMRI study reported impaired activation of the primary motor and ventral premotor cortex rather than the basal ganglia (Dresel et al., 2006).

4.4 The contribution of the cerebellum and its afferent and efferent connections to speech motor control: Ataxic dysarthria

4.4.1 Topographic aspects Speech motor deficits have been observed in a variety of cerebellar disorders, e.g., gunshot injuries, hereditary or sporadic degenerative diseases (atrophy), inflammatory conditions, or ischemic infarctions. Dysarthria seems to be predominantly bound to lesions of superior parts of the cerebellum. However, the available clinical data do not yet provide a coherent picture of the topographic correlates of these communication disorders (Ackermann & Hertrich, 2000; Ackermann, Mathiak, & Riecker, 2007). Besides damage to the cerebellum proper, dysfunctions both of the respective afferent and efferent fiber tracts may compromise speech motor control mechanisms. During early stages of Friedreich's ataxia, the articulatory and phonatory dysfunctions associated with this disease, presumably, reflect a disruption of afferent pathways conveying sensory information arising in vocal tract structures to the cerebellum. Besides the trigeminal nuclei, the frontal lobes project via internal capsule and pontine nuclei to the cerebellum. Conceivably, the so-called dysarthria-clumsy hand syndrome reflects damage to these pathways either at the level of the internal capsule or the basis pontis. In addition, ataxic dysarthria has been observed in a patient suffering from an ischemic meso-diencephalic lesion, encroaching upon efferent projections of the cerebellum to thalamic target nuclei.

4.4.2 Characteristics of ataxic dysarthria Darley, Aronson, and Brown (1975) found imprecise consonants and vowels, irregular articulatory breakdown, excess and equal stress, i.e., scanning speech rhythm, reduced speaking rate as well as harsh voice quality to be the most salient motor speech deficits in cerebellar disorders (Table 16.1). Assuming the same pathomechanisms as in other motor subsystems, the label "ataxic dysarthria" was assigned to this pattern of speech deficits. Relating articulatory and phonatory abnormalities in olivo-ponto-cerebellar atrophy to the distribution of infratentorial glucose metabolism, a later investigation reported, however, a somewhat different profile of perceived speech alterations, emphasizing fluctuations of speaking rate, loudness, and pitch as well as transient changes in voice quality (Kluin et al., 1988).

Acoustic measurements allowed for the objective and parametric characterization of at least some aspects of ataxic dysarthria. For example, voice tremor of a frequency of about 3 Hz and enhanced pitch fluctuations during sustained vowel productions could be documented (see Ackermann & Hertrich, 2000 for a review). Measurements of segment durations, e.g., syllable length, vowel duration, voice onset time (VOT), represent the bulk of the available acoustic data. During fast syllable repetitions ("as fast as possible on a single breath"), a variety of studies found reduced maximum syllable rates (measured at the acoustic signal) in Friedreich's ataxia, in cerebellar diseases and in not further qualified ataxic syndromes. Furthermore, a slowed conversational speech tempo has been observed in cerebellar atrophy and Friedreich's ataxia. Most noteworthy, syllable frequency did not fall below a value of about 3 Hz in these two variants of an ataxia syndrome, both during sentence production and oral diadochokinesis tasks.

A longstanding tenet of clinical neurology considers "scanning speech" a characteristic sign of cerebellar disorders. As an acoustic correlate of this perceptual phenomenon, a tendency toward isochronous syllable durations, predominantly due to a prolongation of short vocalic elements, has been reported. However, the available acoustic data do not yet provide a consistent picture, and some studies suggest increased variability of durational parameters to be bound to ataxic dysarthria – rather than equally spaced syllable lengths. Conceivably, dissolution of verbal utterances in cerebellar disorders evolves across two stages: (a) increased instability of the temporal organization of syllabic sequences develops, finally, into (b) slowed and isochronous syllable pacing (Kent et al., 1997).

Kinematic measurements of articulatory movements documented prolonged movement times and reduced articulatory velocity in cerebellar-ataxic speakers. Similar to an unimpaired control group, cerebellar subjects showed linear peak velocity/amplitude scaling ("mass-normalized stiffness") of lip and jaw speech movements. However, the slope of the regression function was significantly flatter in the cerebellar group, indicating reduced articulatory stiffness, i.e., slower peak velocity for a given amplitude (Ackermann, Hertrich, & Scharf, 1995). Most noteworthy, an influence of movement type and, to a lesser degree, linguistic demands on motor performance could be observed: the higher temporal constraints on movement execution during closing as compared to opening gestures and during short versus long vowels enhanced the inter-group differences in mass-normalized stiffness. Cerebellar dysarthria thus appears to be associated with compromised execution of single vocal tract gestures in terms of, presumably, an impaired ability to generate adequate muscular forces under time-critical conditions. Beyond the specification of kinematic parameters of single orofacial excursions, acoustic studies indicate a contribution of the cerebellum to the co-ordination or the sequencing of vocal tract movements. For example, ataxic speakers show a reduced VOT contrast with respect to the German /t/–/d/ distinction (Ackermann & Hertrich, 1997), and abnormal coarticulation patterns in terms of reduced anticipatory and a tendency toward increased retentive effects – if slowed speech rate is taken into account (Hertrich & Ackermann, 1999).

4.4.3 Transient cerebellar mutism Speechlessness (mutism) after surgical removal of posterior fossa tumors or stereotactic lesions of the dentate nucleus was first reported in the late 1970s. This constellation predominantly emerges in children subsequent to resection of hindbrain tumors (incidence up to 15 percent), but may sporadically occur in adults as well (Ackermann, Mathiak, & Riecker, 2007). Besides surgical interventions, especially at the level of the vermis, mutism also has been observed in patients suffering from traumatic injury or a viral inflammation affecting the cerebellum. Frequently, disrupted speech production is associated with a variety of further behavioral abnormalities and, typically, develops within a time interval of one to several days after surgical intervention. Initial speechlessness may evolve into marked speech motor deficits ("syndrome of cerebellar mutism and subsequent dysarthria"). Based upon these observations, transient cerebellar mutism has been considered the most severe variant of ataxic dysarthria ("anarthria hypothesis"). However, this pattern emerges in a subgroup of patients only. As an alternative – and more plausible – explanation, cerebellar lesions may give rise to reduced cerebral blood flow (hypoperfusion) and, as a consequence, "functional depression" of contralateral mesiofrontal areas ("crossed cerebral diaschisis"). Transient cerebellar mutism, therefore, could reflect a disruption of mesiofrontal "speech initiation mechanisms," resulting in a variant of akinetic mutism. Any dysarthric signs during recovery from transient cerebellar mutism then might reflect a local cerebellar dysfunction subsequent to, for example, the development of an edema after surgery.

4.5   Cranial nerves and (neuro-)muscular diseases: The syndrome of flaccid dysarthria

Dependent upon lesion site, disorders restricted to a single cranial nerve yield dysphonia, velopharyngeal incompetency, impaired tongue motility or oral–facial paresis. More extensive disease processes may encroach upon all cranial nerves supplying the vocal tract, e.g., nasopharyngeal tumors, polyneuritis, or progressive bulbar palsy, i.e., a variant of degenerative motor system diseases. In these instances, a constellation of flaccid dysarthria must be expected. Amyotrophic lateral sclerosis may also present with a similar syndrome prior to its development into a mixed flaccid–spastic constellation. Besides other muscle groups, myasthenia gravis, i.e., a disorder characterized by disrupted synaptic transmission at the level of the neuromuscular junction, may involve the speech apparatus, giving rise to abnormalities of articulation and/or phonation. Rarely, dysphonia or velopharyngeal incompetence even emerge as the initial signs of myasthenia gravis (e.g., Neiman, Mountjoy, & Allen, 1975). Furthermore, muscular dystrophies, e.g., the facioscapulohumeral and oculopharyngeal variants, or polymyositis have been noted to impair orofacial, laryngeal, and/or respiratory functions (Ackermann, 1999).

4.6   Dysarthria in neurological diseases affecting several components of the central-motor system

A variety of disorders of the central nervous system such as multiple sclerosis (e.g., Murdoch & Theodoros, 2000), progressive supranuclear palsy, amyotrophic lateral sclerosis, or multisystem atrophy may compromise several cerebral structures contributing to speech motor control, resulting in a "mixed dysarthria." Depending on the subsystems affected, the profile of performance may vary considerably and – for example, in the case of multisystem atrophy – the initial symptoms and the history of evolving difficulties are hardly predictable.

5   Therapeutic Approaches to Dysarthric Motor Speech Disorders

5.1   Framework of therapeutic intervention

Four approaches to the treatment of dysarthrias are available: behavioral techniques (drill, exercises); instrumental aids including prosthetic and augmentative devices; medication; and surgical procedures. Besides severity and profile of the speech deficits, the planning of therapeutic interventions also must take into account a patient's motor disabilities outside the speech domain, intellectual capabilities, and personal motivation as well as the expected course of the underlying disease. Yorkston and colleagues (1993) proposed an intervention plan for dysarthria in amyotrophic lateral sclerosis that aligns the various therapy procedures to disease stages. This schedule also provides a framework for the approach to other neurogenic disorders of articulatory and phonatory functions. At stage 1, characterized by still unimpaired speech production, treatment is, of course, not necessary. A major role of the clinician is – when requested by the patient – to provide information on the eventual impact of a disease on verbal communication. The facilitation of verbal behavior in natural settings, e.g., minimizing environmental adversity or maximizing the hearing of frequent partners (pragmatic approach), may be helpful in the case of detectable speech disturbances which, however, still allow the intended message to be conveyed at the cost of more or less effort (stage 2). Reduced speech intelligibility (stage 3) requires the use of behavioral modification techniques: for example, patients are encouraged to maintain a slowed speaking rate, to exaggerate articulatory movements, and/or to rely on energy-conserving techniques during verbal communication. Furthermore, instrumental aides or prostheses such as palatal lifts may be beneficial under these conditions. Individuals with mainly unintelligible speech output (stage 4) or patients suffering from a complete loss of useful verbal behavior (stage 5) have to rely on augmentative communication systems. In the absence of medical or surgical intervention acting upon the underlying disease, "compensated intelligibility" rather than "normal speech" must be considered the goal of dysarthria therapy (Rosenbek & LaPointe 1985).

5.2 Behavioral treatment strategies

In severe dysarthria, behavioral treatment begins with exercises acting upon individual components of the speech apparatus or involving even non-speech movements (for further references see Ackermann & Hughes, 2003). As concerns respiration, inefficient use of the breath stream during speech production rather than reduced total air volume in the lungs represents the main problem of dysarthric patients. The goal of therapy, therefore, is to reestablish controlled expiration. Postural adjustments such as lying supine and/or monitoring the amount of air inhaled as well as the evenness of exhalation may improve respiratory support of speech output.

The phonatory abnormalities observed in the various dysarthria types may be classified into three patterns of deviant vocal fold movements: hyper- and hypoadduction as well as incoordination. Since, as a rule, these voice disorders have only a limited impact on speech intelligibility, they do not represent the primary targets for dysarthria intervention. As concerns hypoadduction, therapy focuses on efficient laryngeal closure during speech production. Training aims, for example, at the improvement of voluntary control of vocal fold abduction/adduction through physical maneuvers that elicit glottal closure such as lifting and pushing. As concerns velopharyngeal insufficiency, speaking more slowly and with greater effort, e.g., in terms of increasing jaw opening, can improve intelligibility. By contrast, most non-speech exercises such as blowing and sucking are not effective in restoring velopharyngeal functions.

Articulation drill, as a rule, relies on individualized word lists which improve existing and facilitate lacking motor capabilities. Encouraging the patient to exaggerate intended orofacial gestures can be helpful. Once a patient is able to combine several different sound productions, training proceeds to the level of verbal utterances. In order to improve intelligibility, establishment of an optimum speech rate may be necessary. At later stages of treatment or in the case of less severe speech impairments, exercises aim at a training of coordinated activities of all vocal tract components in order to achieve, for example, voluntary control over stress and rhythm adjustments. Besides rate control and systematic drill based on phonetic principles, movements of the speech apparatus can also be supported by proprioceptive neuromuscular facilitation. This procedure aims at increasing neuronal excitability of vocal tract structures by stimulation such as icing or brushing, or manipulation, e.g., pressure, stretch, or resistance.

Ramig and colleagues introduced a therapy program for Parkinson's disease that focuses on vocal loudness (The Lee Silverman Voice Treatment, LSVT®; e.g., Fox et al., 2006; Ramig, Fox, & Sapir, 2004). Patients are systematically trained to increase phonatory effort during maximum performance tasks. As a rule, subjects receive 16 individual treatment sessions across 4 weeks and perform additional exercises at home. Besides a significant improvement of speech intensity and fundamental frequency variability, this approach also appears to have a significant impact upon articulatory preciseness and speech tempo.

Behavioral techniques have been extended by a so-called pragmatic approach. Rather than articulatory impairment, treatment focuses on the efficacy of verbal communication in various contexts (Kearns & Simmons, 1988). Thus, the patient and his relatives are instructed, for example, to alter the communication environment, to modify the length of utterances, to enhance self-monitoring, and to ensure the orientation of a listener to the topic at hand in order to improve communication.

5.3   *Instrumental aids and prostheses*

Biofeedback, i.e., the transformation of covert physiological processes of speech production into precisely tuned auditory, visual, or tactile signals, has been found to support behavioral exercises: patients focus on key elements of their speech difficulties by means of continuous comparison of actual performance with a given target (e.g., Nemec & Cohen, 1984; see Ackermann & Hughes, 2003 for further references). Besides these procedures, a variety of other instrumental aids as well as specific prostheses have proven valuable for dysarthria therapy. For example, boards segmented into several sections by raised dividers (pacing boards) may help patients to better control their speech rate: the patient moves a finger along the board and produces one syllable per segment. As an alternative, delayed auditory feedback can be used to reduce speech tempo (see, e.g., Adams, 1997). Finally, PD patients may show marked improvement of vocal intensity during application of masking noise (Lombard effect).

Velopharyngeal incompetence, i.e., reduced or missing elevation of the velum during speech production, giving rise to inadequate nasal emission, may significantly impair a patient's intelligibility due to, for example, impaired generation of intra-oral pressure. Dental prostheses such as palatal lifts may improve this condition. Among others, patients suffering from disorders of the upper as well as the lower motor neuron or even myasthenia gravis have been reported to benefit from these devices. Immobilization of the mandible by means of an occlusal splint or bite raiser can be helpful in subjects with involuntary orofacial movements (e.g., Netsell, 1985). Non-verbal systems of communication have to be considered in patients with persistent anarthria or unintelligible speech output if improvement of articulatory or phonatory functions during further follow-up cannot be expected.

5.4 Medication

Some disorders giving rise to dysarthria are susceptible to pharmacological intervention, e.g., myasthenia gravis and multiple sclerosis. Under these conditions, medication may allow for the recovery of "normal spoken language." The motor speech deficits of other neurological disorders show a less pronounced or even missing responsiveness to this therapeutic approach. In patients with Parkinson's disease, dopamine substitution and/or dopamine agonists have a rather limited impact upon hypokinetic dysarthria. These data indicate a significant contribution of non-dopaminergic mechanisms to motor aspects of speech production (Pinto et al., 2004). Similarly, essential voice tremor seems to be less susceptible to pharmacological therapy than essential tremor of the hands (Koller, Graner, & MlCoch, 1985). Several studies indicate drugs such as amphetamine, bromocriptine, or piracetam to enhance the effects of behavioral therapy in aphasic patients (e.g., Huber et al., 1997). It is unsettled so far whether this approach supports the shaping of articulatory skills as well.

Injection of botulinum toxin into the laryngeal muscles has been shown to significantly ameliorate spasmodic dysphonia. This procedure aims either at a unilateral paralysis or at a slight bilateral paresis of the vocal folds (see Chapter 20 for more details). Application of botulinum toxin, therefore, must be restricted to variants of spasmodic dysphonia with glottal hyperadduction.

5.5 Surgical procedures

Rarely, surgical intervention may target the underlying disease process of dysarthria syndromes, e.g., in the case of nasopharyngeal tumors. Unilateral section of the recurrent laryngeal nerve represents an alternative to botulinum toxin injection for the therapy of spasmodic dysphonia. The reported numbers of successfully treated patients in terms of a restoration of effective conversational voice extend from about 30 to 80 percent. Furthermore, recurring spasticity can be corrected by laser thinning of the paralyzed vocal fold via direct laryngoscopy (see Ackermann and Hughes, 2003 for references).

Pharyngeal flaps connect tissue from the posterior pharyngeal wall with the soft palate in order to improve velopharyngeal closure during speech production. This surgical procedure is recommended for patients with velopharyngeal incompetence in the case of unsuccessful alternative therapeutic approaches, given that the lateral pharyngeal wall shows an adequate degree of mobility. Injection of Teflon or similar materials into the posterior pharyngeal walls, producing an anteriorly projecting bulge, provides an alternative in this regard. Usually, these interventions do not allow for the restoration of "normal speech output."

Similar to dopaminergic medication, the more recent technique of deep brain stimulation, again, shows a less beneficial impact upon speech production in PD as compared to other motor domains (Pinto et al., 2004, 2005). In some patients, articulatory and phonatory functions even have been observed to deteriorate after this intervention. Presumably, current spread to the adjacent internal capsule accounts for these adverse side effects.

Oro-facial-cervical dystonia (Meige syndrome) sometimes severely compromises spoken language. In these instances, given pharmacological treatment has proved to be unsatisfactory, bilateral stimulation of the internal segment of the globus pallidus may help to restore normal speech (Taira, 2007, data presented at the 1st International Symposium on Deep Brain Stimulation and Basal Ganglia Speech Disorders, London, June 4–5, 2007).

5.6   Evaluation of treatment efficacy

So far, the effectiveness of dysarthria therapy has been evaluated most widely in PD patients (for reviews of treatment efficacy in speech motor disorders see, e.g., Enderby & Emerson, 1995; Kearns & Simmons, 1990). The first investigations during the 1960s and 1970s failed to document carry-over or maintenance of treatment-related changes during follow-up, once intervention had been discontinued. Therefore, transfer to daily life was considered a significant problem of behavioral treatment in this disease (Comella et al., 1994). As concerns the domain of speech and voice functions, more recent studies, however, were able to document beneficial effects lasting for up to 1 year – the longest period of follow-up so far – in mildly to moderately afflicted PD subjects, receiving intensive daily therapy across 2 to 4 weeks (Fox et al., 2006; Ramig, Fox, & Sapir, 2004; Robertson & Thomson, 1987). A recent Cochrane review identified three studies comparing speech therapy in this disease with placebo application and two studies considering two different intervention strategies (Deane et al., 2006a, 2006b). These data indicate significant improvement of voice intensity, pitch control, and intelligibility in response to specific treatment procedures. Lasting effects seem to be bound, however, to intensive daily interventions across several weeks.

As concerns non-progressive brain damage, no treatment trials of a quality high enough to be included in a Cochrane review are available so far (Sellars, Hughes,

& Langhorne, 2002). However, various case studies were able to document beneficial effects of speech exercises concomitant with instrumental aids – even long after the recognized period of spontaneous recovery in cerebrovascular disorders or closed head injuries (e.g., Simpson, Till, & Goff, 1988; Workinger & Netsell, 1992). Thus, it must be recognized that behavioral treatment supported by instrumental aids may enable dysarthric patients to speak in a more intelligible manner (for further details, see McNeil, 1997).

A number of single- and multiple-case studies demonstrated improved intelligibility and enhanced speech motor functions following adjustment of instrumental aids such as a palatal lift or delayed auditory feedback (see, e.g., the respective chapters in Berry, 1983). Since these procedures may pose considerable demands on compliance and cooperation, patients must be carefully selected in order to achieve long-term treatment effects.

REFERENCES

Ackermann, H. (1999). Acquired disorders of articulation: Classification and intervention. In F. Fabbro (ed.), *Concise encyclopedia of language pathology* (pp. 261–8). Amsterdam: Pergamon/Elsevier.

Ackermann, H. & Hertrich, I. (1997). Voice onset time in ataxic dysarthria. *Brain and Language* 56, 321–33.

Ackermann, H. & Hertrich, I. (2000). The contribution of the cerebellum to speech processing. *Journal of Neurolinguistics* 13, 95–116.

Ackermann, H. & Hertrich, I. (2008). Dysarthrie des Parkinson-Syndroms – klinische Befunde, instrumentelle Daten. In A. Nebel & G. Deuschl (eds.), *Dysarthrie und Dysphagie bei Morbus Parkinson* (pp. 34–51). Stuttgart: Thieme.

Ackermann, H. & Hughes, T. A. T. (2003). Dysarthria and dysphonia. In T. Brandt, L. R. Caplan, J. Dichgans, H. C. Diener, & C. Kennard (eds.), *Neurological disorders: Course and treatment*, 2nd ed. (pp. 245–8). Amsterdam: Academic Press/Elsevier.

Ackermann, H. & Riecker, A. (2009). Cerebral control of motor aspects of speech production: Neurophysiological and functional imaging data. In B. Maassen & P. H. H. M. van Lieshout (eds.), *Speech motor control: New Developments in basic and applied research.* Oxford: Oxford University Press.

Ackermann, H. & Ziegler, W. (1995). Akinetic mutism: A review. *Fortschritte der Neurologie und Psychiatrie* 63, 59–67 [German].

Ackermann, H. & Ziegler, W. (2009). Brain mechanisms underlying speech motor control. In W. J. Hardcastle & J. Laver (eds.), *The handbook of phonetic sciences*, 2nd ed. Malden, MA: Blackwell.

Ackermann, H., Hertrich, I., & Scharf, G. (1995). Kinematic analysis of lower lip movements in ataxic dysarthria. *Journal of Speech and Hearing Research* 38, 1252–59.

Ackermann, H., Konczak, J., & Hertrich, I. (1997). The temporal control of repetitive articulatory movements in Parkinson's disease. *Brain and Language* 56, 312–19.

Ackermann, H., Mathiak, K., & Ivry, R. B. (2004). Temporal organization of "internal speech" as a basis for cerebellar modulation of cognitive functions. *Behavioral and Cognitive Neuroscience Reviews* 3, 14–22.

Ackermann, H., Mathiak, K., & Riecker, A. (2007). The contribution of the cerebellum to speech production and speech perception: Clinical and functional imaging data. *Cerebellum* 6, 202–13.

Ackermann, H., Riecker, A., & Wildgruber, D. (2004). Functional brain imaging of motor aspects of speech production. In B. Maassen, R. D. Kent, H. F. M. Peters, P. H. M. M. van Lieshout, & W. Hulstijn (eds.), *Speech motor control in normal and disordered speech* (pp. 85–111). Oxford: Oxford University Press.

Ackermann, H., Ziegler, W., & Petersen, D. (1993). Dysarthria in bilateral thalamic infarction: A case study. *Journal of Neurology* 240, 357–62.

Ackermann, H., Gräber, S., Hertrich, I., & Daum, I. (1999). Phonemic vowel length contrasts in cerebellar disorders. *Brain and Language* 67, 95–109.

Ackermann, H., Gröne, B. F., Hoch, G., & Schönle, P. W. (1993). Speech freezing in Parkinson's disease: A kinematic analysis of orofacial movements by means of electromagnetic articulography. *Folia Phoniatrica* 45, 84–9.

Ackermann, H., Hertrich, I., Daum, I., Scharf, G., & Spieker, S. (1997). Kinematic analysis of articulatory movements in central motor disorders. *Movement Disorders* 12, 1019–27.

Adams, S. G. (1997). Hypokinetic dysarthria in Parkinson's disease. In M. R. McNeil (ed.), *Clinical management of sensorimotor speech disorders* (pp. 261–85). New York: Thieme.

Ball, M. J. & Lowry, O. M. (2001). *Methods in clinical phonetics*. London: Whurr Publishers.

Benke, T. & Butterworth, B. (2001). Palilalia and repetitive speech: Two case studies. *Brain and Language* 78, 62–81.

Benke, T., Hohenstein, C., Poewe, W., & Butterworth, B. (2000). Repetitive speech phenomena in Parkinson's disease. *Journal of Neurology, Neurosurgery and Psychiatry* 69, 319–24.

Berry, W. R. (ed.) (1983). *Clinical dysarthria*. San Diego, CA: College-Hill Press.

Bohland, J. W. & Guenther, F. (2006). An fMRI investigation of syllable sequence production. *NeuroImage* 32, 821–41.

Botez, M. I. & Barbeau, A. (1971). Role of subcortical structures, and particularly of the thalamus, in the mechanisms of speech and language: A review. *International Journal of Neurology* 8, 300–20.

Comella, C. L., Stebbins, G. T., Brown-Toms, N., & Goetz, C. G. (1994). Physical therapy and Parkinson's disease: A controlled clinical trial. *Neurology* 44, 376–8.

Darley, F. L., Aronson, A. E. and Brown, J. R. (1975). *Motor speech disorders*. Philadelphia, PA: Saunders.

Deane, K. H. O., Whurr, R., Playford, E. D., Ben-Shlomo, Y., & Clarke, C. E. (2006a). *Speech and language therapy versus placebo or no intervention for dysarthria in Parkinson's disease*. Oxford: The Cochrane Library (Update Software).

Deane, K. H. O., Whurr, R., Playford, E. D., Ben-Shlomo, Y., & Clarke, C. E. (2006b). *Speech and language therapy for dysarthria in Parkinson's disease: A comparison of techniques*. Oxford: The Cochrane Library (Update Software).

Dresel, C., Haslinger, B., Castrop, F., Wohlschlaeger, A. M., & Ceballos-Baumann, A. O. (2006). Silent event-related fMRI reveals deficient motor and enhanced somatosensory activation in orofacial dystonia. *Brain* 129, 36–46.

Duffy, J. R. (2005). *Motor speech disorders: Substrates, differential diagnosis, and management*, 2nd ed. St. Louis, MO: Elsevier Mosby.

Duffy, J. R. & Folger, W. N. (1996). Dysarthria associated with unilateral central nervous system lesions: A retrospective study. *Journal of Medical Speech-Language Pathology* 4, 57–70.

Enderby, P. & Emerson, J. (1995). *Does speech and language therapy work?* London: Whurr Publishers.

Fox, C., Ramig, L. O., Ciucci, M. R., Sapir, S., McFarland, D. H., & Farley, B. G. (2006). The science and practice of LSVT/LOUD: Neural plasticity-principled approach to treating individuals with Parkinson disease and other neurological disorders. *Seminars in Speech and Language* 27, 283–99.

Hardcastle, W. J., Gibbon, F., & Jones, W. (1991). Visual display of tongue-palate contact: Electropalatography in the assessment and remediation of speech disorders. *British Journal of Disorders of Communication* 26, 41–74.

Hertrich, I. & Ackermann, H. (1994). Acoustic analysis of speech timing in Huntington's disease. *Brain and Language* 47, 182–96.

Hertrich, I. & Ackermann, H. (1995). Gender-specific vocal dysfunctions in Parkinson's disease: Electroglottographic and acoustic analysis. *Annals of Otology, Rhinology and Laryngology* 104, 197–202.

Hertrich, I. & Ackermann, H. (1997). Acoustic analysis of durational speech parameters in neurological dysarthrias. In Y. Lebrun (ed.), *From the brain to the mouth: Acquired dysarthria and dysfluency in adults* (pp. 11–47). Dordrecht: Kluwer (Neuropsychology and Cognition, Volume 12).

Hertrich, I. & Ackermann, H. (1999). Temporal and spectral aspects of coarticulation in ataxic dysarthria: An acoustic analysis. *Journal of Speech, Language, and Hearing Research* 42, 367–81.

Hertrich, I. & Ackermann, H. (2007). Exploration of orofacial speech movements. In P. Auzou, V. Rolland-Monnoury, S. Pinto, & C. Ozsancak (eds.), *Les Dysarthries* (CD-Version) (pp. 132–9). Marseille: Editions Solal.

Hird, K. & Kirsner, K. (1993). Dysprosody following acquired neurogenic impairment. *Brain and Language* 45, 46–60.

Huber, W., Willmes, K., Poeck, K., van Vleymen, B., & Deberdt, W. (1997). Piracetam as an adjuvant to language therapy for aphasia: A randomized double-blind placebo-controlled pilot study. *Archives of Physical Medicine and Rehabilitation* 78, 245–50.

Kaburagi, T., Wakamiya, K., & Honda, M. (2005). Three-dimensional electromagnetic articulography: A measurement principle. *Journal of the Acoustical Society of America* 118, 428–43.

Kearns, K. P. & Simmons, N. N. (1988). Motor speech disorders: The dysarthrias and apraxia of speech. In N. J. Lass, L. V. McReynolds, J. L. Northern, & D. E. Yoder (eds.), *Handbook of speech-language pathology and audiology* (pp. 592–621). Toronto: B. C. Decker.

Kearns, K. P. & Simmons, N. N. (1990). The efficacy of speech-language pathology intervention: Motor speech disorders. *Seminars in Speech and Language* 11, 273–95.

Kent, R. D. (1997). The perceptual sensorimotor examination for motor speech disorders. In M. R. McNeil (ed.), *Clinical management of sensorimotor speech disorders* (pp. 27–47). New York: Thieme.

Kent, R. D. & Read, C. (2001). *Acoustic analysis of speech*, 2nd ed. San Diego, CA: Singular Press.

Kent, R. D., Vorperian, H. K., & Duffy, J. R. (1999). Reliability of the multi-dimensional voice program for the analysis of voice samples of subjects with dysarthria. *American Journal of Speech-Language Pathology* 8, 129–36.

Kent, R. D., Weismer, G., Kent, J. F., & Rosenbek, J. C. (1989). Towards phonetic intelligibility testing in dysarthria. *Journal of Speech and Hearing Disorders* 54, 482–99.

Kent, R. D., Kent, J. F., Rosenbek, J. C., Vorperian, H. K., & Weismer, G. (1997). A speaking task analysis of the dysarthria in cerebellar disease. *Folia Phoniatrica et Logopaedica* 49, 63–82.

Kent, R. D., Weismer, G., Kent, J. F., Vorperian, H. K., & Duffy, J. R. (1999). Acoustic studies of dysarthric speech:

Methods, progress, and potential. *Journal of Communication Disorders* 32, 141–86.

Koller, W., Graner, D., & MlCoch, A. (1985). Essential voice tremor: Treatment with propranolol. *Neurology* 35, 106–8.

Kluin, K. J., Gilman, S., Markel, D. S., Koeppe, R. A., Rosenthal, G., & Junck, L. (1988). Speech disorders in olivopontocerebellar atrophy correlate with positron emission tomography findings. *Annals of Neurology* 23, 547–54.

Logemann, J. A., Fisher, H. B., Boshes, B., & Blonsky, E. R. (1978). Frequency and cooccurrence of vocal tract dysfunctions in the speech of a large sample of Parkinson patients. *Journal of Speech and Hearing Disorders* 43, 47–57.

Luschei, E. S. & Finnegan, E. M. (1997). Electromyographic techniques for the assessment of motor speech disorders. In M. R. McNeil (ed.), *Clinical management of sensorimotor speech disorders* (pp. 149–76). New York: Thieme.

Marien, P., Engelborghs, S., Fabbro, F., & de Deyn, P. P. (2001). The lateralized linguistic cerebellum: A review and a new hypothesis. *Brain and Language* 79, 580–600.

Mathiak, K., Klose, U., Ackermann, H., Hertrich, I., Kincses, W. E., & Grodd, W. (2000). Stroboscopic articulography using fast magnetic resonance imaging. *International Journal of Language and Communication Disorders* 35, 419–25.

McAuliffe, M. J. & Ward, E. C. (2006). The use of electropalatography in the assessment and treatment of acquired motor speech disorders in adults: Current knowledge and future directions. *NeuroRehabilitation* 21, 189–203.

McNeil, M. R. (1997). Apraxia of speech: Definition, differentiation, and treatment. In M. R. McNeil (ed.), *Clinical management of sensorimotor speech disorders* (pp. 261–85). New York: Thieme.

Müllbacher, W., Artner, C., & Mamoli, B. (1999). The role of the intact hemisphere in recovery of midline muscles after recent monohemispheric stroke. *Journal of Neurology* 246, 250–6.

Müllbacher, W., Boroojerdi, B., Ziemann, U., & Hallett, M. (2001). Analogous corticocortical inhibition and facilitation in ipsilateral and contralateral human motor cortex representation of the tongue. *Journal of Clinical Neurophysiology* 18, 550–8.

Murdoch, B. & Theodoros, D. (eds.) (2000). *Speech and language disorders in multiple sclerosis.* Lonson: Whurr Publishers.

Neiman, R. F., Mountjoy, J. R., & Allen, E. L. (1975). Myasthenia gravis focal to the larynx: Report of a case. *Archives of Otolaryngology* 101, 569–70.

Nemec, R. E. & Cohen, K. (1984). EMG biofeedback in the modification of hypertonia in spastic dysarthria: Case report. *Archives of Physical Medicine and Rehabilitation* 65, 103–4.

Netsell, R. (1985). Construction and use of a bite-block for the evaluation and treatment of speech disorders. *Journal of Speech and Hearing Disorders* 50, 103–6.

Netsell, R. & Rosenbek, J. C. (1985). Treating the dysarthrias. In J. K. Darby (ed.), *Speech and language evaluation in neurology: Adult disorders* (pp. 363–92). Orlando, FL: Grune & Stratton.

Nicola, F., Ziegler, W., & Vogel, M. (2004). Die Bogenhausener Dysarthrieskalen (BODYS): Ein Instrument für die klinische Dysarthriediagnostik. *Forum Logopädie* 2, 14–22.

Ostrem, J. L., Marks Jr., W. J., Volz, M. M., Heath, S. L., & Starr, P. A. (2007). Pallidal deep brain stimulation in patients with cranial-cervical dystonia (Meige syndrome), *Movement Disorders* 22, 1885–91.

Özsancak, C., Auzou, P., Jan, M., & Hannequin, D. (2001). Measurement of voice onset time in dysarthric patients: Methodological considerations. *Folia Phoniatrica et Logopaedica* 53, 48–57.

Perkell, J. S., Cohen, M. H., Svirsky, M. A., Matthies, M. L., Garabieta, I., & Jackson, M. T. T. (1992). Electromagnetic midsagittal articulometer systems for transducing speech articulatory movements. *Journal of the Acoustical Society of America* 92, 3078–96.

Petersen, S. E., Fox, P. T., Posner, M. I., Mintun, M., & Raichle, M. E. (1989). Positron emission tomographic studies of the processing of single words. *Journal of Cognitive Neuroscience* 1, 153–70.

Pinto, S., Ozsancak, C., Tripoliti, E., Thobois, S., Limousin-Dowsey, P., & Auzou, P. (2004). Treatments for dysarthria in Parkinson's disease. *Lancet Neurology* 3, 547–56.

Pinto, S., Gentil, M., Krack, P., Sauleau, P., Fraix, V., Benabid, A. L., & Pollak, P. (2005). Changes induced by levodopa and subthalamic nucleus stimulation on Parkinsonian speech. *Movement Disorders* 20, 1507–15.

Ramig, L. O., Fox, C., & Sapir, S. (2004). Parkinson's disease: Speech and voice disorders and their treatment with the Lee Silverman Voice Treatment. *Seminars in Speech and Language* 25, 169–80.

Riecker, A., Wildgruber, D., Grodd, W., & Ackermann, H. (2002). Reorganization of speech production at the motor cortex and cerebellum following capsular infarction: A follow-up fMRI study. *Neurocase* 8, 417–23.

Riecker, A., Mathiak, K., Wildgruber, D., Erb, M., Grodd, W., & Ackermann, H. (2005). fMRI reveals two distinct cerebral networks subserving speech motor control. *Neurology* 64, 700–6.

Riecker, A., Kassubek, J., Gröschel, K., Grodd, W., & Ackermann, H. (2006). The cerebral control of speech tempo: opposite relationship between speaking rate and BOLD signal changes at striatal and cerebellar structures. *NeuroImage* 29, 46–53.

Robertson, S. J. & Thomson, F. (1987). *Working with dysarthric clients: A practical guide to therapy for dysarthria*. Tucson, AZ: Communication Skill Builders.

Rosenbek, J. C. & LaPointe, L. L. (1985). The dysarthrias: Description, diagnosis, and treatment. In D. F. Johns (ed.), *Clinical Management of Neurogenic Communicative Disorders*, 2nd ed. (pp. 97–152). Boston, MA: Little, Brown & Co.

Rosenbek, J. C. & LaPointe, L. L. (1991). The dysarthrias: Description, diagnosis, and treatment. In D. F. Johns (ed.), *Clinical management of neurogenic communicative disorders*, 2nd ed. (pp. 97–152). Boston, MA: Little, Brown & Co.

Schönle, P. W., Gräbe, K., Wenig, P., Höhne, J., Schrader, J., & Conrad, B. (1987). Electromagnetic articulography: Use of alternating magnetic fields for tracking movements of multiple points inside and outside the vocal tract. *Brain and Language* 31, 26–35.

Sellars, C., Hughes, T., & Langhorne, P. (2002). *Speech and language therapy for dysarthria due to non-progressive brain damage*. In the Cochrane Library. Oxford: Update Software.

Sidtis, J. J., Strother, S. C., & Rottenberg, D. A. (2003). Predicting performance from functional imaging data: methods matter. *NeuroImage* 20, 615–24.

Sidtis, J. J., Gomez, C., Groshong, A., Strother, S. C., & Rottenberg, D. A. (2006). Mapping cerebral blood flow during speech production in hereditary ataxia. *NeuroImage* 31, 246–54.

Simpson, M. B., Till, J. A., & Goff, A. M. (1988). Long-term treatment of severe dysarthria: A case study. *Journal of Speech and Hearing Disorders* 53, 433–40.

Taira, T. (2007). Speech and swallowing disturbance in patients with oro-facial cervical dystonia and effects of pallidal deep brain stimulation. Paper presented at the 1st International Symposium on Basal Ganglia Speech Disorders and Deep Brain Stimulation, London, UK.

Terao, Y., Ugawa, Y., Yamamoto, T., Sakurai, Y., Masumoto, T., Abe, O., Masutani, Y., Aoki, S., & Tsuji, S. (2007).

Primary face motor area as the motor representation of articulation. *Journal of Neurology* 254, 442–7.

Tjaden, K., Rivera, D., Wilding, G., & Turner, G. S. (2005). Characteristics of the lax vowel space in dysarthria. *Journal of Speech, Language, and Hearing Research* 48, 554–66.

Triggs, W. J., Ghacibeh, G., Springer, U., & Bowers, D. (2005). Lateralized asymmetry of facial motor evoked potentials. *Neurology* 65, 541–4.

Turner, G. S., Tjaden, K., & Weismer, G. (1995). The influence of speaking rate on vowel space and speech intelligibility for individuals with amyotrophic lateral sclerosis. *Journal of Speech and Hearing Research* 38, 1001–13.

Urban, P. P., Wicht, S., Hopf, H. C., Fleischer, S., & Nickel, O. (1999). Isolated dysarthria due to extracerebellar lacunar stroke: A central monoparesis of the tongue. *Journal of Neurology, Neurosurgery and Psychiatry* 66, 495–501.

Weismer, G., Martin, R., Kent, R. D., & Kent, J. F. (1992). Formant trajectory characteristics of males with amyotrophic lateral sclerosis. *Journal of the Acoustical Society of America* 91, 1085–98.

Wertz, R. T. (1985). Neuropathologies of speech and language: An introduction to patient management. In D. F. Johns (ed.), *Clinical management of neurogenic communicative disorders*, 2nd ed. (pp. 1–96). Boston, MA: Little, Brown & Co.

Wertz, R. T. (1991). Neuropathologies of speech and language: An introduction to patient management. In D. F. Johns (ed.), *Clinical management of neurogenic communicative disorders*, 2nd ed. (pp. 1–96). Boston, MA: Little, Brown & Co.

Westbury, J. R. (1991). The significance and measurement of head position during speech production experiments using the X-ray microbeam system. *Journal of the Acoustical Society of America* 89, 1782–91.

Whalen, D. H., Iskarous, K., Tiede, M. K., Ostry, D. J., Lehnert-LeHouillier, H., Hailey, D. S., & Vatikiotis-Bateson, E. (2005). The Haskins optically corrected ultrasound system (HOCUS). *Journal of Speech, Language, and Hearing Research* 48, 543–53.

Wise, R. J. S., Greene, J., Büchel, C., & Scott, S. K. (1999). Brain regions involved in articulation. *Lancet* 353, 1057–61.

Workinger, M. S. & Netsell, R. (1992). Restoration of intelligible speech 13 years post-head injury. *Brain Injury* 6, 183–7.

Yorkston, K. M. & Beukelman, D. R. (1984). *Assessment of intelligibility of dysarthric speech*. Philadelphia, PA: C. C. Publications.

Yorkston, K. M., Strand, E., Miller, R., Hillel, A., & Smith, K. (1993). Speech deterioration for the timing of intervention. *Journal of Medical Speech-Language Pathology* 1, 35–46.

Ziegler, W. (2008). Apraxia of speech. In G. Goldenberg & B. Miller (eds.), *Handbook of clinical neurology*, Volume 88 (3rd series): *Neuropsychology and Behavioral Neurology* (pp. 269–85). Elsevier: London.

Ziegler, W. & von Cramon, D. (1986). Spastic dysarthria after acquired brain injury: An acoustic study. *British Journal of Disorders of Communication* 21, 173–87.

Ziegler, W., Vogel, M., Gröne, B., & Schröter-Morasch, H. (2002). *Dysarthrie: Grundlagen, Diagnostik, Therapie*, 2. Aufl. Stuttgart: Thieme.

Ziegler, W. & Zierdt, A. (2008). Telediagnostic assessment of intelligibility in dysarthria: A pilot investigation of MVP-online. *Journal of Communication Disorders* 41, 553–77.

Zyski, B. J. & Weisiger, B. E. (1987). Identification of dysarthria types based on perceptual analysis. *Journal of Communication Disorders* 20, 367–78.

17 Apraxia of Speech

ADAM JACKS AND DONALD A. ROBIN

1 Introduction

Apraxia of speech (AOS) is a motor speech disorder affecting both children and adults. AOS represents a disruption of the translation of linguistic units into actual speech movements. Thus, AOS does not reflect impairment at the linguistic level (aphasia) or the neuromuscular level (dysarthria). As such, AOS is distinct from problems with phonological processing or motor execution and is considered the quintessential disorder of speech motor planning/programming (McNeil, Robin, & Schmidt, 2009).

AOS is a neurogenic motor speech disorder, occurring as a result of identified neurological disease (i.e., *neurological AOS*, also known as acquired AOS), or more commonly in children as either a genetically transmitted *complex neurodevelopmental* form or an *idiopathic* disorder with no clearly identified genetic cause or neurological abnormalities (collectively the latter two are known as *childhood apraxia of speech* [CAS]). Recent works have provided clarity on differential diagnostic criteria and the appropriate methods and principles of treatment to apply in adults with neurological AOS (Wambaugh et al., 2006a, 2006b). The neurological, complex neurodevelopmental, and idiopathic etiologies of AOS are by hypothesis unified by a core of shared behavioral characteristics, although some differences exist relative to interaction with developmental processes (Maassen, 2002). The aim of this chapter is to provide a detailed review of AOS in children and adults from its definition and etiology to its diagnosis and treatment.

2 Definitions

Definitions of any disorder must provide criteria to establish the presence of the disorder and a description of the presumed mechanism representing the fundamental breakdown at a theoretical level (McNeil & Pratt, 2001). A definition must be operational in the sense that it should drive how we describe the disorder

The Handbook of Language and Speech Disorders, First Edition. Edited by Jack S. Damico, Nicole Müller, and Martin J. Ball. © 2013 Blackwell Publishing Ltd except for editorial material and organization © 2013 Jack S. Damico, Nicole Müller, Martin J. Ball. Published 2013 by Blackwell Publishing Ltd.

relative to its underlying cause and its symptomatology. Furthermore, the definition of AOS must encompass the principle that the underlying mechanism of AOS
is distinct from those underlying aphasia or dysarthria. To this end, McNeil, Robin,
and Schmidt (1997) defined AOS as follows:

> Apraxia of speech is a phonetic-motoric disorder of speech production caused
> by inefficiencies in the translation of a well-formed and filled phonologic frame to
> previously learned kinematic parameters assembled for carrying out the intended
> movement, resulting in intra- and interarticulator temporal and spatial segmental
> and prosodic distortions. It is characterized by distortions of segment and interseg-
> ment transitionalization resulting in extended durations of consonants, vowels, and
> time between sounds, syllables and words. These distortions are often perceived as
> sound substitutions and as the mis-assignment of stress and other phrasal and
> sentence-level prosodic abnormalities. Errors are relatively consistent in location
> within the utterance and invariable in type. It is not attributable to deficits of muscle
> tone or reflexes, nor to deficits in the processing of auditory, tactile, kinesthetic,
> proprioceptive, or language information. In its extremely infrequently occurring
> "pure" form, it is not accompanied by the above listed deficits of motor physiology,
> perception, or language. (p. 329)

McNeil and colleagues' description of the mechanism of AOS (see McNeil et al.
2009, p. 264) emphasizes the difficulty in learned movement patterns associated
with speech sounds, but also notably indicates that phonological frames are intact,
differentiating the disorder's mechanism from that of aphasia. Also considered
exclusionary criteria are deficits in muscle tone or reflexes and sensory impairments, thereby differentiating AOS from the dyarthrias.

Direct observation of this mechanism is not readily available to most clinicians
or researchers. As such, a great deal of research has endeavored to determine
behavioral characteristics that unambiguously reflect AOS. In addition to the disorder
mechanism described, McNeil et al. (2009) delineated behavioral characteristics
corresponding to this mechanism, centered on distortions of spatial and temporal
aspects of movement (greater detail of the characteristics is provided in the
Assessment section below). These distortions affect speech production at various
levels, including individual speech sounds (consonant and vowel distortions),
prolongation of intervals between segments (pauses), prolonged duration of speech
segments and prosodic anomalies (particularly the de-stressing of stressed sounds
and syllables).

Another characteristic that deserves mention with respect to the definition and
mechanism of AOS is speech variability, including phonemic variability and acoustic
or kinematic variability. Consistency of error types and locations is now listed
as one of the primary clinical features differentiating neurological AOS from other
disorders (Wambaugh et al., 2006a), but error variability is still listed as a diagnostic
feature of childhood AOS (American Speech-Language-Hearing Association [ASHA],
2007). Still others primarily examine speech variability as it pertains to direct
measures of movement or of acoustic measures of speech, with most findings
suggesting that measures of speech movements or acoustic manifestations of

speech are variable from trial to trial in individuals with AOS (e.g., Jacks, 2008; McNeil, Caligiuri, & Rosenbek, 1989).

This disparity is problematic, but likely stems from different operational definitions of "variability" used in neurological AOS and childhood AOS studies. Further discussion of variability will be provided in the Assessment section relative to recommendations for defining variability for differential diagnosis. Of most relevance here is the question of whether variability or consistency of speech movements or phonemic errors is directly linked to the posited disorder mechanism. Acoustic and kinematic variability appear to be related to this mechanism, with inefficient translation between speech sound representations and learned movement parameters resulting in variable performance on multiple trials. However, the relation between this mechanism and high consistency of phonemic error types and locations is less clear. Conceivably, consistent error types might reflect inability to produce certain more complex articulatory configurations, in which the outcome is a simplified configuration that is relatively invariant at the phonemic level.

The definitions provided by McNeil et al. (1997, 2009) serve as excellent working hypotheses relative to the mechanism and corresponding behavioral characteristics that may be used as diagnostic criteria for AOS. The questions regarding speech error consistency or variability as they relate to the posited mechanism of AOS serve as a reminder that much remains to be learned about the underpinnings of AOS. Improved understanding of the relationship between the disorder mechanism and its behavioral manifestation will result in further refinement to the present definition.

3 Etiology

AOS consists of three separate etiological classifications: (1) neurological, (2) complex neurodevelopmental, and (3) idiopathic (Shriberg, 2006). Neurological AOS also is known as acquired AOS, while the complex neurodevelopmental and idiopathic forms together are termed *childhood apraxia of speech* (ASHA, 2007; previously known as developmental apraxia of speech [DAS]). All three etiological types are considered neurogenic disorders with presumably similar mechanisms; however, much remains unknown about the neurobiology of the disorder (see Robin, Jacks, & Ramage, 2008 for a review). A brief review of the lesion literature for each subtype will be included, when available.

3.1 *Neurological AOS*

Neurological AOS refers to the disorder resulting from known neurological disease. Duffy (2005) reported on the neurological etiologies for cases of AOS seen at the Mayo Clinic from 1969 to 1990 and from 1999 to 2001. Approximately half of the cases resulted from left-hemisphere stroke, including mostly single strokes (41 percent) and an additional 8 percent with multiple strokes. AOS also commonly results from neurosurgery (14 percent) or degenerative diseases (e.g., primary progressive apraxia of speech; Josephs et al., 2006). These cases are important because AOS sometimes may be the initial presenting symptom of neurodegenerative disease (Duffy, Peach, & Strand, 2007).

In cases of neurological AOS seen at the Mayo Clinic (Duffy, 2005), site of lesion most often involved the left frontal lobe, although parietal and temporal lesions often accompanied frontal damage. AOS also occasionally resulted from lesions restricted to the basal ganglia. These findings are consistent with imaging results in the literature, although the specific locale of frontal damage has been a source of debate over the last decade.

Brain regions that have received most attention as candidate sites of lesion for AOS include left anterior insula, Broca's area, as well as other premotor cortical areas (e.g., lateral premotor cortex, Brodmann area [BA] 6). Broca's area (BA 44/45) has been an area of interest for AOS because Broca's patient Leborgne had a speech articulation disorder that largely resembles the modern description of AOS (Broca, 1861/1977). In the years since this report, many other authors also described left cortical lesions, determined at autopsy, as the cause of AOS-like speech disorders.

In the modern era, Mohr (1976) used computed tomography (CT) imaging data to show that damage to Broca's area and adjacent insular cortex and white matter resulted in symptoms similar to AOS. Other reports of CT data in the 1980s yielded a variety of imaging findings, including lesions to temporal and parietal cortex as well as frontal regions (e.g., Deutsch, 1984; Square-Storer & Apeldoorn, 1991) and isolated subcortical damage (Kertesz, 1984; Marquardt & Sussman, 1984). Some difficulties exist interpreting these studies due to the frequent inclusion of participants with aphasia in addition to AOS, lack of consistent diagnostic criteria, or use of diagnostic criteria currently considered non-diagnostic for the disorder (e.g., phonemic paraphasias, see Assessment for current criteria).

Robin et al. (2008) report on MRI lesion data from a series of previous studies with AOS participants diagnosed consistent with the current criteria and without concomitant aphasia (e.g., Hageman et al., 1994; Seddoh et al., 1996). In these studies, brain lesions in participants with AOS were predominantly found in left premotor cortex (BA 6), with frequent involvement of Broca's area as well. By contrast, control participants in these studies with conduction aphasia were found consistently to have temporoparietal and insula involvement.

In the last decade, much interest has surrounded the report of a study by Dronkers (1996) suggesting that anterior insula is a critical site of neurological lesion for AOS. Dronkers found that 100 percent of participants labeled with AOS had structural damage to anterior insular cortex, while 0 percent of participants not labeled with AOS had damage to this area. However, a later study by Hillis and colleagues (2004) using structural and functional lesion analysis techniques (e.g., perfusion-weighted MRI) showed that while the insula is frequently structurally damaged in AOS, cerebral blood flow is most often reduced in Broca's area. They further argue that anterior insula lesions are common in persons with AOS not because they are critical regions involved in articulatory control but because both AOS and insular infarcts commonly occur with large strokes affecting the middle cerebral artery distribution.

The literature on the neurological basis of AOS is still limited; however, existing studies inform us of the importance of several critical issues, including the consistent use of appropriate diagnostic criteria in imaging studies of AOS and the potential for using functional imaging techniques, such as those used by Hillis et al. (2004), to assess the actual functioning of neural tissue in various neural regions in addition to localization of structural lesions. Attention to these two issues has great potential to advance our understanding of the neurobiological mechanism of AOS.

3.2 Complex neurodevelopmental AOS

AOS also is known to occur as a primary symptom among other cognitive and linguistic deficits in people with genetically transmitted syndromes. Complex neurodevelopmental AOS has been explored primarily in a four-generation family with a speech and language disorder (KE family), half of whom present with impaired speech and language, including symptoms of AOS (Vargha-Khadem et al., 1995). In the KE family, a genetic linkage study isolated a point mutation of the *FOXP2* gene as the apparent locus of the disorder (Lai et al., 2001). Further study of brain anatomy and function in the KE family has revealed possible abnormalities in the basal ganglia as well as other regions involved in speech (e.g., supplementary motor area, Broca's area, premotor cortex; Watkins et al., 2002). Apart from the KE family studies, few others have identified specific genetic abnormalities in individuals with non-acquired AOS (although see Shriberg et al., 2006).

3.3 Idiopathic neurogenic AOS

The idiopathic form of the disorder is called thus because the exact cause is unknown. Previously this form has been known by the name of developmental apraxia of speech (DAS, also developmental verbal dyspraxia). Idiopathic AOS likely results from a neurological deficit, although the locus of such a deficit has not been identified to date. Idiopathic AOS is likely present at birth (though diagnosis requires the presence of some speech sounds), initially presenting as late-developing speech, followed by a delayed progression of speech development in which the child's verbal output is often very difficult to understand. A variety of atypical speech development processes may be present, including disturbed prosodic contours, consonant omissions in initial position, and vowel errors. Since idiopathic AOS first occurs in children, development of linguistic representational constructs (e.g., phonological, morphological) progresses in the context of impaired speech motor processes (Maassen, 2002), resulting in various linguistic deficits, including reduced phrase length, grammatical errors, and difficulties with speech perception.

A handful of genetic linkage studies have examined the possibility that idiopathic AOS is genetically transmitted. For example, Lewis and colleagues (2004) found some evidence for familial aggregation of AOS, with 86 percent of children having at least one affected member in their immediate family, and over half having at least one affected parent. However, few children in that study had a sibling with AOS, suggesting that transmission in this population is distinct from that seen in complex neurodevelopmental AOS, in whom 50 percent of offspring are generally affected. To date, the literature on genetic markers for idiopathic AOS is limited, thus limiting comparisons with complex neurodevelopmental AOS.

The working hypothesis that AOS is the same basic disorder in the three etiological classifications described here is based on the premise that the mechanism underlying the disorder is essentially the same regardless of how exactly this mechanism was disrupted. Specifically, it is hypothesized that neural substrates of speech motor planning/programming are impaired in the three distinct forms of AOS. This is a reasonable premise, based on the similarity of behavioral characteristics observed in the different forms and a limited amount of neuroimaging data suggesting that similar brain areas are affected in neurological and complex neurodevelopmental AOS. Clearly, more research is needed to provide more definitive conclusions on this important issue.

4   Assessment

Assessment of AOS may involve the use of a combination of a variety of different types of information, including perceptual judgment of speech as well as instrumental measures of acoustic and kinematic characteristics of speech production. Perceptual judgments remain the most commonly used method of assessing speech characteristics of AOS, as the current diagnostic criteria are perceptual in nature. However, acoustic measures have been developed that are likely to add to our diagnostic acumen in the near future, so some of these will be addressed in this work. Physiological assessment of speech, including a variety of kinematic measurement methodologies as well as airflow assessment and measures of brain function (e.g., electroencephalograms; brain blood flow via PET and fMRI) are limited to a few specialized clinical facilities and research centers.

4.1   *Differential diagnosis criteria for AOS*

The perceived behavioral characteristics of the disorder are at present the standard by which AOS is defined, although some debate has persisted about the symptoms that are critical for diagnosis. Each perceptual criterion must eventually meet rigorous psychometric standards of validity and reliability, which to date have not been well established in motor speech disorders, including AOS. Recently, a panel of experts convened to derive evidence-based practice standards for the treatment of neurological AOS (Wambaugh et al., 2006a, 2006b) delineated the symptoms used to differentially diagnose AOS, based on criteria suggested by McNeil, Robin, & Schmidt (1997).

Critically, the most recent diagnostic standards reported for childhood AOS (e.g., complex neurodevelopmental and idiopathic AOS) differ from neurological AOS in at least one criterion, namely the presence of inconsistent errors, while criteria for neurological AOS include consistency of error types and locations. This difference will be discussed in more detail below; however, we propose that the same behavioral criteria should be used to diagnose the disorder in its different forms. The specific primary and secondary criteria to be used for differential diagnosis of AOS are described as follows.

4.1.1 Primary clinical features of AOS The currently accepted differential diagnostic criteria for AOS include the following speech characteristics:

1 Slow rate of speech (e.g., prolonged segment and intersegment durations; segments are considered individual speech sounds or syllables)
2 Consonant and/or vowel distortions
3 Distorted sounds perceived as sound substitutions
4 Prosodic abnormalities
5 Error types that are consistent in type and location[1]

Further clarification of these characteristics is provided in McNeil et al. (2009). For example, slow rate of speech may be observed in phonemically correct productions of a person with AOS, while they are not able to increase speech rate without experiencing loss of phonemic integrity.

Speech sound errors in AOS are generally distortions or distorted substitutions, but not "clean" substitution errors as may be observed in a person with conduction aphasia. For example, if the target sound is /s/, then an error production in AOS might sound like [s] or [S] that is not quite correct, but it will not sound like a correctly produced [S].

Prosodic abnormalities in AOS are characterized not only by the slowed rate of speech and related increased segment and intersegment durations, but also by errors in stress assignment. Notably, individuals with AOS often have difficulty putting stress on the appropriate syllable, perceived as excess stress on unstressed syllables and generally greater equality in stress among different syllables.

Regarding consistency of errors, McNeil and colleagues (1995) found that when speakers with neurological AOS make repeated errors on production of the same word, the type and location of the error tends to be consistent, a finding that was *not* true for individuals with conduction aphasia. For example, if a speaker with AOS distorted the final vowel of the word "banana" on one production of the word, further errors on the same word were likely to be (a) distortion errors and (b) present in the final vowel position. This error consistency is not to say that individuals with AOS are not variable in some aspects of speech production, as acoustic analyses have shown that durational measures of speech often may be variable on repeated productions, while kinematic analyses of speech also have indicated variability in the speech movements of individuals with AOS (Itoh & Sasanuma, 1984; McNeil, Caligiuri, & Rosenbek, 1989).

Further difficulty with the error consistency criterion stems from the fact that inconsistent articulatory errors are currently used for differential diagnosis of childhood AOS (CAS, ASHA, 2007). This discrepancy may be a result of long-standing differences in how variability is defined in studies of AOS (see Miller, 1992 for a review of definitions). Specifically, in studies of variability in CAS, investigators most often have examined the number of different ways a given word is produced in error (e.g., Marquardt, Jacks, & Davis, 2004; Shriberg, Aram, & Kwiatkowski, 1997), but not specifically whether errors are consistently distortions or substitutions (e.g., error type consistency) or whether errors consistently occur in initial or final position (e.g., error position consistency), as operationalized by McNeil et al. (1995). There is currently a need for research on various types of error consistency across etiological classifications of AOS to resolve the relative importance of this criterion in the differential diagnosis of AOS in its different forms. We recommend the assessment of error consistency on multiple productions of the same words; however, differential diagnosis of AOS should not be based on this criterion alone.

4.1.2 Secondary clinical features of AOS   While the five primary error types previously described are considered to be differential diagnostic criteria for AOS, several other characteristics *may* be present, including several that previously have been considered as critical for diagnosis. These secondary, *non-discriminative* characteristics of AOS are as follows:

1 Articulatory groping
2 Perseverative errors
3 Increasing errors with increasing word length
4 Speech initiation difficulty
5 Awareness of errors (e.g., self-correction)
6 Automatic speech better than propositional speech
7 Islands of error-free speech

Additional characteristics that may occur in conjunction with AOS, but *should not be used for diagnosis* include: anticipatory or transposition errors, limb or oral (non-speech) apraxia, and a gap between expressive and receptive abilities. It is important to recognize that these features may be present in AOS (i.e., their presence does not preclude a diagnosis of AOS); however, they may also be indicative of an aphasic disorder (e.g., conduction aphasia). As such, for the purposes of clinical diagnosis, the more appropriate descriptors are the primary characteristics previously listed.

4.1.3 Exclusionary criteria for AOS   Finally, there are several characteristics which should be an indicator that a person does *not* have AOS, listed as follows:

1 Fast rate
2 Normal rate
3 Normal prosody

4.2 Clinical assessment of AOS

The specific clinical instrument used for evaluation is not of primary importance, as long as the assessment tool enables the clinician to determine the presence of the primary clinical features of the disorder and the instrument does not include procedures or metrics that emphasize characteristics that are not diagnostic for AOS. We recommend a battery that includes the following tasks:

1 Oral motor examination
2 Alternating motion tasks (i.e., diadochokinesis) at comfortable and fast rates
3 Articulation testing
4 Repeated multi-syllable words (see repeated words subtest list from Apraxia Battery for Adults, Dabul, 2000)
5 Connected speech sample
6 Intelligibility testing

Oral motor examination is important to ascertain any neuromuscular weakness of speech structures, including the lips, tongue, and velum. Alternating motion tasks (e.g., repeat "puh-tuh-kuh") provide an opportunity to estimate comfortable speech rate, coordination difficulties, and potential breakdown with increased rate.

Articulation testing can be accomplished using any age-appropriate instrument that includes the speech sounds in the individual's native language. Samples of connected speech may be obtained through phonetically balanced reading passages, single picture description, sequenced picture description (Nicholas & Brookshire, 1993), or elicited monologue (e.g., tell me about your family, what you do at school/work). Finally, speech intelligibility should be assessed to determine a percentage of words that are understandable to a listener. Intelligibility can be rated from connected speech samples by having an unfamiliar listener transcribe words that are understood. Formal testing of intelligibility also may be completed, using the Speech Intelligibility Test (SIT, Madonna Rehabilitation Hospital; see also the Computerized Assessment of Intelligibility of Dysarthric Speech, Yorkston, Beukelman, & Traynor, 1984), or the single word intelligibility test (Kent et al., 1989).

4.2.1 Perceptual rating of speech dimensions Crucial to the use of both articulation testing and connected speech sampling in the diagnosis of AOS is the ability to identify the primary characteristics of the disorder from these sources, including consonant and vowel distortions, distorted substitutions, consistency of errors, slowed speech rate, and prosodic abnormalities. Multidimensional rating scales may be useful for the purpose of making ratings of various perceptual dimensions from speech samples. For example, Darley, Aronson, & Brown's (1975) classification scheme included 38 perceptual dimensions of voice and speech. For each perceptual dimension, listeners make a rating from 0 to 7, with 0 indicating normal performance and 7 indicating profound impairment for that dimension.

For the purpose of identifying AOS, we propose a 7-point rating system including the following dimensions: pitch level, imprecise consonants, distorted vowels, prolonged intervals, excess and equal stress (for inclusionary criteria), as well as separate dimensions for slow rate (inclusionary) and fast rate (exclusionary). While this is a useful clinical tool for identifying the presence of the primary features of AOS, it is necessary for clinicians to be trained in the appropriate identification of each perceptual dimension in order to achieve reliable results (e.g., high inter- and intra-rater reliability) and allow for consistent diagnosis of AOS.

4.2.2 Narrow phonetic transcription of speech   Also critical to the identification of consonant and vowel distortions is the use of narrow phonetic transcription of articulation test results and a representative sample of connected speech samples. Narrow phonetic transcription allows the clinician to capture speech errors not observed using broad transcription, for example vowel distortions (e.g., Odell et al., 1991). Several excellent resources exist for addressing transcription issues specific to disordered populations (e.g., Powell, 2001; see also Pollock & Berni, 2001 regarding vowel transcription) and particularly for AOS (Haley, Bays, & Ohde, 2001). Transcription analyses of multisyllable word repetitions can be used to assess consistency of location and type of speech errors (see McNeil et al., 1995 for a tutorial). Note that current diagnostic standards indicate that "location and type of speech errors should be consistent in individuals with AOS, *and not variable*," as suggested in the Apraxia Battery for Adults – II (Dabul, 2000). See discussion of error consistency in the previous section. Error type consistency and variability are important factors to assess in clinical evaluation of AOS; however, this should not be the sole or primary clinical feature used to diagnose the disorder.

4.2.3 Potential acoustic markers for AOS   A number of acoustic measures also may be useful in the diagnosis of AOS in the future as more data regarding their status as differential markers for the disorder become available. For example, two acoustic measures related to prosodic qualities of word stress and syllable segregation (lexical word stress ratio, coefficient of variation ratio), symptoms present in both adults and children with AOS, have been shown to differentiate children with AOS from children with other speech disorders (Shriberg et al., 2003a; Shriberg et al., 2003b). Another possible acoustic measure that may be useful in the quantification of consonant distortions is the first spectral moment, used in previous studies to examine lack of acoustic differences between [s] or [ʃ] in speakers with AOS (e.g., Shuster & Wambaugh, 2000). However, it is unclear at present whether this measure will prove useful in the differentiation of individuals with AOS and those with aphasia (see Haley, 2002).

4.2.4 Caution in use of apraxia batteries   Several commercial batteries exist for AOS, including the Apraxia Battery for Adults (ABA-II, Dabul, 2000) and the Screening Test for Developmental Apraxia of Speech (STDAS-II, Blakeley, 2001; now out of print). However, these measures are both lacking in a number of psychometric properties, including poor reliability and construct validity, particularly for the STDAS-II (see Clark, 2003; Dean & Brinkman, 2003 for reviews of the ABA-II; and McCauley, 2003; Norris, 2003 for reviews of the STDAS-II).

There may be some benefit to using the ABA-II as it provides a structured tool and appropriate stimuli for the various assessment tasks needed in the evaluation of AOS. However, it is important to note that the ABA-II is specifically geared to identifying characteristics that are no longer considered diagnostic for AOS. For example, subtest 5 is specifically designed to identify speech error variability, while current standards suggest that error consistency is more characteristic of AOS. Additionally, in subtest 6, the inventory of articulation characteristics of apraxia, only two of 15 characteristics are in the primary clinical features list from Wambaugh et al. (2006a), while the remaining are either on the list of non-discriminative features (six of 15), or *features that should not be used for diagnosis of AOS* (three of 15). Although this instrument is convenient for clinicians, it should be used with caution when assessing AOS. The use of a small number of speech tasks from which the presence or absence of primary clinical features of AOS can be ascertained is the best practice for assessment.

5   Treatment

As noted by McNeil and colleagues, apraxia of speech is a treatable motor speech disorder (McNeil, Doyle, & Wambaugh, 2000). The recent evidence-based practice guidelines for adult AOS (see below) show a strong positive effect of various treatments. In general, treatment approaches for AOS fall into four main categories: those focusing on (1) articulatory kinematics, (2) rate and rhythm modification, (3) alternative and augmentative modes of communication (AAC), and (4) intersystemic facilitation or reorganization. A recent review of the treatment literature in AOS found that articulatory kinematic approaches to treatment are most likely to yield substantial benefits in speech production, based on current evidence-based practice standards (Wambaugh et al., 2006a, 2006b). Some patients might benefit from other approaches (e.g., rate/rhythm, AAC, intersystemic reorganization); however, the evidence for these other approaches currently is lacking. A brief description of the different treatment approaches is provided as follows.

Articulatory kinematic (AK) treatments directly address spatial and temporal aspects of speech production, in other words attempting to correct aberrant placement and sequencing of speech structures. Early examples of AK treatments include integral stimulation approaches (e.g., watch me, listen to me, say it with me; Rosenbek, 1973). More recent approaches include "speech production treatment" (SPT), studied extensively by Wambaugh (2004), and the "Prompts for restructuring oral and muscular phonetic targets" program (PROMPT, Square, Martin, & Bose, 2001).

SPT uses a minimal-pair treatment approach in which selected impaired speech sounds are contrasted with minimally different speech sounds. An integrated stimulation approach is applied within a structured treatment hierarchy, focusing on correct production of target sounds at the sound level, word level, and sentence level, with fading of visual and auditory cues as treatment progresses. Several well-controlled case studies have shown this approach to be efficacious in AOS speakers with severity ranging from mild to severe (Wambaugh, 2004; Wambaugh et al., 1996; Wambaugh et al., 1998; Wambaugh et al., 1999). Effect sizes calculated based on the combined treatment data from these studies showed extremely large treatment effects, with Cohen's d = 9.86 for treated speech sounds compared to 0.21 for untreated sounds, based on data from untrained probes (calculations ours). The effect sizes for treated speech sounds are well above levels considered "large effect sizes" by Cohen (1988), providing convincing evidence that this treatment methodology is efficacious for improving speech sound production in individuals with AOS.

PROMPT uses a combination of auditory, visual, tactile, and kinesthetic cues with the aim of heightening sensory awareness of correct movement trajectories and sequences (Square, Martin, & Bose, 2001). The treatment was originally developed for use in children with AOS and has been tested in several adults with neurological AOS; however, most of these reports represent uncontrolled case studies (cf. Bose et al., 2001).

Treatment efficacy data for children with AOS are limited; however, a recent study by Strand and colleagues (Strand, Stoeckel, & Baas, 2006) reports rapid positive gains in speech production in three of four children treated with dynamic temporal and tactile cuing (DTTC), using a multiple baseline design for experimental control. This methodology falls into the class of articulatory kinematic treatments, using a hierarchical framework including visual, tactile, and verbal feedback to shape correct speech production. The treatment is designed to emphasize some principles of motor learning (e.g., gradual reduction of frequency and specificity of feedback), based on the premise that AOS is a disorder of speech motor control.

Motor learning principles are important factors to consider in the design of all articulatory kinematic treatments, whether the affected individual is an adult or a child. Robin and colleagues provided a review of motor learning considerations for treatment, particularly relating to childhood AOS (Robin et al., 2007). Among the critical factors to consider are *the selection of targets, the nature of feedback provided to patients, and the organization of practice*.

In the selection of targets, the clinician should consider which speech sounds to address (e.g., high-frequency sounds in error); whether to focus on production at the speech sound, word, phrase, or sentence level; and the complexity of speech targets. The use of higher-complexity speech targets is preferable to simpler targets, as learning of complex movements tends to generalize to simpler movements, while learning of simpler movements does not generalize to more complex movements.

Treatment may begin with feedback provided in all sensory modalities (e.g., auditory, visual, tactile) and then progress to a limited degree of direct feedback. In addition to sensory feedback, clinicians may provide verbal feedback in the form of knowledge of performance (KP; specific verbal description of the patient's attempt) and knowledge of results (KR; i.e., correct/incorrect). While both types of verbal feedback may be important, providing knowledge of results facilitates greater long-term retention. Other variations that may affect skill retention in motor speech treatment include the frequency and timing of verbal feedback (e.g., infrequent is better than frequent feedback; delayed is better than immediate feedback).

Organization of practice also is an important factor to consider in treatment planning for AOS. Specifically, practice may be organized such that all trials for a particular behavior (e.g., /s/ in the word "safe") are practiced together in a "block" (e.g., blocked practice [BP]), or different target behaviors may be addressed in random order (random practice [RP]) so that the patient practices a given target behavior interspersed with other behaviors. Existing research shows that initial acquisition of target behaviors is better (faster, greater accuracy) with blocked practice; however, retention of performance gains has been shown to be improved following random practice (e.g., Knock et al., 2000). These results suggest that treatment ideally should involve random practice to maximize long-term benefits of treatment, although blocked practice may be useful early in treatment to achieve initial success.

Articulatory kinematic treatment methodologies currently have greater evidence supporting efficacy relative to other approaches. AK treatments directly address the behaviors in error in individuals with AOS, namely incorrect articulatory movements. Principles of motor learning also are readily applied to these treatments in both children and adults, providing a theoretical basis for the treatment aligned with the posited disorder mechanism. Other treatment approaches have received less support from well-controlled efficacy studies, although they might provide benefit for some patients.

One class of alternative treatments includes rate and rhythm modification approaches, typically employing pacing techniques to force slowed rate of speech. The principle underlying this form of treatment may be viewed in two ways, depending on how slowed rate of speech in AOS is thought to relate to the disorder mechanism. First, if slowed rate of speech in AOS results from a direct impairment of temporal parameters of speech production, then rate and rhythm treatments may serve to reestablish aberrant timing patterns. Alternatively, slowed speech rate may be a secondary consequence of speech motor control disruption in AOS. If this is the case, then reduced rate may allow speakers more time for planning movements and processing sensory feedback.

A few well-controlled case studies have provided evidence that rate reduction through the use of metronome pacing or use of a pacing board results in improved speech sound production in patients with mild to severe apraxia (e.g., Dworkin, Abkarian, & Johns, 1988). These results are promising and deserve further study; however, the mechanism by which the treatment operates is less clear than for AK treatments. Furthermore, at least one study (Tjaden, 2000) found that rate modification was not beneficial in a patient with AOS.

Intersystemic reorganization treatment approaches operate by using intact cognitive and linguistic functions as adjuncts to support impaired speech production (Rosenbek, Collins, & Wertz, 1976). These approaches often involve the pairing of verbal production with gestures or with singing. Although a number of studies have examined the effect of intersystemic reorganization treatment on speech production and on gestural use, only two studies provide evidence of internal validity (Raymer & Thompson, 1991; Wertz, 1984). Further investigation is needed to demonstrate the efficacy of these approaches.

Finally, alternative and augmentative communication (AAC) may be appropriate for patients in whom speech production is so severely affected that verbal communication alone is not a viable option. These approaches may include training the use of computerized communication devices, communication books, spelling, drawing, or gestures, or combining one or more of these modalities with residual speech production to optimize communication of wants, needs, and ideas. Although positive treatment effects for AAC methods have been reported by a number of researchers, only one study represented a controlled treatment study (Lustig & Tompkins, 2002). As such, few data exist to indicate whether these approaches are efficacious for the treatment of AOS.

Wambaugh and colleagues' (2006b) review of the treatment literature in AOS underscores the need for greater experimental control in the study of treatment efficacy. Only 39 percent of studies included any of the necessary criteria for scientific adequacy (according to the American Academy of Neurology Evidence Classification Scheme; see Rutschmann, McCrory, & Matchar, 2002), including demonstration of internal validity, replication of methods, replicability across participants, and reliability of outcome measures. To date, no prospective randomized clinical trials for AOS treatment have been performed, and only one prospective matched-group study for AOS treatment has been published (Wertz, 1984).

Notwithstanding the limited status of the treatment literature, a number of studies have shown that articulatory kinematic treatment approaches, particularly minimal-pair based treatment focusing on prominent speech sound errors (e.g., SPT; Wambaugh, 2004), are beneficial for individuals with AOS. Alternative approaches, including rate and rhythm modification, intersystemic reorganization, and alternative and augmentative systems for communication may be helpful, particularly for individuals with severely impaired speech production. Further research into treatment efficacy, including the importance of practice schedule effects (random vs. blocked) and type of feedback, will augment our ability to improve outcomes for speech production in individuals with AOS.

6   Summary and Future Directions

Apraxia of speech (AOS) is an established clinical entity in both adults and children. In the acquired neurological form, consensus has emerged that AOS is a disorder of speech motor planning/programming, resulting from inefficient translation of intact phonological codes into motor plans. A discrete set of behavioral characteristics have been settled upon for differential diagnosis, providing common ground to enable the direct comparison of future research in AOS. At least one class of treatment approaches has been shown to be efficacious for improving speech sound production in individuals with the disorder, suggesting great potential for further understanding the nature of the disorder mechanism.

This progress notwithstanding, a number of challenges face clinicians and researchers engaged with this clinical population. Controversy still exists relative to the question of whether childhood AOS (including complex neurodevelopmental and idiopathic variants) should be considered part of the same disorder class as acquired neurological AOS. As a working hypothesis, we contend that the childhood forms are caused by a similar mechanism as the acquired form and thus should employ the same definitions, diagnostic criteria, and treatment principles. However, further research is needed to demonstrate that the behavioral characteristics of the various etiologies are indeed sufficiently alike to support this claim.

It also remains to be shown that the clinical features exhibited by speakers with AOS are attributable to a particular neurobiological mechanism or set of mechanisms. Growth in the use of neuroimaging technologies in communication sciences and disorders promises improved understanding of the interaction between neurology and behavior in AOS. More importantly, greater knowledge of the disorder mechanism will yield advancements in the clinical arena, with treatment procedures that more directly target the underlying neural dysfunction from which the behavioral disorder arises. The current status of AOS research suggests that we are appropriately poised to address these challenges and ultimately improve functional outcomes for individuals with this disorder.

NOTE

1   Note discussion on error consistency in the text relative to differences in criteria for neurological AOS and childhood AOS.

REFERENCES

American Speech-Language-Hearing Association. (2007). *Childhood apraxia of speech* [Technical report]. Available from http://www.asha.org/policy.

Blakeley, R. W. (2001). *Screening test for developmental apraxia of speech*. Austin, TX: Pro-Ed.

Bose, A., Square, P. A., Schlosser, R., & van Lieshout, P. (2001). Effects of PROMPT therapy on speech motor function in a person with aphasia and apraxia of speech. *Aphasiology* 15 (8), 767–85.

Broca, P. (1977). Remarks on the seat of the faculty of articulate speech, followed by the report of a case of aphemia loss of speech (trans. C. Wasterlain & D. A. Rottenberg). In D. A. Rottenberg & F. H. Hochburg (eds.), *Neurological classics in modern translation* (pp. 136–49). New York, NY: Hafner Press. (Original work published 1861)

Clark, E. (2003). Review of the Apraxia Battery for Adults, second edition. In B. S. Plake, J. C. Impara, & R. A. Spies (eds.), *The fifteenth mental measurements yearbook*. Lincoln, NE: Buros Institute of Mental Measurements.

Cohen, J. (1988). *Statistical power analysis for the behavioral sciences*. Hillsdale, NJ: Lawrence Erlbaum.

Dabul, B. (2000). *Apraxia battery for adults, – second edition*. Austin, TX: Pro-Ed.

Darley, F., Aronson, A., & Brown, J. (1975). *Motor speech disorders*. Philadelphia: W.B. Saunders Inc.

Dean, R. S. & Brinkman, J. J. (2003). Review of the Apraxia Battery for Adults, second edition. In B. S. Plake, J. C. Impara, & R. A. Spies (eds.), *The fifteenth mental measurements yearbook*. Lincoln, NE: Buros Institute of Mental Measurements.

Deutsch, S. (1984). Prediction of site of lesion from speech apraxic error patterns. In J. C. Rosenbek, M. R. McNeil, & A. E. Aronson (eds.), *Apraxia of speech: Physiology, acoustics, linguistics, management* (pp. 113–34). San Diego, CA: College-Hill Press.

Dronkers, N. F. (1996). A new brain region for coordinating speech articulation. *Nature* 384 (6605), 159–61.

Duffy, J. R. (2005). *Motor speech disorders, second edition: Substrates, differential diagnosis, and management*. St. Louis, MO: Elsevier Mosby.

Duffy, J. R., Peach, R. K., & Strand, E. A. (2007). Progressive apraxia of speech as a sign of motor neuron disease. *American Journal of Speech-Language Pathology* 16 (3), 198–208.

Dworkin, J. P., Abkarian, G. G., & Johns, D. F. (1988). Apraxia of speech: The effectiveness of a treatment regimen. *Journal of Speech and Hearing Disorders* 53 (3), 280–94.

Hageman, C. F., Robin, D. A., Moon, J. B., & Folkins, J. W. (1994: Oral motor tracking in normal and apraxic speakers. *Clinical Aphasiology* 22, 219–29.

Haley, K. L. (2002). Temporal and spectral properties of voiceless fricatives in aphasia and apraxia of speech. *Aphasiology* 16 (4), 595–607.

Haley, K. L., Bays, G. L., & Ohde, R. N. (2001). Phonetic properties of aphasic-apraxic speech: A modified narrow transcription analysis. *Aphasiology* 15 (12), 1125–42.

Hillis, A. E., Work, M., Barker, P. B., Jacobs, M. A., Breese, E. L., & Maurer, K. (2004). Re-examining the brain regions crucial for orchestrating speech articulation. *Brain* 127 (7), 1479–87.

Itoh, M. & Sasanuma, S. (1984). Articulatory movements in apraxia of speech. In J. C. Rosenbek, M. R. McNeil, & A. E. Aronson (eds.), *Apraxia of speech: Physiology, acoustics, linguistics, management* (pp. 135–65). San Diego, CA: College-Hill Press.

Jacks, A. (2008). Bite block vowel production in apraxia of speech. *Journal of Speech, Language, and Hearing Research* 51, 898–913.

Josephs, K. A., Duffy, J. R., Strand, E. A., Whitwell, J. L., Layton, K. F., Parisi, J. E., Hauser, M. F., Witte, R. J., Boeve, B. F., Knopman, D. S., Dickson, D. W., Jack, C. R., & Petersen, R. C. (2006). Clinicopathological and imaging correlates of progressive aphasia and apraxia of speech. *Brain* 129 (6), 1385–98.

Kent, R. D., Weismer, G., Kent, J. F., & Rosenbek, J. C. (1989). Toward phonetic intelligibility testing in dysarthria. *Journal of Speech and Hearing Disorders* 54 (4), 482–99.

Kertesz, A. (1984). Subcortical lesions and verbal apraxia. In J. C. Rosenbek, M. R. McNeil, & A. E. Aronson (eds.), *Apraxia of speech: Physiology, acoustics, linguistics, management* (pp. 73–90). San Diego, CA: College-Hill Press.

Knock, T. R., Ballard, K. J., Robin, D. A., & Schmidt, R. A. (2000). Influence of order of stimulus presentation on speech motor learning: A principled approach to treatment for apraxia of speech. *Aphasiology* 14 (5/6), 653–68.

Lai, C. S. L., Fisher, S. E., Hurst, J. A., Vargha-Khadem, F., & Monaco, A. P.

(2001). A forkhead-domain gene is mutated in a severe speech and language disorder. *Nature* 413 (6855), 519–23.

Lewis, B. A., Freebairn, L. A., Hansen, A., Taylor, H. G., Iyengar, S., & Shriberg, L. D. (2004). Family pedigrees of children with suspected childhood apraxia of speech. *Journal of Communication Disorders* 37 (2), 157–75.

Lustig, A. P. & Tompkins, C. A. (2002). A written communication strategy for a speaker with aphasia and apraxia of speech: Treatment outcomes and social validity. *Aphasiology* 16 (4), 507–21.

Maassen, B. (2002). Issues contrasting adult acquired versus developmental apraxia of speech. *Seminars in Speech and Language* 23 (4), 257–66.

Marquardt, T. P. & Sussman, H. (1984). The elusive lesion – apraxia of speech link in Broca's aphasia. In J. C. Rosenbek, M. R. McNeil, & A. E. Aronson (eds.), *Apraxia of speech: Physiology, acoustics, linguistics, management* (pp. 91–112). San Diego, CA: College-Hill Press.

Marquardt, T. P., Jacks, A., & Davis, B. L. (2004). Token-to-token variability in developmental apraxia of speech: Three longitudinal case studies. *Clinical Linguistics and Phonetics* 18 (2), 127–44.

McCauley, R. (2003). Review of the Screening Test for Developmental Apraxia of Speech – second edition. In B. S. Plake, J. C. Impara, & R. A. Spies (eds.), *The fifteenth mental measurements yearbook*. Lincoln, NE: Buros Institute of Mental Measurements.

McNeil, M. R. & Pratt, S. R. (2001). Defining aphasia: Some theoretical and clinical implications of operating from a formal definition. *Aphasiology* 15 (10), 901–11.

McNeil, M. R., Caligiuri, M., & Rosenbek, J. C. (1989). A comparison of labiomandibular kinematic durations, displacements, velocities, and dysmetrias in apraxic and normal

adults. In R. H. Brookshire (ed.), *Clinical aphasiology: Proceedings of the conference* (pp. 173–93). San Diego, CA: College-Hill Press.

McNeil, M. R., Doyle, P. J., & Wambaugh, J. (2000). Apraxia of speech: A treatable disorder of motor planning and programming. In S. E. Nadeau, L. J. Gonzalez Rothi, & B. Crosson (eds.), *Aphasia and language: Theory to practice* (pp. 221–66. New York: Guilford Press.

McNeil, M. R., Odell, K. H., Miller, S. B., & Hunter, L. (1995). Consistency, variability, and target approximation for successive speech repetitions among apraxic, conduction aphasic, and ataxic dysarthric speakers. *Clinical Aphasiology* 23, 39–55.

McNeil, M. R., Robin, D. A., & Schmidt, R. A. (1997). Apraxia of speech: Definition, differentiation, and treatment. In M. R. McNeil (ed.), *Clinical management of sensorimotor speech disorders* (pp. 311–44). New York: Thieme.

McNeil, M. R., Robin, D. A., & Schmidt, R. A. (2009). Apraxia of speech: Definition and differential diagnosis. In M. R. McNeil (ed.), *Clinical management of sensorimotor speech disorders, second edition* (pp. 249–68). New York: Thieme.

Miller, N. (1992). Variability in speech dyspraxia. *Clinical Linguistics and Phonetics* 6 (1/2), 77–85.

Mohr, J. P. (1976). Broca's area and Broca's aphasia. In H. Whitaker (ed.), *Studies in neurolinguistics*, volume 1. New York: Academic Press.

Nicholas, L. E. & Brookshire, R. H. (1993). A system for quantifying the informativeness and efficiency of the connected speech of adults with aphasia. *Journal of Speech, Language, and Hearing Research* 36 (2), 338–50.

Norris, J. (2003). Review of the Screening Test for Developmental Apraxia of Speech – second edition. In B. S. Plake, J. C. Impara, & R. A. Spies (eds.), *The fifteenth mental measurements yearbook*.

Lincoln, NE: Buros Institute of Mental Measurements.

Odell, K., McNeil, M. R., Rosenbek, J. C., & Hunter, L. (1991). Perceptual characteristics of vowel and prosody production in apraxic, aphasic, and dysarthric speakers. *Journal of Speech and Hearing Research* 34 (1), 67–80.

Pollock, K. E. & Berni, M. C. (2001). Transcription of vowels. *Topics in Language Disorders* 21 (4), 22–40.

Powell, T. W. (2001). Phonetic transcription of disordered speech. *Topics in Language Disorders* 21 (4), 52–72.

Raymer, A. M. & Thompson, C. K. (1991). Effects of verbal plus gestural treatment in a patient with aphasia and severe apraxia of speech. *Clinical Aphasiology* 20, 285–98.

Robin, D. A., Jacks, A., & Ramage, A. E. (2008). The neural substrates of apraxia of speech as uncovered by brain imaging: A critical review. In R. J. Ingham (ed.), *Neuroimaging in communication sciences and disorders* (pp. 129–54). San Diego, CA: Plural Publishing.

Robin, D. A., Maas, E., Sandberg, Y., & Schmidt, R. A. (2007). Motor control and learning and childhood apraxia of speech. In P. K. Hall, L. S. Jordan, & D. A. Robin (eds.), *Developmental apraxia of speech – second edition: Theory and clinical practice* (pp. 67–86). Austin, TX: Pro-Ed.

Rosenbek, J. C. (1973). A treatment for apraxia of speech in adults. *Journal of Speech and Hearing Disorders* 38 (4), 462–72.

Rosenbek, J. C., Collins, M. J., & Wertz, R. T. (1976). Intersystematic reorganization for apraxia of speech. In R. H. Brookshire (ed.), *Clinical aphasiology: Proceedings of the conference* (pp. 255–60). Minneapolis, MN: BRK Publishers.

Rutschmann, O. T., McCrory, D. C., & Matchar, D. B. (2002). Immunization and MS: A summary of published evidence and recommendations. *Neurology* 59 (12), 1837–43.

Seddoh, S. A. K., Robin, D. A., Sim, H.-S., & Hageman, C. (1996). Speech timing in apraxia of speech versus conduction aphasia. *Journal of Speech and Hearing Research* 39 (3), 590–603.

Shriberg, L. D. (2006). Research in idiopathic and symptomatic childhood apraxia of speech. *Stem-, Spraak- en Taalpathologie* 14 (Supp.), 121.

Shriberg, L. D., Aram, D. M., & Kwiatkowski, J. (1997). Developmental apraxia of speech: II, Toward a diagnostic marker. *Journal of Speech, Language, and Hearing Research* 40 (2), 286–312.

Shriberg, L. D., Ballard, K. J., Tomblin, J. B., Duffy, J. R., Odell, K. H., & Williams, C. A. (2006). Speech, prosody, and voice characteristics of a mother and daughter with a 7; 13 translocation affecting FOXP2. *Journal of Speech, Language, and Hearing Research* 49 (3), 500.

Shriberg, L. D., Campbell, T. F., Karlsson, H. B., Brown, R. L., McSweeny, J. L., & Nadler, C. J. (2003a). A diagnostic marker for childhood apraxia of speech: The lexical stress ratio. *Clinical Linguistics and Phonetics* 17 (7), 549–74.

Shriberg, L. D., Flipsen, P., Jr., Kwitakowski, J., & McSweeny, J. L. (2003b). A diagnostic marker for speech delay associated with otitis media with effusion: The intelligibility-speech gap. *Clinical Linguistics and Phonetics* 17 (7), 507–27.

Shuster, L. I. & Wambaugh, J. L. (2000). Perceptual and acoustic analyses of speech sound errors in apraxia of speech accompanied by aphasia. *Aphasiology* 14 (5), 635–51.

Square, P. A., Martin, R. E., & Bose, A. (2001). The nature and treatment of neuromotor speech disorders in aphasia. In R. Chapey (ed.), *Language intervention strategies in aphasia and related neurogenic communication disorders* (pp. 847–84). Baltimore, MD: Lippincott, Williams, & Wilkins.

Square-Storer, P. A. & Apeldoorn, S. (1991). An acoustic study of apraxia of speech in patients with different lesion loci. In C. A. Moore, K. M. Yorkston, & D. R. Beukelman (eds.), *Dysarthria and apraxia of speech: Perspectives on management* (pp. 271–88). Baltimore, MD: Paul H. Brookes Publishing Co.

Strand, E. A., Stoeckel, R., & Baas, B. (2006). Treatment of severe childhood apraxia of speech: A treatment efficacy study. *Journal of Medical Speech-Language Pathology* 14 (4), 297.

Tjaden, K. (2000). Exploration of a treatment technique for prosodic disturbance following stroke. *Clinical Linguistics and Phonetics* 14 (8), 619–41.

Vargha-Khadem, F., Watkins, K., Alcock, K., Fletcher, P., & Passingham, R. (1995). Praxic and nonverbal cognitive deficits in a large family with a genetically transmitted speech and language disorder. *Proceedings of the National Academy of Sciences of the United States of America* 92 (3), 930–3.

Wambaugh, J. L. (2004). Stimulus generalization effects of sound production treatment for apraxia. *Journal of Medical Speech-Language Pathology* 12 (2), 77–97.

Wambaugh, J. L., Doyle, P. J., Kalinyak, M. M., & West, J. E. (1996). A minimal contrast treatment for apraxia of speech. *Clinical Aphasiology* 24, 97–108.

Wambaugh, J. L., Duffy, J. R., McNeil, M. R., Robin, D. A., & Rogers, M. A. (2006a). Treatment guidelines for acquired apraxia of speech: A synthesis and evaluation of the evidence. *Journal of Medical Speech-Language Pathology* 14 (2), xv–xxxiii.

Wambaugh, J. L., Duffy, J. R., McNeil, M. R., Robin, D. A., & Rogers, M. A. (2006b). Treatment guidelines for acquired apraxia of speech: Treatment descriptions and recommendations. *Journal of Medical Speech-Language Pathology* 14 (2), xxxv–lxvii.

Wambaugh, J. L., Kalinyak-Fliszar, M. M., West, J. E., & Doyle, P. J. (1998). Effects of treatment for sound errors in apraxia of speech and aphasia. *Journal of Speech, Language, and Hearing Research* 41 (4), 725–43.

Wambaugh, J. L., Martinez, A. L., McNeil, M. R., & Rogers, M. A. (1999). Sound production treatment for apraxia of speech: Overgeneralization and maintenance effects. *Aphasiology* 13 (9), 821–37.

Watkins, K. E., Vargha-Khadem, F., Ashburner, J., Passingham, R. E., Connelly, A., Friston, K. J., et al. (2002). MRI analysis of an inherited speech and language disorder: Structural brain abnormalities. *Brain* 125 (3), 465–78.

Wertz, R. T. (1984). Response to treatment in patients with apraxia of speech. In J. C. Rosenbek, M. R. McNeil, & A. E. Aronson (eds.), *Apraxia of speech: Physiology, acoustics, linguistics, management* (pp. 257–76). San Diego, CA: College-Hill Press.

Yorkston, K. M., Beukelman, D. R., & Traynor, C. (1984). *Computerized assessment of intelligibility of dysarthric speech*. Tigard, OR: C. C. Publications.

18 Augmentative and Alternative Communication:
An Introduction

KATHRYN D. R. DRAGER, ERINN H. FINKE, AND ELIZABETH C. SERPENTINE

Communication is the essence of human life. (Daniel Webster)

1 Introduction

Augmentative and Alternative Communication (AAC) is "the field or area of clinical, educational, and research practice to improve, temporarily or permanently, the communication skills of individuals with little or no functional speech and/ or writing" (American Speech, Language and Hearing Association, 2002, p. 2). It also refers to "a set of procedures and processes by which an individual's communication skills (i.e., production as well as comprehension) can be maximized for functional and effective communication" (ibid.). The need for or use of AAC is not specific to any particular population, age, or cultural background. Individuals who use AAC range across the lifespan and include individuals with congenital impairments (e.g., cerebral palsy, Down syndrome, autism) and acquired impairments (e.g., cerebrovascular accident, traumatic brain injury, Parkinson's disease), as well as individuals with temporary conditions (e.g., shock, surgery/ intubation), which impair or impede the ability to communicate via speech. Combined, these groups make up a significant portion of the population, as well as any speech-language pathology caseload (Beukelman & Mirenda, 2005; Binger & Light, 2006).

In all communicative interactions, regardless of the mode of communication used (e.g., speech, gestures), there are four purposes that are fulfilled: communication of needs and wants, social closeness, information transfer, and social etiquette routines (Light, 1988). The goal of the interaction, as well as specifics about the content and predictability of the messages, are all affected by the purpose of the interaction. For example, the goal of an interaction designed to communicate needs and wants is to regulate the behavior of a listener to a desired action (Light, 1988). Because of this goal, the content of the communication is very important, while the predictability of the communication is high, based on context. In contrast,

The Handbook of Language and Speech Disorders, First Edition. Edited by Jack S. Damico, Nicole Müller, and Martin J. Ball. © 2013 Blackwell Publishing Ltd except for editorial material and organization © 2013 Jack S. Damico, Nicole Müller, Martin J. Ball. Published 2013 by Blackwell Publishing Ltd.

the goal of social closeness communication is to establish, maintain, or develop personal relationships (Light, 1988). The content of these interactions is not as important as the interaction itself, and the content is less predictable than when communicating about needs and wants. Interactions for information transfer have the goal of sharing information. The content is important in these interactions, and not very predictable. Lastly, social etiquette routines are used to conform to social conventions, such as being polite. These interactions are brief and often predictable.

For a person who uses AAC, it is important that all four purposes of communication are accessible. Communication of needs and wants has received a majority of the attention in research investigations and clinical advances, with much less focus on social aspects (Light, Parsons, & Drager, 2002). When conducting research or working clinically with individuals who require AAC, the goal for interventions is the development of communicative competence. Communicative competence involves the ability to transmit messages in all four interaction categories.

Communicative competence can be defined as "the quality or state of being functionally adequate in daily communication, or of having sufficient knowledge, judgment, and skill to communicate" (Light, 1989, p. 138). Based on this definition, there are three major components to the development of competent communication: functionality of communication, adequacy of communication, and sufficiency of knowledge, judgment, and skills (Light, 1989, 1997).

According to Light (1989), the functionality of an individual's communication will be highly affected by the communication demands of the various contexts and environments in which the individual lives and participates. However, individuals do not have to be masters of language in order to be competent communicators. Instead, individuals need to be able to meet the demands of each environment and context in which they communicate (principle of adequacy of communication; Light, 1989, 2003). Finally, individuals require sufficient knowledge, judgment, and skill to be able to communicate with various partners in various environments and to be able to communicate a variety of intents (Light, 1989, 2003).

Knowledge, judgment, and skills need to be acquired in four specific domains – linguistic, operational, social, and strategic (Light, 1989, 2003). Linguistic competence refers to skills in two areas: the native language of the community and in the "language code" of the AAC system. Operational competence is having the skills to technically operate an AAC system or produce gestures and signs. Social competence involves the development of appropriate sociolinguistic skills, such as initiating, maintaining, and terminating conversations, and appropriate sociorelational skills, such as actively participating in interactions, putting partners at ease, etc. Lastly, strategic competence involves compensatory strategies used to bypass limitations in the other three domains, such as asking partners to predict alphabetic messages, or using an introduction strategy to put partners at ease.

There are no prerequisite skills necessary for an individual to be a candidate for AAC. Any individual who does not have the ability to meet daily communication needs using speech alone is an appropriate candidate for AAC systems and strategies. The right to communication should not be denied, "irrespective of the type and/or severity of communication, linguistic, social, cognitive, motor, sensory, perceptual, and/or other disability(ies) they may present" (American Speech, Language, and Hearing Association, 2005, p. 1). This chapter will provide an overview of AAC, including unaided and aided communication, components of aided AAC systems, assessment, and intervention principles.

2   AAC Systems

There are two types of AAC systems: unaided communication systems and aided communication systems. Unaided communication systems utilize only the communicator's body. The communicator must be able to move his/her body but does not require access to equipment or devices that are separate from the body. Unaided communication systems are considered dynamic in that the messages they produce are not enduring and frequently involve movement and change. Examples of unaided communication systems include natural speech and vocalizations, gestures and body language, and sign language and sign systems (Beukelman & Mirenda, 1998; Glennen & DeCoste, 1997; Lloyd & Karlan, 1984; Mirenda, 1985).

As with any intervention option, there are advantages and disadvantages inherent in unaided modes of communication. Advantages to using an unaided communication system include portability, and speed and efficiency. Because no external equipment is required, the communicator can access the system anywhere. Messages can be conveyed with speed and efficiency; however, the success of messages is highly dependent on the communication partner. When conversing with partners familiar with the unaided symbols, communication is relatively fast and efficient. For example, if an individual is using sign language as an unaided communication system, communicating with other individuals who know and understand sign language will be fast and efficient.

There are also several disadvantages associated with use of an unaided communication system. First, in order for the system to be effective, all communication partners must be familiar with the communication system (e.g., the rules of the system). Many communication partners in the community are unfamiliar with formal signs. This creates a situation in which the individual using sign language may have a limited set of communication partners, and may not be able to communicate in all situations or for all communication purposes. Second, the communicator must possess a certain level of physical skill and motor ability to use the system (e.g., he/she must be able to achieve specific hand shapes for sign language). Finally, some unaided communication systems, such as naturally occurring gestures, body language, and vocalizations are finite sets, thereby limiting the number of topics about which the individual can communicate.

In contrast, aided communication systems are those that require equipment in addition to the communicator's body. These systems typically involve graphic symbols and the messages generated are often static (at least for a period of time), meaning the message can be referred back to by both communication partners if not initially understood or transmitted. One advantage to aided communication systems includes potentially readily identifiable and adaptable symbols (depending on how guessable a given symbol is). Aided communication systems also provide a constant visual display, which reduces or accommodates for difficulties with message processing or interpretation for the communicative partner. Finally, minimal motor skills are required to access the system, allowing individuals with even severe motor impairments to independently communicate. Disadvantages include a possible large vocabulary that can make the system cumbersome, a slower rate of communication, and potentially expensive systems.

There are two types of aided communication systems. These are light technology (or low technology) and high technology systems. Light technology systems do not have a computer-based component. Examples include picture communication boards/books, alphabet boards, and eye-point displays. Light technology systems are readily available with excellent picture quality for a relatively low cost in the form of commercially prepared picture sets (e.g., Mayer Johnson's Picture Communication Symbols). Light technology systems can be customized for type and size of picture if the picture sets are constructed by the AAC team.

Advantages associated with employment of a light technology communication system are portability, cost, and durability. These systems tend to be lightweight and relatively small in size and therefore portable between environments. Light technology systems are typically inexpensive to purchase or construct. Finally, because these systems are durable, they can be used in places where high technology systems cannot be employed (e.g., the pool, sandbox, bathtub). The high durability of these systems means that they do not break down and leave the communicator without a system. The primary disadvantage to a light technology system is that the communication partner must always be present (e.g., face to face) for communication to take place.

High technology systems are computer-based systems containing speech synthesizers and/or printers. These systems can be dedicated or non-dedicated communication devices. Dedicated communication devices are used exclusively for communication purposes (e.g., a Dynamo® or Pathfinder®). Non-dedicated devices are not specifically designed for communication but can be used as AAC systems through adaptations (e.g., laptop computers, software).

There are several advantages associated with using high technology systems. The voice output makes it easier to get a listener's attention and to communicate in groups. Hearing the voice output can also facilitate the user's device learning and use. The communicator has greater independence as he/she does not depend on a partner's presence (as with unaided systems). Finally, high technology systems can interface with computers thereby allowing access to the internet, email, and written communication. Disadvantages connected to high technology systems include the cost of the system, lack of portability (e.g., due to weight, connections to outlets, etc.), and possibility for breakdown. It is essential for all communicators who use high technology systems to have a light technology system as a back-up because all high technology systems will break down at one time or another.

3   Components of Aided AAC Systems

There are four components considered when designing aided AAC systems. The first is symbol representation, or how the concepts being communicated will be represented in the system. The second is layout and organization. The symbols that are chosen need to be displayed in physical space, and must be arranged in some format. Third is selection technique. Once in the physical space of the aided system, the individual using AAC must be able to select the desired symbol. Last is output, or the feedback of the system about the selection. Each of these components will be considered in turn.

3.1   *Symbol representation*

When an individual communicates via an AAC modality, he/she is communicating using symbols (Beukelman & Mirenda, 2005). Every communicator uses symbols to express meaning and to relay messages to listeners. A symbol is anything that represents something else (Vanderheiden & Yoder, 1986). The symbols used by a person who requires AAC can be quite varied, and require different amounts of time to learn depending on how easy they are to relate to the concept they represent. Symbols can be spoken, graphic, or manual representations of ideas, affective states, objects, actions, people, relationships, and events.

There are many different kinds of symbols that are used by individuals who require AAC, and the choices should be based on the needs and skills of the individual communicator. Aided symbols include such things as:

- real objects
- miniature objects
- partial objects
- photographs (color and black and white)
- line drawings (color and black and white)
- written text
- Braille
- Morse code.

The use of an aided communication system does not presume the choice of a single symbol representation. An individual may use a combination of objects, photographs, line drawings, and words, as well as unaided symbols, such as gestures and signs. Frequently, communicative competence requires a multi-modal communication system.

3.2   *Layout and organization*

The second component of aided AAC systems is layout and organization. Aided AAC systems require that concepts, which begin as thoughts without dimension, be placed in physical space. When considering this component of aided AAC systems, clinicians must determine the appropriate layout, or type of display, as well as the organization of the symbols on the display.

3.2.1   Display types   There are four major types of display that are generally considered: (a) static displays, (b) dynamic displays, (c) letter-based displays, and (d) iconic encoding-based displays. Most aided AAC systems that have static displays are considered simple digitized AAC systems. Simple digitized systems can be defined as high technology communication devices that support digitized speech with a static, or fixed, display. An aided AAC system with a static display has a series of cells, anywhere between one cell (e.g., BIGmack by Ablenet) and 128 (e.g., Smart/128 by AMDi). On these types of AAC systems the screen does not change; however, some of these may have multiple levels, allowing for additional vocabulary to be stored and accessed by changing the overlay on the AAC system display.

A dynamic display system is defined as a system where a selection on a display results in a new array of graphic symbols (i.e., the screens change based on what is selected, and new choices and items are made available with each selection; Beukelman & Mirenda, 2005). Dynamic display systems are programmable, have touch-screens, and are able to utilize alternative access methods through scanning, joysticks, and switches. Dynamic display systems offer the advantage of being able to have fewer symbols on each page of the display while still allowing the user access to a large vocabulary set.

Dynamic display systems can be set up using either a traditional grid layout or using a visual scene layout (Drager et al., 2003). Traditional grid layouts consist of symbols organized in rows and columns with symbols represented individually within boxes in the rows and columns. A traditional grid layout can be compared to individual student pictures that are organized by class within a yearbook. Another type of layout that is an option for some aided AAC systems are visual scene displays. Visual scene displays can be defined as a picture, photograph, or virtual environment that depicts and represents a situation, place, or experience (Blackstone, 2004). They can include individual elements such as people, actions, and objects that appear within the visual scene (Beukelman & Mirenda, 2005; Blackstone, 2004). In the yearbook example, visual scenes may be compared to the candid photos that depict school events. In these AAC system designs, language concepts are embedded in real-world scenes, and objects integrated within the photo are used as symbols for communication (e.g., selecting a person's dress in the candid prom photo could be used to discuss the dress worn to the event) (Drager et al., 2004; Light et al., 2004).

The third type of display for aided AAC systems is the letter-based display. Letter-based displays can be used with either a static or a dynamic screen. Letter-based displays are displays that are made up of traditional orthography symbols, or in other words, the letters of the alphabet. The display is an alphabet board (in QWERTY layout – the traditional layout of most keyboards – ABC layout, or in frequency of use order, depending on what is most efficient for the individual).

The fourth type of AAC system display is the iconic encoding-based display. Iconic encoding-based displays originated because of the extremely slow nature of communicating via an AAC device. Individuals without disabilities using natural speech to communicate typically converse at a rate of 150 to 250 words per minute. Individuals who require AAC, however, typically converse at a rate of less than 15 words per minute (Beukelman & Mirenda, 2005; Blockberger & Sutton, 2003; Light & Lindsay, 1991, 1992). This is obviously a very significant difference in generative rate for communication. Iconic encoding-based displays contain a communication system in which a finite set of pictures can be combined based on various semantic associations of each picture, allowing for a large vocabulary. For example, a picture of a chef could be used to mean *person, occupation, food, white, cook, eat,* and *chef*, as well as many other things. When using an iconic encoding-based AAC system, an AAC user can produce phrase- and sentence-length messages by combining two or three symbols. The resultant message will take meaning from the combinations of semantic associations of the symbols (for example, combining a picture of a clock and then an apple could mean, "When is lunch?"). This greatly reduces the number of keystrokes required to produce longer messages, which in turn should speed up communication. Minspeak® (Semantic Compaction Systems) is a patented iconic encoding language representation system (Baker, 1982).

3.2.2 Organization of vocabulary   When an individual who requires AAC uses an aided AAC system, the graphic symbols that are used to represent vocabulary must be organized so that the individual can find them efficiently, so he/she can communicate with the AAC system effectively (Beukelman & Mirenda, 2005). This is particularly important, and increasingly difficult, when vocabulary that needs to be stored within the AAC system is large. There are many approaches to organization of vocabulary within aided AAC systems, including (a) schematic organization, (b) taxonomic organization, (c) semantic/grammatical organization, (d) alphabetic organization, and (e) frequency or importance of use.

Schematic organization of vocabulary concepts means that the vocabulary that has been selected for the individual is organized by context or activity (Drager et al., 2003). This type of vocabulary organization can be used with both a traditional grid layout and with a visual scene layout (Beukelman & Mirenda, 2005). When vocabulary is organized in this way, concepts such as people, places, objects, feelings, actions, and descriptors are represented on each page as they apply to individual activities, environments, or contexts. This type of vocabulary organization strategy is most commonly used in AAC systems being constructed for use by children because it may be similar to the way children cognitively organize concepts (Drager et al., 2004).

Taxonomic organization, in contrast, most closely relates to what is widely considered an adolescent and adult conceptualization of how vocabulary should be organized (Fallon, Light, & Achenbach, 2003). When vocabulary is organized in AAC systems using this approach, vocabulary is grouped according to category membership such as people, places, feelings, food, and drinks (Beukelman & Mirenda, 2005). Taxonomic or categorical organization of vocabulary concepts has usually been applied to traditional grid layouts, and is generally reserved for use with individuals functioning cognitively at or above the 6–7-year-old level (Fallon, Light, & Achenbach, 2003).

Semantic/grammatical organization of vocabulary involves organizing concepts according to the parts of speech (Beukelman & Mirenda, 2005). This organization was conceptualized with the hope that it would aid the individual who requires AAC in the language development process. To date, there is no empirical support that this organizational strategy actually serves this purpose (Beukelman & Mirenda, 2005). The most common strategy employed for organizing vocabulary in this manner is the Fitzgerald key (McDonald & Schultz, 1973). The original format for the Fitzgerald key organized symbols from left to right into the following categories: who, doing, modifiers, what, where, when, "with frequently used phrases and letters clustered along the top or bottom of the display" (Beukelman & Mirenda, 2005, p. 336). When this type of display is used, vocabulary items are generally color-coded to match the category, or part of speech, to which they belong.

AAC systems organized using alphabetic organization have vocabulary that is arranged in the same way that a dictionary would be, that is, in alphabetical order. AAC systems that use this strategy are often very similar to dictionaries, but are personalized in that they contain words specifically selected for the individual who requires AAC. This format for organizing vocabulary requires understanding of the alphabet, and alphabetical order. It also requires some basic literacy skills in order to find the desired vocabulary item within the AAC system.

The final vocabulary organization strategy to be discussed is frequency or importance of use. When vocabulary on AAC systems is organized in this way, the words, concepts, phrases, or sentences that are used most frequently by the individual who requires AAC, or that need to be communicated very quickly (e.g., emergency vocabulary), are placed in the areas of the AAC system that are the easiest and most efficient for the individual to access.

3.3   Selection techniques

Regardless of how the symbols are organized on a system, the individual who uses AAC must have a means to access the desired symbol(s). There are two strategies currently used to select symbols: direct selection and scanning. Individuals who are able to use direct selection access the symbols by directly touching the display (e.g., picture board, keyboard, touch-screen, etc.) with a finger or thumb or with an aid (e.g., headstick, chin pointer). While direct selection is an option for some individuals, others have significant motor impairments that preclude accurate and efficient direct selection. The second option, scanning, is available for individuals with significant motor impairments who are unable to use direct selection to accurately target a variety of locations on a system. In a scanning method of access, the items are arranged in an array and highlighted by a communication partner or the computer system one at a time. When the desired item is highlighted, the individual signals a response or activates a switch. Scanning only requires one reliable body movement (e.g., head turn, eyebrow lift). However, scanning is very slow and can be difficult to learn (McCarthy et al.,

2006). Scanning systems are available in a number of different configurations (e.g., circular, linear, or group-item scanning patterns) and can be presented in different ways (e.g., row by row, column by column, or by quadrant, etc.) in an effort to customize the access technique and to speed up communication. See Beukelman and Mirenda (2005) for more information on scanning and options for customizing scanning.

3.4   *Output*

The output of the system is the last component of aided AAC systems to be considered. There are two types of output: activation feedback and message feedback. Activation feedback lets the user know that an item has been selected. It may be auditory, such as a beep or click; visual, such as a change in the display; or tactile feedback, like the keys on a keyboard when depressed. Message feedback provides the user with some information about the selection. For example, upon selection of a key, a high-tech aided AAC system may speak the letter, word, or sentence that was selected, and/or may display the selection visually.

One common form of output is digitized or synthesized speech. Speech output allows for some flexibility in communicating: messages can be sent without first obtaining the partner's attention, communication partners do not need to be attending to the display and do not need to be literate, and communication can occur at a distance. Additionally, speech output provides information in a mode that may be relatively familiar to speaking partners. However, synthesized and digitized speech is less intelligible than natural speech for children and adults (Drager et al., 2006; Mirenda & Beukelman, 1987, 1990). In particular, people with hearing impairments, reduced receptive language, or in a noisy environment may find it difficult to understand.

4   Assessment

To achieve communicative competence, it is critical that an individual have access to an AAC system or systems that are appropriate for his/her skills and needs. Providing communication services to individuals with severe communication disabilities is difficult since a "typical" AAC user does not exist. Individuals utilizing AAC devices come from all socioeconomic groups, age groups, and racial and ethnic backgrounds (Beukelman & Mirenda, 1998). Just as each individual who requires AAC is unique, so too is each assessment process. The assessment process can be likened to a road map in that it twists and turns, and alternate routes are necessary for different individuals, situations, and environments. Because assessments are ongoing and play out differently each time, the field of AAC has yet to develop a consensus concerning best practice procedures to guide assessments (Glennen & DeCoste, 1997; Light, McNaughton, & Parnes, 1994).

Despite utilizing various procedures, clinicians and researchers have a unified goal for AAC interventions. This goal is to assist an individual in becoming communicatively competent to meet the four purposes of communication (wants and needs, social closeness, information exchange, and social etiquette) for the present and future (Glennen & DeCoste, 1997; Beukelman & Mirenda, 1998; Light, 1988; Silverman, 1980). In order to accomplish this, clinicians must assemble a team to engage in an ongoing, dynamic process of determining an individual's needs and capabilities for functional communication in real-world settings, resulting in a profile of the individual's capabilities. Appropriate AAC tools and strategies can then be found to support effective communication (Beukelman & Mirenda, 1998; Reichle, York, & Sigafoos, 1991).

4.1 The AAC assessment team

AAC service delivery has always been practiced as a team effort (Glennen & DeCoste, 1997; Reichle, York, & Sigafoos, 1991). The most central members of any AAC assessment team are the individual for whom the assessment is being conducted and his/her family or caregivers. Other team members might include speech-language pathologists, special educators, rehabilitation engineers, physical therapists, occupational therapists, psychologists, nurses and other persons invested in the individual's communication outcomes. Team membership and size will vary according to the environments and needs of the individual requiring AAC (Beukelman & Mirenda, 1998; Glennen & DeCoste, 1997). While it might seem reasonable to include as many team members as possible in order to gain as much information as possible, it may be difficult to coordinate meetings according to the schedules of all team members. In addition, a large team may produce too much information to sort through in a timely manner (Beukelman & Mirenda, 1998; Glennen & DeCoste, 1997; Rainforth, York, & Macdonald, 1992). It may be more practical and effective to utilize the concept of "core" and "expanded" teams. Core teams are comprised of a small number of persons that interact with the individual requiring AAC on a daily basis. Expanded teams are comprised of the core team members and persons that interact with the individual on a less frequent basis. All members of core and expanded teams work collaboratively to contribute information that is critical to the assessment process (Beukelman & Mirenda, 1998; Glennen & DeCoste, 1997; Thousand & Villa, 1990).

4.2 Primary components of AAC assessment

Comprehensive AAC assessments have three primary components. First, teams must identify client needs and participation patterns. Needs assessment involves the identification of specific communication tasks that the individual must perform in order to function optimally in particular communication environments (Yorkston & Karlan, 1986). The team identifies with whom, when, where, how, what and about what the individual needs to communicate. The current participation patterns are recorded to detect communication needs that are and are not adequately met at the present time. Finally, priority communication needs for the individual and his/her family are determined.

The second component is to assess the individual's strengths and abilities by means of a capability assessment. Capability assessment is the process of gathering information about an individual's competencies in a variety of areas (e.g., motor, natural speech, receptive and expressive language, literacy, cognitive organization, seating and positioning, and sensory-perceptual), which will assist the team in selecting AAC system components and intervention strategies to optimize the individual's performance within his/her range of capabilities (Beukelman & Mirenda, 1998).

The third component is to identify opportunity barriers and facilitative strategies in the individual's environment. Opportunity barriers are obstacles imposed by society or by the individual's partners that limit participation in communication in daily life. Opportunity barriers include both the official and unofficial policies that affect use of AAC devices in the classroom (policy barriers), the attitudes and opinions of persons who interact with the individuals using AAC (attitude barriers), lack of knowledge regarding AAC practices (knowledge barriers), and the skills of the communication partners interacting with the individual (skill barriers) (Baumgart, Johnson, & Helmstetter, 1990; Beukelman & Mirenda, 1998; Glennen & DeCoste, 1997). The interaction strategies used by partners to facilitate communication should also be examined as participants influence each other throughout the course of communication interaction (Light, McNaughton, & Parnes, 1994).

4.3   Assessment procedures

A number of general methods are utilized to assess the aforementioned primary components. First, team members should review past reports to obtain relevant background information. Baumgart, Johnson, and Helmstetter (1990) suggested that clinicians review client records in order to familiarize themselves with the individual's documented status in the areas of cognition, motor skills, vision and hearing, medical, communication skills, speech and language, and social-emotional or interpersonal behavior. While past reports do provide teams with essential background information, Light, McNaughton, and Parnes (1994) warn that reports "often fail to provide the clinician with relevant information regarding the client's functional communication skills" (p. 14). Therefore, reviewing past reports should be considered an initial step in the assessment process.

Conducting interviews with the individual and his/her facilitators provides some indication of the environment's responsiveness to the individual's communicative intentions (Schuler et al., 1989). The individual's current methods of communication and the relative success of those methods is explored, and current and potential communication partners, environments, and topics are identified (Glennen & DeCoste, 1997). The information gathered during interviews allows team members to formulate clearly defined instructional objectives that are relevant to communicative functioning in the individual's typical daily environments (Schuler et al., 1989).

Ecological inventories provide detailed information about communication needs by way of direct observation of the individual and his/her peers. Observations can be conducted in person, or by setting up a video camera and letting it record for an extended period of time. These observations assist the team in identifying the individual's typical environments, activities, communication partners, seating/positioning, communication needs, and vocabulary needs.

Finally, formal and informal tests are often employed throughout the assessment process. It is critical that professionals adapt these measures as individuals requiring AAC may be unable to respond verbally, may have difficulty manipulating pictures and objects, and may require extended time to complete tasks. Alternatives to standard testing formats might include cutting test pages apart, rearranging or decreasing the number of responses to accommodate visual or motor limitations, offering yes/no verbal scanning, or providing multiple choice formats. While providing these accommodations for a typical individual would render the resulting score invalid, they can provide valuable information about the strengths and capabilities of the individual requiring AAC. If such tests are administered, it is important that the results are not compared to those of peers of the same age.

4.4   Assessing the individual's skills

4.4.1 Sensory-perceptual skills In order to determine a client's sensory-perceptual function, it is necessary to examine the individual's visual, hearing, and tactile abilities. "The degree of intactness of a person's auditory, visual, and tactile-kinesthetic systems partially determines the non-speech communication modes it is possible for him to use" (Silverman, 1980, p. 199). For example, if an individual has poor visual acuity, he/she may require larger graphic symbols, which may in turn limit the number of concepts per "page" of a dynamic device.

4.4.2 Linguistic skills The goals of receptive language assessment are to determine the type of spoken language input that is appropriate (e.g., single words vs. whole sentences), to determine when and how augmentation of spoken input is required, and to identify discrepancies between comprehension and expression. Commonly used procedures to assess receptive language include standardized language tests, observations in the natural environment, informal, clinician-developed tasks, and dynamic assessment (e.g., teach and test) of augmented input (Beukelman & Mirenda, 1998).

The purposes of expressive language assessment are to determine how the individual currently expresses him/herself in daily interactions, and to investigate the expressive skills that the client has but does not typically use in daily interactions. Turn-taking patterns, initiations and response patterns, range and frequency of communicative functions, modes of communication, and the content and form of communication should all be examined. Commonly used procedures to assess expressive language skills include interviews with the individual and/or his/her facilitators, structured observation, and informal eliciting contexts to probe specific skills (Beukelman & Mirenda, 1998).

Literacy assessment involves careful consideration of a person's reading, spelling, and writing skills. The assessment of literacy skills is conducted to determine whether the individual has sufficient literacy ability to consider using written language as a communication modality (Glennen & DeCoste, 1997). Specific skills to address include print and phoneme awareness, word recognition, reading comprehension and spelling skills.

4.4.3 Cognitive skills The purpose of cognitive assessment in AAC is to determine how the individual understands the world and how the AAC team can best facilitate communication within this understanding. Symbol assessment should assist in selecting the types of symbols that will meet the individual's current communication needs, matching his current abilities, and identifying symbol options that might be used in the future. Symbols should be assessed according to levels of abstraction (from concrete objects to abstract representations of objects and concepts). It is important to consider both aided symbol representation (pictures, objects, words) and unaided symbol representation (signs and gestures). A dynamic approach (e.g., teach then test) is required and may involve receptive language tasks (verbal label matching), yes/no tasks, visual matching tasks, and/or requesting tasks (Beukelman & Mirenda, 1998).

The goal of an organization assessment it to determine how the individual organizes semantic information and to determine the best organization for aided AAC systems (Blackstone, 1991; Light & Lindsay, 1991). Assessment tasks may include sorting or grouping vocabulary items multiple times, pairing tasks using relevant vocabulary, and trial and error systems of evaluation (e.g., develop trial systems using different organizations and assess the best fit for the individual based on the ease of use, speed, preference, and accuracy).

4.4.4 Natural speech skills Assessment of natural speech is important as the majority of individuals requiring AAC do have some vocalizations and/or speech productions that can be utilized for communication. Speech samples are collected to calculate word intelligibility (number of words understood correctly by the partner divided by the number of words communicated) and message intelligibility (number of messages understood by partners divided by the number of messages communicated). Clarification strategies for natural speech (e.g., proper positioning and stabilization, pacing, repetition, use of gestures, etc.) should also be assessed.

4.4.5 Motor skills Assessment of motor control is conducted to identify optimum means of accessing an AAC aid or to determine possible constraints of using a gestural communication system (Blackstone, 1986). The expertise of an occupational therapist and/or a physical therapist is required to probe the production of an individual's hand shapes, orientations, positions, and movements. Accuracy and efficiency of access techniques to control aided systems is also assessed. Finally, assessment for functional seating and positioning is an integral part of motor skill assessment.

4.5   Vocabulary selection

Vocabulary selection is defined as the dynamic process attempting to capture the changing experiences, interests, and knowledge of the individual using the AAC system (Beukelman, McGinnis, & Morrow, 1991). It is an ongoing process that begins with assessment, but needs to be sensitive to developmental, environmental, and cultural changes. Selecting vocabulary for a system is a difficult and time-consuming task as all decisions made must consider equipment features and the individual's unique capabilities, communicative needs, goals, listening partners, personal experiences, and environments (Blackstone, 1988; Glennen & DeCoste, 1997).

Several techniques are utilized to select vocabulary that meets an individual's communicative needs across many environments, including interviews and direct observation. Interviews with family, professionals, and other primary communication partners present the speech-language pathologist with data regarding the AAC user's communicative partners, environments, demands, and activities. Direct observations provide information about the user's communicative needs in certain settings that contribute directly to selecting vocabulary to meet expressive communicative needs (Carlson, 1981; Glennen & DeCoste, 1997).

Vocabulary selection techniques range from blank sheet methods, where individuals (AAC users and/or communication partners) simply record words they think may be valuable, to categorical formats, where general category headings are supplied to the individual completing the form, ecological inventories, and standard vocabulary lists. These methods provide the professional with both general overviews and specific details regarding the needs of the AAC user (Glennen & DeCoste, 1997).

4.6   Types of vocabulary

Vocabulary selected for individuals using AAC systems can be broken down into several categories: core and fringe vocabularies. Core vocabularies are comprised of words that are used by a variety of individuals, occur frequently, and have some universal utility (Blackstone, 1988; Beukelman & Mirenda, 1998; Glennen & DeCoste, 1997). Core vocabularies are generally highly functional words and phrases related to basic needs, brief social exchanges, and other necessary information. The objective of a core vocabulary is to provide the individual with the ability to communicate most effectively and about the widest possible range of topics (Vanderheiden & Kelso, 1987). Core vocabularies are successful in meeting the basic communicative needs of the individual only if the selected words are highly reinforcing to the AAC user (Glennen & DeCoste, 1997).

Fringe vocabularies consist of words and expressions that are unique to the individual AAC user. These content-rich and topic-related words relate directly to the user's activities and environments. Fringe vocabularies enhance participation in activities through their diversity and language richness. Fringe vocabularies should allow the user to expand on communication topics and be accessible across activities (Blackstone, 1988; Glennen & DeCoste, 1997).

The dynamic and ongoing nature of vocabulary selection demands that the vocabulary be maintained and updated. Updating an individual's vocabulary requires that a list of vocabulary and its locations be maintained. This list should note items that are used and unused, how frequently items are used, in what environments items are used, and items that are needed for the future. Objective data can be provided to the individual and his/her caregivers by taking language samples across environments at regular intervals (Blackstone, 1988).

Vocabulary is often viewed as an obstacle in AAC (Blackstone, 1988). Without the appropriate vocabulary, an individual is unable to express his/her thoughts and is therefore limited in his/her ability to participate in communicative interactions. Therefore, vocabulary selection is a crucial step in developing an effective and individualized AAC system.

5   AAC Intervention

Assessment, although ongoing, must ultimately lead to intervention. The primary goals of AAC interventions are to maximize language and communication (Beukelman & Mirenda, 2005). In order for AAC interventions to maximize language and communication, intervention must focus on the development of communicative competence and the ability to communicate for all four purposes of communication (Light, 2003). Frequently, AAC systems are focused on making requests, not sustaining communication and social interactions. It is common to see communication aids in the field that focus primarily on topics that address basic wants and needs only, such as food, grooming, clothing, toys, and people (Fallon, Light, & Kramer-Paige, 2001; Light, Parsons, & Drager, 2002). When communication systems only contain vocabulary within these restricted areas, it is difficult to engage in meaningful social communication. AAC interventions should help to develop breadth of vocabulary concepts to support more diverse communication and build greater complexity of language structure in order to support more complex communication (Fallon, Light, & Kramer-Paige, 2001). AAC interventions should also support semantic-syntactic development, morphological development, as well as build phonological awareness/foundations for literacy development (Bedrosian, 1997).

Communicative competence allows us to define who we are, to establish meaningful relationships with others and realize the essence of our humanity (Light, 2003). The development of communicative competence is the ultimate goal in AAC interventions. The acquisition, or development, of an AAC system is not the final goal, far from it. AAC systems are merely tools that help individuals who cannot use speech to communicate to realize their dreams and participate in their lives.

In order to meet the goal of increasing communicative competence in domains, a two-pronged approach to AAC intervention is necessary: instruction that will be provided to the individual who requires AAC as well as instruction that will be provided to their communication partners, or facilitators (McNaughton & Light,

1989). There are several steps to the intervention process: (1) Identify situations that are priorities for the individual; (2) ensure required vocabulary and means of communication are available (tools); (3) teach partners to support the individual in learning the new skill (as required); (4) teach the target skill(s) to the individual who uses AAC in naturally occurring interactions in order to enhance communicative competence; (5) check to ensure generalization and maintenance of the skill(s); and (6) evaluate the outcomes of intervention (Light & Binger, 1998).

The first step in the AAC intervention process is to identify contexts and/or situations that are priorities for intervention. There are several factors to consider when trying to prioritize contexts for intervention. Contexts or situations selected as priorities for intervention should (adapted from Light & Binger, 1998):

- be valued by the client and be motivating
- be valued by facilitators (communication partners) and society
- be meaningful to the client
- benefit the client and enhance real-world function
- be important (high frequency, emergency) to the individual
- address the individual's greatest needs
- be interactive and/or provide multiple communicative opportunities
- have a strong probability of success
- be age appropriate

It is critical to involve the individual who requires AAC, his/her family, and other facilitators, in the decision-making process. Making these decisions as a team will ensure that the contexts and situations that are chosen as priorities for intervention will truly address the needs of the individual who requires AAC, and thus facilitate increasing the communicative competence of that individual (Light & Binger, 1998). After the context(s) for intervention have been chosen, specific goals need to be set to outline the skills that need to be taught in order to help the individual to be communicatively competent within the environments and/or contexts selected.

When identifying appropriate goals for intervention, assessment results need to be summarized to determine: (a) the communication needs (i.e., when, where, why, how, with whom, and about what) of the individual who requires AAC; (b) the communication skills (i.e., knowledge, judgment, and skills to communicate) of the individual who requires AAC; (c) the needs that are unmet by the current skills of the individual who requires AAC (Light & Binger, 1998).

The second step in the intervention process is to ensure that the vocabulary and means of communication needed by the individual to communicate in the context chosen are available (Light & Binger, 1998). For the purposes of an AAC intervention clinicians should specifically consider and ensure that the vocabulary chosen for the AAC system is appropriate for meeting the goal that has been set for interaction within the specific context. The clinician also needs to ensure that the vocabulary chosen is worded appropriately for the individual – that is, that the messages sound like the individual using the AAC system (e.g., a 5-year-old boy) and not like the individual putting the vocabulary into the AAC system (e.g., a

30-year-old female). Clinicians also need to ensure that the vocabulary is represented appropriately for the individual using the AAC system (Light & Binger, 1998).

The third step in the AAC intervention process is to teach facilitators, or communication partners, strategies to support the communication of the individual who requires AAC (Light & Binger, 1998). When teaching facilitators to support communication, clinicians want to make sure the facilitators understand how to provide communicative opportunities to the individual so that he/she may use the skills that he/she is learning in intervention to increase their functional participation in daily life and improve their communicative competence (Light et al., 1992; McNaughton & Light, 1989). Facilitators may need to learn how to adapt or change their interaction strategies in order to be able to provide the support to the individual that is needed. There are several approaches to teaching facilitators the skills needed to allow them to better support communication with individuals who require AAC. Kent-Walsh and McNaughton (2005) and Light and Binger (1998) describe strategies for teaching the facilitators of individuals who require AAC.

The fourth step in an AAC intervention is to teach the target skill(s) to the individual who uses AAC in naturally occurring interactions. Light and Binger (1998) describe the following instructional procedures when teaching a target skill to an individual who requires AAC. First, the clinician should explain the target skill to the individual. This part of the instructional procedure will only be appropriate for individuals with the necessary metalinguistic skills that would be needed to understand this explanation out of context. When explaining the target skill to the individual who requires AAC it is important to highlight why the skill is important for him/her to learn, and how it will help them to be more successful in interacting and in meeting their daily communication needs. Second, the clinician should demonstrate how to use the target skill to the individual. He or she should be provided with repeated opportunities to practice the target skill in the natural environment. Because opportunities to practice the target skill may not occur with as much frequency as is necessary initially for the individual to learn the target skill, natural opportunities for using the target skill should be supplemented with role plays (simulations of interactions in the natural environment) for additional opportunities to learn and practice the target skill. A "least to most" prompting hierarchy is recommended so that the individual is always afforded the opportunity to use the target skill spontaneously before a prompt is provided. Data should be collected on the individual's use of the target skill(s) and feedback should be continually provided until the individual who requires AAC is able to use the skills targeted in the intervention to the criterion level (i.e., adequate level of skill use) specified at the goal-setting stage of the intervention process.

The fifth step in the intervention process is to check to ensure that the individual and his/her communication partners have generalized and maintained the use of the target skill(s) taught throughout the intervention process (Light & Binger, 1998). Generalization means that the individual is able to use the skill that was taught in a context or environment that is different than the one where the skill was originally taught. Maintenance means that the individual continues to use the target skill with a high level of accuracy over a long period of time (e.g., months, years). In order to ensure generalization and maintenance, the clinician needs to observe the individual in various real-life situations at regular intervals (e.g., 1 month, 2 months, 3 months, etc.) after instruction. The clinician should determine: (a) if the individual who requires AAC is being provided with opportunities to use the skills that have been taught; (b) if the individual is able to use the target skill(s) spontaneously in naturally occurring interactions; and (c) if the individual is communicatively competent within that context. If any of these areas is not adequate, then provision of additional intervention is required.

The sixth and final step in the AAC intervention process is to evaluate the outcomes of the intervention. The clinician should evaluate: (a) the individual's, and the communication partner's, acquisition of the target skill(s); (b) the individual's, and the communication partner's, generalization and maintenance of the target skill(s); (c) the satisfaction of individual who uses AAC, their communication partners, and society regarding the effectiveness of the intervention in increasing the communicative competence and meaningful interaction skills of the individual and his/her partners; and (d) the impact of the use of the target skill on daily functioning (Light & Binger, 1998). From this evaluation, specific action plans can be developed to resolve any problems that are still evident or address further needs to increase the communicative competence of the individual who requires AAC.

6   Summary

The field of AAC is a rich, dynamic area of research and practice. This chapter has provided an overview of the terminology, current systems, and some clinical aspects. While the chapter has presented the current state of practice in AAC, there is a need for continued research in this area. There are many areas of research that are required to maximize the communicative competence of individuals who cannot rely on speech to communicate. Given the heterogeneity of the population of individuals who require AAC, each system will ultimately be as different as the individuals themselves. More research is required to address best approaches for individuals based on their needs and skills, as well as to advance technological developments. With these concerted efforts, it will be possible to attain the power of communication for all persons.

REFERENCES

American Speech, Language, and Hearing Association. (2002). *Augmentative and alternative communication: Knowledge and skills for service delivery* [Knowledge and Skills]. Available from www.asha.org/policy.

American Speech, Language, and Hearing Association. (2005). *Roles and responsibilities of speech-language pathologists with respect to augmentative and alternative communication: Position statement* [Position Statement]. Available from www.asha.org/policy.

Baker, B. (1982). Minspeak: A semantic compaction system that makes self-expression easier for communicatively disabled individuals. *Byte 7*, 186–202.

Baumgart, D., Johnson, J., & Helmstetter, E. (1990). *Augmentative and alternative communication systems for persons with moderate and severe disabilities*. Baltimore, MD: Paul H. Brookes Publishing.

Bedrosian, J. L. (1997). Language acquisition in young AAC system users: Issues and directions for future research. *Augmentative and Alternative Communication 13*, 179–85.

Beukelman, D. & Mirenda, P. (1998). *Augmentative and alternative communication: Management of severe communication disorders in children and adults*. Baltimore, MD: Paul H. Brookes Publishing.

Beukelman, D. R. & Mirenda, P. (2005). *Augmentative and alternative communication: Supporting children and adults with complex communication needs*, 3rd ed. Baltimore, MD: Paul H. Brookes Publishing.

Beukelman, D., McGinnis, J., & Morrow, D. (1991). Vocabulary selection in augmentative and alternative communication. *Augmentative and Alternative Communication 7*, 171–85.

Binger, C. & Light, J. (2006). Demographics of preschoolers who require AAC. *Language, Speech, and Hearing Services in Schools 37*, 200–8.

Blackstone, S. (1986). *Augmentative communication: An introduction*. Rockville, MD: American Speech, Language, and Hearing Association.

Blackstone, S. (1988). Vocabulary selection: Issues, techniques and tips. *Augmentative Communication News 1*, 1–5.

Blackstone, S. (1991). Telecommunication technologies. *Augmentative Communication News 4*, 3–8.

Blackstone, S. (2004). Clinical news: Visual scene displays. *Augmentative Communication News 16* (2), 1–8.

Blockberger, S. & Sutton, A. (2003). Toward linguistic competence: Language experiences and knowledge of children with extremely limited speech. In J. Light, D. Beukelman, & J. Reichle (eds.), *Communicative competence for individuals who use AAC: From research to effective practice*. Baltimore, MD: Paul H. Brookes Publishing.

Carlson, F. (1981). A format for selecting vocabulary for the nonspeaking child. *Language, Speech and Hearing Services in the Schools 12*, 140–5.

Drager, K. D. R., Clark-Serpentine, E. A., Johnson, K. E., & Roeser, J. L. (2006). Accuracy of repetition of digitized and synthesized speech for young children in background noise. *American Journal of Speech-Language Pathology 15*, 155–64.

Drager, K. D. R., Light, J. C., Carlson, R., D'Silva, K., Larsson, B., Pitikin, L., & Stopper, G. (2004). Learning of dynamic display AAC technologies by typically developing 3-year-olds: Effect of different layouts and menu approaches. *Journal of Speech, Language, and Hearing Research 47*, 1133–48.

Drager, K. D. R., Light, J. C., Speltz, J. C., Fallon, K. A., & Jeffries, L. Z. (2003). The performance of typically developing $2^1/_2$-year-olds on dynamic display AAC technologies with different system layouts and language organizations. *Journal of Speech, Language, and hearing Research 46*, 298–312.

Fallon, K., Light, J., & Achenbach, A. (2003). The semantic organization patterns of young children: Implications for augmentative and alternative communication. *Augmentative and Alternative Communication 19*, 74–85.

Fallon, K. A., Light, J. C., & Kramer-Paige, T. (2001). Enhancing vocabulary selection for preschoolers who require augmentative and alternative communication (AAC). *American*

Journal of Speech-Language Pathology 10, 81–95.

Glennen, S. L. & DeCoste, D. C. (1997). *Handbook of augmentative and alternative communication*. San Diego, CA: Singular Publishing Group.

Kent-Walsh, J. & McNaughton, D. (2005). Communication partner instruction in AAC: Present practice and future directions. *Augmentative and Alternative Communication* 21, 195–204.

Light, J. (1988). Interaction involving individuals using augmentative and alternative communication systems: State of the art and future directions. *Augmentative and Alternative Communication* 4, 66–82.

Light, J. (1989). Toward a definition of communicative competence for individuals using augmentative and alternative communication systems. *Augmentative and Alternative Communication* 5, 137–44.

Light, J. (1997). "Communication is the essence of human life": Reflections on communicative competence. *Augmentative and Alternative Communication* 13, 61–70.

Light, J. (2003). Shattering the silence: Development of communicative competence by individuals who use AAC. In J. Light, D. Beukelman, & J. Reichle (eds.), *Communicative competence for individuals who use AAC* (pp. 3–38). Baltimore, MD: Paul H. Brookes Publishing.

Light, J. & Binger, C. (1998). *Building communicative competence with individuals who use augmentative and alternative communication*. Baltimore, MD: Paul H. Brookes Publishing.

Light, J. & Lindsay, P. (1991). Cognitive science and augmentative and alternative communication. *Augmentative and Alternative Communication* 7, 186–203.

Light, J. & Lindsay, P. (1992). Message encoding techniques for augmentative communication systems: The recall

performance of adults with severe speech impairments. *Journal of Speech & Hearing Research* 35, 853–64.

Light, J., McNaughton, D., & Parnes, P. (1994). *A protocol for the assessment of the communicative interaction skills of non-speaking severely handicapped adults and their facilitators*. Toronto, Canada: Augmentative Communication Service.

Light, J. C., Parsons, A. R., & Drager, K. (2002). "There's more to life than cookies": Developing interactions for social closeness with beginning communicators who use AAC. In J. Reichle, D. Beukelman, & J. Light (eds). *Exemplary practices for beginning communicators: Implications for AAC* (pp. 187–218). Baltimore, MD: Paul H. Brookes Publishing.

Light, J., Dattilo, J., English, J., Gutierrez, L., & Hartz, J. (1992). Instructing facilitators to support the communication of people who use augmentative communication systems. *Journal of Speech and Hearing Research* 35, 865–75.

Light, J. C., Drager, K. D. R., McCarthy, J., Mellott, S., Millar, D., Parrish, C., Parsons, A., Rhoads, S., Ward, M., & Welliver, M. (2004). Performance of typically developing four- and five-year-old children with AAC systems using different language organization techniques. *Augmentative and Alternative Communication* 20, 63–88.

Lloyd, L. & Karlan, G. (1984). Nonspeech communication symbols and systems: Where have we been and where are we going? *Journal of Mental Deficiency Research* 38, 3–20.

McCarthy, J., Light, J., Drager, K., McNaughton, D., Grodzicki, L., Jones, J., Panek, E., & Parkin, E. (2006). Re-designing scanning to reduce learning demands: The performance of typically developing 2-year-olds. *Augmentative and Alternative Communication* 22, 269–83.

McDonald, E. & Schultz, A. (1973). Communication boards for cerebral palsied children. *Journal of Speech and Hearing Disorders* 38, 73–88.

McNaughton, D. & Light, J. (1989). Teaching facilitators to support the communication skills of an adult with severe cognitive disabilities: A case study. *Augmentative and Alternative Communication* 5, 35–41.

Mirenda, P. (1985). Designing pictorial communication systems for physically able-bodied students with severe handicaps. *Augmentative and Alternative Communication* 1, 58–64.

Mirenda, P. & Beukelman, D. R. (1987). A comparison of speech synthesis intelligibility with listeners from three age groups. *Augmentative and Alternative Communication* 3, 120–8.

Mirenda, P. & Beukelman, D. R. (1990). A comparison of intelligibility among natural speech and seven speech synthesizers with listeners from three age groups. *Augmentative and Alternative Communication* 6, 61–8.

Rainforth, B., York, J., & Macdonald, C. (1992). *Collaborative teams for students with severe disabilities*. Baltimore, MD: Paul H. Brookes Publishing.

Reichle, J., York, J., & Sigafoos, J. (1991). *Implementing augmentative and alternative communication: Strategies for learners with severe disabilities*. Baltimore, MD: Paul H. Brookes Publishing.

Schuler, A. L., Peck, C. A., Willard, C., & Theimer, K. (1989). Assessment of communicative means and functions through interview: Assessing the communicative capabilities of individuals with limited language. *Seminars in Speech and Language* 10, 51–63.

Silverman, F. H. (1980). *Communication for the speechless*. Englewood Cliffs, NJ: Prentice Hall Publishing Co.

Thousand, J. & Villa, R. (1990). Sharing expertise and responsibilities through teaching in teams. In W. Stainback & S. Stainback (eds.), *Support networks for inclusive schooling: Independent integrated education* (pp. 151–66). Baltimore: Brookes Publishing Co.

Thousand, J. S. & Villa, R. A. (1992). Collaborative teams: A powerful tool in school restructuring. In R. A. Villa, J. S. Thousand, W. Stainback, & S. Stainback (eds.), *Restructuring for caring and effective education: An administrative guide to creating heterogeneous schools* (pp. 73–108). Baltimore, MD: Paul H. Brookes Publishing.

Vanderheiden, G. & Yoder, D. (1986). Overview. In S. Blackstone (ed.), *Augmentative communication: An introduction* (pp. 1–28). Rockville, MD: American Speech, Language, and Hearing Association.

Vanderheiden, G. & Kelso, D. (1987). Comparative analysis of fixed-vocabulary communication acceleration techniques. *Augmentative and Alternative Communication* 3, 196–206.

Yorkston, K. & Karlan, G. (1986). Assessment procedures. In S. Blackstone (ed.), *Augmentative communication: An introduction* (pp. 163–96). Rockville, MD: American Speech, Language, Hearing Association.

19   Fluency and Fluency Disorders

JOHN A. TETNOWSKI AND KATHY SCALER SCOTT

1   Introduction

We begin this chapter with some information on just how prevalent stuttering is within the world. There have been many studies that examine the prevalence of stuttering and, with few exceptions, prevalence numbers remain within a range of about 1 percent (see Bloodstein & Bernstein Ratner, 2008 for a review). Although that number may seem small, it translates into about 3 million people who stutter (PWS) in the United States, or about 600,000 PWS in the United Kingdom.

Throughout this chapter, we will use the terms "stutterer" and "PWS" interchangeably. The term "stutterer" (also "stammerer") appears in research papers and texts prior to the mid- to late 1990s and is slowly being replaced by the "person first" term, "person who stutters" (PWS).

1.1   Background, philosophy, and definition

Cases of stuttering have been documented for a very long time. For example, the biblical figure Moses is described as being "slow of speech and tongue" (Exodus 4:10). However, despite its long documentary history, stuttering is still not entirely understood.

Within the realm of stuttering disorders, there appears to be a key philosophical division that is driving both research and clinical interests. This issue is the cause of opposing points of view in establishing validity for both research agendas and clinical applications. This key issue has caused strong debate and several points of view when considering therapy approaches, evidence-based practice, and documentation of change, assessment tool use and development, and even general theories relating to definition, onset, progression, and cause. This issue that drives current thought, theory, and research in fluency and fluency disorders is the dilemma regarding the impact of behaviorism versus social constructivism. With regard to stuttering, behaviorism relates to aspects of stuttering that can be directly observed, that is, behaviors that can be seen and heard. From this perspective,

The Handbook of Language and Speech Disorders, First Edition. Edited by Jack S. Damico, Nicole Müller, and Martin J. Ball. © 2013 Blackwell Publishing Ltd except for editorial material and organization © 2013 Jack S. Damico, Nicole Müller, Martin J. Ball. Published 2013 by Blackwell Publishing Ltd.

stuttering is viewed as the motor movements that produce the stuttered speech. The stuttering may be a result of a person's genetic composition, neurological makeup, or motor speech patterns, but adherents to this approach are most interested in the observable aspects of speech, that is, the stuttering behaviors themselves. From this standpoint, these observable characteristics are what define stuttering.

The opposing view looks at the issues related to stuttering from a social constructivist view, that is, the question of how stuttering affects an individual as they operate within a social system. Of interest is primarily how stuttering affects a person's ability to communicate, or *inability* to communicate in a functional setting. Adherents to this philosophy are interested in the outward speech symptoms of stuttering, but are more interested in the inner emotions and anxieties associated with stuttering and how the stuttering impacts a person's ability to live and communicate with others in real-life scenarios. The stuttering itself can be easily observed and documented, but the internal fears, avoidances, frustration, or reluctance to speak with others as a result of the stuttering – and how they impact on social interaction – are the real interest of the social constructivist.

Each philosophy has its merits and detractions, and they will be pointed out whenever possible. Using this controversy as a backdrop, this chapter will review information relating to the definition, onset, development, treatment, and theory surrounding fluency and fluency disorders.

1.2   *Definition of stuttering (behavioral)*

A definition of stuttering may appear to be a simple construct; however, this is not the case. From a behavioral standpoint, a definition of stuttering is based upon clearly defined and measurable symptoms. For example, one of the most widely used definitions of stuttering comes from the work of Marcel Wingate (1964, p. 488), who defined stuttering as "(a) Disruption in the fluency of verbal expression, which is (b) characterized by involuntary, audible or silent, repetitions or prolongations in the utterance of short speech elements, namely: sounds, syllables, and words of one syllable. These disruptions (c) usually occur frequently or are marked in character and (d) are not readily controllable." In this definition, all of the behaviors are observable, except for the final point that relates to the "readily controllable" aspects of stuttering. From this viewpoint, stuttering is a speech disorder that can be observed and documented by a listener. Wingate's definition does make special note of the issue of "readily controllable," and this warrants explanation. Although there are many techniques that can quickly eliminate or reduce stuttering (see Andrews et al., 1983; see Table 19.1 for examples), the long-term efficacy of treatments that eliminate stuttering is unclear and poorly defined, especially in older children and adults (Cordes, 1998). A meta-analysis of results showed some positive trends, particularly in young children, but these reports were mostly limited to behaviorally based interventions (Bothe et al., 2006). Clinically, we have heard many parents ask (or tell) their children to stop stuttering, or to control their speech. This implies that they could stop stuttering if they

Table 19.1 Examples of fluency-inducing strategies

Choral reading	Johnson & Rosen (1937)
Delayed auditory feedback	Goldiamond (1965)
Fluency altered feedback	Kalinowski et al. (1993)
Operant techniques	Martin & Siegel (1966)
Reduced rate	Adams, Lewis, & Besozzi (1973)
Rhythmic speech	Brady (1969)
Singing	Johnson & Rosen (1937)
White noise masking	Shane (1955)
Whispering	Johnson & Rosen (1937)

wished, and contrary to the "not readily controllable" portion of Wingate's definition. Further testimonials from people who stutter include stories of how they had practiced their fluency for an important event and were highly successful in practicing, only to fail when the actual situation arose (St. Louis, 2001). This indicates that PWS may not stutter on the same words in all conditions, and their stuttering may vary from day to day and situation to situation. If there is one thing that is certain about stuttering, it is that there is significant variance in the way that the observable symptoms present themselves.

Also within this genre of behavioral/observable symptoms, there have been numerous attempts to quantify exactly what stuttering is, and what it is not. One of the first attempts at defining and describing these speech behaviors came from the work of Wendel Johnson and his associates (1959), later modified by Williams, Silverman and Kools (1968); see Darley and Spriestersbach (1978). Their works defined all of the types of speech breakdowns that were reported in the speech of American speakers. They then classified which speech behaviors were considered to be stuttering and which ones were considered to be "other types of disfluency" (see Table 19.2). Throughout this chapter, we will use the term *non-fluency* to define any breakdown in fluency, whether stuttering or not. We will use the terms *stuttering*, or stuttering-like disfluency to define the breakdowns in fluency that would be defined as stuttering. And finally, we will use the term *disfluency* to define the breakdowns in fluency that would not be considered stuttering. This terminology is consistent with studies that must differentiate between stuttering and other types of non-fluencies that occur in a variety of speech and language disorders (Van Borsel & Tetnowski, 2007). In this classification system, stuttering and disfluency are both subsets of non-fluency.

Based on the work of Ham (1989), we might infer that any non-fluency that takes the form of a part-word repetition, single-syllable word repetition, prolongation, or block is considered to be stuttering. All other types of non-fluency, including interjections, multi-syllable word repetitions, phrase repetitions, revisions, incomplete phrases, and broken words are considered to be a disfluency (i.e., *not stuttering*). More recently, this concept was renewed in the epidemiological

Table 19.2   All types of non-fluencies. The non-fluency is in *bold italics*

Non-fluency type	Example	Stuttering or disfluency
Interjections	My *um* dog's name is Sherry.	Disfluency
Part-word repetition	My *d-d-d-d*-dog is a poodle.	Stuttering
Word repetition	*She-she-she* is silver.	Stuttering*
	She is *silver-silver-silver*.	Disfluency*
Phrase repetition	*She likes-she likes* to play.	Disfluency
Revision	*I like-I love* my dog.	Disfluency
Incomplete phrase	*She is*-oh I forgot how old.	Disfluency
Broken word	The dog is *ru[pause]-nning* fast.	Disfluency
Prolonged sounds	*Sssssssssss*ilver is a pretty color.	Stuttering
Tense pause**	*... [pause with tension]*I'm done.	Stuttering

*In further studies, it has been determined that word repetitions of one syllable are generally considered as stuttering and word repetitions of multi-syllable words are disfluencies (Ham, 1989).
** Also referred to as blocks, stoppages, or fixations.

research of Yairi and Ambrose (2005) who coined the term "stuttering-like disfluencies" (SLD), which separated those behaviors that were likely to occur with a higher degree of frequency and consistency in children who stutter. These SLDs include part-word repetitions, monosyllabic word repetitions, and dysrhythmic phonations, which consist of prolongations and blocks. These behaviors are consistent with research carried out on expert judges (Ham, 1989), and the criteria set by the American Speech-Language-Hearing Association (1999). The key factor from a behavioral point of view is that these behaviors can be readily observed and documented.

1.3   Definition of stuttering (constructivist)

An alternative definition of stuttering is based on the World Health Organization's International classification of functioning, disability and health (ICF; WHO, 2001). Within this definition of functionality (and thus how it is related to stuttering), Yaruss and Quesal (2004) have defined stuttering by its impact on how stuttering affects the ability of a person to function in their everyday environment. In this definition, stuttering is defined by how much it may "handicap" an individual in their ability to function in their everyday environment. That is, a person may stutter overtly in their speech, but this may not impact how they function in daily life, whereas another person may stutter mildly, yet never leave home, have a relationship, or hold a job due to their stuttering. The range of "functional limitations" due to stuttering may vary greatly. This limitation to functionality is real to the social constructivist, but can only be defined through measures other than the outward blocks, prolongations, and repetitions. Within a constructivist point of view, stuttering symptoms would include far more than just overt stuttering and would include constraints that stuttering would place on the functional and social activities carried out by the PWS. If this were true of stuttering, a valid definition of stuttering would include the observable speech symptoms, but also must include the social activities that the PWS would not or could not carry out. It might include an assessment of fears, avoidances, feelings, attitudes, and other cognitive and emotional issues that cannot be readily observed. For example, when asked his name in a casual, social setting the first author of this chapter might answer, "They call me Dr. Tetnowski," when "John" would be the preferred answer. The shift from "John" to "Dr. Tetnowski" is an adjustment to the fear of saying his first name (a common fear among PWS). Other examples of social limitations might include being underemployed due to stuttering, avoidance of social relationships due to stuttering, and other choices made to not communicate, fear communication, alter communication, and any other adjustments made as a reaction to stuttering. These behaviors may be difficult to observe and document in a behavioral paradigm, but are highly valid in a constructivist paradigm and require different types of research designs and data collection strategies (Tetnowski & Damico, 2001). Thus, the constructivist view would say that a valid definition of stuttering must include the internal fears, avoidances, word substitutions, functional limitations, and social anxieties that are present in many PWS.

A common critique of this philosophy is that these behaviors cannot be easily observed (Ingham, 2005). Alternatively, others feel that the documentation of stuttering can only be accomplished by the PWS themselves. Some researchers have gone as far as to say that the only person who can identify stuttering is the PWS themselves and only within a short period of time after the stuttering (and emotional reaction) has occurred. Research has shown that the PWS can be an accurate judge of their own stuttering (Moore & Perkins, 1990; Tetnowski & Schagen, 2001). Based on these findings, Perkins, Kent, and Curlee (1991) believe that stuttering is a response to internal time pressures, which is certainly difficult to observe in behavioral paradigms. Others have claimed that the most valid assessment of stuttering is only made in social settings where communication breakdowns can be studied in their true contexts (Tetnowski & Damico, 2001). Within this paradigm of social constructivism, stuttering is far more than just the behavioral observations of stuttered speech.

From this discussion, clinicians and researchers should understand that there are at least two distinct paradigms on how stuttering should be labeled, evaluated, and treated. In summary, these two opposing views of stuttering present the case that stuttering is either (a) an outward manifestation of speech that can be reliably judged by observers or precise physical measurement tools, or (b) the opinion, inner feelings, attitudes, and reactions of the PWS and how it affects their daily life in authentic communication settings. Stuttering, therefore, must be evaluated differently by people who hold these opposing points of view.

2   Stuttering Evaluation and Assessment

The method by which speech-language pathologists evaluate stuttering is defined by the paradigm of stuttering to which they subscribe. Behaviorists will evaluate stuttering within observable paradigms, whereas social constructivists will evaluate stuttering on its overall impact on communication in authentic settings.

2.1   Behavioral assessment of stuttering

Stuttering has traditionally been evaluated by how many instances of stuttering have been observed within a given time frame, or as a percentage of total words or syllables spoken. The most common means of identifying stuttering is simply counting the number of instances of stuttering and dividing that by the total number of syllables spoken, then multiplying that number by 100 in order to calculate a percentage of stuttered syllables (%SS). Thus, six instances of stuttering in a sample of 100 total syllables spoken would yield a total of 6%SS. These types of calculations have been consistently used by clinicians and researchers for many years and serve as the basis for most stuttering assessment batteries including the highly popular Stuttering Severity Instrument – 3 (Riley, 1994). In this assessment tool, a stuttering severity score is calculated by combining the totals of three subscores. The three subscores are (a) the percentage of stuttered syllables (calculated from a monologue task in younger children and a combination of monologue and reading tasks by adults and older children); (b) the length of stuttering events (calculated by averaging the three longest stuttering events within the sample); and (c) physical concomitants, i.e., the documentation of physical movements that may accompany stuttering, such as eye blinks, foot tapping, facial grimaces, distracting sounds, or other observable behaviors (based on a total of four 0–5 subscore ratings relating to distracting sounds, facial grimaces, head movements, and movements of the extremities). The stuttering frequency, duration, and physical concomitants scores are totaled to determine an overall score that is transposed to provide a severity rating and percentile score. Most observation-type stuttering evaluation scales and protocols are based upon similar models to the Stuttering Severity Instrument – 3, that is, they evaluate stuttering on the basis of observable behaviors of speech and other movements.

The use of behaviorally based stuttering evaluation tools has been invaluable to researchers and practicing clinicians; however, their reliability has been called into question by several researchers (Ingham, Cordes, & Gow, 1993; Lewis, 1995). The biggest point of concern for this type of scoring method is whether judges, even expert judges, could reliably indicate the precise point where stuttering actually occurred. In response to this argument, Ingham, Cordes, and colleagues (Ingham, Cordes, & Finn, 1993; Ingham, Cordes, & Gow, 1993) have developed an alternative method for determining the occurrence of stuttering. Rather than using percentage of stuttered syllables as the dependent measure for stuttering, they used time intervals as the basis for counting the occurrence of stuttering.

That is, judges listened to a short period of speech and simply made a binary decision as to whether stuttering occurred or not within a given time period. In a series of experiments, Ingham, Cordes, and colleagues investigated the shortest interval of time by which stuttering could be reliably identified, and determined that time intervals of 4 seconds were the shortest durations in which a listener could reliably judge the occurrence of stuttering. Therefore, they subscribe to the theory that accurate observation of stuttering should take place with judges listening to 4-second intervals of speech and then determine whether stuttering has occurred or not. This method has been shown to bring about reliable judgments of stuttering across different types of stuttering (Cordes & Ingham, 1994), individuals with different backgrounds and from different training programs (Ingham & Cordes, 1992), and individuals with various levels of expertise and experience (Cordes & Ingham, 1995). In spite of the high levels of reliability provided by this method, its use has not been universally adopted due to questions of practicality, clinical importance, and validity. For most observable assessments of stuttering, most speech-language pathologists continue to use the percentage of stuttered syllables method.

2.2 Alternative methods for assessing stuttering behaviors

In response to the reliability issues brought up by behaviorists, other clinicians and researchers have taken a totally different route when assessing stuttering. They believe that stuttering is not a condition that can be reliably observed, and that the most salient features of stuttering are internal, such as emotions and feelings. Thus, another set of diagnostic tools have been developed that challenge the validity of behavioral assessments as the sole diagnostic criteria by which stuttering is evaluated. These measures have been used for a number of years, and include tools such as the Modified Erickson, S-24 Scale (Andrews and Cutler, 1974), the Perceptions of Stuttering Inventory (PSI; Woolf, 1967), the Communication Attitude Test – Revised (CAT-R; DeNil & Brutten, 1991), the Profile of Stutterers' and Nonstutterers' Affective, Cognitive, and Behavioral Communication Attitudes (Watson, 1987), and other similar protocols. The common link between these assessment tools are that they are paper and pencil tests where the PWS, with the help of the clinician, indicates how they feel about their stuttering. These tools assess the feelings, attitudes, and emotions of stuttering and how it affects their life. The behaviorists have often questioned both the reliability and validity of these tests and, in response, a new wave of more carefully designed tools have been devised in recent years. These tests include the Wright and Ayer Stuttering Self-Assessment Profile (WASSP; Wright and Ayer, 2000) and the Overall Assessment of the Speaker's Experience of Stuttering (OASES; Yaruss and Quesal, 2006). These tools, especially the OASES, have been put through more stringent evaluations and have been shown to be considerably more valid and reliable than their predecessors.

In conclusion, there are a large number of tests, profiles and protocols for the assessment of stuttering. Most clinicians and researchers employ a combination of these tools to evaluate both the observable and the emotional and cognitive aspects of stuttering.

3 Epidemiological Issues Related to Stuttering

In most cases, adults who stutter can readily identify themselves as such. However, diagnosis of stuttering in early childhood is not as straightforward. Since most children go through periods of disfluency as they learn to use language, it may appear to the casual observer that they are really stuttering, and research has shown that the non-fluent behaviors observed in young children who stutter are also observed in children who do not stutter (Ambrose & Yairi, 1999). Since it is well known that the prevalence of stuttering in children is 5 percent, while the prevalence in adults is only 1 percent, it would be valuable to know why and how this change takes place. Either many children who stutter are getting better spontaneously or with therapy before adulthood, or there is a dramatic miscounting of school-age children who truly stutter. It would be advantageous to know which speech behaviors and what frequency of these speech behaviors differentiate chronic stuttering from developmental episodes of disfluency. If this distinction could be made readily in young children, it would be possible to get young children into stuttering therapy at an early age before emotional scars of stuttering can develop. Again, the importance of accurately predicting which children are likely to recover and which children are likely to continue stuttering cannot be overestimated.

In order to answer these and similar questions, a group of researchers at the University of Illinois, under the direction of Ehud Yairi, have set out to track stuttering from a very early age to determine its course and accurately describe its symptoms. In a series of longitudinal studies, Yairi and his associates have tracked at least 89 young children who were reported to stutter. They tracked the PWS across many years, beginning at the time when stuttering was most likely to have its onset. Prior studies have placed the mean age of onset at around 3 years of age, with a majority of cases having their onset before the age of 6 (2;7 years old, Bernstein Ratner & Silverman, 2000; 3;0 years old, Milesen & Johnson, 1936; 2;7 years old, Yairi & Ambrose, 1992). In the vast majority of these types of studies, date of onset was reported by parent interviews and was not directly observed. The purpose of the longitudinal studies by Yairi and colleagues was to plot the course of stuttering (or its recovery/remission) from near the time of onset. Monitoring the symptoms from this early time would allow clinicians to make informed decisions about which children are likely to continue to stutter (and thus need intervention) and which children are likely to recover. The results of the data are very compelling and should be used as a metric for determining the early course and intervention strategies for those children who may develop into chronic people who stutter, i.e., those who are unlikely to recover without intervention.

In this series of studies, participants were considered to be "recovered" if they were free of clinical symptoms of stuttering and were judged to be free of stuttering by parental interview. These criteria had to be met and maintained for a period of over 12 months in order to be labeled "recovered." In addition, they had to maintain this label of "recovered" for 4 years in order to be classified as such (Yairi & Ambrose, 2005). Thus, those labeled as "recovered" very likely were truly recovered.

3.1 Early childhood stuttering: Persistence and recovery

Among the factors that were considered in the series of studies by Yairi and colleagues were: (1) age at onset of stuttering and (2) age of remission of symptoms. Once these factors could be determined, they also considered these important variables: (a) types of stuttering behaviors observed, (b) gender of recovered and persistent children who stutter, (c) change in stuttering behaviors over time, (d) characteristics of stuttering symptoms observed, and (e) types of physical behaviors observed.

A great deal of investigation of the development of stuttering has led to increased understanding of stuttering's development and possible factors related to its persistence and remission. Whereas we once considered linear tracks along which stuttering progressed, we now realize that stuttering can begin at any level of severity. The majority of cases, however, do follow some pattern of progression, beginning with little tension and/or avoidances and increasing along all of these dimensions. It is clear, however, that this is still not a linear pattern. Yairi suggested this in 1990 when he called for subtyping CWS (children who stutter) for the purposes of research. Due in large part to the work of Yairi and colleagues, we have now pinpointed several specific prognostic indicators that help us to make potential predictions about recovery and therefore to plan intervention.

Prognostic parameters serve as a guideline to professionals for determining whether or not stuttering intervention is warranted. Because there is an overlap between types of disfluency in those who will become chronic stutterers and those who will spontaneously recover, and because some studies indicate that as many as 80 percent of preschoolers who stutter will achieve spontaneous recovery (Yairi & Ambrose, 2005), knowing what risk factors are more associated with those who do not stutter becomes critical for timing of intervention. Thanks to ongoing epidemiological work, we now know that children who have a family history of stuttering (particularly those family members who did not recover), children who have concomitant speech and/or language disorders (in particular, phonological disorders), children who have been stuttering at a stable level for at least a year prior to referral, and boys are more at risk to continue to stutter (Yairi & Ambrose, 2005). This information becomes even more valuable when we consider the fact that Yairi and Ambrose were among the first to correct mistakes in previous studies of early childhood stuttering. That is, the 89 children in these researchers' studies were selected closer to the onset of stuttering (i.e., within 12 months of onset), were followed for longer periods of time (i.e., at least 4 years, many for longer), and did not receive any speech-language intervention that might serve as a confounding variable. These 89 children were followed for 4 to 12 years after stuttering onset to obtain the recovery and persistence data we currently have available to us today.

Researchers have become more accurate in measurement of disfluency and have developed some measurement markers that enable them to begin to differentiate between typical disfluency and stuttering. Although there is more than one approach to counting disfluencies adopted for research and/or evaluation purposes, one of the most commonly adopted systems is that of Yairi and Ambrose (2005), in which childhood disfluency is divided into the categories of "stuttering-like disfluencies" and "other disfluencies." Such a classification system recognizes the fact that children who do not stutter (CWNS) may in fact exhibit stuttering that is more typical of children who do stutter. Yairi and Ambrose argue that their classification system is based upon the idea that those disfluencies classified as "stuttering-like disfluencies" are ones that are more frequently a part of the disfluencies of those who stutter, and that "other disfluencies" are those that are more frequently occurring in those who do not stutter, while taking into account that both groups can exhibit both types of disfluency. In other words, the difference is not so much in the types of disfluency exhibited, but rather in the degree to which each type is exhibited. This involves a more qualitative analysis of the disfluencies once they are identified. For example, Yairi and Ambrose argue that children who stutter tend to have a greater number of iterations of a sound repetition than children who do not stutter, who might experience only one iteration.

Most researchers use a cut-off point to determine when a child can be classified as stuttering: that is, a child must exhibit at least 3 percent syllables or words stuttered. Although there are slight variations in the cut-off points for those moments defined as stuttering and those defined as normal disfluency, this 3 percent is most accepted among researchers as one criterion for differentiating CWS from CWNS. Other criteria include parental concern and diagnosis by a speech-language pathologist. A slight distinction exists between Conture's (2001) and Yairi and Ambrose's (2005) definitions in that Conture includes within-word disfluencies, whereas Yairi and Ambrose include stuttering-like disfluencies; however, the rest of their definitions are the same (i.e., parental concern and 3 disfluencies per 100 syllables for Yairi and Ambrose and per 100 words for Conture). Within the past 10 years in the *Journal of Speech, Language, and Hearing Research*, the definitions researchers most based their own definitions upon were these criteria of Yairi and Ambrose and Conture. Thus, our procedures for clearly defining stuttering in order to conduct research studies have been slowly tightening.

Within this context, Yairi and his colleagues have looked to indicators that indicate recovery from stuttering, in contrast to persistent stuttering. Through their studies, they have found that recovery is more likely in females than males (1.8:1.0 ratio for females; 4.5:1.0 ratio for males; Yairi & Ambrose, 2005), and that if recovery does occur, it happens faster in females than in males (12–30 months in females; 24–36 months in males; Yairi & Ambrose, 2005). However, a major point of their research was to identify the specific speech behaviors that are most commonly seen in young children who truly stutter. These behaviors are specifically labeled by Yairi and colleagues as "stuttering-like disfluencies" (SLD) and specifically include part-word repetitions ("bu-bu-bu-bu-butter tastes really good"), single-syllable word repetitions ("I-I-I-I-I love butter"), dysrhythmic phonations that include prolongations ("I llllllllllllllllllllllove to eat butter"; the word "love" is stretched out over an abnormal period), and blocks (".........butter tastes really good"; the speech mechanism becomes rigid and no phonation occurs). The important part of this definition is that these behaviors have served to become a predictor of recovery or persistency of stuttering. Specifically, the concept of the SLD has progressed to a concept called weighted SLD, and the weighted SLD has been shown to be a powerful predictor of recovery from stuttering in young children, as noted in Figure 19.1; as indicated there, the recovered stutterers showed dramatic changes in stuttering behaviors, i.e., weighted SLD within a relatively short time after onset. It should also be noted that the route to recovery from stuttering can take as long as 4 years or longer. Just as importantly, the persistent stutterers showed a gradual decrease in weighted SLD, and in some cases, an increase was noted. In summary, Yairi and his colleagues have provided parents and clinicians with valuable information regarding the likelihood of stuttering spontaneously resolving itself.

In addition to the information on recovery, Yairi and colleagues have provided many other valuable insights into what stuttering looks like very close to its onset, how it develops over time, and how it is either different from, or similar to, non-stuttering disfluent children. The findings are summarized in Table 19.3.

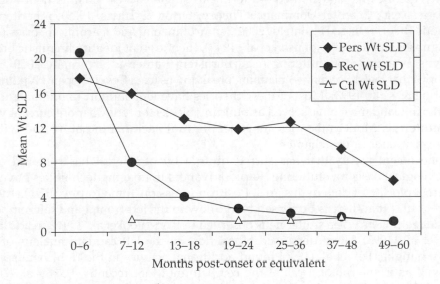

Figure 19.1   Trends in recovery from stuttering.

Table 19.3   Other contributions of Yairi, Ambrose, and the Illinois Longitudinal Studies (Yairi & Ambrose, 2005)

- CWS have more non-fluencies than children who do not stutter.
- CWS have more repetitions per unit than children who do not stutter.
- CWS have more prolongations than children who do not stutter.
- All disfluency types noted in CWS were also noted in normally disfluent children.
- Children have a significant awareness of their stuttering as early as 5 or 6, and many even earlier.
- Children who develop into CWS have faster speech rates than children who do not stutter.
- The proportion of SLD to overall disfluency is about 65 percent in CWS.
- Stuttering may begin in any mode (mild, moderate, or severe).
- The majority of stuttering begins near a period of stress (emotional, linguistic, physical, etc.).
- Secondary symptoms may accompany early stuttering, but were noted in only about 50 percent of cases.
- Parental ratings of stuttering (of their children) change in the same manner that %SLD changes.

4   Causes of Stuttering

There has been a tremendous interest in the cause of stuttering for many years. Many theories have attributed stuttering to single causes, such as neurological theories (e.g., Cerebral Dominance Theory; Orton & Travis, 1929), inheritance/ genetic theories (e.g., Felsenfeld, 2002), environmental and learning theories (e.g., Diagnosogenic Theory; Johnson et al., 1942), theories that identify linguistic break-downs as a cause of stuttering (e.g., Bernstein Ratner & Silverman, 2000), and theories that look to cognitive/planning breakdowns (e.g., Covert Repair Hypothesis; Postma & Kolk, 1993). Most of these theories have lent support to understanding stuttering, and most have served as building blocks for today's more current view of stuttering. Modern theories are generally multifactorial in nature and will be discussed later in this chapter.

One recent theory that has stirred quite a bit of interest has centered on a neurological basis for stuttering. Rapid advances in imaging techniques have led to an explosion of data in this area. Positron Emission Tomography (PET) studies have found that there is decreased blood flow in the left frontal and left temporal language centers when stuttering is observed in PWS (Pool et al., 1991). In addition, Wu et al. (1995) found decreased blood flow in the left caudate nucleus of the basal ganglia. Fox et al. (1996) found additional activity in the right hemisphere as well as in the motor areas of the cerebellum. More recently, Fox et al. (2000) noted decreased activation in the right superior and middle temporal gyri. These studies all seem to indicate an underlying neurological cause for stuttering. At this point, however, it is not perfectly clear whether these differences are a cause of stuttering, or whether they are a reaction to stuttering.

4.1 Multifactorial theories

As noted earlier, today's most popular theories of stuttering are multifactorial in nature. One of the earliest, yet simplest, of these is called the Demands and Capacities Model (Starkweather & Gottwald, 1990). In this model, the genetic contribution to stuttering is considered as the inherited capacity of an individual to speak fluently. In this model, each individual is born with various levels of innate capacity to speak fluently. Some have considerably less of this fluent speech capacity than others, which is consistent with studies that show higher prevalence of stuttering within family groups (Felsenfeld, 2002; Howie, 1981). This genetic predisposition then interacts with varying degrees of environmental demand. This demand can come from increased linguistic demand to use longer and more complex utterances, increased social demands to speak in more demanding and difficult situations, increased motor demands to speak faster or with more rapid movements, or any other type of environmental demand. In this model, whenever environmental demand exceeds genetic capacity, fluency can break down (see Figure 19.2). Thus, a person with little genetic capacity for fluent speech could never develop stuttering if environmental demands were kept very low. On the other hand, a person with quite a bit of genetic capacity for fluent speech could develop stuttering if they continuously faced very high environmental demands.

The simple model proposed by Starkweather and Gottwald is a forerunner to the many other multifactorial models that exist today. These include the Neuropsycholinguistic Model (Perkins, Kent, & Curlee, 1991), which expands upon the multiple factors leading to stuttering but adds a component of internal time pressure to produce fluent speech as a key to whether non-fluent speech

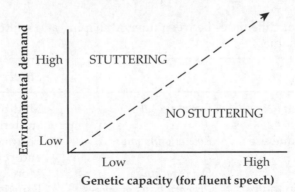

Figure 19.2 The demands and capacities model. Whenever demand exceeds capacity, stuttering can occur.

will be either stuttered or disfluent. Smith and Kelly (1997), in their multifactorial, dynamic model of stuttering, add the synergistic aspect of various levels of breakdown that can lead to stuttering, and Conture et al. (2006) add emotional and temperamental components to the genetic capacities and environmental demands described earlier to provide a more thorough model of how stuttering develops. In summary, today's theories of stuttering account for more factors, and view stuttering as a more complex phenomenon than earlier theories of stuttering.

5   Treatment Techniques and Efficacy

With current theories of stuttering becoming more complex in nature, there are multiple measures to treat stuttering and document success. Within this context, there is also a great deal of emphasis on "evidence-based" practice, treatment outcomes, and other hallmarks of effective and efficient therapy (e.g., Sackett, 1998). This has certainly had a significant influence in the treatment of stuttering and other fluency disorders. This is magnified in the debate between behaviorally based therapy versus more constructivist-based interventions. Traditionally, stuttering therapies have been broken into two categories: fluency shaping and stuttering modification (see Table 19.4).

5.1   Fluency shaping

Fluency-shaping strategies of therapy are based on the premise that the clinician should guide the PWS through a hierarchy of tasks while speaking in a manner that is "incompatible" with stuttering. Many of these strategies are listed in Table 19.1. The efficacy of this treatment model is dependent upon the success of the client using the selected form of speech throughout *all* of their communication. These techniques may be a slowing of the rate by prolonging speech, taking longer pauses, modifying breathing patterns or other changes in the act of producing

Table 19.4   Major differences between fluency shaping and stuttering modification therapies

Fluency shaping		Stuttering modification
Modify all speech	*Primary goal*	Modify moments of stuttering
Reinforce technique use	*Role of clinician*	Educate, desensitize, and counsel
Highly objective	*Data tracking*	More qualitative
Reduction/elimination of stuttering	*Primary basis of success*	Functional communication

speech. Some therapies have used artificial devices to assist in this role. These devices include the use of delayed auditory feedback (DAF), frequency altered feedback (FAF), masking, rhythmic speech, and combinations of these techniques. These devices include microphone and speaker combinations that through the advancement in microprocessor technologies have become as small as the tiniest "in-the-canal" hearing aids. These devices are used to simply change speech to a pattern that reduces stuttering. Consistent with fluency-shaping approaches, the goal is simply to modify the way a person speaks so that they can eliminate or greatly reduce stuttering. The role of the clinician is simply to reinforce correct use of the technique, build therapeutic hierarchies, and track data.

The issue of treatment efficacy is handled in a very straightforward manner in fluency-shaping therapies. The validity of the therapy is simply ensured by the reduction and/or elimination of stuttering events that can be readily detected by observers. There has been a great deal of attention paid to the documentation of outcomes using fluency-shaping therapies in the literature. A great deal of this data comes from the efforts of the Lidcombe therapy consortium in Australia (Onslow, Packman, & Harrison, 2003). The Lidcombe Program is a behaviorally based stuttering intervention program that lists its primary goal as the elimination of stuttering (Onslow, Packman, & Harrison, 2003). This is accomplished through a parent-training program that teaches parents to reinforce unambiguous fluent speech. The reinforcement of fluent speech by parents has shown to be highly successful in eliminating stuttering in young children. A meta-analysis of the success of the program (Jones et al., 2000) indicated that 250 out of 261 children who began the Lidcombe treatment program before the age of 6 met the objective of near zero stuttering. Furthermore, the median number of sessions to meet this goal was 11 sessions. Based upon the success of this model, it is clear that fluency-shaping strategies can be effective for the treatment of young children who stutter. Other successful fluency-shaping strategies include Extended Length of Utterance (ELU; Costello, 1983), Gradual Increase in the Length and Complexity of Utterances (GILCU; Ryan, 1974), and Prolonged Speech (the Camperdown Program; O'Brian et al., 2003). Although assorted other measures were used to evaluate success, the primary component validating success in these programs was a decrease in %SS.

5.2   *Stuttering modification*

Stuttering modification refers to a group of therapies initiated by Charles Van Riper (see Van Riper, 1973 for a review) that was based upon the concept of limiting the effects of stuttering. To many individuals, this may mean stuttering less severely, while to others it may mean understanding and coping with stuttering. The key components in stuttering modification therapies include the *identification* of stuttering and associated behaviors, *desensitization* to stuttering, variation, or *modification* of the speech signal to a method that greatly reduces the degree, severity, and tension of stuttering, and *stabilization* of the techniques. As noted in Table 19.4, the role of the clinician is to provide education and counseling for the PWS. Following the identification phase of therapy, the client is trained to become desensitized to the effects of stuttering. This takes place through a series of exercises to reduce the impact of stuttering. This may include tasks such as advertising stuttering (telling others that you may stutter) or voluntary stuttering (stuttering on purpose without loss of control; Dunlap, 1932) to minimize the anxiety and fear of stuttering. In the stabilization phase the PWS modifies their speech to lessen the severity of stuttering through cancellations (regrouping and modifying stuttering after it occurs), pullouts (modifying stuttering during the moment when it occurs), and preparatory sets (changing speech to lessen the likelihood and severity of stuttering just prior to stuttering occurrences). These strategies are then stabilized and used in increasingly more challenging tasks and situations.

The efficacy of these types of treatments is not entirely uncontroversial, in that efficacy is not measured only as a decrease of stuttering, but effectiveness may also be judged by factors that are internal to the PWS. For example, the PWS may be feeling better about themselves, avoiding fewer communication opportunities, having increased self-esteem, or other improvements that are not as readily observable. Programs that have been evaluated in this manner include the Successful Stuttering Management Program (SSMP; Blomgren et al., 2005), the ISTAR Comprehensive Stuttering Program (Kully, Langevin, & Lomheim, 2007), and the family-focused treatment approach for children (Yaruss, Coleman, & Hammer, 2006). Although these programs did not all meet the strict criteria of eliminating stuttering as established by most fluency-shaping programs, they did show gains in fluency and also showed improvements in other measures including anxiety and avoidance measures. In summary, this method showed successful therapeutic outcomes in the goals that were established by each program's philosophy: that is, the effectiveness of these programs was measured by their clients' ability to stutter less severely and eliminate various handicapping conditions of stuttering.

5.3   *Pharmacological treatment*

In recent years, various different pharmaceutical agents were introduced to treat stuttering. These drug therapies can be grouped into several classifications that include dopamine D2 receptor blockers, such as haloperidol; norepinephrine reuptake inhibitors, such as desipramine; serotonin selective reuptake inhibitors, such as clomipramine; and GABA selective receptor modulators, such as pagaclone. A review of the effectiveness of these drugs (Maguire et al., 2004) indicates that although they may either moderate stuttering or decrease anxiety surrounding stuttering, most are not recommended at this time due to limited effectiveness or substantial negative side effects. The drug therapy that appears to show the most promise at this time is pagaclone, which has shown some effectiveness after completing multi-center phase II trials. At this point, there are some promising, but still unconfirmed, effectiveness issues regarding pharmaceutical intervention for the treatment of stuttering.

5.4 Fluency-enhancing devices

As noted earlier in this chapter, there are devices that improve fluency in many PWS. Over the years, these have been used as adjuncts to therapy (e.g., Ryan & Van Kirk, 1974); however, recent advances in microelectronics have brought about devices that are used all of the time, rather than just as an aid to assist in achieving fluency. The most popular of these devices is the SpeechEasy, which combines DAF and FAF in a very small portable package that can fit entirely in the ear. A series of studies by the developers report impressive gains of fluency (e.g., Stuart et al., 2006). But reports by others (Molt, 2007; O'Donnell, Armson, & Kiefte, 2008) indicate less than impressive long-term results and limitations on out-of-clinic success. Although fluency-enhancing devices can serve as a valuable adjunct to speech therapies, their long-term efficacy has yet to be established.

6 Developmental Trends in Stuttering and Stuttering Theory: Yesterday and Today

It is clear from this discussion that there are multiple factors that lead to the present understanding of stuttering. Theories of the past have tried to find a single cause for stuttering, while today's theories are multifactorial in nature. A result of this is that today's stuttering researchers are exploring multiple contributing factors of stuttering and subgroups of stuttering. Within this exploration, the contributions of early pioneers such as Charles Van Riper and Oliver Bloodstein are still relevant.

Van Riper (1982) classified the development of stuttering into tracks, based upon the course of development he and his workers observed among the records of 300 stuttering clients first seen in childhood, 44 of whom he followed longitudinally. Although his work lacked the scientific rigor called for in today's refereed journals, Van Riper identified significant patterns of development that are echoed in the current epidemiological research. From his client files, Van Riper was able to identify four tracks of stuttering development. Parallels can be seen between each of the tracks and types of stuttering that clinicians and researchers alike have identified in their work today. Van Riper's Track I stutterers appear to be the same as what is today known as resolved and unresolved cases of developmental stuttering. Track II mirrors what to some today would be known as cluttering (Van Riper even suggests that some of the cases in Track II, whom he says all turn out to be stutterers, might in fact have cluttering characteristics as well), and to others, who do not include language difficulties as a component of cluttering, perhaps children who stutter with concomitant speech and/or language disorders. Track III in some cases bears similarity to psychogenic stuttering, yet is more reflective of Track I stutterers who begin stuttering with severe blocks rather than easy repetitions. Track IV by description mirrors what we know today as a conversion reaction for secondary gain. It is important to note, however, that Van Riper is clear that his tracks are merely reflecting *patterns* of stuttering development rather than possible etiology. Nonetheless, Van Riper saw trends that researchers continue to see today. In the current stuttering literature, possible subgroups of stutterers are suggested in the discussion and/or conclusion sections of many research articles (Schwartz & Conture, 1988; see Yairi, 2007, for a review).

Bloodstein (1995) also proposed four phases of stuttering, after following 418 stutterers over a 6-year period. However, his phases are less a reflection of specific subtypes of stuttering, and more a tracing of stuttering's development from early stages in preschool to more confirmed and severe cases of stuttering in adulthood. Although stuttering's development can certainly be traced through such stages today in many cases, Bloodstein's continuity hypothesis may have reflected the most foresight into how we view non-fluencies today, particularly during preschool development, when the lines between disfluency and chronic patterns of stuttering can often become blurred:

> The question, quite simply, is whether we are dealing with a problem like a broken collarbone or a case of pneumonia, in which the diagnosis is either yes or no, or whether stuttering is more like hearing loss, high blood pressure, emotional maladjustment, mental retardation, or innumerable other ills that merge by fine degrees of normal. The continuity hypothesis holds that stuttering belongs to the second group. (1995, p. 404)

Both Van Riper and Bloodstein saw anticipatory struggle playing some role in stuttering, but not explaining the entire disorder, as was originally proposed by Sheehan (1953). Bloodstein (1995) pointed out that speech pressures may (or may not) come from within a child's personality. Following this trend, stuttering researchers today recognize the contribution of multiple factors to the development and maintenance of stuttering (e.g., Conture et al., 2006; Perkins, Kent, & Curlee, 1991; Smith & Kelly, 1997). Currently, research has been ongoing regarding the possible sensitive temperaments of individuals who stutter, and significant differences in the sensitivity traits of preschoolers who stutter. Specifically, Anderson et al. (2003) administered a behavioral checklist to parents of 31 children who stutter (CWS) between 3 years and 5 years, 4 months of age, and 31 age-matched controls. Significant differences were found in parental responses of CWS in three areas: hypervigilance, non-adaptability to change, and irregular biological functions. The authors contend that these three differentiating temperamental factors may be related to differences in those preschoolers who recover from stuttering and those who do not. As with Van Riper and Bloodstein, the authors recognize the contribution of such factors as temperament as significant, but not complete enough to explain the development of stuttering in all children who stutter.

In later years, Bloodstein (2002) proposed incipient stuttering as a language disorder, possibly related to retrieval, syntax, or "motor planning of a phrase or sentence." He based this suggestion on two factors: first, the fact that when children repeat words, it indicates that they are not having difficulty saying the word; and second, the fact that stuttering rarely occurs at ends of words; therefore, incipient stuttering must be related to some type of formulation issue, be it syntactical or lexical. This concept seemed to arrive in the midst of the ongoing research regarding the relationship between mean length of utterance, utterance complexity, and stuttering (Bernstein Ratner & Sih, 1987; Gaines, Runyan, & Meyers, 1991; Tetnowski, 1998; Zackheim & Conture, 2003). While much of what Bloodstein contends is true in that the majority of stuttering does not occur at the ends of words, increased incidences of cases of word-final disfluencies, including word-final syllable and sound repetitions, prolongations and blocks, are emerging in the literature. Many of these cases are emerging among those who in fact would have concomitant language disorders, such as those with mental retardation (Stansfield, 1995) or autism spectrum disorders (Hietala & Spillers, 2005; Scott et al., 2006; Sisskin, 2006). While it has been proposed that perhaps these instances of word-final disfluencies occurring in the middle of formulation may be related to difficulties with formulation (Humphrey, 1997), the concept fails to hold when these same individuals exhibit patterns of word-final disfluencies in tasks that require no formulation, such as on the last sound of a sentence repetition task (Scott et al., 2006). Thus, although some cases of incipient stuttering may indeed be language-related, we know that many cases are not related to language. In fact, researchers have been identifying patterns of precocious language development among incipient stutterers, based upon both results of standardized testing and spontaneous language samples (Yairi & Ambrose, 2005). However, continued work is needed in this area: Hakim and Bernstein Ratner (2004) point out that the measures used thus far to measure language development in children who stutter may not be specific enough to detect subtle difficulties.

7 Summary

In summary, the field of stuttering has advanced dramatically in recent decades. Improvements in neurological and genetic causes of stuttering dominate the new findings in causality. The findings of the Illinois Longitudinal Studies have laid new foundations for the prediction of recovery or persistence of stuttering. The Lidcombe Program has gathered a large collection of results relating to efficacy of treatment in young children. At the same time, more psychometrically advanced tools such as the OASES are finding ways to evaluate stuttering that look at factors other than just the overt symptoms that mark stuttering. As a result of this wealth of information, stuttering theories, and even the factors that define stuttering, are rapidly changing and developing to encompass these new advances.

REFERENCES

Adams, M. R., Lewis, J. I., & Besozzi, T. E. (1973). The effect of reduced reading rate on stuttering frequency. *Journal of Speech and Hearing Research* 16, 671–5.

Ambrose, N. G. & Yairi, E. (1999). Normative disfluency data for early childhood stuttering. *Journal of Speech, Language, and Hearing Research* 42, 895–909.

American Speech-Language-Hearing Association Special Interest Division 4: Fluency and Fluency Disorders. (1999, March). Terminology pertaining to fluency and fluency disorders: Guidelines. *ASHA*, 41 (Suppl. 19), 29–36.

Anderson, J. D., Pellowski, M. W., Conture, E. G., & Kelly, E. M. (2003). Temperamental characteristics of young children who stutter. *Journal of Speech, Language, and Hearing Research* 46, 1221–33.

Andrews, G. & Cutler, J. (1974). Stuttering therapy: The relation between changes in symptom level and attitudes. *Journal of Speech and Hearing Disorders* 39, 312–19.

Andrews, G., Craig, A., Feyer, A. M., Hoddinott, S., Howie, P., & Neilson, M. (1983). Stuttering: A review of research findings and theories circa 1982. *Journal of Speech and Hearing Disorders* 48, 226–46.

Bernstein Ratner, N. & Sih, C. C. (1987). Effects of gradual increases in sentence length and complexity on children's disfluency. *Journal of Speech and Hearing Disorders* 52, 278–87.

Bernstein Ratner, N. & Silverman, S. (2000). Parental perceptions of children's communicative development at stuttering onset. *Journal of Speech, Language, and Hearing Research* 43, 1252–63.

Blomgren, M., Roy, N., Callister, T., & Merrill, R. M. (2005). Intensive stuttering modification therapy: A multidimensional assessment of treatment outcomes. *Journal of Speech, Language, and Hearing Research* 48, 509–23.

Bloodstein, O. (1995). *A handbook of stuttering*, 5th ed. San Diego, CA: Singular Publishing Group.

Bloodstein, O. (2002). Commentary. Early stuttering as a type of language difficulty. *Journal of Fluency Disorders* 27, 163–7.

Bloodstein, O. & Bernstein Ratner, N. (2008). *A handbook on stuttering*, 6th ed. Clifton Park, NY: Delmar.

Bothe, A. K., Davidow, J. H., Bramlett, R. E., & Ingham, R. J. (2006). Stuttering treatment research 1970–2005: I. Systematic review incorporating trial quality assessment of behavioral, cognitive, and related approaches. *American Journal of Speech-Language Pathology* 15, 321–41.

Brady, J. P. (1969). Studies on the metronome effect on stuttering. *Behavior Research Therapy* 7, 197–204.

Conture, E. G. (2001). *Stuttering: Its nature, diagnosis, and treatment*. Boston, MA: Allyn & Bacon.

Conture, E. G., Walden, T. A., Arnold, H. S., Graham, C. G., Hartfield, K. N., & Karrass, J. (2006). A communication-emotional model of stuttering. In N. Bernstein Ratner & J. A. Tetnowski (eds.), *Current issues in stuttering research and practice*. Mahwah, NJ: Lawrence Erlbaum.

Cordes, A. K. (1998). Current status of the stuttering treatment literature. In A. K. Cordes & R. J. Ingham (eds.), *Treatment efficacy for stuttering: A search for empirical bases*. San Diego, CA: Singular.

Cordes, A. K. & Ingham, R. J. (1994). Time interval measurement of stuttering: Effects of training with highly-agreed or poorly-agreed exemplars. *Journal of Speech and Hearing Research* 37, 1295–307.

Cordes, A. K. & Ingham, R. J. (1995). Judgments of stuttered and nonstuttered intervals by recognized authorities in stuttering research. *Journal of Speech and Hearing Research* 38, 33–41.

Costello, J. M. (1983). Current behavioral treatments for children. In D. Prins & R. J. Ingham (eds.), *Treatment of stuttering in early childhood*. San Diego, CA: College Hill Press.

Darley, F. L. & Spriestersbach, D. C. (1978). *Diagnostic methods in speech pathology*. New York: Harper & Row.

De Nil, L. F. & Brutten, G. J. (1991). Speech associated attitudes of stuttering and nonstuttering children. *Journal of Speech and Hearing Research* 34, 60–6.

Dunlap, K. (1932). *Habits: Their making and unmaking.* New York: Liverright.

Felsenfeld, S. (2002). Finding susceptibility genes for developmental disorders of speech: The long and winding road. *Journal of Communication Disorders* 35, 329–45.

Fox, P. T., Ingham, R. J., Ingham, J. C., Hirsch, T. B., Downs, J. H., Martin, C. et al. (1996). A PET study of the neural systems of stuttering. *Nature* 382, 158–61.

Fox, P. T., Ingham, R. J., Ingham, J. C., Zamarripa, F., Xiong, J. H., & Lancaster, J. L. (2000). Brain correlates of stuttering and syllable production. A PET performance-correlation analysis. *Brain* 123, 1985–2004.

Gaines, N. D., Runyan, C. M., & Meyers, S. C. (1991). A comparison of young stutterers' fluent versus stuttered utterances on measures of length and complexity. *Journal of Speech and Hearing Research* 34, 37–42.

Goldiamond, I. (1965). Stuttering and fluency as manipulative operant response classes. In L. Kraner & L. P. Ullmann (eds.), *Research in behavior modification.* New York: Holt, Rinehart, & Winston.

Hakim, H. B. & Bernstein Ratner, N. (2004). Nonword repetition abilities of children who stutter: An exploratory study. *Journal of Fluency Disorders* 29, 179–99.

Ham, R. E. (1989). What are we measuring? *Journal of Fluency Disorders* 14, 231–43.

Hietala, A. & Spillers, C. (2005, November). Disfluency patterns in children with autism spectrum disorders. Poster session presented at the Annual Convention of the American Speech-Language-Hearing Association, San Diego, CA.

Howie, P. M. (1981). Concordance for stuttering in monozygotic and dizygotic twin pairs. *Journal of Speech and Hearing Research* 24, 317–21.

Humphrey, B. D. (1997). Unusual dysfluency: Repetitions in final position in an adolescent boy. *Florida Association of Speech-Language Pathologists Audiologists* 17, 41–2.

Ingham, R. J. (2005). Clinicians deserve better: Observations on a clinical forum titled "What Child Language Research May Contribute to the Understanding and Treatment of Stuttering." *Language, Speech, and Hearing Services in Schools* 36, 152–6.

Ingham, R. J. & Cordes, A. K. (1992). Interclinic differences in stuttering-event counts. *Journal of Fluency Disorders* 17, 171–6.

Ingham, R., Cordes, A., & Finn, P. (1993). Time-interval measurement of stuttering: Systematic replication of Ingham, Cordes, & Gow. *Journal of Speech and Hearing Research* 36, 1168–76.

Ingham, R. J., Cordes, A. K., & Gow, M. L. (1993). Time-interval measurement of stuttering: Modifying interjudge agreement. *Journal of Speech and Hearing Research* 36, 1168–76.

Johnson, W. & Associates (1942). A study of the onset and development of stuttering. *Journal of Speech Disorders* 7, 251–7.

Johnson, W. & Associates (1959). *The onset of stuttering.* Minneapolis: University of Minnesota Press.

Johnson, W. & Rosen, L. (1937). Studies in the psychology of stuttering: VII. Effects of certain changes in speech pattern upon frequency of stuttering. *Journal of Speech Disorders* 2, 105–9.

Jones, M., Onslow, M., Harrison, E., & Packman, A. (2000). Treating stuttering in young children: Predicting treatment time in the Lidcombe Program. *Journal of Speech, Language and Hearing Research* 43, 1440–50.

Kalinowski, J., Armson, J., Roland-Mieszkowski, M., Stuart, A., & Gracco, V. J. (1993). Effects of alteration in auditory feedback and speech rate on stuttering frequency. *Language and Speech* 36, 1–16.

Kully, D., Langevin, M., & Lomheim, H. (2007). Intensive treatment of adolescents and adults who stutter. In E. G. Conture & R. F. Curlee (eds.), *Stuttering and related disorders of fluency*, 3rd ed. New York: Thieme.

Lewis, K. E. (1995). Do SSI-3 scores adequately reflect observations of stuttering behaviors? *American Journal of Speech-Language Pathology* 4, 46–59.

Maguire, G. A., Yu, B. P., Franklin, D. L., & Riley, G. D. (2004). Alleviating stuttering with pharmacological interventions. *Expert Opinion on Pharmacotherapy* 5, 1565–71.

Martin, R. R. & Siegel, G. M. (1966). The effects of simultaneously punishing stuttering and rewarding fluency. *Journal of Speech and Hearing Research* 9, 340–52.

Milesen, R. & Johnson, W. (1936). A comparative study of stutterers, former stutterers, and normal speakers whose handedness has been changed. *Archives of Speech* 1, 61–86.

Molt, L. (2007). Speecheasy AAF device long-term clinical trial: 24-month outcomes. Poster presented to the American Speech-Language-Hearing Association, Boston, MA.

Moore, S. E. & Perkins, W. H. (1990). Validity and reliability of judgments of authentic and simulated stuttering. *Journal of Speech and Hearing Disorders* 55, 383–91.

O'Brian, S., Onslow, M., Cream, A., & Packman, A. (2003). The Camperdown Program: Outcomes of a new prolonged-speech treatment model. *Journal of Speech, Language, and Hearing Research* 46, 933–46.

O'Donnell, J. J., Armson, J., & Kiefte, M. (2008). The effectiveness of SpeechEasy during situations of daily living. *Journal of Fluency Disorders* 33, 99–119.

Onslow, M., Packman, A., & Harrison, E. (2003). *The Lidcombe Program of early stuttering intervention*. Austin, TX: Pro-Ed.

Orton, S. & Travis, L. E. (1929). Studies in stuttering: IV. Studies of action currents in stutterers. *Neurology and Psychiatry* 21, 61–8.

Perkins, W., Kent, R., & Curlee, R. (1991). A theory of neuropsycholinguistic function in stuttering. *Journal of Speech and Hearing Research* 34, 734–52.

Pool, K. D., Devous, M. D., Freeman, F. J., Watson, B. C., & Finitzo, T. (1991). Regional cerebral blood flow in developmental stutterers. *Archives of Neurology* 48, 509–12.

Postma, A. & Kolk, H. (1993). The Covert Repair Hypothesis: Prearticulatory repair processes in normal and stuttered disfluencies. *Journal of Speech and Hearing Research* 36, 472–87.

Riley, G. D. (1994). *Stuttering severity instrument for children and adults*, 3rd. ed. Austin, TX: Pro-Ed.

Ryan, B. P. (1974). *Programmed therapy for stuttering in children and adults*. Springfield, IL: Charles C. Thomas.

Ryan, B. P. & Van Kirk, B. (1974). The establishment, transfer, and maintenance of fluent speech in 50 stutterers using delayed auditory feedback and operant procedures. *Journal of Speech and Hearing Disorders* 39, 3–10.

Sackett, D. L. (1998). Evidence-based medicine. *SPINE* 23, 1085–86.

Scaler Scott, K., Grossman, H., Abendroth, K., Tetnowski, J. A., & Damico, J. S. (2006). Asperger Syndrome and Attention Deficit Disorder: Clinical disfluency analysis. *Proceedings of the 5th World Congress on Fluency Disorders*, Dublin, Ireland.

Schwartz, H. D. & Conture, E. G. (1988). Subgrouping young stutterers: Preliminary behavioral observations. *Journal of Speech and Hearing Research* 31, 62–71.

Shane, M. L. S. (1955). Effect on stuttering of alteration in auditory feedback. In

W. Johnson & R. R. Leutenegger (eds.), *Stuttering in children and adults.* Minneapolis: University of Minnesota Press.

Sheehan, J. G. (1953). Theory and treatment of stuttering as approach-avoidance conflict. *Journal of Psychology* 36, 27–49.

Sisskin, V. (2006). Speech disfluency in Asperger's Syndrome: Two cases of interest. *Perspectives on Fluency and Fluency Disorders* 16 (2), 12–14.

Smith, A. & Kelly, E. (1997). Stuttering: A dynamic, multifactorial model. In R. F. Curlee & G. M. Siegel (eds.), *Nature and treatment of stuttering: New directions*, 2nd ed. Needham Heights, MD: Allyn & Bacon.

St. Louis, K. O. (2001). *Living with stuttering: Stories, basics, resources, and hope.* Morgantown, WV: Populore Publishing.

Stansfield, J. (1995). Word-final disfluencies in adults with learning difficulties. *Journal of Fluency Disorders* 20, 1–10.

Starkweather, C. W. & Gottwald, S. R. (1990). The demands and capacities model II: Clinical applications. *Journal of Fluency Disorders* 15, 142–57.

Stuart, A., Kalinowski, J., Saltuklaroglu, T., & Guntupalli, V. K. (2006). Investigations of the impact of altered auditory feedback in-the-ear devices on the speech of people who stutter: A one-year follow-up. *Disability and Rehabilitation* 28, 757–65.

Tetnowski, J. A. (1998). Linguistic effects on disfluent speech. In R. Paul (vol. ed.), The speech/language connection. A volume in the Communication and Language Intervention Series. Baltimore, MD: Paul H. Brookes Publishers.

Tetnowski, J. A. & Damico, J. S. (2001). A demonstration of the advantages of qualitative methodologies in stuttering research. *Journal of Fluency Disorders* 26, 17–42.

Tetnowski, J. A. & Schagen, A. M. (2001). A comparison of listener and speaker

perception of stuttering events. *Journal of Speech-Language Pathology and Audiology* 25, 8–18.

Van Borsel, J. & Tetnowski, J. A. (2007). Stuttering in genetic syndromes. *Journal of Fluency Disorders* 32 (4), 279–96.

Van Riper, C. (1973). *The treatment of stuttering.* Englewood Cliffs, NJ: Prentice-Hall.

Van Riper, C. (1982). *The nature of stuttering*, 2nd ed. Prospect Heights, IL: Waveland Press, Inc.

Watson, J. B. (1987). Profiles of stutterers' and nonstutterers' affective, cognitive, and behavioral communication attitudes. *Journal of Fluency Disorders* 12, 389–405.

Williams, D. E., Silverman, F. H., & Kools, J. A. (1968). Disfluency behavior of elementary-school stutterers and nonstutterers: The adaptation effect. *Journal of Speech and Hearing Research* 11, 622–30.

Wingate, M. E. (1964). A standard definition of stuttering. *Journal of Speech and Hearing Disorders* 29, 484–9.

Woolf, G. (1967). The assessment of stuttering as struggle, avoidance, and expectancy. *British Journal of Disorders of Communication* 2, 158–71.

World Health Organization (2001). *The international classification of functioning, disability and health.* Geneva: World Health Organization.

Wright, L. & Ayre, A. (2000). *Wright and Ayre Stuttering Self-Rating Profile.* Bicester, UK: Winslow Press.

Wu, J. C., Maguire, G. Riley, G., Fallon, J., LaCasse, L., Chin, S. et al. (1995). A positron emission tomography [18F] deoxyglucose study of developmental stuttering. *Neuroreport* 6, 501–5.

Yairi, E. (1990). Subtyping child stutterers for research purposes. *ASHA Reports* 18, 50–7.

Yairi, E. (2007). Subtyping stuttering I: A review. *Journal of Fluency Disorders* 32, 165–96.

Yairi, E. & Ambrose, N. (1992). Onset of stuttering in preschool children: A preliminary report. *Journal of Speech and Hearing Research* 35, 782–8.

Yairi, E. & Ambrose, N. G. (2005). *Early childhood stuttering: For clinicians by clinicians*. Austin, TX: Pro-Ed.

Yaruss, J. S., Coleman, C., & Hammer, D. (2006). Treating preschool children who stutter: Description and preliminary evaluation of a family-focused treatment approach. *Language, Speech, and Hearing Services in Schools* 37, 118–36.

Yaruss, J. S. & Quesal, R. W. (2004). Stuttering and the International Classification of Functioning, Disability, and Health (ICF): An update. *Journal of Communication Disorders* 37, 35–52.

Yaruss, J. S. & Quesal, R. W. (2006). Overall Assessment of the Speaker's Experience of Stuttering (OASES): Documenting multiple outcomes in stuttering treatment. *Journal of Fluency Disorders* 31, 90–115.

Zackheim, C. T. & Conture, E. G. (2003). Childhood stuttering and speech disfluencies in relation to children's mean length of utterance: A preliminary study. *Journal of Fluency Disorders* 28, 115–42.

20 Describing Voice Disorders

RICHARD MORRIS AND ARCHIE BERNARD HARMON

1 Introduction

The human voice serves as a window into each person. While providing the main vehicle for our spoken and sung messages, it also indicates our emotional state. A voice disorder occurs when the voice itself becomes a focus of the listener. Voice disorders are laryngeally based problems of speech physiology, acoustics, and perception. This definition indicates that the anatomy and/or physiology of the larynx in a person with a voice disorder differ in some manner from what is typical for the people in a given speech community. These anatomic and/or physiologic differences then cause the acoustic signal from the larynx to sound different. The acoustic differences can be in frequency, amplitude, duration, or spectrum. The listener perceives the acoustic differences as a voice disorder.

Voice disorders can result from a variety of laryngeal changes. Anatomically, the edge of the vocal folds can be characterized by bumps or projections of tissue, or conversely, erosion or furrows. Another anatomic change would be vocal fold muscle atrophy. Physiologically, the muscles may not move in a normal bilateral vibrating pattern. For example, the vocal folds can be too tight or too loose; or one vocal fold can move faster than the other one; or anatomic differences can cause parts of the same vocal fold to move at different rates; or the nerve impulses to the muscles can create vocal fold tremors, rigidity, or erratic movements.

The structural or movement differences in the vocal folds and larynx can result in a voice produced with acoustic differences. First, the anatomic and physiologic changes might affect the rate at which the vocal folds vibrate, resulting in alterations in the fundamental frequency and harmonics of the acoustic signal. The fundamental frequency can be too low, causing a perception of a low-pitch voice; or the fundamental frequency can be too high, causing a perception of a high-pitch voice. Another possibility is that the fundamental frequency can be too steady so that the normal melody of speech is absent, as in a monotone voice. The opposite of this could also occur so that the fundamental frequency varies

The Handbook of Language and Speech Disorders, First Edition. Edited by Jack S. Damico, Nicole Müller, and Martin J. Ball. © 2013 Blackwell Publishing Ltd except for editorial material and organization © 2013 Jack S. Damico, Nicole Müller, Martin J. Ball. Published 2013 by Blackwell Publishing Ltd.

excessively. Any of these fundamental frequency differences can distract a listener from the speaker's message.

Second, the anatomic and physiologic differences in the vocal folds and larynx can result in voice problems associated with amplitude and its percept, loudness. These problems occur in a manner similar to the voice problems associated with fundamental frequency and pitch. The amplitude can be too low for the speaking situation so that the voice is too soft, or it can be too high for the situation so that the voice is perceived as too loud. As was true for frequency differences, the person's vocal amplitude can vary too little, so that it sounds monoloud, or it may vary excessively.

When the anatomic and physiologic differences in the vocal folds and larynx cause airflow to be wasted, the third acoustic parameter, duration of the voice, is affected. These differences may not be easily perceived in running speech, but can be detected during singing and during prolonged vowels.

Anatomic and physiologically based differences in the fourth acoustic parameter, spectrum, will affect how the voice is perceived. If there are different vibration rates between the two vocal folds or different areas on the same vocal fold, then there will be acoustic energy between the harmonics of the vocal tone. This acoustic energy is heard as noise; a noisy voice is perceived as rough or hoarse. If the vocal folds are closing too tightly, then there will be greater energy in the harmonics in the higher frequencies of the spectrum. This spectral variation is perceived as a strained or pressed voice. If the vocal folds close too loosely, there will be less energy in the harmonics of the higher frequencies of the spectrum. This variation is perceived as breathy voice. Finally, if the vocal folds are closed before the person breathes out to speak, the resulting voice is characterized by hard glottal attacks.

Differences in these four acoustic parameters result in voicing differences that listeners perceive as abnormal or disordered voices. However, no clear boundary exists for any of the acoustic parameters between a normal deviance and a mildly dysphonic voice. Some speech communities tolerate wider variations than others, so that a given level of vocal difference will be perceived as a normal voice in one speech community and be perceived as dysphonic in another.

2   Prevalence of Voice Disorders

The number of people exhibiting voice disorders varies with the age and sex of the population. Although investigators have reported data from various samples of individuals, the actual prevalence of voice disorders is not known (Roy et al., 2004). Differences among the studies include the target population, sample size, voice disorder definitions, and data collection methods (Simberg, Sala, & Rönnemaa, 2004).

Beginning with the youngest speakers, Duff, Proctor, and Yairi (2004) found a voice disorder incidence rate of 3.9 percent among 2,445 preschool-aged children. They found no difference in prevalence between African-American and European

American children. The 3.9 percent incidence level came from the perceptions of speech-language pathologists. When the parents and teachers of the children were questioned about the identified voices, only 25.7 percent agreed with the judgment (Duff, Proctor, & Yairi, 2004). Thus, the prevalence of voice disorders, which varies from 1.0 to 3.9 percent, among preschool-aged children depends on the listener. When a sample of Australian teachers identified children with voice disorders, they found only 0.12 percent of a population of 10,425 elementary school children (McKinnon, McLeod, & Reilly, 2007). In contrast, when speech-language pathologists have identified the children with voice disorders, the percentage of children identified varied from 2.4 percent to 23.8 percent (Baynes, 1966; Carding, Roulstone, Northstone, & ALSPAC Study Team, 2006; Powell, Filter, & Williams, 1989; Senturia & Wilson, 1968; Silverman & Zimmer, 1975; Yairi et al., 1974). The lowest percentage was reported by Yairi et al. (1974), who required that listeners rate the voice as at least moderately hoarse. This criterion level for a voice disorder may be closer to the definition used by the general population than the criteria used in the other studies. For several of the studies, voice disorders were found more often among boys than girls (Carding et al., 2006; Senturia & Wilson, 1968; Silverman & Zimmer, 1975).

Three to ten percent of adults in the United States exhibit voice disorders (Ramig & Verdolini, 1998). Voice disorders are more common among women than men (Roy et al., 2004; Stemple, Glaze, & Klaben, 2000). Among adults, the prevalence of voice disorders varies with occupation, with higher levels among those who use their voice extensively in their work (Titze, Lemke, & Montequin, 1997). For example, two studies comparing schoolteachers to non-teachers for self-reported voice disorders found rates of 11 percent and 14.6 percent among the schoolteachers in contrast to 6.2 percent and 5.6 percent among the non-teachers (Roy et al., 2004; Smith et al., 1997). Other studies of the prevalence of voice disorders among teachers have revealed rates of 9 percent to 15.9 percent (Russell, Oates, & Greenwood, 1998; Smith et al., 1998a; Smith et al., 1998b).

The incidence of voice disorders appears to be higher among older adults. For example, a survey of self-reported voice disorders among 117 people over 65 years of age found a prevalence of 29.1 percent (Roy et al., 2007). In addition, 47 percent of this sample indicated that they had experienced a voice disorder at some time in their life. However, only 14.6 percent of them had sought professional help to treat the voice problem. Roy et al. (2007) found that these older participants reported that physical sensations of laryngeal discomfort and increased effort to speak were the main complaints concerning their voices as opposed to perceptions such as breathiness or hoarseness.

3   Recent Developments in Voice and Voice Disorders

Recent research and development concerning voice disorders generally has focused on diagnostic issues. Developments in the technology for observing the vocal folds and larynx include the use of high-speed video and videokymography to view the vocal folds as they vibrate. These technologies provide different enhancements to the viewing of vocal folds that can assist accurate diagnosis of glottal differences. High-speed video endoscopy represents a significant improvement in endoscopic evaluation of glottal function because it allows the professional to view actual cycle-to-cycle patterns of vocal fold motion (Deliyski, 2007). The currently used stroboscopic laryngeal endoscopy depicts vocal fold motion as shown by samples taken across multiple vocal fold cycles. The advantages of high-speed video endoscopy include the ability to view the vocal folds during initiation of vocal fold motion and the ability to view aperiodic vocal fold motion. Severely rough or strained voices often have aperiodic vocal fold motions. The across-cycle sampling used during stroboscopic observations is incapable of tracking vocal fold motion during either of these vocal events.

By focusing on the events at a single location along the glottis in real time, videokymography also provides information not available during stroboscopic laryngeal endoscopy (Schutte, Švec, & Šram, 1998). The plane to be scanned by videokymography can be selected by the user, allowing focus on a suspected lesion or place of immobility (ibid.). Like high-speed video stroboscopy, this equipment allows observation of vocal fold movement during the aperiodic vocal fold vibration that characterizes moderate and severe voice disorders and phonation onsets and offsets. Qui and Schutte (2006) demonstrated the utility of this method when used in conjunction with stroboscopic laryngeal endoscopy.

During the late 1990s scales were developed for people with voice disorders to report the degree to which they perceived their voice disorder to be a handicap (Benninger et al., 1998; Gliklich, Glovsky, & Montgomery, 1999; Hogikyan & Sethuraman, 1999; Hogikyan et al., 2001; Hogikyan et al., 2000). These scales have been useful in rating the effectiveness of treatment, as they provide information from the patient's perspective that supplements visual perceptual, auditory perceptual, acoustic, and aerodynamic data. These self-perception data often reinforce findings from the other measures. However, these data are unique since they indicate the effectiveness of the treatment from the perspective of the patient and help voice clinicians determine the effectiveness of voice therapy.

The medial edge of the vocal folds includes a layer of loose, gelatinous material called Reinke's space. Reinke's space is a part of the lamina propria of the vocal folds that contains a matrix of extracellular tissue. One substance that has received attention is hyaluronic acid. This molecule is important for the viscosity of the lamina propria. Researchers have determined that hyaluronic acid has similar viscoelastic properties as the outer layer or cover of the vocal folds (Chan, Gray, & Titze, 2001). The roles assigned to this material include absorbing shock from the impact of vocal fold vibration and wound healing in the superficial layer of the vocal folds after scarring or other lamina propria damage (Huang et al., 2007; Ward, Thibeault, & Gray, 2002;). Lower levels of hyaluronic acid in the lamina propria of women have been considered to be a reason for the higher prevalence of voice disorders among women (Butler, Gray, & Hammond, 2001). Since hyaluronic acid is an important component in wound healing, women may be more susceptible to lamina propria damage and less capable of repairing tissue damage that can occur from vocal fold trauma (Ward, Thibeault, & Gray, 2002).

Recent animal studies indicate that injecting hyaluronic acid into the vocal folds after injury helps wound healing. Under normal wound conditions the level of hyaluronic acid drops during the days just after the wound occurs (Rousseau et al., 2004; Thibeault et al., 2004). Increasing the amount of hyaluronic acid during the acute stage of wound repair reduces the extent of scarring (Hansen et al., 2005). This occurs because the hyaluronic acid helps carry cells needed for repair to the wound and it prevents the build-up of scar tissue. Thus, treatments of this type may prove useful in enhancing the speed and degree of vocal fold healing (Hansen et al., 2005). Because of its viscosity and space-filling properties, hyaluronic acid may be injected in the vocal fold to augment the tissue in people who have glottal insufficiency (Butler, Gray, & Hammond, 2001; Chan & Titze, 1999; Finck & Lefebvre, 2005; Ward, Thibeault, & Gray, 2002).

4 Etiologies of Voice Disorders

There are a variety of differences in laryngeal structure and function that can result in voice disorders. These can be the result of congenital differences in the tissues such as laryngomalacia; disruptions of neuromuscular systems such as vocal fold paralysis or spasmodic dysphonia; or neoplastic tissue developments such as laryngeal papilloma and laryngeal cancer. In addition, ineffective muscle use patterns that stress the tissues of the vocal folds can result in structural changes in the vocal folds such as vocal nodules and vocal polyps. Finally, people can learn behaviors that result in vocal differences like a breathy voice or too low a fundamental frequency. Diagnosis of the laryngeal difference underlying a voice disorder is the responsibility of the otolaryngologist (ENT). For many of these disorders the primary treatment is voice therapy. Interestingly, almost all of the laryngeal differences, from mild swelling in the vocal fold cover to laryngeal cancer, result in some degree of vocal roughness. Morrison et al. (1994) developed a decision tree for diagnosing the cause of vocal roughness among those with voice disorders.

Other etiologic factors that the speech-language pathologist evaluates can be considered to be predisposing, precipitating, or perpetuating factors for the voice disorder (Morrison et al., 1994). These include issues such as stress level, occurrence of major life events, reflux problems, allergies, and behaviors such as vocal habits, smoking tobacco, diet, and hydration. Although the other etiologic factors may not appear to have the direct impact that a laryngeal difference does, they must be considered in an effective treatment plan.

5 Voice Diagnostics

When a speech-language pathologist undertakes to determine if a person's voice is in need of treatment, there are many decisions to be made. As Nation and Aram

(1984) stated, the process has three main components. First the clinician must examine the characteristics of the voice and compare those characteristics to those of other, similar speakers. Second, the clinician must use the information available to evaluate, as best as possible, the causal factors for any observed vocal differences. Finally, the clinician must use the observations and perceptions from the first two components to develop a proposed program for treating any observed vocal differences. The diagnostic process includes input from other professionals as well as subjective and objective observations of the person and the person's voice. From these data the speech-language pathologist determines the etiologic factors responsible for any disorder, compares the person's data to published normative data, and develops an efficacious treatment plan. The ability to consistently make these systematic observations generally develops with training and practice.

The speech-language pathologist must keep in mind that she needs as much data as possible from as many perspectives as possible to make accurate clinical decisions. A single diagnostic session provides a brief moment in time perspective of the person's vocal behavior (Verdolini & Lee, 2004). The brief view may or may not be representative of how that person typically uses her or his voice. Similarly, clinicians have been cautioned against using a single measure (i.e., visual perceptual, auditory perceptual, or acoustic) to assess vocal function (Bless & Hicks, 1996; Colton, Casper, & Leonard, 2006). As these authors noted, one should not consider the results from one vocal measure a reason not to complete other vocal assessments that may provide confirming or conflicting information. In addition, the perspectives of the patient, the ENT, the speech-language pathologist, and other relevant professionals are all needed to completely and accurately assess the person's vocal status. Likewise, the speech-language pathologist must consider every treatment session with the patient as an opportunity to reassess and better understand that person's vocal behavior.

The diagnostic process for a person with suspected voice disorder consists of several steps. The steps in the process include: a medical examination and diagnosis by an ENT, completion of case history information, an intake interview, an auditory perceptual evaluation, a visual perceptual evaluation, an acoustic evaluation, an aerodynamic evaluation, clinical decision making and planning, and an exit interview. Both the auditory perceptual evaluation and the visual perceptual evaluation have been considered the "gold standard" of voice evaluations. Whichever is the "standard," both provide important evaluation information that will help guide the treatment process.

5.1   Voice diagnostic and treatment team

According to Woodson (1996), the most effective evaluation of the voice occurs when the speech-language pathologist and ENT work together to complete the diagnosis. Ongoing teamwork between these professionals enhances the effectiveness of the treatment of the voice patient. Many voice problems have hoarseness as one of the features, but there are many etiologies for hoarseness. For example, Belafsky, Postma, and Koufman (2001, 2002) reported that as many as 50 percent of people with vocal nodules also have laryngopharyngeal reflux problems that must be medically treated along with voice therapy from a speech-language pathologist.

In addition to the speech-language pathologist and ENT, the team to treat people with voice disorders may include other professionals such as voice coach, singing teacher, pulmonologist, neurologist, or psychologist (Colton, Casper, & Leonard, 2006; Morrison et al., 1994; Sataloff, 2005; Stemple, Glaze, & Klaben, 2000; Woodson, 1996).

5.1.1 Case history The first part of the voice evaluation by the speech-language pathologist involves a thorough and extensive interview with the patient and/or significant others in order to determine the possible etiology. To help the speech-language pathologist make this interview as effective as possible, the patient and/or family members complete a history form prior to the evaluation appointment. The case history and interview should reveal the etiologic factors that may influence the nature of the voice difference. The case history provides background information on the person to help the speech-language pathologist know the relevant facts to help inform the diagnostic process and clarify the focus of the initial interview.

5.1.2 Quality of life measures Over the past decade several questionnaires have been developed to determine the impact the voice difference has on the person's quality of life. Researchers have shown that questionnaires of this sort can effectively gauge the person's perception of the effect of the voice difference on daily living (Benninger et al., 1998; Gliklich, Glovsky, & Montgomery, 1999; Hogikyan & Sethuraman, 1999; Hogikyan et al., 2001; Hogikyan et al., 2000; Murry & Rosen, 2000; Rosen & Murry, 2000; Rosen et al., 2000). As might be predicted, people who use their voice more intensively in their lives perceived their voice disorders as more handicapping than those who used their voices less (Behrman, Sulica, & He, 2004). The two most commonly used questionnaires are the Voice Handicap Index (VHI) (Jacobson et al., 1997) and the Voice Related Quality of Life (V-RQOL) (Hogikyan & Sethuraman, 1999). Scores on these tests correlate well to changes in vocal function as the result of treatment (Benninger et al., 1998; Hogikyan et al., 2001; Hogikyan et al., 2000; Murry & Rosen, 2000; Rosen & Murry, 2000; Rosen et al., 2000). These correlations indicate that voice treatment can significantly improve a person's perceived quality of life.

5.1.3 Initial interview During the initial interview the speech-language pathologist first has the opportunity to listen to the person's voice. Being with the person allows the speech-language pathologist to make initial auditory perceptual judgments, observe the person for posture, breathing, and behavioral habits, and receive clarification concerning information on the case history form. While interacting with the person the speech-language pathologist is also making initial determinations as to the adequacy of the pitch, loudness, and quality of the person's voice in relation to what is typical for someone who is similar to the patient's age and sex. When listening to the pitch and loudness, the speech-language pathologist is listening to the typical pitch and loudness level as well as the extent of variations and the grammatical appropriateness of those variations. In contrast, the quality judgments involve impressions of breathiness, roughness, nasality, and whether the voice seems to be placed high, low, front, or back in the vocal tract. The speech-language pathologist also should be observing whether the person is moving her/his shoulders up and down to breathe, or whether all of the movement is anterior and posterior in the thorax, or the movement low in the thorax and abdominal. Low thoracic and abdominal movement with no shoulder movement is the most desirable.

5.1.4 Auditory perceptual observations   Once the interview is completed, the speech-language pathologist will begin to collect data by directing the patient to complete specified tasks. The systematic collection of these data includes perceptual, physiologic, and aerodynamic measures. The perceptual activities include both auditory and visual perceptions. As Bless and Hicks (1996) stated, "clinicians need to keep their ears keenly trained and be aware of factors known to affect perception such as expectation bias, recency effects, experience with wide range of dysphonias, case history bias, and clinician training" (p. 137). When listening to voices, ratings made from sustained vowel productions appear to be more reliable than those obtained from connected speech (de Krom, 1994). Therefore, de Krom (1994) suggested that completion of a rating scale be based primarily on prolonged vowel productions.

In 2002, Special Interest Division 3, Voice and Voice Disorders, of the American Speech-Language-Hearing Association (ASHA) brought together a team of voice specialists to create a scale that would be used by all speech-language pathologists for the auditory perceptual component of voice evaluations, the Consensus Auditory-Perceptual Evaluation of Voice (CAPE-V). The CAPE-V includes both the utterances to be rated – spontaneous speech, sentences, and sustained vowels – and a scale for rating the person's voice. The voice features rated are overall severity, roughness (hoarseness), breathiness, strain (pressed or harsh), pitch, and loudness. Procedures for administration and scoring of this scale are still being standardized. Once the CAPE-V scale has been normalized with data from multiple test sites and a large number of voices, a method of standardized training for using it will be developed. The current version of the CAPE-V form can be downloaded from the ASHA website.

5.1.5 Maximum phonation time and counting   In addition to the items on the CAPE-V form two other items are often part of the non-instrumental voice evaluation: maximum phonation time (MPT) and counting. These tasks can indicate the interaction of vocal fold activity with respiratory and articulatory function. Kent, Kent, and Rosenbek (1987) cautioned against using MPT as the only measure to distinguish between reduced respiratory support and inefficient laryngeal control of airflow. MPT is dependent upon the flow of air through the glottis; hence the speech-language pathologist should view it as an indication of the interaction of the two. The second task conducted during the voice recording is counting. For most patients, it is sufficient to ask them to count from 75 to 90. This structured activity is an automatic task that provides the speech-language pathologist with an idea of the patient's phrasing, breath support, and habitual pitch level. It can also serve as a guide for the next step in the evaluation process. For example, evidence of a hard glottal onset in the patient's speech may indicate the need for a few trial therapy techniques (e.g., precede phonation of a vowel-initial utterance with /h/), to determine if the individual is capable of modifying the hard glottal onset.

5.1.6 Visual perceptual measures The principal visual perceptual measure is viewing the vocal folds using laryngeal videostroboscopy. Laryngeal stroboscopy provides a view of vocal fold motion that is averaged across many cycles; thus it does not depict the actual motion of the vocal folds within any cycle. Voice specialists incorporate laryngeal stroboscopy in 81 percent of their voice evaluations and 94 percent of them consider it important for determining treatment goals (Patel & Bless, 2007). The use of laryngeal stroboscopy has enhanced the accuracy of voice evaluations by confirming uncertain diagnoses (Casiano, Zaveri, & Lundy, 1992; Woo et al., 1991). Since stroboscopic views provide a signal that is averaged over repeated vibrations, the patient must be able to produce relatively periodic vocal fold vibration for it to work. Because of their aperiodicity, moderately to severely dysphonic voices cannot be viewed via laryngeal stroboscopy. Patel (2007) reported that the voice disorders secondary to neuromuscular conditions are the most difficult to judge from laryngeal stroboscopic images.

Developments in high-speed digital video endoscopy and videokymography promise to overcome the limitations of laryngeal stroboscopy. These imaging systems allow observation of aperiodic voices. They can also record the onset and offset of voice, whisper, cough, and other vocal fold actions that can have clinical importance. As clinical interest in these vocal features increases, high-speed digital images may replace laryngeal stroboscopy as the main visual perceptual tool for voice evaluations (Deliyski, 2007). It should be noted that even these systems cannot be used to measure vocal fold activity and glottal width. The distance from the endoscope to the vocal folds, the exact position of the endoscope from the left and right sides of the vocal tract, and the rotation of the endoscope can all affect what the clinician perceives without any changes in vocal fold activity or glottal width.

5.1.7 Acoustic measures and electroglottography Acoustic measures provide information that can help quantify aurally and visually perceived events. Thus, they can be helpful in documenting initial performance level and improvement across treatment sessions. Unfortunately, most acoustic measures require signal periodicity; therefore they cannot be used when the person exhibits a moderate or severe dysphonia. Among the available acoustic parameters are measures of fundamental frequency, signal amplitude, cycle-to-cycle perturbation of those two measures (jitter and shimmer respectively), noise to harmonic ratios, long-term average spectrum, and acoustic correlates of glottal function. Tables showing normal values for most of these measures are available (see Baken & Orlikoff, 2000; Colton, Casper, & Leonard, 2006).

Voice disorders affect many of these acoustic measures. In particular, jitter, shimmer, and noise to harmonic ratios change, with higher values for jitter and shimmer and lower values for noise to harmonic ratios. Typically, jitter and shimmer values are reported as percentages of the fundamental frequency (Baken & Orlikoff, 2000), with values of under 1 percent for jitter and 3 percent for shimmer being normal. Perturbation values that are over 20 percent indicate aperiodic vocal fold vibration or a voice that will be perceived as dominated by noise.

The acoustic correlates of glottal function are affected by voice disorders; these measures include the duration of the open phase of the glottal cycle, the glottal width during vocal fold vibration, and the speed of vocal fold closure. Changes in the duration of the open phase will affect the peak amplitudes of the first two harmonics and change the difference between them (H1–H2), with a shorter open phase resulting in a greater difference with H1 higher, and a longer open phase can result in H2 being higher than H1 (Stevens & Hanson, 1995). A wider glottal opening will result in a small difference between the amplitude of the first harmonic and that of the first formant (H1–A1) and a narrow glottal opening will result in a large H1–A1 difference (Stevens & Hanson, 1995). A fast-closing glottis will result in greater amplitudes in the harmonics through those in the region of the third formant so that the difference between the first harmonic and third formant (H1–A3) is small. In contrast, a slow-closing glottis will result in a rapid energy drop across the harmonics so that the H1–A3 difference will be great (Stevens & Hanson, 1995).

Buder (2000) reported several other frequency, spectral, amplitude, and time-based acoustic measures that have been used in research. However, those measures have not become part of the voice clinician's array of diagnostic tools. In particular, the temporally based and the chaos-based measures have the potential to be developed for widespread clinical utility.

Electroglottography (EGG) is a physiologic measure that is often used with laryngeal video stroboscopy in the assessment of voice. EGG involves the transmitting of a weak high-frequency signal from an electrode on the skin over one side of the thyroid cartilage to a receiving electrode on the skin over the other side. When the vocal folds are closed, more of the signal is received. In this manner the pattern of vocal fold opening and closing is depicted (Baken & Orlikoff, 2000). Some manufacturers incorporate the EGG image onto the laryngeal video stroboscopy image so that both can be viewed simultaneously.

5.1.8 Aerodynamic measures   The aerodynamic parameters of voice include measures of air volume such as vital capacity and tidal volume; measures of airflow such as peak glottal airflow, the varying or AC airflow, the constant or DC airflow, and the first derivative maximum flow declination rate; and subglottal air pressure. Because these aerodynamic parameters vary with speech amplitude and with speaking fundamental frequency, their normal values have a wide range.

These normal data are reported in several places (see Baken & Orlikoff, 2000; Colton, Casper, & Leonard, 2006). Values outside the normal ranges correlate with observed physiologic changes in glottal activity (Hillman et al., 1989).

6 Voice Therapy

6.1 Goals of voice therapy

The goal of voice therapy is highly dependent on the individual who possesses the voice disorder. Ideally, a patient's voice should be functional for all activities of daily living including employment, home life, and recreation. As the person performing these activities, it is imperative that the patient become the custodian of his/her own vocal health. The voice clinician provides education and techniques when implementing treatment plans that provide respiratory, phonatory, and resonatory patterns that will replace vocally ineffective behaviors and facilitate optimum voice production. Treatments of voice disorders can be classified into three distinct goals: (a) teach/instruct a vocal behavior that is absent; (b) reduce or eliminate inappropriate behaviors and substitute an appropriate behavior; (c) strengthen appropriate vocal behaviors that are weak or inconsistent (Andrews & Summers, 2002). The treatment goals are established to dissolve or decrease the three etiological factors related to dysphonia (ineffective muscle use, organic disease, and/or psychological stressors).

Successful vocal rehabilitation needs to address all of the lifestyle, emotional, and technical issues that may be factors in the vocal difference (Morrison et al., 1994). Investing time and energy in the psychosocial aspects that often accompany voice disorders will aid the clinician and the patient in accomplishing the above-referenced goals. Rosen and Sataloff (1997) emphasized the concept that the anxiety that may follow vocal injury may exacerbate established vocal problems, which may result in disturbances of memory, concentration, and the patient's overall well-being. The voice clinician must recognize possible stressors and anxieties that the patient experiences that may reduce vocal quality. The voice clinician must be prepared to refer the patient to the appropriate professional (i.e., psychologist) that provides counsel to such patients.

6.2 Indirect/behavioral voice therapy approach

Behavior modification therapy concentrates on treating and maintaining the indirect aspects of the voice difficulty, including issues such as ineffective muscle use patterns and poor vocal hygiene (Carding, Horsley, & Docherty, 1999). The goal of this type of voice therapy is to direct the patient to develop an informed rational approach to his/her voice use pattern and provide a foundation for improved voice use (ibid.). Behavior modification does not involve specific focus on correcting the voice problem. However, when used by themselves, vocal hygiene programs can result in improved voice use (Roy et al., 2001).

Indirect therapies include activities focused on eliminating vocally abusive behaviors such as frequent throat clearing, as well as deleterious lifestyle choices such as smoking and dietary habits such as eating just before going to bed at night (Roy et al., 2001). Indirect voice therapy is implemented to educate the patient about the dangers of poor voice management and encourage proper vocal hygiene. Hicks and Milstein (2007) stated that many people with voice disorders have a poor understanding of how the voice mechanism works. They stated that vocal hygiene training can help these people use their voices more appropriately. Implementing this change requires the patient to replace vocally abusive behaviors with ones that are more conducive to good vocal function. The emphasis is placed on teaching proper habits to reduce future voice problems. Vocal education is provided to help the patient develop a better understanding of the anatomy and physiology of the speech mechanism. Those with voice disorders respond individually to vocal hygiene instruction for a wide range of reasons (van Leer, Hapner, & Connor, 2008). Thus, the clinician must discuss vocal hygiene with the patient using a variety of instruction techniques until the patient can explain the anatomic and physiologic effects of vocally abusive behaviors. Then the clinician can be confident that the patient understands the importance of good vocal hygiene and how to implement it. Since approximately 10–20 percent of the workforce use their voices as their primary occupational tools, it is imperative that therapy programs address functional behavioral modification techniques (Titze, Lemke, & Montequin, 1997). Vocal hygiene is an effective treatment tool for both professional voice users and others (Chan, 1994; Yiu & Chan, 2003). However, Roy et al. (2001) found it to be less effective than direct voice therapy techniques such as vocal function exercises. Thus, vocal hygiene should be considered an effective method that must be combined with other therapy techniques.

Drinking adequate water to keep the entire body hydrated has been shown to help vocal function. Maintaining adequate hydration can delay the onset of vocal fatigue symptoms (Solomon & DiMattia, 2000; Solomon et al., 2003). In addition, maintaining adequate hydration allows the vocal folds to be set into vibration with a minimum of effort, as measured using phonation threshold pressure (Solomon & DiMattia, 2000; Verdolini, Titze & Fennell, 1994; Verdolini et al., 2002). The phonation threshold pressure is the minimum subglottal pressure needed to set the vocal folds into motion for quiet phonation.

6.3   Common direct voice therapy approaches

6.3.1   Easy onset technique   This technique is designed to reduce the effects of abrupt vocal fold closure on the vocal folds. Hard glottal attack is a by-product of improper vocal fold adduction wherein the patient delays voicing until sub-glottic pressure builds to a point where the vocal folds are abruptly blown apart. This method of phonation taxes the margins of the vocal folds. The patient should be instructed to voice in a relaxed, effortless manner, using abdominal breath support. Initial treatment is implemented using single syllables that are comprised of the phoneme /h/ and a vowel. Once the clinician determines that the patient is using easy voicing onsets consistently, the patient is instructed to shift hierarchically from vowels, phrases, sentences, monologues, and ultimately to conversational speech. The patient may be also instructed to contrast between hard glottal attack voicing and easy onset voicing, which facilitates kinesthetic feedback that the patient may use to increase the use of the easy onset technique. Data are needed to demonstrate the efficacy of this treatment method.

6.3.2 Lip/tongue trills Lip trills are used in the clinical voice care setting as a warm-up before more strenuous exercises are performed. Menezes, de Campos Duprat, and Costa (2005) stated that the production of the trill balances resonance, fosters normal laryngeal tension by equalizing the aerodynamic and myoelastic forces, and enhances coordination of respiration, phonation, and resonance. Lip trills are to be performed at a comfortable loudness and pitch level. Patients should be instructed to place their lips loosely together while releasing the air steadily to create a trill or raspberry sound on the consonant [h] or [b]. The resulting production should be held steady while the air passes through the lips in a controlled manner. Descending and ascending pitch variation (sustaining or gliding up and down the patient's pitch range) can be introduced to extend the exercise after mastering the proper technique. Tongue trills can be performed in the same fashion by instructing the patient to place their tongue behind the upper teeth, gently blowing air over the top of the blade of the tongue. The patient should repeat this action several times, alternating between voice and voiceless productions.

6.3.3 Yawn/sigh technique Boone and McFarlane (1993) described the yawn/ sigh as a treatment technique that is useful for the patient who desires to develop optimal phonation with far less effort. These authors reported evidence that patients with functional dysphonia will benefit from this facilitating approach. Generally, when a person produces a yawn, a period of prolonged inspiration with maximum widening of the supraglottal structures is experienced. The sigh phase of this technique is performed by prolonged, easy, open-mouthed exhalation. The voice clinician should explain how a yawn feels and demonstrate an exaggerated yawn. It is important that the patient is able to rely on imagery to maintain a relaxed approach to phonation. After the patient is able to produce this technique, he or she should be instructed to use the technique while saying a series of words beginning with the /h/ phoneme. All words should be produced with easy onset phonation in order to eliminate hard glottal attack.

6.3.4 Lessac's Y-buzz resonance exercises This exercise is a resonance training technique that helps patients associate facial postures with specific resonance sensations in the lips, cheeks, and nose to improve vocal quality features. The theoretical framework that underlies these exercises is that kinesthetic awareness of the vibratory structures within the face will yield increased resonance. Once this referent is established, it can be used during vowel and non-nasal voiced phonemes. Eventually, carry-over is expected throughout running speech. Relaxed articulatory movements of the articulators are incorporated to facilitate maximum oral resonance sensations in sound sequences. This activity is used in both vocal function exercises (Roy et al., 2001; Stemple, Lee, D'Amico, & Pickup, 1994) and resonant voice therapy (Roy et al., 2003; Verdolini-Marston et al., 1995). Both of these voice treatment programs have been demonstrated to be effective treatment systems.

6.3.5   Laryngeal manual therapy   Laryngeal manual therapy has been shown to be beneficial in managing cases of muscle tension dysphonia and in the improvement of the overall voice quality and relief of the pain associated with laryngeal hypertension (Roy et al., 1997). In addition, Roy and Leeper (1993) concluded that perceptual measures of severity were consistently more likely to be rated as normal following laryngeal manual therapy. They also reported that the acoustic measures of voice (jitter, shimmer, and signal-to-noise ratio) all significantly improved. The therapist is to initiate laryngeal manual therapy superiorly at the level of the hyoid bone and progress inferiorly to the level of the thyroid cartilage. It is recommended that the voice therapist/pathologist administer laryngeal manual therapy rather than the patient, to ensure the proper technique is used.

6.4   Eclectic voice therapy/merging indirect and direct approaches

Eclectic voice therapy is an approach that combines behavioral modification techniques and direct voice therapy techniques. Eclectic voice therapy techniques allow the voice clinician to merge indirect and direct voice therapy techniques to shape an individualized treatment program that will yield maximum voice rehabilitation. Traditional voice therapy programs tend to focus on either behavioral modification therapy or direct voice therapy, but not both. Because effective vocal rehabilitation must address a variety of factors including making conscious efforts to change the current manner in which patients produce voice, the ways in which patients use their voice (conversational speech, singing, lecturing), and the environments that patients use voice (classroom, concert halls, home, noisy environments), eclectic voice therapy may satisfy all of the primary goals of vocal rehabilitation.

6.5   Evidenced-based decision making

Because many clinicians have anecdotally reported success with patients using various therapy approaches, it is imperative that voice care professionals have empirical evidence to support or refute their use. Since knowledge of theoretical framework and clinical experience in the field of voice disorders are the primary means by which vocal rehabilitation decisions are made, it behooves voice clinicians to incorporate the results of therapy efficacy studies while developing individualized treatment plans. Since measuring the effectiveness of voice treatment is now a basic requirement of health care delivery, more studies of voice therapy practices need to be conducted and integrated into diagnostic and treatment plans. With the recent focus on evidence-based practice in the field of speech pathology, developing reliable methods to evaluate, monitor, and treat voice disorders will ensure that the profession withstands internal as well as external scrutiny. In addition, proper documentation of voice therapy outcomes (both objective and perceptual measures) may reduce the amount of therapy time needed to improve the voice. Alison Behrman, a clinician and researcher within the field of voice science, put it best when she stated, "The most common practice is not always the best practice."

REFERENCES

Andrews, M. & Summers, A. (2002). *Voice treatment for children and adolescents.* San Diego, CA: Singular Publishing.

Baken, R. & Orlikoff, R. (2000). *Clinical measures of speech and voice*, 2nd ed. San Diego, CA: Singular Publishing.

Baynes, R. A. (1966). An incidence study of chronic hoarseness among children. *Journal of Speech and Hearing Disroders* 31, 172–6.

Behrman, A., Sulica, L., & He, T. (2004). Factors predicting patient perception of dysphonia caused by benign vocal fold lesions. *Laryngoscope* 114, 1693–700.

Belafsky, P. C., Postma, G. N., & Koufman, J. A. (2001). Laryngopharyngeal reflux symptoms improve before changes in physical findings. *Laryngoscope* 111, 979–81.

Belafsky, P. C., Postma, G. N., & Koufman, J. A. (2002). Validity and reliability of the reflux symptom index (RSI). *Journal of Voice* 16, 274–7.

Benninger, M. S., Ahuga, A. S., Gardner, G., & Grywalski, C. (1998). Assessing outcomes for dysphonic patients. *Journal of Voice* 12, 540–50.

Bless, D. M. & Hicks, D. M. (1996). Diagnosis and measurement: Assessing the "WHs" of voice function. In W. S. Brown, Jr., B. P. Vinson, & M. A. Crary (eds.), *Organic voice disorders: Assessment and treatment* (pp. 119–71). San Diego, CA: Singular Publishing.

Boone, D. & McFarlane, S. (1993) A critical view of the yawn-sigh as a voice therapy technique. *Journal of Voice* 7, 75–80.

Buder, E. (2000). Acoustic analysis of voice quality: A tabulation of algorithms. In R. Kent & M. Ball (eds.) *Voice quality measurement* (pp. 119–244). San Diego, CA: Singular Publishing.

Butler, J. E., Gray, S. D., & Hammond, T. H. (2001). Gender-related differences of hyaluronic acid distribution in the human vocal fold. *Laryngoscope* 111, 907–11.

Carding, P. N., Horsley, I. A., & Docherty, G. (1999). A study of the effectiveness of voice therapy in the treatment of 45 patients with non-organic dysphonia. *Journal of Voice* 13, 72–104.

Carding, P. N., Roulstone, S., Northstone, K., & ALSPAC Study Team. (2006). The prevealence of childhood dysphonia: A cross-sectional Study. *Journal of Voice* 20, 623–30.

Casiano, R., Zaveri, V., & Lundy. D. (1992). Efficacy of videostroboscopy in the diagnosis of voice disorders. *Otolaryngology – Head and Neck Surgery* 107, 95–100.

Chan, R. W. K. (1994). Does the voice improve with vocal hygiene education? A study of some instrumental voice measures in a group of kindergarten teachers. *Journal of Voice* 8, 279–91.

Chan, R. & Titze, I. (1999). Hyaluronic acid (with fibronectin) as a bioimplant for the vocal fold mucosa. *The Laryngoscope* 109 (7), 1142–49.

Chan, R. W., Gray, S. D., & Titze, I. R. (2001). The importance of hyaluronic acid in vocal fold biomechanics. *Otolaryngology-Head and Neck Surgery* 124, 607–14.

Colton, R. H., Casper, J. K., & Leonard, R. (2006). *Understanding voice problems: A physiologic perspective for diagnosis and treatment*, 3rd ed. Baltimore, MD: Lippincott, Williams & Wilkins.

Deliyski, D. (2007). Clinical feasibility of high-speed videoendoscopy. *Perspectives on Voice and Voice Disorders* 17 (1), 12–16.

Duff, M. C., Proctor, A., & Yairi, E. (2004). Prevalence of voice disorders in African American and European American preschoolers. *Journal of Voice* 18, 348–53.

Finck, C. & Lefebvre, P. (2005). Implantation of esterified hyaluronic acid in microdissected Reinke's space after vocal fold microsurgery: First clinical experiences. *Laryngoscope* 115, 1841–47.

Gliklich, R. E., Glovsky, R. M., & Montgomery, W. W. (1999). Validation of a voice outcome survey for unilateral vocal cord paralysis. *Otolaryngology – Head & Neck Surgery* 120, 153–8.

Hansen, J., Thibeault, S., Walsh, J., Shu, X., & Prestwich, G. (2005). In vivo engineering of the vocal fold extracellular matrix with injectable hyaluronic acid hydrogels: Early effects on tissue repair and biomechanics in a rabbit model. *Annals of Otlology, Rhinology & Laryngology* 114, 662–70.

Hicks, D. M. & Milstein, C. F. (2007). Laryngeal hygiene. In A. L. Merati & S. A. Bielamowicz (eds.), *Textbook of voice disorders* (pp. 83–8). San Diego, CA: Plural Publishing.

Hillman, R. E., Holmberg, E., Perkell, J. S., Walsh, M., & Vaughan, C. (1989). Objective assessment of vocal hyperfunction: A theoretical framework and preliminary results. *Journal of Speech and Hearing Research* 32, 373–92.

Hogikyan, N. D. & Sethuraman, G. (1999). Validation of an instrument to measure voice-related quality of life (V-RQOL). *Journal of Voice* 13, 557–69.

Hogikyan, N. D., Wodchis, W. P., Spak, C., & Kileny, P. R. (2001). Longitudinal effects of botulinum toxin injections on voice-related quality of life (V-RQOL) for patients with adductory spasmodic dysphonia. *Journal of Voice* 15, 576–86.

Hogikyan, N. D., Wodchis, W. P., Terrell, J. E., Bradford, C. R., & Esclamado, R. M. (2000). Voice-related quality of life (V-RQOL) following type I thyroplasty for unilateral vocal fold paralysis. *Journal of Voice* 14, 378–86.

Huang, C.-C., Sun, L., Dailey, S., Wang, S.-H., & Shung, K. (2007). High frequency ultrasonic characterization of human vocal fold tissue. *Journal of the Acoustical Society of America* 122, 1827–32.

Jacobson, B. A., Johnson, A., Grywalski, C., Silbergleit, A. Jacobson, G., Benninger, M., & Newman, C. (1997). The voice handicap index (VHI): Development and validation. *American Journal of Speech-Language Pathology* 6, 66–70.

Kent, J. F., Kent, R. D., & Rosenbek, J. C. (1987). Maximum performance tests of speech production. *Journal of Speech and Hearing Disorders* 52, 367–87.

de Krom, G. (1994). Some spectral correlates of breathy and rough voice quality for different types of vowel fragments. *Journal of Speech and Hearing Research* 37, 985–1000.

van Leer, E., Hapner, E., & Connor, N. (2008) Transtheoretical model of health behavior change applied to voice therapy. *Journal of Voice* 22, 688–98.

McKinnon, D. H., McLeod, S., & Reilly, S. (2007). The prevalence of stuttering, voice and speech-sound disorders in primary school students in Australia. *Language, Speech, and Hearing Services in Schools* 38, 5–15.

Menezes, M., de Campos Duprat, A., & Costa, H. (2005). Vocal and laryngeal effects of voiced tongue vibration technique according to performance time. *Journal of Voice* 19, 61–70.

Morrison, M., Rammage, L., Nichol, H., Pullan, B., May, P., & Salkeld, L. (1994). *The management of voice disorders*. San Diego, CA: Singular Publishing.

Murry, T. & Rosen, C. A. (2000). Outcome measurements and quality of life in voice disorders. *Otolaryngological Clinics of North America* 33, 905–16.

Nation, J. E. & Aram, D. M. (1984), *Diagnosis of speech and language disorders*, 2nd ed. San Diego, CA: College-Hill.

Patel, R. (2007). Visual perceptions in laryngeal imaging. *Perspectives on Voice and Voice Disorders* 17 (2), 7–10.

Patel, R. & Bless, D. (2007). Laryngeal high-speed digital imaging and kymography. In A. Merati & S. Beiamowicz (eds.), *Text of voice disorders*. San Diego, CA: Plural.

Powell, M., Filter, M., & Williams, B. (1989). A longitudinal study of the prevalence of voice disorders in children from a rural school district. *Journal of Communication Disorders* 22, 375–82.

Qui, Q. & Schutte, H. (2006). A new generation videokymography for routine clinical vocal fold examination. *Laryngoscope* 116, 1124–28.

Ramig, L. & Verdolini, K. (1998). Treatment efficacy: Voice disorders. *Journal of Speech, Language, and Hearing Research* 41, S101–S116.

Rosen, C. A. & Murry, T. (2000). Voice handicap index in singers. *Journal of Voice* 14, 370–7.

Rosen, D. C. & Sataloff, R. T. (1997). *Psychology of voice disorders*. San Diego, CA: Singular Publishing.

Rosen, C. A., Murry, T., Zinn, A., Zullo, T., & Sonbolian, A. (2000). Voice handicap index change following treatment of voice disorders. *Journal of Voice* 14, 619–23.

Rousseau, B., Sohn, J., Montequin, D., Tateya, I., & Bless, D. (2004). Functional outcomes of reduced hyaluronan in acute vocal fold scar. *Annals of Otology, Rhinology & Laryngology* 113, 767–76.

Roy, N. & Leeper, H. (1993). Effects of the manual laryngeal musculoskeletal tension reduction technique as a treatment for functional voice disorders: Perceptual and acoustic measures. *Journal of Voice* 7, 242–9.

Roy, N., Bless, D., Heisey, D., & Ford, C. (1997). Manual circumlaryngeal therapy for functional dysphonia: An evaluation of short- and long-term treatment outcomes. *Journal of Voice* 11, 321–31.

Roy, N., Gray, S. D., Simon, M., Dove, H., Corbin-Lewis, K., & Stemple, J. C. (2001). An evaluation of the effects of two treatment approaches for teachers with voice disorders: A prospective randomized clinical trial. *Journal of Speech, Language, and Hearing Research* 44, 286–96.

Roy, N., Merrill, R. M., Thibeault, S., Parsa, R. A., Gray, S. D., & Smith, E. M. (2004). Prevalence of voice disorders in teachers and the general population. *Journal of Speech-Language-Hearing Research* 47, 281–93.

Roy, N., Stemple, J., Merrill, R., & Thomas, L. (2007). Epidemiology of voice disorders in the elderly: Preliminary findings. *The Laryngoscope* 117, 628–33.

Roy, N., Weinrich, B., Gray, S., Tanner, K., Stemple, J., & Sapienza, C. (2003). Three treatments for voice-disordered teachers: A randomized clinical trial. *Journal of*

Speech, Language, and Hearing Research 46, 670–88.

Russell, A., Oates, J., & Greenwood, K. M. (1998). Prevalence of voice problems in teachers. *Journal of Voice* 12, 467–97.

Sataloff, R. T. (2005). *Vocal assessment.* San Diego, CA: Plural Publishing.

Schutte, H., Švec, J., & Šram, F. (1998). First results of clinical application of videokymography. *Laryngoscope* 108, 1206–10.

Senturia, B. & Wilson, F. (1968). Otorhinolaryngic findings in children with voice deviations. *Annals of Otology Rhinology and Laryngology* 77, 1027–41.

Silverman, E. M. & Zimmer, C. H. (1975). Incidence of hoarseness among school-age children. *Journal of Speech and Hearing Disorders* 40, 211–15.

Simberg, S., Sala, E., & Rönnemaa, A.-M. (2004). A comparison of the prevalence of vocal symptoms among teacher students and other university students. *Journal of Voice* 18, 363–8.

Smith, E., Gray, S., Dove, H., Kirch, L., & Heras, H. (1997). Frequency and effects of teachers' voice problems. *Journal of Voice* 11, 81–7.

Smith, E., Kirchner, H. L., Taylor, M., Hoffman, H., & Lemke, J. (1998). Voice problems among teachers: Differences by gender and teaching conditions. *Journal of Voice* 12, 328–34.

Smith, E., Lemke, J., Taylor, M., Kirchner, H. L., & Hoffman, H. (1998). Frequency of voice problems among teachers and other occupations. *Journal of Voice* 12, 480–8.

Solomon, N. & DiMattia, M. (2000). Effects of a vocally fatiguing task and systemic hydration on phonation threshold pressure. *Journal of Voice* 14, 341–62.

Solomon, N., Glaze, L., Arnold, R., & van Mersbergen, M. (2003). Effects of a vocally fatiguing task and systemic hydration on men's voices. *Journal of Voice* 17, 31–46.

Stemple, J., Glaze, L., & Klaben, B. (2000). *Clinical voice pathology: Theory and*

management, 3rd ed. San Diego, CA: Singular Publishing.

Stemple, J., Lee, L., D'Amico, B., & Pickup, B. (1994). Efficacy of vocal function exercises as a method of improving voice production. *Journal of Voice* 8, 271–8.

Stevens, K. & Hanson, H. (1995). Classification of glottal vibration from acoustic measurements. In O. Fujimura & M. Hirano (eds.), *Vocal fold physiology: Voice quality control* (pp. 147–70). San Diego, CA: Singular Publishing.

Thibeault, S., Rousseau, B., Welham, N., Hirano, S., & Bless, D. (2004). Hyaluronan levels in acute vocal fold scar. *Laryngoscope* 114, 760–4.

Titze, I., Lemke, J., & Montequin, D. (1997). Populations in the U.S. workforce who rely on voice as a primary tool of trade: A preliminary report. *Journal of Voice* 11, 254–9.

Verdolini, K. & Lee, T. D. (2004). Optimizing motor learning in speech interventions: Theory and practice. In C. M. Sapienza & J. K. Casper (eds.), *Vocal rehabilitation for medical speech-language pathology* (pp. 403–46). Austin, TX: Pro-Ed.

Verdolini, K., Min, Y., Titze, I., Lemke, J., Brown, K., van Mersbergen, M., Jiang, J., & Fisker, K. (2002). Biologic mechanisms underlying voice changes due to dehydration. *Journal of Speech, Language, and Hearing Research* 45, 268–81.

Verdolini, K., Titze, I. R., & Fennell, A. (1994). Dependence of phonatory effort on hydration level. *Journal of Speech and Hearing Research* 37, 1001–7.

Verdolini-Marston, K., Burke, M., Lessac, A., Glaze, L., & Caldwell, E. (1995). Preliminary study of two methods of treatment for laryngeal nodules. *Journal of Voice* 9, 74–85.

Ward, P. D., Thibeault, S. L., & Gray S. D. (2002). Hyaluronic acid: Its role in voice. *Journal of Voice* 16, 303–9.

Woo, P., Colton, R., Casper, J., & Brewer, D. (1991). Diagnostic value of stroboscopic examination in hoarse patients. *Journal of Voice* 5, 231–8.

Woodson, G. E. (1996). The voice care team. In W. S. Brown, Jr., B. P. Vinson, & M. A. Crary (eds.), *Organic voice disorders: Assessment and treatment* (pp. 112–17). San Diego, CA: Singular Publishing.

Yairi, E., Currin, L. H., Bulian, N., & Yairi, J. (1974). Incidence of hoarseness in school children over a one-year period. *Journal of Communication Disorders* 7, 321–8.

Yiu, E. & Chan, R. (2003). Effect of hydration and vocal rest on the vocal fatigue in amateur karaoke singers. *Journal of Voice* 17, 216–27.

21   Orofacial Anomalies

JANE RUSSELL

1   Introduction

Speech disorders associated with orofacial anomalies present a fascinating challenge to the researcher and the clinician alike. As Howard (2004, p. 314) comments with regard to cleft palate, speech production in this condition is subject to a "complex constellation of influences." For any individual with an orofacial anomaly, their speech will be the result of the inter-relationship between structure and the dynamic function of the vocal tract and subject to any number of associated and influencing factors relating to their condition. This "means that each speaker will, at any point in their development, present with a unique profile of skills and difficulties linked in a complex way to underlying aetiology" Howard (2004, p. 313).

Historically, speech disorders arising from orofacial anomalies were primarily considered to be articulatory in nature, potentially affecting consonant production with associated resonance and airflow features. However, this view, though still very applicable in conditions where a physical defect affects the structures of the mouth and face, ignored other factors such as hearing and psychosocial factors which may have linguistic as well as articulatory sequelae. In addition, the importance of the developmental dimension and the need to consider phonological as well as the phonetic implications of orofacial anomalies was largely ignored until the 1980s, when Crystal (1989) highlighted the need to study the speech of children with cleft palate using phonetic and phonological analyses. He stressed the importance of identifying whether there are phonological as well as phonetic deviations in cleft speech and, if there are phonological deviations, whether these are unusual phenomena or typical of developmental phonological disorders. Similarly, Hewlett (1990, p. 35), highlighted the need to address the relationship between "phonological representation and phonetic implementation" in order to provide a psycholinguistic explanation of speech disorders arising from structural anomalies. Hewlett (1990) proposes that speech disorders associated with structural anomalies occur at the lowest level of his model of speech production, that is, at

The Handbook of Language and Speech Disorders, First Edition. Edited by Jack S. Damico, Nicole Müller, and Martin J. Ball. © 2013 Blackwell Publishing Ltd except for editorial material and organization © 2013 Jack S. Damico, Nicole Müller, Martin J. Ball. Published 2013 by Blackwell Publishing Ltd.

the vocal tract shape/movements level. There is, therefore, the possibility of an unimpaired phonology underlying a primary phonetic disorder which results in compensatory strategies in "the intact remainder of the speech production system" (Hewlett, 1990, p. 34).

In the last two decades, considerable advances have been made in understanding the effect of a structural abnormality on phonetic and phonological development. Research in cleft palate has confirmed that although there are some common tendencies, there is also considerable heterogeneity. Some individuals do have an unimpaired phonology underlying a primary phonetic disorder but there can also be persisting phonetic influence on phonological development and, overall, there is considerable individual variability. In addition, in the field of cleft palate in particular, significant progress has been made with developing improved methods of perceptual assessment and analysis that have facilitated clinical management as well as the reporting of audit and research. However, as Sell (2005) points out, outcome measurements need to be further extended to include more functional issues, which affect the individual's quality of life. Furthermore, with regard to clinical management, it is important to take an holistic approach to the assessment and treatment of individuals with orofacial anomalies. Children, in particular, may present with developmental communication disorders that are unrelated to the structural defect. Therefore they require a comprehensive assessment of speech and language development which must be evaluated in the light of any physical, psychosocial, and linguistic factors associated with the structural abnormality. Conversely, though, with regard to therapy, even children who will benefit from input focusing on receptive and expressive language skills may also require direct work on speech production, and it is important that this is not overlooked. If it is not addressed, speech problems can persist into adolescence and adulthood.

This chapter describes speech disorders associated with cleft palate, craniofacial anomalies, and non-cleft velopharyngeal dysfunction in both the pediatric and adult populations. The potential influences of a structural abnormality on speech and language development are discussed and the characteristics of speech patterns described. In addition, information is provided about assessment, intervention, and cross-linguistic aspects.

2 Cleft Lip and Palate

Cleft lip and palate is one of the most common congenital deformities. It is difficult to obtain exact figures but the incidence is estimated to be in the region of one in 750 live births (McWilliams, Morris, & Shelton, 1990). This estimate is based on overt clefts which are diagnosed at birth and on a Caucasian population. Watson (2001, pp. 13–14), citing evidence from Denmark, suggests that the incidence may be slowly increasing. He proposes that this may partly be due to better reporting but that it may also be the result of factors such as "an increase in environmental teratogens, lower neonatal maturity and increased marriage and childbearing among cleft patients." There are some racial differences, with a higher incidence reported for American Indians and Chinese/Oriental people and the lowest incidence for Afro-Caribbean people (McWilliams, Morris, & Shelton, 1990; Watson, 2001). There are two genetically distinct groups: that is, cleft lip with or without cleft palate and isolated cleft palate. Clefts most often present as isolated anomalies but they may be associated with other congenital defects and can occur as part of a syndrome. In fact cleft lip and/or cleft palate is a component of over 400 syndromes (Lees, 2001). Some of the most common of these syndromes are 22q11 deletion (velocardiofacial syndrome), Stickler syndrome, Van der Woude syndrome, CHARGE association, Treacher–Collins syndrome and fetal alcohol syndrome (Lees, 2001; Saal, 2001). In addition, babies may present with Pierre Robin sequence, which includes a small chin, a retro-positioned tongue and cleft palate with associated breathing and feeding difficulties. In some cases Pierre Robin sequence ultimately proves to be Stickler syndrome.

Facial clefts originate in the first 3 months *in utero*, when the anatomical processes which will ultimately form the face fail to fuse at the appropriate stage in embryological development (Watson, 2001). The resultant defect ranges from slight to severe and can affect the lip, alveolus, hard palate, and soft palate. Clefts may be unilateral, bilateral or median and can occur in different combinations, as described by McWilliams, Morris, and Shelton (1990) and Watson (2001). Submucous clefts of the palate, in which there are muscle and bone defects underlying what appears to be an intact palate, may remain undiagnosed unless they give rise to feeding and/or associated speech disorders. Similarly, other congenital defects resulting in velopharyngeal dysfunction and hypernasal speech, in the absence of cleft palate, are identified from speech characteristics. They are not identified routinely in early life but may be detected when there are difficulties with speech development and/or resonance disorders.

In advanced countries, clefts of the lip and palate are routinely repaired surgically, usually in early childhood. However, surgery to repair submucous clefts of the palate and "speech surgery" to remediate velopharyngeal insufficiency may occur in older children and adults. There is considerable variation in the timing and type of surgical procedures and a continuing debate concerning the resultant effects of early surgery on facial growth and speech development. Speech is one of the primary outcome measures for cleft palate repair particularly with regard to adequate velopharyngeal function.

3   Craniofacial Anomalies

In addition to cleft lip and palate there are other orofacial anomalies which may affect speech development. Craniofacial anomalies are anatomical deviations which may or may not include cleft palate. They are rare but, as McWilliams (1984, p. 187) comments, they "constitute a major group of handicaps in children." Such abnormalities can affect the oral and facial structures, the cranium or both. They are often complex and, as indicated above, may occur with cleft palate, as features of a particular syndrome. Although it is possible for similar physical features to occur as a result of trauma, they are usually congenital and often of genetic origin (Sparks, 1984). Craniosynostosis (premature fusion of one or more of the cranial sutures) is a feature associated with some of the most commonly occurring craniofacial syndromes, for example, Apert, Crouzon, Pfeiffer, and Saethre–Chotzen syndromes (Thompson & Britto, 2004). These conditions may present with communication disorders associated with the physical defect or particular syndrome. These can be further complicated by associated conditions such as hearing loss, learning difficulties, and psychosocial factors.

Considerable advances have been made in the management and treatment of craniofacial anomalies, particularly with regard to surgical correction. However, the surgery required can be complex and challenging. As Tessier (2004, p. x) comments, "the main goals are to improve the vital functions and to give the cranium, midface and mandible a better chance of development, but this is not always achieved." He also states that, surgically, the brain, respiratory and ocular functions are the most important features to consider first, followed by speech and the relationship between the jaws, and that some of these overlap.

4   Influences of Orofacial Anomalies on Communication Development

The presence of a cleft palate or other craniofacial condition may influence the earliest stages of communication development because of physical factors which may also disrupt parent/child interaction and social development. In addition, there may be associated conditions such as visual, hearing, and cognitive impairment which can also adversely affect speech and language development.

One of the initial consequences of a cleft palate is early feeding difficulties. These infants are more prone to wind and can take longer to feed, at least until an appropriate feeding method is established. This can create anxiety and distress for both mother and child. Both abnormal feeding patterns and the physical defect itself can affect both oral motor and oro-sensory development. Bzoch (1979) suggests that abnormal neuromotor patterns may develop because both decoding and encoding skills are learned while the vast majority of infants with clefts have an abnormal (speech) mechanism. Both the abnormal physical structures and neuromotor patterns may result in delayed or deviant pre-speech development.

In some types of cleft palate, especially when there is Pierre Robin sequence or where the cleft is part of a syndrome and also in children with syndromic craniosynostosis, there may be respiratory difficulties. This is due to upper airway obstruction secondary to the abnormal orofacial structures. Shipster (2004) describes how severe respiratory difficulties may lead to developmental delay, impaired cognitive function and failure to thrive, all of which can impact on speech and language development.

A further effect of early feeding and respiratory difficulties is the disruption of normal mother–child interaction. This relationship is inevitably vulnerable when a baby is born with a facial deformity (Bradbury, 2001). At the same time as having to cope with feeding and respiratory problems, some mothers grieve over the lost opportunity to breastfeed. This sorrow, combined with the practical difficulties and fatigue of coping with respiratory and feeding difficulties, may limit the mother's motivation to communicate with her baby. As Nieman and Savage (1997, p. 223) comment in their study of the development of children with clefts from birth to 3 years of age, the feeding context helps to shape early communicative sequences. The authors suggest that feeding difficulties and environmental adjustments may account for "early cognitive lags (in the cleft lip and palate group) and language lags (in the cleft palate group)." Some mothers, however, seem to fear that their baby might feel rejected and actively compensate for their own reactions by consciously interacting intensively with their cleft palate infant. This can result in more advanced communicative abilities.

In addition to the effect of early feeding and respiratory difficulties on parent–child interaction, it is also possible that the presence of a physical defect will affect the parents' attitude to the child and thus their response to and initiation of communication. This is compounded in syndromic craniosynostosis when visible differences are even more severe. Parents may be struggling to come to terms with a child who looks different and in some cases may have special needs. This may mean that parents underrate their child's potential and make fewer demands on them to participate in communication. Attempts by the child to communicate may not be recognized as words because of the effects of the orofacial anomaly on articulation development. Additional stress may also be placed on the parent–child relationship and early communicative interaction by hospitalization, surgery, and outpatient clinic appointments.

Another physical consequence of cleft palate is the frequent occurrence of otitis media due to Eustachian tube malfunction. This results in a conductive hearing loss which may fluctuate and can seriously affect auditory skills and communication development. Conductive hearing loss is also frequently associated with syndromic synostosis, particularly in Apert syndrome. Sensorineural hearing loss is rarer but is more prevalent that in the normal population. Any hearing loss, together with the sequelae of difficulties with listening, attention control, and concentration may, of course, be a contributory factor to speech and language impairment. An additional factor with regard to craniofacial anomalies is that hearing loss in young children may not be diagnosed and treated effectively because severe craniofacial and neurosurgical factors require more immediate consideration. In addition, there is the danger of communication impairment being attributed to learning difficulties rather than poor hearing.

The impact of visual impairment on speech and language development in children with craniosynostosis also needs to be considered. Shipster (2004) describes the different types of visual impairments and abnormal eye movements that can occur in this population and explains how these may impact on language learning and social interaction.

Cognitive impairment is also a potential influence in craniofacial anomalies. Shipster (2004) comments that cognitive impairment has been found in differing degrees of frequency and severity in several syndromes including Apert and

Crouzon. This appears to be related to abnormalities and damage in the central nervous system, raised intracranial pressure and hydrocephalus. Shipster (2004) also highlights the lack of studies of intellectual functioning and the limitations of the studies that have been undertaken, and emphasizes the importance of appropriate test selection and differentiating between performance and verbal IQ scales.

As children with orofacial anomalies develop, psychosocial factors may further influence their acquisition of communication skills. In particular those with visible disfigurement may be treated differently by their peers and others in social situations. Children may avoid interacting with them and adults and siblings may talk for them in an attempt to avert embarrassing situations. As Shipster (2004) points out, delayed communication development may lead to false assumptions that these children will have great difficulty learning to talk or even be unable to speak. This can lead to fewer demands being made on them to communicate and can lead to distorted social interaction and social avoidance.

It is evident from the preceding discussion that there are multiple factors that can influence the development of communication in children with orofacial anomalies. Furthermore, the coexistence of predisposing factors increases children's vulnerability to communication impairments and can result in complex cases requiring detailed assessment and careful management to enable each child to reach their potential. There is also the danger of assumptions being made because of the appearance of the child. However, as Shipster emphasizes, there is not a direct correlation between the severity of physical problems and aspects of development and function. She comments that, "Children who have mild craniofacial abnormalities may have severe functional difficulties and, conversely, some children with relatively severe physical findings exhibit cognitive, social and communicative skills within normal limits" (Shipster, 2004, p. 279). This is also true of the cleft palate population, in which the severity and type of cleft does not correlate with the incidence and nature of speech difficulties. A child with, for example, a severe bilateral cleft of the lip and palate may develop normal speech production with minimal or no intervention.

4.1 Language impairment

There is general agreement that the language skills of cleft palate children tend to be delayed, particularly in the development of expressive language. This has also been reported in children with syndromic craniosynostosis. There is, however, considerable variation in the aspects of language investigated and the variables taken into account. The causes of any delay, for example, may be more closely related to hearing loss, linguistic environment, and other psychosocial factors rather than to direct effects of the physical defect itself. However, in children with syndromic synostosis, significant discrepancies between levels of language function and levels of non-verbal cognitive skills suggest that there may be specific language impairment (Shipster, 2004). The psychosocial effects described above also have the potential to result in pragmatic language difficulties. It has also been suggested that poor speech production in cleft palate children results in them being less conversationally assertive, thus impacting on their language performance (Frederickson, Chapman, & Hardin-Jones, 2006). Pamplona, Ysunza, and Espinosa (1999) also demonstrate that children with "compensatory articulation disorder" in addition to VPI (velopharyngeal insufficiency) evidenced a significantly higher frequency of language delay than children with only VPI.

Although the focus of this chapter is on the speech production aspects of orofacial anomalies, it is evident that receptive and expressive language skills are also very much at risk and need to be considered alongside speech difficulties. Language abilities will, therefore, need to be comprehensively assessed when necessary and taken into account when implementing appropriate management strategies.

4.2   The potential effects of orofacial anomalies on speech production

Russell and Harding (2001) describe how specific structural deficiencies can impose articulatory constraints on the developing speech patterns of children with cleft palate. Such constraints can also continue to affect established speech production. Shipster (2004) provides information about the articulatory constraints resulting from structural malformations in syndromic craniosynostosis and provides more detail about different syndromes. Structural conditions that may impose articulatory constraints include velopharyngeal insufficiency (VPI), residual clefts or fistulae, nasal obstruction, and dental and occlusal anomalies.

Prior to any operation to close a cleft palate, the infant will be developing feeding and pre-speech skills with an inadequate intra-oral mechanism. Although the purpose of surgery is to provide an intact palate and functioning velopharyngeal sphincter, this may not be achievable in some cases. There may be a residual hole or fistula in the palate and some surgical regimes deliberately leave the hard palate unrepaired until the child is older. Even when the palate appears to be intact it may be unable to function adequately to provide sufficient intra-oral pressure for speech. This velopharyngeal insufficiency may be characterized by hypernasal resonance, weak pressure consonants and/or nasal emission accompanying pressure consonant production (Wyatt et al., 1996). In severe VPI oral consonants may be realized as nasals, but this could also be a result of abnormal learned neuromotor patterns (Bzoch, 1979).

A fistula or residual cleft palate has the potential to affect articulatory placement as well as velopharyngeal function. In some cases, backing of alveolar consonants to velar or even uvular placements may occur, because oral pressure can be built up more easily behind the fistula. However, it should be noted that backing can also be evident in the speech of children who do not have fistulae. The quality of alveolar fricative consonants may also be affected by fistulae. This is due to difficulty in establishing the central grooved airflow between the tongue tip and the hard palate because of air loss through the fistula.

Whilst cleft palate is most commonly associated with VPI and excessive nasal resonance, nasal obstruction can precipitate hyponasal resonance in developing cleft palate speech. Nasal obstruction can lead to mouth breathing, snoring, slow eating, and disturbed sleep patterns. There is also the potential for growth to be affected because normal facial growth is dependant on nose breathing and sustained lip closure (Moss, 1969; Oblak & Kozelj, 1984). Hyponasality is also a feature in some of the craniosynostosis syndromes, especially Apert syndrome, due to the abnormal structures of the oro- and nasopharynx which reduce the volume of the resonating cavities. This can be compounded by the presence of adenoids and tonsils which further reduce the available space. Shipster (2004) comments that, even when tonsils and adenoids have been removed, hyponasality persists because of the abnormal structures. In addition, hyponasal resonance may be present in children with Apert syndrome who also have a cleft palate or submucous cleft palate. This may be deliberately left unrepaired to help maintain the child's airway.

Voice impairment may also be associated with orofacial anomalies (Grunwell & Sell, 2001; Shipster, 2004; Shprintzen, 2000). In particular, dysphonia can occur when there is VPI. It is hypothesized that this is a result of the speaker using excessive laryngeal effort in an attempt to compensate for inadequate velopharyngeal closure. However, as Grunwell and Sell (2001) point out, voice disorders are probably multifactorial and can relate to physical, physiological, functional, and psychological factors. Shprintzen (2000, p. 201) also comments with regard to craniosynostosis that "abnormalities in voice production may be caused by structural anomalies, behavioural problems or a combination of both." Abnormal voice production is reported in Apert syndrome but an increased prevalence in the other craniosynostosis syndromes is not evident (Shipster et al., 2002).

Occlusal and dental anomalies may influence speech production in both cleft palate and craniofacial conditions. In some individuals who have had repaired cleft lip and palate, facial growth may be affected so that there is under-development of the maxilla and relatively greater growth of the mandible (Mars, 2001). This midface retrusion or Class III occlusion is also a predominant feature in syndromic craniosynostosis. This type of occlusion and an anterior open bite may make it difficult for the individual to achieve lip closure for bilabial consonants. These may, therefore, be realized as lingualabial productions. There may also be reverse articulation of the labiodental consonants with the upper, not the lower, lip approximating with the mandibular rather than the maxillary incisors. Tongue-tip consonants are also affected, resulting in blade articulation or, in milder cases, dental articulation of alveolar and palato-alveolar consonants. Dental anomalies may also affect these consonants, resulting particularly in palatalization and lateralization (Albery & Grunwell, 1993). However, palatalization and lateralization may also result from atypical phonetic development (Russell & Grunwell, 1993).

With regard to phonetic development, the effect of the cleft palate condition may result in an atypical order of consonant acquisition from that which occurs in the non-cleft child (Harding, 1993; O'Gara & Logemann, 1998; Russell & Grunwell, 1993). In particular, velar plosives may occur prior to alveolar plosives, and voiceless may occur before voiced consonants. In addition, the early speech of children with cleft palate may contain a vocabulary which reflects a limited repertoire of consonants, for example a predominance of nasal versus oral consonants.

5   Speech Development in Orofacial Anomalies

5.1   *Babbling and early phonetic development*

It is self-evident that the physical defect of a cleft palate will, in addition to affect-ing the child's ability to form an intra-oral seal for effective feeding, have an effect on the child's ability to develop the oro-motor skills required for articulation and the future development of consonants. Studies have confirmed that there is atypical development in the pre-speech vocalizations of cleft palate children both pre- and postoperatively (Chapman, Hardin-Jones, & Halter, 2003; Russell & Grunwell, 1993). In comparison with non-cleft infants there is a lack of labial and lingual articulations and a predominance of nasals and glottal and pharyngeal articula-tions. It should be remembered, however, that early vocalizations in non-cleft children are also glottal and pharyngeal and that neonatal vocalizations are hypernasal. This is due to physiological influences; but by 6 months of age, when the larynx has lowered and the tongue has dropped, facilitating mouth breathing, there is increased velopharyngeal control and the emergence of oral contoid (consonant-like) productions. The marked difference from normal babble in the cleft population is, therefore, undoubtedly physically based and results from the structural inadequacy of the intra-oral mechanism. Postoperatively there is grad-ual progress toward more normal articulatory patterns as the infants begin to discover the potential of their improved intra-oral structure. However, even in those with normal velopharyngeal function, there is still a delay in articulatory development in comparison with the non-cleft children. Studies have shown that there is normal development of the structure of babble in that there is no dif-ference in the production of canonical syllables or the size of the contoid phonetic inventory, but there are significant differences in manner of articulation, with cleft children producing more sounds requiring less intra-oral pressure (Jones, Chapman, & Hardin-Jones, 2003; Willasden & Albrechtsen, 2006).

As in normal children, it has also been established that there is a link between the phonetic repertoire of babbling and the basic sound system of a child's lan-guage in the cleft palate population. An absence of plosives, for example, indicates that there may be a delay in plosive consonant acquisition in the child's future speech development. A lack of labial and lingual articulations in babbling may result in a backing process in early speech, although this could also be related to an articulatory constraint (see above) and phonetic deviance may also persist (Russell & Grunwell, 1993).

5.2   *Phonological development*

As the child continues to develop, cleft palate articulatory simplifications are to some extent superimposed on the non-cleft immaturities that occur in normal speech development. However, for children with cleft palate, they can continue to be directly associated with specific structural conditions which have the potential to impose articulatory constraints. Similarly, the speech development of children with craniofacial synostosis who may not have clefts of the palate but have other structural abnormalities, may also be affected by articulatory constraints. These physical constraints can result in articulation errors that have the potential to be integrated into the developing phonological system (Chapman, 1993).

Literature relating to speech development in syndromic craniosynostosis is very limited. However, in her study of the children attending the Craniofacial Unit at Great Ormond Street Hospital in London, Shipster (2004, p. 282) reports that these children have "a more reduced range of consonants in their babble and early word attempts when compared to the normal child." In this population there is also a very high incidence of phonological impairment due to a delay in the development of phonological skills. Common patterns observed in an audit of 6-year-olds with syndromic craniosynostosis included stopping of fricatives and affricates, word final consonant deletion, voicing of voiceless consonants, and fronting of velar and palato-alveolar consonants (Shipster, 2004). It is interesting to contrast this with patterns that may be found in the developing speech of (younger) children with cleft palate. Any of the same patterns may occur but backing is more likely than the normal developmental pattern of fronting. In addition, particularly when there is VPI, voiceless consonants may be more prevalent and develop before voiced consonants. Children with cleft palate, therefore, may exhibit patterns that are atypical of normal development but children with craniosynostosis tend to show a more general pattern of delay.

In cleft palate speech, whole groups of consonants may be affected by articulatory constraints in addition to normal immature patterns (Harding & Grunwell, 1996). Russell and Harding (2001) describe how the backing process employed by a child with a cleft palate who realizes alveolar /d/ as a velar /g/ affects all the consonants grouped with /d/ in normal development. This process can persist and subsequently affect fricative development so that /s/ and /z/ are also backed to velar. Furthermore, as Morris and Ozanne (2003) point out, sounds such as nasals that would not be considered difficult for a cleft palate speaker may also be affected. Existing processes in a child's phonological system are sufficiently strong that realizations of a new target, such as /s/, which might be produced accurately in sound play, would always conform to the existing phonological rules, whether cleft related or developmental. Grundy and Harding (1995) describe this effect of an articulatory constraint on the phonological system as a phonological consequence of an articulation disorder. It is important to identify when this occurs in a child's speech, because whereas normal immaturities usually resolve spontaneously, cleft-type processes can stabilize and require therapeutic intervention.

Employing phonological techniques of analysis to cleft palate speech may, therefore, contribute by identifying the extent and nature of any deviance or delay and determining whether these result primarily from phonetic or phonological bases (Crystal, 1989). Broen, Felsenfield, and Kittleson-Bacon (1986) illustrate how phonological analysis helped to identify children at the age of 2;6 who required secondary surgery for velopharyngeal insufficiency. Lynch, Fox, and Brookshire (1983) studied the developing phonological systems of two cleft palate children. One of their subjects evidenced cleft-type characteristics associated with structural inadequacy whereas the other showed evidence of developmental delay. Both these subjects, and those in the non-surgical group studied by Broen et al., differed from non-cleft subjects with regard to consonant development. Russell and Grunwell (1993) report considerable individual variation but also common tendencies in the developing phonological systems of eight subjects. Character-istics of cleft palate speech were detected in the data of all their subjects at some stage but the number and types of characteristics varied. The results of this study indicated that more normal phonetic development leads to normal phonological development but delay in phonetic development causes further delay in the establishment of a child's phonological system.

With regard to following a normal or atypical pattern, a similar finding is reported by Morris and Ozanne (2003), who compared two groups of cleft palate children, one with normal language development and the other with significantly delayed expres-sive language development at 2 years. At 3 years the delayed group continued to have delayed language and also a disordered profile of phonological development.

It is evident, therefore, that cleft palate children are "at risk" for both phonetic and phonologically based disorders of speech production (Peterson-Falzone, Hardin-Jones, & Karnell, 2001), and that these can be identified in early speech development. Phonological problems may be related to early language delays or result from physically based articulation errors interacting with the developing phonological system.

Some authors argue that the phonological perspective contributes little to our understanding of cleft palate speech per se (Golding-Kushner, 2001; Peterson-Falzone, Hardin-Jones, & Karnell, 2001). However, it does contribute another dimension to our understanding of the origins of different cleft-type speech pat-terns and facilitates the early identification of children who require secondary surgery and/or early therapeutic intervention. Although Russell and Grunwell (1993, p. 46) conclude that "children with cleft palate can achieve more or less normal phonological systems, but the process and pattern of phonological develop-ment is affected by the sequelae of the cleft palate condition," they also emphasize the individual variation between children and also the influence of fluctuating hearing loss. This is a further indication of the complex interaction between the different physical, functional, and developmental aspects of the cleft palate condi-tion and associated influencing factors such as hearing.

5.3   Speech patterns

Despite all the potential hazards described above, it is important to remember that many children with cleft palate will achieve normal speech production with no further surgical intervention and with little or no speech therapy. However, as Grunwell and Sell (2001) point out, there is agreement that there is a high risk of disordered articulation in this population. The nature of the disordered articula-tion is heterogeneous in presentation but there are some common tendencies such as backing of anterior consonants and the vulnerability of the "pressure consonants," particularly when there is VPI. The early identification and appropriate management of those who do have difficulties is, therefore, essential, so that they are provided with every opportunity to achieve intelligible and acceptable speech. It is recognized that the severity of speech problems increases with the severity of cleft type (Grunwell & Sell, 2001). In addition, there is an increase in the likelihood of speech difficulties if the cleft is associated with a syndrome and if there are other identifiable malformations (Persson, Lohmander, & Elander, 2006). Similarly, children with craniofacial conditions are more at risk of speech problems when there are additional influencing factors such as hearing or visual difficulties.

Speech patterns associated with orofacial anomalies have been described as obligatory, compensatory, active and passive (Golding-Kushner, 1995; Grunwell & Sell, 2001; Harding & Grunwell, 1998; Hutters & Bronsted, 1987; Shprintzen, 2000). Obligatory errors are those that relate directly to an anatomical defect that makes it impossible or very unlikely for the target sound to be produced (Grunwell & Sell, 2001; Shprintzen, 2000). Obligatory errors are "not amenable to therapy and often self correct when the underlying structural anomaly is corrected. For example, the incorrect realizations of / b d / as their nasal equivalents [m n] spontaneously correct" when secondary surgery has provided an efficient velopharyngeal mechanism (Grunwell & Sell, 2001, p. 79). Compensatory errors are "abnormalities of articulation employed by patients with structural anomalies designed to approximate the correct acoustic production by altering the place or manner of articulation" (Shprintzen, 2000, p. 200). Examples include the use of labiolingual consonants to realize bilabial consonants when lip approximation cannot be achieved, and the use of a reversed labiodental fricative for a dentolabial fricative because of abnormal occlusion. Grunwell and Sell (2001, p. 79) comment that these errors may or may not resolve spontaneously when an underlying anatomical anomaly is corrected, "but may be a reasonable functional compensation sometimes until the correct placement can be taught."

With regard to the active/passive distinction, active articulatory processes are considered to be "alternative articulations thought to have been actively generated to establish the necessary phonemic distinctions between consonant targets" (Harding & Grunwell, 1998, p. 332). Active alternatives to target consonants may include dentalization, lateralization/lateral articulation, palatalization/palatal articulation, double articulation, backing to velar or uvular, pharyngeal articulation, glottal articulation, and active nasal fricatives. In contrast, passive processes do not involve any change in place of articulation for the target consonant but there is accompanying nasal air flow and some targets may be realized as nasals. Passive characteristics include weak/nasalized consonants, nasal realizations of fricatives and plosives, absent pressure consonants, and gliding of fricatives/affricates. Both the active and passive features are described as speech cleft-type characteristics (Grunwell & Sell, 2001).

5.4 Persisting speech problems

There is considerable variation in the figures reported for the incidence of speech problems and/or velopharyngeal insufficiency in cleft palate. Different cleft groups have been studied and different methodologies employed so that it is difficult to compare outcomes (Grunwell & Sell, 2001). It is apparent, however, that following primary surgery up to 50 percent of children may need some form of speech therapy and/or further surgery. There does seem to be some improvement in articulation with age but the rate of improvement tends to slow down after 10 years of age (CSAG Report, 1998; Harding & Grunwell, 1993). Patterns of incorrect articulation may then become firmly established and prove resistant to therapy (D'Antonio & Scherer, 1995).

In adolescence and adulthood, clients may continue to present with speech difficulties associated with orofacial anomalies. Some of these will be those with unoperated cleft palate living in or originating from undeveloped countries where multidisciplinary care is not available. Others will have persisting speech problems resulting from inadequate primary surgery or speech therapy or other factors such as non-compliance with treatment. The UK CSAG study of 5- and 12-year-old children with unilateral cleft lip and palate found that 15 percent of 12-year-olds still had serious errors of consonant production (CSAG, 1998). Adults do, therefore, present with the types of articulation errors that could and should have been successfully remedied when they were younger. The challenges these pose to the success of intervention are explored below. In addition, some adult clients may still have obligatory articulation errors resulting from underlying structural anomalies such as VPI and dental/occlusal abnormalities.

6 Assessment

As stated above, it is important to undertake a comprehensive assessment of communication skills and to relate the results to influencing factors that may include the underlying structural abnormality. In this chapter, however, the focus is primarily on the assessment of articulatory ability and speech production. As Sell (2005, p. 103) comments with regard to cleft palate, "perceptual speech assessment is recognized to be of the utmost importance." However, such assessment has advanced considerably from the traditional framework of error analysis that was used in early studies of cleft palate speech. New methods for assessing, analyzing, and recording speech that facilitate clinical management and also the reporting and comparison of speech results have been developed.

With the knowledge that characteristics of later speech difficulties can be identified in the pre-speech patterns of children with orofacial anomalies and that early intervention can help to prevent or alleviate such difficulties, it is evident that monitoring and assessment of early phonetic output is appropriate (Russell & Harding, 2001). The child's phonetic repertoire can be assessed through the transcription of babble and parent report. Consonant production can be recorded using a phonetic inventory or diagram enabling the speech/language clinician to identify any indicators for early intervention: for example, an absence of plosive articulations, a predominant pattern of non-oral glottal and pharyngeal articulations, and/or a lack of labial and front-of-tongue plosives. As the child gets older and is producing more language, a systematic phonological assessment such as PACS TOYS (Grunwell & Harding, 1995) can be useful and will help to identify any atypical processes that are developing. In addition, more spontaneous language will facilitate the perceptual assessment of resonance and airflow, thus giving more information about velopharyngeal function.

From about the age of 3 years, many children will happily respond to the picture stimuli and sentence repetition tasks used for obtaining data for the GOS.SP. ASS.98 (Sell, Harding, & Grunwell 1994, 1999). This is an assessment tool that provides a systematic framework for the evaluation of all the different aspects of cleft palate speech. Although specifically designed for assessing children with cleft palate and/or velopharyngeal dysfunction, the parameters included mean that it is also appropriate for the speech assessment of other non-cleft orofacial anomalies. It is a practical and time-efficient procedure that enables the clinician to identify speech characteristics that require further investigation. In addition, the procedure can be used to measure progress over time and it also facilitates comparison between different clients. When the initial assessment indicates that there are specific speech problems, and/or a potential inter-relationship with developmental patterns, it may also be necessary to carry out a full phonetic and phonological analysis.

The framework of GOS.SP.ASS.98 facilitates the recording of resonance and nasal airflow characteristics and the phonetic representation of consonant production. These aspects can then be compared and summarized to confirm whether there are specific cleft type characteristics (CTCs), which are categorized as anterior oral, posterior oral, non-oral, and passive CTCs. Additional sections of the GOS. SP.ASS.98 include voice, the visual appearance of speech, a comprehensive oral examination, language and etiological factors. When completed, therefore, it enables the clinician to fully evaluate the presenting speech pattern and to relate it to etiological and other influencing factors, thus enabling the identification of areas requiring further assessment and the formulation of a management plan.

GOS.SP.ASS.98 has been adopted as the clinical tool used for the perceptual evaluation of speech in the UK and Ireland. However, it is considered too detailed for the purpose of audit and the inter-center comparison of speech outcomes and for that purpose the Cleft Audit Protocol for Speech – Augmented (CAPS-A) – has been developed (John et al., 2006). Based on a small sample, CAPS-A is proven to be a valid, reliable, and acceptable audit tool. A cohort of specialist speech and language therapists from cleft palate centers in the UK and Ireland have now been trained in the use of this tool, including phonetic transcription and procedures for capturing, documenting, and analyzing the data. These therapists participate in regular consensus listening sessions within their own teams but also, more importantly, with trained listeners from other teams,which facilitates unbiased inter-center audit.

6.1   *Further assessment of velopharyngeal function*

In the clinical setting, the perceptual evaluation of speech production in orofacial anomalies is paramount but instrumentation may also contribute to assessment.

Instrumentation has been developed to provide aerodynamic and acoustic measures of nasal resonance and airflow. The instrument most commonly used to measure the relative amount of nasal versus oral acoustic energy in an individual's speech is the nasometer. For detailed descriptions of the nasometer and its application see Kummer (2001) and Peterson-Falzone, Hardin-Jones, and Karnell (2001). One drawback of the nasometer is that it has been shown that nasalance scores vary according to different accents and dialects. This means that normative data is required for reliable and valid use on clinical populations and such data is limited (Sell & Grunwell, 2001). However, at an individual level, nasometry is useful in contributing to the assessment of velopharyngeal function and comparison of pre- and postoperative assessments.

Aerodynamic measures of airflows and air pressures may also be used to study velopharyngeal function. These range from simple sensing devices such as manometers and the mirror test to more sophisticated systems using combinations of pressure transducers and airflow meters. The most advanced of these is the PERCI-SARS system; its pressure flow measurements have been shown to have a moderate to good relationship with perceptual judgments of nasal emission (Kummer 2001; Peterson-Falzone, Hardin-Jones, & Karnell, 2001; Sell & Grunwell 2001).

When the results of perceptual assessment indicate that there is hypernasality and/or nasal emission and passive cleft-type characteristics, further investigations of palate function are required to determine the cause of this velopharyngeal dysfunction. Such investigations are multi-view videofluoroscopy and nasendoscopy, which are used to establish the size and shape of any velopharyngeal defect and also the range of movements of the palate and the posterior and lateral walls of the pharynx (Mercer & Pigott, 2001). The speech and language clinician has an important role in interpreting these investigations by relating the anatomical structure and function to the patient's speech production. In addition, multi-disciplinary discussion will determine whether surgery, prosthetic management (Sell, Mars, & Worrell 2006), and/or speech and language therapy is indicated.

7   Intervention for Speech Disorders

7.1   *Early intervention*

Part of the speech and language clinician's role in the multidisciplinary team is to provide information about speech and language development and the potential effects of the orofacial anomaly. In addition, advice is given to parents regarding how to encourage normal development and minimize possible adverse effects. With regard to cleft palate in particular, it is important for the carers to understand that the goal is always normal speech and that they have an important part to play in facilitating sound development. This commences even prior to palate repair when engaging in vocal play and stimulation helps establish early patterns of turn taking and vocal response (Russell & Harding, 2001).

The aims of early intervention are to facilitate the development of normal babbling and to try and prevent the establishment of patterns that could result in cleft-type characteristics, as described above. In the pre-speech stage of development, early intervention is recommended when there is evidence of a lack of plosive articulations, a predominance of glottal and pharyngeal articulations, a lack of labial and front-of-tongue plosives, and/or any other evidence of deviant or delayed communication development. Techniques for implementing early intervention usually involve training parents how to model target consonants and to reinforce appropriate responses. As Russell and Harding (2001, p. 201) comment, "through this approach, the acquisition of new sounds may be completely effortless for the child." Such indirect therapy approaches and home programs for cleft palate children are described by Golding-Kushner (1995, 2001), Peterson-Falzone et al. (2001), and Russell and Albery (2005). Unfortunately, the success of such programs is largely anecdotal and some may argue that it is not justified on the grounds of cost and burden to the parents. However, an opposing view is that putting time into adequately training parents could be more cost effective since it can reduce the number of visits to the speech and language clinician and prevent the need for future therapy that can be lengthy and an even greater burden to the child and parents. In addition, reports regarding the success of early intervention programs have begun to appear in the literature. Peterson-Falzone, Hardin-Jones, and Karnell (2001) comment that the impact of early intervention together with improved surgical techniques has resulted in a decline over the years in the number of children with cleft palate who have severe articulation and resonance disorders. Blakely and Brockman (1995) describe a 4-year project in which 41 children aged between 12 and 24 months were seen for speech and hearing assessments at 3- to 4-monthly intervals. These sessions included parental advice and training in direct and indirect techniques to facilitate sound development. Direct articulation therapy with a speech and language clinician was provided for 27 of the children. Impressively, when the children were reassessed at the age of 5 years, 88 percent had achieved normal articulation and resonance. In addition, a recent study by Scherer, Antonio, and McGahey (2008) demonstrates that parent training can be effective and the results indicate increased sound inventories, increased speech accuracy, and reduced use of glottal stops for children with clefts.

7.2 Direct intervention

Depending on the age and ability of the child, intervention may continue to be a combination of the indirect approach used with younger children and more direct articulation therapy, together with other approaches such as Metaphon, Cued Articulation, and phonological therapy (Russell & Albery, 2005). Even when direct intervention is provided, parent involvement and support continues to be crucial to the success of therapy. It is also important for activities to be motivating, and specific individual reward systems may be required.

Intervention should obviously be based on the results of comprehensive assessment as described above and appropriate individual or group therapy provided as indicated to help with language and other communication difficulties. However, when the speech disorder is directly related to the orofacial anomaly, in particular cleft palate, it is most likely that direct focused articulation therapy is required. Unfortunately, in the UK and also in the USA (Golding-Kushner, 2001; Peterson-Falzone, Hardin-Jones, & Karnell, 2001) children may be included in intervention that does not meet their specific needs, for example phonological awareness groups or classroom-based programs. Such therapy will be of limited value and will not help children who need to be taught how to articulate oral consonants and subsequently to establish them in their phonological systems. However, as Howell and McCartney (1990, p. 39) describe, "speech and language therapists are remarkably successful in changing child speech patterns which deviate from the norm," and good progress can be made when correctly focused therapy is provided.

The frequency of therapy and length of intervention are also important issues to consider. The literature strongly recommends intensive therapy, that is, three to five times a week. However, positive changes can be achieved with weekly or less frequent sessions provided that therapy is correctly targeted, motivation is in place, and there is appropriate daily home practice and support. Therapy usually needs to continue for much longer than a 6- to 8-week block model in order to consolidate and maintain changes that are beginning to occur and to avoid intervention being unsuccessful. Stopping therapy too soon is one of the reasons that children with cleft palate stay on the caseloads of speech and language clinicians for unacceptably long periods of time without progressing (Russell & Albery, 2005). It is also inappropriate to leave children with speech disorders relating to orofacial anomalies "on review" with the anticipation that articulation therapy will be more effective when they are older. These children have physically based articulation disorders that have phonological consequences. If they do not receive the intervention they require, their incorrect patterns become firmly established and resistant to therapy (D'Antonio & Scherer, 1995). In addition, progress with articulation therapy is often part of the decision-making process when velopharyngeal surgery is being considered. It is also important to continue to work toward accurate articulation and manner of production even when VPI is suspected or confirmed. The only time when this is not necessary is where normal articulation patterns have developed and the client has intelligible speech despite the presence of hypernasality and/or nasal emission.

Adult clients can make changes to their speech patterns even after years of incorrect production. However, they need to be highly motivated and strongly committed to invest considerable time and effort into learning and maintaining new articulatory gestures while inhibiting habitual patterns. It may be necessary to explore in depth psychological aspects of therapy related to self-image, the expectations of friends and family, and the intrinsic desire of the individual to change (Russell & Albery, 2001).

Both adults and children with persisting articulation problems that are not responding to conventional therapy procedures may benefit from treatment using electropalatography (EPG). This computer-based system provides a visual record of the timing and location of tongue contacts with the hard palate during continuous speech (Hardcastle & Gibbon, 1997). It can, therefore, provide important information about lingualpalatal contact patterns that have not been identified by perceptual assessment, thus improving the understanding of both clinician and patient (Howard, 2004). EPG is considered expensive because it requires a custom-made palatal plate for each individual. However, this is outweighed by the effectiveness of intervention with appropriately selected clients (Gibbon et al., 1998). EPG should be one of the treatment options available in a multidisciplinary cleft palate/craniofacial center.

8 Cross-linguistic Aspects

Not only has considerable progress been made with the development of procedures for clinical assessment and audit in the UK, but there have also been significant advances with regard to developing tools that will enable the comparison of results across languages. These are the result of extensive international collaborations between speech and language specialists in the field of cleft palate.

The Eurocleft Speech Study was the first multilingual, multicenter comparison of speech outcomes in cleft palate speakers and represents a major methodological landmark (Eurocleft Speech Group, 1994, 2000). This study investigated the speech of children with repaired unilateral cleft lip and palate (UCLP) from six different centers and from five different language backgrounds (all Germanic languages). The group developed a research protocol that would provide comparable information about the speech of children from different backgrounds and an analytical framework taking account of the phonetic characteristics of the five target languages and their vulnerability to the cleft palate condition. In addition, the group established that consensus listening panels of three individuals, which included one native speaker of the language samples being analyzed, resulted in an acceptable level of agreement (Eurocleft Speech Group, 1993).

Hutters and Henningsson (2004) highlight the methodological problems involved in undertaking cross-linguistic studies of cleft palate speech with reference to both the Eurocleft and Scandcleft Studies. The latter is an ongoing cross-linguistic multicenter study of speech outcome following cleft palate repair. It involves four Germanic languages and Finnish, a Finno-Ugric language, and focuses on pressure consonants and nasal resonance on vowels. In contrast to the Eurocleft Study in which the subjects were about 10 years old, the Scandcleft Project is collecting data at 3 and 5 years of age, thus introducing a complicating developmental dimension. Hutters and Henningsson (2004) illustrate how this affects the selection of speech assessment materials and discuss how developmental and other factors mean that the requirement of speech units that are phonetically identical across languages may not be met. Furthermore, they emphasize the need for detailed information about the interaction between the cleft palate condition and speech sound production in order to fully understand the consequences of any compromises on the validity of data.

More recently, a further exciting advance in the field of cleft palate has been the development of universal parameters with the aim of achieving consistency and uniformity in reporting speech outcomes "regardless of the language or languages spoken" (Henningsson et al., 2008, p. 1). This is the result of years of collaborative work undertaken by a dedicated team of researchers from Sweden, the USA, the UK, Ireland, and Hong Kong (the steering group), with additional input from individuals from a further seven countries who attended a workshop in 2004. The parameters include five universal parameters which are hypernasality, hyponasality, nasal emission and/or turbulence, consonant production errors, and voice disorder. Each of these parameters is clearly defined with specific descriptors given for severity ratings. These authors have also addressed the difficulties of using ratings of intelligibility (Whitehill, 2002) to measure speech outcomes and this is one of the most exciting aspects of this work. They have achieved this by developing two global parameters for speech understandability and speech acceptability. It is, therefore, possible to identify those individuals who, although they can be understood by the listener, still have speech characteristics that makes their speech distinctive and "cleft-like."

9   Conclusion

The end of the twentieth and beginning of the twenty-first century has been an exciting time to be involved in the field of speech disorders associated with orofacial anomalies. This chapter outlines advances that have been made with understanding, assessing, and treating such disorders. The future promises to be equally fruitful for the researcher and clinician alike. The results of longitudinal studies such as Eurocran will soon be available and will contribute new knowledge. It is anticipated that new studies will investigate different types of cleft palate (rather than focusing solely on UCLP, for example) including syndromic clefts, and also that there will be more studies of speech development and disorder in craniofacial conditions. In addition, the development of standardized speech recording and assessment together with the use of universal parameters will facilitate inter-center and cross-linguistic comparison of outcomes. Further work is also needed to demonstrate the effectiveness of all types of speech therapy intervention so that individuals with orofacial anomalies receive appropriate help at the optimum time in order to help them achieve their maximum potential.

REFERENCES

Albery, E. & Grunwell, P. (1993). Consonant articulation in different types of cleft palate. In P. Grunwell (ed.), *Analysing cleft palate speech* (pp. 83–111). London: Whurr.

Blakely, R. W. & Brockman, J. H. (1995). Normal speech and hearing by age 5 as a goal for children with cleft palate: a demonstration project. *American Journal of Speech-Language Pathology* 4, 25–32.

Bradbury, E. (2001). Growing up with a cleft: the impact on the child. In A. C. H. Watson, D. A. Sell, & P. Grunwell (eds.), *Management of cleft lip and palate* (pp. 365–78). London: Whurr.

Broen, P. A., Felsenfield, S., & Kittleson-Bacon, C. K. (1986). Predicting from the phonological patterns observed in children with cleft palate. Paper presented at the Symposium on Research in Child Language Disorders, Madison, Wisconsin.

Bzoch, K. R. (1979). *Communicative disorders related to cleft lip and palate.* Boston, MA: College Hill Press.

Chapman, K. L. (1993). Phonologic processes in children with cleft palate. *Cleft Palate-Craniofacial Journal* 30, 64–72.

Chapman, K. L., Hardin-Jones, M., & Halter, K. A. (2003). The relationship between early speech and later speech and language performance for children with cleft lip and palate. *Clinical Linguistics and Phonetics* 17 (3), 173–97.

Crystal, D. (1989). *Clinical linguistics.* London: Whurr.

CSAG Report – Clinical Standards Advisory Group (1998). *Cleft Lip and/or Palate.* London: HMSO.

D'Antonio, L. L. & Scherer, N. J. (1995). The evaluation of speech disorders associated with clefting. In R. J. Shprintzen & J. Bardach (eds.), *Cleft palate speech management: A multidisciplinary approach to the management of cleft palate* (pp. 176–220). St. Louis, MO: C. V. Mosby.

Eurocleft Speech Group (1993). Cleft palate speech in a European perspective: Eurocleft Speech Project. In P. Grunwell (ed.), *Analysing cleft palate speech* (pp. 48–82). London: Whurr.

Eurocleft Speech Group: Grunwell, P., Bronsted, K., Henningsson, G., Jansonius, K., Karling, J., Meijer, M., Ording, U., Wyatt, R., Sell, D., & Vermeij-Zieverink, E. (1994). A phonetic framework for the cross-linguistic analysis of cleft palate speech. *Clinical Linguistics and Phonetics* 8, 109–25.

Eurocleft Speech Group: Grunwell, P., Bronsted, K., Henningsson, G.,

Jansonius, K., Karling, J., Meijer, M., Ording, U., Wyatt, R., Sell, D., & Vermeij-Zieverink, E. (2000). A six-centre international study of treatment outcome in patients with clefts of the lip and palate. *Scandinavian Journal of Plastic Reconstructive Hand Surgery* 34, 219–29.

Frederickson, M. S., Chapman, K., & Hardin-Jones, M. (2006). Conversational skills of children with cleft lip and palate: a replication and extension. *Cleft Palate-Craniofacial Journal* 43 (2) (March), 179–88.

Gibbon, F., Crampin, L., Hardcastle, W., Nairn, M., Razzell, R., Harvey, L., & Reynolds, B. (1998). Cleft Net (Scotland): a network for the treatment of cleft palate speech using EPG. *International Journal of Language and Communication* 33 (Supplement, December), 44–9.

Golding-Kushner, K. J. (1995). Treatment of articulation and resonance disorders associated with cleft palate and VPI. In R. J. Shprintzen & J. Bardach (eds.), *Cleft palate speech management: A multidisciplinary approach to the management of cleft palate* (pp. 327–52). St Louis, MO: C. V. Mosby.

Golding-Kushner, K. J. (2001). *Therapy techniques for cleft palate speech and related disorders.* San Diego, CA: Singular.

Grundy, K. & Harding, A. (1995). Disorders of speech production. In K. Grundy (ed.), *Linguistics in clinical practice*, 2nd ed. London: Taylor & Francis.

Grunwell, P. & Harding, A. (1995). *PACS TOYS: A screening assessment of phonological development.* Windsor: NFER-Nelson.

Grunwell, P. & Sell, D. (2001). Speech and cleft palate/velopharyngeal anomalies. In A. C. H. Watson, D. A. Sell, & P. Grunwell (eds.), *Management of cleft lip and palate* (pp. 68–86). London: Whurr.

Hardcastle, W. J. & Gibbon, F. (1997). Electropalatography and its clinical applications. In M. J. Ball & C. Code

494 *Jane Russell*

(eds.), *Instrumental clinical phonetics* (pp. 149–93). London: Whurr.

Harding, A. (1993). Speech development related to timing of cleft palate repair. Unpublished PhD thesis, De Montfort University.

Harding, A. & Grunwell, P. (1993). Relationship between speech and timing of hard palate repair. In P. Grunwell (ed.), *Analysing cleft palate speech* (pp. 48–82). London: Whurr.

Harding, A. & Grunwell, P. (1996). Characteristics of cleft palate speech. *European Journal of Disorders of Communication* 31, 331–57.

Harding A. & Grunwell P. (1998). Active versus passive cleft-type speech characteristics. *International Journal of Disorders of Communication and Language* 33, 329–52.

Henningsson, G., Kuehn, D. P., Sell, D., Sweeney, T., Trost-Cardamone, J. E., & Whitehill, T. L. (2008). Universal parameters for reporting speech outcomes in individuals with cleft palate. *Cleft Palate-Craniofacial Journal* 45 (1) (January), 1–17.

Hewlett, N. (1990). Processes of development and production. In P. Grunwell (ed.), *Developmental speech disorders* (pp. 15–38). London: Whurr.

Howard, S. (2004). Compensatory articulatory behaviours in adolescents with cleft palate: comparing the evidence. *Clinical Linguistics & Phonetics* 18 (4–5), 313–40.

Howell, J. & McCartney, E. (1990). Approaches to remediation. In P. Grunwell (ed.), *Developmental speech disorders* (pp. 15–38). London: Whurr.

Hutters, B. & Bronsted, K. (1987). Strategies in cleft palate speech – with special reference to Danish. *Cleft Palate Journal* 24, 126–36.

Hutters, B. & Henningsson, G. (2004). Speech outcome following treatment in cross-linguistic cleft palate studies: Methodological implications. *Cleft Palate-Craniofacial Journal* 41 (5) (September), 544–9.

John, A., Sell, D., Sweeney, T., Harding-Bell, A., & Williams, A. (2006). The Cleft Audit Protocol for Speech – Augmented: A validated and reliable measure for auditing cleft palate speech. *Cleft Palate-Craniofacial Journal* 43 (3) (May), 272–88.

Jones, C. E., Chapman, K., & Hardin-Jones, M. A. (2003). Speech development of children with cleft palate before and after surgery. *Cleft Palate-Craniofacial Journal* 40 (1) (January), 19–31.

Kummer, A. W. (2001). *Cleft palate and craniofacial anomalies the effects on speech and resonance.* San Diego, CA: Singular.

Lees, M. (2001). Genetics of cleft lip and palate. In A. C. H. Watson, D. A. Sell, & P. Grunwell (eds.), *Management of cleft lip and palate* (pp. 87–104). London: Whurr.

Lynch, J. L., Fox, D. R., & Brookshire, B. L. (1983). Phonological proficiency of two cleft palate toddlers with school-age follow up. *Journal of Speech and Hearing Disorders* 48, 274–85.

McWilliams, B. J. (1984). Speech problems associated with craniofacial anomalies. In W. H. Perkins (ed.), *Recent advances: Speech disorders.* San Diego, CA: College Hill.

McWilliams, B. J., Morris, H. L., & Shelton, R. L. (1990). *Cleft palate speech,* 2nd ed. Philadelphia: B. C. Decker.

Mars, M. (2001). Facial growth. In A. C. H. Watson, D. A. Sell, & P. Grunwell (eds.), *Management of cleft lip and palate* (pp. 44–67). London: Whurr.

Mercer, N. S. G. & Pigott, R. W. (2001). Assessment and surgical management of velopharyngeal dysfunction. In A. C. H. Watson, D. A. Sell, & P. Grunwell (eds.), *Management of cleft lip and palate* (pp. 258–85). London: Whurr.

Morris, H. & Ozanne, A. (2003). Phonetic, phonological, and language skills of children with a cleft palate. *Cleft Palate-Craniofacial Journal* 40 (5), 460–9.

Moss, M. L. (1969). The primary role of functional matrices in facial growth. *American Journal of Orthodontics* 55, 566–77.

Nieman, G. S. & Savage, H. E. (1997). Development of infants and toddlers from birth to three years of age. *Cleft Palate-Craniofacial Journal* 34, 218–25.

Oblak, P. & Kozelj, V. (1984). Basic principles in the treatment of cleft at the University Clinic for Maxillofacial Surgery in Lubljana and their evolution in 30 years. In M. Hotz, W. M. Gnoinski, M. A. Perko, H. Nussbaumer, & E. Hof (eds.), *Early treatment of cleft lip and palate. Proceedings of the Third International Symposium.* Zurich: Hans Huber.

O'Gara, M. M. & Logemann, J. A. (1998). Phonetic analysis of the development of babies with cleft palate. *Cleft Palate Journal* 25, 122–34.

Pamplona, M. C., Ysunza, A., & Espinosa, J. (1999). A comparative trial of two modalities of speech intervention for compensatory articulation in cleft palate children, phonologic approach versus articulatory approach. *International Journal of Pediatric Otorhinolaryngology* 49, 21–6.

Persson, C., Lohmander, A., & Elander, A. (2006). Speech in children with an isolated cleft palate: a longitudinal perspective. *Cleft Palate-Craniofacial Journal* 43 (3) (May), 295–309.

Peterson-Falzone, S. J., Hardin-Jones, M. A., & Karnell, M. P. (2001). *Cleft palate speech*, 3rd ed. St. Louis, MO: Mosby.

Russell, J. & Albery, E. (2005). *Practical intervention for cleft palate speech*. Bicester, UK: Speechmark.

Russell, J. & Grunwell, P. (1993). Speech development in children with cleft lip and palate. In P. Grunwell (ed.), *Analysing cleft palate speech* (pp. 19–47). London: Whurr.

Russell, J. & Harding, A. (2001). Speech development and early intervention. In A. C. H. Watson, D. A. Sell, & P. Grunwell (eds.), *Management of cleft lip and palate* (pp. 191–209). London: Whurr.

Saal, H. M. (2001). The genetics evaluation and common craniofacial syndromes. In A. W. Kummer (ed.), *Cleft palate and craniofacial anomalies: The effects on speech and resonance.* San Diego, CA: Singular.

Scherer, N. J, Antonio, L. L., & McGahey, H. (2008). Early intervention for speech impairment in children with cleft palate. *Cleft Palate-Craniofacial Journal* 45 (1) (January), 18–31.

Sell, D. (2005). Issues in perceptual speech analysis in cleft palate and related disorders: a review. *International Journal of Language & Communication Disorders* 40, 103–21.

Sell, D. & Grunwell, P. (2001). Speech assessment and therapy. In A. C. H. Watson, D. A. Sell, & P. Grunwell (eds.), *Management of cleft lip and palate* (pp. 227–57). London: Whurr.

Sell, D., Harding, A., & Grunwell, P. (1994). A screening assessment of cleft palate speech: GOS.SP.ASS (Great Ormond Street Speech Assessment). *European Journal of Disorders of Communication* 29 (1), 1–15.

Sell, D., Harding, A., & Grunwell, P. (1999). Revised GOS.SP.ASS (98): Speech assessment for children with cleft palate and/or velopharyngeal disorders. *International Journal of Language and Communication Disorders* 34 (1), 17–33.

Sell, D., Mars, M., & Worrell, E. (2006). Process and outcome study of multidisciplinary prosthetic treatment for velopharyngeal dysfunction. *International Journal of Language and Communication Disorders* 41 (5), 495–511.

Shipster, C. (2004). Speech and language characteristics of children with craniosynostosis. In R. Hayward, B. Jones, D. Dunaway, & R. Evans (eds.),

The clinical management of craniosynostosis (pp. 270–98). London: MacKeith Press.

Shipster, C. Hearst, D., Dockrell, J. E., Kilby, E., & Hayward, R. (2002). Speech and language skills and cognitive functioning in children with Apert syndrome: A pilot study. *International Journal of Language and Communication Disorders* 37 (3), 325–43.

Shprintzen, R. J. (2000). Speech and language disorders in syndromes of craniosynostosis. In M. M. Cohen Jr. & R. M. MacLean (eds.), *Craniosynostosis diagnosis, evaluation and management*, 2nd ed. (pp. 197–203). New York: Oxford University Press.

Sparks, S. N. (1984). *Birth defects and speech-language disorders*. San Diego, CA: College Hill Press.

Tessier, P. (2004). Preface to R. Hayward, B. Jones, D. Dunaway, & R. Evans (eds.), *The clinical management of craniosynostosis* (pp. ix–xii). London: MacKeith Press.

Thompson, D. N. P. & Britto, J. (2004). Classification and clinical diagnosis. In R. Hayward, B. Jones, D. Dunaway, & R. Evans (eds.), *The clinical management of craniosynostosis* (pp. 12–44). London: MacKeith Press.

Watson, A. C. H. (2001). Embryology, aetiology and incidence. In A. C. H. Watson, D. A. Sell, & P. Grunwell (eds.), *Management of cleft lip and palate* (pp. 3–15). London: Whurr.

Whitehill, T. L. (2002). Assessing intelligibility in speakers with cleft palate: A critical review of the literature. *Cleft Palate-Craniofacial Journal* 39 (1) (January), 50–8.

Willasden, E. & Albrechtsen, H. (2006). Phonetic description of babbling in Danish toddlers born with and without cleft lip and palate. *Cleft Palate-Craniofacial Journal* 43 (1) (March), 189–200.

Wyatt, R., Sell, D., Russell, J., Harding, A., Harland, K., & Albery, E. (1996). Cleft palate speech dissected: A review of current knowledge and analysis. *British Journal of Plastic Surgery* 49, 143–9.

22 Speech Disorders Related to Head and Neck Cancer

Laryngectomy, Glossectomy, and Velopharyngeal and Maxillofacial Deficits

TIM BRESSMANN

1 Introduction

Head and neck cancer is a serious medical condition that can very quickly become life threatening. The diagnosis and the subsequent treatment will often drastically affect the patient's quality of life. The speech-language pathologist is an integral part of the patient's rehabilitation team. He or she can often have a significant positive impact on the patient's communicative function and well-being. The speech-language pathologist will also be involved in making important medical decisions related to the functional and communicative rehabilitation of the patient.

The speech disorders related to head and neck cancer are structurally related disorders of the speech mechanism. The focus of this chapter will be mainly on speech production. However, a short introduction to cancer and treatment approaches will be provided because many of the treatment sequelae are directly relevant to the work of the speech-language pathologist. It will also be necessary to refer to related areas such as swallowing and respiratory rehabilitation because, in many clinical settings, these will also be the responsibility of the speech-language pathologist (Logemann, 1994).

The medical treatment and the rehabilitation of the head and neck cancer patient require a multidisciplinary treatment team. In such a treatment team, all necessary professional disciplines are represented. The team members hold regular patient conferences and share information to achieve the best outcome for each patient. The team members typically consist of head and neck surgeons (including specialists for plastic and reconstructive surgery), radiation oncologists, radiologists, physical therapists, oncological nurses, dieticians, dentists, prosthodontists, psychologists, and speech-language pathologists (Machin & Shaw, 1998).

The Handbook of Language and Speech Disorders, First Edition. Edited by Jack S. Damico, Nicole Müller, and Martin J. Ball. © 2013 Blackwell Publishing Ltd except for editorial material and organization © 2013 Jack S. Damico, Nicole Müller, Martin J. Ball. Published 2013 by Blackwell Publishing Ltd.

1.1   Treatment philosophy and quality of life

Historically, cancer treatment was dominated by the intent to save the patient's life and to fight the cancer at all costs. Cancer surgery in the 1960s and 1970s was often radical, and the treatment team would accept serious sequelae and functional limitations if only the patient would survive. The development of reconstruction techniques with rotated flaps meant that even large defects could be covered and rebuilt. Older surgical textbooks sometimes demonstrate incredibly extensive resections with severely disfiguring and functionally extremely limiting recon-structions. As the surgeons and radiation oncologists were pushing their envelopes to the extremes, it became clear that the treatment "costs" to the patient in terms of function and general well-being often out-weighed the benefit of a slightly extended life span.

In the past two decades, the concept of "quality of life" has led to a paradigm shift in the concepts of cancer care. Obviously, patient survival is still paramount. However, the current philosophy is that the patient's survival and the resulting quality of life should be weighed against each other. This approach has coincided with a new generation of less invasive and more specific cancer treatments. Current cancer treatment is dominated by the concern for the well-being and dignity of the cancer patient (Chandu, Smith, & Rogers, 2006; Mehanna, 2007; Myers, 2005).

The treatment team is responsible for helping the patient make informed choices about the cancer treatment and the rehabilitation options. This involves a careful weighting of the patient survival and the expected functional limitations. The best treatment choices are individually different and depend on the patient's personal circumstances and preferences.

1.2   Cancer

In order to understand the nature of cancer, it is necessary to say a few words about cell biology. Cells in the body become cancerous because of changes to their deoxyribonucleic acid (DNA), which contains the genetic code. A cell propagates by copying its DNA and dividing itself into two new cells (mitosis). In order to shuffle out of each other's way or to fit into an anatomical structure, cells can move themselves around. Cell division, growth, differentiation, and movement are the basis of life (Kleinsmith, 2006). The DNA is copied millions of times throughout the cells in the body. Every cell relies on the information in the DNA to carry out its functions. The DNA also tells the cell when to self-terminate and to initiate the process of mitosis. Since the DNA is copied so many times, cells may sometimes end up with a faulty DNA. Usually, this is not a problem. The immune system recognizes faulty and atypical cells and destroys them. However, if a genetic mutation goes undetected or can withstand the immune system, the cells can propagate and a tumor may form.

Tumors can be benign or malignant. Benign tumors are characterized by uncon-trolled growth. The tumor is self-contained and does not invade other structures or metastasize. However, the unchecked growth of the tumor can lead to compression and damage in adjacent structures, so that treatment, such as a surgical resection, is often necessary. Malignant tumors are more complex and sinister. Like the benign tumors, these lesions are characterized by uncontrolled growth. However, these tumors also invade and infiltrate adjacent tissue. Malignant tumor cells can travel in the lymphatic system or the bloodstream to transport themselves to other organs in the body and cause distant metastases. This way, cells that are characteristic for a head and neck tumor can metastasize in the lungs and other internal organs. Because of their tendency to invade and infiltrate healthy tissue and their ability to migrate and metastasize, malignant tumors can quickly become life-threatening (Kleinsmith, 2006).

1.3   Causative factors

Head and neck tumors are relatively rare, and the tumor genesis is multifactorial. The main exogenic factors are often summarized as a triad of smoking, alcohol abuse, and poor oral hygiene (Brouha et al., 2005). Indeed, some patients with head and neck cancer have significant alcohol problems. This will sometimes lead to unfortunate stereotyping and generalizations about head and neck cancer patients by professionals. Casper and Colton (1998) summarize this stereotype as follows: "The typical person diagnosed with laryngeal cancer is a 60-year-old man who is a heavy smoker with moderate to heavy alcohol intake." We see little value in such sweeping generalizations and would urge the reader to treat each case of head and neck cancer on its own merit and without prejudice. There is evidence that at least a subgroup of patients will show an atypical etiology (Farshadpour et al., 2007; Goldstein & Irish, 2005). There are other factors that have been linked to the onset of head and neck cancer. These tumors may be caused by prolonged exposure to noxious substances such as chemicals or wood dust. Squamous cell carcinomas may also occur as a late effect of a syphilis infection.

1.4   Tumor diagnosis and staging

The diagnosis of cancer is always based on a biopsy and a histological evaluation of the tumor. Most head and neck carcinomas are of the malignant squamous cell type. These tumors will grow aggressively and invade and infiltrate the surrounding tissue. Squamous cell carcinomas also use the lymphatic system to migrate and metastasize in other organs. The severity of a tumor is classified according to the international tumor–node–metastasis (TNM) system (Wittekind & Sobin, 2002). The tumor is labeled as T0 (absent) to T4 (severe), depending on its size and location. Regional lymph node involvement is rated as N0 (absent) to N3 (large metastasis of one or more lymph nodes). Distant metastases are assessed as M0 (absent) or M1 (present). The tumor stage is then determined as a combination of the scores on the three scales, with Stage IV as the most severe category. The classification of a tumor on the TNM system helps the treatment team determine the optimum treatment plan for the patient. However, the TNM system cannot be used to make any predictions about functional limitations that may be associated with the tumor or its treatment.

1.5   Principles of cancer treatment

The focus of cancer treatment can be curative or supportive. Curative treatment aims at eradicating the tumor. Supportive treatment aims to reduce the patient's suffering from the illness. The curative treatment of cancer follows two general approaches. One approach is to resect the tumor. In this case, the surgeon also takes a safety margin in order to ensure that any cancer cells that have spread into the surrounding healthy tissue are removed. This approach is useful for tumors that are confined and that are in a location that is accessible for the surgeon. The alternative is to render the cancer cells useless. This is the treatment principle in radiation therapy or chemotherapy. The approach is useful for cancers that are surgically inaccessible, that have a diffuse location, or that have spread throughout the body. The treatment capitalizes on the fact that the DNA in cancer cells is inherently unstable and more vulnerable than in healthy cells. Since the cancer cells grow uncontrollably, they are in a constant state of mitosis. This means that their DNA is more often uncoiled and opened for transcription. If the cell is exposed to radiation or a noxious chemotherapeutic agent during mitosis, there is a higher likelihood that the DNA will be damaged beyond repair, which will effectively terminate the life cycle of the cell (Washington & Leaver, 2003). However, the radiation or chemotherapy will also stress and affect the surrounding healthy tissue. The art of radiation and chemotherapy is to stop the treatment at exactly the point when maximum damage has been inflicted on cancer cells but the side effects for the healthy tissue are still tolerable. The theoretical relationship between tumor control and tissue necrosis is often illustrated with a double sigmoid curve as shown in Figure 22.1. The figure shows that tissue necrosis increases exponentially as the radiation dose begins to show an effect on the tumor.

While the radiation damage of the surrounding healthy tissue is instantaneous, the effect is delayed by the mitotic cycles of the affected tissue. For example, skin and mucosa cells are undergoing very frequent cell division cycles. As a result, radiation dermatitis and mucositis are seen very soon during and after the treatment. On the other hand, muscle and bone tissue have considerably slower mitotic cycles. Consequently, it will often take years for muscle fibrosis or osteoradionecrosis to become apparent. The radiation treatment will usually be limited to a certain dosage. It is important to note that a dosage of 60–70 Gy constitutes a life limit. Once the patient has reached the life limit, he or she must not receive any more radiation therapy in this part of the body. If the cancer should recur, radiation therapy will no longer be a treatment option (Washington & Leaver, 2003).

In head and neck cancer, the choice of treatment is determined by the extent and location of the cancer. For example, the tongue is easily accessible for the surgeon, so that tongue tumors would usually be resected surgically. On the other hand, the larynx is more difficult to access. For small cancers of the larynx, the primary treatment approach is often a course of radiation therapy. Often, both approaches are used jointly: following the surgery, the patient undergoes a course of adjuvant radiation therapy to minimize the risk of recurrence. The radiation dose is usually delivered via external beam from an X-ray accelerator. The radiation

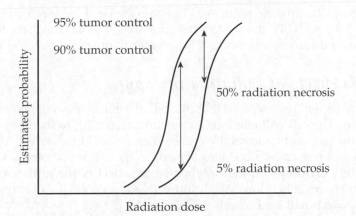

Figure 22.1 The double sigmoid curve model. The model illustrates the fine balance between tumor control and long-term radiation side effects. As the radiation dose increases over time, the cells in the radiated tissue start dying. This process can be expressed as a sigmoid function. The tumor cells are more vulnerable to the radiation. However, the surrounding healthy tissue is equally stressed by the radiation. The double sigmoid curve model allows the radiation oncologist to determine a theoretical cut-off point at which the tumor is largely controlled but the side effects are still tolerable for the patient.

oncologist will carefully determine the radiation fields and the doses in order to maximize the effect on the tumor while keeping the effect on the surrounding healthy tissue as low as possible. The treatment approach is sometimes changed for nasopharyngeal cancer. Nasopharyngeal tumors are often located deep in the skull and close to the brain. Radiating such a tumor with an external beam would cause unacceptable damage to the structures around the tumor. In such a case, loaded gold pellets are surgically implanted to deliver the radiation in situ (brachytherapy).

The overwhelming majority of head and neck cancers that affect structures in the vocal tract are squamous cell carcinomas. These tumors use the lymphatic system to spread and metastasize. When the tumor is removed surgically, the lymph nodes in the patient's neck are evaluated. If there is evidence that the cancer has spread to the lymph nodes, the surgeon performs a neck dissection. Based on the extent of the lymph node metastasis, the surgeon will perform a radical neck dissection and remove the lymph nodes, the associated veins, and the adjacent neck muscles (Cummings et al., 2004).

In recent years, highly localized chemotherapy and combined chemo-radiotherapy have been found to be effective new tools of treatment. Rather than exposing the patient to a generalized chemotherapy that will affect the whole body, these new approaches use cytostatic agents that have a very short half-life. This way, the chemotherapeutic agents deliver a maximum treatment effect to the tumor site while the effects on the rest of the organism are limited. High-dose radiation or radio-chemotherapy can reduce or eliminate the need for surgery and preserve the organ (Kelly, 2007). However, the potential loss of function following a high-intensity treatment can actually be greater than after a surgical resection.

1.6   Side effects of radiation therapy

When the radiation destroys the DNA in a cell, the effect does not become apparent immediately. The cell will continue to function according to its designation until it reaches the end of its normal life cycle, when mitosis is initiated. At this point, the DNA cannot be transcribed and copied, so the cell must perish. Cancer cells are constantly dividing and multiplying, so the effect of the radiation therapy is seen relatively quickly. However, healthy tissue adjacent to the tumor will be irradiated, which will lead to side effects for the patient.

Some of the side effects occur during or very early after the radiation therapy, such as mucositis, dermatitis, xerostomia (dry mouth), and dysgeusia (distorted taste). The mucositis and dermatitis are painful but usually resolve relatively quickly. The dysgeusia and xerostomia can be particularly bothersome to the patient. The dysgeusia causes foods to have an overly sweet taste, which can detract from the pleasurability of eating. The xerostomia is caused by damage to the salivary glands. The patient's mouth becomes dry and food cannot be properly lubricated for chewing and swallowing. The patient's mucous becomes stringy and sticky (Brosky, 2007). The dry mucous membranes can be colonized by fungi such as *Candida albicans*. Xerostomia can resolve after a few months but it can also be an unfortunate and irreversible long-term side effect. A number of manufacturers make artificial saliva sprays based on extracts of slippery elm bark. However, these products are expensive. Most patients contend themselves with constantly carrying a bottle of water, often laced with a pinch of baking powder to reduce the acidity in the dry mouth. The dry, irritated mouth is incredibly bothersome for the patient. It is possible to surgically relocate one of the sublingual salivary glands into the anterior oral cavity (Rieger et al., 2005; Seikaly, 2003; Seikaly et al., 2004). This procedure moves the gland out of the radiation field and ensures some salivary flow. However, the technique cannot be used for patients whose anterior oral cavity is in the radiation field.

Other radiation side effects take much longer to become manifest, such as muscle fibrosis, trismus (lockjaw), osteoradionecrosis (brittle and fragile bone), and radiation caries. Muscle and bone tissue have relatively slow cell cycles. If muscle tissue has been irradiated, it can become fibrotic and indurated over time. The muscle loses its flexibility and becomes stiff. In the case of the tongue, muscle fibrosis can lead to significant problems with speech, swallowing, and other oral motor functions (Harrison et al., 2003; Miller & Quinn, 2006). Muscle fibrosis of the masseter muscle can lead to trismus (lockjaw). This is a painful and bothersome condition for the patient. Stretching exercises can bring some relief (Cohen et al., 2005). However, the masseter is a very strong muscle and it will often be necessary to cut the muscle surgically in order to relieve the fibrosis. Osteoradionecrosis may weaken bones over time and lead to inflammations and fractures. The mandible in particular is very prone to osteoradionecrotic fractures.

Unfortunately, the irradiated bone loses the ability to heal on its own. It is possible to repair a fracture with a transplant but the results are often mixed. Irradiation of the teeth can lead to radiation caries, which is an extremely unfortunate condition. The enamel of the teeth becomes brittle and the teeth become impacted. It becomes very difficult to pull affected teeth because the dental root and the alveolar ridge will often be osteoradionecrotic so that pulling a tooth may break the patient's jaw. In order to avoid radiation caries, the patient's teeth must be carefully shielded with a customized mouth guard. If it is not possible to avoid exposure of the teeth, it is preferable to extract the teeth before the radiation therapy begins (Schweiger & Salcetti, 1986).

2 Total Laryngectomy

The larynx plays an important role in the regulation of airflow to and from the lungs. It also protects the airway against aspiration during eating and drinking. These are the primary, life-supporting functions of the larynx – voice production and speech are only secondary functions. In a total laryngectomy, the hyoid bone, the epiglottis, thyroid, arytenoid and cricoid cartilages are removed together with the upper one to three tracheal cartilages. In addition, a radical neck dissection may be performed. To ensure adequate ventilation of the lungs, the trachea is bent forward, and a permanent tracheostoma is created in the patient's lower neck, near the sternum (Figure 22.2). The pharyngeal walls are medialized and surgically joined with the hypopharynx and the upper esophageal sphincter.

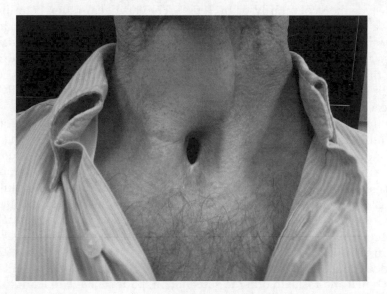

Figure 22.2 Permanent tracheostoma following total laryngectomy. The trachea and the esophagus have been completely separated, and the patient breathes exclusively through the tracheostoma.

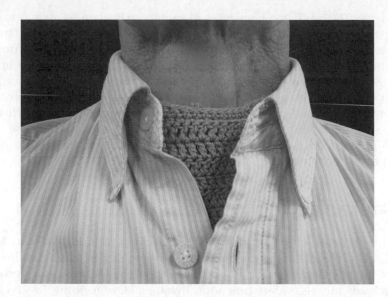

Figure 22.3   Tracheostoma cover. In order to protect the trachea from irritants and particles in the air, the stoma should be covered with a light, breathable fabric.

As a result of the total laryngectomy, the airway and the digestive tract are completely separated. This changes the physiology of the upper aerodigestive tract considerably. The consequences are most marked for respiration. The patient now breathes exclusively through the neck. This means that he or she cannot close the airway, either voluntarily or by reflex. The laryngeal reflex is an important protective mechanism to keep the airway patent. Laryngeal closure is also important to achieve thoracic fixation. Thoracic fixation is used to tense the body and build up muscle force during heavy lifting or to evacuate the bowel during defecation. Finally, thoracic fixation has an important role in maneuvers such as coughing. To cough out phlegm or secretions, the laryngectomee has to manually occlude and release the stoma.

Since the tracheostoma is always open, the patient has to be mindful of protecting the lungs from dust, particles, and bugs (Figure 22.3). The patient has to learn to take showers and wash hair in a different way because he or she could drown. A simple infectious respiratory disease such as a cold may quickly become a full-blown pneumonia. The patient has lost the filtering and humidifying functions of the upper aerodigestive tract. As a result, cold, dry weather will evaporate the heat and moisture from the lungs. Hot, humid weather may flood the lungs. Heat-moisture exchangers may alleviate these problems. These devices provide a barrier between the warm, moist air in the lungs and the colder, dry air outside (see Figure 22.4). Since the air does not pass through the nose or the mouth anymore, the patient loses the sense of smell and taste. In order to smell again, patients have to learn to circulate air between their oral and nasal cavities (Ackerstaff, Zuur, & Hilgers, 2007; Hilgers & Ackerstaff, 2005; Hilgers et al., 1991; Ward, Acton, & Morton, 2007).

Figure 22.4 Heat and moisture exchanger ("artificial nose"). A foam cushion inside the plastic casing of the heat and moisture exchanger serves as a barrier between the warm, moist air inside the lungs and the colder, drier air outside.

Following the laryngectomy, the patient will continue to eat orally. McConnel (1988) describes normal swallowing as a two-pump process. The first pump is a pressure pump. It is comprised of the tongue and the pharyngeal walls which empty the oral cavity and press the bolus into the hypopharynx. The second pump is a suction pump. During the swallow, the hyoid bone and the larynx move upward and forward. This stretches the upper esophageal sphincter (cricopharyngeus) and opens the esophagus. The esophagus has a negative resting pressure. The joint action of the two pumps ensures that the bolus is moved along quickly and that the pharyngeal phase of the swallow is completed in about a second. In the laryngectomee, the larynx and the hyoid have been removed. As a result, the cricopharyngeus cannot be opened actively. The patient loses the negative pressure pump and has to rely on the positive pressure from the tongue and the pharynx to empty the pharynx. If there is resistance in the upper esophageal segment, swallowing may become laborious, and multiple swallows may be required. On the other hand, if the upper esophageal sphincter is hypotonic, the patient may experience reflux.

2.1   Speech rehabilitation in total laryngectomy – artificial larynges

The electrolarynx was historically considered the default rehabilitation for laryngectomy patients. Today, many patients still rely on an electrolarynx as their main means of communication, and even patients who use esophageal or tracheo-esophageal speech will keep an electrolarynx as a back-up. The most common type of electrolarynx is the transcervical variety (Figure 22.5). The patient holds this electrolarynx against the neck. The device has an oscillator with a soft diaphragm that produces a low-frequency buzzing noise. When the diaphragm is held against the neck, the sound is transmitted into the vocal tract, and the patient can produce speech (Figure 22.6). The ideal coupling spot for the best sound transmission is different for every patient (Figure 22.7). It is important that the patient uses the residual air in the oral cavity to clearly articulate fricatives and plosives. The patient also has to learn to coordinate the buzzing of the electrolarynx with the phrasing (Doyle, 1994; Graham, 1997).

A limitation of the electrolarynx is its sound quality. The pitch is monotonous and unnatural (Meltzner & Hillman, 2005). Some electrolarynges offer two buttons with different frequencies that will allow the patient to place minimal prosodic accents. Nevertheless, the sound of electrolarynx speech is relatively robotic and may attract attention in social situations.

Not all patients can use transcervical electrolarynges because of scarring, induration, or tissue irritation related to the surgery or the radiation therapy. For these patients, an oral electrolarynx may be an appropriate choice (Figure 22.8). In this device, the sound is transmitted into the oral cavity through a plastic tube (Figure 22.9). The patient positions the end of the tube on the dorsum of the tongue

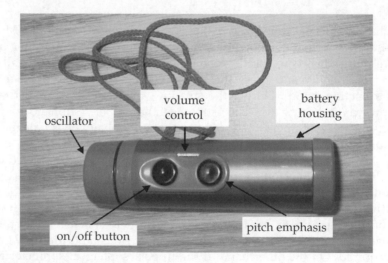

Figure 22.5   Transcervical electrolarynx.

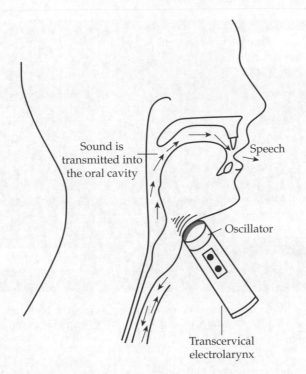

Sound is transmitted into the oral cavity

Speech

Oscillator

Transcervical electrolarynx

Figure 22.6 Sound production with a transcervical electrolarynx.

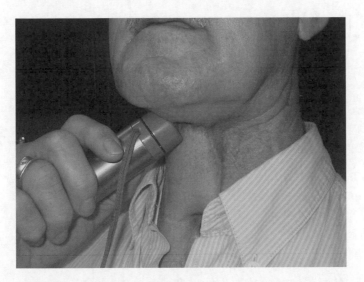

Figure 22.7 Position of the transcervical electrolarynx. Many laryngectomy patients have tissue scarring or radiation fibrosis on their neck, which may impede the sound transmission. The ideal coupling spot is individually different, and some patients may even prefer to hold the electrolarynx to the cheeks or the lips.

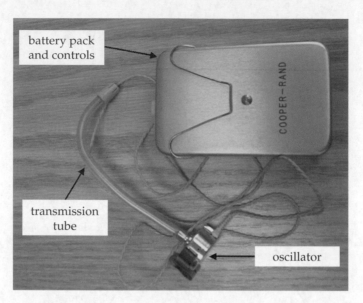

Figure 22.8   An oral electrolarynx. The metal box contains the batteries and the controls for the external oscillator. A tube is used to transmit the sound from the oscillator into the oral cavity.

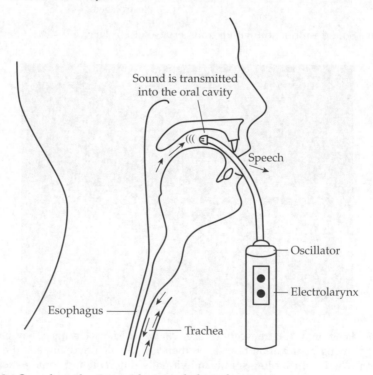

Figure 22.9   Sound production with an oral electrolarynx.

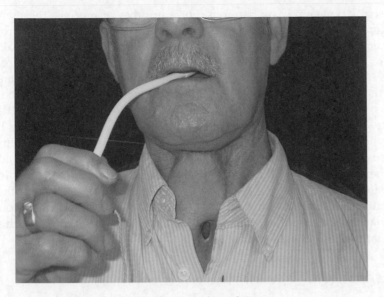

Figure 22.10 A laryngectomee using an oral electrolarynx.

and uses the sound from the oral electrolarynx to speak (Figure 22.10). The oral electrolarynx is more difficult to handle than the transcervical type. The movement of the tongue can attenuate the sound, so the patient will have to practice harder to achieve intelligible speech. Since the mouthpiece goes into the oral cavity, the patient has to be mindful of hygiene when he or she is around other people.

The design of the transcervical and the oral electrolarynx has remained remarkably unchanged since the first mass-produced models (Keith, Shanks, & Doyle, 2005). Since the sound waves from the electrolarynx have to penetrate the tissue of the neck, the signal has to be relatively loud and low in frequency to minimize signal attenuation. It would be possible to make an electrolarynx with multiple pitches and intonation contours. However, most laryngectomees prefer a simple on/off solution. Many of the patients are elderly and experience problems with eyesight and dexterity.

There also different designs for intra-oral electrolarynges. This device is integrated into a dental prosthesis, so the patient is usually edentulous. A handheld remote control regulates pitch and loudness of the device. The sound oscillator and the rechargeable battery are integrated into the prosthesis. Although the idea for such a device has been around for some time (Knorr & Zwitman, 1977), the intra-oral electrolarynx is currently not a common intervention. The cost of the device is high, and the sound projection is not better than that of a standard oral electrolarynx. Another recent line of research relates to the development of a hands-free electrolarynx. This device is worn like a collar and reads the electromyographic signals of the strap muscles of the neck, so that the device switches on automatically when the patent begins to speak (Goldstein et al., 2007).

All electrolarynges rely on batteries. For a number of models, these are expensive custom-made rechargeables. Like all battery-operated devices, electrolarynges may go flat at the wrong time and leave the patient in the lurch. An alternative design for an artificial larynx is the pneumatic larynx, which is powered by the patient's lungs. The patient covers the tracheostoma with a special adapter. The air flow that is diverted into the device moves a mechanical rattle, which produces a buzzing sound not unlike an electrolarynx. The sound from this rattle is then transmitted into the oral cavity via a plastic tube. The patient speaks as he or she would when using an oral electrolarynx. The pneumatic artificial larynx (sometimes also called a Tokyo larynx; Nelson, Parkin, & Potter, 1975) has the advantage that it does not rely on batteries. An added benefit is that the air pressure can be used to slightly modulate the pitch and loudness of the rattle, so that the patient has a better dynamic speaking range. Despite these advantages, the pneumatic artificial larynx is currently not in very wide use. It is more popular with speakers of tonal languages (Chalstrey et al., 1994).

2.2   *Esophageal[1] speech*

The larynx is the main sound generator in the hypopharynx. However, it is also possible to generate sound with the upper esophageal sphincter. One may normally experience this if gas has formed in the stomach and an air bubble forces its way up the esophagus. As the air passes through the upper esophageal sphincter, the airflow moves the edges of the cricopharyngeus, which results in a ructus, more commonly known as a burp. Esophageal speech uses a similar principle of sound production. An esophageal speaker insufflates the upper esophagus, just below the level of the upper esophegeal sphincter, and then expels the air in a controlled fashion (Figure 22.11). The resulting voice is rough and has a low pitch. The speaker has very little control over the volume and the pitch of the voice.

It should be noted that the sound production mechanism of esophageal speech is different from the common eructation. A ructus releases gas that has formed in the stomach and that is potentially foul-smelling and unpleasant. An esophageal speaker injects a small amount of air from the oral cavity into the upper esophagus. This air is then expelled in a voluntary and controlled fashion. The upper esophagus is just as clean and free of food as the pharynx or the mouth, so this method of sound production is not in any way unhygienic or unpleasant. It is important that this is properly explained to the patient and his or her caregivers to avoid prejudice or resistance against this method of speech rehabilitation.

There are two methods of insufflating air into the upper esophagus. Air can either be injected, using active pressure build-up in the oral cavity by maneuvers such as air swallows, glossopharyngeal pumping, or forceful articulation of an unreleased plosive such as [k]. If the patient seals the lips and the velum, the esophageal sphincter becomes the point of least resistance for the air pressure, and a bubble of air is injected into the upper esophagus. Alternatively, the patient can use an inhalation maneuver to fill the esophagus with air. Remember that the airway and the esophagus are completely separated in a laryngectomee, and that

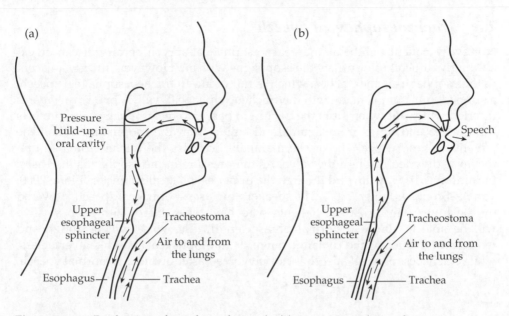

(a)

Pressure
build-up in
oral cavity

Upper
esophageal
sphincter

Tracheostoma

Air to and from
the lungs

Esophagus

Trachea

(b)

Speech

Upper
esophageal
sphincter

Tracheostoma

Air to and from
the lungs

Esophagus

Trachea

Figure 22.11 Production of esophageal speech. (a) Air is injected into the upper esophagus by building up pressure in the oral cavity; (b) as the air is ejected from the upper esophagus, it vibrates the upper esophageal segment and generates sound.

the patient breathes through the neck. The esophagus has a negative pressure at rest. When the patient inhales, the trachea expands, which stretches the esophagus and increases the negative pressure so that some air may flow below the level of the upper esophageal sphincter. Fluent esophageal speakers will use a combination of all these methods. An excellent speaker on a good day will produce up to ten syllables upon a single insufflation. A very good speaker will produce four to five syllables with ease. As in electrolarynx speech, the residual air in the oral cavity is used to differentiate plosives and fricatives (Doyle, 1994; Graham, 1997, 2005).

Speech-language pathologists often find that they are not very good models and teachers for esophageal speech. As a result, in many treatment centers, laryngectomees will work as esophageal voice teachers. This form of peer teaching is a very successful and motivating model. In North America, esophageal voice teachers are certified by the International Association of Laryngectomees. The standards and scope of the esophageal voice teacher's practice may vary between countries.

Esophageal speech requires regular practice, even in proficient speakers. Unfortunately, not every laryngectomee is able to produce good esophageal speech. The differences between good and poor esophageal speakers are the result of morphological differences rather than of practice. Fluent esophageal speech is simply not possible for many patients, and it is usually not for want of trying. It is important that the therapist recognizes when the patient has reached his or her physiological limit in order to avoid frustration (Doyle, 1994; Graham, 2005, 1997).

2.3   *Tracheoesophageal speech*

Not every patient will be able to learn esophageal speech because it can be exceedingly difficult to insufflate the esophagus with air. However, directly adjacent to the esophagus is the trachea, which is full of air. In tracheoesophageal speech, a surgical puncture is made into the tracheoesophageal wall. A one-way valve is inserted which allows air from the trachea to pass into the esophagus and protects the trachea and lungs from liquids and solids from the esophagus. When the patient wishes to speak, he or she manually occludes the tracheostoma so that the air is diverted through the valve. As the pressure in the esophagus increases, the air forces its way upward through the upper esophageal sphincter (Blom, 2000; Van As-Brooks & Fuller, 2007). The speaker now uses esophageal speech, powered by the lungs (Figure 22.12). Patients who have been fitted with such a valve will be able to speak in normal phrase length. The voice will be rough and reduced in frequency and dynamic range, as in esophageal speech. Nevertheless, while tracheoesophageal speech is not perceived as equivalent to normal speech,

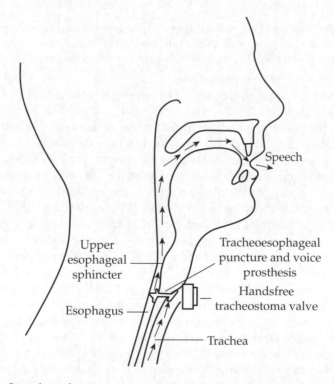

Figure 22.12   Sound production using a tracheoesophageal voice prosthesis. When the speaker occludes the tracheostoma (manually or with a hands-free speaking valve), the one-way valve inside the voice prosthesis allows air from the trachea to go into the esophagus and vibrate the upper esophageal sphincter.

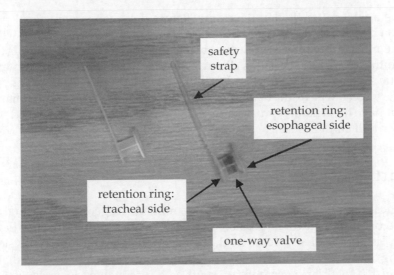

Figure 22.13   Tracheoesophageal voice prostheses.

it compares favorably to electrolarynx and esophageal speech (Clements et al., 1997; Williams & Watson, 1987).

The patient will only require minimal instruction on the use of the new voice. The main focus of the speech-language pathologist will be on device maintenance and safety. The tracheoesophageal puncture and the prosthesis need to be maintained meticulously in order to avoid aspiration. There are many different types of tracheoesophageal voice prostheses (Figure 22.13). These prostheses may differ in terms of the pressure required to open the one-way valve, and in terms of how long they can be worn. Tracheoesophageal voice prostheses are made by a number of different manufacturers. The type and size of the prosthesis is determined individually for every patient, so the speech-language pathologist should have a good understanding of the products available.

Unfortunately, there are a number of potential complications that may make it impossible for some patients to continue using a tracheoesophageal puncture prosthesis. A frequent complication is candidiasis, which leads to irritation of the tissue and can clog the tracheoesophageal prosthesis. Other severe complications may involve the formation of fistulas and granulomas (Izdebski et al., 1994). The tracheoesophageal prosthesis must have a certain opening resistance in order to prevent aspiration. As a result, a relatively high air pressure is needed in the trachea to open the prosthesis and insufflate the esophagus. Over time, the trachea and the neck of the patient may dilate, which may require additional corrective surgery.

Tracheoesophageal punctures can be performed as primary or secondary procedures. The primary tracheoesophageal puncture operations are performed together with the laryngectomy (Hamaker et al., 1985). The secondary operations are done a while after the laryngectomy. Before the tracheoesophageal puncture operation is performed, the surgeon or the speech-language pathologist will determine the muscle tone of the upper esophageal sphincter by injecting air through a tube into the upper esophagus (Blom, Singer, & Hamaker, 1985). A hypertonic or spastic segment will result in a laborious, strained voice quality. A hypotonic cricopharyngeus will result in a low, flaccid voice quality. If the cricopharyngeus does not have the desirable muscle tone, an operation can be performed to either loosen or tighten the muscle.

3   Partial Laryngectomies

As surgical techniques are becoming more refined, surgeons increasingly try to preserve organs as much as possible (Zeitels, 2005). The goal of a partial laryngectomy is to effectively remove the cancer while maintaining physiological breathing, swallowing, and voice production. From the perspective of the speech pathologist, a total laryngectomy presents as a reasonably clear scenario with a fixed set of rehabilitation options. Partial laryngectomies are more complex, and the surgical techniques and the outcomes are more variable. The learning curve may be steep for both the patient and the speech-language pathologist. The matter is further complicated by the fact that there are many different types of partial laryngectomies. While there are some general definitions, most surgeons will develop their own personal variations. The following descriptions of surgical procedures are listed as examples of the more typical procedures.

Unilateral cordectomy is a very circumscribed procedure. In this procedure, a carcinoma on a vocal fold is removed with a safety margin. This operation will usually not affect the anterior commissure or the ipsilateral arytenoid cartilage. Since the surgery is limited, the impact on voice quality and quantity is usually comparatively minor. If the tumor is more extended, it may spread around the anterior commissure, which requires a more extensive surgery. In an anterior commissure resection, the arytenoids are left in place. Most of the intrinsic laryngeal muscles attach to the arytenoid cartilage. Even if the vocal and muscular part of the thyroarytenoid are affected by a cordectomy or an anterior commissure resection, the patient can still control the position of the arytenoid and achieve some degree of laryngeal closure through the lateral cricoarytenoids and the interarytenoids. This will usually allow the patient to preserve relatively good function for speech and swallowing. If the tumor has spread too far posteriorly, the surgeon may choose to resect half of the larynx, which is called a hemilaryngectomy. In a hemilaryngectomy, the arytenoid is resected together with a complete vocal fold. The patient still has one vocal fold to interact with the scar tissue on the operated side. A more confined version of the hemilaryngectomy procedure where the arytenoid is left in place is sometimes called a vertical partial laryngectomy. The surgical results of these procedures may vary. Patients will often experience considerable glottal leakage, which may decrease the utterance length. If the residual vocal fold cannot achieve adequate glottal approximation, supraglottal compensation with false fold phonation may occur. The resected side will scar over time, which may lead to a decrease of the glottal opening. The most extensive form of partial laryngectomy is the supraglottic subtotal laryngectomy. In this procedure, all laryngeal structures above the vocal folds are removed (i.e., epiglottis, ventricular folds, hyoid bone, thyroid cartilage, and false folds). This leaves only the vocal folds and the arytenoids as the sole protection of the airway and as a source for voice production. However, the procedure changes the structure and function of the larynx drastically. Airway management and aspiration are frequent concerns, and many patients require a permanent tracheostoma. Despite the fact that the vocal folds and the arytenoids are left in place, voice quality and quantity are often poor. A more recent variation of this surgery is the supracricoid partial laryngectomy with cricohyoidoepiglottopexy. This surgery is a variation of the supraglottic laryngectomy in which the hyoid and the epiglottis are preserved. By pulling up the cricoid cartilage to the hyoid, patients achieve better swallowing safety and voice quality (Doyle, 1994).

3.1 Rehabilitation of the partial laryngectomee

Patients with partial laryngectomies require voice therapy in order to reestablish good phonation. Doyle (1994) observed that many patients react to a resection with hyperfunctional compensation. It is therefore important to use phonation and speech exercises that promote easy, relaxed phonation so that the hyperfunctional compensation will not consolidate. Most speech-language pathologists working with partial laryngectomees will use classic symptomatic voice exercises as described by Boone & McFarlane (2000). Appropriate exercises include tasks such as gentle humming, voiced lip trills, and chanting. If the patient cannot achieve complete glottal closure, activating exercises such as gentle pushing, hard vocal onsets, or the so-called "half-swallow boom" (a maneuver that attempts to transfer the vocal fold closure from swallowing to phonation) may be used. Some patients may benefit from posture adjustments such as head turns or from gentle digital manipulation of the larynx to achieve a better vocal quality. The voice therapy will usually start with vocalizations of single sounds (such as long vowels). Over time, therapy will progress to the word and sentence level. The therapist should also work on aspects of the vocal plasticity and the dynamic range. Secondary techniques, such as consonant over-articulation, can be used to promote better speech intelligibility despite a poor voice quality. Especially for patients with more extensive partial laryngectomies, the goals of the voice therapy are adjusted according to the severity of the defect, and a hoarse vocal quality is often an acceptable goal.

Another important phenomenon that partial laryngectomees often exhibit after the surgery is spontaneous glottal-ventricular phonation (also called oblique or crossed phonation). This phonation style can be compared to the singing voice of Louis Armstrong. In general, the speech-language pathologist should first attempt to re-establish phonation of the proper vocal folds. If the patient finds the mixed glottal-ventricular phonation easier to produce and if the resulting voice quality projects better than the true vocal fold phonation, the focus of the therapy should shift accordingly. Mixed glottal-ventricular or true ventricular fold phonation are effective for everyday communication and may constitute an appropriate therapy goal for patients with extensive partial laryngectomies.

4   Glossectomy

Cancer of the tongue is typically localized on the lateral tongue (Figure 22.14), on the underside of the tongue, on the anterior-lateral floor of the mouth, or in the retromolar trigone. Most lingual cancers are squamous cell carcinomas. The main treatment approach for cancer of the tongue or floor of the mouth is surgery. The tumor is removed *in toto*, if possible. In order to make sure that all pseudo-podia of the tumor are removed and to avoid recurrence, the surgeon also resects a safety margin around the tumor. Total glossectomy surgery (ablation of the complete tongue) is rarely performed today, and the term "glossectomy" is often used to denote a partial glossectomy.

When the tumor has been resected, a defect remains. The surgeon has a number of different options how such a defect could be closed. The surgeon may choose to let the resection site heal over by itself. A granuloma will form over the defect, and the tissue will scar over time. The orientation of the muscle fibers in the tongue will remain unchanged. This technique is used with relatively small defects. Alternatively, the surgeon may close the margins of the wound over

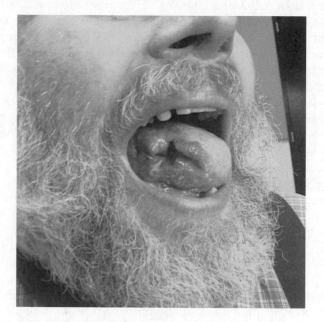

Figure 22.14   A large lateral lingual carcinoma.

the defect (primary closure). Since the defect margins are pulled together in the reconstruction, the orientation of muscle fibers may be altered. As a result, the direction of movement of the affected parts of the tongue may change. In a local flap closure, the surgeon uses tissue in the immediate or close vicinity of the defect. For example, the surgeon could use palatal or buccal mucosa to graft over very small defects. To close bigger defects, the surgeon can take larger muscles such as the platysma (a skin muscle in the neck), or the pectoralis muscle in the chest. These muscles can be rotated and brought up around the mandible to close lingual defects. It should be noted that one end of a local flap always remains attached to the point of origin. This ensures the blood supply of the flap tissue. Local flaps are an effective way to close a defect. The orientation of the muscles in the tongue is not changed. However, the flap adds dead weight to the tongue. Since the flap needs to remain attached to its point of origin, a poorly made local flap could potentially have a tethering effect. Finally, defects can also be closed with free flaps. The tissue for a free flap is lifted in another part of the body, such as the radial forearm or the inside of the thigh. Together with the flap tissue, the surgeon also takes several blood vessels from the donor site. These blood vessels are connected to the blood vessels in the resection site (anastomosis). This ensures the blood flow and survival of the free flap. The free flap allows the surgeon to recreate the shape and bulk of the original tongue. However, as in the local flap, the transplanted tissue does not have any active function and adds weight to the tongue (Matthews & Lampe, 2005). Figure 22.15 shows two lateral lingual defects with different defect reconstructions.

There are different theories about the surgical variables that determine post-operative speech and tongue function. It has been suggested that the extent (Rentschler & Mann, 1980), the site (Logemann et al., 1993; Michiwaki et al., 1993), or the reconstruction of the defect are the crucial factors (Konstantinovic & Dimic, 1998). While Imai and Michi (1992) argue that maintaining the motility of the tongue is more important than replacing its original volume, Kimata et al. (2003) state that the surgeon must create bulk. Pauloski et al. (1998) assessed the speech

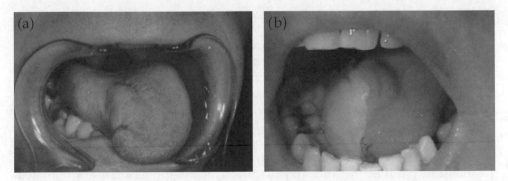

Figure 22.15 Comparison of two patients with lateral lingual resections of similar sizes. (a) Reconstruction using a local closure approach; (b) reconstruction using a radial forearm free flap.

and surgical results from 142 patients and concluded that the extent of the resection correlated with the decrease in articulatory precision, and that flap reconstructions lead to poorer outcomes than local closures. However, the defects that were closed with flaps were considerably larger than those closed locally. In over a decade's worth of data, Nicoletti et al. (2004) used an automated speech analyzer to assess speech production in 196 patients. Using correlation analyses, the authors demonstrated that larger resections lead to poorer speech results. Local reconstructions lead to better results than flap reconstructions when the group was analyzed as a whole but comparisons in location subgroups failed to differentiate between reconstructive techniques.

It is often difficult to predict the results of a glossectomy surgery (Mackenzie-Beck et al., 1998). It is expected that the resection will lead to a loss of lingual movement range, which will in turn result in articulatory undershoot and speech distortions (Korpijaakko-Huuhka, Söderholm, & Lehtihalmes, 1998). In a series of studies, Bressmann et al. (2005a, 2005b) used three-dimensional ultrasound to assess the impact of a partial glossectomy on the lingual biomechanics. Bressmann et al. (2007) found that a lateral lingual resection resulted in increased asymmetry and decreased midsagittal grooving of the tongue. The degree of decreased concavity for the individual speaker correlated moderately with the decrease in speech acceptability. Rastadmehr et al. (2008) demonstrated that a lateral resection led to an increased raising of the tongue in the oral cavity during speech. It was also found that the velocity of the tongue during a standardized reading passage increased after the operation. These findings were contrary to expectations because the loss of lingual tissue was thought to result in a loss of lingual movement range (Korpijaakko-Huuhka, Söderholm, & Lehtihalmes, 1998). However, it appears that the patients compensate with more speed and articulatory effort. This mirrors the process of hyperfunctional compensation that is often observed in patients with partial laryngectomies (Doyle, 1994). This increased effort may correspond to the changed patterns of cerebral activation in post-glossectomy speakers that were described by Mosier et al. (2005).

4.1   Rehabilitation of the partial glossectomee

The outcomes of glossectomy surgery are difficult to predict. The resulting defect is complex. Since the structure of the tongue is changed so drastically, some of the concepts of traditional phonetic articulation therapy (Bauman-Waengler, 2004) do not apply. As a result, the literature on glossectomy speech therapy is lamentably scant and there are almost no guidelines for therapy. Skelly's (1973) landmark book *Glossectomee Speech Rehabilitation* focuses on the acquisition of compensatory articulations in speakers with total or near-total glossectomies (see also Skelly et al., 1971). However, total glossectomy surgery is rarely performed these days, so many of the therapy strategies discussed in this publication are outdated. For patients with partial glossectomies, Skelly recommended the use of secondary compensatory strategies aimed at increasing speech intelligibility, such as modification of the vowel duration, intensity, rate and pitch range. None of these recommendations is geared toward an improvement of the articulatory skills. Appleton and Marchin (1995) inform about general aspects of head and neck cancer but dedicate only a few pages to speech rehabilitation. The authors recommend improving non-speech oral motor function by tongue exercises because better tongue motility is thought to result in better speech. Leonard (1994) gives a number of general recommendations on the improvement of speech intelligibility following glossectomy surgery. She recommends maximizing the mobility and motility of residual tissue. Articulatory targets must be reestablished within the movement capabilities of the partially resected tongue in order to improve the speaker's ability to achieve speech sound differentiation. Lazarus, Ward, and Yiu (2007) also stress the importance of non-speech tongue motility exercises. We would agree that tongue motility exercises are a good way to orient the patient to structures in the oral cavity. Unfortunately, in many health care systems, the time that the speech-language pathologist can spend with a glossectomy patient is limited. As a result, the tongue exercises will often be the only treatment patients will receive. We would argue that the specific and effective treatment of glossectomy speech is an area of speech-language pathology that still requires development and refinement.

While speech therapy for glossectomees aims at improving tongue function, prosthodontists have tried to compensate for the loss in speech and swallowing function through the design of individualized palatal augmentation (or palatal drop) prostheses. These prostheses facilitate linguo-palatal contact (Gillis & Leonard, 1983; Leeper et al., 2005; Leonard & Gillis, 1990; Logemann et al., 1989; Shimodaira et al., 1998). However, this approach has not become a standard treatment. In a systematic review, Marunick and Tselios (2004) found only nine studies that had evaluated the outcomes for a combined total of 50 patients between 1969 and 2003. The authors concluded that the use of palatal augmentation prostheses is not substantiated by enough scientific evidence.

5 Velopharyngeal Defects

The velopharyngeal sphincter is crucially important for the oral–nasal balance in speech. A number of muscles contribute to velopharyngeal closure in speech. According to the classic description by Fritzell (1969), the levator veli palatini elevates the velum and pulls it in a cranio-dorsal direction toward the posterior pharyngeal wall. Activity of the palatopharyngeus and palatoglossus medializes the lateral walls, which narrows the pharyngeal space (Moon et al., 1994). A number of patients also exhibit muscle bulges in the posterior pharyngeal wall. This phenomenon is called "Passavant's ridge" and is attributed to the pharyngeal constrictor muscles (Glaser, Skolnick, & Shprintzen, 1979). If a tumor affects the velum or the faucial arches, the tumor ablation may leave a defect, resulting in a hypernasal resonance disorder (Figure 22.16). Velopharyngeal dysfunction can be treated surgically, using procedures such as velopharyngoplasties or pharyngoplasties. However, many patients will have radiation damage in the

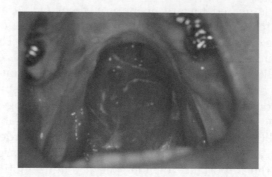

Figure 22.16   Patient with a complete resection of the velum.

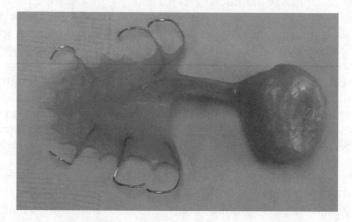

Figure 22.17   Speech bulb appliance.

velopharyngeal tract. The resection defects may often be quite extensive so that these patients are usually not considered good candidates for a surgical reconstruction. Therefore, the main approach to hypernasality in head and neck cancer patients is prosthodontic treatment. There are two types of prosthodontic appliances to support velopharyngeal closure. Palatal lifts are shoehorn-shaped appliances that serve to elevate a velum that is sufficiently long but does not raise adequately. Speech bulbs are used to partially fill the velopharyngeal space, so that the patient can use the lateral pharyngeal walls to make contact with the speech bulb and close off the pharynx (Figure 22.17). Often, the two designs are combined to maximize the effectiveness of the appliance. Neither palatal lifts nor speech bulbs can be made so big that they would fill the complete velopharyngeal sphincter because this would interfere with the nasal air passage and be exceedingly uncomfortable during swallowing. Therefore, speech therapy has a vital role following the fitting of a palatal appliance because the patient has to learn to actively use the appliance (Lazarus, Ward, & Yiu, 2007; Leeper et al., 2005).

6 Maxillofacial and Facial Defects

These areas are usually only of tangential interest to the speech-language pathologist. However, surgeons or dentists may sometimes wish to involve a speech-language pathologist in the rehabilitation of these patients. Maxillary defects involve the hard palate, with or without the alveolar ridge and the teeth. A maxillary fistula will result in nasal regurgitation and a hypernasal resonance disorder. The standard therapy for these patients is a maxillary obturator that fills the defect completely. This will usually solve the problem, often without further need for speech therapy (Rieger et al., 2003).

Maxillofacial cancers may sometimes affect the face. In rare cases, this may lead to large facial resection, sometimes including enucleation of an eye (Figure 22.18). Since the face is an important instrument for social interaction, the immediate impact on the patient's quality of life is often devastating. However, clinical experience shows that many patients will bounce back over time and regain an acceptable quality of life, despite the extreme severity of the defect. These patients will normally be treated with epitheses that cover the defect and normalize the facial appearance. Unless other structures in the vocal tract are affected as well, patients with facial resections will have normal articulation and communicate with good intelligibility. However, the resonatory characteristics of the skull can be changed as a result of the operation. The normal signal attenuation by the facial bones and tissue is missing and the patient has a new resonating chamber behind the epithesis.

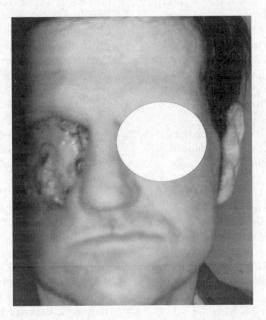

Figure 22.18 Patient with an extensive facial resection, including enucleation of the right eye.

Filling the space with gauze will provide a dampening effect and improve the sound of the voice quality to some extent.

ACKNOWLEDGMENTS

The author would like to thank Mr. Laurie Gallant, Ms. Rebecca Fleming, and Ms. Michelle Racine for their assistance with the drawings and the photography.

NOTE

1   Also found with the spelling *oesophageal*.

REFERENCES

Ackerstaff, A. M., Zuur, J. K. & Hilgers, F. M. (2007). Pulmonary function and rehabilitation. In E. C. Ward & C. J. van As-Brooks (eds.), *Head and neck cancer: Treatment, rehabilitation, and outcomes* (pp. 313–24). San Diego, CA: Plural.

Appleton, J. & Marchin, J. (1995). *Working with oral cancer*. Bicester, UK: Winslow.

Bauman-Waengler, J. (2004). *Articulatory and phonological impairments: A clinical focus*, 2nd ed. Boston, MA: Allyn & Bacon.

Blom, E. D. (2000). Tracheoesophageal voice restoration: origin – evolution – state-of-the-art. *Folia Phoniatrica et Logopaedica* 52 (1–3), 14–23.

Blom, E. D., Singer, M. I., & Hamaker, R. C. (1985). An improved esophageal insufflation test. *Archives of Otolaryngology – Head & Neck Surgery* 111 (4), 211–12.

Boone, D. & McFarlane, S. (2000). *The voice and voice therapy*. Boston, MA: Allyn & Bacon.

Bressmann, T., Uy, C., & Irish, J. C. (2005a). Analysing normal and partial glossectomee tongues using ultrasound.

Clinical Linguistics and Phonetics 19 (1), 35–52.

Bressmann, T., Thind, P., Uy, C., Bollig, C., Gilbert, R. W., & Irish, J. C. (2005b). Quantitative three-dimensional ultrasound analysis of tongue protrusion, grooving and symmetry: Data from 12 normal speakers and a partial glossectomee. *Clinical Linguistics and Phonetics* 19 (6–7), 573–88.

Bressmann, T., Ackloo, E., Heng C. L., & Irish, J. C. (2007). Quantitative three-dimensional ultrasound imaging of partially resected tongues. *Otolaryngology – Head and Neck Surgery* 136 (5), 799–805.

Brosky, M. E. (2007). The role of saliva in oral health: Strategies for prevention and management of xerostomia. *The Journal of Supportive Oncology* 5 (5), 215–25.

Brouha, X., Tromp, D., Hordijk, G. J., Winnubst, J., & De Leeuw, R. (2005). Role of alcohol and smoking in diagnostic delay of head and neck cancer patients. *Acta Oto-Laryngologica* 125 (5), 552–6.

Casper, J. K. & Colton, R. H. (1998). *Clinical manual for laryngectomy and head & neck cancer rehabilitation*, 2nd ed. San Diego, CA: Singular.

Chalstrey, S. E., Bleach, N. R., Cheung, D., & van Hasselt, V. A. (1994). A pneumatic artificial larynx popularized in Hong Kong. *The Journal of Laryngology and Otology* 108 (10), 852–4.

Chandu, A., Smith, A. C., & Rogers, S. N. (2006). Health-related quality of life in oral cancer: A review. *The Journal of Oral and Maxillofacial Surgery* 64 (3), 495–502.

Clements, K. S., Rassekh, C. H., Seikaly, H., Hokanson, J. A., & Calhoun K. H. (1997). Communication after laryngectomy. An assessment of patient satisfaction. *Archives Otolaryngology – Head Neck Surgery* 123 (5), 493–6.

Cohen, E. G., Deschler, D. G., Walsh, K., & Hayden, R. E. (2005). Early use of a mechanical stretching device to improve mandibular mobility after composite resection: A pilot study. *Archives of Physical Medicine and Rehabilitation* 86 (7), 1416–19.

Cummings, C. W., Haughey, B. H., Thomas, J. R., Harker, L. A., Robbin, K. T., Schuller, D. E., Flint, P. W., & Richardson, M. A. (2004). *Otolaryngology – head and neck surgery*, 4th ed. St. Louis, MO: Mosby.

Doyle, P. C. (1994). *Foundation of voice and speech rehabilitation following laryngeal cancer.* San Diego, CA: Singular.

Farshadpour, F., Hordijk, G. J., Koole, R., & Slootweg, P. J. (2007). Non-smoking and non-drinking patients with head and neck squamous cell carcinoma: A distinct population. *Oral Diseases* 13 (2), 239–43.

Fritzell, B. (1969). The velopharyngeal muscles in speech: An electromyographic and cineradiographic study. *Acta Otolaryngologica* 250, Supplement, 1–81.

Gillis, R. E. & Leonard, R. J. (1983). Prosthetic treatment for speech and swallowing in patients with total glossectomy. *Journal of Prosthetic Dentistry* 50 (6), 808–14.

Glaser, E. R., Skolnick, M. L., & Shprintzen, R. J. (1979). The dynamics of Passavant's ridge in subjects with and without velopharyngeal insufficiency. A multi-view videofluoroscopic study. *Cleft Palate Journal* 16 (1), 24–33.

Goldstein, D. P. & Irish, J. C. (2005). Head and neck squamous cell carcinoma in the young patient. *Current Opinion in Otolaryngology and Head and Neck Surgery* 13 (4), 207–11.

Goldstein, E. A., Heaton, J. T., Stepp, C. E., & Hillman, R. E. (2007). Training effects on speech production using a hands-free electromyographically controlled electrolarynx. *Journal of Speech, Language and Hearing Research* 50 (2), 335–51.

Graham, M. S. (1997). *The clinician's guide to alaryngeal speech therapy.* Boston, MA: Butterworth-Heinemann.

Graham, M. S. (2005). Taking it to the limits: Achieving proficient esophageal speech. In P. C. Doyle & R. L. Keith (eds.), *Contemporary considerations in the treatment and rehabilitation of head and neck cancer* (pp. 379–430). Austin, TX: Pro-Ed.

Hamaker, R. C., Singer, M. I., Blom, E. D., & Daniels, H. A. (1985). Primary voice restoration at laryngectomy. *Archives of Otolaryngology – Head and Neck Surgery* 111 (3), 182–6.

Harrison, J. S., Dale, R. A., Haveman C. W., & Redding, S. W. (2003). Oral complications in radiation therapy. *General Dentistry* 51 (6), 552–60.

Hilgers F. J. M. & Ackerstaff, A. H. (2005). Respiratory consequences of total laryngectomy and the need for pulmonary protection and rehabilitation. In P. C. Doyle & R. L. Keith (eds.), *Contemporary considerations in the treatment and rehabilitation of head and neck cancer* (pp. 503–20). Austin, TX: Pro-Ed.

Hilgers. F. J., Aaronson, N. K., Ackerstaff, A. H., Schouwenburg, P. F., & van Zandwikj, N. (1991). The influence of a heat and moisture exchanger (HME) on the respiratory symptoms after total laryngectomy. *Clinical Otolaryngology and Allied Sciences* 16 (2), 152–6.

Imai, S. & Michi, K. (1992). Articulatory function after resection of the tongue and floor of the mouth: Palatometric and perceptual evaluation. *Journal of Speech and Hearing Research* 35 (1), 68–78.

Izdebski, K., Reed, C. G., Ross, J. C., & Hilsinger, R. L. (1994). Problems with tracheoesophageal fistula voice restoration in totally laryngectomized patients. A review of 95 cases. *Archives of Otolaryngology – Head and Neck Surgery* 120 (8), 840–5.

Keith, R. L., Shanks, J. C., & Doyle, P. C. (2005). Historical highlights: Laryngectomy rehabilitation. In P. C. Doyle & R. L. Keith (eds.), *Contemporary considerations in the treatment and rehabilitation of head and neck cancer* (pp. 17–57). Austin, TX: Pro-Ed.

Kelly, L. E. (2007). Radiation and chemotherapy. In E. C. Ward & C. J. van As-Brooks (eds.), *Head and neck cancer: Treatment, rehabilitation, and outcomes* (pp. 57–86). San Diego, CA: Plural.

Kimata, Y., Sakuraba, M., Hishinuma, S., Ebihara, S., Hayashi, R., Asakage, T., Nakatsuka, T., & Harii, K. (2003). Analysis of the relations between the shape of the reconstructed tongue and postoperative functions after subtotal or total glossectomy. *Laryngoscope* 113 (5), 905–9.

Kleinsmith, L. J. (2006). *Principles of cancer biology.* San Francisco, CA: Pearson Benjamin Cummings.

Knorr, S. G. & Zwitman, D. H. (1977). The design of a wireless-controlled intra-oral electrolarynx. *Journal of Bioengineering* 1 (3), 165–71.

Konstantinovic, V. S. & Dimic, N. D. (1998). Articulatory function and tongue mobility after surgery followed by radiotherapy for tongue and floor of the mouth cancer patients. *British Journal of Plastic Surgery* 51 (8), 589–93.

Korpijakko-Huuhka, A. M., Söderholm, A. L., & Lehtihalmes, M. (1998). Long-lasting speech and oral-motor deficiencies following oral cancer surgery: A retrospective study. *Logopaedics, Phoniatrics and Vocology* 24 (3), 97–106.

Lazarus, C. L., Ward, E. C., & Yiu, E. M. (2007). Speech and swallowing following oral, oropharyngeal, and nasopharyngeal cancers. In E. C. Ward & C. J. van As-Brooks (eds.), *Head and neck cancer: Treatment, rehabilitation, and outcomes* (pp. 103–22). San Diego, CA: Plural.

Leeper, H. A., Gratton, D. G., Lapointe, H. J., & Armstrong, J. E. A. (2005). Maxillofacial rehabilitation for oral cancer: Surgical, prosthodontic and communication aspects of management. In P. C. Doyle & R. L. Keith (eds.), *Contemporary considerations in the treatment and rehabilitation of head and neck cancer* (pp. 261–314). Austin, TX: Pro-Ed.

Leonard, R. J. (1994). Characteristics of speech in speakers with glossectomy and other oral/oropharyngeal ablation. In J. E. Bernthal & N. W. Bankson (eds.), *Child phonology: Characteristics, assessment, and intervention with special populations* (pp. 54–78). New York: Thieme.

Leonard, R. J. & Gillis, R. (1990). Differential effects of speech prostheses in glossectomized patients. *Journal of Prosthetic Dentistry* 64 (6), 701–8.

Logemann, J. A. (1994). Rehabilitation of the head and neck cancer patient. *Seminars in Oncology* 21 (3), 359–65.

Logemann, J. A., Kahrilas, P. J., Hurst, P., Davis, J., & Krugler, C. (1989). Effects of intraoral prosthetics on swallowing in patients with oral cancer. *Dysphagia* 4 (2), 118–20.

Logemann, J. A., Pauloski, B. R., Rademaker, A. W., McConnel, F. M., Heiser, M. A., Cardinale, S., Shedd, D., Stein, D., Beery, Q., Johnson, J., & Lewin, J. (1993). Speech and swallow function after tonsil/base of tongue resection with primary closure. *Journal of Speech and Hearing Research* 36 (5), 918–26.

Machin, J. & Shaw, C. (1998). A multidisciplinary approach to head and neck cancer. *European Journal of Cancer Care* 7 (2), 93–6.

Mackenzie-Beck, J., Wrench, A., Jackson, M., Soutar, D., Robertson, A. G., & Laver, J. (1998). Surgical mapping and phonetic analysis in intra-oral cancer. In W. Ziegler & K. Deger (eds.), *Clinical phonetics and linguistics* (pp. 481–92). London: Whurr.

Marunick, M. & Tselios, N. (2004). The efficacy of palatal augmentation prostheses for speech and swallowing in patients undergoing glossectomy: A review of the literature. *Journal of Prosthetic Dentistry* 91 (1), 67–74.

Matthews, T. W. & Lampe, H. B. (2005). Treatment options in oral cancer. In P. C. Doyle & R. L. Keith (eds.), *Contemporary considerations in the treatment and rehabilitation of head and neck cancer* (pp. 153–70). Austin, TX: Pro-Ed.

McConnel, F. M. (1988). Analysis of pressure generation and bolus transit during pharyngeal swallowing. *Laryngoscope* 98 (1), 71–8.

Mehanna, H. M. (2007). Will measuring quality of life in head and neck cancer alter individuals' treatment? *Current Opinions in Otolaryngology – Head and Neck Surgery* 15 (2), 57–62.

Meltzner, G. S. & Hillman, R. E. (2005). Impact of aberrant acoustic properties on the perception of sound quality in electrolarynx speech. *Journal of Speech, Language and Hearing Research* 48 (4), 766–79.

Michiwaki, Y., Schmelzeisen, R., Hacki, T., & Michi, K. (1993). Functional effects of a free jejunum flap used for reconstruction in the oropharyngeal region. *Journal of Craniomaxillofacial Surgery* 21 (4), 153–6.

Miller, E. H. & Quinn, A. I. (2006). Dental considerations in the management of head and neck cancer patients. *Otolaryngological Clinics of North America* 39 (2), 319–29.

Moon, J. B., Smith, A. E., Folkins, J. W., Lemke, J. H., & Gartlan, M. (1994). Coordination of velopharyngeal muscle activity during positioning of the soft palate. *Cleft Palate-Craniofacial Journal* 31 (1), 45–55.

Mosier, K., Liu, W. C., Behin, B., Lee, C., & Baredes, S. (2005). Cortical adaptation following partial glossectomy with primary closure: Implications for reconstruction of the oral tongue. *Annals of Otology, Rhinology and Laryngology* 114 (9), 681–7.

Myers, C. (2005). Quality of life in head and neck cancer. In P. C. Doyle & R. L. Keith (eds.), *Contemporary considerations in the treatment and rehabilitation of head and neck cancer* (pp. 697–736). Austin, TX: Pro-Ed.

Nelson, I. W., Parkin, J. L., & Potter, J. F. (1975). The modified Tokyo larynx: An improved pneumatic speech aid. *Archives of Otolaryngology* 101 (2), 107–8.

Nicoletti, G., Soutar, D. S., Jackson, M. S., Wrench, A. A., Robertson, G., & Robertson, C. (2004). Objective assessment of speech after surgical treatment for oral cancer: Experience from 196 selected cases. *Plastic and Reconstructive Surgery* 113 (1), 114–25.

Pauloski, B. R., Logemann, J. A., Colangelo, L. A., Rademaker, A. W., McConnel, F. M., Heiser, M. A., Cardinale, S., Shedd, D., Stein, D., Beery, Q., Myers, E., Lewin, J., Haxer, M., & Esclamado, R. (1998).

Surgical variables affecting speech in treated patients with oral and oropharyngeal cancer. *Laryngoscope* 108 (6), 908–16.

Rastadmehr, O., Bressmann, T., Smyth, R., & Irish, J. C. (2008). Increased tongue velocity indicates articulatory compensation in speakers with partial glossectomies. *Head and Neck*.

Rentschler, G. J. & Mann, M. B. (1980). The effects of glossectomy on intelligibility of speech and oral perceptual discrimination. *Journal of Oral Surgery* 38 (5), 348–54.

Rieger, J., Seikaly, H., Jha, N., Harris, J., Williams, D., Liu, R., McGaw, T., & Wolfaardt, J. F. (2005). Submandibular gland transfer for prevention of xerostomia after radiation therapy: Swallowing outcomes. *Archives of Otolaryngology – Head and Neck Surgery* 131 (2), 140–5.

Rieger, J. M., Wolfaardt, J. F., Jha, N., & Seikaly, H. (2003). Maxillary obturators: The relationship between patient satisfaction and speech outcome. *Head and Neck* 25 (11) (November), 895–903.

Schweiger, J. W. & Salcetti, M. A. (1986). Dental management of the geriatric head and neck cancer patient. *Gerodontology* 5 (2), 119–22.

Seikaly, H. (2003). Xerostomia prevention after head and neck cancer treatment. *Archives of Otolaryngology – Head and Neck Surgery* 129 (2), 250–1.

Seikaly, H., Jha, N., Harris, J. R., Barnaby, P., Liu, R., Williams, D., McGaw, T., Rieger, J., Wolfaardt, J. F., & Hanson, J. (2004). Long-term outcomes of submandibular gland transfer for prevention of postradiation xerostomia. *Archives of Otolaryngology – Head and Neck Surgery* 130 (8), 956–61.

Shimodaira, K., Yoshida, H., Yusa, H., & Kanazawa, T. (1998). Palatal augmentation prosthesis with alternative palatal vaults for speech and swallowing: A clinical report. *Journal of Prosthetic Dentistry* 80 (1), 1–3.

Skelly, M. (1973). *Glossectomee speech rehabilitation*. Springfield, IL: Thomas.

Skelly, M., Spector, D. J., Donaldson, R. C., Brodeur, A., & Paletta, F. X. (1971). Compensatory physiologic phonetics for the glossectomee. *Journal of Speech and Hearing Disorders* 36 (1), 101–14.

Van As-Brooks, C. & Fuller, D. P. (2007). Prosthetic tracheoesophageal voice restoration following total laryngectomy. In E. C. Ward & C. J. van As-Brooks (eds.), *Head and neck cancer: Treatment, rehabilitation, and outcomes* (pp. 229–66). San Diego, CA: Plural.

Ward, E. C., Acton, L. M., & Morton, A.-L. (2007). Stoma care and appliances. In E. C. Ward & C. J. van As-Brooks (eds.), *Head and neck cancer: Treatment, rehabilitation, and outcomes* (pp. 229–66). San Diego, CA: Plural.

Washington, C. M. & Leaver, T. (2003). *Principles and practice of radiation therapy*. St. Louis, MO: Mosby.

Williams, S. E. & Watson, J. B. (1987). Speaking proficiency variations according to method of alaryngeal voicing. *Laryngoscope* 97 (6), 737–9.

Wittekind, C. & Sobin, L. H. (2002). *TNM classification of malignant tumours*. New York: Wiley-Liss.

Zeitels, S. M. (2005). Recent advances in the surgical treatment of laryngeal cancer. In P. C. Doyle & R. L. Keith (eds.), *Contemporary considerations in the treatment and rehabilitation of head and neck cancer* (pp. 171–94). Austin, TX: Pro-Ed.

Part IV Cognitive and Intellectual Disorders

23 ADHD and Communication Disorders

CAROL WESTBY AND SILVANA WATSON

1 Introduction

The incidence and increasing awareness of attention-deficit/hyperactivity disorder (ADHD) in our educational systems and the expectation that speech-language pathologists have a role in its intervention ensure that clinicians will encounter many children with ADHD. Children identified initially as having specific language impairments frequently are later identified as also having ADHD. Many children with ADHD exhibit delays in language development and later communication difficulties that affect their social and academic performance. Understanding the inter-relationships of language and ADHD requires an understanding of the nature of both ADHD and types of language impairments. Neither ADHD nor language impairments are single constructs. Different types of language impairments are associated with different types of ADHD.

2 What Is ADHD?

2.1 Diagnosis of ADHD

The Diagnostic and Statistical Manual (DSM IV-TR) (American Psychiatric Association, 2000) lists nine characteristics of inattention and nine characteristics of hyperactivity/impulsivity (see Table 23.1). Diagnosis of ADHD requires that children exhibit at least six of these 18 behaviors in either the inattention category or the hyperactivity/impulsivity category. The symptoms must have been present for at least 6 months, occur to a degree that is developmentally deviant, and must have developed before the age of 7 years. The type of ADHD that is diagnosed depends on whether criteria are met for inattention, hyperactivity/impulsivity, or both – the predominantly inattentive type (ADHD-PI), the predominantly hyperactive-impulsive type (ADHD-PHI), or the combined type (ADHD-C).

The Handbook of Language and Speech Disorders, First Edition. Edited by Jack S. Damico, Nicole Müller, and Martin J. Ball. © 2013 Blackwell Publishing Ltd except for editorial material and organization © 2013 Jack S. Damico, Nicole Müller, Martin J. Ball. Published 2013 by Blackwell Publishing Ltd.

Table 23.1   DSM-IV-TR criteria for ADHD

A. Either (1) or (2)

(1)   Six (or more) of the following symptoms of inattention have persisted for at least 6 months to a degree that is maladaptive and inconsistent with developmental level:

Inattention
(a)   Often fails to give close attention to details or makes careless mistakes in schoolwork, work, or other activities.
(b)   Often has difficulty sustaining attention in tasks or play activities.
(c)   Often does not seem to listen when spoken to directly.
(d)   Often does not follow through on instructions and fails to finish schoolwork, chores, or duties in the workplace (not due to oppositional behavior or failure to understand instructions).
(e)   Often has difficulty organizing tasks and activities.
(f)   Often avoids, dislikes, or is reluctant to engage in tasks that require sustained mental effort (such as schoolwork or homework).
(g)   Often loses things necessary for tasks or activities (e.g., toys, school assignments, pencils, books, or tools).
(h)   Is often easily distracted by extraneous stimuli.
(i)   Is often forgetful in daily activities.

(2)   Six (or more) of the following symptoms of hyperactivity-impulsivity have persisted for at least 6 months to a degree that is maladaptive and inconsistent with developmental level:

Hyperactivity
(a)   Often fidgets with hands or feet or squirms in seat.
(b)   Often leaves seat in classroom or in other situations in which remaining seated is expected
(c)   Often runs about or climbs excessively in situations in which it is inappropriate (in adolescents or adults, may be limited to subjective feelings of restlessness).
(d)   Often has difficulty playing or engaging in leisure activities quietly.
(e)   Is often "on the go" or often acts as if "driven by a motor."
(f)   Often talks excessively.

Impulsivity
(g)   Often blurts out answers before questions have been completed.
(h)   Often has difficulty awaiting turn.
(i)   Often interrupts or intrudes on others (e.g., butts into conversations or games).

Table 23.1 *(Cont'd)*

B. Some hyperactive-impulsive or inattentive symptoms that caused impairment were present before 7 years.

C. Some impairment from symptoms is present in two or more settings (e.g., at school [or work] and at home).

D. There must be clear evidence of clinically significant impairment in social, academic, or occupational functioning.

E. The symptoms do not occur exclusively during the course of a pervasive developmental disorder, schizophrenia, or other psychotic disorder, and are not better accounted for by another mental disorder (e.g., mood disorder, anxiety disorder, dissociative disorder, or a personality disorder).

Specify type:

- *Attention-Deficit/Hyperactivity Disorder, Combined Type*: if both Criteria A1 and A2 are met for the past 6 months.
- *Attention-Deficit/Hyperactivity Disorder, Predominantly Inattentive Type*: if Criterion A1 is met but Criterion A2 is not met for the past 6 months.
- *Attention-Deficit/Hyperactivity Disorder, Predominantly Hyperactive-Impulsive Type*: If Criterion A2 is met but Criterion A1 is not met for the past 6 months.

At the time of writing this chapter, work is beginning on the DSM-V. High on the list of changes to the diagnostic criteria for ADHD are separation of the inattentive subtype of ADHD from other subtypes (Milich, Balentine, & Lynam, 2001) and a liberalizing of the age-of-onset criteria (McGough & Barkley, 2004). The two symptom clusters as described in DSM-IV-TR (inattention and hyperactivity-impulsivity) are thought to be distinct in terms of their etiology, clinical course, associated/co-morbid conditions, response to treatment, and outcomes. There is some indication that the inattention in ADHD-C is not exactly the same as the inattention in ADHD-PHI. Children with ADHD-PI have more problems with focused/selective attention, lethargy, daydreaming, social withdrawal, and sluggish information processing, whereas children with ADHD-C have more problems with persistence of effort and distractibility (McBurnett, Pfiffner, & Frick, 2001). All types of ADHD are associated with executive dysfunction. In general, the inattentive type of ADHD is thought to be more associated with processing disorders and internalizing disorders such as reading, language-learning disabilities, and anxiety; and the impulsive-hyperactive type is thought to be more associated with externalizing disorders such as oppositional defiant disorder and conduct disorders. The combined hyperactivity/impulsive and inattentive groups demonstrate the most severe problems in all areas.

2.2   ADHD across cultures

ADHD, one of the most common neurobehavioral disorders of childhood, exists across cultures (Remschmidt, 2005). Although different cultures have different interpretations, tolerance, expectations, and perceptions of behaviors, studies conducted with participants from different ethnic, geographic, and cultural backgrounds strongly suggest that ADHD is a disorder that has cross-cultural validity (Bauermeister et al., 2004; Meyer et al., 2004; Rohde et al., 2005). The diagnostic symptoms of ADHD are listed in the *International Classification of Diseases*, now in its 10th revision (ICD-10; World Health Organization, 2005), under the term *hyperkinetic disorder* (HKD). Those symptoms are very similar to the symptoms of ADHD listed in the *Diagnostic and Statistical Manual of Mental Disorders, 4th edition – Revised* (DSM-IV-TR), the official categorization system of the American Psychiatric Association (American Psychiatric Association, 2000). ICD-10 criteria for the diagnosis of HKD are more severe and conservative than the DSM-IV-TR, requiring at least 10 of the 18 symptoms for a diagnosis. The HKD diagnosis is similar to the DSM-IV-TR diagnosis of the combined-type of ADHD without co-morbid conditions (Remschmidt, 2005; Yang, Schaller, & Parker, 2000). Although criteria for normal and deviant behaviors are culturally determined, the patterns of ADHD/HKD symptoms that form the basis for diagnosis share many similarities in both systems, showing cross-cultural agreement on the classification of the ADHD/HKD behaviors (Meyer et al., 2004; Remschmidt, 2005; Rohde et al., 2005; Yang, Schaller, & Parker, 2000).

Notwithstanding the strong supportive evidence for the validity of ADHD as a neurobehavioral disorder across cultures, it continues to be under-diagnosed and untreated in many countries and cultures (Minnis et al., 2003; Remschmidt, 2005). As part of the search for an explanation, researchers from the USA and other countries (e.g., Leslie et al., 2005; Minnis et al., 2003; Perry, Hatton, & Kendall, 2005; Roberts et al., 2005) have investigated the barriers encountered by different ethnic/racial, cultural, and geographic groups to assessment, diagnosis, and treatment of ADHD and other mental health services. The findings of those studies suggest as possible causes for under-utilization of mental health services (a) lack of parental understanding and recognition of a child's problems, (b) cultural differences on which behaviors are considered dysfunctional or deviant, (c) financial difficulties and lack of insurance or benefits, (d) language barriers, (e) lack of culturally sensitive services, and (f) lack of belief in the effectiveness of treatments. Certainly these findings have important implications for those working with children with ADHD and their families. It is important to understand the children and their families within the context of their culture, values, beliefs, and financial abilities.

3   The Nature of ADHD

Despite the designation of attention deficit, ADHD is not primarily a disorder of attention. Barkley (1997) noted a number of behaviors associated with ADHD that cannot be explained by poor attention:

- poor persistence of effort;
- poor compliance to parental and teacher commands;
- diminished delay of gratification;
- reduced tolerance for delay periods;
- excessive activity;
- greater variability of behavior and work;
- hyper-responsive to environmental events;
- delayed internalization of speech;
- poor working memory;
- delayed motor coordination and motor control;
- deficient verbal fluency;
- diminished sensitivity to reinforcement and punishment;
- poor emotional self-regulation.

Barkley (1990) concluded that poor regulation and inhibition are the hallmarks of ADHD. Based on this conceptualization, Barkley (1990, p. 71) defined ADHD as consisting of "developmental deficiencies in the regulation and maintenance of behavior by rules and consequences. These deficiencies give rise to problems with inhibiting, initiating, or sustaining responses to tasks or stimuli and adhering to rules or instructions, particularly in situations where consequences for such behavior are delayed, weak, or nonexistent."

   This definition of ADHD has significant implications for how the social and academic deficits of children with ADHD are understood and treated. Barkley (2005) proposed a theory to explain the link that exists between poor behavioral inhibition (hyperactivity-impulsivity) and inattention. Barkley's theory links the dimensions of hyperactivity-impulsivity and inattention with the concept of executive or metacognitive functions because most, if not all, of the impairments associated with ADHD are in the realm of self-regulation or executive functions (Brown, 2006; Denkla, 1994; Pennington & Ozonoff, 1996; Wilcutt et al., 2005). Behavioral inhibition is the first component in Barkley's model and the foundation for executive functions that shift control of behavior from the external environment to control of behavior by internally represented information. Behavioral inhibition enables individuals to:

- inhibit the urge to act on the moment;
- inhibit ongoing responses that are proving to be ineffective – being sensitive to errors and shifting to more effective responses;

- inhibit responses to task-irrelevant events, known as interference control or avoiding distractibility.

These aspects of behavioral inhibition provide the critical support for the use of four components of executive function (non-verbal working memory, verbal working memory, emotional control, and problem solving) that are essential for management or self-regulation of behavior. Working memory enables the ability to hold several facts or pieces of information in mind while solving a problem or performing a task (Baddeley, 1986). These four executive functions are interactive and hierarchical, with a deficit in one executive function contributing to deficits in other executive functions. Table 23.2 shows the four components of executive functioning and the results of deficits in each component. All four of these executive functions serve the same purpose – the internalization of behavior that enables individuals to anticipate change and guide their future behaviors. Many of the behaviors manifested in children with ADHD can be understood in terms of deficits in these executive functions.

Table 23.2   Interventions to promote language in children with ADHD

Executive function	Deficits	Goals/interventions
Non-verbal working memory	<ul><li>Inability to remember events or information</li><li>Poor schema formation</li><li>Poor sense of time</li><li>Limited self-awareness</li><li>Deficits in anticipatory set/hindsight and forethought</li></ul>	<ul><li>Train visual imagery strategies</li><li>Support working memory with visual cues and schedules</li><li>Use graphic organizers to teach text structure</li><li>Use clocks, calendars to show passage of time</li></ul>
Internalization of self-directed speech (verbal working memory)	<ul><li>Reduced description and reflection</li><li>Difficulty self-questioning</li><li>Deficient rule-governed behavior</li><li>Delayed moral reasoning</li><li>Impaired reading comprehension</li></ul>	<ul><li>Develop expressive language skills to describe sequences of actions and events:<ul><li>develop dependent clauses to express relationships</li><li>develop use of cohesive strategies</li></ul></li><li>Increase range of language functions to include self-directing, reporting, reasoning, predicting, and projecting</li></ul>

Table 23.2   *(Cont'd)*

Executive function	Deficits	Goals/interventions
Emotional control (self-regulation of mood, motivation, and level of arousal)	• Inability to regulate emotions • Difficulty with self-motivation • Poor perspective taking • Poor self-regulation of arousal and goal-directed action	• Develop a vocabulary of emotions • Develop theory of mind skills – projecting into thoughts and feelings of others • Provide social skills instruction • Use social stories
Problem solving	• Limited analysis and synthesis of tasks and behaviors	• Develop narrative and expository discourse skills • draw attention to conflict resolution/ problem solving in narratives • Model problem solving in realistic activities • Coach in problem-solving activities (i.e., scaffolding and questioning students during interactions)

3.1   *Types of executive functions*

3.1.1   Non-verbal working memory   This executive function represents non-verbal schemas or imagery for events. The retention of a sequence of events in working memory provides the basis for the human sense of time, which in turn, sensitizes persons to potential cause–effect relationships. The ability to activate these schemas allows for hindsight and forethought. With hindsight, an individual can evaluate what worked and did not work and why. With forethought, an individual can predict what might happen and take action to make a positive event occur or avoid a negative event. Such hindsight and forethought underlies pragmatic skills, enabling persons to engage in expected, appropriate social interactions. A sense of time also sensitizes persons to potential cause–effect relationships that are critical to developing mental schemas or mental models for texts. Such mental models enable the inferencing that is essential in comprehending texts that are heard or read (Baddeley, 1986; Barkley, 1997; Perfetti, 1997). This reduced sense of time may contribute to the greater difficulty children with ADHD have in understanding the causal relationships in stories compared to children without ADHD (Lorch et al., 2007).

The human sense of time also underlies time management abilities. Because of a poor sense of time, students with non-verbal working memory deficits may forget important responsibilities, such as deadlines for assignments, or they may not adequately judge the time needed to complete assignments. Calvin, in the cartoon series Calvin and Hobbes, often exhibited many characteristics of ADHD. He frequently had difficulty managing time. For example, he approaches his mother, asking her for a shoebox for a school project. He explains that he is studying ecosystems and he is going to make a desert diorama. He'll need glue and paper to build a cactus and roadrunner. When his mother asks when the project is due, Calvin explains that it was due today, but he told the teacher he wasn't quite finished.

3.1.2   Internalization of language (verbal working memory)   This function enables the control of behavior from within the individual rather than by others or the environment. Language is used to code many of the schemas in non-verbal memory. It is used to talk with oneself to provide reflection, description, instruction, and questioning, which in turn facilitates problem solving, the development of rules to guide behavior, and moral reasoning. Without internalized speech, one fails to develop appreciation of rule-governed behavior and, without this, one lacks self-regulation. Persons with poor internalized language do not talk themselves through activities. They lack an "inner voice" or "conscience" that tells them right from wrong. (As Dolly in a Family Circus cartoon explains, "Conscience is e-mail your head gets from heaven.") When a parent or teacher leaves the room, the rules leave with them. Persons with deficits in internalized language depend on others to control their behavior by providing clear rules and immediate rewards when the rules are obeyed and punishments when they are not obeyed.

Many children with ADHD exhibit delays in language development. Even those children who do not exhibit obvious delays in language development are likely to exhibit difficulty in formulating sentences and delays in the internalization of language. For typically developing children, language increasingly controls their behavior during their preschool and early elementary school years. Children under 3 years of age are dependent on the language of others to stop their inappropriate or ineffective behavior or to change or initiate a new behavior. In later preschool years, children begin to manage their behavior by talking aloud to themselves. The process toward the internalization of speech evolves from more conversational, task-irrelevant speech to more descriptive, task-relevant forms, then to more prescriptive and self-guiding speech, then to more private, inaudible speech, and finally to fully private subvocal speech (Berk, 1992; Diaz, Neal, & Amaya-Williams, 1990). Children with ADHD have consistently been found to be less mature in their self-speech and delayed in the sequence from public to private self-speech. Berk and Potts (1991) observed children with ADHD and children without ADHD in their classrooms, recording their use of private speech (self-directed but publicly observable) while engaged in math work at their desks. Three developmental levels of private speech were noted:

Level I: Task-irrelevant utterances.
Level II: Task-relevant externalized speech such as describing one's own actions and giving self-guiding comments; asking task-relevant, self-answered questions, and expressing task-relevant affect.
Level III: Task-relevant external manifestations of inner speech, including inaudible muttering, mouthing of words related to the task.

Greater amounts of level III speech, which reflects greater maturity, were significantly correlated with degree of focused attention and negatively associated with amount of off-task behavior. Both children with and without ADHD showed a similar pattern of development, but children with ADHD at all ages engaged in more level II speech than children without ADHD. Both groups declined in use of level II speech, but children without ADHD in the oldest group (10–11 years) declined in use of level III speech, which was interpreted as their move to fully internalized, unobservable speech. Children with language learning disabilities (LLD) alone (without ADHD) also exhibit delays in internalization of speech, but ADHD appears to contribute more to delays in internalization of speech than LLD (Berk & Landau, 1993).

Internalization of speech/language is essential if persons are to regulate their own behavior. Deficits in internalization of speech or verbal working memory will result in social and academic difficulties and lead to deficits in self-regulation. Children with ADHD are less able than same-aged peers to resist forbidden temptations. Such rule following is particularly difficult for children with ADHD when the rules compete with rewards available for committing rule violations. They are also less likely to use organizational rules and strategies in their performance of memory tasks, and they are less likely to transfer the rules they have acquired on a prior task to a new task. Deficits in verbal working memory also affect reading comprehension. What is read must be held in mind as it is processed. Persons with ADHD report that when they read, they often forget what was read at the top of the page by the time they have reached the middle or bottom of the page. They tend to retain only the most obvious and concrete aspects of the texts and consequently fail to comprehend more complex and subtle features (Barkley, 2006).

3.1.3 Self-regulation or emotion control   Deficits in self-regulation are a hallmark of executive function deficits. As a result of their executive function deficits, children with ADHD seem to have more trouble doing what they know than knowing what to do. Internalized language enables the self-regulation of affect, motivation, and arousal. Individuals with deficits in emotional control are less able to moderate their initial feelings, motivate themselves in the absence of external consequences, and arouse themselves in the service of future goals.

Persons with deficits in self-regulation may show quick frustration and anger. Calvin often exhibits this frustration and anger. Looking at the instructions for a model plane, he comments, "I can't get this model airplane to look right. These instructions are impossible!" He then takes a hammer, screams, and smashes the plane, saying to Hobbes, "Hit by antiaircraft guns." Hobbes notes, "Your planes seem to run into those, don't they?" This frustration and anger compromises the interactions children with ADHD have with their peers. Studies of peer interactions have found children with ADHD to be more negative and emotional in their social communication. This tends to be most marked in children who have high levels of co-morbid aggression (Hinshaw & Melnick, 1995). In a frustrating peer competition activity, boys with and without ADHD were asked to try to hide their feelings if they felt upset. Each boy was informed that he would win a prize if he constructed a Lego model faster than his competitor (an alleged boy in the next room). The puzzles were, however, insoluble due to missing parts. Boys with ADHD were less effective in hiding their emotions than control boys (Walcott & Landau, 2004).

Persons with deficits in self-regulation of emotion fail to persist with a task they perceive as difficult or boring, and tasks that do not have quick and frequent rewards are perceived as difficult and boring. Calvin exhibits difficulty with persistence on a task. Calvin and his tiger Hobbes are building a snowman. As Calvin rolls the first snowball, he announces, "I'm making a monumental, heroic snow sculpture. It will be called 'The Triumph of Perservence.'" Hobbes comments, "Very inspiring. What will it look like?" As Calvin points to the single snowball, he says, "This." When Hobbes asks, "Are you through?" Calvin walks away saying "I'm bored."

Deficits in self-regulation or emotional control can account for some of the behavior that appears to reflect attentional problems. Problems with alertness, arousal, selectivity, sustained attention, or distractibility frequently occur not only in classroom activities that children may perceive as dull and boring (Luk, 1985; Milich, Loney, & Landau, 1982), but also in self-selected free-play settings in which, compared to children without ADHD, children with ADHD display shorter durations of play with each toy and frequent shifts in play across various toys (Barkley & Ullman, 1975; Routh & Schroeder, 1976). Although parents and teachers perceive children with ADHD as being easily distracted by extraneous stimulation in the environment, research is contradictory and in general finds that children with ADHD are not more distractible than normal children (Campbell, Douglas, & Morgenstern, 1971; Steinkamp, 1980). The problem appears to be not so much one of distractibility, but of less persistence or effort on tasks that have little intrinsic appeal or minimal immediate consequences for completion (Barkley, 2006).

If persons are to manage their emotional responses in social situations, they must be able to recognize and interpret emotional expressions of others – they must have an adequate "theory of mind" (the ability to understand that others have beliefs, desires, and intentions that are different from one's own). Children with ADHD (and no co-morbid disorders) have exhibited a general deficit in decoding of emotional expressions (Cadesky, Mota, & Schachar, 2000; Pelc et al., 2006). Cadesky and colleagues (2000) reported that 7–13-year-old children with ADHD were less accurate than typical children in identifying the emotions of happiness, sadness, anger, and fear in pictures and in the tone of voice of an adult reading a sentence. Pelc and colleagues reported that when shown photographs depicting joy, anger, disgust, and sadness in varying intensities, children with ADHD aged 7–12 years exhibited particular difficulty in identifying anger and sadness. There was a significant correlation between interpersonal problems and impairment in decoding emotional facial expressions. This deficit appears to continue into adulthood. In a study in which adults with and without ADHD viewed faces displaying one of six emotions and identified the emotions using a forced-choice procedure, adults with ADHD had more difficulty identifying the emotions compared to those adults without ADHD (Rapport et al., 2002).

Without the ability to interpret emotional expressions correctly and an adequate theory of mind, persons exhibit pragmatic deficits. They misinterpret or are insensitive to the thoughts and feelings of others and are likely to say whatever comes to mind, regardless of the consequences. Hence, they frequently make comments that alienate them from peers and family members. Deficits in emotional control as a result of an inadequate decoding of emotional expression and theory of mind also affect reading comprehension, because readers do not recognize the intentions and goals of characters. Consequently, they are likely to miss the plots and themes of narratives they read. Deficits related to emotional regulations could contribute to the story comprehension impairments of children with ADHD – difficulty understanding causal relations among story events; difficulty using goal structures of a story to build a coherent story representation; difficulty recalling the most important information in stories; and difficulty making appropriate inferences about the story (Lorch et al., 2007).

3.1.4 Reconstitution or problem solving   Persons must be able to adapt to changing environmental demands by engaging in problem solving. If one is to engage in creative problem solving, one must have some degree of behavioral inhibition, be able to reflect on one's behavior, and be able to regulate one's own arousal. In problem solving, individuals must be able to analyze behaviors and synthesize new behaviors; they must take apart and recombine behavioral sequences so as to create novel, complex, and organized response patterns that are goal directed. Problem solving taxes working memory because one must keep the task in mind while simultaneously generating, implementing, and evaluating strategies. Calvin has difficulty developing effective strategies. As he sits before his homework, he proclaims, "Hocus, pocus, abracadabra, I command my homework to do itself. Homework be done!" He looks down at his papers and realizes his strategy has not worked. Norman Drabble, a cartoon college student, has difficulty with problem solving. In class, his girlfriend asks him, "What are you writing on?" Norman answers, "A magic slate. It conserves paper! I write my class notes on it and when it's filled up, I erase it and start over." Unlike Norman, his girlfriend can visualize the consequence of such an approach: "I can't wait to see the look on his face when it comes time to study for finals." In contrast to Drabble, in another cartoon, Wayne Merlman develops a strategy that may be effective for his problem: Unable to find a hi-liter pen, Wayne uses a black magic marker to cross out all the stuff he doesn't want to read again. If Wayne has been able to determine what is important and unimportant in the text, the strategy could work.

Verbal fluency is one manifestation of reconstitution. Children with ADHD have been noted to perform more poorly on tests of verbal fluency that typically require them to generate a diversity of verbal responses within a short time period (usually 1 minute). To accomplish the task, they must keep the requirements of the task in mind while searching their memory for relevant responses and keeping track of the responses they have already given. Tests that require children to generate words within semantic categories (Weyandt & Willis, 1994), such as names for animals and fruits, are easier and thus not as likely to discriminate children with ADHD from control children as those using more subtle or abstract organizing cues such as letters (Grodzinsky & Diamond, 1992; Reader et al., 1994). With limited reconstitution or problem-solving skills, persons also do not readily generalize something learned in one context to a new situation. Persons with deficits in this executive function will have difficulty analyzing reading tasks and selecting and implementing the appropriate strategies to facilitate comprehension.

4   ADHD and Language Learning Disabilities

Research shows that ADHD is closely associated both with speech and language problems and with mental health and behavioral problems (Cantwell, Baker, & Mattison, 1979, 1981; Chess & Rosenberg, 1974; Love & Thompson, 1988; Trautman, Giddan, & Jurs, 1990). Many studies have found children with ADHD to be somewhat more delayed in the onset of talking in early childhood than normal children (6 to 35 percent versus 2 to 25 percent of typically developing children (Hartsough & Lambert, 1985; Szatmari, Offord, & Boyle, 1989). Psychiatric problems are correlated more strongly with the type and severity of language disorders than with any other variable considered (Baker & Cantwell, 1982). Children who are initially diagnosed with speech and language impairments are highly likely to also be diagnosed with ADHD (Baker & Cantwell, 1987; Cohen, Menna, & Vallance, 1998). Studies concerning psychiatric problems of children referred to community clinics found that attention deficit disorder was the most frequently found psychiatric diagnosis for children with language impairments (Baker & Cantwell, 1982; Cantwell et al., 1981). Tirosh and Cohen (1998) reported 45 percent co-morbidity between language deficits and ADHD in a sample of 3,208 children aged 6 to 11 years old.

Not all studies have found increased rates of delayed speech/language development in children with ADHD (Barkley, DuPaul, & Murray, 1990). Two factors may account for the variation in research results on the relationship between language impairment and ADHD: systematic language assessment is rarely completed on children with ADHD, and, until recently, language assessments have focused on the structural (grammatical) aspects of language and have not included the social language (pragmatic) and extended discourse domains (Cohen, Menna, & Vallance, 1998). Whether or not speech is delayed, children with ADHD are more likely to have expressive language than receptive language problems, with 10–54 percent having expressive difficulties compared to 2–25 percent of typically developing children. In numerous studies, children with ADHD have exhibited particular difficulty on tasks requiring them to recall or formulate complex sentences (even when their performance on other semantic and grammatical/syntactic measures are age appropriate) (Kim & Kaiser, 2000; Oram et al., 1999; Redman, 2005). Children with ADHD may not exhibit obvious expressive language deficits characterized by grammatic, syntactic, and semantic deficits, but most children with ADHD will exhibit difficulties with discourse organization and conversational pragmatics of language (Bruce, Thernlund, & Nettelbladt, 2006; Humphries et al., 1994; Kim & Kaiser, 2000; Tannock & Schachar, 1996). Because there is a significant overlap between ADHD and language impairment, it is important to determine which deficits in speech and language are attributable to ADHD and which are attributable to a specific language impairment.

ADHD rarely occurs in isolation. Between 50 percent and 80 percent of children with ADHD also meet diagnostic criteria for other disorders. Persons with ADHD will exhibit *associated disorders* that are directly related to the executive dysfunction/working memory deficits of ADHD itself; and many persons with ADHD will also exhibit *co-morbid disorders* that are not part of the ADHD, but exist in addition to it. Co-morbid disorders include externalizing conditions such as oppositional defiant disorder and conduct disorder; and internalizing disorders such as anxiety/depression, language learning disability, and dyslexia. The nature of language and learning difficulties exhibited by children with ADHD differs in associated and co-morbid disorders.

4.1 Associated language/literacy disorders in ADHD-only

The language disorders of children with ADHD-only are not always easily recognized. Children with ADHD-only typically have age-appropriate scores on traditional tests of intelligence and language. Although ADHD-only is not accompanied by significant general language delays, evidence shows a strong association between ADHD and communication disorders, particularly expressive, pragmatic, and discourse organization deficits (Baker & Cantwell, 1992; Beitchman, Tuckett, & Bath, 1987; Berk & Potts, 1991; McInnes, et al., 2003). These deficits are evident in both interpersonal and intrapersonal domains (i.e., in language used for social communication and in that used for self-regulation). Students with ADHD-only are also likely to have age-appropriate scores on reading tests that focus on decoding or reading of sentences or very short passages, but have difficulty with comprehension of longer texts. These higher-level language deficits are considered associated disorders because they are viewed as part of the primary

ADHD. The associated disorders are directly related to the impairments in executive function and working memory. The executive function deficits result in deficits in pragmatic interactions, discourse organization/cohesion, inferencing, monitoring of communication and comprehension, and problem solving.

4.2   *Pragmatic deficits*

The DSM-IV criteria for ADHD reveal a set of communication problems characteristic of pragmatic dysfunction (e.g., difficulty awaiting turns, talking excessively, interrupting others, not listening to what is being said, and blurting out answers to questions before they are completed) (Camarata & Gibson, 1999; Westby & Cutler, 1994). Children with ADHD are likely to talk more than typical children during spontaneous conversations (Barkley, Cunningham, & Karlsson, 1983; Zentall, 1988). When they must organize and generate language in response to specific task demands, however, they are likely to talk less, to be dysfluent (using pauses, fillers such as "uh," "er," and "um"), and to be less organized (Hamlett, Pelligrini, & Conners, 1987; Purvis & Tannock, 1997; Zentall, 1985). Compared with typically developing children, children with ADHD tend to produce excessive verbal output during spontaneous conversations, task transitions, and in play settings; yet they tend to produce less speech in response to confrontational questioning than do children without ADHD (Baker & Cantwell, 1992; Tannock & Schachar, 1996). They are also less competitive in verbal problem-solving tasks and less capable of communicating task-essential information to peers in cooperative tasks (Whalen et al., 1979). Children with ADHD exhibit difficulties in introducing, maintaining, and changing topics appropriately, in negotiating smooth interchanges or turn taking during conversation, and in adjusting language to the listener in specific contexts (Hamlett, Pelligrini, & Conners, 1987).

Deficits in rule-governed behavior and self-regulation affect children's social skills. Children with ADHD have also been shown to have less knowledge about social skills and appropriate behavior with others. They seem to lack self-talk critical to the control and organization of interpersonal behavior. They do not read essential verbal, non-verbal, and situational cues, or make decisions based on that evidence in accordance with social expectations. Lack of private, self-directed speech also affects their ability to modulate their emotional reactions. Because negative emotions prove more socially unacceptable, students' difficulties in managing these emotions is problematic in relationships with teachers, peers, and parents.

4.3   *Discourse/reading deficits*

Language difficulties of children with ADHD are primarily in the higher-order cognitive processes involved in organizing and monitoring narrative and expository discourse. Narrative and explanatory language require more careful thought and organization than do spontaneous conversational or descriptive language, and consequently, they require greater degrees of working memory.

Children with ADHD produce less information and less organized information in tasks that require planning and verbal organization such as story narratives (Baker & Cantwell, 1992; Tannock, Purvis, & Schachar, 1992; Whalen et al., 1979) or in describing the strategies they use during task performance (Zentall, 1988).

Narrative production demands efficient working memory. When producing spoken or written narratives, one must keep the goal of the story in mind, while simultaneously linking each utterance to the goal and to the preceding and following utterances in temporal and causal relationships. Narrators must also monitor the clarity of their stories to ensure that they are cohesive and coherent to listeners. A number of studies have revealed that children with ADHD have difficulty with narrative discourse. Purvis and Tannock (1997) investigated the relationship of language abilities of ADHD children with and without reading disabilities (RD). Students were required to retell a lengthy narrative and to complete tests assessing semantic knowledge. Children with ADHD (ADHD-only and ADHD+RD) exhibited difficulties in organizing and monitoring their story retelling. They made numerous sequence errors and ambiguous references in their stories. Children with RD (RD-only and ADHD+RD) also demonstrated deficits in receptive and expressive language abilities. Purvis and Tannock concluded that the deficiencies of children with ADHD were consistent with higher-order executive function deficits, while the deficits of RD children were consistent with deficits in the basic semantics of language processing.

Studies of narrative discourse have also shown that children with ADHD have greater difficulty using causal, goal-based story structures to guide their ongoing comprehension and later recall than children without ADHD (Flory et al., 2006; Renz et al., 2003). This was true, even though the children with and without ADHD told stories of similar length. Renz et al. (2003) had children tell the story in the wordless picture book, *Frog, Where Are You?* (Mayer, 1969). In this story, a boy's pet frog escapes from its jar. The boy encounters a number of obstacles as he searches and finally finds the frog. Children without ADHD, ages 9 to 11, were better able than children with ADHD to maintain a goal plan throughout the narration as indicated by more frequent mention of the overall goal and specific linked attempts. In addition, children with ADHD made more errors by repeating themselves and using more ambiguous references. In a similar study with younger children, ages 7 to 9, children with ADHD had even greater difficulties in telling the story from the wordless picture book (Flory et al., 2006). They exhibited deficits in establishing the goal plan as indicated by less frequent mention of the initiating event (e.g., the frog is missing from its jar) that gave rise to the boy's goal to find the frog and bring it home. The children with ADHD differed from their peers without ADHD by more frequently failing to complete the story goal (bringing the frog home) and also in mentioning the story's final positive outcome (finding the frog). Furthermore, the younger children with ADHD included even more repetitions, ambiguous references, and extraneous information not supported by the pictures.

Difficulties in understanding cause–effect relationships and goals affect students' abilities to make inferences essential for text comprehension. McInnes et al. (2003)

had typically developing students (TD), students with ADHD-only, and students with ADHD+language impairment (LI) listen to expository passages and answer factual and inferential questions. For example, the students read a passage about mummies. They responded to factual questions that were explicitly answered in the text, e.g., "Who turned the king's body into a mummy?" or "What was used to dry the king's body?" They answered inferential questions such as, "What did the mummy smell like when it was put in the tomb?" or "What did the king think he would need in his afterlife?" They also responded to true/false questions requiring inferencing and explained the basis for their answers. The ADHD+LI students correctly answered fewer explicit and inferential questions than the TD and ADHD-only students. The ADHD-only students correctly answered as many explicit questions as the TD students, but they answered fewer inferential questions. Answering explicit questions requires short-term memory (STM), whereas answering inferential questions requires working memory. The inferencing deficits students with ADHD-only exhibit in listening tasks are also exhibited in their reading.

Students with ADHD-only also exhibit deficits in monitoring what they are reading (Hamlett, Pelligrini, & Conners, 1987; McInnes et al., 2003). They fail to notice inconsistencies in texts, particularly when the inconsistent pieces of information are separated in the text. They have difficulty differentiating the important from unimportant aspects of stories (Lorch et al., 2006); they may attend to insignificant details when reading and consequently fail to understand the main ideas of the text (Baker & Cantwell, 1992; Brock & Knapp, 1996; Pennington et al., 1996). Because they fail to monitor their comprehension, students with ADHD often are unaware that they are not comprehending. Even when they do recognize their failure to comprehend, they may not possess, or use, appropriate strategies to repair their comprehension failure. The nature of the reading difficulties in students with ADHD may be misinterpreted as due to attention or motivational issues. As a consequence, the students do not receive the appropriate interventions.

4.4 Language/literacy in ADHD with co-morbid disorders

In addition to the communication deficits specifically related to the executive function deficits of ADHD, many students with ADHD also exhibit co-morbid language-learning and literacy disabilities defined in classic ways – that is, phonological disorders, morphosyntactic/semantic delays, word-finding difficulties, and decoding difficulties. Estimates of the overlap between ADHD and specific language impairment (SLI) vary from a low of 8 percent to a high of 90 percent depending on the precise definitions of SLI, the nature of the SLI, and the methods used to diagnose ADHD (Baker & Cantwell, 1992). Children whose early language impairments persist beyond 5.5 years exhibit increased incidence of attention and social difficulties (Beitchman, Brownlie, & Wilson, 1996; Snowling et al., 2006). The language profile most commonly associated with attention disorder was expressive language impairment; the profile most associated with social difficulties was combined receptive and expressive language impairment.

Reading impairments in children with ADHD who have co-morbid reading disabilities are characterized by deficits in phonological awareness and/or rapid automatic naming (RAN). These students exhibit particular difficulty in mastering the phonologic and orthographic codes needed for fluent reading of English. A number of children with co-morbid reading disabilities also exhibit co-morbid syntactic and semantic deficits related to broader-based language disorders that affect their reading comprehension (McInnes et al., 2003; Szatmari, Offord, & Boyle, 1989).

5 Implications for Assessment and Intervention

5.1 Language assessment of children with ADHD

The results of the research on language impairments in children with ADHD provide support for the need to conduct language assessments on all children with ADHD. The language impairments associated with ADHD can have a significant impact on children's social and academic success. Speech-language pathologists (SLPs) will want to assess the language factors related to the executive function deficits associated with ADHD – pragmatics, discourse organization, inferencing, monitoring, and problem solving.

Standardized language tests typically do not assess the pragmatic and discourse deficits associated with ADHD. Even standardized tests that purport to assess these factors may not capture the difficulties exhibited by children with ADHD. Standardized tests assess discrete pieces of behaviors out of context. For many students with ADHD, it is not a matter of knowing what to do, but of knowing when and how to do – they may have the necessary factual information, but not know how to use it in context. This is particularly true for aspects of social cognition. For example, children with ADHD did not differ from typically developing children on the Test of Pragmatic Language (Phelps-Terasaki & Phelps-Gunn, 1992), yet produced significantly more inappropriate pragmatic behaviors in conversational interactions. Consequently, children's pragmatic skills should be evaluated in naturalistic situations during play or in conversations with adults or peers. Damico (1985) and Kim and Kaiser (2000) have proposed protocols that can be used for documenting inappropriate pragmatic behaviors. Using Damico's protocol (1985), the SLP considers inappropriateness in four types of behaviors:

- *Quantity category*
  - Failure to provide important information to listeners.
  - Use of non-specific vocabulary (e.g., use of vague words such as "thing," "stuff," or ambiguous pronouns).
  - Informational redundancy (continuing to return to a topic that has been covered).
  - Need for repetition of information in order to participate in the conversation.

- *Quality category*
  - Incorrect or untrue information.
- *Relation category*
  - Poor topic maintenance (rapid and inappropriate changes in topic without providing transitional cues to the listener).
  - Contributions not related to the topic of conversation.
  - Failure to seek clarification of information that is unclear.
  - Violation of social conventions of politeness and appropriateness.
  - Failure to change the structural, lexical, or prosodic nature of utterances to accommodate different listeners.
- *Manner category*
  - Linguistic non-fluency/revisions.
  - Delays before responding.
  - Failure to structure discourse.
  - Turn-taking difficulty.
  - Gaze inefficiency.
  - Inappropriate intonational contour.

The Kim and Kaiser (2000) protocol includes the elements in the Damico protocol and in addition considers the variety of speech acts the child uses.

Narrative assessment is essential for children with ADHD. Students with ADHD are likely to have difficulty simultaneously centering and chaining in discourse. They are particularly likely to begin discussing the topic, but then to chain a series of associated ideas, forgetting the original topic; consequently, their narratives lack overall coherence and cohesion. Their stories tend to consist of chaining of events and to lack clear plans to achieve goals. The Test of Narrative Language (TNL) (Gillam & Pearson, 2004) is a standardized test that may be useful for identifying children in early elementary grades. The TNL is structured to assess a range of narrative difficulties that children with SLI are known to exhibit. It requires that a child retell a short story they listen to without picture support; answer literal and inferential questions about stories they listen to while looking at a sequence of five pictures and a single picture of a dragon guarding a treasure; and generate a story about a five-picture sequence and about a single picture of an alien spaceship landing in a park. Scoring of generated narratives considers both grammatic/syntactic and narrative content/structure. Children receive points for grammatic correctness, syntactic complexity, indicating temporal and causal relationships among the events; providing consequences and an ending; and producing a coherent story that makes sense. The TNL has not been used with children with ADHD. Although it assesses discourse elements that have been shown to be problematic in children with ADHD (understanding causal relationships and goals, story coherence, answering inferencing questions), only a few points on each subtest measure these components.

Although the TNL has good sensitivity and specificity for children with SLI, it may not be as effective for children with ADHD-only. This is because the tool may not sufficiently sample the narrative components and inferencing difficulties

Table 23.3 Examples of dependent clauses

Dependent clauses that work as adverbs:
- *While Max went to the store*, the bird ate all the food in the house.
- Max fed the bird *until he had no more food*.
- *After the bird was full grown*, it took off with Max's house.
- *Although Max fed the bird a lot of food*, the bird was still crying.
- Max kept feeding the bird *because he wanted it to be quiet*.
- The bird took off into the sky *as Max stepped onto his porch*.

Dependent clauses that work as adjectives:
- The yellow bird *that had eaten all of Max's food* flew off with the house.
- Once there was a mouse named Max *who found a little yellow bird*.
- The bird flew to Mexico *where Max got a job making sombreros*.

Dependent clauses that work as nouns:
- Max explained to his girlfriend Maxine *how the bird had eaten all his food*.
- Max's friends didn't know *what happened to him*.

that are associated with ADHD-only. Further, it is appropriate for only elementary school children. Consequently, SLPs will need to consider other ways to conduct narrative assessments. Students can be asked to tell or write about stories in wordless picture books or from wordless videos (e.g., the *Max the Mouse* videos available from Clearvue & SVE, Inc.: http://www.clearvue.com), from single pictures, or from story-started statements. The narratives produced should be evaluated for:

- *Complexity of narrative structure* – are all elements of the story included (setting, characters, initiating events, response, plan/goal/attempts, consequence, resolution)?
- *Syntactic complexity*, particularly use of dependent clauses that show the temporal and causal relationships between events (see examples in Table 23.3).
- *Cohesive strategies* (see examples in Table 23.4).

Beyond third grade, students should be able to include cause–effect sequences of behaviors, goals, and plans for characters; consequences; and a conclusion that relates back to the events at the beginning of the story.

The inferencing required to comprehend oral and written texts can be assessed in two ways:

- *By asking students about characters' thoughts and feelings*: what are the characters' feelings; why do they feel that way (what caused their feelings); what will they do because they feel that way? (How did Max feel when he found the

Table 23.4   Examples of cohesion

Category	Type	Examples
Conjunction	Additive	The boy saw the present *and* he read the tag.
	Adversative	The boy took his dog and baby frog on the raft, *but* the big frog wasn't allowed to come.
	Causal	The big frog bit the little frog *because* he didn't want another frog in his life.
	Temporal	*When* the baby frog saw the big frog on the raft, he was worried.
Referential	Pronominal	The boy got a present. *He* opened it.
	Demonstrative	The big frog kicked the little frog. He shouldn't do *that*.
	Comparative	The boy had two frogs. *The bigger one* was mean.
	Lexical	
	same word	Max got a *thistle* for a shell. The *thistle* hurt the snail's back.
	synonym	Max was *mad* at the bird. He was *furious*.
	superordinate	Max tried a *thistle*, *rose*, and a *mushroom*. None of the *plants* worked.
Impaired cohesion	Ambiguous	
	exophoric	The little frog hid *there*.
	can't retrieve from text	Max picked *it* and gave *it* to the snail.
	Wrong relation	Max took the bird home *when* he liked him.
	Inappropriate voice (abrupt shift in role)	*I* like these videos. *We* see them a lot.
	Incorrect determiner	Use of "the" on first reference or "a" on second reference, e.g., The boy picked up *the* baby frog. He showed *a* baby frog to his pets.

baby bird crying? What do you think Max will do about the baby bird? Why did Max run out of the house?)

- *By using informal reading inventories* such as the Qualitative Reading Inventory – 4 (Leslie & Caldwell, 2005). This assessment provides narrative and expository passages from pre-primer to high school levels. Multiple passages at each level allow for students both to listen to and read texts. Explicit and inferential questions are asked about each passage. Because expository texts generally have a less familiar structure and content than narrative texts, they place greater demands on working memory. Consequently, students may perform better on narrative passages than on expository passages.

The Qualitative Reading Inventory – 4 can also be used to assess the monitoring strategies students use when they are attempting to comprehend a passage. Students are given a text at their instructional level. The evaluator asks the student to stop at designated segments of the text and explain what he or she is thinking at that point. Ideally, the evaluator models how to "think aloud" about a text.

The ability to generate a variety of means to an end, suggest alternative solutions to problems, and think of multiple consequences correlates well to children's problem-solving abilities in social situations (Shure, 1997). In means–ends thinking, the person plans a step-by-step, sequenced means to reach a goal. The person also identifies potential obstacles that could interfere with reaching the goal. Alternative solution thinking is the ability to name unconnected, alternative solutions to a stated problem (instead of connecting sequenced plans). Consequential thinking is the ability to think of the different things that might happen in certain situations. Using tasks like those that follow will enable the SLP to assess these skills:

- *Means–end thinking*: The child is told the beginning and end of a story and is asked to fill in the middle, tell what happens in between, or tell how the ending got to be that way:

  Al (Joyce) moved into the neighborhood. He (she) didn't know anyone and felt very lonely. The story ends with Al (Joyce) having many good friends and feeling at home in the neighborhood. What happens in between Al's (Joyce's) moving in and feeling lonely, and when he (she) ends up with many good friends?

- *Alternative solution thinking*: Someone pushes you on the playground. What are all the things you might do if this happened?
- *Consequential thinking*: David was at Kevin's house and when Kevin wasn't looking, David put Kevin's new ball in his pocket and later took it home with him. What might happen next – give all the ideas you can think of.

5.2 Interventions for ADHD

Any discussion of interventions for ADHD must consider the use of medication. The news media frequently raise concerns about the frequency of use of medications to manage ADHD. Many parents are hesitant or even resistant to recommendation for medication use and prefer more behavioral interventions. The National Institutes of Health's Multimodal Treatment study (MTA) was designed to investigate the long-term effects of medication and behavioral interventions for ADHD (Multimodal Cooperation Group, 1999, 2004). Children were randomly assigned to one of four treatment groups: medication alone, behavior modification alone, the combination of medication and behavior modification, and a community comparison group. It was hypothesized that a combination of treatments would result in greater symptom reduction and less impairment. Treatment conditions using medication resulted in significantly greater lasting results than behavioral treatments alone. At the 24-month follow-up, the combined treatment yielded significantly greater improvement in social skills than medical management alone, but there was no significant difference in reading achievement across the treatments.

Researchers emphasize that these results were for students with ADHD-only and students who were responders to medication. They caution that "pills will not substitute for skills," so medication is highly unlikely to be sufficient for students with co-morbid language learning disabilities or with disruptive behavioral disorders. There is no indication that the behavioral program targets specific reading or language difficulties. Interventions should address the underlying executive function deficits and nature of the specific working memory and language impairments that are characteristic of persons with ADHD. Table 23.2 (see above) shows goals for intervention that address the problems arising from deficits in executive function in students with ADHD. The intended outcomes of language interventions are facilitation of students' pragmatic, discourse, monitoring, and problem-solving skills.

6   Conclusion

The increasing incidence of ADHD and our changing understanding of its causes and nature place new demands and challenges on professionals working with children and adults with ADHD. Clinical practice should be based on current research evidence. Intervention choice and planning are influenced by one's beliefs. If educators and SLPs believe that the learning difficulties of students with ADHD are due primarily to attention deficits, they will fail to provide students with the most appropriate interventions. Current research on ADHD indicates that language impairment is a component of all types of ADHD, even the type that has been termed ADHD-only. All students with ADHD, whether or not they have diagnosed co-morbid reading and language disabilities, exhibit deficits in aspects of higher-order discourse. This is in accord with Barkley's postulate that a core impairment in ADHD involves deficits in self-directed speech and the internalization of language used for the development of mental representation and self-regulation.

REFERENCES

American Psychiatric Association (2000). *Diagnostic and statistical manual of mental disorders*, 4th ed., text rev. Washington, DC: Author.

Baddeley, A. (1986). *Working memory*. Oxford: Clarendon.

Baker, L. & Cantwell, D. P. (1982). Psychiatric disorder in children with different types of communication disorders. *Journal of Communicative Disorders* 15, 113–26.

Baker, L. & Cantwell, D. P. (1987). A prospective psychiatric follow-up of children with speech/language disorders. *Journal of the American Academy of Child and Adolescent Psychiatry* 26, 545–53.

Baker, L. & Cantwell, D. P. (1992). Attention deficit disorder and speech/language disorders. *Comprehensive Mental Health Care* 2, 3–16.

Barkley, R. A. (1990). *Attention-deficit hyperactivity disorder: A handbook for diagnosis and treatment.* New York: Guilford Press.

Barkley, R. A. (1997). Behavioral inhibition, sustained attention, and executive functions: Constructing a unifying theory of ADHD. *Psychological Bulletin* 121, 65–94.

Barkley, R. A. (2005). *ADHD and the nature of self-control.* New York: Guilford.

Barkley, R. A. (2006). A theory of ADHD. In R. A. Barkley (ed.), *Attention-deficit hyperactivity disorder* (pp. 297–334). New York: Guilford.

Barkley, R. A., Cunningham, C., & Karlsson, J. (1983). The speech of hyperactive children and their mothers: Comparisons with normal children and stimulant drug effects. *Journal of Learning Disabilities* 16, 105–10.

Barkley, R. A., DuPaul, G. J., & McMurray, M. B. (1990). A comprehensive evaluation of attention deficit disorder with and without hyperactivity. *Journal of Consulting and Clinical Psychology* 58, 775–89.

Barkley, R. A. & Ullman, D. G. (1975). A comparison of objective measures of activity and distractibility in hyperactive and nonhyperactive children. *Journal of Abnormal Psychology* 3, 213–44.

Bauermeister, J. J., Matos, M., Reina, G., Salas, C. C., Martinez, J. V., Cumba, E., & Barkley, R. A. (2004). Comparison of DSM-IV combines and inattentive types of ADHD in a school-based sample of Latino/Hispanic children. *Journal of Child Psychology and Psychiatry* 46, 166–79.

Beitchman, J. H., Brownlie, E. B., & Wilson, B. (1996). Linguistic impairment and psychiatric disorder: Pathways to outcomes. In J. H. Beitchman, N. J. Cohen, M. Konstantareas, & R. Tannock (eds.), *Language, learning and behavior disorders* (pp. 493–514). Cambridge: Cambridge University Press.

Beitchman, J., Tuckett, M., & Bath, S. (1987). Language delay and hyperactivity in preschoolers: Evidence for a distinct group of hyperactives. *Canadian Journal of Psychiatry* 32, 683–7.

Berk, L. E. (1992). Children's private speech: An overview of theory and the status of research. In R. M. Diaz & L. E. Berk (eds.), *Private speech: From social interaction to self-regulation* (pp. 17–54). Mahwah, NJ: Lawrence Erlbaum.

Berk, L. E. & Landau, S. (1993). Private speech of learning disabled and normally achieving children in classroom academic and laboratory contexts. *Child Development* 64, 556–71.

Berk, L. E. & Potts, M. K. (1991). Development and functional significance of private speech among attention-deficit hyperactivity disorder and normal boys. *Journal of Abnormal Child Psychology* 19, 357–77.

Brock, S. W. & Knapp, P. K. (1996). Reading comprehension abilities of children with attention-deficit/ hyperactivity disorder. *Journal of Attention Disorders* 1, 173–86.

Brown, T. E. (2006). Executive functions and attention deficit hyperactivity disorder: Implications of two conflicting views. *International Journal of Disability, Development and Education* 53 (1), 35–46.

Bruce, B., Thernlund, G., & Nettelbladt, U. (2006). ADHD and language impairment. *European Child and Adolescent Psychiatry* 15, 52–60.

Cadesky, E. B., Mota, V. L., & Schachar, R. (2000). Beyond words: How do children with ADHD and/or conduct disorder process nonverbal information about affect? *Journal of the American Academy of Child & Adolescent Psychiatry* 39 (9), 1160–67.

Camarata, S. M. & Gibson, T. (1999). Pragmatic language deficits in attention-deficit hyperactivity disorder (ADHD). *Mental Retardation and Developmental Disabilities Research Reviews* 5, 202–14.

Campbell, S. B., Douglas, V. I., & Morganstern, G. (1971). Cognitive styles in hyperactive children and the effect of methylphenidate. *Journal of Child Psychology and Psychiatry* 12, 55–67.

Cantwell, D. P., Baker, L., & Mattison, R. E. (1979). The prevalence of psychiatric disorder in children with speech and language disorder: An epidemiological study. *Journal of the American Academy of Child Psychiatry* 18, 450–9.

Chess, S. & Rosenberg, M. (1974). Clinical differentiation among children with initial language complaints. *Journal for Autism and Childhood Schizophrenia* 4, 99–109.

Cohen, N., Menna, R., & Vallance, D. (1998). Language, social cognitive processing, and behavioral characteristics of psychiatrically disturbed children with previously identified and unsuspected language impairments. *Journal of Child Psychology and Psychiatry* 39, 853–64.

Damico, J. S. (1985). Clinical discourse analysis: A functional approach. In C. S. Simon (ed.), *Communication skills and classroom success*. San Diego, CA: College-Hill.

Denkla, M. B. (1994). Measurement of executive function. In G. R. Lyon (ed.), *Frames of reference for the assessment of learning disabilities: New views on measure issues* (pp. 117–42). Baltimore, MD: Brookes.

Diaz, R., Neal, C. J., & Amaya-Williams, M. (1990). The social origins of self-regulation. In L. C. Moll (ed.), *Vygotsky and education: Instructional implications and applications of sociohistorical psychology* (pp. 127–54). New York: Cambridge University Press.

Flory, K., Milich, R., Lorch, E. P., Hayden, A. N., Strange, C., & Welsh, R. (2006). Online story comprehension among children with ADHD: Which core deficits are involved? *Journal of Abnormal Child Psychology* 34, 850–62.

Gillam, R. B. & Pearson, N. A. (2004). *Test of narrative language*. Austin, TX: Pro-Ed.

Grodzinsky, G. M. & Diamond, E. (1992). Frontal lobe functioning in boys with attention-deficit hyperactivity disorder. *Developmental Neuropsychology* 8, 427–45.

Hamlett, K. W., Pelligrini, D. S., & Conners, C. K. (1987). An investigation of executive processes in the problem-solving of attention deficit disorder-hyperactivity children. *Journal of Pediatric Psychology* 12, 227–40.

Hartsough, C. S. & Lambert, N. M. (1985). Medical factors in hyperactive and normal children: Prenatal, developmental, and health history findings. *American Journal of Orthopsychiatry* 55, 190–210.

Hinshaw, S. P. & Melnick, S. M. (1995). Peer relationships in boys with attention-deficit hyperactivity disorder with and without comorbid aggression. *Development and Psychopathology* 7, 627–47.

Humphries, T., Koltun, H., Malone, M., & Roberts, W. (1994). Teacher-identified oral language difficulties among boys with attention problems. *Journal of Developmental and Behavioral Pediatrics* 15, 92–8.

Kim, O. H. & Kaiser, A. P. (2000). Language characteristics of children with ADHD. *Communication Disorders Quarterly* 21 (3), 154–65.

Leslie, L. & Caldwell, J. (2005). Qualitative reading inventory – 4. Boston, MA: Allyn & Bacon.

Leslie, L. K., Canino, G., Landsverk, J., Wood, P. A., Chavez, L., Hough, R. L., Bauermeister, J. J., & Ramirez, R. (2005). ADHD treatment patterns of youth served in public sectors in San Diego and Puerto Rico. *Journal of Emotional and Behavioral Disorders* 13, 224–36.

Lorch, E. P., Berthiaume, K. S., Milich, R., & van den Broek, P. (2007). Story comprehension impairments in children with attention-deficit/hyperactivity disorder. In K. Cain & J. Oakhill (eds.), *Children's comprehension problems in oral and written language* (pp. 128–56). New York: Guilford.

Lorch, E. P., Milich, R., Astrin, C. C., & Berthiaume, K. S. (2006). Cognitive engagement and story comprehension in typically developing children and children with ADHD from preschool through elementary school. *Developmental Psychology* 42, 1206–19.

Love, A. & Thompson, M. G. G. (1988). Language disorders and attention deficit disorders in young children referred for psychiatric services. *American Journal of Orthopsychiatry* 58, 52–63.

Luk, S. (1985). Direct observations studies of hyperactive behaviors. *Journal of the American Academy of Child Psychiatry* 24, 338–44.

Mayer, M. (1969). *Frog, where are you?* New York: Dial.

McBuernett, K., Pfiffner, L. J., & Frick, P. J. (2001). Symptom properties as a function of ADHD type: An argument for continued study of sluggish cognitive temp. *Journal of Abnormal Child Psychology* 29, 207–13.

McInnes, A., Humphries, T., Hogg-Johnson, S., & Tannock, R. (2003). Listening comprehension and working memory are impaired in attention-deficit hyperactivity disorder. *Journal of Abnormal Child Psychology* 31 (4), 427–43.

McGough, J. J. & Barkley, R. A. (2004). Diagnostic controversies in adult attention deficit hyperactivity disorder. *American Journal of Psychiatry* 161, 1948–56.

Meyer, A., Eilertsen, D.-E., Sundet, J. M., Tshifularo, J., & Sagvolden, T. (2004). Cross-cultural similarities in ADHD-like behaviour amongst South African primary school children. *South African Journal of Psychology* 34, 122–38.

Milich, R., Balentine, A. C., & Lyman, D. R. (2001). ADHD/combined type and ADHD/predominantly inattentive type are distinct and unrelated disorders. *Clinical Psychology: Science and Practice* 8, 463–88.

Milich, R., Loney, J., & Landau, S. (1982). The independent dimensions of hyperactivity and aggression: A validation with playroom observation data. *Journal of Abnormal Psychology* 91, 183–98.

Minnis, H., Kelly, E., Bradby, H., Oglethorpe, R., Raine, W., & Cockburn, D. (2003). Cultural and language mismatch: Clinical complications. *Clinical Child Psychology and Psychiatry* 8, 179–86.

Multimodal Cooperative Group (1999). A 14-month randomized clinical trial of treatment strategies for attention-deficit/hyperactivity disorders. *Archives of General Psychiatry* 56, 1073–86.

Multimodal Cooperative Group (2004). National Institute of Mental Health Multimodal Treatment Study of ADHD follow-up: Changes in effectiveness and growth after the end of treatment. *Pediatrics* 113, 762–9.

Oram, J., Fine, J., Okamoto, C., & Tannock, R. (1999). Assessing the language of children with attention deficit hyperactivity disorder. *American Journal of Speech-Language Pathology* 8, 72–80.

Pelc, K., Kornreich, C., Foisy, M. L., & Dan, B. (2006). Recognition of emotional facial expressions in attention-deficit hyperactivity disorder. *Pediatric Neurology* 35 (2), 93–7.

Pennington, B. F. & Ozonoff, S. (1996). Executive functions and developmental psychopathology. *Journal of Child Psychology and Psychiatry* 37, 51–87.

Pennington, B. F., Bennetto, L., McAleer, O., & Roberts, R. J. (1996). Executive functions and working memory: Theoretical and measurement issues. In G. R. Lyon & N. A. Krasnegor (eds.), *Attention, memory and executive function*. Baltimore, MD: Brookes.

Perfetti, C. (1997). Sentences, individual differences, and multiple texts: Three issues in text comprehension. *Discourse Processes* 23, 337–55.

Perry, C. E., Hatton, D., & Kendall, J. (2005). *Journal of Transcultural Nursing* 16 (4), 312–21.

Phelps-Terasaki, D. & Phelps-Gunn, T. (1992). *Test of pragmatic language*. Austin, TX; Pro-Ed.

Purvis, K. L. & Tannock, R. (1997). Language abilities in children with attention deficit hyperactivity disorder, reading disabilities, and normal controls. *Journal of Abnormal Child Psychology* 25, 133–44.

Rapport, L. J., Friedman, S. L., Tzelepis, A., & Van Voorhis, A. (2002). Experienced emotion and affect recognition in adult attention-deficit hyperactivity disorder. *Neuropsychology* 16, 102–10.

Reader, M. J., Harris, E. L., Schuerholz, L. J., & Denkla, M. B. (1994). Attention deficit hyperactivity disorder and executive dysfunction. *Developmental Neuropsychology* 10, 493–512.

Redman, S. M. (2005). Differentiating SLI from ADHD using children's sentence recall and production of past tense morphology. *Clinical Linguistics & Phonetics* 19 (2), 109–27.

Remschmidt, H. (2005). Global consensus on ADHD/HKD. *European Child & Adolescent Psychiatry* 14, 127–37.

Renz, K., Lorch, E. P., Milich, R., Lemberger, C., Bodner, A., & Welsh, R. (2003). Online story representation in boys with attention deficit hyperactivity disorder. *Journal of Abnormal Child Psychology* 31, 93–104.

Roberts, R. E., Alegria, M., Roberts, C. R., & Chen, I. G. (2005). Mental health problems of adolescents as reported by their caregivers: A comparison of European, African, and Latin Americans. *The Journal of Behavioral Health Services and Research* 32, 1–13.

Rohde, L. A., Szobot, C., Polancczyk, G., Schmitz, M., Martins, S., & Tramontina, S. (2005). Attention-deficit/hyperactivity disorder in a diverse culture: Do research and clinical findings support the notion of a cultural construct for the disorder? *Biological Psychiatry* 57, 1436–41.

Routh, D. K. & Schroeder, C. S. (1976). Standardized playroom measures as indices of hyperactivity. *Journal of Abnormal Child Psychology* 4, 199–207.

Shure, M. B. (1997). Interpersonal cognitive problem solving: Primary prevention of early high-risk behaviors in the preschool and primary years. In G. W. Albee & T. P. Gullotta (eds.), *Primary prevention works* (pp. 167–88). Thousand Oaks, CA: Sage.

Snowling, M. J., Bishop, D. V. M., Stohard, S. E., Chipchase, B., & Kaplan, C. (2006). Psychosocial outcomes at 15 years of children with a preschool history of speech-language impairment. *Journal of Child Psychology and Psychiatry* 47 (8), 759–65.

Steinkamp, M. W. (1980). Relationships between environmental distractions and task performance of hyperactive and normal children. *Journal of Learning Disabilities* 13, 40–5.

Szatmari, P., Offord, D. R., & Boyle, M. H. (1989). Correlates, associated impairments, and patterns of service utilization of children with attention deficit disorder: Findings from the Ontario child health study. *Journal of Child Psychology and Psychiatry* 30, 205–17.

Tannock, R. & Schachar, R. (1996). Executive dysfunction as an underlying mechanism of behaviour and language problems in attention deficit hyperactivity disorders. In J. H. Beitchman, N. J. Cohen, M. M. Konstantareas, R. R. Tannock (eds.), *Language learning and behavior disorders: Developmental, biological, and clinical perspective* (pp. 128–55). New York: Cambridge University Press.

Tannock, R., Purvis, K. L., & Schachar, R. J. (1992). Narrative abilities in children with attention deficit hyperactivity disorder and normal peers. *Journal of Abnormal Child Psychology* 21, 103–17.

Tirosh, E. & Cohen, A. (1998). Language deficit with attention-deficit disorder: A prevalent comorbidity. *Journal of Child Neurology* 13, 493–7.

Trautman, R., Giddan, J., & Jurs, S. (1990): Language risk factor in emotionally disturbed children within a school and day treatment program. *Journal of Childhood Communication Disorders* 13, 123–33.

Walcott, C. M. & Landau, S. (2004). The relation between disinhibition and emotion regulation in boys with attention deficit hyperactivity disorder. *Journal of Clinical Child and Adolescent Psychology* 33, 772–82.

Westby, C. E. & Cutler, S. (1994). Language and ADHD: Understanding the bases and treatment of self-regulatory behaviors. *Topics in Language Disorders* 14 (4), 58–76.

Weyandt, L. L. & Willis, W. G. (1994). Executive functions in school-aged children: Potential efficacy of tasks in discriminating clinical groups. *Developmental Neuropsychology* 19, 27–38.

Whalen C., Henker, B., Collins B., McAuliffe, S., & Vaux, A. (1979). Peer interactions in a structured communication task. Comparison of normal and hyperactive boys and methylphenidate (Ritalin) and placebo effect. *Child Development* 50, 338–401.

Willcutt, E. G., Doyle, A. E., Nigg, J. T., Faraone, S. V., & Pennington, B. (2005). Validity of the executive function theory of attention-deficit/hyperactivity disorder: A meta-analytic review. *Biological Psychiatry* 57 (11), 1336–46.

World Health Organization (2005). *International classification of diseases and health related problems: ICD-10*, 2nd ed. Geneva: World Health Organization.

Yang, K. N., Schaller, J. L., & Parker, R. (2000). Factor structures of Taiwanese teachers' ratings of ADHD: A comparison with U.S. studies. *Journal of Learning Disabilities* 33, 72–82.

Zentall, S. S. (1985). A context for hyperactivity. In K. D. Gamow & I. Bailer (eds.), *Advances in learning and behavioral disabilities*, Vol. 4 (pp. 273–343). Greenwich, CT: JAI Press.

Zentall, S. S. (1988). Production deficiencies in elicited language but not in spontaneous verbalization of hyperactive children. *Journal of Abnormal Child Psychology* 16, 657–73.

24 Communication Deficits Associated with Right Hemisphere Brain Damage

MARGARET LEHMAN BLAKE

1 Introduction

Damage to the right cerebral hemisphere (RHD) may cause a variety of disorders involving communication, attention, and executive functions. Most of the research on cognitive and communication deficits has been conducted with adults who have had a stroke with relatively focal lesions. RHD also may be caused by tumors, traumatic brain injuries, or other neurological insults or diseases. Right-hemisphere (RH) strokes occur with approximately the same frequency as those in the left hemisphere, but may not be recognized or treated as quickly. Foerch and colleagues (Foerch et al., 2005) examined hospital admissions for over 11,000 stroke patients and found that those with left-hemisphere strokes had a shorter amount of time between the onset of symptoms and the time of admission. This difference was most apparent for patients with mild to moderate symptoms; for severe strokes, the timing of admission was similar for right- and left-hemisphere strokes. The authors suggested that impairments in language function and/or of dominant hand function due to left-hemisphere strokes were more obvious and easier for individuals to identify. Additionally, the reduced awareness of deficits (anosognosia) that can accompany RHD may prevent individuals from recognizing symptoms of a RH stroke.

Disorders commonly associated with RHD include impairments in attention, including visuo-spatial neglect; cognitive deficits apparent in executive functions; and difficulties with effective and efficient communication. The focus of this chapter will be on disorders of communication, theoretical underpinnings of those disorders, and suggestions for intervention.

2 Overview of Disorders of Communication

Communication deficits resulting from RHD may not initially be apparent to an examiner and are quite different from aphasic language disorders. While adults with aphasia have difficulty with linguistic aspects of communication, adults with RHD have difficulty with extralinguistic and pragmatic aspects. Extralinguistic aspects include organization and content of discourse, use of prosody and non-verbal communication, and interpretation of intent as opposed to literal interpretation of linguistic content.

Discourse can generally be defined as two or more connected sentences. Adults with RHD often exhibit deficits in comprehension of discourse. They may seem to miss the "gist" or overall theme of a story or have difficulty generating a title for a picture or story that conveys the theme (Benowitz, Moya, & Levine 1990; Gardner et al., 1983; Hough, 1990; Joanette et al., 1986; Mackisack, Myers, & Duffy, 1987; Moya et al., 1986; Myers & Brookshire, 1994, 1996; Rehak et al., 1992).

Discourse production also often is affected. Discourse can be disorganized, rambling, and tangential with no apparent purpose or topic (Brady, Mackenzie, & Armstrong, 2003; Chantraine, Joanette, & Ska, 1998; Cherney, Drimmer, & Halper, 1997; Glosser, 1993; Joanette et al., 1986; Lojek-Osiejuk, 1996; Mackenzie et al., 1999; Marini et al., 2005; Wapner, Hamby, & Gardner, 1981). The topic may not be appropriate for the situation or communication partner. There may be poor cohesion (individual sentences are not clearly related or linked) or poor coherence (the topic or purpose is unclear). Pragmatic deficits also may be apparent. Individuals with RHD may exhibit poor eye contact and poor turn taking. They also may not appear to have a sense of a listener's knowledge in terms of what the listener knows and does not know about a particular topic, or that the listener may have different beliefs or viewpoints. This is referred to as theory of mind (e.g., Brownell & Martino, 1998; Griffin et al., 2006; Happé, Brownell, & Winner, 1999; Winner et al., 1998). Adults with RHD may not be able to recognize breakdowns in conversations, nor be able to repair them if the breakdown is noticed. Some may be very animated, talk a lot, and provide too much information (Hillis Trupe & Hillis, 1985; Mackisack, Myers, & Duffy, 1987); others may display little emotion or affect, say very little, and provide minimal information in response to questions (Mackenzie, Begg, & Brady, 1997; Uryase, Duffy, & Liles, 1991). Some adults with RHD have difficulties interpreting non-verbal cues, such as facial expressions or prosody (Blonder et al., 2005; Bloom et al., 1990; Bloom et al., 1992; Borod et al., 2000; Ross, 1981). They may not be able to determine speakers' intents or emotional states based on facial expressions or tone of voice. They also may not effectively convey their own emotional states, either through word choice or prosody.

Adults with RHD are a heterogeneous group. There is a wide range of deficits associated with damage to the RH. No obvious patterns of broadly defined cognitive and communication deficits have been observed (Blake et al., 2002). However, Côté and colleagues (Côté et al., 2007) reported four clusters of communication deficits in a small group of participants. One group had a broad range of deficits in many areas of communication; a second had no obvious deficits in any one area; a third group had specific problems with lexical-semantic processing; and the fourth was characterized by relative preservation of discourse processing compared to the other areas. More extensive research is needed to confirm these results.

Approximately 50 percent of all adults with RHD exhibit cognitive-communicative deficits (Benton & Bryan, 1996; Joanette & Goulet, 1994), while 80–90 percent of those admitted to a rehabilitation unit following RHD demonstrate such deficits (Blake et al., 2002; Côté et al., 2007). Prevalence estimates suggest that attention/ perception and learning/memory deficits are the most commonly diagnosed, while communication deficits such as aprosodia and pragmatic deficits are less frequently observed (Blake et al., 2002). These findings may be due in part to the fact that (at least in the United States) speech-language pathologists, who are most likely to observe and diagnose communication deficits, do not always receive referrals to assess and/or treat these individuals.

The ensuing discussion will focus on communication deficits associated with RHD, themes underlying these deficits that recur in the RHD literature, and clinical implications. Readers should remember that not all adults with RHD have the deficits discussed, and although there are suggested or logical links between many of the proposed underlying deficits, little research has been done to specifically evaluate the existence of those links.

3   Themes Underlying Comprehension Disorders

Several themes have surfaced in the understanding of communication disorders associated with RHD. These include (a) impairments in activation of less-frequent or less-familiar meanings, (b) difficulties with multiple meanings, and (c) difficulties integrating contextual cues to determine the most appropriate interpretation. These three areas are closely intertwined: activation of less-frequent meanings is one component of dealing with multiple meanings, and the use of contextual cues is necessary to determine the appropriate interpretation when several are possible.

3.1   Activation of distantly related meanings

One theme that has arisen from work with RHD is the activation of less-familiar or less-frequent meanings or features of words. Beeman (1993, 1998; Beeman, Bowden, & Gernsbacher, 2000; Jung-Beeman, 2005) first proposed a fine-coding vs. coarse-coding hypothesis to explain processing styles within the intact right hemisphere. According to this account, the intact left hemisphere uses "fine coding" in which small, circumscribed representations of words are activated. These representations include frequent or familiar, and often concrete, meanings or features. In contrast, the right hemisphere uses "coarse coding" in which broad representations of words are activated. These include abstract or metaphorical meanings, distantly related meanings, or less-familiar or less-frequent features of a word (e.g., glass can cut). The broad activations are maintained within the right hemisphere until the correct interpretation (derived from semantic and syntactic analyses) is selected by the left hemisphere. Beeman proposed that RHD would abolish this coarse coding and resulting interpretations would reflect the fine coding of the left hemisphere, which would be devoid of inferences and non-literal or abstract interpretations.

This and other accounts based on normal functioning of the intact right hemisphere must be used cautiously in generating predictions about disorders resulting from RHD (e.g., Tompkins & Lehman, 1998; Tompkins, Fassbinder, et al., 2002). Many reports of performance by adults with RHD do not match the predictions. This may be in part because predictions either implicitly or explicitly suggest that damage to the right hemisphere results in loss of functioning of the entire hemisphere. Additionally, it is not known what resulting deficits may be a result of loss of excitation versus inhibition of remaining right or intact left hemisphere functions.

While the predictions about performance by adults with RHD based on the coarse-coding hypothesis were overly general and directly tested in only one study of eight individuals with RHD (Beeman, 1993), some components of the coarse-coding hypothesis have been confirmed in an independent study. Tompkins and colleagues (Tompkins, Fassbinder et al., 2008; Tompkins, Scharp et al., 2008) reported a coarse-coding deficit for activation and maintenance of distantly related features (e.g., "rotten" for apple). Adults with RHD were less likely to exhibit activation of distantly related features (Tompkins, Fassbinder et al., 2008), and failure to maintain the activation of such features was related to inferential discourse comprehension performance (Tompkins, Scharp et al., 2008).

3.2 Multiple meanings

Multiple meanings occur in ambiguous words or sentences and non-literal language such as idioms, metaphors, indirect requests, and sarcasm. Sarcasm and "white lies" both involve multiple meanings, but in contrast to idioms and metaphors, they convey direct contradictions of meaning. Various studies of language disorders in adults with RHD suggest that adults with RHD are overly literal, and are unable to infer meanings or intents that are not explicitly stated (Brownell et al., 1984; Kaplan et al., 1990; Kempler et al., 1999; McDonald, 2000b; Myers & Linebaugh, 1981; Sabbagh, 1999; Van Lancker & Kempler, 1987; Wapner, Hamby, & Gardner, 1981). Many of these conclusions were derived from studies in which comprehension of non-literal language was tested without context: participants were asked to match an idiom with a picture, or asked to describe what an idiom meant. The results indicated that adults with RHD were more likely to select literal interpretations, or to provide a literal retelling of idioms/ metaphors, as compared to adults with LHD or without brain damage. In picture description tasks, adults with RHD were less likely to generate inferential concepts (e.g., Myers & Brookshire, 1994, 1996). The "overly literal" characteristic became engrained in the RHD stereotype.

In contrast to those reports of deficits in processing non-literal language, adults with RHD have been reported to generate multiple meanings for ambiguous sentences. Tompkins and colleagues (Tompkins et al., 2001) demonstrated that given a sentence with a lexical ambiguity such as "She picked up the spade," adults with RHD were able to indicate that both "card" and "shovel" were potential interpretations. Similarly, participants were able to accept multiple meanings of inferential ambiguities such as: "The customer asked Joe to trim carefully in the back," in which they indicated both "barber" and "gardener" were possible interpretations (Tompkins, Lehman-Blake et al., 2002).

One explanation for the deficits in processing non-literal meanings is the impairment in activation of distant meanings, described above. It is not yet clear what the boundaries are for defining "distant" meanings of words. Previous work has demonstrated that in online tasks, adults with RHD activate non-literal meanings of idioms (Tompkins, Boada, & McGarry, 1992), and have difficulty primarily with features that are fairly distant from common word meanings (e.g., "rotten" for apple) (Tompkins, Fassbinder et al., 2008; Tompkins, Scharp et al., 2008). These results indicate that the activation deficit does not prevent *all* access to non-literal meanings. Further work is needed to determine what should be considered "distant" meanings.

Another factor to be considered is the complexity of the tasks (e.g., Tompkins & Lehman, 1998). For tasks that involve matching lexical items to pictures or picture description, visuo-perceptual skills should be accounted for to ensure that misperceptions are not a contributor to poor performance. Defining non-literal language is a metalinguistic task, which adds a variety of demands to the process of interest, and may obscure the results. Support for this explanation was provided by Tompkins and colleagues (Tompkins, Boada, & McGarry, 1992), who reported that adults with RHD demonstrated recognition of idioms in an online, implicit task, even though the same participants were unable to accurately define those same items in an offline task. Defining non-literal language may be more difficult than defining an unambiguous statement because there are two potential meanings. If the idiom is presented without any context, participants may activate both meanings, and then have difficulty selecting which meaning they think is the intended meaning prior to defining the statement. This will be discussed below in terms of a suppression deficit.

A critical problem with the "overly literal" characteristic is that examination of responses by adults with RHD from prior studies indicates that they do not respond only with concrete information that was explicitly stated or presented; on the contrary, many responses contain inferences. For example, Wapner and colleagues (1981) asked participants to describe the mood of characters in stories. Adults with RHD were able to generate moods, although the emotions did not always match with the story. Thus, the problem is not with the ability to generate inferences (infer someone's mood), but to integrate contextual cues in order to generate the most appropriate. Similarly, Stemmer, Giroux, and Joanette (1994) reported that adults with RHD were able to appropriately produce and interpret most direct and indirect requests following short vignettes, with deficits confined to one type of indirect requests (hints).

3.3   *Using context to facilitate comprehension*

A third theme that has emerged is the use of context in comprehension. The RHD literature is replete with conflicting results and conclusions. Some studies suggest that adults with RHD are unable to use context to generate inferences (Beeman, 1993; Purdy, Belanger, & Liles, 1992; Rehak et al., 1992) and identify main ideas (Hough, 1990; Wapner, Hamby, & Gardner, 1981). In contrast, other studies indicate that use of context is not abolished (Blake & Lesniewicz, 2005; Lehman-Blake & Tompkins, 2001; Leonard, Waters, & Caplan, 1997a, 1997b; Leonard et al., 2001; Leonard & Baum, 1998, 2005; Rehak et al., 1992). For example, using a word-monitoring task, adults with RHD exhibited normal context effects given a semantically anomalous statement as opposed to a semantically appropriate sentence (Leonard & Baum, 1998). For example, they responded faster to the word "store" when it appeared in a semantically appropriate sentence (1a) than when it appeared in a semantically anomalous sentence (1b):

(1a)   They were relieved to find that a *store* was near.
(1b)   They were impressed to feel that a *store* was gradual.

These context effects were maintained even in cognitively demanding conditions, including compressed speech rate (Leonard et al., 2001) and divided attention conditions (Leonard & Baum, 2005). Additionally, although individuals with RHD may provide a literal interpretation of an indirect request that is posed without context (e.g., answering "yes" to "Can you pass the salt?"), they respond appropriately when the requests occur within natural conversation settings (Vanhalle et al., 2000).

4   The Use of Context

Three components of the ability to use context will be discussed. One is the ability to use context to generate inferences. A second is the ability to determine the most appropriate interpretation if two are possible. A third component is the ability to integrate *multiple* contextual cues to determine the most likely interpretation.

4.1   Using context to generate inferences

There are a variety of types of inferences. One basic classification scheme divides them into inferences that are necessary for comprehension and those that elaborate or expand upon understanding, but are not required for basic comprehension (McKoon & Ratcliff, 1992). The former are referred to as coherence or bridging inferences, because they are required for maintaining local coherence or for bridging consecutive sentences. Bridging inferences are generated quickly by most comprehenders (including young adults, older adults, and adults with RHD), and are considered to be "automatic" in that they require few mental resources (e.g., McKoon & Ratcliff, 1992). Mapping pronouns onto referents can be considered a very basic form of bridging inference. Elaborative inferences, on the other hand, are not required for comprehension. These include inferences about tools used but not specified, character moods and motivations, and predictions about what will happen in a story. In example (2a), comprehenders may infer that Kristy used a spoon to stir her coffee, but this inference is not needed to understand the sentence as it is (e.g., Graesser, Singer & Trabasso, 1984):

(2a) Kristy stirred her coffee and then took a small sip.
(2b) As she put the cup down she knocked the spoon onto the floor.
(2c) As she put the cup down she knocked the fork onto the floor.

Generation of elaborative inferences can be beneficial if subsequent information refers to an inferred event or item. For example, if (2a) was followed by (2b), and if comprehenders had inferred that Kristy stirred with a spoon, they would quickly comprehend this second sentence, as they already had a spoon in their mental representation of the story. Elaborative inferences also can disrupt comprehension if they are not validated. If (2c) followed (2a), comprehenders may have to revise their initial inference about the spoon to determine how the fork fit into the story.

Beeman (1993) reported RHD impairments in generating bridging inferences, but there have been multiple studies that have suggested otherwise. Leonard and colleagues (Leonard, Waters, & Caplan, 1997a, 1997b) reported that adults with RHD were able to use semantic cues within a sentence to disambiguate pronouns, as in (3a) (Leonard et al., 1997a):

(3a) Mark lost to Paul because he was a poor player.
(3b) Mark lost to Paul because he was a great player.

They also were able to use semantic cues to override syntactic preferences in assigning pronouns to referents, as in (3b). Verbs have an implicit causality property in which the action or emotion of a verb typically is assigned to either the subject or object. Implicit causality has a strong effect on the determination of referents for ambiguous pronouns (see Leonard, Waters, & Caplan, 1997a for a brief review). An ambiguous pronoun accompanying the verb "lost" is typically linked to the subject, rather than the object of a sentence. However, in sentence (3b), the context indicates that the object (Paul) is the more appropriate referent. Together, these results suggest that adults with RHD maintain the ability to use semantic contextual cues within single sentences, and can even use these cues to override syntactic preferences.

Adults with RHD also are able to use semantic cues and world knowledge to assign ambiguous pronouns to referents across sentences (Leonard, Waters, & Caplan, 1997a, 1997b). In one study (Leonard et al., 1997a) the disambiguating information appeared in the first sentence (4a). Adults with RHD were faster to identify the correct referent for the ambiguous pronoun when the context was present versus without the context. This result was found even when the semantically appropriate referent did not agree with the implicit causality bias of the verb. In a second study (Leonard et al., 1997b), the researchers created ambiguities that had to be resolved using world knowledge (4b). Again, in this case, adults with RHD were able to correctly resolve the pronoun ambiguity and their performance patterns matched those of a control group without brain damage:

(4a) Mark knew that Paul was an understanding priest and would grant absolution. Mark confessed to Paul because he offered forgiveness.

(4b) Henry spoke at a meeting while John drove to the beach. He brought along a surfboard.

Adults with RHD also can use context to generate certain types of elaborative inferences, particularly predictive inferences. Blake and colleagues (Blake & Lesniewicz, 2005; Lehman-Blake & Tompkins, 2001) demonstrated that adults with RHD can use strong contextual cues to generate predictive inferences. Given the sentence "Beth took out a broom and began to clean," evidence suggests that they predict that she is going to sweep (Lehman-Blake & Tompkins, 2001). Adults with RHD also are able to generate predictive inferences from longer texts in which several contextual cues have to be integrated to determine the outcome (Blake & Lesniewicz, 2005). In one stimulus story, a retired widow is barely living off her social security check, has a valuable anniversary ring, does not want to ask family for help, and goes to a local jeweler. The target outcome was that she would sell the ring. Adults with RHD were able to generate the target inference as frequently as adults without brain damage. They generated the target inference even in a second, less strongly biasing condition, in which the woman's social security check was late, she had a valuable but damaged ring that she wanted to have fixed, and had family that she could ask for help in a crisis. Both adults with RHD and those without brain damage repeated the target inference (sell) more often and were more confident of the outcome ("she *will* sell the ring" versus "she *might* sell the ring") for the strongly biasing condition as compared to the less strongly biased condition.

4.2   *Determining appropriate interpretations*

Tompkins and colleagues (Tompkins et al., 2000; Tompkins et al., 2001; Tompkins et al., 2004; Tompkins, Lehman-Blake et al., 2002) proposed the suppression deficit hypothesis to explain RHD deficits in comprehending lexical and inferential ambiguities. Results of the studies indicated that the problem was not in the initial activation of multiple meanings, as described above. Rather, the deficit appeared in suppressing the less likely meaning when an ambiguous word was inserted into a disambiguating context (5a). Adults with RHD accepted the correct meaning (shovel), but were slower to reject the alternate meaning (card) as being unrelated to the sentence (Tompkins et al., 2001):

(5a) She *dug* with a spade.

(5b) The customer asked Joe to trim carefully in the back. She wanted her entire yard to look perfect.

Again, the effects were replicated in stimuli that contained inferential ambiguities (Brownell et al., 1986; Tompkins, Lehman-Blake et al., 2002). In (5b) the preferred interpretation of the first sentence – that Joe was a barber – had to be revised once the second sentence was introduced. Again, adults with RHD were able to accept the correct (revised) meaning, but were slower than adults without brain damage to confirm that "barber" was not related to the story as a whole. The results indicated that suppression was inefficient but not eliminated after RHD, and that poor suppression may impact overall comprehension.

Interpretation of jokes or verbal humor often relies on the ability to revise an initial interpretation. In the joke below (6) a disconnect is detected between the question and the answer, sparking a reinterpretation of the question, in which the word "flies" is reinterpreted from the original interpretation (movement) to one that coheres with the answer (bugs).

(6)   Q: What has four wheels and flies?
       A: A garbage truck.

Adults with RHD may have difficulty with the process of identifying a disconnect and reinterpreting their initial interpretation. A difficulty with the reinterpretation process was reported by Brownell and colleagues (Brownell et al., 1983). They examined whether or not adults with RHD could correctly identify a punchline to a joke. The results indicated that the participants generally selected a punchline that created a disconnect or surprise ending, but that the answer did not cohere with the body of the joke. Thus, they were unable to reinterpret the story so that it would cohere with the surprising ending.

Theory of mind, the ability to understand another's ideas, views, and emotions, and understand that they can differ from one's own, has been implicated in the communication deficits caused by RHD (Brownell & Martino, 1998; Griffin et al., 2006; Happé, Brownell, & Winner, 1999; Winner et al., 1998). More broadly, Sabbagh (1999, p. 56) suggested that RHD communication problems are due to "a fundamental deficit in the ability to think about mental states." A critical issue with the theory of mind explanation is the complexity of the stimuli. The correct interpretation of the outcome depends on what each character knows, and if they know what the other character knows. Happé and colleagues (1999) reported that adults with RHD had particular difficulty with stories that hinged on social interactions (7). However, when the complexity of comparison stories was carefully matched to the social stories, no differences were found (Tompkins, Scharp, Fassbinder et al., 2008). This suggests that complexity may be a factor in interpretation of social interactions, and the deficits may not be restricted to processing social aspects of communication:

(7)   A soldier taken prisoner during a war is interrogated. The interrogators are convinced that the soldier will lie about the location of his army's tanks. The prisoner is clever, and does not want the interrogators to know

that the tanks are really in the mountains. When asked, the prisoner states, "the tanks are in the mountains."

4.3 Integrating multiple cues

As suggested above, the problem with inferencing may not lie in the basic ability to use context, or being able to use individual, strongly suggestive contextual cues, but rather in the ability to integrate *multiple* cues to determine the most appropriate meaning out of several possible meanings (e.g., Tompkins & Lehman, 1998).

In the "thinking out loud" study discussed above (Blake & Lesniewicz, 2005), both groups demonstrated activation of target predictive inferences. The difference between groups appeared in the number of alternative predictive inferences generated: individuals without brain damage made few alternative inferences in the strongly biasing condition, and more in the weakly biased condition. The RHD group, in contrast, made the same number of alternative predictions in the strongly and the weakly biasing stories. This result suggested that although they were able to use context to generate the predictions, they had difficulty integrating the multiple cues in order to narrow down their interpretation to the most likely outcome.

Myers (1999; Myers & Brookshire, 1994) provided examples of difficulties integrating multiple cues in response to picture description tasks. Adults with RHD asked to describe Norman Rockwell prints often generated inferences about a scene, but were not able to integrate all of the relevant cues to determine the overall theme or meaning. For example, in the painting "Breaking Home Ties," a farmer and a teenaged boy are sitting on the running board of an old truck. The boy is dressed in a suit with a look of eager anticipation on his face and a suitcase with a university sticker on it. Some participants responded that the men were waiting for someone to help fix a flat tire, or they were trying to hitch a ride somewhere. Another suggested that they had run over a chicken. All of these responses are inferences about what is happening in the picture, but none represent an integration of all of the relevant cues needed to determine the overarching theme.

Integration of multiple cues also may be a factor in difficulties with interpreting intent. Cues to intent are conveyed in a variety of modalities. In addition to choice of words and syntactic arrangement, prosodic cues, facial expressions, relationships between communicators, and world knowledge often add to intent. If I said to a student wearing a bright pink shirt, "That's a nice shirt," it could be interpreted either as complimentary or sarcastic. The prosodic contours (tone of voice) I used would help convey that intent. It also may help to know my relationship with the student: if I knew her well, then I may be more likely to joke with her about a garish-looking outfit, as opposed to if I did not know her well. My facial expression also would help convey my intent. An additional cue might be what I was wearing: if I had on a shirt the exact same color, I might be complimenting both of us on our choice of attire. Adults generally are able to quickly integrate all potential cues and determine the correct intention. If some of those cues are missing, misinterpretations may occur. One common example is communicating via email. Given the absence of non-verbal cues such as prosody and facial expression, the intent of email messages can be misconstrued. A joke can be interpreted literally without the associated smile or emotional prosody signaling a "joking" intent that would be conveyed in person.

Brownell and colleagues (Brownell et al., 1997; Kaplan et al., 1990) have examined interpretation of intent of comments or responses in short vignettes in which various cues are manipulated. In one study (Kaplan et al., 1990), a character's comment could be interpreted as either a lie or a joke (sarcasm) based on the relationship between the characters (friendly or hostile) and how well one of them performed (well or poorly). While adults without brain damage used both factors (relationship and performance) to interpret the responses, adults with RHD generally used only the performance. Unable to integrate multiple cues, they focused on only one of them. The authors suggested that problems with understanding relationships or characters' shared knowledge could have contributed to the difficulties.

An inability to integrate multiple cues also was demonstrated in a study of the use of formal versus informal personal references (Brownell et al., 1997). In each stimulus vignette, two characters were interacting, and referred to a third, absent person. Three variables were manipulated: how well a character knew the person he was referring to, the status of the person he was referring to, and the relationship between the two people interacting. Adults without brain damage used all three cues to determine whether to refer to the absent person formally (e.g., Mr. Joseph) or informally (e.g., Peter). In contrast, adults with RHD generally used the status variable, choosing formal titles for characters that had a high occupational status (e.g., a boss). Again, they were unable to integrate multiple cues and so relied on only one. As with the Kaplan et al. (1990) study, RHD participants had the most difficulty using relationship variables (e.g., choosing to refer to the boss by his first name if the character was close friends with the boss).

For adults with RHD several factors may contribute to problems correctly determining intent. As described above, they may have difficulty integrating multiple cues and they may select one interpretation based on only one or two of the possible cues. Second, RHD often results in difficulties interpreting prosody (aprosodia). If adults with RHD are not able to interpret a happy versus serious tone of voice they would lose that cue for determining intent. Similarly, RHD can cause difficulties with visuo-perceptual skills and interpreting facial expressions. Again, this would eliminate or distort another potential cue. These factors result in a reduction of potential cues, and difficulties integrating those that are processed correctly. Carefully controlled research is needed to determine whether there are certain types of cues that are more difficult to process (e.g., relationship cues), whether there is a "breaking point" at which adults with RHD cannot integrate any more cues (e.g., can they integrate two or three, but not four or more?), or other factors that influence performance, such as modality (visual versus verbal stimuli or tasks).

5 Discourse Production Deficits

Less attention has been paid to problems with discourse production. Studies have been conducted to elicit discourse and to examine characteristics of RHD discourse, but there have been no direct explorations of hypotheses to explain the discourse deficits. A variety of problems have been described. Marini and colleagues (Marini et al., 2005) examined story retelling by adults with RHD. Tasks included retelling a written story, telling a story based on a cartoon sequence, and telling a story based on a cartoon sequence that first had to be put into the correct order. The RHD group had no apparent difficulties with the story retelling, in which they were able to construct cohesive, coherent stories that were complete and accurate. Problems surfaced with the cartoon sequence conditions in all areas examined. The stories produced by participants in the RHD group were less cohesive and less coherent, and relevant details were omitted. In the third task, in which a sequence had to be correctly ordered first, the RHD group had difficulties with the ordering task as well as in constructing a story. The results generally supported previous reports of difficulties with story structure (macrostructure; Joanette et al., 1986), extracting a theme or main idea around which to construct a story (Delis et al., 1983; Hough, 1990; Joanette & Goulet, 1994), and deficits that are more apparent on story construction from pictures than from verbal retelling tasks (Davis & Coelho, 2004). Marini and colleagues suggested that deficits may lie in the ability to create mental models, while others have suggested it is based on the ability to generate a theme or structure (e.g., Sabbagh, 1999). These explanations are more descriptive than prescriptive, and need to be systematically examined.

The suppression deficit hypothesis (Tompkins et al., 2000, 2001, 2002), while developed and tested for comprehension deficits, may explain some discourse deficits. If adults with RHD generate multiple possible interpretations and then are slow to suppress those that are not relevant, the irrelevant concepts may be verbalized in their discourse productions, appearing as tangential or irrelevant comments. A study of suppression and its relationship to discourse production characteristics is needed to explore this potential correlation.

Another explanation for poor discourse production is the presence of executive function deficits. Deficits in organization, planning, and sequencing, along with other components of executive function, have been reported in the RHD literature (e.g., Martin & McDonald, 2003; McDonald, 2000a; Tompkins, 1995). Such deficits could have logical implications for organizing and sequencing discourse in a story generation task, although there is little supportive evidence. Marini and colleagues (2005) screened participants on a variety of cognitive tests to exclude participants with general cognitive disorders, yet still observed discourse deficits in the RHD group. Martin and McDonald (2003) failed to find clear relationships between executive functioning tasks and pragmatic deficits.

Sabbagh (1999) suggests that production deficits may arise from difficulties with "communicative intentions" and the ability to tailor a conversation to a specific communication partner. This involves an understanding of the partner's goals, knowledge, and intentions, and how they fit with one's own. It also includes interpreting the other person's intentions, such as when a conversational partner introduces an apparently irrelevant piece of information. While adults without brain damage typically interpret this as a desire to change the topic of conversation, adults with RHD are more likely to believe that it is somehow related to the original topic (Rehak et al., 1992). The communicative intention explanation, similar to many others, is fairly broad and vague, and has not been objectively defined or systematically examined to determine the usefulness of the concept in assessing and treating adults with RHD.

6 Assessment

Assessment of communication disorders associated with RHD typically involves observation, informal testing, and formal measures. There are a few batteries specifically designed for adults with RHD. These include the Burns Brief Inventory of Communication and Cognition (Burns, 1997), the Mini Inventory of Right Brain Injury (MIRBI; Pimental & Kingsbury, 1989); the Rehabilitation Institute of Chicago Evaluation Clinical Management of Right Hemisphere Dysfunction – Revised (RICE-R; Halper, Cherney & Burns, 1996); the Right Hemisphere Language Battery (RHLB; Bryan, 1989); and the Protocole Montreal d'Evaluation de la Communication (Protocole MEC; Joanette, Ska & Côté, 2004; currently available in French with an English translation in progress). These all include subtests of non-literal language comprehension. The Burns Inventory includes one subtest that assesses inference revision processes. The deficits in inference revision reported by Tompkins and colleagues (2001) were apparent in reaction times, but not necessarily accuracy. Participants with RHD were able to revise interpretations, but were slower to do so than adults without brain damage. Thus, an offline, untimed comprehension task such as that included in the Burns Inventory likely will not be sensitive to suppression deficits. Only the Protocole MEC tests comprehension of lengthy discourse. Assessment of pragmatics (where included) is based on subjective judgments from small conversational samples. In general, these measures are not sensitive to mild deficits.

7 Treatment

There is minimal evidence regarding the efficacy of treatments for discourse and pragmatic deficits in adults with RHD. Current suggestions generally are based on treating the symptoms. While some have a theoretical basis, others do not (e.g., Myers, 1999; Tompkins, 1995). Preliminary data from one treatment study have been published. Lundgren and colleagues (2006) constructed a treatment to facilitate comprehension of metaphors (e.g., "some jobs are jails"). Partial data from three participants indicated that the treatment led to improvements in using the treatment strategy for determining metaphorical meanings. However, the authors did not assess generalization to other tasks, or whether benefits facilitated other communication abilities (e.g., discourse comprehension or production). In the absence of evidence for treatment efficacy or effectiveness, one option is to use existing theories and accounts to develop treatments (see Blake, 2007 for other treatment suggestions).

7.1 Treatment for impaired activation of distantly related meanings and multiple meanings

Traditional treatment approaches based on the "overly literal" stereotype of adults with RHD suggest encouraging generation of multiple meanings and non-literal meanings of stimuli; however, the evidence does not support their use. While the coarse-coding hypothesis (Beeman, 1993; 1998; Jung-Beeman 2005) suggests extensive deficits in activation of secondary or more distantly related meanings, research specifically with adults with RHD suggests the problems are specific to meanings or features that are quite distant (Tompkins, Scharp, Meigh et al., 2008). Further research is needed to determine the effect of such activation deficits on discourse comprehension and communicative interactions, and whether treatment for these deficits would have an effect on communicative competency.

7.2 Treatment using context to facilitate comprehension

The use of context to guide appropriate interpretations and determine intent may be fruitful. Context can facilitate interpretations when multiple meanings are activated, such as with an inefficient suppression function, and can facilitate interpreting intent in social interactions. These treatment suggestions are theoretically based, but currently have not been tested to determine their efficacy or effectiveness.

Blake (2007) provides a variety of examples of treatment stimuli that can be used to emphasize the use of context (see also Myers, 1999; Tompkins & Baumgaertner, 1998). At the most basic level, ambiguous words can be paired with related words to bias interpretations (8a). Ambiguous words also can be inserted into sentences that provide contextual disambiguation (8b). Ambiguous sentences also can be used, and then an additional, disambiguating sentence can be added either by the clinician or by the client (8c):

(8a) ball – dance vs. ball – catch
(8b) The prince danced at the ball; The prince threw the ball to his dog; The prince hosted a ball to celebrate his engagement.
(8c) The prince threw a ball. He invited the entire kingdom to celebrate his engagement.

Contextual cues also can be used to determine appropriate meanings of non-literal language, particularly if clients are unfamiliar with the idioms or similes used. In increasingly multicultural societies, some clients may not be familiar with

Table 24.1   Example of identifying multiple contextual cues to facilitate interpretation of social interactions

Setting: College classroom. Instructor sees student wearing a bright pink shirt. The instructor says "That's a nice shirt."

Additional linguistic cues to help determine intended meaning
  Male vs. female student

Non-linguistic cues
  Facial expression
  Prosody

Other cues
  Relationship between instructor and student
  The instructor's attire (e.g., wearing the same color)

culturally specific idioms or non-literal language (9a). Clinicians can guide interpretation by putting idioms into contexts and helping the client to identify relevant cues (9b). Particularly for interpreting social interactions (e.g., theory of mind stimuli) and integrating multiple contextual cues, a clinician can guide a client through identifying cues, determining which cues are relevant and which are not, and how intent may change with the addition of multiple cues (see Table 24.1):

(9a)   That's the way the cookie crumbles.
(9b)   John and Rosanne were participating in a raffle, eagerly looking at their ticket stubs. At the end of the evening, when neither of their ticket numbers had been called, John exclaimed, "Oh well, that's the way the cookie crumbles."

7.3   Treatment for discourse production

There is no evidence for efficacy of treatment for discourse production deficits associated with RHD. There are a few studies of treatment for young adults with discourse deficits due to traumatic brain injury (Cannizzaro & Coelho, 2002; Cannizzaro, Coelho, & Youse, 2002), but these have not been very successful at creating lasting improvements in discourse organization or coherence. Myers (1999) provides suggestions for treatments designed to improve construction and use of macrostructures and themes for discourse production. Examples of stimuli and tasks consistent with a theory of mind deficit also are provided.

8   Conclusions

Adults with RHD frequently have difficulties with communication, particularly determining communicative intent. Similar to adults with dementia, these individuals "talk better than they communicate." Recurrent themes in the RHD literature suggest that problems occur with multiple meanings and when interpretations rely on integration of multiple cues. These communication processes all are quite complex, which may negatively affect performance and obscure the processes of interest. Much work is needed to identify underlying deficits, to develop psychometrically sound, sensitive measures of those deficits, and develop and test efficacy and effectiveness of treatments for communication deficits in adults with RHD.

REFERENCES

Beeman, M. (1993). Semantic processing in the right hemisphere may contribute to drawing inferences from discourse. *Brain and Language* 44, 80–120.

Beeman, M. (1998). Coarse semantic coding and discourse comprehension. In M. Beeman & C. Chiarello (eds.), *Right hemisphere language comprehension: Perspectives from cognitive neuroscience* (pp. 255–84). Mahwah, NJ: Lawrence Erlbaum.

Beeman, M. J., Bowden, E. M., & Gernbacher, M. A. (2000). Right and left hemisphere cooperation for drawing predictive and coherence inferences during normal story comprehension. *Brain and Language* 71, 310–36.

Benowitz, L. I., Moya, K. L., & Levine, D. N. (1990). Impaired verbal reasoning and constructional apraxia in subjects with right hemisphere damage. *Neuropsychologia* 28, 231–41.

Benton, E. & Bryan, K. (1996). Right cerebral hemisphere damage: Incidence of language problems. *International Journal of Rehabilitation Research* 19, 47–54.

Blake, M. L. (2007). Perspectives on treatment for communication deficits associated with right hemisphere brain damage. *American Journal of Speech-Language Pathology* 16, 331–42.

Blake, M. L., Duffy, J. R., Myers, P. S., & Tompkins, C. A. (2002). Prevalence and patterns of right hemisphere cognitive/ communicative deficits: Retrospective data from an inpatient rehabilitation unit. *Aphasiology* 16, 537–48.

Blake, M. L., Duffy, J. R., Tompkins, C. A., & Myers, P. S. (2003). Right hemisphere syndrome is in the eye of the beholder. *Aphasiology* 17, 423–32.

Blake, M. L. & Lesniewicz, K. (2005). Contextual bias and predictive inferencing in adults with and without right hemisphere brain damage. *Aphasiology* 19, 423–34.

Blonder, L. X., Heilman, K. M., Ketterson, T., Rosenbek, J., Raymer, A., Crosson, B., et al. (2005). Affective facial and lexical expression in aprosodic versus aphasic stroke patients. *Journal of the International Neuropsychological Society* 11, 677–85.

Bloom, R. L., Borod, J. C., Obler, L. K., & Gerstman, L. J. (1992). Impact of emotional content on discourse production in patients with unilateral brain damage. *Brain and Language* 42, 153–64.

Bloom, R. L., Borod, J. C., Obler, L. K., & Koff, E. (1990). A preliminary characterization of lexical emotional expression in right and left brain-damaged patients. *International Journal of Neuroscience* 55, 71–80.

Borod, J. C., Rorie, K. D., Pick, L. H., Bloom, R. L., Andelman, F., Campbell, A. L., et al. (2000). Verbal pragmatics following unilateral stroke: Emotional content and valence. *Neuropsychology* 14, 112–24.

Brady, M., Mackenzie, C., & Armstrong, L. (2003). Topic use following right hemisphere brain damage during three semi-structured conversational discourse samples. *Aphasiology* 17, 881–904.

Brownell, H. H. & Martino, G. (1998). Deficits in inference and social cognition: The effects of right hemisphere brain damage on discourse. In M. Beeman & C. Chiarello (eds.), *Right hemisphere language comprehension: Perspectives from cognitive neuroscience* (pp. 309–28). Mahwah, NJ: Lawrence Erlbaum.

Brownell, H. H., Michel, D., Powelson, J., & Gardner, H. (1983). Surprise but not coherence: Sensitivity to verbal humor in right-hemisphere patients. *Brain and Language* 18, 20–7.

Brownell, H. H., Pincus, D., Blum, A., Rehak, A., & Winner, E. (1997). The effects of right-hemisphere brain damage on patients' use of terms of personal reference. *Brain and Language* 57, 60–79.

Brownell, H. H., Potter, H. H., Bihrle, A. M., & Gardner, H. (1986). Inference deficits in right brain-damaged patients. *Brain and Language* 27, 310–21.

Brownell, H. H., Potter, H. H., Michelow, D., & Gardner, H. (1984). Sensitivity to lexical denotation and connotation in brain damaged patients: A double dissociation? *Brain and Language* 22, 253–65.

Bryan, K. L. (1989). *The right hemisphere language battery*. Kibworth, UK: Far Communications.

Burns, M. S. (1997). *Burns brief inventory of communication and cognition*. San Antonio, TX: Psychological Corporation.

Cannizzaro, M. S., & Coelho, C. (2002). Treatment of story grammar following traumatic brain injury: A pilot study. *Brain Injury* 16, 1065–73.

Cannizzaro, M. S., Coelho, C. A., & Youse, K. (2002). Treatment of discourse deficits following TBI. *Perspectives on Neurophysiology and Neurogenic Speech and Language Disorders* 12, 14–19.

Chantraine, Y., Joanette, Y., & Ska, B. (1998). Conversational abilities in patients with right hemisphere damage. *Journal of Neurolinguistics* 11, 21–32.

Cherney, L. R., Drimmer, D. P, & Halper, A. S. (1997). Informational content and unilateral neglect: A longitudinal investigation of five subjects with right hemisphere damage. *Aphasiology* 11 (4/5) (April/May), 351–63.

Côté, H., Payer, M., Giroux, F., & Joanette, Y. (2007). Towards a description of clinical communication impairment profiles following right-hemisphere damage. *Aphasiology* 21, 739–49.

Davis, G. A. & Coelho, C. (2004). Referential cohesion and logical coherence of narration after closed head injury. *Brain and Language* 89, 508–23.

Delis, D. C., Wapner, W., Gardner, H., & Moses, J. A. (1983). The contribution of the right hemisphere to the organization of paragraphs. *Cortex* 19, 43–50.

Foerch, C., Misselwitz, B., Sitzer, M., Berger, K., Steinmetz, H., & Neumann-Haefelin, T. (2005). Difference in recognition of right and left hemisphere stroke. *Lancet* 366 (9483) (Jul/Aug), 349–51.

Gardner, H., Brownell, H. H., Wapner, W., & Michelow, D. (1983). Missing the point: The role of the right hemisphere in the processing of complex linguistic materials. In E. Perecman (ed.), *Cognitive processing in the right hemisphere* (pp. 169–91). New York: Academic.

Glosser, G. (1993). Discourse patterns in neurologically impaired and aged populations. In H. H. Brownell & Y. Joanette (eds.), *Narrative discourse in neurologically impaired and normal aging adults* (pp. 191–212). San Diego, CA: Singular.

Graesser, A. C., Singer, M., & Trabasso, T. (1994). Constructing inferences during narrative text comprehension. *Psychological Review* 101, 371–95.

Griffin, R., Friedman, O., Ween, J., Winner, E., Happé, F., & Brownell, H. (2006). Theory of mind and the right cerebral hemisphere: Refining the scope of impairment. *Laterality: Asymmetries of Body, Brain and Cognition* 11, 195–225.

Halper, A. S., Cherney, L. R., & Burns, M. S. (1996). *Clinical management of right hemisphere dysfunction*, 2nd ed. Gaithersburg, MD: Aspen Publishers.

Happé, F., Brownell, H., & Winner, E. (1999). Acquired "theory of mind" impairments following stroke. *Cognition* 70, 211–40.

Hillis Trupe, E. & Hillis, A. (1985). Paucity vs. verbosity: Another analysis of right hemisphere communication deficits. In R. H. Brookshire (ed.), *Clinical aphasiology: Conference proceedings*, Vol. 15 (pp. 83–96). Minneapolis, MN: BRK Publishers.

Hough, M. (1990). Narrative comprehension in adults with right and left hemisphere brain-damage: Theme organization. *Brain and Language* 38, 253–77.

Joanette, Y. & Goulet, P. (1994). Right hemisphere and verbal communication: Conceptual, methodological, and clinical issues. *Clinical Aphasiology* 22, 1–23.

Joanette, Y., Goulet, P., Ska, B., & Nespoulous, J.-L. (1986). Informative content of narrative discourse in right-brain-damaged right-handers. *Brain & Language* 29, 81–105.

Joanette, Y., Ska, B., & Côté, H. (2004). *Protocole Montreal d'Evaluation de la Communication (MEC)*. Isbergues: Ortho Edition.

Jung-Beeman, M. (2005). Bilateral brain processes for comprehending natural language. *Trends in Cognitive Sciences* 9, 512–18.

Kaplan, J. A., Brownell, H. H., Jacobs, J. R., & Gardner, H. (1990). The effects of right hemisphere damage on the pragmatic interpretation of conversational remarks. *Brain and Language* 28, 315–33.

Kempler, D., Van Lancker, D., Marchman, V., & Bates, E. (1999). Idiom comprehension in children and adults with unilateral brain damage. *Developmental Neuropsychology* 15, 327–49.

Lehman-Blake, M. T. & Tompkins, C. A. (2001). Predictive inferencing in adults with right hemisphere brain damage. *Journal of Speech, Language and Hearing Research* 44, 639–54.

Leonard, C. L. & Baum, S. R. (1998). On-line evidence for context use by right-brain-damaged patients. *Journal of Cognitive Neuroscience* 10, 499–508.

Leonard, C. L. & Baum, S. R. (2005). Research note: The ability of individuals with right-hemisphere damage to use context under conditions of focused and divided attention. *Journal of Neurolinguistics* 18, 427–41.

Leonard, C. L., Baum, S. R., & Pell, M. D. (2001). The effect of compressed speech on the ability of right-hemisphere-damaged patients to use context. *Cortex* 37 (3), 327–44.

Leonard, C. L., Waters, G. S., & Caplan, D. (1997a). The use of contextual information by right-brain damaged individuals in the resolution of ambiguous pronouns. *Brain and Language* 57, 309–42.

Leonard, C. L., Waters, G. S., & Caplan, D. (1997b). The use of contextual information related to general world knowledge by right brain-damaged individuals in pronoun resolution. *Brain and Language* 57, 343–59.

Lojek-Osiejuk, E. (1996). Knowledge of scripts reflected in discourse of aphasics and right-brain-damaged patients. *Brain and Language* 53, 58–80.

Lundgren, K., Brownell, H. H., Roy, S., & Cayer-Meade, C. (2006). A metaphor comprehension intervention for patients with right hemisphere brain damage:

A pilot study. *Brain and Language* 99, 69–70.

Mackenzie, C., Begg, T., & Brady, M. (1997). The effects on verbal communication skills of right hemisphere stroke in middle age. *Aphasiology* 11, 929–45.

Mackenzie, C., Begg, T., Brady, M., & Lees, K. R. (1999). The effects on verbal communication skills of right hemisphere stroke in middle age. *Aphasiology* 11, 929–46.

Mackisack, E. L., Myers, P. S., & Duffy, J. R. (1987). Verbosity and labeling behavior: The performance of right hemisphere and non-brain-damaged adults on an inferential picture description task. In R. H. Brookshire (ed.), *Clinical aphasiology*, Vol. 17 (pp. 143–51). Minneapolis, MN: BRK.

Marini, A., Carlomagno, S., Caltagirone, C., & Nocentini, U. (2005). The role played by the right hemisphere in the organization of complex textual structures. *Brain and Language* 93, 46–54.

Martin, I. & McDonald, S. (2003). Weak coherence, no theory of mind, or executive dysfunction? Solving the puzzle of pragmatic language disorders. *Brain and Language* 85, 451–66.

McDonald, S. (1999). Exploring the process of inference generation in sarcasm: A review of normal and clinical studies. *Brain and Language* 68, 486–506.

McDonald, S. (2000a). Exploring the cognitive basis of right-hemisphere pragmatic language disorders. *Brain and Language* 75, 82–107.

McDonald, S. (2000b). Neuropsychological studies of sarcasm. *Metaphor and Symbol* 15, 85–98.

McKoon, G. & Ratcliff, R. (1992). Inference during reading. *Psychological Review* 99, 440–66.

Moya, K. L., Benowitz, L. I., Levine, D. N., & Finklestein, S. P. (1986). Covariant deficits in visuospatial abilities and recall of verbal narrative after right hemisphere stroke. *Cortex* 22, 381–97.

Myers, P. S. (1991). Inference failure: The underlying impairment in right-hemisphere communication disorders. *Clinical Aphasiology* 20, 167–80.

Myers, P. S. (1999). *Right hemisphere disorder: Disorders of communication and cognition*. San Diego, CA: Singular.

Myers, P. S. & Brookshire, R. H. (1994). The effects of visual and inferential complexity on the picture descriptions of non-brain-damaged and right-hemisphere-damaged adults. *Clinical Aphasiology* 22, 25–34.

Myers, P. S. & Brookshire, R. H. (1996). The effect of visual and inferential variables on scene descriptions of right-hemisphere-damaged and non-brain-damaged adults. *Journal of Speech and Hearing Research* 39, 870–80.

Myers, P. S. & Linebaugh, C. W. (1981). Comprehension of idiomatic expressions by right-hemisphere-damaged adults. In R. H. Brookshire (ed.), *Clinical aphasiology*, Vol. 11 (pp. 254–61). Minneapolis: BRK Publishers.

Pimental, P. A. & Knight, J. A. (2000). *Mini inventory of right brain injury – revised*. Nerang East, QLD: Pro-Ed Australia.

Purdy, M. H., Belanger, S., & Liles, B. Z. (1992). Right-hemisphere-damaged subjects' ability to use context in inferencing. *Clinical Aphasiology* 21, 135–43.

Rehak, A., Kaplan, J. A., Weylman, S. T., Kelly, B., Brownell, H. H., & Gardner, H. (1992). Story processing in right-hemisphere-brain damaged patients. *Brain and Language* 42, 320–36.

Ross, E. D. (1981). The aprosodias. Functional-anatomic organization of the affective components of language in the right hemisphere. *Archives of Neurology* 38 (9) (Sept), 561–9.

Sabbagh, M. (1999). Communicative intentions and language: Evidence from right-hemisphere damage and autism. *Brain* and *Language* 70, 29–69.

Stemmer, B., Giroux, F., & Joanette, Y. (1994). Production and evaluation of requests by right hemisphere brain-damaged individuals. *Brain and Language* 47, 1–31.

Tompkins, C. A. (1995). *Right hemisphere communication disorders: Theory and management.* San Diego, CA: Singular.

Tompkins, C. A. & Baumgaertner, A. (1998). Clinical value of online measures for adults with right hemisphere brain damage. *American Journal of Speech-Language Pathology* 7, 68–74.

Tompkins, C. A., Baumgaertner, A., Lehman, M. T., & Fassbinder, W. (2000). Mechanisms of discourse comprehension impairment after right hemisphere brain damage: Suppression and enhancement in lexical ambiguity resolution. *Journal of Speech, Language, and Hearing Research* 43, 62–78.

Tompkins, C. A., Bloise, C. G. R., Timko, M. L., & Baumgaertner, A. (1994). Working memory and inference revision in brain-damaged and normally aging adults. *Journal of Speech and Hearing Research* 37, 896–912.

Tompkins, C. A., Boada, R., & McGarry, K. (1992). The access and processing of familiar idioms by brain-damaged and normally aging adults. *Journal of Speech and Hearing Research* 35, 626–37.

Tompkins, C. A., Fassbinder, W., Blake, M. L., Baumgaertner, A., & Jayaram, N. (2004). Inference generation during text comprehension by adults with right hemisphere brain damage: Activation failure versus multiple activation. *Journal of Speech, Language, and Hearing Research* 47, 1380–95.

Tompkins, C. A. & Lehman, M. T. (1998). Interpreting intended meanings after right hemisphere brain damage: An analysis of evidence, potential accounts, and clinical implications. *Topics in Stroke Rehabilitation* 5, 29–47.

Tompkins, C. A., Fassbinder, W., Lehman-Blake, M. T., & Baumgaertner, A. (2002). The nature and implications of right hemisphere language disorders: Issues in search of answers. In A. Hillis (ed.), *Handbook of adult language disorders: Integrating cognitive neuropsychology, neurology, and rehabilitation* (pp. 429–48). Philadelphia: Psychology Press.

Tompkins, C. A., Fassbinder, W., Scharp, V. L., & Meigh, K. M. (2008). Activation and maintenance of peripheral semantic features of unambiguous words after right hemisphere brain damage in adults. *Aphasiology* 22, 119–38.

Tompkins, C. A., Lehman-Blake, M. T., Baumgaertner, A., & Fassbinder, W. (2001). Mechanisms of discourse comprehension impairment after right hemisphere brain damage: Suppression in inferential ambiguity resolution. *Journal of Speech, Language, and Hearing Research* 44, 400–15.

Tompkins, C. A., Lehman-Blake, M., Baumgaertner, A., & Fassbinder, W. (2002). Characterizing comprehension difficulties after right brain damage: Attentional demands of suppression function. *Aphasiology* 16, 559–72.

Tompkins, C. A., Scharp, V. L., Meigh, K. M., & Fassbinder, W. (2008). Coarse coding and discourse comprehension in adults with right hemisphere brain damage. *Aphasiology* 22, 204–23.

Tompkins, C. A., Scharp, V. L., Fassbinder, W., Meigh, K. M., & Armstrong, E. M. (2008). A different story on "theory of mind" deficit in adults with right hemisphere brain damage. Aphasiology 22, 1–20.

Urayse, D., Duffy, R. J., & Liles, B. Z. (1991). Analysis and description of narrative discourse in right-hemisphere-damaged adults: A comparison with neurologically normal and left-hemisphere-damaged aphasic adults. In T. Prescott (ed.), *Clinical aphasiology*, Vol. 19 (pp. 125–38). Austin, TX: Pro-Ed.

Vanhalle, C., Lemieux, S., Joubert, S., Goulet, P., Ska, B., & Joanette, Y. (2000). Processing of speech acts by right hemisphere-damaged patients: An ecological approach. *Aphasiology* 14, 1127–42.

Van Lancker, D. R. & Kempler, D. (1987). Comprehension of familiar phrases by left- but not by right hemisphere damaged patients. *Brain and Language* 32, 265–77.

Wapner, W., Hamby, S., & Gardner, H. (1981). The role of the right hemisphere in the apprehension of complex linguistic material. *Brain and Language* 14, 15–32.

Weylman, S., Brownell, H. H., Roman, M., & Gardner, H. (1989). Appreciation of indirect requests by left- and right-brain-damaged patients: The effects of verbal context and conventionality of wording. *Brain and Language* 62, 89–106.

Winner, E., Brownell, H. H., Happé, F., Blum, A., & Pincus, D. (1998). Distinguishing lies from jokes: Theory of mind deficits and discourse interpretation in right hemisphere brain-damaged patients. *Brain and Language* 62, 89–106.

25   Traumatic Brain Injury

JENNIFER MOZEIKO, KAREN LÉ, AND CARL COELHO

1   Introduction

In this chapter we provide a brief overview of traumatic brain injury (TBI) before discussing the cognitive communication disorders that tend to follow such injury. We then discuss potential cognitive interpretations for communication deficits, focusing on the areas of attention and information processing, memory, and executive functions. Pragmatic deficits, their pervasive nature and their effect on social reintegration are also reviewed. Management of cognitive communication disorders following TBI is beyond the scope of this chapter and touched upon only briefly within each of the aforementioned sections.

2   Overview

Traumatic brain injury (TBI) occurs when there is damage to the brain caused by the impact of external forces. TBI is not to be confused with damage occurring to the brain as a result of cerebrovascular accidents, disease, or toxins, which are etiologies of an internal nature. TBI can result from penetrating head injuries (PHI), such as when a bullet or other object penetrates the skull and enters the brain. Closed head injuries (CHI) are more common and often caused by the rapid acceleration and deceleration of the head such as occurs in falls or motor vehicle accidents. For the remainder of this chapter, the term "TBI" will refer to closed head injuries unless otherwise noted.

2.1   Incidence

The incidence of TBI in the US is approximately 538.2 per 100,000 people (Rutland-Brown et al., 2006). This rate is considered to be low since mild brain injuries are not always accounted for or reported. The percentage of deaths due to TBI has declined from as high as 24.6 per 100,000 in 1979 to an estimated 17.5 per 100,000

The Handbook of Language and Speech Disorders, First Edition. Edited by Jack S. Damico, Nicole Müller, and Martin J. Ball. © 2013 Blackwell Publishing Ltd except for editorial material and organization © 2013 Jack S. Damico, Nicole Müller, Martin J. Ball. Published 2013 by Blackwell Publishing Ltd.

in 2003 (Rutland-Brown et al., 2006). This is a result of improved medical care and injury prevention strategies. (See Brown et al., 2008 for a review on brain injury epidemiology and pathophysiology.)

The global "war on terrorism" has contributed to an even greater increase in the number of TBI survivors. TBI has been called the "signature injury" of the Iraq War, with some experts reporting the incidence of TBI among wounded soldiers to be as high as 22 percent (Martin et al., 2008). Weapons used by the insurgents tend to be those that produce powerful blasts thought to cause shear and stress forces that cause concussion, subdural hematoma, and diffuse axonal injury (DePalma et al., 2005). Blast injuries are classified by the mechanism of injury and typically categorized as primary, secondary, tertiary, quaternary, or quinary (see Rutland-Brown et al., 2008 for descriptions of each).

Body armor and advanced medical care prevent injuries that would have been fatal in previous wars and have contributed to an increase in the number of brain-injured survivors. The need for specific and efficacious brain injury rehabilitation has thus become all the more pressing.

2.2   *Consequences of TBI*

The consequences of TBI vary greatly between individuals, depending on the extent of the injury and the individual who sustained it. There is great variability in symptom presentation even among individuals who appear to have similar brain injuries.

TBI can result in psychosocial symptoms, cognitive deficits, and/or communication difficulty, all of which are obstacles to social reintegration. Unresolved symptoms, even in those with mild TBI, have been associated with limitations in functional outcome including the return to work and engaging in important life activities (Evered et al., 2003). In severe brain injury, even when independence of activities of daily living is achieved, psychosocial outcome is poor. Tate and colleagues (1989) found that nearly 50 percent of patients suffering a severe TBI had limited social contact and few leisure activities one year post injury. Ten years after severe injury, patients' social participation reportedly continues to decline, and close relatives report a decrease in their own quality of life due primarily to the neurobehavioral and emotional factors they must endure (Koskinen, 1998).

Persistent cognitive deficits are the most common complaint after TBI. Most predictably impaired are executive or self-regulation functions; attention and speed of information processing; and short-term memory and learning. There is generally much overlap in function of these cognitive constructs: that is, deficits in attention will impact working memory; deficits in executive function will affect attention, etc. Complaints that result from these cognitive deficits can include difficulty in thinking clearly and efficiently or problems with planning and organizing.

Altered behavior and personality changes are also frequent symptoms following TBI and include altered emotional experience (blunting, lability, or irritability), insensitivity to others' emotions, deficient decision making, poor social and non-social judgment, impulsivity, lack of self-monitoring, and/or inflexibility and deficient goal-directed behavior characterized by apathy, depression, disinhibition, task impersistency, and general disorganization (McAllister, 2008; Rankin, 2007). Behavioral changes tend to be complicated by lack of awareness of changes by the brain-injured individual (McAllister, 2008), making remediation of behavior, including communicative behavior, more difficult.

2.3   *Profile of an injury*

Before beginning a discussion on cognitive-communicative disorders following TBI, it is important to understand the typical profile of injury. TBI resulting from primary blast injuries sustained in war zones such as Iraq and Afghanistan have a somewhat different overall profile but the damage described below applies to all, including those resulting from falls, motor vehicle accidents, and all blast injuries.

1   Certain brain regions have been found to be particularly vulnerable to injury, regardless of whether the damage is diffuse or multifocal (see McAllister, 2008 for more information).
2   Neurotransmitters essential to maintaining cognitive and behavioral homeostasis are altered in TBI (McAllister, 2008).
3   Diffuse axonal injury (DAI) is a disruption of axonal transport, meaning that connections of brain areas to other brain areas are compromised. DAI occurs when the brain is exposed to stretch and torque forces, typically in acceleration and deceleration events (Brown et al., 2008). DAI is the leading cause of morbidity including impairment in cognition, behavior, and arousal (Gennarelli, 1996), and yet recent evidence suggests that its extent has been underestimated due to limitations of imaging techniques (Brown et al., 2008; Rankin, 2007).

This chapter will focus on the cognitive-communicative disorders following TBI, particularly within the domain of pragmatics, arguably the most common, pervasive, and debilitating of the cognitive-communicative disorders. Aphasic deficits following TBI are relatively rare and often show rapid recovery. For example, Richardson (2000) reviewed several studies on TBI and found the incidence of aphasia to range from 2 to 35 percent of individuals. The range is likely a consequence of sample size considering that studies with the smallest samples report the larger percent of cases of aphasia and vice versa. Larger sample sizes may be more representative of the aphasia population. Aphasic deficits will not be discussed in this chapter but are discussed in detail in a variety of other sources (readers should refer to Richardson, 2000 and Togher, McDonald, & Code, 1999 for a summary). Motor speech disorders, which may also be a communicative deficit following TBI, are discussed in the Speech Disorders section of this handbook.

3   Cognitive-Communicative Disorders Following TBI

According to the American Speech-Language-Hearing Association (2005),

> Cognitive-communication disorders encompass difficulty with any aspect of communication that is affected by disruption of cognition. Communication may be verbal or nonverbal and includes listening, speaking, gesturing, reading, and writing in all domains of language (phonologic, morphologic, syntactic, semantic, and pragmatic). Cognition includes cognitive processes and systems (e.g., attention, perception, memory, organization, executive function). Areas of function affected by cognitive impairments include behavioral self-regulation, social interaction, activities of daily living, learning and academic performance, and vocational performance.

3.1   *Discourse impairments*

Discourse impairments are a hallmark of the cognitive-communicative disorders associated with TBI. Disruption of discourse ability is a common problem in individuals with TBI. By and large, individuals with TBI are not aphasic. They do indeed have trouble with communication, but their deficits are not categorized as being purely linguistic. Assessments at the word and sentence level, usually tapping linguistic form and content, typically pose little difficulty for individuals with TBI. However, communication encompasses the use of language as well. Individuals with TBI appear to get their words across, but not their message. Discourse is complex language use that depends on linguistic and non-linguistic cognitive abilities. It is at the level of discourse that individuals with TBI struggle. Given that linguistic ability is adequate, discourse impairments following TBI have been attributed to damage in underlying cognitive systems.

Discourse is dynamic language functioning that can be defined as a series of linguistic units that communicate a message. There are different types of discourse, which fall into two main genres – monologues and conversation. *Monologic discourse* is non-interactive. Procedural discourse (e.g., providing directions to a destination), descriptive discourse (e.g., describing a childhood memory), and story narratives are all types of monologic discourse. *Conversational discourse* is interactive, taking place in a communicative dyad. Both monologic and conversational discourse pose communicative challenges for individuals with TBI. Discourse deficits will be examined by level of analysis within each discourse genre.

3.1.1   Monologic discourse impairments   Measures of monologic discourse are hierarchically categorized according to the level at which the analysis occurs. Monologic discourse may be examined at the *microlinguistic, microstructural, macrostructural,* or *superstructural* level.

3.1.1.1   Microlinguistic discourse impairments   Monologic discourse deficits at the microlinguistic level are inconsistently observed in the TBI literature. Micro-linguistic measures of monologic discourse are within-sentence analyses that tap lexical, semantic, and grammatical processes. These measures are typically concerned with lexical productivity, grammatical complexity and accuracy, or counts of propositional information and content units. *Propositions* refer to units of meaning derived from an utterance's predicate and associated arguments. With regard to syntactic processing and production of propositions, evidence from research studies is equivocal. Some researchers have found that individuals with TBI perform normally on syntactic indices, such as the proportion of T-units with dependent clauses (Chapman et al., 1992) and the number of subordinate clauses per T-unit (Liles et al., 1989), and propositional measures (Chapman et al., 1992). In contrast, other studies have found support for impaired grammatical complexity and accuracy following TBI (Glosser & Deser, 1991) and a reduction in the production of propositions (Coelho et al., 2005).

Evidence has been less variable for measures of productivity, efficiency, and production of content units. A review of several studies found that reduced verbal output and communicative efficiency consistently characterized the discourse of individuals with TBI (Coelho, Ylvisaker, & Turkstra, 2005). Additionally, narratives of TBI subjects may be reduced in conveying essential communicative content (Stout, Yorkston, & Pimentel, 2000). These findings suggest that lexical productivity, communicative efficiency, and identification of relevant story information are more susceptible to cognitive deficits following TBI than other microlinguistic measures and, thus, more sensitive to detecting microlinguistic discourse impairments.

3.1.1.2 Microstructural discourse impairments *Microstructural* analyses, such as cohesion measures, examine discourse across sentences. *Cohesion* refers to how well utterances within a discourse are meaningfully connected to one another. The connections occur through the use of cohesive markers or ties, which establish the local organization of discourse from one sentence to the next. A cohesive marker is identified as an element that cannot be understood without referring to another utterance for its meaning. Cohesive ties are categorized as references (e.g., his, that), conjunctions (e.g., then, and, because), and lexical markers (e.g., "Merlin" in reference to "the magician"). The cohesion of a text is typically assessed through tallies of cohesive devices used and adequacy ratings. A cohesive marker may be judged as complete, incomplete, or erroneous (Liles, 1985).

Studies at the microstructural level of discourse in TBI have yielded mixed results with reports of normal and impaired cohesion. Performance on cohesion measures has been found to be normal across different age groups (Ewing-Cobbs et al., 1998). By contrast, a number of studies have reported impairments in cohesion (Davis & Coelho, 2004; Mentis & Prutting, 1991). Impairments of cohesion have been shown to be influenced by the elicitation task, suggesting that some caution is warranted in extrapolating diagnostic information from cohesion measures using only one mode of story elicitation (Liles et al., 1989).

3.1.1.3 Macrostructural discourse impairments *Macrostructural* analyses involve assessments of coherence at local and global levels. The thematic unity of a text is referred to as *coherence*, reflected locally, in meaningful relationships between utterances, or globally, between an utterance and the text in its entirety. Rating scales are typically employed to evaluate coherence (Glosser & Deser, 1991; Van Leer & Turkstra, 1999a). As such, most of the currently available macrostructural procedures have a strong subjective component, which may account for the lower reliability of coherence indices in comparison to other types of monologic discourse analysis (Coelho, 1995). A more quantitative approach to coherence analysis has been taken using ratio scores that combined a count of causal connections and the number of propositions within a discourse sample (Davis & Coelho, 2004).

There is general agreement that coherence is disrupted in the TBI population, although a few studies have emerged with contrary results. A few investigations have shown no difference between TBI and non-brain-injured participants on coherence measures (Van Leer & Turkstra, 1999b). However, several studies have demonstrated that individuals with TBI have poorer coherence than non-brain-injured controls on both rating scales and more quantitative measures of coherence (Davis & Coelho, 2004; Hough & Barrow, 2003). Emerging evidence casts global coherence, rather than local coherence, as the more affected process in TBI (Glosser & Deser, 1991; Hough & Barrow, 2003), which may reflect the need for increased cognitive resources in producing text that is thematically unified.

3.1.1.4   Superstructural discourse impairments   Superstructural analyses of monologic discourse target the overarching organizational structure, which provides a foundation for semantic information in story narratives. Stories are governed by causal and temporal rules that facilitate comprehension and production of discourse, which are referred to as *story grammar rules*. The episode functions as the critical unit of analysis in story grammar measures. An episode comprises three main components – an initiating event, an attempt, and a direct consequence. Information from story grammar analyses usually pertains to episode completeness, productivity, and efficiency.

The inability of individuals with TBI to organize discourse at the superstructural level has been widely supported in the research literature. Studies have found that TBI participants are less productive with respect to key story elements and often fail to address implied meanings within a story (Tucker & Hanlon, 1998). Reduced storytelling efficiency in the TBI group has been noted, evidenced by a lower proportion of T-units in episodic structure (Coelho, 2002). The findings suggest that TBI participants are less able to organize semantic content.

3.1.2   Conversational discourse impairments   Analyses of conversational discourse are numerous in type and function. Conversational measures may take the form of pragmatic rating scales, checklists, or highly structured types of analyses. The communicative abilities examined may include response appropriateness, topic management, turn taking, and appropriateness of verbal and non-verbal behaviors during interaction.

3.1.2.1   Response appropriateness   Blank and Franklin's (1980) protocol for analyzing response appropriateness in children has been used to examine conversational ability in the TBI population. Conversational partners typically alternate roles as initiators and responders. The response appropriateness procedure involves marking initiator utterances as obliges (i.e., utterances that summon a response from the conversational partner, such as a question) or comments (i.e., utterances that do not necessitate a response). Speaker responses are then coded for adequacy.

It has been noted that TBI participants have a greater number of turns per conversation, decreased adequacy of response and that their conversational partners have a higher proportion of obliges than those paired with normal subjects (Coelho, Liles & Duffy, 1991). During interactions with TBI participants, one study indicated that the onus of communication was carried by the conversational partner, as evidenced by their higher frequency of turns as initiators (Coelho, Youse, & Lé, 2002).

3.1.2.2 Topic management   *Topic management* is an important aspect of conversational ability and has been analyzed using structured approaches. The *intonation unit* is the metric of information in Mentis and Prutting's procedure (1991). Each intonation unit measures the production of a concept. *Ideational intonation units* delineate a concept and are propositional in nature. Ideational units are classified based on their contribution of information to the topic during conversation interaction. Ideational unit analysis has yielded conflicting results (Mentis & Prutting, 1991).

Another structured approach to studying topic management is to examine how the topic is introduced and changed during conversational discourse. Topics may be classified as a (1) *novel introduction* when a new topic is introduced, (2) *smooth shift* when the topic is subtly altered, and (3) *disruptive shift* when the topic is abruptly or illogically changed to another (Brinton & Fujiki, 1989). It has been noted that a general characteristic of conversational discourse in TBI is deficient topic initiation and topic management (Coelho, Ylvisaker, & Turkstra, 2005).

3.1.2.3 Pragmatic rating scales and checklists for conversational discourse   *Pragmatic rating scales* and *checklists* are less structured alternatives to the formal methods described in the previous sections. A variety of these measures are available, ranging in breadth and depth of the conversational skills assessed. These include Clinical Discourse Analysis (CDA; Damico, 1985), the Pragmatic Protocol (Prutting & Kirchner, 1987), the Profile of Functional Impairment in Communication (PFIC; Linscott, Knight, & Godfrey, 1996), and the La Trobe Communication Questionnaire (Douglas, O'Flaherty, & Snow, 2000). Some measures focus on particular verbal features, such as intelligibility and coherence, while both non-verbal (e.g., eye contact, gesture) and verbal (e.g., turn taking, topic maintenance) communication skills are evaluated on others. Rating scales and checklists are less labor intensive than formal conversational procedures and allow more naturalistic evaluations of conversational ability. However, the use of these measures requires training to ensure reliable administration (Coelho, Ylvisaker, & Turkstra, 2005). Overall, the application of rating scales and checklists to conversational discourse analysis has shown that individuals with TBI have difficulty with topic initiation, management, and engaging conversation partners, and the information they contribute to the interaction is often redundant or insufficient (Coelho, 1998; Ehrlich & Barry, 1989; Snow, Douglas, & Ponsford, 1997).

The complex and cognitive nature of discourse renders it vulnerable to the effects of TBI. Cognitive-communicative impairments are evident in both monologic and interactive discourse and at various levels of examination. In a review of 18 monologic discourse studies, consistent findings in the TBI population were diminished productivity, efficiency, and coherence as well as reduced essential content and poor organization (Coelho, Ylvisaker, & Turkstra, 2005). The most consistent problems in conversational discourse for individuals with TBI were poor topic initiation and management and content errors.

4 Potential Cognitive Explanations for Communication Deficits Following TBI

4.1 *Attention and information processing*

4.1.1 Definition of attention and attentional components affected by TBI
Attention is a multifaceted cognitive function that serves as the basis for other cognitive processes, but how the various facets are divided and labeled is inconsistent. The following terms are fairly common within the TBI literature. *Orienting attention* is the most basic component and involves allocating attention to sensory information. *Attention span* refers to the amount of information which can be processed at one time. *Selective attention* is the ability to attend to specific information while ignoring irrelevant or distracting information. *Divided attention* requires the processing of more than one source of information at a time. *Sustained attention* refers to an ability to maintain focus over a long period of time. Finally, *supervisory attentional control* is responsible for allocation of resources in demanding situations in order to optimize performance.

Attention is one of the most studied cognitive constructs following TBI; it is assessed as a matter of course and included in treatment plans. It is reported as one of the primary problems by clinicians, family members, and even patients themselves. These individuals are easily distracted, lose their train of thought, and complain of difficulty in concentrating. Complaints are more frequent and persistent for those who have suffered a more severe TBI (Ponsford & Kinsella, 1992). And yet, recent research struggles to find measures that clearly identify all but the most severe attentional deficits, and treatments attempting to contribute to remediation have fallen short. This is not to suggest that attention is not compromised but rather that the processes contributing to and overlapping with attention processes make it difficult to isolate this single process.

4.1.2 Cognitive processes underlying attention in TBI
There is some debate as to whether deficits in attention reflect a discrete cognitive deficit or whether

they are the result of a more pervasive reduction in information processing, which is one of the most frequent and persistent outcomes of TBI (van Zomeren & Brouwer, 1994). Studies of attention following TBI have consistently shown a decreased rate of processing (Ríos Lago, Periáñez, & Muñoz-Céspedes, 2004; Spikman, Deelman, & Van Zomeren, 2000). Furthermore, slowing of information processing has been shown to remove most of the differences between TBI patients and control subjects in attention performance (Spikman, Deelman, & Van Zomeren, 2000).

Studies that have sought to identify measures most sensitive to deficits in attention following TBI found those that tap into processing speed (usually timed measures) were those with the strongest results (Mathias & Wheaton, 2007; Ponsford & Kinsella, 1992). Some researchers also indicate deficits in attention span, selective attention, sustained attention, and supervisory attentional control but many of these tests yield scores that reflect a time component. Attentional measures have been shown to depend not only on speed of processing but also on cognitive flexibility, interference control, and working memory (Ríos Lago, Periáñez, & Muñoz-Céspedes, 2004).

4.1.3 Working Memory Theory Subjects with TBI are known to be impaired in dual-task conditions when both tasks require controlled processes involving working memory (Perbal et al., 2003). Several studies have suggested that both attention *and* working memory deficits in TBI patients are due to a slowing of information processing (Perbal et al., 2003).

Problems attending to complex information following TBI may be explained, in part, by Baddeley's (1990) Working Memory Theory (Serino et al., 2006). Those tasks that can be done semi-automatically (i.e., habitual tasks like driving) do not require much in the way of conscious attentional resources, so a second task (e.g., eating a sandwich) could be performed without disrupting the first. However, when the task requires conscious attention, the addition of a second task requires working memory in order to switch between needed cognitive resources. Within Baddeley's theory, a "central executive" processes information in working memory, regulates allocation of attentional resources, and coordinates cognition. When the central executive limits are exceeded, task performance decreases (Baddeley, 1990; Baddeley & Hitch, 1974). This theory was applied to participants with TBI (Serino et al., 2006) since they are known to have slower response times and are inaccurate in their performance on demanding tasks. Researchers concluded that cognitive impairment following TBI is more likely caused by impairment to the central executive than to a processing speed deficit (Serino et al., 2006).

4.1.4 Communication deficits Selective attention, sustained attention, alternating or shifting attention, and divided attention are seen as the major areas of attentional impairment among individuals with TBI (Brookshire, 2007). A deficit in selective attention means that an individual may have difficulty separating what is important from what is not important in spoken and printed materials. It follows that if a listener is not attending to the important elements in a speaker's conversation, a response would likely be perceived as inappropriate. This hypothesis may be partly supported by a recent pilot study (Lé et al., 2008) in which completeness of story elements was measured and compared to a non-brain-injured group. Only 42 percent of the brain-injured individuals were considered to have told a "complete" story comprising its essential elements compared with nearly 90 percent of the non-brain-injured group. One might infer that a selective attention deficit is responsible for difficulty in retelling the story accurately. Information processing deficits might also play a role in identifying the important elements of a story (or a conversation).

Sustained attention, in which performance deteriorates over longer periods of required attention, would seem also to impact communicative performance. It is known that longer and more complex utterances are more difficult to comprehend following brain injury. Sustained attention deficits would explain this, as would decreased information processing.

Individuals with TBI are slow to shift attention from one stimulus to another and perform poorly on tasks in which response requirements change. Conversational interactions are a good example of changing response requirements and tend to be particularly difficult for these patients (Brookshire, 2007). Once again, slowed information processing would also make it difficult to follow the varying response requirements in conversation.

Van Zomeren (1994) postulates that due to reduced information processing resources, individuals with TBI cannot store information in memory with the efficiency they had before the injury so they must use pragmatics-challenging compensatory devices such as averting eye gaze in order to maximize concentration during conversation. He reasons that the laborious verbal production, struggle to find a word, and intense concentration needed to grasp a concept are proof that these patients have no spare "capacity" to pay attention to mood, facial expression or other non-verbal cues in the behavior of their communication partner. This would lead to the pragmatic deficits discussed later in this chapter, including difficulty making mental states inferences (theory of mind).

There are limited studies linking communicative inefficiency to attentional deficits or reduced information processing but it is reasonable to suggest that greater deficits in these areas would have greater impact on the speed and efficiency with which individuals with TBI can comprehend and produce communication. It follows that more complex discourse in more distracting environments would likely have a greater negative impact on communication.

4.2   Memory

Memory is composed of several functional systems, which are classified by their temporal characteristics and content. Memory is divided along the time axis into *short-term memory* (STM) and *long-term memory* (LTM). STM refers to the temporary storage of limited information, typically up to a few minutes. *Working memory* (WM) is a type of STM that functions in manipulation of information in addition to temporary storage operations and is inextricably linked with attention (see section 4.1.3). LTM is a durable store with an unlimited capacity. LTM is subdivided into *declarative memory*, referring to explicitly acquired and recalled knowledge, and *non-declarative memory*, referring to implicit learning that is based on performance. Declarative memory comprises *episodic memory*, pertaining to knowledge of events tied to a specific time and place (e.g., recall of one's graduation from college), and *semantic memory*, relating to factual knowledge (e.g., knowing that penguins are a type of bird). Non-declarative memory includes procedural memory, which is learning of skills and sequences, and priming, which relates to the accurate retrieval of information by implicit cues or prompts.

The processing of information in memory occurs in stages. *Encoding*, the first stage, is the processing of information to be recalled. *Consolidation* refers to the organization and binding of information in preparation for permanent retention, which is *storage*. *Retrieval* involves activation of stored knowledge for use. For a more in-depth treatment of memory processes and systems, the reader is referred to Tulving (1995) and Markowitsch (2000).

4.2.1 Communication deficits Memory deficits are a reliable and pervasive corollary of traumatic brain injury (TBI). While TBI symptomatology is extensive and diverse, the leading subjective complaint among patients and caregivers is difficulty remembering, reflecting the functional consequences of impaired memory. Research evidence supports the persistence of memory deficits extending to 10 years post injury (Vanderploeg, Curtiss, & Belanger, 2005). As widespread as memory difficulties are in TBI, the relationship between memory deficits and cognitive-communicative disorders and pragmatics is equivocal. The research has yet to establish that deficits of memory play a primary role in social communication (Marsh & Knight, 1991).

4.2.2 Working memory WM impairments appear to impact communication more directly than other types of memory (Murray, Ramage, & Hopper, 2001). Modest correlations between WM and monologic discourse measures have been noted (Youse & Coelho, 2005). Most of the significant correlations involved story retelling tasks as opposed to story generation, suggesting that story retelling taps into WM's dual roles in information processing and storage. Similarly, problems in comprehension of both concrete and abstract proverbs have been correlated with WM (Moran, Nippold, & Gillon, 2006). Thus, impaired WM may limit the ability of individuals with TBI to understand figurative language. There is also some evidence to show that when WM demands of a task are reduced, individuals with TBI perform better (Turkstra & Holland, 1998).

4.2.3 Amnesia *Post-traumatic amnesia* (PTA), a transient period marked by confusion and disorientation and an inability to form new memories, frequently occurs in recovery after TBI. Individuals in the PTA period are unable to consolidate new information in LTM. Patients in PTA will likely demonstrate difficulty in social interactions because they are unable to tap into memory for recent events.

"Small talk," which presents virtually no trouble for non-brain-injured subjects and is usually of little consequence, may prove particularly difficult for those experiencing PTA (McDonald, Togher, & Code, 1999). These informal exchanges often involve a barrage of particulars about recent events for which individuals with PTA may have no record. Since PTA also causes confusion, patients may repeatedly ask for clarifications or repetitions of information.

As PTA resolves, the true nature of the memory impairment manifests. *Retrograde amnesia* (RA) is an inability to recall information acquired prior to the injury. Neuropsychological evidence suggests that RA is specifically an episodic memory impairment (Richardson, 2000). *Source amnesia*, the inability to remember how and when information was acquired, is a type of RA has been associated with TBI (Aharon-Peretz & Tomer, 2007). Recollection of temporal and situational context in which information is learned underlies episodic memory. Source amnesia may account for some of the problems individuals with TBI encounter with recall of episodic information. *Anterograde amnesia* (AA) refers to the inability to learn new information and occurs frequently after TBI. In mild cases, AA does not usually extend beyond the period of PTA. In more severe cases, the inability carry out new learning can impact daily functioning.

4.2.4 Episodic and semantic memory Considering that narrative discourse revolves around episode structure and that narratives comprise much of daily communication, memory deficits may potentially disrupt discourse ability. Difficulties with tagging events appropriately may affect how they are bound together into a complete memonic record and later expressed during a social exchange. These memory disruptions may explain why the discourse of individuals with TBI appears disorganized and lacking in essential content information.

Deficits in semantic memory can affect retrieval of words already learned and new verbal learning. Word retrieval difficulties can slow the pace of communication, which may account for depressed efficiency on some discourse measures, and result in imprecise language use. An inability to learn new verbal information will likely have direct effects on the individual's ability to return to school or work.

4.3 Self-regulation and executive functions

Executive functioning is a construct of central importance in TBI. In broad terms, executive functions are higher-level cognitive control processes. There are a number of different definitions of executive functions. The numerous renderings of executive functioning seem only to add to the nebulousness of the construct. Researchers have yet to come to a consensus. Perhaps Barkley (1996) put it best in stating that "a greased pig by any other name is still a greased pig" (p. 310), in reference to the iterations of ambiguous definitions and terms that continue to muddle the concept of executive functions. In the following sections, the term "executive functions" is eschewed in favor of "self-regulation," a term that captures the dynamic nature of control processes.

4.3.1 Definitions of self-regulation and its components Three components appear to be present in many models of executive functioning: task analysis, strategy selection, and strategy monitoring (Borkowski & Burke, 1996). A model of self-regulation proposed by Kennedy and Coelho (2005) comprises these three components. *Self-regulation* is viewed as the process that takes place in the interactions among metacognitive knowledge and beliefs, self-monitoring, self-control (strategy decision), and strategy execution. *Metacognition* refers to knowledge and beliefs regarding one's own cognition. *Self-monitoring* is online assessment of one's behavior. The internal feedback from the self-monitoring assessment is incorporated into one's metacognitive content and is used to decide upon a strategy to navigate the current task, referred to as *strategy decision*. Strategy decision is a part of self-control. Once a strategy has been selected, it then must be executed. The self-regulatory cycle then begins anew with self-monitoring of the behavior put into action.

4.3.2 Communication deficits Most individuals with severe TBI experience communication problems as direct consequences of impaired self-regulation (Ylvisaker & Szekeres, 1989). The following are areas of self-regulation that can impact communicative function:

1 *Self-awareness and goal setting.* Patients who do not have insight into their deficits may not be willing to use compensatory strategies or engage in treatment because they do not understand the need for them.
2 *Planning.* Planning impairments can impact a variety of daily activities if individuals cannot appropriately organize steps to carry out tasks.
3 *Self-directing/initiating.* Individuals with difficulty self-directing may not initiate conversation even though they can sustain one once they have been prompted.
4 *Self-inhibiting.* Deficits of self-inhibition may result in hyperverbosity, socially inappropriate language, perseverations, ineffective use of verbal and non-verbal social cues, and tangential discourse.
5 *Self-monitoring.* Individuals who have difficulty self-monitoring may result in inappropriate language use because of failure to take into account the communicative context (e.g., communicative partner, social situation) or comprehension problems if individuals do not ask for clarification.
6 *Self-evaluation.* Individuals who cannot self-evaluate adequately may not be able to learn from their communicative breakdowns in one situation to apply a better approach to communication in the next social interaction.
7 *Flexible problem solving.* Social interactions may be disrupted if individuals with TBI cannot modify their communication styles to adapt to the social context or use alternatives ways of expressing an idea when clarification is requested.

4.3.3 Prefrontal cortex function and communication With its extensive network of connections to other areas of the brain, the prefrontal cortices are in a unique position to carry out self-regulatory activities. Models of prefrontal cortex functioning differ somewhat in the functions assigned to particular prefrontal areas. However, most models share a common theme in attributing prefrontal regions with mediation of automatic and controlled processing. Three models of prefrontal cortex function are discussed along with their implications for communication dysfunction in TBI.

4.3.4 Supervisory attentional system   The supervisory system acts upon lower-level cognitive processing, such as those implemented during routine activities, and mediates higher-level processing, which are required in novel situations (Norman & Shallice, 1986). Lower-level automatic processes involve the deployment of schemas to carry out the task at hand. When there is damage to the supervisory system, there is no regulation of the schemas. As such, the ones activated are likely to be the schemas that have been overlearned, such as those implemented in routines. Such processing may suffice for routine activities, but will not for non-routine and novel situations when the "default" schema does not fit the requirements and goals of the task. Breakdowns in the supervisory system have been attributed to discourse impairment. Discourse dysfunction may result as a failure to select and apply the organizing schema that would best fit the context of communication (Ylvisaker, Szekeres, & Feeney, 2001).

4.3.5 Structured event complex   Grafman (1995) has postulated that the prefrontal cortex houses plan-specific knowledge. This information is represented in the form of memory units, referred to as *structured event complexes* (SEC). SECs contain goal-oriented event information that is ordered in sequence. For example, grocery shopping with the goal of obtaining all items on the shopping list in a certain amount of time would call upon the appropriate SEC for that task. The sequence of events would likely involve selecting the closest store, leaving the house, parking the car, navigating the store efficiently, and so on. SECs are very similar to other organizational structures, such as story grammar and scripts. SECS may function as the knowledge representation for various discourse comprehension and production tasks, such as following a conversation or telling a story (Frattali & Grafman, 2005).

4.3.6 Somatic marker hypothesis and communication   The ability to make an appropriate decision is crucial in social communication. The somatic marker hypothesis describes the decision-making process as being mediated by somatic signals that facilitate response selection by tagging potential choices (Bechara, Damasio, & Damasio, 2000). The presence of the emotional or sensory tags serves to automate part of the decision-making mechanism. The somatic marker hypothesis may explain conversational impairments following TBI (Body, 2007). Given the myriad potential utterances from which one could choose to say and the speed at which conversation takes place, it has been argued that deliberation and conscious decision making cannot guide conversational decisions alone. Somatic signals are thought to aid conversation by steering individuals toward "socially advantageous" choices. Without an intact guidance system, individuals with TBI may make poor communicative decisions that manifest as inappropriate conversational moves.

4.3.7 Measures of executive function and communication Superstructural narrative discourse measures (e.g., story grammar analysis) have been significantly correlated to performance on the Wisconsin Card Sorting Test (WCST), which assesses the ability to shift attentional set and adopt new sorting strategies (Coelho, Liles, & Duffy, 1995). Modest correlations have also been found between performance on word fluency, trail making, and verbal learning tests and conversational discourse measures (Snow, Douglas, & Ponsford, 1998). However, given the magnitude of the correlations, caution is warranted in attributing discourse dysfunction solely to impairments of self-regulation.

The dynamic nature of communication calls for mental flexibility, self-monitoring of the communicative exchange, and the ability to make changes according to the communicative context. It is not surprising that impaired self-regulation would have an impact on communication. There is consensus in the research literature that impaired self-regulatory processes underlie, at least, in part, the cognitive-communicative deficits seen following TBI. Theories of prefrontal cortex function may offer insights into the cognitive-communicative and pragmatic deficits observed in TBI.

5   Cognitive-communicative Deficits Following TBI Viewed as a Dysfunction in Pragmatics

Pragmatics, most broadly defined, "constitute a comprehensive set of skills required for competence in naturalistic, functional use of language" (Sohlberg & Mateer, 2001, p. 308). Pragmatic behaviors make up the system of rules employed for language use in social context and can vary depending on culture and situation. These "rules" are inherent in normal discourse comprehension and production and include an attempt toward clarity, brevity, relevance, truth, and organization (Grice, 1975). They also require an ability to use language correctly (e.g., knowing when to use a request instead of a demand) and to change language use when necessary (e.g., knowing that an unfamiliar listener may need more background information than a familiar listener.) Understanding the way another speaker uses language is also critical to partaking in conversation. Language is often indirect or non-literal, requiring a communication partner to make inferences in order to respond appropriately. Finally, the ability to read non-verbal social cues, such as a sarcastic tone or a raised eyebrow, is critical to language competence.

Many of the cognitive-communicative deficits following TBI, described in the previous section, are observed in both production and comprehension of discourse as well as in *extralinguistic* (i.e., gesture) and *paralinguistic* (i.e., voice and facial expression) communication and, since they violate the aforementioned language rules, are considered pragmatic deficits.

In conversation, individuals with TBI have been found to have difficulty taking account of others' interests, use fewer politeness markers (Togher & Hand, 1998), have disorganized discourse, increased turn taking (Coelho, 2002), increased reliance on a conversational partner to keep conversations focused and meaningful (Coelho, Liles, & Duffy, 1991), extreme verbosity or paucity of speech (Coelho, 1995), and topic repetitiveness (Body & Parker, 2005).

Pragmatics is affected via receptive language as well. This is seen in decreased ability to make inferences (Ferstl et al., 2005) and difficulty understanding proverbs and idioms (Moran, Nippold, & Gillon, 2006). Individuals with brain injury struggle with comprehension and production of deceit and more so with the comprehension of irony (Angeleri et al., 2008). Finally, this population's ability to process literal meaning was found to be insufficient in detecting sarcasm (Channon, Pellijeff, & Rule, 2005).

The inability to make accurate communicative inferences is a well-established pragmatic deficit following TBI (Bara, Cutica, & Tirassa, 2001) that may be related to theory of mind (ToM), referring to difficulty making inferences about others' mental states (Channon, Pellijeff, & Rule, 2005). The overlap with many of the aforementioned pragmatic deficits with the social difficulties associated with ToM has led to recent examination of ToM in the TBI population (see, e.g., Bibby & McDonald, 2005; Havet-Thomassin et al., 2006; Henry et al., 2006; Martin & McDonald, 2003) in which individuals with TBI consistently perform more poorly than controls on most ToM tasks. The precise relationship of ToM to the pragmatic deficits of TBI subjects is still unclear but evidence to date suggests that they are highly related.

5.1   Social reintegration

Deficits in communication production, comprehension, and ToM may be glaring but in many cases communication with an individual with TBI may only be perceived by a listener as slightly odd or disconcerting. Although there is heterogeneity in the types of pragmatic deficits observed within this population, all types are pervasive, persistent, and potentially ostracizing. Some authors suggest that communicative inappropriateness following TBI represents one of the greatest obstacles to patients' social reintegration (Milton, Prutting, & Binder, 1984). This is one reason why discussion must revolve around the term "pragmatics" despite the variation in how the word is used and the fact that approaches to assessment, management, and even discussion of pragmatics remain difficult to compare. A clear understanding and consensus of the components of pragmatics is necessary in order to determine whether pragmatics is equivalent to a cognitive construct that can be addressed as a whole or whether an individual is better served by focusing on specific, individual deficits (e.g., disorganized discourse); or whether potential underlying cognitive deficits such as attention, memory or executive function should be treated directly.

5.2 Cognitive bases

Neuropragmatics is a field of study interested in mapping pragmatic language skills to corresponding neuroanatomical regions. This is a relatively new sub-discipline of pragmatics and there is little definitive evidence for specific locations corresponding to specific pragmatic deficits. There is, however, an established connection between TBI and dysexcutive syndrome due to axonal shearing; thus it is a fairly common assertion that pragmatic deficits are due to underlying cognitive deficits resulting from frontal lobe pathology (Henry et al., 2006; McDonald, 1992). Henry et al. (2006) believe aspects of executive functioning may at least partially underlie pragmatic deficits. Body (1999) suggests overlap with memory, attention, and executive function and postulates that some key cognitive skills from these systems play into social communication, while others do not.

There is some evidence to support that ToM, on the other hand, is its own separate cognitive model within the frontal lobes (Stuss, Gallup Jr., & Alexander, 2001) but the issue remains controversial (Havet-Thomassin et al., 2006). Henry and colleagues (2006) found ToM to be substantially related to performance on one measure of executive function but not emotional recognition. This suggests that social dysfunction following TBI can be partly explained by underlying executive function deficits.

5.3 Intervention

While it is now clear that pragmatics must not be viewed as secondary to cognitive deficits and must be a primary target of intervention, it remains enigmatic as to how best to approach this since there is disagreement as to whether we deal with potential underlying etiology or with the symptom observed in each individual. Adding to the confusion is the fact that cognitive-communicative symptoms following TBI vary greatly between individuals and neuropsychological testing is insufficient to determine the extent of the underlying deficits, unless they are very severe.

In 1982, Prutting (1982) described pragmatics as "social competence" and provided a summary of the contributions made by the addition of pragmatics to speech language pathology. She conceived of pragmatics within an "interactional framework" overlapping with social and cognitive knowledge and with our linguistic rules. More recently, it has been suggested that discourse and pragmatics are to some extent interdefinable, and that the difference between the two is a matter of focus and emphasis (Body, Perkins, & McDonald, 1999). They reason that pragmatics (contextualized language) must include discourse (a series of utterances) and that discourse includes pragmatics since utterances will depend on context. This raises the question of validity in sampling discourse acontextually.

Individuals with pragmatic deficits frequently violate language rules and thereby isolate themselves from family, friends, and new social contacts. Pragmatic deficits include inappropriate expressive language, decreased receptive language and also impaired extralinguistic and paralinguistic skills. Deficits are most evident in conversational discourse, when all of these communication skills come into play. The precise underpinnings of pragmatic deficits are unclear but it is generally believed that frontal lobe pathology plays a distinct role.

6   Conclusion

Cognitive-communicative disorders following TBI are common and pervasive. The complex and dynamic nature of discourse places it at the nexus of cognition and communication. Discourse impairments associated with TBI are typically attributed to non-linguistic underlying causes. In this chapter, potential explanations for discourse deficits were proposed. Cognitive-communicative impairments may be ascribed to disruptions in cognitive systems, such as attention, memory, and self-regulatory processes. Alternatively, they may be viewed as manifestations of underlying pragmatic impairments. The potential causes are not only of theoretical importance but have clinical implications as well. If one attributes the cognitive-communicative disorder to cognitive dysfunction, then treatment should focus on remediation of the cognitive systems. Likewise, if the disorder is interpreted as a pragmatic deficit, then the approach should target pragmatic skills. While specific management approaches were not discussed in this chapter, it is critical that the approach taken reflect what the clinician considers to be the underlying cause.

REFERENCES

Aharon-Peretz, J. & Tomer, R. (2007). Traumatic brain injury. In B. L. Miller & L. Cummings (eds.), *The human frontal lobes* (pp. 540–51). New York: The Guilford Press.

American Speech-Language-Hearing Association. (2005). *Knowledge and skills needed by speech-language pathologists providing services to individuals with cognitive-communication disorders* [Knowledge and Skills]. Available from www.asha.org/policy.

Angeleri, R., Bosco, F. M., Zettin, M., Sacco, K., Colle, L., & Bara, B. G. (2008). Communicative impairment in traumatic brain injury: A complete pragmatic assessment. *Brain and Language*.

Baddeley, A. (1990). The development of the concept of working memory:

Implications and contributions of neuropsychology. 54.

Baddeley, A. D. & Hitch, G. H. (1974). Working memory. *Recent Advances in Learning and Motivation* 8, 47–89.

Bara, B. G., Cutica, I., & Tirassa, M. (2001). Neuropragmatics: Extralinguistic communication after closed head injury. *Brain and Language* 77 (1), 72–94.

Barkley, R. A. (1996). Linkages between attention and executive functions. In G. R. Lyon & N. A. Krasnegor (eds.), *Attention, memory, and executive function* (pp. 307–25). Baltimore, MD: Paul H. Brookes Publishing Co.

Bechara, A., Damasio, H., & Damasio, A. R. (2000). Emotion, decision making and the orbitofrontal cortex. *Cerebral Cortex* 10 (3), 295–307.

Bibby, H. & McDonald, S. (2005). Theory of mind after traumatic brain injury. *Neuropsychologia* 43 (1), 99–114.

Blank, M. & Franklin, E. (1980). Dialogue with preschoolers: A cognitively-based system of assessment. *Applied Psycholinguistics* 1 (2), 127–50.

Body, R. (2007). Decision making and somatic markers in conversation after traumatic brain injury. *Aphasiology* 21 (3–4), 394–408.

Body, R. & Parker, M. (2005). Topic repetitiveness after traumatic brain injury: An emergent, jointly managed behaviour. *Clinical Linguistics and Phonetics* 19 (5), 379–92.

Body, R., Perkins, M., & McDonald, S. (1999). Pragmatics, cognition, and communication in traumatic brain injury. In S. McDonald, L. Togher, & C. Code (eds.), *Communication disorders following traumatic brain injury* (pp. 81–112). Hove, UK: Psychology Press.

Borkowski, J. G. & Burke, J. E. (1996). Theories, models, and measurements of executive functioning. In G. R. Lyon & N. A. Krasnegor (eds.), *Attention, memory, and executive function* (pp. 235–61). Baltimore, MD: Paul H. Brookes Publishing Co.

Brinton, B. & Fujiki, M. (1989). *Conversational management with language-impaired children*. Rockville, MD: Aspen.

Brookshire, R. H. (2007). *Introduction to neurogenic communication disorders*. St. Louis, MO: Mosby Elsevier.

Brown, A. W., Elovic E. P., Kothari, S., Flanagan, S. F., & Kwasnica, C. (2008). Congenital and acquired brain injury: Epidemiology, pathophysiology, prognostication, innovative treatments, and prevention. *Archives of Physical Medicine and Rehabilitation* 89 (3) Suppl 1, S3–8.

Channon, S., Pellijeff, A., & Rule, A. (2005). Social cognition after head injury: Sarcasm and theory of mind. *Brain and Language* 93 (2), 123–34.

Chapman, S. B., Culhane, K. A., Levin, H. S., Harward, H., Mendelsohn, D., Ewing-Cobbs, L., Fletcher, J. M., & Bruce, D. (1992). Narrative discourse after closed head injury in children and adolescents. *Brain and Language* 43 (1), 42–65.

Coelho, C. A. (1995). Discourse production deficits following traumatic brain injury: A critical review of the recent literature. *Aphasiology* 9 (5), 409–29.

Coelho, C. A. (1998). Analysis of conversation. In L. R. Cherney, B. B. Shadden, & C. A. Coelho (eds.), *Analyzing discourse in communicatively impaired adults* (pp. 123–50). Gaithersburg, MD: Aspen.

Coelho, C. A. (2002). Story narratives of adults with closed head injury and non-brain-injured adults: Influence of socioeconomic status, elicitation task, and executive functioning. *Journal of Speech, Language, and Hearing Research* 45 (6), 1232–48.

Coelho, C. A., Grela, B., Corso, M., Gamble, A., & Feinn, R. (2005). Microlinguistic deficits in the narrative discourse of adults with traumatic brain injury. *Brain Injury* 19 (13), 1139–45.

Coelho, C. A., Liles, B. Z., & Duffy, R. J. (1991). Analysis of conversational discourse in head-injured adults. *Journal of Head Trauma Rehabilitation* 6 (2), 92–9.

Coelho, C. A., Liles, B. Z., & Duffy, R. J. (1995). Impairments of discourse abilities and executive functions in traumatically brain-injured adults. *Brain Injury* 9 (5), 471–7.

Coelho, C., Ylvisaker, M., & Turkstra, L. S. (2005). Nonstandardized assessment approaches for individuals with traumatic brain injuries. *Seminars in Speech and Language* 26 (4), 223–41.

Coelho, C. A., Youse, K. M., & Lé, K. N. (2002). Conversational discourse in closed-head-injured & non-brain-injured adults. *Aphasiology* 16 (4–6), 659–72.

Damico, J. (1985). Clinical discourse analysis: A functional language assessment technique. In C. S. Simon (ed.), *Communication skills and classroom success: Assessment of language-learning disabled students* (pp. 165–204). San Diego, CA: College-Hill.

Davis, G. A. & Coelho, C. A. (2004). Referential cohesion and logical coherence of narration after closed head injury. *Brain and Language* 89 (3), 508–23.

DePalma, R. G., Burris, D. G., Champion, H. R., & Hodgson, M. J. (2005). Current concepts: Blast injuries. *New England Journal of Medicine* 352 (13), 1335–42 & 1399.

Douglas, J. M., O'Flaherty, C., & Snow, P. C. (2000). Measuring perception of communicative ability: The development and evaluation of the La Trobe communication questionnaire. *Aphasiology* 14 (3), 251–68.

Ehrlich, J. & Barry, P. (1989). Rating communication behaviours in the head-injured adult. *Brain Injury* 3 (2), 193–8.

Evered, L., Ruff, R., Baldo, J., & Isomura, A. (2003). Emotional risk factors and postconcussion disorder. *Assessment* 10 (4), 420–7.

Ewing-Cobbs, L., Brookshire, B., Scott, M. A., & Fletcher, J. M. (1998). Children's narratives following traumatic brain injury: Linguistic structure, cohesion, and thematic recall. *Brain and Language* 61 (3), 395–419.

Ferstl, E. C., Guthke, T., & Von Cramon, D. Y. (2002). Text comprehension after brain injury: Left prefrontal lesions affect inference processes. *Neuropsychology* 16 (3), 292–308.

Ferstl, E. C., Walther, K., Guthke, T., & Von Cramon, D. Y. (2005). Assessment of story comprehension deficits after brain damage. *Journal of Clinical and Experimental Neuropsychology* 27 (3), 367–84.

Frattali, C. & Grafman, J. (2005). Language and discourse deficits following prefrontal cortex damage. In L. L. LaPointe (ed.), *Aphasia and related neurogenic language disorders* (pp. 51–67). New York: Thieme.

Gennarelli, T. A. (1996). The spectrum of traumatic axonal injury. *Neuropathology and Applied Neurobiology* 22 (6), 509–13.

Glosser, G. & Deser, T. (1991). Patterns of discourse production among neurological patients with fluent language disorders. *Brain and Language* 40 (1), 67–88.

Grafman, J. (1995). Similarities and distinctions among current models of prefrontal cortical functions. *Annals of the New York Academy of Sciences* 769, 337–68.

Grice, H. P. (1975). Logic and conversation. In P. Cole & J. L. Morgan (eds.), *Syntax and semantics* (p. 41). New York: Academic Press.

Havet-Thomassin, V., Allain, P., Etcharry-Bouyx, F., & Le Gall, D. (2006). What about theory of mind after severe brain injury? *Brain Injury* 20 (1), 83–91.

Henry, J. D., Phillips, L. H., Crawford, J. R., Ietswaart, M., & Summers, F. (2006). Theory of mind following traumatic brain injury: The role of emotion recognition and executive dysfunction. *Neuropsychologia* 44 (10), 1623–28.

Hough, M. S. & Barrow, I. (2003). Descriptive discourse abilities of traumatic brain-injured adults. *Aphasiology* 17 (2), 183–91.

Kennedy, M. R. T. & Coelho, C. (2005). Self-regulation after traumatic brain injury: A framework for intervention of memory and problem solving. *Seminars in Speech and Language* 26 (4), 242–55.

Koskinen, S. (1998). Quality of life 10 years after a very severe traumatic brain injury (TBI): The perspective of the injured and the closest relative. *Brain Injury* 12 (8), 631–48.

Lé, K. N., Coelho, C. A., Mozeiko, J. L., & Grafman, J. (2008). Quantifying story goodness: Development of a new narrative discourse tool. Research Colloquium, Storrs, CT.

Liles, B. (1985). Narrative ability in normal and language-disordered children. *Journal of Speech and Hearing Research* 23, 123–33.

Liles, B. Z., Coelho, C. A., Duffy, R. J., & Rigdon Zalagens, M. (1989). Effects of elicitation procedures on the narratives of normal and closed head-injured adults. *Journal of Speech & Hearing Disorders* 54 (3), 356–66.

Linscott, R. J., Knight, R. G., & Godfrey, H. P. D. (1996). The profile of functional impairment in communication (PFIC): A measure of communication impairment for clinical use. *Brain Injury* 10 (6), 397–412.

Markowitsch, H. J. (2000). The anatomical bases of memory. In M. S. Gazzaniga (ed.), *The new cognitive neurosciences*, 781–795. Cambridge, MA: MIT Press.

Marsh, N. V. & Knight, R. G. (1991). Relationship between cognitive deficits and social skill after head injury. *Neuropsychology* 5 (2), 107–17.

Martin, E. M., Lu, W. C., Helmick, K., French, L., & Warden, D. L. (2008). Traumatic brain injuries sustained in the Afghanistan and Iraq wars. *American Journal of Nursing* 108 (4), 40–7.

Martin, I. & McDonald, S. (2003). Weak coherence, no theory of mind, or executive dysfunction? Solving the puzzle of pragmatic language disorders. *Brain and Language* 85 (3), 451–66.

Mathias, J. L. & Wheaton, P. (2007). Changes in attention and information-processing speed following severe traumatic brain injury: A meta-analytic review. *Neuropsychology* 21 (2), 212–23.

McAllister, T. W. (2008). Neurobehavioral sequelae of traumatic brain injury: Evaluation and management. *World Psychiatry* 7 (1), 3–10.

McDonald, S. (1992). Communication disorders following closed head injury: New approaches to assessment and rehabilitation. *Brain Injury* 6 (3), 283–92.

McDonald, S., Togher, L., & Code, C. (1999). The nature of traumatic brain injury: Basic features and neuropsychological consequences. In S. McDonald, L. Togher, & C. Code (eds.), *Communication disorders following traumatic brain injury* (pp. 19–54). Hove, UK: Psychology Press.

Mentis, M. & Prutting, C. A. (1991). Analysis of topic as illustrated in a head-injured and a normal adult. *Journal of Speech and Hearing Research* 34 (3), 583–95.

Milton, S. B., Prutting, C. A., & Binder, G. M. (1984). Appraisal of communicative competence in head injured adults. *Clinical Aphasiology Conference Proceedings* 114–23.

Moran, C. A., Nippold, M. A., & Gillon, G. T. (2006). Working memory and proverb comprehension in adolescents with traumatic brain injury: A preliminary investigation. *Brain Injury* 20 (4), 417–23.

Murray, L. L., Ramage, A. E., & Hopper, T. (2001). Memory impairments in adults with neurogenic communication disorders. *Seminars in Speech and Language* 22 (2), 127–36.

Norman, D. A. & Shallice, T. (1986). Attention to action: Willed and automatic control of behavior. *Consciousness and Self-Regulation* 4, 1–18.

Perbal, S., Couillet, J., Azouvi, P., & Pouthas, V. (2003). Relationships between time estimation, memory, attention, and processing speed in patients with severe traumatic brain injury. *Neuropsychologia* 41 (12), 1599–610.

Ponsford, J. & Kinsella, G. (1992). Attentional deficits following closed-head injury. *Journal of Clinical and Experimental Neuropsychology* 14 (5), 822–38.

Prutting, C. A. (1982). Pragmatics as social competence. *Journal of Speech and Hearing Disorders* 47 (2), 123–34.

Prutting, C. A. & Kirchner, D. M. (1987). A clinical appraisal of the pragmatic aspects of language. *Journal of Speech and Hearing Disorders* 52 (2), 105–19.

Rankin, K. P. (2007). Social cognition in frontal injury. In B. L. Miller & J. L. Cummings (eds.), *The human frontal lobes* (pp. 345–60). New York: Guilford Press.

Richardson, J. T. E. (2000). *Clinical and neuropsychological aspects of closed head injury*. Hove, UK: Psychology Press.

Ríos Lago, M., Periáñez, J. A., &. Muñoz-Céspedes, J. M. (2004). Attentional control and slowness of information processing after severe traumatic brain injury. *Brain Injury* 18 (3), 257–72.

Rutland-Brown, W., Langlois, J. A., Bazarian, J. J., & Warden, D. (2008). Improving identification of traumatic brain injury after nonmilitary bomb blasts. *Journal of Head Trauma Rehabilitation* 23 (2), 84–91.

Rutland-Brown, W., Langlois, J. A., Thomas, K. E., and Xi, Y. L. (2006). Incidence of traumatic brain injury in the United States, 2003. *Journal of Head Trauma Rehabilitation* 21 (6), 544–8.

Serino, A., Ciaramelli, E., Di Santantonio, A. , Malagù, S., Servadei F., & Làdavas, E. (2006). Central executive system impairment in traumatic brain injury. *Brain Injury* 20 (1), 23–32.

Snow, P., Douglas, J., & Ponsford, J. (1997). Conversational assessment following traumatic brain injury: A comparison across two control groups. *Brain Injury* 11 (6), 409–29.

Snow, P., Douglas, J., & Ponsford, J. (1998). Conversational discourse abilities following severe traumatic brain injury: A follow-up study. *Brain Injury* 12 (11), 911–35.

Sohlberg, M. M. & Mateer, C. A. (2001). Cognitive rehabilitation: An integrative neuropsychological approach. *Cognitive Rehabilitation: An Integrative Neuropsychological Approach*. New York: Guilford Press.

Spikman, J. M., Deelman, B. G., & Van Zomeren, A. H. (2000). Executive functioning, attention and frontal lesions in patients with chronic CHI. *Journal of*

Clinical and Experimental Neuropsychology 22 (3), 325–38.

Stout, C. E., Yorkston, K. M., & Pimentel, J. I. (2000). Discourse production following mild, moderate, and severe traumatic brain injury: A comparison of two tasks. *Journal of Medical Speech-Language Pathology* 8 (1), 15–25.

Stuss, D. T., Gallup Jr., G. G., & Alexander, M. P. (2001). The frontal lobes are necessary for "theory of mind." *Brain* 124 (2), 279–86.

Tate, R. L., Lulham, J. M., Broe, G. A., Strettles, B., & Pfaff, A. (1989). Psychosocial outcome for the survivors of severe blunt head injury: The results from a consecutive series of 100 patients. *Journal of Neurology, Neurosurgery, and Psychiatry* 52 (10), 1128–34.

Togher, L. & Hand, L. (1998). Use of politeness markers with different communication partners: An investigation of five subjects with traumatic brain injury. *Aphasiology* 12 (7–8), 755–70.

Togher, L., McDonald, S., & Code, C. (1999). Communication problems following traumatic brain injury. In S. McDonald, L. Togher, & C. Code (eds.), *Communication disorders following traumatic brain injury* (pp. 1–18). Hove, UK: Psychology Press.

Tucker, F. M. & Hanlon, R. E. (1998). Effects of mild traumatic brain injury on narrative discourse production. *Brain Injury* 12 (9), 783–92.

Tulving, E. (1995). Organization of memory: Quo vadis? In M. S. Gazzaniga (ed.), *The cognitive neurosciences* (pp. 839–53). Cambridge, MA: MIT Press.

Turkstra, L. S. & Holland, A. L. (1998). Assessment of syntax after adolescent brain injury: Effects of memory on test performance. *Journal of Speech, Language, and Hearing Research* 41 (1), 137–49.

Van Leer, E. & Turkstra, L. (1999a). The effect of elicitation task on discourse coherence and cohesion in adolescents with brain injury. *Journal of Communication Disorders* 32 (5), 327–49.

Van Leer, E. & Turkstra, L. (1999b). The effect of elicitation task on discourse coherence and cohesion in adolescents with brain injury. *Journal of Communication Disorders* 32 (5), 327–49.

van Zomeren, A. H. & Brouwer, W. H. (1994). *Clinical neuropsychology of attention*. New York: Oxford University Press.

Vanderploeg, R. D., Curtiss, G., & Belanger, H. G. (2005). Long-term neuropsychological outcomes following mild traumatic brain injury. *Journal of the International Neuropsychological Society* 11 (3), 228–36.

Ylvisaker, M. & Szekeres, S. F. (1989). Metacognitive and executive impairments in head-injured children and adults. *Topics in Language Disorders* 9 (2), 34–49.

Ylvisaker, M., Szekeres, S. F., & Feeney, T. (2001). Communication disorders associated with traumatic brain injury. In R. Chapey (ed.), *Language intervention strategies in aphasia and related neurogenic communication disorders* (pp. 745–808). Baltimore, MD: Lippincott William & Wilkins.

Youse, K. M. & Coelho, C. A. (2005). Working memory and discourse production abilities following closed-head injury. *Brain Injury* 19 (12; 12), 1001–9.

26 Dementia

NICOLE MÜLLER

1 Introduction

Dementia and dementing conditions have in recent years had a high visibility in popular culture and the media. It can be argued that this has led to a higher public awareness about dementing conditions, and quite possibly a higher level of public knowledge concerning risk factors, disease progressions, effects on daily living and independence, and the like. On the other hand, it could also be argued that dominant ideologies of aging and cognitive functioning in the industrialized world, in tandem with dementia as a highly visible "bad news" threat, might lead to unease and fear.

Given the multifarious effects of dementing conditions on physical, cognitive, and communicative abilities, care for persons with dementia is always a multidisciplinary effort. Among those involved are family members, family physicians, geriatricians, neurologists, nurses, speech-language pathologists, medical social workers, and others. This chapter is an attempt to situate dementia and dementing conditions into various contexts relevant for students, practitioners, and researchers in the field of speech and language disorders, many of whom work with and care for persons with dementia. The chapter begins with an overview of memory systems and impairments, discusses definitions and categorizations of dementia and dementing conditions, and then narrows down its focus to Alzheimer's disease, as the most common progressive dementing condition.

2 Memory Systems and Memory Impairments

Memory impairments are a predominant consequence of dementing diseases. Therefore, a brief summary of the components of memory is warranted. Most recent research in dementia and other memory impairments makes reference, with small variations, to a model of human memory as sketched in the following paragraphs (much more detailed accounts can be found in e.g. Squire, 1987; Squire & Kandel, 1999; Baddeley, 2002).

The Handbook of Language and Speech Disorders, First Edition. Edited by Jack S. Damico, Nicole Müller, and Martin J. Ball. © 2013 Blackwell Publishing Ltd except for editorial material and organization © 2013 Jack S. Damico, Nicole Müller, Martin J. Ball. Published 2013 by Blackwell Publishing Ltd.

The fact that *memory* is not a unitary phenomenon, but rather a system of distinct components, is by now well established. A basic distinction is that between *short-term memory* (STM) and *long-term memory* (LTM). Two major components can be distinguished in STM: *immediate memory* (IM), and *working memory* (WM). IM has very limited capacity (an upper limit of seven distinct items is often given), and unless rehearsed, this content is lost within a span of 30 seconds or less (Squire & Kandel, 1999). The work of Baddeley and colleagues (see e.g. Baddeley, 2002, with references to earlier work) has established the notion of *working memory* (WM). The working memory faculty is conceptualized as including a number of storage units, or buffers, that can contain limited amounts of information. The buffers commonly distinguished are the phonological input store and articulatory loop, the visuo-spatial sketchpad, and the episodic buffer. The phonological input store and articulatory loop serve to hold auditory traces for a few seconds, and as a subvocal rehearsal faculty. The visuo-spatial sketchpad holds visual and spatial information. The episodic buffer is conceptualized as an intermediary processor, between the different components of WM and long-term memory. In addition to these WM components, there is a central executive system that enables a person to actively use information, for example to hold incoming information in consciousness, to encode information or activate and access stored knowledge, to rehearse input received. This system is held to underlie the ability to form intentions, monitor expression and plan action.

Within the long-term memory systems, declarative and non-declarative, or implicit and explicit subsystems are distinguished. Declarative memory essentially refers to stored factual information of several types. *Semantic* memory is the memory for concepts, or entities. *Lexical* memory is the memory for words and patterns of word use. *Episodic* memory is the memory for specific events. Thus, the knowledge that in the state of Louisiana, a species of medium-sized mammal can be found that looks as though it wears a bandit's mask and that likes to rummage through domestic trashcans is an instantiation of semantic memory. The knowledge that "raccoon" and "Waschbär" are the words in English and German, respectively, for that type of mammal, and that some people in Louisiana call it "chaoui," are examples of lexical memory. Remembering the last time one saw a raccoon in one's yard is an instance of episodic memory.

Non-declarative, or implicit memory is non-volitional, and generally held to be unavailable for conscious review. The term *procedural* memory describes abilities such as, for example, riding a bicycle: this ability is often used as the prototypical example of a procedural skill, in that it is something that is learned (that is, committed to the non-declarative memory system) by doing it rather than by conscious cognitive effort; it is highly automatized such that once it is learned, it is highly unlikely that anyone will "unlearn" it. It is open for discussion to what extent some interactional skills, such as turn taking in conversation, are also procedural in nature. *Conditioned habits* or *reflexes* are another facet of non-declarative memory, as is *priming*, that is, the circumstance that responses to tasks are influenced by previous exposure to either the target response itself, or to an item that is related to the target.

It is not entirely clear or uncontroversial at this stage to what extent memory systems interact and precisely how they relate to each other. As regards episodic and semantic memory, one view is that semantic memory represents the accumulation of exemplars, memories of largely overlapping episodes that have over time lost their specific contextual cues; in other words, semantic memory is seen as emerging from episodic memory. Another view regards episodic and semantic memory as two separate systems. A widely accepted view is that we are dealing with two functionally distinct systems that do, however, interact with each other. Further, it is widely held that the memory dysfunctions that are observed, for example in dementia of the Alzheimer's type (DAT), result from the breakdown of neurologically, or anatomically, separate systems (see Becker & Overman, 2002, for discussion).

In addition to an, as it were, diachronic dimension in memory, we can distinguish different stages in memory, which in turn may be differentially disrupted in various neurological conditions. The encoding stage, that is, the laying down of new memories, is studied in the laboratory by varying the material that study participants are to learn. The ability to store information is measured through the opposite of storage, that is, forgetting. In memory retrieval, recall is distinguished from recognition, the former typically being more difficult in memory-impairing conditions than the latter. In the study of memory and memory impairments, Baddeley (2002) draws an important distinction between what he calls laboratory memory and everyday memory. Classical laboratory techniques use, for example, tasks that require participants to recall complex figures, or paired associative learning. However, people with memory impairments are concerned about forgetting people's names, or whether they've turned the stove off after cooking a meal, or about no longer finding their way around their neighborhoods or their homes. Baddeley (2002) draws attention to the tension between, on the one hand, the laboratory scientist's desire to gain a precise picture of various types of memory function and dysfunction and, on the other hand, the need to map measures of memory function onto a person's ability to cope in their daily lives. While the former is firmly embedded in classical science using decontextualized tasks, the latter requires a holistic and contextualized approach. Typically, memory assessments tend to use decontextualized tasks, for instance paired associative learning. However, as Baddeley (2002) points out, patients' concerns are not the lack of success in learning pairs of unrelated words, but rather that they forget appointments, or lose their way around the hospital. For example, it has been found that normally aging older adults can show significant defects in laboratory investigations of prospective memory. This term refers to the process whereby an individual forms an intention to carry out an action at some future time, and at the appropriate time remembers to carry out that intention. However, it has also been found that older adults tend to perform better in real-life prospective memory demands than on laboratory tasks (an example of a real-life prospective memory demand would be to make plans for dinner with a friend on the weekend, and then to remember to keep that date). This illustrates that decontextualized measures of memory components in aging populations do not necessarily map easily onto how individuals manage the memory demands in their daily lives. This is significant in the study of memory impairments in relation to individuals' ability to live independently (see Baddeley, 2002; also Clare, 2002, and Kester et al., 2002, for detailed discussions of changes in memory functions in normal aging).

3 Dementia and Dementing Diseases

3.1 *Definitions and diagnostic criteria of dementia*

The *Diagnostic and Statistical Manual of Mental Disorders* (4th edition, text revision; DSM-IV TR; American Psychiatric Association, 2000) defines the diagnostic criteria for dementia as follows:

A. The development of multiple cognitive deficits manifested by both:
    (1) Memory impairment (impaired ability to learn new information or to recall previously learned information).
    (2) One (or more) of the following cognitive disturbances:
         (a) aphasia (language disturbance);
         (b) apraxia (impaired ability to carry out motor activities despite intact motor function);
         (c) agnosia (failure to recognize or identify objects despite intact sensory function);
         (d) disturbance in executive functioning (e.g., planning, organizing, sequencing, abstracting).
B. The cognitive deficits in Criteria A1 and A2 each cause significant impairment in social or occupational functioning and represent a significant decline from a previous level of functioning. (American Psychiatric Association, 2000, pp. 147–50; 157)

The World Health Organization's definition of dementia as published in the 10th edition of the *International Classification of Diseases* (ICD-10; World Health Organization, 1992) reads as follows:

> Dementia is a syndrome due to disease of the brain, usually of a chronic or progressive nature, in which there is disturbance of multiple higher cortical functions, including memory, thinking, orientation, comprehension, calculation, learning capacity, language, and judgement. Consciousness is not clouded. Impairments of cognitive function are commonly accompanied, and occasionally preceded, by deterioration in emotional control, social behaviour, or motivation. Dementia produces an appreciable decline in intellectual functioning, and usually some interference with personal activities of daily living, such as washing, dressing, eating, personal hygiene, excretory and toilet activities.

In addition to this definition, the following inclusions and exclusions are applied to categorize symptoms as those of dementia: insidious in onset; not caused by delirium, schizophrenia, or major depression; acquired; persistent; affecting several areas of mental function; severe enough to interfere with work, social activities, and relationships with others (Brookshire, 2007, p. 532).

Thus dementia is defined diagnostically as a constellation of symptoms including cognitive, psychological/emotional, and behavioral impairments. For professionals working with persons with dementia, it is important to keep in mind that dementia is not a disease process with a single cause and easily predictable course. Rather, dementia is a syndrome or cluster of symptoms that is the consequence of one of several degenerative diseases of the central nervous system. Therefore, professionals must expect considerable variation in the nature and progression of dementing symptoms (though "core" symptoms that characterize various dementing diseases can be identified), as well as co-morbidity with other impairments, depending on the nature of the underlying disease.

3.2   Dementia categories and dementing diseases

The dementia conditions most commonly discussed both in the popular media and the scientific literature are irreversible dementias. However, dementia symptoms are not all necessarily progressive and irreversible. They can be reversible, and some of the causes of reversible dementing symptoms are drug toxicity; major clinical depression (this is an exclusion criterion for the definition of dementia under ICD-10; see above); metabolic or endocrine disorders (for instance, thyroid dysfunction); severe deficiency states (e.g., of vitamin B12); normal-pressure hydrocephalus; or subdural hematoma. The term *reversible* should, however, be used with caution. Research has found that in many individuals with a diagnosis of a reversible dementing condition, treatment does not really result in a return to pre-morbid levels of functioning. However, it is important to note that some conditions that lead to dementing symptoms are treatable, and that treatment can lead to genuine, significant, and lasting improvement of function (rather than in a slowing down or temporary halting of deterioration) (see Bayles & Tomoeda, 2007, and Molloy & Lubinski, 1995 for more detailed discussion of reversible dementias).

A commonly used classification system is the categorization of dementias into *cortical*, *subcortical*, and *mixed* dementias, depending on the location of the brain areas primarily affected by the degenerative process. Although of wide currency, this categorization is not entirely unproblematic, since brain damage in progressive dementing conditions spreads, and thus will typically involve both cortical and subcortical brain regions (see e.g., Osimani & Friedman, 1995). An example of a subcortical dementia is dementia associated with Parkinson's disease, whereas dementia of the Alzheimer's type (see below) illustrates the category of cortical dementia. Depending on the lesion sites, a vascular dementia (formerly usually referred to as multi-infarct dementia, that is, dementia caused by multiple CVAs, or cerebrovascular accidents) is an example of a mixed dementia. Alzheimer's disease is by far the most common cause of dementia in countries for which reliable statistics are available, and in public and media discourses about dementia, the terms "Alzheimer's" and "dementia" are frequently used as synonyms. Because dementia of the Alzheimer's type dominates dementia statistics, the primary focus of the remaining discussion in this chapter is on this type of dementia; however, several other dementing conditions will also be described briefly. The details in the following paragraphs are based on DSM-IV-TR (American Psychiatric Association, 2000), Baddeley et al. (2002), Bayles and Tomoeda (2007), Brookshire (2007), Guendouzi and Müller (2006), and Molloy and Lubinski (1995), any of which readers may wish to consult for more detailed descriptions.

Parkinson's disease (PD) leads to dementia in approximately 20 to 60 percent of persons thus diagnosed. Characteristics of PD include tremors, rigidity, brady-kinesia, and postural instability. Symptoms of dementia in PD are the slowing of motor and cognitive function. Persons with dementia owing to PD typically have difficulties with executive function and with memory retrieval. In addition, a high proportion of persons with PD suffer from depression. Post-mortem examination of brains of persons diagnosed with PD and dementia sometimes show patho-logical signs associated with Alzheimer's disease, or Lewy body disease (see below). PD was first described by James Parkinson (1755–1824), an English physician, in his "Essay on the shaking palsy" (Parkinson, 1817).

Huntington's disease is an inherited degenerative condition that affects move-ment, emotion, and the control of movement. Among typical early symptoms are depression, as well as emotional anxiety and increasingly frequent irritability. In addition, persons with Huntington's disease have problems with memory retrieval, executive function, and judgment.

Dementing symptoms associated with *HIV infection* have in recent years expe-rienced increasing interest, one reason being that the availability of highly active anti-retroviral treatments (HAART) have dramatically increased the lifespan of many persons living with HIV (Mantie-Kozlowski, 2008 gives an overview of the recent history of HIV treatments). Infection of the brain with HIV initially adversely affects the subcortical white matter and the basal ganglia, the damage eventually progressing to the cerebral cortex. Among early symptoms are a general weakness and slowness, as well as rigidity and dyskinesia. Later symptoms include language and memory impairment, difficulties with concentrating and problem solving. Persons with *HIV encephalopathy* may experience hallucinations, delirium, and delusions, and among the behavioral symptoms encountered are social withdrawal and apathy. There are other degenerative conditions related to HIV/AIDS that are indirectly related to HIV infection by way of the severe and persistent weak-ening of an individual's immune system. An example is *progressive multifocal leukoencephalopathy* (PML), a demyelinating disease caused by the JC virus. This virus is estimated to be carried by around 70 percent of adults (Wyen et al., 2005), but it remains dormant in persons with healthy immune systems. In individuals with severely compromised immune systems, as in AIDS consequent to HIV infection, the JC virus causes PML. Brain lesions characteristic of PML affect primarily the hemispheric white matter, but have also been found in the basal ganglia, the brain stem, and more rarely in the spinal cord. Owing to the multi-focal and progressive nature of the condition, a wide variety of cognitive, motor, and behavioral symptoms may occur, including dysarthria, and executive function and memory problems (see Mantie-Kozlowski, 2008, and Müller, Kozlowski, & Doody, 2007, for further discussion and relevant literature).

The term *frontotemporal dementia* (FTD) covers several degenerative conditions of the central nervous system affecting primarily the frontal and temporal lobes, such as *Pick's disease, primary progressive aphasia, semantic dementia*, and *amyotrophic lateral sclerosis* (or *motor neuron disease*). McKhann et al. (2001) subcategorize FTD into a behavioral and a language variant, the distinction resting on the early symptoms with which a patient presents. Later on in disease progression, the behavioral variant will likely also include language and communication difficulties, and vice versa. Pick's disease represents the behavioral variant of FTD, while the language variant includes fluent and non-fluent primary progressive aphasia, and semantic dementia.

Pick's disease was first described in 1892 by Arnold Pick, a psychiatrist at the University of Prague. He noted the characteristic structures found at autopsy, namely tangles of protein, which came to be named Pick bodies. Early symptoms include so-called personality changes (such as a deterioration of behavioral inhibition and in social skills, and emotional blunting). Memory for day-to-day events is typically preserved until late in the disease progression. Many patients with Pick's disease eventually develop symptoms of non-fluent aphasia and apraxia.

Individuals diagnosed with primary progressive aphasia (PPA) experience progressive aphasia, but initially no cognitive or behavioral problems. A defining criterion for PPA is that a progressive aphasia is noted at least 2 years prior to the occurrence of behavioral changes. Persons with PPA often experience no difficulty in general, day-to-day problem solving or the recall of events in their daily lives.

The language impairment presented by persons with semantic dementia is typically fluent, but empty of content; these patients experience a progressive loss of conceptual knowledge, which entails the loss of word meaning. In addition, perceptual difficulties occur: impaired recognition of faces (prosopagnosia) and of object identity (associative agnosia). In contrast, episodic memory is typically preserved in persons with semantic dementia, as are executive function, non-verbal reasoning, and spatial abilities.

Dementia due to *Lewy body disease* is difficult to distinguish from DAT. So-called Lewy bodies are abnormal protein deposits that occur in the cell bodies of neurons, in both cortical and subcortical structures. These lead to the loss of dopamine-producing neurons in the substantia nigra (similar to what is found in Parkinson's disease; see above), as well as of acetylcholine-producing neurons (similar to Alzheimer's disease; see below).

Vascular dementia (in earlier sources more often referred to as multi-infarct dementia) is one of the more commonly occurring patterns of dementia in elderly populations. The dementing symptoms are caused by multiple infarcts in sub-cortical and cortical structures of the brain. Molloy and Lubinski (1995, p. 6) summarize the major characteristics of vascular dementia as follows: "abrupt onset, stepwise deterioration, fluctuating course, nocturnal confusion, relative preservation of personality, depression, somatic complaints, emotional lability, history of hypertension and strokes, atherosclerosis, and focal neurological symptoms and signs."

Head trauma has also been identified in some patients as a so-called "trigger event" for dementing symptoms. The impairments owing to head trauma depend on the severity, location, and extent of brain injury. Often encountered are post-traumatic amnesia, and persistent memory impairment. In addition, other impairments may occur, such as aphasia, problems with attention, emotional and affective stability, anxiety, or depression.

4 Alzheimer's Disease: The "Poster Child" of Dementing Conditions

The remainder of this chapter will focus largely on Alzheimer's disease (AD) and dementia of the Alzheimer type (DAT). Many issues surrounding, for example, caregiving, increasing loss of independence and the social role reversal that comes with it, or the need for institutionalized care, are common to the experience of many, if not all, progressive dementing conditions. Others, such as focused pharmacological treatment, are specific to AD/DAT, and will be discussed as such. Distinctions are drawn where necessary. A narrowing down of our focus on AD/DAT is justified, given that AD is by far the most common form of irreversible, progressive dementing condition in elderly people, as witnessed by disease statistics in countries for which reliable data exist (see incidence and prevalence, below). Brookshire (2007, p. 541) describes persons with AD as the "fastest growing and most expensive clinical population in the United States." This statement sums up two pressing concerns, which in turn lend themselves to a (sometimes sensationalist) portrayal of AD/DAT in media, public, and political discourses: First, a steady increase in numbers of people diagnosed with a disease for which there is no cure, nor, at the present time, preventive treatment (such as a vaccine), but only treatment which can, in a reasonable proportion of patients, slow down symptom progression, but is costly. Second, this tendency coincides (at least in part causally) with demographic trends in most if not all industrialized nations of "aging" populations. In a country such as the United States, where substantial numbers of citizens do not have sufficient health care coverage, and in a climate of economic decline, these factors make for an emotionally and politically charged, and potentially alarming picture.

Prevalence and incidence statistics support the cliché of what is on occasion referred to as the "Alzheimer's epidemic" (see for example, Hyman, 2008). At the time of writing, it is estimated that the prevalence (that is, the number of cases that exist at a specified point in time) amounts to up to four million people in the United States diagnosed with AD. Increasing age correlates with increasing prevalence such that one person in ten over the age of 65 and nearly half of those over 85 years of age in the United States are predicted to be affected by AD (Brookshire, 2007). Incidence (that is, the number of new cases of a condition identified during a specified time period) runs to an estimated 360,000 or more people in the United States who are diagnosed with AD; around 50,000 people annually are reported to die from the disease (National Institute of Neurological Disorders and Stroke [NINDS], 2008). Similarly, a steady increase of cases of dementia, with DAT being the most common form, is predicted worldwide: Ferri et al. (2005) give estimates of dementia prevalence for each WHO world region. With the caveat that reliable epidemiological evidence is not readily available in many regions, they estimate that in 2001, 24.3 million people had dementia, with 4.6 million new cases every year. This number is projected to rise to 81.1 million by 2040. The majority of people with dementia live in developing countries, and the rate of increase in dementia cases is projected to be larger in developing countries, as well (a projected 300 percent increase between 2001 and 2040 in India, China, and neighboring south Asian and western Pacific countries, compared to a 100 percent projected increase in developed countries).

Two subtypes of DAT are distinguished, the chief criterion being age of onset: DAT with early onset is defined as the occurrence of symptoms before age 65. In early onset DAT (also referred to as pre-senile dementia), cognitive deterioration progresses relatively quickly, and typically with simultaneous multiple disorders of higher cortical functions. In DAT with late onset, in contrast, symptoms begin to occur after the age of 65. Progression is slower, and the main characteristic is gradually worsening memory loss (World Health Organization, 2007). It is difficult to predict the life span of a patient with AD after onset of symptoms, or after diagnosis. Onset of symptoms may precede a final diagnosis of "probable Alzheimer's disease," or "probable dementia of the Alzheimer's type" by several years, depending on the rate of decline. Some authorities give an average of 8 years of life post diagnosis (see e.g., Bayles & Tomoeda, 2007), but many patients may live far longer than that. This means that care for persons with AD, whether institutionalized or in the home, is a long-term proposition, and therefore has a profound effect on families and communities.

4.1   A brief historical excursion: Frau Auguste D., and Dr. Alois Alzheimer

On November 25, 1901, a 51-year-old woman was admitted to the Hospital for the Mentally Ill and Epileptics in Frankfurt am Main, Germany. She was to remain there until she died, on April 8, 1906. Among the symptoms noted over the course of her illness were progressive deterioration of cognition and impairment of memory function, hallucinations and delusions, and increasing psychosocial incompetence (Maurer, Volk & Gerbaldo, 1997). Mrs. Auguste D., as she is known from her hospital file, was born on May 16, 1850, in the town of Kassel. She had three siblings and spent her childhood in Kassel. She could read and write, and the conclusion is that she experienced at least a rudimentary primary education. She married Karl D., a railway clerk, in 1873, and moved to Frankfurt, approximately 115 miles to the south of Kassel. They had one daughter, and were married for 33 years. Mr. D. described the marriage as "happy and harmonious," his wife as of an amiable disposition, and an orderly and hardworking person (Maurer & Maurer, 2003; Page & Fletcher, 2006). In early 1901, changes in behavior and demeanor became noticeable: Mrs. D. began to voice suspicions about her husband having an affair with a neighbor. She began to make mistakes in the running of the household, and became more and more restless and erratic in her behavior. Eventually, the family physician was approached, and he referred her to the mental hospital, describing her as having been "suffering for a long time from weakening of memory, persecution mania, sleeplessness, restlessness. She is unable to perform any physical or mental work" (admission note, 1901; translated in Maurer & Maurer, 2003, p. 19; see also Page & Fletcher, 2006, p. 578).

Alois Alzheimer was born in 1864, in the village of Marktbreit, near Würzburg, Germany. He studied medicine at Berlin, Tübingen, und Würzburg. In 1888, he was appointed as a resident at the Frankfurt mental hospital, with Emil Sioli as senior physician, and was later appointed senior physician. While at Frankfurt, Alzheimer examined Mrs. D. repeatedly. A translation of part of Alzheimer's case notes can be found in Maurer, Volk, and Gerbaldo (1995). What follows are brief extracts (italics indicate Mrs. D.'s answers to Alzheimer's questions).

Extracts from case notes, November 26, 1901
She sits on the bed with a helpless expression. What is your name? *Auguste*. Last name? *Auguste*. What is your husband's name? *Auguste, I think*. Your husband? *Ah, my husband*. . . . What is this? I show her a pencil. *A pen*. A purse and key, diary, cigar are identified correctly. At lunch she eats cauliflower and pork. Asked what she is eating she answers *spinach*.

Extracts from case notes, November 29, 1901
Writing: she does it as already described [that is, holding the paper in such a way to give the impression of loss in the right visual field]. When she has to write Mrs Auguste D, she writes Mrs and we must repeat the other words because she forgets them. The patient is not able to progress in writing and repeats, *I have lost myself*. (Maurer, Volk, & Gerbaldo, 1995, pp. 1547–8)

In 1903, Alzheimer moved to Heidelberg and shortly thereafter to Munich, where he worked at the Royal Psychiatric Clinic, under the direction of Emil Kraepelin. However, he continued to follow the development of Auguste D.'s illness until her death in 1906, and requested permission to examine her brain after her death, which was duly granted (Maurer, Volk, & Gerbaldo, 1995; Page & Fletcher, 2006). It is worth mentioning here that the late nineteenth and early twentieth century also saw the invention of important histopathological techniques, for example by Alzheimer's colleague Franz Nissl. These techniques for the preparation and preservation (for example, the slicing and staining) of brain tissue for microscopic examination made it possible to link pre-mortem observation of behavioral and cognitive changes with post-mortem examination of structural changes of brain tissue.

The article in which Alzheimer published his findings (Alzheimer, 1907) summarizes the cognitive and behavioral deterioration of Mrs. D. as that of a

51-year-old woman who presented with "as one of her first disease symptoms a strong feeling of jealously towards her husband. Very soon she showed rapidly increasing memory impairments; she was disoriented carrying objects to and fro in her flat and hid them. Sometimes she felt that someone wanted to kill her and began to scream loudly . . . After $4\frac{1}{2}$ years of sickness she died" (Maurer, Volk, & Gerbaldo, 1995, p. 1548; translated from Alzheimer, 1907). The results of the post-mortem histopathological investigation are reported as involving both changes to the neurofibrils, and plaques of what later became known as beta amyloid. The former, Alzheimer describes as follows: "In the centre of an otherwise almost normal cell there stands out one or several fibrils due to their characteristic thickness and peculiar impregnability" (ibid., p. 1548, translated from Alzheimer, 1907). The plaques he characterizes as "[n]umerous small miliary foci are found in the superior layers. They are determined by the storage of a peculiar material in the cortex."

At around the same time, Perusini examined four cases (including a reexamination of Auguste D.'s case history and brain tissue) which showed amyloid plaques and neurofibrillary tangles (Maurer et al., 1995; Perusini, 1909). Kraepelin associates Alzheimer's name with the disease in his textbook of psychiatry (10th ed.) (Kraepelin, 1910), and draws attention to the fact that although the disease pattern investigated by Alzheimer and others suggests the most severe form of senile dementia, a patient may experience the onset of symptoms as early as in the late forties. As mentioned above, it is conventional to distinguish in diagnostic practice between early onset and late onset dementia of the Alzheimer's type. It appears that in Alzheimer's day, the symptoms presented by Mrs. D. were so noteworthy particularly because she was comparatively young at age of onset. While the concept of "senile dementia," and senility as a property of old age, was accepted medically and socially, a comparatively young, otherwise healthy individual showing signs of dementing was unusual enough to warrant in-depth investigation. The notions of early and late onset dementia, and whether they are to be equated in terms of not only the brain pathologies involved but also their status of "disease" or "aging," have not been entirely uncontroversial (see e.g., Chen & Fernandez, 2001; Goodwin, 1991).

4.2   The neuropathology of Alzheimer's disease

The "plaques and tangles" identified by Alzheimer and others can be said to have become part of the modern-day "folklore" of AD. *Neurofibrillary tangles* are twisted, threadlike structures that are found in the cell bodies, dendrites, axons, and occasionally also in the synaptic endings of neurons in brains affected by AD. The *neuritic plaques* identified by Alzheimer and other contemporary researchers, as mentioned above, have been found to be concentrations of beta-amyloid protein. In addition, other pathological changes have been found: *Granulovacuolar degeneration* is the term used to describe the appearance of fluid-filled cavities containing granular debris inside nerve cells. This degenerative process mainly affects the hippocampus. In the later stages of AD, cortical shrinkage can be made visible on CT or MRI scans (unlike the other brain abnor-malities associated with the disease). This shrinkage is clearly visible as progres-sively larger ventricles and wider sulci, attesting to the loss of neurons. Neurotransmitter abnormalities have also been associated with AD, chiefly mark-edly lower levels of acetylcholine. The *cortical* brain areas primarily affected by AD are the temporoparietal–occipital junctions and the inferior temporal lobes. The frontal lobes, the motor and sensory cortex, and the occipital lobes are more typically spared. The *subcortical* brain region most heavily implicated in AD is the hippocampus. (For a more detailed discussion of the neuropathology of AD, see e.g. Brookshire, 2007; Osimani and Friedman, 1995.)

4.3   Causes of and risk factors for AD

Every professional or volunteer working with persons with dementia or their caregivers sooner or later is asked the question, "But what's the cause?" The short, and often frustrating answer is, "We don't know," or, for those of a more optimistic inclination, "We don't know yet." Over the years, various environmental factors have been identified as potential contributors to Alzheimer risk, among them aluminum absorbed through the use of antiperspirants, toothpaste, or cookware, or mercury leaching from amalgam tooth fillings. A link between Alzheimer's disease and aluminum was first advanced in the 1960s (Alzheimer's Society, 2008; see e.g. Terry & Pena, 1965). However, there is no conclusive scientific or medical evidence that a causal connection exists between exposure to aluminum and Alzheimer's disease. The role of mercury, as absorbed from amalgam tooth fillings, as a causal factor in AD has also been investigated in recent years. For example, Mutter et al. (2004) hypothesize that mercury, with apolipoprotein E as a moderating factor, may increase the risk for Alzheimer's disease. However, they acknowledge that findings from studies targeting the amount of mercury in brain cells of persons with or without pre-mortem AD symptoms have been neither consistent nor conclusive.

The search for causes of adversity, especially external causes we can precisely identify (and by implication, avoid), appears to be a facet of human nature. The way that scientific research agendas and results (with all their caveats, relativiza-tions, demonstration of probabilities, possibilities, and tendencies, rather than certainties) are transformed into sound bites and thence into health scares is an important lesson, however, in the enormous responsibility carried by researchers and professionals toward the public at large.

Over the past decades, well-documented risk factors, that is, statistical patterns emerging from studies of the populations diagnosed with AD, have been described (see Bayles & Tomoeda, 2007; Brookshire, 2007 for further discussion). Chief among these risk factors are gender and age. Women are more likely to be diagnosed with AD than men, and older age groups are at far greater risk than younger ones. Bickel (2000) attributes the fact that the majority of persons diagnosed with AD are women to the higher life expectancy of women, although this is not universally accepted. As regards the age factor (see also above, incidence and prevalence), some calculations predict that after age 60, the number of people with AD doubles in every 10-year age bracket (Khatchaturian & Radebaugh, 1998).

Another question that regularly arises in the context of caregiver support is, "Does it run in families?" The familial profile of AD is somewhat more complicated than the aging factor. The majority of cases of diagnosed AD are sporadic; in other words, occurrence in families within and across generations is no more frequent than would be expected by chance. Only a small number (5 percent approximately) of cases of AD have been found to have a familial link of autosomal dominant inheritance; that is, inheritance is not sex-linked, and the responsible gene dominates its counterpart from the unaffected parent. Documented familial histories of AD are more often early onset than late onset AD, which circumstance may point toward a difference between early and late onset AD as regards its genetic inheritance. Three genes have been implicated in early onset AD. One of these, the amyloid precursor protein gene on chromosome 21, is found on the same chromosome that plays the key role in Down syndrome (trisomy-21). Indeed, there is a strong documented likelihood for individuals with Down syndrome to show symptoms of AD in their forties and fifties (see e.g. Bayles & Tomoeda, 2007; Chen & Fernandez, 2001; Zigman et al., 1995).

While familial AD is more often early onset AD, another genetic factor has been identified as a risk factor for late onset AD: significant numbers of persons with AD have been found to have a particular allele of apolipoprotein E (ApoE4), and for persons who have two copies of ApoE4, the risk of developing late onset AD has been calculated to be particularly high. But again, a genetic link has been documented in only a small proportion of diagnosed cases of AD (Bayles & Tomoeda, 2007).

Several studies that have investigated social variables in the lives of people with AD have identified education as a significant factor. In the USA, Fitzpatrick et al. (2004) found poor education to be a risk factor for AD in Caucasians, but not African Americans. A low level of education also emerged as a risk for AD (but not vascular dementia) in an Italian study (Ravaglia et al., 2005), and a study in rural China (Zhou et al., 2006). One explanation has been, according to Bayles and Tomoeda (2007), that persons with higher levels of education have greater cognitive reserves owing to more densely connected neural networks. In other words, symptoms of cognitive decline, if mild, might not manifest as warning signs of underlying brain pathologies during their lifetimes. If, in future research, levels of education emerge as solidly correlated with risk of manifesting AD, then this point takes on increased social and political significance. In societies where income levels determine not only access to quality health care, but equally, access to quality education, poverty represents multiple long-term risk factors.

Bayles & Tomoeda (2007) also mention a history of head trauma as a possible risk factor for AD. The exact processes involved have not been well explained as yet. Given that in recent years, war veterans have, thanks to advances in acute medical care and medical battlefield evacuation, survived head injuries that in earlier decades would have proved fatal, a potential link between head trauma and AD in later life is a concern for this population.

4.4 Impairments of memory, cognition, and communication in AD/DAT

The available literature on the progressively worsening impairments that arise out of AD typically makes reference to "stages" of AD and concomitant impairment levels. Most commonly, a three-stage categorization is used, which distinguishes between early or mild, middle stage or moderate, and late stage or severe AD/DAT. These categories are used here for the sake of convenience; however, readers should keep in mind that the "staging" of dementia represents the averaging of many observed cases, and that the multiple impairments of DAT do not necessarily progress at the same rate. Therefore, any one person's individual symptom profile does not necessarily fit into any one specific stage at any given time.

Persons with *early* or *mild* DAT have been shown to have problems with working memory (WM), as well as episodic memory (EM) for recent events. Experimental research investigating WM points toward an intact phonological store and articulatory loop, but to impairment of the central executive system (Becker & Overman, 2002). This has an impact, among other things, in situations that require "multi-tasking" and would manifest in the laboratory as reduced performance when participants simultaneously carry out, for example, a manual tracking task and a digit span task.

In the absence of other conditions that impair speech and language (e.g., stroke), speech intelligibility, language form (syntax, morphology, phonology), and fluency are preserved until late in the progression of DAT. Typically the earliest language problem in DAT is word-finding difficulty. Comprehension appears largely intact, but the comprehension of language that requires a lot of inferences, as well as comprehension of complex discourse such as multi-party conversations, becomes difficult. A combination of word-finding difficulties, the use of non-specific place-holder nouns and verbs such as "stuff," or "do," and frequent circumlocutions and the repetition of ideas leads to the production of discourse that has been characterized as "empty" of content (see e.g. Kempler, 1995; Salmon, Heindel, & Butters, 1995; Ulatowska & Chapman, 1995; also Guendouzi & Müller, 2006 for a summary of earlier research). The five most frequently named problems that emerged out of Bayles & Tomoeda's (1991) investigation of caregiver reports on the appearance of language and communication symptoms were difficulties with word finding, naming objects, writing a letter, comprehending instructions, and sustaining a conversation.

Persons with *moderate* or *mid-stage* DAT essentially experience a worsening of all the cognitive and communicative difficulties identified above: WM and EM functioning becomes weaker. In addition, SM memory begins to deteriorate, which in turn leads to a loss of concepts, and words. However, it has been shown that some procedural memory skills remain relatively intact until quite late in the disease progression (see e.g. Salmon, Heindel, & Butters, 1995, on the learning of motor skills; also Bayles & Kim, 2003; Becker & Overman, 2002). Persons with mid-stage AD/DAT increasingly also have attentional difficulties and are therefore more easily distracted from tasks that are becoming more cognitively demanding. Visuo-spatial problems also become more common. The language difficulties that begin to manifest at the early stage gradually become more severe. While speech output remains intelligible and language intact as regards syntax and morphology, meaning and content errors become more frequent, and increasing difficulties with topic maintenance as well as reference errors such as inaccurate pronoun use may make the language output of a person with moderate DAT difficult to comprehend. Individuals with moderate DAT also become increasingly less aware of communication problems, less aware of both linguistic and non-linguistic context (which makes, for example, jokes harder to interpret), and less able to monitor their output. Language comprehension becomes more difficult, of both spoken and written language (see e.g. Bayles & Tomoeda, 2007; Kempler, 1995). Personal experience with caregivers has shown that the time when avid readers give up what used to be an absorbing activity because text becomes too difficult to understand is often perceived as a milestone in disease progression that is emotionally difficult to negotiate.

The *late* or *severe* stage of DAT is characterized by the collapse of declarative memory systems as well as WM. This manifests in, among other things, one's loss of orientation in the here and now, including the loss of recognition of one's nearest and dearest, and the inability to retain information that is intended to reorient one to reality. In terms of language and communication, there is great variation between individuals. While some lose the use of language altogether and become mute, in some patients language output is restricted to repetitive behaviors such as echolalia, or perseverative repetition of their own utterances. Some, though by no means all, patients manifest dysarthria, and hence reduced intelligibility. On the other hand, some persons with DAT retain some conversational language (Bayles & Tomoeda, 2007; Kempler, 1995).

As Kempler (1995) points out, it is also useful to mention that there are some language and speech deficits that we do not (in the absence of other neurological conditions) find in persons with DAT. Suprasegmental aspects of speech such as prosody typically remain intact, as does segmental phonology. Syntax and morphology are preserved until very late in the disease, and spoken language output remains fluent; the agrammatic deficits of non-fluent aphasia are absent from DAT. In addition, it is worth emphasizing that turn-taking skills remain intact in many persons even in the presence of severe cognitive impairment. It is also important to reiterate that language, communication, and cognitive skills do not necessarily deteriorate at the same rate, and that therefore the multiple observable impairments do not always map evenly onto any one stage of disease progression. In addition, we also need to keep in mind that communicative success is as much a function of the context in which communication happens, as of a bundle of skills, or impairments, pertaining to any one individual. (A detailed investigation of what in fact constitutes communicative skills, or otherwise, would go beyond the scope of this chapter. See Clark, 1996; Clark, 2003; Guendouzi & Müller, 2006; Perkins, 2007, for discussions of communicative, and cognitive, processes as distributed and emergent entities.)

The example below illustrates some of the skills and deficits that are encountered in persons with DAT. It is an extract from a transcript of conversation between a person with a diagnosis of DAT, Ms. FM, and two graduate students, MH and R. Ms. FM was also a cancer patient, receiving palliative care. She was a resident in a nursing home, and no recent cognitive or communicative evaluation had been administered. At the time the conversation was recorded, she showed cognitive symptoms consistent with mid- to late-stage DAT, such as marked deficits in immediate memory and memory for recent events, lack of orientation to person, time, and space. She never, over the course of two years, established recognition of either myself or any of the students working with me. However, she was a keen and skilled conversationalist, described in more detail elsewhere (Guendouzi & Müller, 2006, contains the full transcript).

Example 1: Conversation between Ms. FM, and MH and R (two graduate students)

475 MH: how old are your brothers.
476 FM: my brothers.
477 R: mhm,
478 FM: o:h, (7.0) I'm tryin to think, (4.0) I'm older than them. (17.0) it must be like sixteen, (.) and a- (.) eighteen somethin like this. one must be sixteen the other one eighteen. (3.0) they still in school they're not (1.5) out of school yet. (14.0) and where you live,
479 MH: O,
480 FM: O. that's not far from L,
481 MH: no. about half an hour, (2.0)
482 FM: and where you live honey.

(From Guendouzi & Müller, 2006, pp. 272–3)

Looking at deficits, we find that long stretches of silence, timed in seconds in the transcript, attest to the fact that Ms. FM clearly has difficulties expressing her thoughts. Further, she is clearly not oriented to the present time, stating that her brothers are still at school: long-established knowledge about her family (that she has brothers and is older than they are) is preserved, but how it relates to the present is not. She also demonstrates vagueness of expression ("like," "something like"), and repetition of ideas within one turn (turn 479), and an unflagged topic shift ("where you live").

Looking at skills, we find that Ms. FM clearly has preserved language form, as well as turn-taking skills: she effectively uses a clarification question (turn 477), and questions eliciting information from her interlocutors (end of 479, and 483). These questions are highly repetitive (see Müller & Guendouzi, 2005; Guendouzi & Müller, 2006, for detailed discussion), but they are also *functional* interactionally, in that they continue the conversation, and allow Ms. FM to hand over her turn to someone else. She also demonstrates that given enough time, she can construct a statement that has internal logic (older – sixteen, eighteen – in school), and she effectively uses discourse markers ("o:h", "I'm trying to think") to give herself time at the beginning of a turn. Finally, she evidences intact interactional politeness in the way she addresses her interlocutors (asking questions, the term of address "honey," which in the local culture is entirely appropriate).

The language and communication skills and difficulties of *bilingual* persons with dementia have thus far been investigated in less detail than those of monolinguals, or of bilingual persons with aphasia. There is published work on language mixing and code switching in bilingual persons with dementia, as well as on issues of caregiving and access to persons speaking familiar or preferred languages (see Friedland & Miller, 1999; Hyltenstam & Stroud, 1989; Obler, de Santi, & Goldberger, 1995); however, much remains to be done in these areas, particularly in "aging" societies that are inherently and increasingly multilingual. A recently published study that found a correlation between being bilingual and later onset of dementing symptoms (compared to monolingual individuals) also presents intriguing food for thought (Bialystok, Craik, & Freedman, 2007).

4.5   Assessment and diagnosis

As Clare (2002, p. 717) points out, a diagnosis of dementia is "reasonably straightforward" in the later stages of disease progression. However, a reliable identification of early dementia in general and DAT in particular is rather more challenging. In particular, it is important to distinguish the effects of normal aging, or depression, from the effects of a dementing condition. Assessment is an integral part of the diagnostic process, as well as of the monitoring of disease progression. Given that AD is not associated with tell-tale metabolic or chemical deficit states that could be positively identified via blood tests, and that the characteristic structural changes in the brain only appear in non-invasive brain imaging late in the disease, the path to a diagnosis is as much a process of elimination as of identification. Further, given that the brain pathology, that is, AD, manifests as a complex of symptoms in multiple behavioral and cognitive domains, that is, DAT, the assessment process is of necessity also complex.

Dementia rating scales are used in clinical research and practice in order to track and quantify the progression of dementia severity. They rate various domains of a person's functioning, cognitive as well as behavioral. Examples of dementia rating scales often referred to in the anglophone world are the Blessed Dementia Scale (Blessed, Tomlinson, & Roth, 1968), the Global Deterioration Scale (Reisberg et al., 1982), and the Clinical Dementia Rating Scale (Morris, 1993). The Blessed Dementia Scale evaluates changes in the performance of eight activities of daily living (e.g., ability to perform household tasks, cope with small amounts of money, or remember short lists), and changes in 14 habits, behaviors, and personality traits, ranging from eating, to purposeless hyperactivity. The Global Deterioration Scale requires a trained clinical professional to rate behavior descriptions that emerge out of a clinical interview with the patient and caregiver(s), on a seven-point scale that ranges from 1 (no cognitive decline; clinical stage: normal) to 7 (very severe cognitive decline; clinical stage: late dementia). The Clinical Dementia Rating Scale uses a standardized interview protocol, on the basis of which six domains of cognition and functioning are evaluated. Raters use scores ranging from 0 to 3 to calculate impairment levels of none, mild, moderate, or severe; a rater can assign a score or 0.5 to any one dimension or descriptor when impairment is questionable.

Dementia screening procedures are a frequently employed first step in the diagnostic process. In English-speaking contexts, probably the most widely used such screening procedure is the Mini-Mental State Examination (MMSE; Folstein, Folstein, & McHugh, 1975). A variety of brief tasks targeting for example orientation, registration, attention and recall, as well as various language functions, are presented to a patient and scored by the examiner. The MMSE continues to be widely used, but concerns have been raised because MMSE scores have been found to correlate strongly with level of education, and if the test is administered repeatedly, practice effects may inflate scores (see Clare, 2002).

Another dementia screening procedure, the Saint Louis University Mental Status (SLUMS) examination, has been claimed to be a more sensitive tool than the MMSE for the detection of early dementia, or mild cognitive disorder. The SLUMS consists of a 30-point questionnaire that probes orientation, memory, attention, and executive functions (Tariq et al., 2006). The SLUMS is available online at the Saint Louis University Medical School website (http://medschool.slu.edu/agingsuccessfully/pdfsurveys/slumsexam_05.pdf).

As mentioned above, the areas of dysfunction in AD are multiple and varied, and, therefore, both the diagnostic process and the monitoring of progressive deterioration involve a wide array of assessment procedures. Diagnostic assessments typically include blood analyses and brain imaging to detect deficiency states and neuro-anatomical abnormalities, as well as a series of tests addressing multiple domains of neuropsychological functioning. Clare (2002, p. 715) outlines the domains of cognitive functioning that should be addressed in neuropsychological assessment: General cognitive functioning (current and estimated prior IQ); long-term memory (episodic, semantic, autobiographical, prospective); working memory, attention, and executive function; perception (object and spatial perception); and expressive and receptive language. In addition, a patient's mood and the potential presence of depression should be assessed, as well as their functional ability in daily living (which should also include an investigation of his or her living environment). It is also important to gain insight into the knowledge and attitudes of family members and caregivers (see Clare, 2002, for a detailed list of assessments suitable to assess these domains).

Tests specifically developed for the assessment of cognition and communication in dementia are the Arizona Battery for Communication Disorders in Dementia (ABCD; Bayles & Tomoeda, 1993), and the Functional Linguistic Communication Inventory (FLCI; Bayles & Tomoeda, 1994). The ABCD is designed for the assessment of individuals with mild to moderate dementia, whereas the FLCI is targeted at persons with severe dementia. There are other tools that are geared toward assessing functional communication skills of persons with various acquired impairments of communication and cognition, for example the Communicative Abilities in Daily Living (CADL; Holland, 1980), or the Functional Assessment of Communication Skills for Adults (ASHA FACS; Frattali et al., 1995). The Montreal

Evaluation of Communication Questionnaire for use in Long-term Care (MECQ-LTC; Le Dorze et al., 2000) is a protocol aimed at residents in institutional care, such as nursing homes.

An example from a case study may serve as an illustration of the path toward a diagnosis of DAT (Wilson, 2007). The patient in question was a well-educated woman who consulted her family physician at the age of 54 because of concerns with short-term memory and word finding. The family physician had blood analyses performed in order to test for metabolic abnormalities or deficiency states. Once such abnormalities were excluded, the patient was referred to a neuropsychologist, who after an initial interview performed a battery of seven tests addressing multiple areas of cognitive and language functioning, as follows: The Kaufman Brief Intelligence Test, the MicroCog Assessment of Cognitive Functioning, the Reitan Indiana Aphasia Screening Test, the Vigil Continuous Performance Test, The Halstead–Reitan Neuropsychological Test Battery, the Babcock Story Recall Test, and the Rey–Osterrieth Complex Figure. This series of tests was administered over a period of approximately a month, and the patient performed below normal on all of them. The patient was referred to a neuropathologist, who performed new blood tests and a lumbar puncture to detect possible abnormalities in the cerebrospinal fluid. These having been excluded, the patient was referred further to a neurologist, who had MRI, CAT, and PET scans performed. None of these imaging techniques revealed visible brain abnormalities. The neurologist finally made a diagnosis of probably DAT with early onset (Wilson, 2007, pp. 55–8; see also Clare, 2002, for a detailed discussion of neuropsychological testing as applicable in DAT). Multiple referrals, as experienced by this patient, are not necessarily the rule for all persons with dementia. However, the case illustrates the complexity of interaction of multiple levels of cognition that needs to be addressed in the diagnosis and assessment of DAT/AD.

4.6   Intervention

At the present time, there is no cure for AD/DAT, nor are there interventions that can reliably prevent the onset of AD (whether it is even realistic to expect that research will, at some time in the future, discover a cure for AD/DAT depends to an extent on one's conceptualization of AD/DAT). *Pharmacological intervention* aims to slow down the progression of cognitive symptoms that are a consequence of AD. The US Federal Food and Drug Administration has approved the use of two types of medications to target AD: cholinesterase inhibitors, and glutamate regulators. Cholinesterase inhibitors are used to reduce the breakdown of acetylcholine; by maintaining high acetylcholine levels, communication between brain cells is supported. In the US, three cholinesterase inhibitors are commonly prescribed to patients with a diagnosis of AD: donepezil, rivastagmine, and galantamine. While the latter two are approved for use by patients with mild to moderate DAT, the former is also prescribed for patients with severe DAT. The focus on early prescription, that is, the use of these drugs for patients with mild DAT, has in turn fueled an increased interest in early detection and diagnosis of

DAT. The glutamate regulator memantine has been approved for moderate to severe DAT. Anecdotal evidence (caregiver reports) shows that donepezil and memantine are increasingly prescribed together in the US. It is not easy to measure the beneficial effects of dementia drugs in any one individual. While patients may show improvements clinically evidenced by, for example, a 2- to 3-point increase on the MMSE (Folstein et al., 1975), this may only represent a slowing down of cognitive deterioration by 6 months. Where performance does not improve, but remains constant over a given period of time, it is not possible to reliably determine whether this temporary halting of deterioration is entirely due to the drug administered (see Clare, 2002, for further discussion).

A plethora of both direct and indirect interventions for persons with dementia have been discussed in the literature, and a detailed review would far exceed the scope of this chapter (see Bayles & Tomoeda, 2007; Clare, 2002; Kasl-Godley & Gatz, 2000; Woods, 2002). *Direct interventions* are implemented directly with individuals with dementia; they may address, for example, cognitive rehabilitation, coping skills, and the maintenance of a positive self-image and identity and self-esteem. *Indirect interventions* address the environment of the person with dementia, and include the modification of the physical environment, as well as training, counseling, and support of caregivers.

As detailed above, the different subsystems of memory do not deteriorate uniformly in DAT. Procedural memory systems are preserved longer than declarative memory, and early in disease progression, episodic memory (especially for recent events) is affected more severely than semantic memory; and encoding, rather than rates of forgetting, presents the greatest difficulties. Cognitive rehabilitation interventions in early DAT need to be designed to take the best possible advantage of preserved memory systems, as well as tailored to the skills and impairments of each individual. Clare (2002) reviews three categories of individually targeted interventions: *compensation using external memory aids, skills training to optimize procedural memory functioning,* and *facilitating residual long-term memory performance.* Compensation with external memory aids involves the use of, for instance, memory wallets or personalized notebooks, or video and computer equipment to monitor an individual's movements and behaviors and prompt for certain activities (e.g., taking medications, washing hands). Research has shown that individuals with dementia typically require training in the use of memory aids, but that these tools can be beneficial in enhancing conversation ability, and in prolonging independent functioning (see Bourgeois, 1992).

Some studies have shown that intensive training building on procedural memory to enhance independent functioning in activities of daily living can be beneficial for persons with mild to moderate DAT, on tasks that are part of individuals' daily routine, and which they are motivated to perform. Such training programs involve high levels of prompting, with gradual fading out of prompts.

An example of a strategy aimed at facilitating residual long-term memory performance is the spaced retrieval technique, or expanding rehearsal (e.g., Vance & Farr, 2007). In this technique, an individual is presented with an item to be remembered, and prompted to recall the item immediately, and then at gradually increased intervals. Spaced retrieval can be beneficial in teaching factual information (e.g., face–name associations, the location of an object), prospective memory tasks, or procedures (such as remembering to use a memory aid).

5   Outlook: Dementing and Aging

Thus far, this chapter has treated dementia in essence as the property of a person, that is, of the individual diagnosed with a dementing disease, such as AD, and the process of dementing as a property of a disease. Public and medical discourses of dementia, and in particular of DAT, are dominated by a disease model which views the decline in functioning experienced by persons with a diagnosis of DAT as the consequence of a diagnosed disease which is qualitatively different from processes to be expected in normal aging. It is time to relativize, and expand, this perspective.

A disease focus is useful from a number of angles: among other things, research focused on disease processes in AD has led to diagnostic categories, and pharmacological interventions. In addition, it is a useful political stance for agencies among whose aims is the lobbying for funds for medical research: conceptualizing a condition as a "disease" brings with it the implications that there may be a cure waiting to be discovered, or treatment that may, if not cure, then substantially alleviate symptoms, and that potentially, said disease may be prevented if only risk factors can be pinned down with sufficient precision, or preventive treatment be developed.

In this context, it is worth recalling the well-documented increase in incidence and prevalence of AD in old age: if we have to expect that, according to some sources, approximately half of those aged 85 or over will develop AD, do we in fact need to treat AD as "normal" for people of advanced age? Dominant ideologies of successful aging have led to the expectation that "normal" cognitive functioning in old age is indeed the norm. A prominent example from public life is the nomination by his party, in 2008, of a 72-year-old for the office of President of the United States. Given that people in their mid-seventies are at considerable risk of developing AD, this nomination might have given many people pause for thought if an age-related dementing process (in other words, "senility", see e.g. Goodwin, 1991) were considered as normal. If, however, the cognitive deterioration that comes with AD is regarded strictly as a disease process (and which in many quarters is regarded as categorically separable from normal aging; see again Goodwin, 1991), and, moreover, a disease for which there will, eventually, be found either a cure or prevention or both, then the picture is subtly different, since disease is, by definition, not "normal," and therefore by implication, exceptional, whereas aging is not, of course.

However, a disease focus alone does not do justice to the experience of Alzheimer's disease (to borrow Sabat's phrase), or dementia (Sabat, 2001). Various authors have discussed problems with a straightforward mapping of pre-mortem cognitive and behavioral symptoms of DAT thus diagnosed, and post-mortem identification of the brain pathologies typical of AD (see Kitwood, 1997; Sabat, 2001; Snowden, 2001). Further, a person's functioning (whether in terms of cognition, emotional stability and happiness, or independence in activities of daily living, to name only a few) is the product of multiple interacting factors, among which neurological impairment is one, but by no means the only, nor necessarily the decisive one. The work of the late Tom Kitwood, identifying factors constituting what he labeled "malignant social psychology," is important here (Kitwood, 1997; Kitwood & Bredin, 1992); the term refers to social interactions that undermine a person's sense of integrity, self-esteem, and personhood. Among the elements of malignant social psychology identified by Kitwood are, for example, labeling, infantilization, and disempowerment: for instance, the diagnosis of "probable DAT" may be foregrounded by others in the way a person with this diagnosis is treated, to the detriment of other, more positively loaded aspects of her or his identity. The person is dealt with in a patronizing fashion, as someone dependent and incompetent whose life is controlled by others, and even tasks that the individual can carry out are done for her/him, thus further reducing independent living. A person thus treated may well become either apathetic and withdrawn, exhibiting signs of depression, or else react with frustration and become aggressive. However, owing to the foregrounding of DAT as the overriding factor in the person's life, these reactions are interpreted as symptomatic of the disease, rather than examined in their own right and identified as consequences of malignant social psychology. Malignant social psychology is closely linked with excess disability and learned helplessness, that is, a person's functioning at a level that is lower than what the individual is capable of, and the acceptance of increased dependence. This in turn has a detrimental effect on quality of life and well-being, as well as leading to an increased burden on caregivers. Therefore, a perspective on dementia as the exclusive property of a disease, which in turn colors the perception of all other domains of a person's life, is likely to become, in fact, counterproductive (see also Chapter 1 this volume).

6 Conclusion

Improved medical care and healthier living conditions have led to increased life spans for large parts of the world's population. Older age groups now make up larger proportions of many societies than even a few decades ago, and therefore the need to provide for the social and medical needs of these populations is becoming a more pressing need. Given the stated correlation between longer life spans and dementing conditions, these conditions will feature prominently on the agenda of health professionals, as the "baby boomer" generation in the industrialized world reaches the sixth decade and beyond. Dementia is a multifaceted condition that goes far beyond the sphere of physical, or medical, health, which has wide-ranging ramifications for cognitive and communicative functioning of an individual within her or his social environment. Practicing speech-language pathologists will increasingly be expected to provide services to this population.

SLPs are involved in the diagnostic process, provide interventions and counseling to persons with dementia and their caregivers, and are advocates for this growing clinical population. Therefore, SLPs can make an important positive contribution to the lives of persons with dementia. This chapter has provided an overview of important issues and content in this growing field of research and clinical practice, and it is intended as a first step toward learning about dementia. Given the scope of the topic, it would have been unrealistic to attempt complete coverage of all relevant issues. However, armed with the information presented here, and using the references provided, practicing SLPs, students, and researchers should be able to develop a basis of knowledge that will allow them to better serve the needs of individuals with dementia.

REFERENCES

Alzheimer, A. (1907). Über eine eigenartige Erkrankung der Hirnrinde [On a peculiar disease of the cerebral cortex]. *Allgemeine Zeitschrift für Psychiatrie und Psychisch-Gerichtliche Medizin* 64, 146–8.

Alzheimer's Society. (2008). *Aluminium and Alzheimer's disease*. On-line factsheet. London: Alzheimer's Society. Accessed November 2008, at: http://www.alzheimers.org.uk/site/scripts/documents_info.php?documentID=99

American Psychiatric Association. (2000). *Diagnostic and statistical manual of mental disorders*, 4th ed., text revision. Washington, DC: American Psychiatric Association.

Baddeley, A. D. (2002). The psychology of memory. In A. D. Baddeley, M. D. Kopelman, & B. A. Wilson (eds.), *The handbook of memory disorders* (pp. 3–15). New York: Wiley.

Baddeley, A. D., Kopelman, M. D., & Wilson, B. A. (2002). *The handbook of memory disorders*. New York: Wiley.

Bayles, K. A. & Kim, E. S. (2003). Improving the functioning of individuals with Alzheimer's disease: Emergence of behavioral interventions. *Journal of Communication Disorders* 36, 327–43.

Bayles, K. A. & Tomoeda, C. K. (1991). Caregiver report of prevalence and appearance order of linguistic symptoms in Alzheimer's patients. *The Gerontologist* 31, 210–16.

Bayles, K. A. & Tomoeda, C. K. (1993). *Arizona battery for communication disorders of dementia*. Austin, TX: Pro-Ed.

Bayles, K. A. & Tomoeda, C. K. (1994). *Functional linguistic communication inventory*. Austin, TX: Pro-Ed.

Bayles, K. A. & Tomoeda, C. K. (2007). *Cognitive-communication disorders of dementia*. San Diego, CA: Plural.

Becker, J. T. & Overman, A. A. (2002). The memory deficit in Alzheimer's disease. In A. D. Baddeley, M. D. Kopelman, & B. A. Wilson (eds.), *The handbook of memory disorders* (pp. 569–89). New York: Wiley.

Bialystok, E., Craik, F. I. M., & Freedman, M. (2007). Bilingualism as a protection against the onset of symptoms of dementia. *Neuropsychologia* 45, 459–64.

Bickel, H. (2000). Dementia syndrome and Alzheimer disease: An assessment of morbidity and annual incidence in Germany. *Gesundheitswesen* 62, 211–18.

Blessed, G., Tomlinson, B. E., & Roth, M. (1968). The association between quantitative measures of dementia and senile change in the cerebral gray matter of elderly subjects. *British Journal of Psychiatry* 114, 791–811.

Bourgeois, M. S. (1992). Evaluating memory wallets in conversations with persons with dementia. *Journal of Speech and Hearing Research* 34, 831–44.

Brookshire, R. H. (2007). *Introduction to neurogenic communication disorders*, 7th ed. St Louis, MO: Mosby Elsevier.

Chen, M. & Fernandez, H. L. (2001). Alzheimer movement re-examined 25 years later: Is it a "disease" or a senile condition in medical nature? *Frontiers in Bioscience* 6, e30–40.

Clare, L. (2002). Assessment and intervention in dementia of the Alzheimer's type. In A. D. Baddeley, M. D. Kopelman, & B. A. Wilson (eds.), *The handbook of memory disorders* (pp. 711–39). New York: Wiley.

Clark, A. (2003). *Natural-born cyborgs.* New York: Oxford University Press.

Clark, H. H. (1996). *Using language.* Cambridge: Cambridge University Press.

Ferri, C. P., Prince, M., Brayne, C., Brodaty, H., Fratiglioni, L., Ganguli, M., Hall, K., Hasegawa, K., Hendrie, H., Huang, Y., Jorm, A., Mathers, C., Menezes, P. R., Rimmer, E., & Scazufca, M., Alzheimer's Disease International. (2005). Global prevalence of dementia: A Delphi consensus study. *Lancet* 366, 2112–17.

Fitzpatrick, A. L., Kuller, L. H., Ives, D. G, Lopez, O. L., Jagust, W., Breitner, J. C., Jones, B., Lyketsos, C., & Dulberg, C. (2004). Incidence and prevalence of dementia in the Cardiovascular Health Study. *Journal of the American Geriatrics Society* 52 (2), 195–204.

Folstein, M. F., Folstein, S. E., & McHugh, P. R. (1975). "Mini-mental State": A practical method for grading the mental state of patients for the clinician. *Journal of Psychiatric Research* 12, 189–98.

Frattali, C. M., Thompson, C. M., Holland, A. L., Whol, C. B., & Ferketic, M. M. (1995). *Functional assessment of communication skills for adults (ASHA FACS).* Rockville, MD: ASHA.

Friedland, D. & Miller, N. (1999). Language mixing in bilingual speakers with Alzheimer's dementia: A conversation analysis approach. *Aphasiology* 13, 427–44.

Goodwin, J. S. (1991). Geriatric ideology: The myth of the myth of senility. *Journal of the American Geriatrics Society*, 39, 627–31.

Guendouzi, J. A. & Müller, N. (2006). *Approaches to discourse in dementia.* Mahwah, NJ: Lawrence Erlbaum.

Holland, A. L. (1980). *Communicative abilities in daily living.* Baltimore, MD: University Park Press.

Hyltenstam, K. & Stroud, C. (1989). Bilingualism in Alzheimer's dementia: Two case studies. In K. Hyltenstam & L. Obler (eds.), *Bilingualism across the lifespan: Aspects of acquisition, maturity and loss* (pp. 205–24). Cambridge: Cambridge University Press.

Hyman, R. (2008). *America's frightening Alzheimer's epidemic.* Accessed October 2008 at: http://www.alternet.org/healthwellness. Alternet.org: Author

Kasl-Godley, J. & Gatz, M. (2000). Psychosocial interventions for individuals with dementia: An integration of theory, therapy, and a clinical understanding of dementia. *Clinical Psychology Review* 20, 755–82.

Kempler, D. (1995). Language changes in dementia of the Alzheimer type. In R. Lubinski (ed.), *Dementia and communication* (pp. 98–114). San Diego, CA: Singular.

Kester, J. D., Benjamin, A. S., Castel, A. D., & Craik, F. M. (2002). Memory in elderly people. In In A. D. Baddeley, M. D. Kopelman, & B. A. Wilson (eds.), *The handbook of memory disorders* (pp. 543–67). New York: Wiley.

Khatchaturian, Z. S. & Radebaugh, T. S. (1998). AD: Where are we now? Where are we going? *Alzheimer Disease and Related Disorders* 12 (Suppl 3), 24–8.

Kitwood, T. (1997). *Dementia reconsidered: The person comes first*. Philadelphia, PA: Open University Press.

Kitwood, T. & Bredin, K. (1992). Towards a theory of dementia care: Personhood and well-being. *Ageing and Society* 10, 177–96.

Kraepelin, E. (1910). *Psychiatrie: Ein Lehrbuch für Studierende und Ärzte* [Psychiatry: a text for students and physicians]. Leipzig: Barth.

Le Dorze, G., Julien, M., Généreux, S., Larfeuil, C., Navennec, C., Laporte, D., & Champagne, C. (2000). The development of a procedure for the evaluation of communication occurring between residents in long-term care and their caregivers. *Aphasiology* 14, 17–51.

Mantie-Kozlowski, A. (2008). Repetitive verbal behaviors in free conversation with a person with progressive multifocal leucoencephalopathy. Doctoral dissertation, University of Louisiana at Lafayette.

Maurer, K. & Maurer, U. (2003). *Alzheimer: The life of a physician and the career of a disease*. New York: Columbia University Press.

Maurer, K., Volk, S., & Gerbaldo, H. (1997). Auguste D and Alzheimer's disease. *The Lancet* 349, 1546–49.

McKhann, G. M., Albert, M. S., Grossman, M., Miller, B., Dickson, D., & Trojanowski, J. Q. (2001). Clinical and pathological diagnosis of frontotemporal dementia. *Archives of Neurology* 58, 1803–9.

Molloy, D. W. & Lubinski, R. (1995). Dementia: impact and clinical perspectives. In R. Lubinski (ed.), *Dementia and communication* (pp. 2–21). San Diego, CA: Singular.

Morris, J. C. (1993). The clinical dementia rating scale (CDR): Current version and scoring rules. *Neurology* 43, 2412–14.

Müller, N. & Guendouzi, J. A., (2005). Order and disorder in conversation: Encounters with dementia of the Alzheimer's type. *Clinical Linguistics and Phonetics* 19, 393–404.

Müller, N., Kozlowski, A., & Doody, M. P. (2007). Repetitive verbal behaviors in PML: An exploratory study of conversation. In M. J. Ball & J. S. Damico (eds.), *Clinical aphasiology – future directions. A festschrift for Chris Code* (pp. 168–80). Hove, UK: Psychology Press.

Mutter, J., Naumann, J., Sadaghiani, C., Schneider, R., & Walach, H. (2004). Alzheimer disease: Mercury as pathogenetic factor and apolipotrotein E as a moderator. *Neuroendocrinology Letters* 25, 331–9.

National Institute of Neurological Disorders and Stroke (NINDS) (2008). *Dementia: Hope through research*. Bethesda, MD: National Institute of Neurological Disorders and Stroke. Accessed October 2008 at: http://www.ninds.nih.gov/disorders/dementias/detail_dementia.htm

Obler, L., de Santi, S., & Goldberger, J. (1995). Bilingual dementia: Pragmatic breakdown. In In R. Lubinski (ed.), *Dementia and communication* (pp. 133–41). San Diego, CA: Singular.

Osimani, A. & Friedman, M. (1995). Functional anatomy. In R. Lubinski (ed.), *Dementia and communication* (pp. 22–36). San Diego, CA: Singular.

Page, S. & Fletcher, T. (2006). Auguste D 100 years on: "The person" not "the case." *Dementia* 5, 571–83.

Parkinson, J. (1817). *Essay on the shaking palsy*. London: Sherwood, Neely & Jones.

Perkins, M. R. (2007). *Pragmatic impairment*. Cambridge: Cambridge University Press.

Perusini, G. (1909). Über klinisch und histologisch eigenartige psychische Erkrankungen des späteren Lebensalters. [On clinically and histologically peculiar diseases of the later life span]. In F. Nissl & A. Alzheimer (eds.), *Histologische und Histopathologische Arbeiten* (pp. 297–351). Jena: Verlag G. Fischer.

Ravaglia, G., Forti, P., Maioli, F., Martelli, M., Servadei, L. Brunetti, N., Dalmonte, E., Bianchin, M., & Mariani, E. (2005). Incidence and etiology in a large elderly Italian population. *Neurology* 64 (9), 1525–30.

Reisberg, B., Ferris, S. H., DeLeon, M. J., & Crooke, T. (1982). The global deterioration scale for assessment of primary degenerative dementia. *American Journal of Psychiatry* 139, 1136–39.

Ripich, D. N. & Terrell, B. Y. (1988). Patterns of discourse cohesion and coherence in Alzheimer's disease. *Journal of Speech and Hearing Disorders* 53, 8–19.

Sabat, S. R. (2001). *The experience of Alzheimer's disease: Life through a tangled veil*. Oxford: Blackwell.

Salmon, D. P., Heindel, W. C., & Butters, N. (1995). Patterns of cognitive impairment in Alzheimer's disease and other dementing disorders. In R. Lubinski (ed.), *Dementia and communication* (pp. 37–46). San Diego, CA: Singular.

Snowden, D. (2001). *Aging with grace*. New York: Bantam Books.

Squire, L. R. (1987). *Memory and brain*. New York: Oxford University Press.

Squire, L. R. & Kandel, E. R. (1999). *Memory: From mind to molecules*. New York: Scientific American Library.

Tariq, S. H., Tumosa, N., Chibnall, J. T., Perry, M. H., & Morley, J. E. (2006). Comparison of the Saint Louis University Mental Status Examination and the Mini-Mental State Examination for detecting dementia and mild neurocognitive disorder: A pilot study. *American Journal of Geriatric Psychiatry* 14, 900–10.

Terry, R. D. & Pena, C. (1965). Experimental production of neurofibrillary pathology: Electron microscopy, phosphate histochemistry and electron probe analysis. *Journal of Neuropathology and Experimental Neurology* 24, 200–10.

Ulatowska, H. & Chapman, S. B. (1995). Discourse studies. In R. Lubinski (ed.), *Dementia and communication* (pp. 115–32). San Diego, CA: Singular.

Vance, D. E. & Farr, K. F. (2007). Spaced retrieval for enhancing memory: Implications for nursing practice and research. *Journal of Gerontological Nursing* 33 (9), 46–52.

Wilson, B. T. (2007). A functional exploration of discourse markers by an individual with dementia of the Alzheimer's type: A conversation analytic perspective. Unpublished doctoral dissertation, University of Louisiana at Lafayette.

Woods, B. (2002). Reducing the impact of cognitive impairment in dementia. In A. D. Baddeley, M. D. Kopelman, & B. A. Wilson (eds.), *The handbook of memory disorders* (pp. 741–55). New York: Wiley.

World Health Organization (1992). *The ICD-10 classification of mental and behavioural disorders*. Geneva: World Health Organization.

World Health Organization (2007). *ICD-10 online, version for 2007*. Geneva: World Health Organization. Accessed February 2008 at: http://www.who.int/classifications/apps/icd/icd10online/

Wyen, C., Lehmann, C., Fatkenheuer, G., & Hoffmann, C. (2005). AIDS-related progressive multifocal leukoencephalopathy in the era of HAART: Report of two cases and review of the literature. *AIDS Patient Care and STDs* 19, 486–94.

Zhou, D. F., Wu, C. S., Qi, H., Fan, J. H., Sun, X. D., Como, P., Qiao, Y. L., Zhang, L., & Kieburtz, K. (2006). Prevalence of dementia in rural China: Impact of age, gender and education. *Acta Neurologica Scandinavica* 114 (4), 273–80.

Zigman, W. B., Schupf, N., Sersen, E., & Silverman, W. (1995). Prevalence of dementia in adults with and without Down syndrome. *American Journal on Mental Retardation* 100, 403–12.

Author Index

Aaron, P. G., 252
Abbeduto, L., 122, 123
Abberley, P., 12, 16
Ackermann, H., 362, 363, 365, 367, 369, 371, 374, 376, 377, 378, 379, 380, 381, 382, 384
Ackerstaff, A. M., 504
Adams, C., 133
Adams, C. V., 299
Adams, G., 261
Adams, M., 276, 277, 278, 433
Adams, S. G., 106, 376, 383
Addler, S., 115, 116
Ahlsén, E., 145, 229
Aharon-Peretz, J., 588
Ainsworth, M., 168
Airasian, P., 22
Akefeldt, A., 115
Albery, E., 481
Algeria, J., 74
Allen, C., 103
Allington, R. L., 268, 279, 282, 286
Almond, G. A., 269
Al-Mondhiry, R., 58
Almor, A., 233
Alt, M., 180
Alzheimer, A., 609, 610
Alzheimer's Society, 319, 611
Ambrose, N. G., 438
American Psychiatric Association, 529, 532, 603, 605

American Speech-Language-Hearing Association, 392, 393, 397, 410, 412, 434, 580
Amorosa, H., 346
Amsel, A., 273, 274
Anderson, D., 69, 76
Anderson, E., 79, 81, 82, 83
Anderson, J. D., 448
Anderson, K., 78
Anderson, P., 39
Anderson, R., 45, 46
Andrews, G., 432, 437
Andrews, M., 465
Angeleri, R., 592
Anglin, J., 164
Annegers, J. F., 319
Apel, K., 276
Apfel, H., 187
Apple, M. W., 16
Applebee, A., 182
Applegate, J., 341
Appleton, J., 519
Aram, D., 211
Archer, M., 15
Archibald, S., 297
Ardila, A., 323, 325
Armstrong, D. F., 324
Armstrong, E. M., 229
Artiles, A. J., 14, 16
Aspel, A. D., 11, 26
Astley, S. J., 297, 298, 299

Subject Index

African-American English (AAE), 40–3
Alzheimer's disease (AD), 24, 600, 602,
    604–26
  communication impairment, 613–4, 616
  early onset, 608, 610–12, 618
  intervention, 618–20, 622
  memory impairment, 600, 602–3,
    608–10, 613–15, 618–19
  neuropathology, 610–11
  risk factors, 600, 611–12, 620
  stages, 610, 613–16
  see also dementia
American Sign Language (ASL), 58–9, 61,
    65, 69, 73, 75–7, 85
aphasia, 28, 391, 557, 579, 603, 606–7, 614,
    616, 618
  agrammatism, 324
  anomia, 323
  aphemia, 320
  conduction aphasia, 325
  definition, 317
  dysgraphia, 324
  dyslexia, 324
  expressive or motor aphasia, 325
  fluent versus non-fluent, 323–4, 616, 614
  history, 320–2
  incidence and prevalence, 318–20
  jargon, 323
  paraphasia, 323
  psychosocial and emotional response,
    329–32
  receptive or sensory aphasia, 325
  recovery, 326–7

recurrent utterances, 325
  therapy, 327–9
  transcortical motor aphasia, 365, 369
  Wernicke–Lichtheim model, 321
  Wernicke–Lichtheim–Geschwind model,
    321, 322
aphonia, 317
  see also voice disorders
apraxia of speech (AOS), 11, 365, 367, 375,
    391–409
  acquired, 391–5
  assessment, 396–401
  childhood AOS, 348, 391–3, 397, 398,
    402–5
  clinical features, 396–9
  definitions, 391–3
  diagnosis, 396–9
  neurological AOS, 393–6
  treatment, 401–4
Asperger's syndrome, 14, 27, 155, 157
  see also pervasive developmental
    disorder
attention-deficit/hyperactivity disorder
    (ADHD), 15, 23–4, 232, 257, 299,
    529–50
  across cultures, 532
  co-morbid disorders, 531–2, 538, 540–2,
    544–5, 550
  diagnosis, 13, 25, 529, 532, 540
  discourse deficits, 535, 541–3, 545–6, 550
  executive function, 531, 533–5, 537,
    540–5, 550
  intervention, 529, 53–5, 544–5, 549, 550